6783

Afro-American Writers from the Harlem Renaissance to 1940

Dictionary of Literary Biography

Documentary Series

Yearbooks

Afro-American Writers from the Harlem Renaissance to 1940

6783

Edited by
Trudier Harris
University of North Carolina at Chapel Hill

Associate Editor
Thadious M. Davis
University of North Carolina at Chapel Hill

A Bruccoli Clark Layman Book
Gale Research Company • Book Tower • Detroit, Michigan 48226

Manufactured by Edwards Brothers, Inc.
Ann Arbor, Michigan
Printed in the United States of America

Library of Congress Cataloging-in-Publication Data

Afro-American writers from the Harlem Renaissance to
    1940.

    (Dictionary of literary biography; v. 51)
    "A Bruccoli Clark book."
    Includes index.
    1. American literature—Afro-American authors—History and criticism. 2. American literature—20th century—History and criticism. 3. Afro-American authors—Biography—Dictionaries. 4. Authors, American—20th century—Biography—Dictionaries. 5. American literature—Afro-American authors—Bio-bibliography. 6. American literature—20th century—Bio-bibliography. 7. Harlem Renaissance. 8. Afro-Americans in literature. I. Harris, Trudier. II. Series.
PS153.N5A396   1987   810'.9'896   [B]   86-26954
    ISBN 0-8103-1729-X

For
Blyden Jackson
Unareed Harris

Contents

Plan of the Series

The advisory board, the editors, and the publisher of the *Dictionary of Literary Biography* are joined in endorsing Mark Twain's declaration. The literature of a nation provides an inexhaustible resource of permanent worth. It is our expectation that this endeavor will make literature and its creators better understood and more accessible to students and the literate public, while satisfying the standards of teachers and scholars.

To meet these requirements, *literary biography* has been construed in terms of the author's achievement. The most important thing about a writer is his writing. Accordingly, the entries in *DLB* are career biographies, tracing the development of the author's canon and the evolution of his reputation.

The publication plan for *DLB* resulted from two years of preparation. The project was proposed to Bruccoli Clark by Frederick G. Ruffner, president of the Gale Research Company, in November 1975. After specimen entries were prepared and typeset, an advisory board was formed to refine the entry format and develop the series rationale. In meetings held during 1976, the publisher, series editors, and advisory board approved the scheme for a comprehensive biographical dictionary of persons who contributed to North American literature. Editorial work on the first volume began in January 1977, and it was published in 1978.

In order to make *DLB* more than a reference tool and to compile volumes that individually have claim to status as literary history, it was decided to organize volumes by topic or period or genre. Each of these freestanding volumes provides a biographical-bibliographical guide and overview for a particular area of literature. We are convinced that this organization—as opposed to a single alphabet method—constitutes a valuable innovation in the presentation of reference material. The volume

plan necessarily requires many decisions for the placement and treatment of authors who might properly be included in two or three volumes. In some instances a major figure will be included in separate volumes, but with different entries emphasizing the aspect of his career appropriate to each volume. Ernest Hemingway, for example, is represented in *American Writers in Paris, 1920-1939* by an entry focusing on his expatriate apprenticeship; he is also in *American Novelists, 1910-1945* with an entry surveying his entire career. Each volume includes a cumulative index of subject authors and articles. The final *DLB* volume will be a comprehensive index to the entire series.

With volume ten in 1982 it was decided to enlarge the scope of *DLB*. By the end of 1985 twenty-one volumes treating British literature had been published, and volumes for Commonwealth and Modern European literature were in progress. The series has been further augmented by the *DLB Yearbooks* (since 1981) which update published entries and add new entries to keep the *DLB* current with contemporary activity. There have also been occasional *DLB Documentary Series* volumes which provide biographical and critical background source materials for figures whose work is judged to have particular interest for students. One of these companion volumes is entirely devoted to Tennessee Williams.

The purpose of *DLB* is not only to provide reliable information in a convenient format but also to place the figures in the larger perspective of literary history and to offer appraisals of their accomplishments by qualified scholars.

We define literature as the *intellectual commerce of a nation:* not merely as belles lettres but as that ample and complex process by which ideas are generated, shaped, and transmitted. *DLB* entries are not limited to "creative writers" but extend to other figures who in this time and in this way influenced the mind of a people. Thus the series encompasses historians, journalists, publishers, and screenwriters. By this means readers of *DLB* may be aided to perceive literature not as cult scripture in the keeping of cultural high priests but as at the center of a nation's life.

DLB includes the major writers appropriate to each volume and those standing in the ranks immediately behind them. Scholarly and critical counsel has been sought in deciding which minor figures to include and how full their entries should be. Wherever possible, useful references are made to figures who do not warrant separate entries.

Each *DLB* volume has a volume editor responsible for planning the volume, selecting the figures for inclusion, and assigning the entries. Volume editors are also responsible for preparing, where appropriate, appendices surveying the major periodicals and literary and intellectual movements for their volumes, as well as lists of further readings. Work on the series as a whole is coordinated at the Bruccoli Clark editorial center in Columbia, South Carolina, where the editorial staff is responsible for the accuracy of the published volumes.

One feature that distinguishes *DLB* is the illustration policy—its concern with the iconography of literature. Just as an author is influenced by his surroundings, so is the reader's understanding of the author enhanced by a knowledge of his environment. Therefore *DLB* volumes include not only drawings, paintings, and photographs of authors, often depicting them at various stages in their careers, but also illustrations of their families and places where they lived. Title pages are regularly reproduced in facsimile along with dust jackets for modern authors. The dust jackets are a special fea-

ture of *DLB* because they often document better than anything else the way in which an author's work was launched in its own time. Specimens of the writers' manuscripts are included when feasible.

A supplement to *DLB*—tentatively titled *A Guide, Chronology, and Glossary for American Literature*—will outline the history of literature in North America and trace the influences that shaped it. This volume will provide a framework for the study of American literature by means of chronological tables, literary affiliation charts, glossarial entries, and concise surveys of the major movements. It has been planned to stand on its own as a vade mecum, providing a ready-reference guide to the study of American literature as well as a companion to the *DLB* volumes for American literature.

Samuel Johnson rightly decreed that "The chief glory of every people arises from its authors." The purpose of the *Dictionary of Literary Biography* is to compile literary history in the surest way available to us—by accurate and comprehensive treatment of the lives and work of those who contributed to it.

The *DLB* Advisory Board

Foreword

DLB 51, Afro-American Writers from the Harlem Renaissance to 1940, is the second in a series of three volumes covering the work of black American authors up to 1955. The first volume, *DLB 50,* covers *Afro-American Writers Before the Harlem Renaissance,* and the third treats *Afro-American Writers, 1940-1955.*

The one period in black letters that stands out above all others is the one commonly referred to as the Harlem Renaissance. Not easily reducible to exact dates, the Harlem Renaissance is defined as that flowering of Afro-American creativity beginning around World War I and extending into the early days of the 1930s. Coming from Florida and Idaho, California and Jamaica, Missouri and Ohio, Boston and Washington, D.C., black artists and writers flocked into Harlem, making it the race capital of the world; they arrived there to begin a decade of self-conscious striving to change popular perceptions of their people. Langston Hughes, Countee Cullen, Claude McKay, Zora Neale Hurston, Nella Larsen, Jessie Fauset, and many others worked to claim a place for themselves in a literary history that had narrow meaning before their contributions in the 1920s.

While Harlem was perhaps the center of events during the 1920s, it should not be viewed as the *only* place in which creative activity among Afro-Americans was proliferating. Washington, D.C., for example, proved to be a nurturant environment for the black arts renaissance. From her home on S Street, Georgia Douglas Johnson encouraged a number of writers, including Marita Bonner Occomy, who was contemporary with her, as well as later writers such as Mary Miller and Ted Shine. Jean Toomer and Rudolph Fisher used Washington as a beginning place for their literary careers, and Alain Locke had his based there as a professor of philosophy at Howard University. It was to Washington that writers such as Langston Hughes came for their breaks from Harlem, and the city proved to be one of the literary meccas of the years of the renaissance and after.

Chicago and Memphis, among other places, also served as beacons for aspiring writers, some of whom had ties to Harlem and others not. George Washington Lee, who set his novels along the Mississippi, was inspired in part to write because he did not like Walter White's evaluation of his works;

to an extent, therefore, he wrote in reaction to the Harlem group. Frank Marshall Davis wrote his most important works in Chicago, as did Occomy. Richard Wright, who flourished in the period immediately after the Harlem Renaissance, drew heavily from his Chicago experiences for his best-known works.

The Harlem Renaissance was spurred by a variety of factors. The depletion of southern soil and the industrial opportunities afforded by World War I encouraged more black Americans than ever to leave the country for the city. Visible black communities were therefore emerging in a number of urban areas, including Chicago, Detroit, and Philadelphia. Returning black veterans had also made it clear that, after fighting for democracy on foreign soil, they were no longer content to accept second-class citizenship in their own country. Consequently, there was a renewed spirit of racial mobility in the country, as well as a series of riots that indicated the extent to which blacks were willing to go to bring about change.

The era represented the emergence of "the New Negro," a phrase Alain Locke coined to describe the drastic changes taking place on all strata of black American life. This was the era when prominent black people, such as W. E. B. Du Bois, who now had public outlets for their opinions, encouraged renewed fervor against lynchings. It was also the era of Charles S. Johnson, Jessie Fauset, and others who consciously sought to encourage an artistic renaissance in an effort to change the public conception of Afro-Americans by fostering more contact between the races. These years were also the era of bohemianism, when many young black writers, like their white counterparts Ernest Hemingway, F. Scott Fitzgerald, and others, wanted to establish a new direction for themselves, dramatically different from that of their forefathers. These "New Negroes," then, were a provocative mix; they sought to change but they also sought to preserve—to change racist attitudes but to preserve African heritage, to diminish isolation between races but to nurture distinctive racial characteristics.

Many of these younger writers were aided by the older, more established critics and writers. William Stanley Braithwaite, through his annual selections of poetry, and W. E. B. Du Bois and other editors of the *Crisis,* through their liberal publication policies, consistently brought to the public some of these younger voices. Charles S. Johnson, editor of *Opportunity,* sponsored literary contests to encourage creativity among these writers; Johnson also sponsored annual awards dinners in the mid-1920s at which he celebrated current literary achievements within the younger group. Although these older critics, editors, and scholars may at times have disagreed with the young writers who were eager to depict the masses of blacks instead of the privileged "talented tenth," they nevertheless played important roles in providing outlets for publishing and encouraging discussion on the direction black writing should take.

In his first autobiography, *The Big Sea* (1940), Langston Hughes credited Jessie Fauset and Alain Locke with midwifing the Harlem Renaissance into existence. Certainly Fauset's position as literary editor at the *Crisis* was a help to many of the young writers. Alain Locke, cultural connoisseur and cosmopolitan citizen of the world, guided many of the young writers, including Cullen and Hughes, into more broadly based appreciations of culture than they had experienced in their youthful years. Non-literary figures, such as a hair-straightener heiress A'Lelia Walker, also played a role in the creative atmosphere. Through her infamous parties, where the well-known and the budding, the artistic and the nonartistic rubbed elbows, Walker made her contribution to the shaping of the renaissance.

The young black writers also provided their own publishing outlet. Langston Hughes, Wallace Thurman, Zora Neale Hurston, Gwendolyn Bennett, Richard Bruce Nugent, and others joined together to produce *Fire!!* in 1926. The one issue of the journal, which has now become a collector's item, featured most of the writers whose names we identify with the renaissance. Two of the younger writers, Countee Cullen and Gwendolyn Bennett, had the opportunity to write columns for one of the more established journals; Cullen provided criticism in "The Dark Tower" for more than two years in *Opportunity,* and Bennett provided similar analysis and commentary on the arts in "Ebony Flute," her two-year column in the same journal.

The new writers were concerned with burning up some of the old ideas associated with Afro-American writing. They turned away from the themes that usually defined works in the genteel tradition and they experimented with different forms. Jean Toomer's *Cane* (1923), received with fervor in black intellectual circles, is an amalgam

of poems, prose, and drama which epitomizes the stylistic experimentation of the period while it defies easy categorization. Claude McKay raised many an establishment eyebrow, by crowding militant emotions into the Shakespearean sonnet form. Langston Hughes took advantage of the possibilities of free verse; he turned to jazz and blues rhythms to depict the lifestyles and activities of and for the masses of blacks, whom he preferred over the "talented tenth" usually depicted by black writers of the preceding generations. Toomer, Sterling A. Brown, Zora Neale Hurston, and Waters E. Turpin were among the writers who extended the focus on the folk, the black masses. In his depictions of the restrictions of the sharecropping system, Brown anticipated the treatments of rural blacks that would form the focus of Richard Wright's *Uncle Tom's Children* (1938). Hurston's emphasis on the folk in her fiction parallels some of the prevailing trends of the time, captured in the folk plays of Ridgely Torrence, Paul Green, and Willis Richardson and in the folk novels of Julia Peterkin. Rudolph Fisher experimented with the detective novel, and Walter White joined Fisher in using his fiction to comment on current affairs; Fisher concentrated on Harlem nightlife and White depicted the lynchings that he had investigated for the NAACP.

The 1920s were an age of focus on color, and the volumes published during that period attest to that fact. McKay's *Harlem Shadows* (1922) led the way, followed by Cullen's *Color* (1925) and *Copper Sun* (1927), Bennett's *Bronze* (1922), Thurman's *The Blacker the Berry* (1929), and George Schuyler's *Black No More* (1931). There were "dark towers," "ebony flutes," "weary blues," and many other indications that the writers were captivated with a sense of their own people.

The theme continued in some of the anthologies of the era, including Cullen's *Caroling Dusk* (1927) and Charles S. Johnson's *Ebony and Topaz: A Collectanea* (1927). Alain Locke's *The New Negro* (1925) captured the iconoclastic spirit of the era that Hughes had penned in "The Negro Artist and the Racial Mountain"; the same was true of the special issue of *Survey Graphic* (March 1925) devoted to black American writers.

The 1920s were also the age of patronage; the most famous benefactor of the period was Charlotte Osgood ("godmother") Mason to Langston Hughes and Zora Neale Hurston. Though Hurston was more temperamentally suited to such an arrangement than Hughes, they both nevertheless were given free time and support to produce some of their most important works. Whites who did not provide direct financial support to the up-and-coming black writers and artists frequently served as sources of contact for possible publications. Of this group, Carl Van Vechten led the way. Having made blacks his special area of concern since the 1890s, Van Vechten began, in the 1920s, introducing writers to publishers and to each other and slumming in Harlem. More lastingly, he encouraged the establishment of collections with the photographs that have now become essential to any study of the renaissance. H. L. Mencken also found his way to Harlem, and Max Eastman of the *Liberator* was instrumental in offering McKay opportunities to move up in the publishing world.

Greater opportunities were also available to black writers for international travel, sometimes with white compatriots, as in the case of McKay, who traveled to the Soviet Union during the 1920s. He also spent extensive periods in England, France, and northern Africa. Hughes and Cullen also spent time in Africa, and Hughes toured various parts of Europe, serving as a correspondent in Spain in the late 1930s. Jean Toomer spent a summer in France at the Gurdjieff Institute, immersed in the philosophy that he would try unsuccessfully to transplant to Harlem. Such cultural exposure outside the United States provided a unique perspective from which the writers viewed race relations and anticipated the attraction to the left that many of them developed in the late 1920s and early 1930s.

Not all of the writers covered in this volume are identifiably associated with the aims of the Harlem Renaissance; indeed, some were far removed from it. Novelist Waters Edward Turpin, for example, was busy producing his works in the Baltimore area and tended to turn his concern toward academic issues. Although Frank Horne contributed to the journals of the day, he spent a large part of the 1920s in Georgia. Ted Poston, though in New York, focused his attention on journalism more than cultural politics. Eric Walrond, who, like Claude McKay, came from the Caribbean, was writing in the United States during the peak of the Harlem Renaissance, but his affiliation was temporary, and he left America to pursue other intellectual aims. George Schuyler seems to have spent most of his time decrying what the younger writers hoped to achieve. Though Anne Spencer knew many of the writers of this period, it was only because they came to her home in Virginia, not because she sought them out in New York; only through the intervention of her friend James Weldon Johnson did she publish a few poems during the 1920s. Leslie Pinckney Hill spent the time as an educational administrator in Pennsylvania. Despite the geographical and sometimes intellectual diversity of these writers, they formed a complex unit of progression that changed the shape and conception of Afro-American literature.

Some writers included here, such as Langston Hughes and Zora Neale Hurston, will be familiar to the American public. Others, such as Ray Garfield Dandridge and Helene Johnson, are probably being introduced. Yet all of these writers shared a vision of Afro-American creativity and a hope that literature could be more liberal than elitist, equally as reflective of the masses as the upper classes. The ties that bound them together also bound them to later generations of writers; their collective achievement offers to scholars, teachers, and students an intricate view of their philosophy of art.

—*Trudier Harris*

Acknowledgments

This book was produced by Bruccoli Clark Layman, Inc. Karen L. Rood is senior editor for the *Dictionary of Literary Biography* series. Ellen Rosenberg Kovner was the in-house editor.

Art supervisor is Patricia M. Flanagan. Copyediting supervisor is Patricia Coate. Production coordinator is Kimberly Casey. Typesetting supervisor is Laura Ingram. The production staff includes Rowena Betts, David R. Bowdler, Tara P. Deal, Mary S. Dye, Kathleen M. Flanagan, Joyce Fowler, Pamela Haynes, Judith K. Ingle, Judith E. McCray, Janet L. Phelps, Joyce Rogers, Joycelyn R. Smith, and Lucia Tarbox. Jean W. Ross is permissions editor. Joseph Caldwell, photography editor, and Joseph Matthew Bruccoli did photographic copy work for the volume.

Walter W. Ross and Rhonda A. Marshall did the library research with the assistance of the staff at the Thomas Cooper Library of the University of South Carolina: Lynn Barron, Daniel Boice, Connie Crider, Kathy Eckman, Michael Freeman, Gary Geer, David L. Haggard, Jens Holley, Marcia Martin, Dana Rabon, Jean Rhyne, Jan Squire, Ellen Tillett, and Virginia Weathers.

Thomas Battle, Maricia Battle Bracey, and Esme Bhan at the Moorland-Spingarn Research Center, Howard University; and Howard Dodson, Mary Yearwood, Cheryl Shackelton, and Natasha Russell at the Schomburg Center for Research in Black Culture, New York Public Library, Astor, Lenox and Tilden Foundations, provided invaluable assistance with illustrations for this volume.

Afro-American Writers from the Harlem Renaissance to 1940

Dictionary of Literary Biography

Gwendolyn Bennett

(8 July 1902-30 May 1981)

Walter C. Daniel
University of Missouri, Columbia
and
Sandra Y. Govan
University of North Carolina at Charlotte

WORKS: "Nocturn," in *The Book of American Negro Poetry*, edited by James Weldon Johnson (New York: Harcourt, Brace, 1922; revised, 1931);

"Moon Tonight" and "Song," in *Anthology of Magazine Verse for 1927 and Yearbook of American Poetry*, edited by William Stanley Braithwaite (Boston: B. J. Brimmer, 1927), pp. 31, 32;

"Advice," "Fantasy," "Hatred," "Lines Written at the Grave of Alexander Dumas," "Quatrains," "Secret," "Sonnet I," "Sonnet II," "To a Dark Girl," and "Your Songs," in *Caroling Dusk: An Anthology of Verse by Negro Poets*, edited by Countee Cullen (New York & London: Harper, 1927);

"Tokens," in *Ebony and Topaz: A Collectanea*, edited by Charles S. Johnson (New York, 1927), pp. 149-150.

PERIODICAL PUBLICATIONS:
POETRY
"Heritage," *Opportunity*, 1 (December 1923): 371;

"To Usward," *Crisis*, 28 (May 1924): 19; *Opportunity*, 2 (May 1924): 143-144;

"Wind," *Opportunity*, 2 (November 1924): 335;

"Purgation," *Opportunity*, 3 (February 1925): 56;

"On a Birthday," *Opportunity*, 3 (September 1925): 276;

"Street Lamps in Early Spring," *Opportunity*, 4 (May 1926): 152;

"Hatred," *Opportunity*, 4 (June 1926): 190;

"Lines Written at the Grave of Alexander Dumas," *Opportunity*, 4 (July 1926): 225;

"Song," "Dear Things," and "Dirge," *Palms*, 4 (October 1926): 21-22;

"Epitaph," *Opportunity*, 12 (March 1934): 76.
FICTION
"Wedding Day," *Fire!!* (November 1926): 26-28.
NONFICTION
"The Future of the Negro in Art," *Howard University Record*, 19 (December 1924): 65-66;

"Negroes: Inherent Craftsmen," *Howard University Record*, 19 (February 1925): 172;

"The Ebony Flute," column in *Opportunity*, 4 (August 1926)-6 (May 1928);

"The American Negro Paints," *Southern Workman*, 57 (January 1928): 111-112;

"Never the Twain Shall Meet," review of *Salah and His American* by Leland Hall, *Opportunity*, 12 (March 1934): 92;

"I Go to Camp," *Opportunity*, 12 (August 1934): 241-243;

"Rounding the Century: Story of the Colored Orphan Asylum and Association for the Benefit of Colored Children in New York City," *Crisis*, 42 (June 1935): 180-181, 188.

Gwendolyn B. Bennett, a minor literary figure and graphic artist, is often mentioned almost in passing in association with other Harlem Renaissance writers whose reputations surpassed hers. Yet in the midst of the Harlem Renaissance Bennett was widely recognized by her peers as one of the more active and promising authors of the New Negro movement.

Gwendolyn Bennett (courtesy of the Prints and Photographs Collection, Moorland-Spingarn Research Center, Howard University)

published story, appeared in Charles S. Johnson's *Ebony and Topaz: A Collectanea* (1927).

Bennett was born in Giddings, Texas, on 8 July 1902 to Joshua and Maime Bennett. She spent her earliest years in Nevada where both of her parents taught at an Indian reservation. When Bennett was four or five, the family moved to Washington, D.C., where Joshua Bennett studied law, and his wife became a manicurist and beautician at a finishing school. Shortly thereafter the Bennetts divorced, and Maime Bennett was awarded custody of her daughter. When Gwendolyn was seven, her father kidnapped her on the pretext of taking her to see George Washington's Mt. Vernon home. Bennett would be a teacher at Howard University before she saw her mother again. Of her parents' struggle, Bennett merely said: "It was not the problem of a child that wasn't loved enough, it was a child that was loved too much." She and her father moved frequently, staying mostly in the cities and small towns of Pennsylvania. In Harrisburg, where Bennett was a high school honors student for two years, Joshua Bennett married Marechal Neil. The family finally settled in Brooklyn, New York.

Bennett attended Brooklyn's Girl's High School, where she won the school art contest, was the first black student elected to both the literary and drama societies, and wrote both the class graduation speech and the lyrics to the graduation song. Upon her graduation in 1921, against the advice of her family (who wanted to see her established in a stable profession), Bennett began preparing herself for a career in fine arts. For the next three years she studied at Pratt Institute and took courses at Columbia University. Her training at Pratt and additional work in Paris in 1925 led to Bennett's career as a graphic artist in watercolor, oil, woodcuts, pen and ink, and batik. While at Howard University, where she had gone in 1924 to teach in the year-old fine arts department, she exhibited some of her works. Unfortunately many of her pictures and batiks were destroyed in a fire at her stepmother's Brooklyn home in 1926.

Bennett had also shown an early interest in creative writing. She had written and acted in her high school class play and had composed several poems that had been read in the circles of the new young writers in Harlem in the 1920s.

In 1923 *Opportunity* had published Bennett's poem "Heritage," a piece that tapped Afro-American cultural images—Africa, "lithe Negro girls" dancing at dusk, "sad people's soul/hidden by a minstrel smile"—two years before Cullen's cele-

While only a small amount of Bennett's poetry was published and her work was never collected into a single volume, twenty-two of her poems appeared between 1923 and 1931, in black journals of the day such as *Crisis, Opportunity, Palms,* and *Gypsy.* Several poems were collected in major anthologies of the period: James Weldon Johnson's *The Book of American Negro Poetry* (1922), Countee Cullen's *Caroling Dusk: An Anthology of Verse by Negro Poets* (1927), and William Stanley Braithwaite's *Anthology of Magazine Verse for 1927 and Yearbook of American Poetry* (1927). Bennett also illustrated the front cover of *Crisis* twice and *Opportunity* three times between 1923 and 1930. Between 1925 and 1927 Bennett focused her creative attention on writing short stories. "Wedding Day," her first published story, appeared in *Fire!!,* the ill-fated black arts journal founded by Bennett, Wallace Thurman, Langston Hughes, and several other notable New Negro artists. "Tokens," Bennett's second

brated poem of the same title addressed some of the same themes and images.

Bennett was only twenty-two years old when Charles S. Johnson, editor of *Opportunity*, the National Urban League's new magazine, introduced her to a wider literary public. Johnson invited her to a literary dinner in honor of Jessie Redmon Fauset, held 21 May 1924 at the Civic Club in New York. Among those who attended were the older generation of black literati, W. E. B. Du Bois, Alain Locke, and James Weldon Johnson, and radical young writers, Cullen, Hughes, Thurman, and Zora Neale Hurston, who wanted their work published in an arena free from the constraints of the house organs of the racial uplift organizations. Although their poetry and fiction had reached a national audience through the pages of *Crisis* and *Opportunity*, they wanted entrée into the publishing establishment. Johnson helped them by bringing to that dinner representatives from *Harper's Survey Graphic, World Tomorrow, Nation,* and the *New York World.* Bennett became a member of the younger literary "group," as Johnson referred to them, who

met occasionally at the headquarters of the Urban League. In a 1979 interview Bennett recalled the significance of that period for her: "It was fun to be alive and to be part of this . . . like nothing else I've ever been a part of. . . . there's been nothing exactly like this . . . nothing like this particular life in which you saw the same group of people over and over again. You were always glad to see them. You always had an exciting time when you were with them."

In May 1924 Bennett's commemorative poem, "To Usward," dedicated to Fauset in honor of the publication of *There is Confusion,* appeared simultaneously in the *Crisis* and in *Opportunity;* it had been selected as the dedication piece at the official dinner "debut" for Harlem's artists sponsored by Johnson. "To Usward" captures a unity in the loosely woven Renaissance aesthetic through its central metaphor, a ginger jar. The poem identifies and sanctions the diversity of vision and the variety of thematic concerns animating the collective muse of Harlem's writers. It celebrates youth and diversity: "If any have a song to sing/That's

Covers illustrated by Bennett

different from the rest/Oh let them sing/Before the urgency of youth's behest!" Alluding to cultural riches of Africa ("jungle heat and fires") and to folk culture ("crooning Negro lullabies"), it proclaims: "We claim no part of racial dearth,/We want to sing the songs of birth!" The last stanza of the poem returns to the delicate and central emblem: "And so we stand like ginger jars/Like ginger jars bound round/With dust and age;/Like jars of ginger we are sealed/By nature's heritage."

Contemporary criticism of Bennett's poetry was complimentary. James Weldon Johnson said of her: "Miss Bennett is the author of a number of fine poems, some of them in the freer forms, but she is at her best in the delicate poignant lyrics that she has written." Playwright Theodore Ward called Bennett one of the "most promising of the poets out of the Harlem Renaissance" and observed that she was a "dynamic figure . . . noted for her depth and understanding." J. Mason Brewer, perhaps from a kind of romanticized state chauvinism, alleged that Bennett had become a "nationally known artist and poetess"; he further suggested that Bennett's Texas origin made "Texans feel that they have a claim on her and that the beautiful and poignant lyrics she writes resulted partially from the impression of her early Texas surroundings."

After her sojourn in Paris, Bennett returned to New York in the summer of 1926. She was hired by *Opportunity* to serve as assistant to the editor; she was also the recipient of an Alfred C. Barnes Foundation fellowship. That fall Bennett returned to Howard, though she continued her association with *Opportunity*, performing her duties by mail and during periodic visits to New York.

But she was never happy in staid, caste-conscious Washington nor at Howard, both so unlike fast-paced New York where she knew everybody and was part of everything going on. However, she was gratified by her position as an assistant editor of *Opportunity* and her charge to write a literary and fine arts column. Johnson wrote in an editorial announcing the column that ran monthly for nearly two years: "The growth of Negro literary groups throughout the country and the manifest concern about the activities of other writers prompts the introduction this month of a column carrying informal literary intelligence." He went on to note that Bennett was "one of the most versatile and accomplished of the younger poets" who had published poetry. Her "Song" had appeared in Alain Locke's important anthology, *The New Negro* (1925), and she had reviewed books for *Opportunity*. Like Johnson, Bennett would relate significantly to

the "old heads" as well as to the new writers.

"I want to sing Harlem on an ebony flute," Bennett wrote in titling her column after the first line of William Rose Benét's poem "Harlem." The brief comments, 1,200 to 1,500 words, made the metaphor appropriate; they celebrated black creative artists and their works. Bennett announced Eric Walrond's *Tropic Death*, short fiction due out in the fall of 1926, and a black magazine, *American Life*, scheduled for publication in Chicago. She mentioned Maude Cuney Hare's *Musical Observer* article on Creole folksongs, noted that Aaron Douglass's illustrations would appear in Carl Van Vechten's *Nigger Heaven* and that the English version of Langston Hughes's *Weary Blues* had appeared, and commented that Alain Locke was planning a second edition of *The New Negro*. She reported, too, that Hall Johnson and Langston Hughes were collaborating in writing an operetta, as were Hughes and Hurston. Jean Toomer was spending the summer at the Gurdjieff Institute in France, and Countee Cullen and his father were traveling through Europe. Charles S. Johnson held a reception for Negro summer school students studying at universities in New York, where he spoke and called on several winners of *Opportunity*'s 1926 literary contests to share their writing. Arna Bontemps had read his "Golgotha Is a Mountain," and Hughes had read his "Brass Spittoons."

"Ebony Flute" represents the bulk of Bennett's published work. It is a significant piece of Afro-American cultural history because it provided regular news about the writers, painters, sculptors, actors, and musicians who shaped the Harlem Renaissance into the most important artistic movement in Afro-American history. "Ebony Flute" and Cullen's "From the Dark Tower," a column of literary criticism published in *Opportunity* for two years, constituted the only organized chronicles of their kind in Afro-American letters.

Bennett also continued writing and publishing her own poetry. Her poem "Hatred" received second honorable mention in *Opportunity*'s 1926 literary contest. Typical of Bennett's lyrical verse, "Hatred" is deeply personal, projects high emotion, and does not in any way emphasize the prevailing sense of the "New Negro." The speaker of the poem states: "I shall hate you/Like a dart of singing steel/Shot through still air/At even-tide." The motivation for hating is not revealed, but the persona declares: "Memory will lay its hand/Upon your breast/And you will understand/My hatred." In "To a Dark Girl," she expresses a pride in black beauty reminiscent of Cullen and Hughes. The fi-

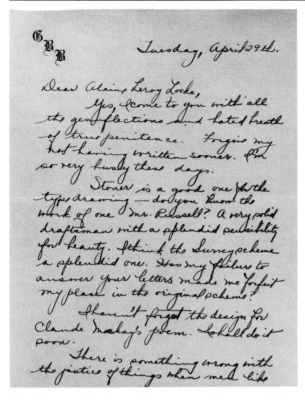

The "Survey scheme" to which Bennett refers in this 1924 letter became the March 1925 issue of Survey Graphic, *which was devoted to Afro-American literature (courtesy of the Alain Locke Papers, Moorland-Spingarn Research Center, Howard University)*

nal stanza's admonition to the little brown girl, "brown for sorrow's mate," is to keep all her queenliness; "forgetting that you once were slave" is part of the vogue. "Heritage," a poem in the atavistic mode of the time, expresses a longing to "see the slim palm trees/Pulling at the clouds/With little pointed fingers" etched dark against the sky at sunset.

Bennett's "Lines Written at the Grave of Alexander Dumas," written in Paris and published in *Opportunity* in 1926, mixes recognition of the black author Dumas with unrequited personal love. Denying the secrecy of the grave, the poem asks Dumas to "stir the lucid waters" of his sleep and tell a tale of happy loves and "gems of joyous limbs." "Lines" is a "graveyard" poem that carries a racial identification only because of the name of Dumas in its title.

During the course of her career, Bennett published only two short stories, "Wedding Day" and "Tokens." "Wedding Day," a popularly anthologized piece, appeared in *Fire!!* It explores the universal and eternal question black Americans face: "Who am I?" The story's hero is Paul Watson. Nei-

ther a soldier nor an artist, Watson was a black American who believed he could escape racial prejudice in the United States by living as an expatriate in Europe.

The story recounts Watson's superhuman exploits against rednecked Americans who call him "nigger." Rue Pigalle, Paris's equivalent to Harlem's Seventh Avenue, is his metier. His music makes him well known, but he becomes heroic because of the strength and fierce pride that will not let him accept racial slurs from anyone. Before the war he had been sentenced to prison for maiming prejudiced white Americans. Released to fight alongside Frenchmen in the war, he is in limbo when peace comes and the large numbers of Americans make him less exotic. His lack of experience with women leaves him unprepared for a conniving white American woman who uses him when she is down on her luck. He falls in love with her, much to the surprise of all who knew him in the Pigalle. His wedding day, the occasion that gives the story its title, is his movement from innocence to experience. When he calls on his "betrothed" the morning of that fateful day, she has simply left a note stating that white women do not marry black men. Paul is enraged, but he cannot resort to the violence he would have so quickly and effectively used at another time. Stunned, he goes into the subway and finds himself holding a pink first-class ticket while riding a second-class car, which becomes symbolic of that stoical endurance required of black people in coping with contradictory and absurd situations, even outside the United States. In this first-person narrative, Bennett makes explicit the ironies and agony associated with black people living with white prejudices.

"Tokens," which appeared in *Ebony and Topaz* in 1927, also focuses on a black American in Paris. Jenks Barnett, along with other musicians, remained in France after World War I. Now dying from tuberculosis, he recalls singing with Will Marion Cook in the heyday of Negro entertainers. In his last days, he is bitter and suspicious. Only his memories of his childhood, his music, and the French girl he had loved remain. "See I'm dyin' . . . get me. They keep stickin' that needle in me but I know damn well I'm dyin'. Now what I want you to do is this . . . I wrote a letter to Tollie when I first came here . . . it's in her picture in my suitcase. . . . Well when I die I want you to give it to her, if it's a thousand years from now," he tells the one friend who still visits him occasionally. Ironically, Tollie had died of tuberculosis a month earlier. Jenks dies, and the story ends with the comment: "Funny how the first kind thing Jenks had done for anybody since Tollie left him should be done for a person who was dead."

Bennett remained active in the Harlem Renaissance even when she was away from Harlem. She not only wrote poetry and fiction, but also scholarly articles on the Negro and the arts, journalistic social essays, critical reviews, and "Ebony Flute," her literary "chit-chat" or literary gossip column. While Bennett was able to sustain the chatty art "news" quality of her "Flute" column from her post as an arts and design instructor at Howard University, she was not able to continue the column from rural Florida, where she moved following her marriage.

In the spring of 1927 Bennett resigned from Howard University amid a minor scandal. She had met Alfred Jackson, a graduate of Morehouse College, on her return from Paris. Jackson was studying medicine at Howard and interning at the Freedman's Hospital. They fell in love and were engaged by early 1927. Apparently news of their engagement and subsequent marriage was not approved of by the authoritarian administration.

Bennett therefore offered her resignation. It was not forced; she was not fired. But when she asked if she could reconsider, she was told "No; it was just as well."

During the summer of 1927 Bennett taught art education and English at Tennessee State College, then joined her husband in the fall at Eustis, Florida, where he had established his practice. In contrast to what she had expected, she found herself trapped in a "very unhappy" marriage. Florida was not her element, even though the surrounding black community tried hard to entertain the new doctor and his wife. "Jack" accused her of no longer being productive and badgered her with "We need money. Why don't you earn some money? You were a writer before we were married." In turn, she pushed him to take the licensing exams in New York and establish a practice in the city. In Florida she did not have that necessary "leaven" of " 'what did you write today' and 'you ought to do this' or 'you ought to do the other.' "

In Florida no "news" from the large urban centers filtered down, and without essential input Bennett's column ended abruptly. Psychologically the Florida move stifled her creative muse. She gained sixty-nine pounds in a three-year period and published very little. When the Jacksons finally returned to Hemstead, Long Island, in 1930, the Harlem Renaissance had given way to the Great Depression. Yet, in spite of the financial crunch created by the bank holiday closings in 1932-1933, the Jacksons lived reasonably well, and Bennett returned to a semblance of the life she had known. She channeled her energies into work with New Deal era federal support programs such as the WPA's Federal Writers Project and Federal Art Project. Friends came out to the Jacksons' "country place" to visit and to party, but much of the Jackson gaiety was false because of strained relations.

An untitled, unfinished, autobiographical short story dramatized the Jacksons' domestic problems. The protagonist's husband, a doctor, is drinking himself to death; his wife is on the verge of killing him or killing herself. Like the Jacksons, this fictional couple suffers financial losses and fears being unable to make house payments or repay their loan. "Each night they went to bed sick with worry. That we must not lose our home became an obsession." But the Jacksons did lose their home, and Alfred "Jack" Jackson died young, in the early 1930s.

In 1937, when the Harlem Community Art Center, the largest of the Federal Art Projects, opened, Bennett served as assistant to Director Au-

Anna Williams, Fannie Keene, Ruth E. Steber, Gwendolyn Bennett, Geraldine Sweeney, and Ollie De Loach at a benefit dance for the Harlem Art Center at the Savoy Ballroom on 24 May 1939 (Morgan and Marvin Smith photo, courtesy of the Schomburg Center for Research in Black Culture, the New York Public Library, Astor, Lenox and Tilden Foundations)

gusta Savage. Within a year she was director of a thriving center. Her success ended when headlines such as the following appeared in several newspapers: "Suspend the HAC Head in Red Probe!" "Miss Gwendolyn Bennett Suspended on Word from Washington!" (*Amsterdam News*, 26 April 1941).

Following her suspension as director of the Harlem Community Art Center in 1941, Bennett taught and served on the administrative staff of the Jefferson School for Democracy. In 1943 she became director of the George Washington Carver School. Jefferson and Carver, both accused of being subversive "Communist front" organizations, were investigated by the House Committee on Un-American Activities. The negative publicity nearly destroyed Bennett's spirit and forced her from public life permanently. In the mid 1940s Bennett worked anonymously as a secretary for the Consumers Union. Upon her retirement, she moved to Kutztown, Pennsylvania, where she spent her re-

maining years as an antique collector and dealer with her second husband, Richard Crosscup. One year after Crosscup's death, Bennett died on 30 May 1981.

Few artists can work, let alone work well, under the kinds of pressure that beset Gwendolyn Bennett. She started out with three strikes against her: she was black, a woman, and an artist. She compounded her problems by being an artist divided, unable to find a center within and unable to secure the ones she built outside. As a consequence, Bennett's talents, as either writer or painter, never had a chance to mature. Her activities and her accomplishments cannot be neatly separated; the tensions animating her private life color all her public productions, all her art.

References:

Elton C. Fax, *Seventeen Black Artists* (New York: Dodd, Mead, 1971), pp. 23-24, 173;

Gloria Hull, "Black Women Poets from Wheatley to Walker," *Negro American Literature Forum,* 9 (Fall 1975): 91-96;

Abby Arthur Johnson and Ronald Maberry Johnson, *Propaganda and Aesthetics: The Literary Politics of Afro-American Magazines in the Twentieth Century* (Amherst: University of Massachusetts Press, 1979), pp. 55-56;

Charles S. Johnson, "A Note on the New Literary Movement," *Opportunity,* 4 (March 1926): 80;

David Levering Lewis, *When Harlem was in Vogue* (New York: Knopf, 1981), pp. 94-95, 105, 122-123;

William F. McDonald, *Federal Relief Administration and the Arts* (Columbus: Ohio State University Press, 1969);

Margaret Perry, *Silence to the Drums: A Survey of the Literature of the Harlem Renaissance* (Westport, Conn.: Greenwood Press, 1976);

James A. Porter, *Modern Negro Art* (New York: Dryden Press, 1943), p. 130.

Papers:

Bennett's papers are housed at the Schomburg Center for Research in Black Culture, the New York Public Library. Letters from Gwendolyn Bennett are included in the Countee Cullen papers at Dillard University, the James Weldon Johnson Collection at Yale University, and the Moorland-Spingarn Research Center at Howard University.

Arna Bontemps

Kirkland C. Jones
Lamar University

See also the Bontemps entry in *DLB 48, American Poets, 1880-1945, Second Series.*

BIRTH: Alexandria, Louisiana, 13 October 1902, to Paul Bismark and Maria Carolina Pembroke Bontemps.

EDUCATION: A.B., Pacific Union College, 1923; M.L.S., Graduate School of Library Science, University of Chicago, 1943.

MARRIAGE: 26 August 1926 to Alberta Johnson; children: Joan Marie, Paul Bismark, Poppy Alberta, Camille Ruby, Constance Rebecca, and Arna Alexander.

AWARDS AND HONORS: *Opportunity* magazine Alexander Pushkin Poetry Prize, 1926, 1927; *Crisis* poetry prize, 1927; *Opportunity* magazine short story prize, 1932; Rosenwald Fellowships, 1938, 1942; Guggenheim Fellowships, 1949, 1954; Jane Addams Children's Book Award for *The Story of the Negro* (1948), 1956; James L. Dow Award, with Jack Conroy, for *Anyplace But Here,* 1967; L.H.D., Morgan State College, 1969; L.H.D., Berea College, 1973.

DEATH: Nashville, Tennessee, 4 June 1973.

BOOKS: *God Sends Sunday* (New York: Harcourt, Brace, 1931);

Popo and Fifina, Children of Haiti, by Bontemps and Langston Hughes (New York: Macmillan, 1932);

You Can't Pet a Possum (New York: Morrow, 1934);

Black Thunder (New York: Macmillan, 1936);

Sad-Faced Boy (Boston: Houghton Mifflin, 1937);

Drums at Dusk (New York: Macmillan, 1939; London: Harrap, 1940);

The Fast Sooner Hound, by Bontemps and Jack Conroy (Boston: Houghton Mifflin, 1942);

They Seek A City, by Bontemps and Conroy (Garden City: Doubleday, 1945); revised and enlarged as *Anyplace But Here* (New York: Hill & Wang, 1966);

We Have Tomorrow (Boston: Houghton Mifflin, 1945);

Slappy Hooper, the Wonderful Sign Painter, by Bontemps and Conroy (Boston: Houghton Mifflin, 1946);

Story of the Negro (New York: Knopf, 1948; enlarged, 1955);

Arna Bontemps (courtesy of the Prints and Photographs Collection, Moorland-Spingarn Research Center, Howard University)

George Washington Carver (Evanston, Ill.: Row, Peterson, 1950);

Chariot in the Sky; A Story of the Jubilee Singers (Philadelphia: Winston, 1951);

Sam Patch, the High, Wide, & Handsome Jumper, by Bontemps and Conroy (Boston: Houghton Mifflin, 1951);

The Story of George Washington Carver (New York: Grosset & Dunlap, 1954);

Lonesome Boy (Boston: Houghton Mifflin, 1955);

Frederick Douglass: Slave, Fighter, Freeman (New York: Knopf, 1959);

100 Years of Negro Freedom (New York: Dodd, Mead, 1961);

Personals (London: Breman, 1963);

Famous Negro Athletes (New York: Dodd, Mead, 1964);

I Too Sing America, by Bontemps and Hughes (Dortmund: Verlag Lambert Lensing, 1964);

Mr. Kelso's Lion (Philadelphia: Lippincott, 1970);

Free At Last; The Life of Frederick Douglass (New York: Dodd, Mead, 1971);

Young Booker; Booker T. Washington's Early Days (New York: Dodd, Mead, 1972);

The Old South; "A Summer Tragedy" and Other Stories of the Thirties (New York: Dodd, Mead, 1973).

PLAY PRODUCTIONS: *St. Louis Woman,* by Bontemps and Countee Cullen, New York, Martin Beck Theatre, 30 March 1946;

Free and Easy, Amsterdam, Theatre Carré, 15 December, 1949.

OTHER: *Father of the Blues: An Autobiography by W. C. Handy,* edited by Bontemps (New York: Macmillan, 1941);

Golden Slippers: An Anthology of Negro Poetry for Young Readers, edited by Bontemps (New York & London: Harper, 1941);

The Poetry of the Negro, 1746-1949, edited by Bontemps and Langston Hughes (Garden City: Doubleday, 1949); revised and enlarged as *The Poetry of the Negro, 1746-1970* (Garden City: Doubleday, 1970);

The Book of Negro Folklore, edited by Bontemps and Hughes (New York: Dodd, Mead, 1958);

James Weldon Johnson, *The Autobiography of an Ex-Colored Man,* introduction by Bontemps (New York: Hill & Wang, 1960);

American Negro Poetry, edited by Bontemps (New York: Hill & Wang, 1963; revised, 1974);

"The Negro Renaissance: Jean Toomer and the Harlem Writers of the 1920's," in *Anger, and Beyond,* edited by Herbert Hill (New York: Harper & Row, 1966), pp. 20-36;

Hold Fast to Dreams: Poems Old and New, edited by Bontemps (Chicago: Follett, 1969);

Great Slave Narratives, edited, with an introduction, by Bontemps (Boston: Beacon, 1969);

St. Louis Woman, by Bontemps and Countee Cullen, in *Black Theatre,* edited by Lindsay Patterson (New York: Dodd, Mead, 1971);

The Harlem Renaissance Remembered: Essays, edited, with a memoir, by Bontemps (New York: Dodd, Mead, 1972).

PERIODICAL PUBLICATIONS:
POETRY
"Hope," *Crisis,* 28 (August 1924): 176;

"Spring Music," *Crisis,* 30 (June 1925): 93;

"Dirge," *Crisis,* 32 (May 1926): 25;

"Holiday," *Crisis,* 32 (July 1926): 121;

"Nocturne at Bethesda," *Crisis,* 33 (December 1926): 66;

"Tree," *Crisis,* 34 (April 1927): 48.

FICTION

"A Summer Tragedy," *Opportunity,* 11 (June 1933): 174-177, 190;

"Barrel Staves," *New Challenge,* 1 (March 1934): 16-24.

NONFICTION

"Who Recreates Significant Moments in History," *Opportunity,* 22 (Summer 1944): 126-139;

"Two Harlems," *American Scholar,* 14 (April 1945): 167-173;

"Langston Hughes," *Ebony,* 2 (October 1946): 19-23;

"White Southern Friends of the Negro," *Negro Digest* (August 1950): 13-16;

"Buried Treasures of Negro Art," *Negro Digest* (December 1950): 17-21;

"How I Told My Child About Race," *Negro Digest* (May 1951): 80-83;

"Chesnutt Papers at Fisk," *Library Journal,* 77 (1952): 1288;

"Facing a Dilemma," *Saturday Review,* 35 (16 February 1952): 23ff;

"Bud Blooms," *Saturday Review,* 35 (20 September 1952): 15ff;

"Harlem Renaissance," *Saturday Review,* 36 (28 March 1953): 15-16;

"Three Portraits of the Negro," *Saturday Review,* 36 (28 March 1953): 15-16;

"New Black Renaissance," *Negro Digest* (November 1961): 52-58;

"Evolution of Our Conscience," *Saturday Review,* 44 (9 December 1961): 52-53;

"Minority's New Militant Spirit," *Saturday Review,* 45 (14 July 1962): 30;

"Harlem: the Beautiful Years: A Memoir," *Negro Digest* (January 1965): 62-65;

"Why I Returned," *Harper's,* 230 (April 1965): 176-182;

"Harlem in the Twenties," *Crisis,* 73 (October 1966): 431-434ff;

"Langston Hughes: He Spoke of Rivers," *Freedomways,* 8 (Spring 1968): 140-143.

Poet, critic, playwright, novelist, historian, educator, librarian, writer of children's books, Arna Bontemps was also a voracious reader, devoted family man, pioneering Afro-American literary figure, and, above all, a champion of freedom for all people and of dignity for the individual. A writer who began to achieve prominence in the late days of the Harlem Renaissance, the multifaceted Bontemps exercised his productive genius into the 1970s, touching black and white reading audiences with a wide range of works that draw from his experience of black American culture and from his own life. Nine months younger than one of his closest friends, Langston Hughes, whom he first met in Harlem in 1924, Bontemps was not only Hughes's physical look-alike and his intellectual twin, but their names are often linked in twentieth-century literary history as coauthors, anthologists, and like-minded innovators of black American literature.

Arnaud Wendell Bontemps was born in Alexandria, Louisiana, on 13 October 1902 to Paul Bismark and Maria Carolina Pembroke Bontemps. His parents were of Creole stock, the source for the dialect Bontemps used in some of his early writing and that he liked to employ in his correspondence with Langston Hughes. As a result of several racially motivated incidents, including one in which a group of white men threatened to beat him up, Paul Bontemps moved his family to Los Angeles, California; Arna was only three at the time. When Bontemps was twelve, his mother died, but not before she had instilled in her son a love for books. A schoolteacher until the time of her marriage, she introduced young Arna to a world beyond the skilled labor that dominated his father's life.

The older of two children, Bontemps would experience recurring conflict with his father, who wanted him to continue the brick masonry trade into a fourth generation of Bontempses; he could never understand why the son for whom he had so many hopes wanted to write literature. Bontemps's father and his Uncle Buddy, his grandmother's younger brother who had moved to California to live with the family, would prove to be significant influences upon the young Arna after his mother's death. Bontemps's father was negative toward his writing; however, Uncle Buddy exercised the most wholesome influence upon his personal and literary development. Buddy's warmth and sense of humor were a sharp and welcome contrast to the conservative Paul Bontemps. Though Paul respected Buddy's ability to quote Thomas Hood's "The Vision of Eugene Aram" and frequently praised him for his ability to spell and read, he was horrified by Buddy's alcoholism and his association with the lower classes. Bontemps admired Buddy enough to use him as the model for one of the characters in his first novel. Through Buddy, Bontemps was able to embrace the folk heritage that would form the basis for many of his works, for he loved dialect stories, preacher stories, and ghost stories. Buddy "half-believed in signs and

FISK UNIVERSITY
NASHVILLE 8, TENNESSEE

OFFICE OF THE LIBRARIAN   May 25, 1951

Miss Jean Blackwell, Curator
Schomburg Collection
The New York Public Library
104 West 136th Street
New York, New York

Dear Jean:

Eric Waldron was alive and kicking at the last report. My
impression is that he is in London. In any case, I believe
it was Wallace Thurman who died about the same time Bud
Fisher did.

Survival qualities are not necessarily synonymous with
excellence. Some good books live and some don't. Most bad
books die, but now and then one survives. Another thing
to remember is that literary tastes change. The popularity
of a writer of the past is likely to rise and fall with
these changes in public taste. Bud's case can probably be
explained within these generalities.

We would certainly be interested in an exhibition of Fisher
materials at some time during the next school year if Pearl
Fisher or anyone else would be interested in cooperating. I
think institutions like Fisk are the natural places in which
to perpetuate literary reputations like Bud's A first rate
showing of relevant materials would promote lively class discussion.

Perhaps it is our role as university library that causes us to
receive a steady stream of questions about Negro literature and
history. Your leaflet can be sent in answer to inquiries about
other Negro collections - since I am running out of reprints of
my article.

Ever sincerely,

Arna Bontemps
Librarian

AB:j

Bontemps's response to Jean Blackwell's queries includes an evaluation of Rudolph Fisher's work that was largely shared by Harlem Renaissance writers (courtesy of the Schomburg Center for Research in Black Culture, the New York Public Library, Astor, Lenox and Tilden Foundations)

charms and mumbo-jumbo, and he believed whole-heartedly in ghosts."

As an adolescent, Bontemps helped to support himself after his mother's death by working as a newsboy and a gardener. Between 1917 and 1920 his father sent him to San Fernando Academy, a white boarding school, with the admonition not to "go up there acting colored," which was a frequent, embarrassing memory for Bontemps. He viewed his father's decision and the subject matter as efforts to make him forget his blackness, and he suspected—as he confirmed during his college years—that he was being "miseducated." While a student at Pacific Union College in Angwin, California, in the early 1920s, Bontemps worked as a post office clerk and was in the glee club. His singing was perhaps a conscious attempt to combat the miseducation, to retain something that he could identify as distinctly black. Of his college experience, Bontemps later asserted: "Had I not gone home summers and hobnobbed with Negroes, I would have finished college without knowing that any Negro other than Paul Laurence Dunbar ever wrote a poem. I would have come out imagining that the story of the Negro could be told in two short paragraphs: a statement about jungle people in Africa and an equally brief account of the slavery issue in American history."

Bontemps graduated from Pacific Union in 1923, the year before he launched his literary career. Although he had plans to complete a Ph.D. degree in English, the Depression years, family responsibilities, and the demands of his writing contracts with publishing houses, coupled with the rigors of full-time employment, prevented him from following that course. He eventually earned a masters degree in library science from the University of Chicago in 1943.

In the summer of 1924, at twenty-one, Bontemps published a poem, "Hope," in *Crisis*, a journal which was instrumental in advancing the careers of most of the young writers associated with the Harlem Renaissance. Reminiscent of the works of Countee Cullen in its introspective bent, the poem favors the personal over the communal or nationalistic concerns of the Renaissance:

Lone and dismal; hushed and dark,
    Upon the waves floats an empty bark.

The stars go out; the raindrops fall,
    And through the night comes a ghostly call—

My lone and dismal life's a-float

Upon the seas like an empty boat.
. . . .
And just beyond my bark that drifts,
    Moonbeams steal through the kindly rifts.

Clearly the publication of the poem reflected the prevailing trend of encouraging young writers, for it seems slight from a later vantage point.

In addition to making his literary debut in 1924, Bontemps moved from California to New York to accept a teaching job at the Harlem Academy. In 1926 and again in 1927, he won *Opportunity* magazine's Alexander Pushkin Poetry Prize. The winning piece in 1926 was "Golgotha Is a Mountain," an atavistic poem connecting Bontemps to other poets of the Harlem Renaissance who expressed a longing for their roots in Africa. Civilizations rise and fall, the poet asserts, and under each mountain, there is a pile of wreckage representing one of them or lost treasures to be derived from them.

There are mountains in Africa too.
Treasure is buried there:
gold and precious stones
and moulded glory.
Lush grass is growing there
sinking before the wind.
Black men are bowing
naked in that grass
digging with their fingers.
I am one of them:
Those mountains should be ours. . . .
Oh, brothers, it is not long!
Dust shall yet devour the stones
but we shall be here when they are gone.

As in Hughes's "The Negro Speaks of Rivers," Bontemps points to the enduring quality of black people as the trait that will enable them to survive, even if in quiet, contained ways, when others are more conspicuously succeeding.

Bontemps's winning *Opportunity* poem in 1927 was "The Return," which combines the personal and the racial in making a returned lover a symbol of atavism: "Darkness brings the jungle to our room:/the throb of rain is the throb of muffled drums/This is a night of love/retained from those lost nights our fathers slept/in huts." The repeated phrase "let us go back" suggests the alien-and-exile theme apparent in much of the poetry from Harlem Renaissance writers. Jungles, rain, the throbbing sound of drums, and sensuousness combine to create the new world longing for a more primitive time.

While winning poetry contests in 1926, Bontemps paused for a more personal event; on 26 August, he married Alberta Johnson. Over the years, they would have six children.

Bontemps continued his winning streak in poetry contests by claiming first place in the 1927 *Crisis* contest for "Nocturne at Bethesda." The poem depicts a black man waiting at that ancient pool for some kind of revelation or cleansing. Ultimately he reflects the twentieth-century demise in faith in concluding that previously sustaining forces no longer have the power to heal or transform:

> You do not hear, Bethesda.
> O still green water in a stagnant pool!
> Love abandoned you and me alike.
> There was a day you held a rich full moon
> upon your heart and listened to the words
> of men now dead and saw the angels fly.
> There is a simple story on your face:
> years have wrinkled you. I know, Bethesda!
> You are sad. It is the same with me.

The poem continues Bontemps's concern for older times and ancient places, characteristic of a romantic vein that runs throughout his works.

Although he did not live in Harlem for long, Bontemps met, worked with, influenced, and was influenced by several of the important figures of the Harlem Renaissance, including Langston Hughes, Jean Toomer, Claude McKay, James Weldon Johnson, and Countee Cullen. He also knew W. E. B. Du Bois and Zora Neale Hurston. But his association with literary figures was not confined to writers of color. He formed friendships with Willa Cather, Katherine Anne Porter (whose farm he visited), Carson McCullers, Sinclair Lewis, Ernest Hemingway, Robert Lowell, and Carl Van Vechten. During and after the 1940s and 1950s, Bontemps was also acquainted with Owen Dodson, Chester Himes, and Melvin Tolson, and he heartily praised the advent of young James Baldwin, asserting that Baldwin "couldn't write badly if he tried."

Bontemps taught at Harlem Academy until 1931, the year that also saw the publication of his first book. *God Sends Sunday,* published by Harcourt, Brace, is the story of the most successful black jockey in St. Louis. Little Augie, who likes fast money and flashy clothes, pursues an epicurean life-style until he dilutes his own success. He earns notoriety for his luck during the 1890s, then loses his ability to win and becomes a penniless wanderer. The book's language is unusually rhythmic, bordering, at times, on the poetic. One critic commented that "there is an undulating movement to this prose that is closely kin to the author's dignified, well-turned poems." Critics recognized the authentic rendering of the "Negro language" as Bontemps's most outstanding talent. That emotion-charged economy of speech peculiar to Louisiana Creoles imparts uniqueness to Bontemps's fiction. Life in "the quarter" is always vividly and economically depicted, and the dialogue is always faithful. Though set in the "Gay Nineties," the story does not degenerate into a minstrel show. The characters are real, never maudlin.

Taking an unusual approach in Afro-American literature, the novel offers a look at the sporting life of blacks as well as at the temptations that invariably alter their successes. Not all of the reviews of *God Sends Sunday* were positive, however; in a 1931 *Crisis* article Du Bois condemned the novel for its portrayal of the less complimentary side of life in black America. The reviewer for the *Boston Transcript* asserted that the book "is less narrative than descriptive and has no great significance," but he commented that Bontemps deserved "to be encouraged." Still, most critics, led by the reviewer for *Books,* hailed Bontemps as "one of the most important writers of his race."

Critical acclaim notwithstanding, Bontemps liked the story well enough to collaborate with Countee Cullen on turning it into a play. *St. Louis Woman,* written in 1939, combines song and folk beliefs to illustrate the precarious state of luck surrounding Little Augie's racing success as well as his romantic endeavors. Augie wins consistently and prances like a bantam rooster until a rival, killed by a jealous girlfriend, curses him as he dies. Augie cannot win any longer and disappears for a period of regeneration, after which he is able to overcome superstition, reclaim the hand of the woman he loves, and win again. The play premiered at the Martin Beck Theatre in New York on 30 March 1946 and ran for 113 performances.

Bontemps moved from Harlem Academy to Huntsville, Alabama, in 1931 to teach at Oakwood Junior College, where he was on the faculty until 1934. His success with *Opportunity* continued, and he won the 1932 prize for his short story "A Summer Tragedy." Often anthologized, the story depicts an elderly couple who, unable to escape the cycle of poverty and indebtedness endemic to the sharecropping system, calmly drive their old Ford into a river one day. Jeff Patton has had a paralytic stroke after forty-five years of growing cotton; his

Arna Bontemps (courtesy of the Schomburg Center for Research in Black Culture, the New York Public Library, Astor, Lenox and Tilden Foundations)

condition, combined with his wife Jennie's blindness, makes their future uncertain if not desolate. Having outlived five children, all of whom died in their adult years and within two years of each other, the Pattons cannot expect familial comfort in their aged infirmity. They approach their double suicide by donning their Sunday finery, conquering their last-minute doubts, and driving stoically into the water. They consistently refer to their journey as a "trip," bringing to mind the black folk religious connection of crossing the Jordan River into heaven, and the car itself has connotations of the "chariot" mentioned in the spiritual "Swing Low Sweet Chariot." The horror of the Pattons' act belies their final quiet dignity, thereby painting a bleak vision of lives lived under a system that Richard Wright would graphically imprint upon the minds of Americans a few years later in *Uncle Tom's Children* (1938).

Bontemps's situation in Alabama epitomized his career: he was always short of funds and rarely found a comfortable place to work. In Huntsville, he and his family lived through almost insufferable summer heat and damp and piercing winter cold.

Their frame cottage had its hot water tank situated above the ceiling, attached to the roof, to give "plenty of hot water without any fire" as the builder explained it. Bontemps was forced to type out-of-doors on the house's shady side, on a round table, armed with a large bath towel and a flyswatter. Yet his persistence brought results.

While in Huntsville, Bontemps turned his attention to the writing of children's books, partly out of a belief that the younger audience was more reachable: "I began to suspect that it was fruitless for a Negro in the United States to address serious writing to my generation, and I began to consider the alternative of trying to reach young readers not yet hardened or grown insensitive to man's inhumanity to man, as it is called." He believed that through his juvenile books he could contribute more positive images of blacks to American literature. Through these books he was able to minister to the needs of youth, while satisfying his own need to write something that was lasting.

His first juvenile book, *Popo and Fifina* (1932), a story of two black children in Haiti, was written in collaboration with Langston Hughes. It recounts the everyday occurrences in the children's lives, including a move from the farm to a village where their father hopes to earn a living as a fisherman. The reviewer for the *New York Times* lauded the simplicity and innocence of the story as well as the obvious hand of Bontemps as poet: "The book has some of the simple homelike atmosphere that has made 'The Dutch Twins' such a favorite. Older readers will recognize that the beauty of the style has much to do in holding the reader's attention, and younger readers will unconsciously be held by the same quality. 'Popo and Fifina' tempts us to wish that all our travel books for children might be written by poets. The illustrations are charmingly childlike and humorous."

In 1934, his last year in Huntsville and at Oakwood Junior College, Bontemps published *You Can't Pet a Possum,* the second of his juvenile books. It is the story of the adventures of Shine Boy and his dog Butch, who manage to get in and out of trouble in Birmingham, Alabama, and who are frequently rescued by Shine Boy's Aunt Cindy.

Over the next forty years, Bontemps continued writing for children and editing more than

fifteen works for children and adolescent readers. Among his books for older girls and boys, *We Have Tomorrow* (1945), a collection of career stories of successful blacks, offers positive adult models. *Frederick Douglass: Slave, Fighter, Freeman* (1959), a biography Bontemps wrote for a youthful audience, refers to Douglass as the first great Negro abolitionist. The work stresses his boyhood and youth with only slight attention to his adult life. Bontemps wrote a sequel to this biography, *Free at Last; The Life of Frederick Douglass* (1971), which follows Douglass from the time that he escaped from slavery, at about age twenty, through his career as an abolitionist and political reformer. Some critics accused Bontemps of neglecting the intellectual side of Douglass's character. Possibly they did not account for the fact that Bontemps aimed this work at a secondary school audience. A 1972 biography by Bontemps is aimed at a similar audience. *Young Booker; Booker T. Washington's Early Days* is an account of Washington's early life and his rise to prominence. It ends with his 1895 address at the Atlanta Exposition. Although the work does give some attention to the forces that shaped Washing-

Dust jacket for Bontemps's 1970 children's book

ton's personality and determined his social and educational decisions, the reader detects Bontemps's genuine striving to appeal to the juvenile reader. The book's abrupt ending bothered critics, but many of them liked its readable, lively style.

A new teaching assignment took Bontemps from Huntsville and Oakwood Junior College to Chicago and Shiloh Academy, where he taught from 1935 until his resignation in 1937. He then went to work for the Illinois Writer's Project, a division of the Works Progress Administration. It was here that he met Jack Conroy, also a member of the Writer's Project, who became his frequent literary collaborator, mostly on the children's books. This acquaintance developed into a lifelong friendship.

In 1936 Bontemps published *Black Thunder,* his most celebrated novel. It is a historical novel dealing with the theme of revolt through the recounting of a slave narrative. The novel fictionalizes the "Gabriel Insurrection" that occurred in 1800 in Henrico County, Virginia, near Richmond. The hero of *Black Thunder* is Gabriel Prosser, an eighteenth-century insurrectionist in the state of Virginia. A mischievous slave is subjected to punishment that exceeds the usual limits of cruelty; as a result, Gabriel plans a rebellion and is able to gain widespread support for it from slaves and free blacks as well as from a few whites. His intention is to take over the arsenal at Richmond, confiscate the weapons, and seize the town. Following the court records from the historical case, Bontemps depicts the failure of the rebellion due to a torrential rainstorm coupled with a last minute betrayal. The rebellion is suppressed about halfway through the novel, and the remainder of the story is devoted to describing the capture and punishment of those involved in it.

When the novel appeared, Wright praised it as the only novel of its kind that dealt forthrightly with the black American's historical and revolutionary traditions. Other reviewers considered it "good and powerful," "truer than most history," and "a sort of prose spiritual . . . movingly sung." Again Bontemps's use of language was a critical focus, and his dialect was called "exceptionally accurate."

Although *Black Thunder* is Bontemps's best and most popular novel, it was not written under the most congenial of circumstances. Bontemps and his family were "temporarily and uncomfortably quartered" in California with his father and stepmother. He did not have space for his typewriter and had written the book in longhand on top of a folded-down sewing machine in the extra bedroom of his parents' house, listening to his father's admonition that he should have done something more "solid" with his life, like become a brick mason. Such conditions must have made writing even harder for the man who continually castigated himself for being a slow producer.

In his private correspondence, Bontemps frequently referred to the difficulty he experienced throughout his career in meeting his writing deadlines as being the result of his own "plodding" style (especially when he compared himself to Hughes); however, the pressure under which Bontemps wrote was not the result of slow, laborious thinking, but it was the direct result of having to write under unfavorable conditions, many much worse than those he experienced in Alabama. In 1937 he remarked in a letter to Hughes, "I suppose I'm cut out to write under persecution, if I write at all." Of his part in a 1939 collaborative writing project with Hughes he expressed the hope that he could do his "end of the work a bit more swiftly than I usually do." And during the following year he was still not satisfied with his rate of production: "I'm working hard (as I have time) but progressing slowly on my novel. My New Year's resolve is to perk up."

Bontemps ended his early teaching endeavors in 1938 to pursue more actively his possibilities as a writer. He accepted a Rosenwald Fellowship for a study tour in the Caribbean and continued to write and travel when the grant was renewed. His third novel, *Drums at Dusk,* came out that year. Also devoted to a slave uprising, the novel depicts the revolt of blacks in Haiti which occurred simultaneously with the French Revolution. The hero is a young Frenchman who is in sympathy with the blacks. With the help of his black friend Toussaint, he is able to avoid the revenge of the rebellious blacks and escapes to safety with the girl he loves.

Drums at Dusk is less skillfully developed than *Black Thunder,* and it did not fare as well with the critics. Bontemps is at times more interested in creating a Haitian ambience than in following his narration. One reviewer commented that "the book as a whole suffers from a style that is too lush and romantic and from writing that is often careless." Another wished for something "larger in scale" on an obviously rich subject matter.

In 1943, upon the completion of his masters degree in library science, Bontemps became librarian at Fisk University in Nashville, Tennessee, a post he would hold continuously until 1965, after which time he would return intermittently to the school. As head librarian at Fisk, Bontemps pur-

Charles S. Johnson and Arna Bontemps (courtesy of the Schomburg Center for Research in Black Culture, the New York Public Library, Astor, Lenox and Tilden Foundations)

chased early materials on the black experience that are now classics in the field. He enlarged the black collection started when the school was founded and which had been strengthened by Arthur Schomburg. His friendship with Hughes also enabled him to establish a Langston Hughes Collection, and he succeeded in getting the papers of such Harlem Renaissance figures as Jean Toomer, James Weldon Johnson, Charles S. Johnson, and Countee Cullen. One of Bontemps's finest accomplishments at Fisk was his collection honoring George Gershwin, an effort he began shortly after taking the job. He succeeded, therefore, in making the Fisk University Library an essential resource for the study of Afro-American life and culture.

Perhaps Bontemps's most lasting contribution to Afro-American literary history is the number of scholarly anthologies he compiled and edited, alone and in collaboration with Hughes. These anthologies primarily appeal to secondary school students and college undergraduates, a fact that has

kept them in use since they were first issued. *Golden Slippers* (1941) is a collection of poems by black authors that are suitable for young readers.

In 1958 Bontemps and Hughes published *The Book of Negro Folklore,* a collection of animal tales, animal rhymes, slave narratives, superstitions and magic, preacher stories, ghost stories, sermons, prayers, and folk songs, including blues, spirituals, work songs, and gospel songs. The volume also includes essays written by novelist Julia Peterkin (on black burial societies), Sterling Brown (on poetry in the blues), and Zora Neale Hurston (on folk hero High John de Conqueror). In an effort to connect past and present, Bontemps and Hughes also include a section on contemporary urban humor (Harlem jive); anecdotes from jazz musicians; and tales, songs, and short stories told, sung, or written in the folk manner. The book has frequently been used in college courses.

American Negro Poetry, edited by Bontemps, came out in 1963 and was revised posthumously in

1974. It includes selected works of fifty-six poets of the seventy years leading up to the date of publication. This anthology breaks only a minimum of new ground, for more than a third of the poems had appeared in the 1949 volume by Bontemps and Hughes (*The Poetry of the Negro, 1746-1949*). The 1963 volume does, of course, include many later poets: Robert Hayden, Margaret Danner, Samuel Allen, LeRoi Jones (Amiri Baraka), and Gwendolyn Brooks. The verses of Richard Wright and Frank Yerby are also included.

In 1969 Bontemps published *Hold Fast to Dreams: Poems Old and New,* an anthology of poetry selected from English and American authors; the title was lifted from a poem by Hughes. The volume has no notes to tell the reader where, specifically, the poets are from or to which periods they belong. No doubt Bontemps wanted to let the poems speak for themselves, because the absence of chronological and biographical structuring seems deliberate. The volume appeals to all ages and is a unique blend of works by blacks and whites; Countee Cullen, Owen Dodson, and Gwendolyn Brooks appear with William Shakespeare, Amy Lowell, and Ezra Pound. *Great Slave Narratives,* an anthology of reactions to slavery seen through black eyes, also appeared in 1969. *The Harlem Renaissance Remembered* was published in 1972. It consists of edited essays with a memoir by Bontemps. He provides an eyewitness description of the period and includes discussions by a dozen other writers of the 1920s.

Bontemps also collected his own poetry later in his life, publishing *Personals* in London in 1963. The volume contains an introductory comment on the poet's arrival in New York in 1924 and his reaction in the 1940s to the Harlem he had known in the 1920s. He also comments on what the young writers of the 1920s saw themselves trying to accomplish and how they were guided—and sometimes misguided—by the opinions of individuals outside the race.

Personals contains twenty-three poems, many of which had appeared earlier. Among them are Bontemps's most well-known poems, including "Gethsemane," "Southern Mansion," "Golgotha Is a Mountain," "Nocturne at Bethesda," and "A Black Man Talks of Reaping," the latter two perhaps the most frequently anthologized. "A Black Man Talks of Reaping" explores the question of labor without reward that has so characterized the status of blacks in America. Although the speaker has "scattered seed enough to plant the land/in rows from Canada to Mexico," there is no healthy

Dust jacket for Bontemps's retrospective anthology covering the Harlem Renaissance

yield that he can pass on to his children:

Yet what I sowed and what the orchard yields
my brother's sons are gathering stalk and root;
small wonder then my children glean in fields
they have not sown, and feed on bitter fruit.

The sentiment Bontemps expresses here echoes that of Countee Cullen in "From the Dark Tower," in which he asserts: "We shall not always plant while others reap/The golden increment of bursting fruit,/Not always countenance, abject and mute,/That lesser men should hold their brothers cheap."

In 1964, eight years before he reached the mandatory retirement age of seventy, Bontemps retired from his job at Fisk. For about a year after leaving this post he served as director of university relations and acting librarian until a new head librarian could be found. In 1966 he taught courses in black history and black literature at the University of Illinois, Chicago Circle, and in 1969 he accepted a position at Yale as lecturer and curator of the James Weldon Johnson Collection, where he remained through the 1971 school term. Returning afterwards to Nashville, he began writing his autobiography, a work he never finished. He died of a heart attack in Nashville, Tennessee, on 4 June 1973.

Arna Bontemps, perhaps as overshadowed by Langston Hughes as Zora Neale Hurston was by Richard Wright, contributed to the perpetuation of what, in his early years, was a small interest in Afro-American life and culture. His pioneering collecting efforts have allowed later scholars and writers easier access to research materials, and his early interest in children's literature stretches forth to contemporary writers like Virginia Hamilton. As critic Arthur P. Davis asserts, Bontemps "kept flowing that trickle of interest in Negro American literature—that trickle which is now a torrent."

Letters:

Arna Bontemps-Langston Hughes Letters, 1925-1967, edited by Charles Nichols (New York: Dodd, Mead, 1980).

Bibliographies:

James A. Page, *Selected Black American Authors: An Illustrated Bio-Bibliography* (Boston: G. K. Hall, 1977), p. 19;

Robert E. Fleming, *James Weldon Johnson and Arna Wendell Bontemps: A Reference Guide* (Boston: G. K. Hall, 1978).

References:

Robert A. Bone, *The Negro Novel in America* (New Haven & London: Yale University Press, 1958), pp. 120-123;

Jack Conroy, "Memories of Arna Bontemps: Friend and Collaborator," *American Libraries,* 5 (December 1974): 602-606;

Hugh M. Gloster, *Negro Voices in American Fiction* (Chapel Hill: University of North Carolina Press, 1948);

James M. McPherson, et al., *Blacks in America: Bibliographical Essays* (Garden City: Doubleday, 1971);

Ione Rider Morrison, "Arna Bontemps," *Horn Book,* 15 (January 1939): 13-19;

Darwin T. Turner, *Black American Literature: Poetry* (Columbus, Ohio: Merrill, 1969);

Dorothy Weil, "Folklore Motifs in Arna Bontemps' *Black Thunder*," *Southern Folklore Quarterly,* 35 (March 1971): 1-14;

Roger Whitlow, *Black American Literature: A Critical History* (Chicago: Nelson-Hall, 1973);

James D. Young, *Black Writers in the Thirties* (Baton Rouge: Louisiana State University Press, 1973).

Papers:

A collection of Arna Bontemps's papers is located in the George Arents Research Library, Syracuse University. Several oral history audiotapes, interviews, correspondence, photographs, and manuscripts are located in the Fisk University Library Special Collections. The Bontemps-Hughes letters are located in the James Weldon Johnson Collection at Yale University.

Sterling A. Brown

Joanne V. Gabbin
James Madison University

See also the Brown entry in *DLB 48, American Poets, 1880-1945.*

BIRTH: Washington, D.C., 1 May 1901, to Sterling Nelson and Adelaide Allen Brown.

EDUCATION: B.A., Williams College, 1922; M. A., Harvard University, 1923; Harvard, 1931-1932.

MARRIAGE: September 1927 to Daisy Turnbull; child: John L. Dennis (adopted).

BOOKS: *Outline for the Study of Poetry of American Negroes* (New York: Harcourt, Brace, 1931);
Southern Road (New York: Harcourt, Brace, 1932);
The Negro in American Fiction (Washington, D.C.: Associates in Negro Folk Education, 1937);
Negro Poetry and Drama (Washington, D.C.: Associates in Negro Folk Education, 1937);
The Last Ride of Wild Bill and Eleven Narrative Poems (Detroit: Broadside Press, 1975);
The Collected Poems of Sterling A. Brown, edited by Michael S. Harper (New York: Harper & Row, 1980).

OTHER: "The Blues as Folk Poetry," in *Folk-Say,* volume 1, edited by Benjamin A. Botkin (Norman: University of Oklahoma Press, 1930);
American Stuff; an Anthology of Prose and Verse by Members of the Federal Writers' Project, with Sixteen Prints by the Federal Art Project (New York: Viking, 1937);
"The Negro in Washington," in *Washington City and Capital,* Federal Writers' Project (Washington, D.C.: U.S. Government Printing Office, 1937);
"Long Gone," "Slim in Hell," "Southern Road," "Old Lem," "Break of Day," and "Strong Men," in *The Negro Caravan, Writings by American Negroes,* edited by Brown, Arthur P. Davis, and Ulysses Lee (New York: Dryden Press, 1941);

"Athletics and the Arts," in *The Integration of the Negro into American Society,* Papers of the Fourteenth Annual Conference. Division of Social Sciences, Howard University, edited by E. Franklin Frazier (Washington, D.C.: Howard University Press, 1951), pp. 117-147;
Entries on Matthew Arnold, Charles Baudelaire, Emily Brontë, Robert Burns, Emily Dickinson, Ralph Waldo Emerson, Benjamin Franklin, Robert Frost, Heinrich Heine, A. E. Housman, Thomas Jefferson, Abraham Lincoln, Henry Wadsworth Longfellow, Herman Melville, *Moby-Dick,* Edgar Allan Poe, Henry David Thoreau, Mark Twain, and Walt Whitman, in *The Reader's Companion to World Literature,* edited by Lillian D. Hornstein, G. D. Percy, and others (New York: New American Library, 1956);
Langston Hughes and Arna Bontemps, eds., *The Book of Negro Folklore,* includes poetry by Brown (New York: Dodd, Mead, 1958);
"And/Or," in *American Negro Short Stories,* edited by John Henrik Clarke (New York: Hill & Wang, 1966).

PERIODICAL PUBLICATIONS: "Roland Hayes," *Opportunity,* 3 (June 1925): 173-174;
"Our Literary Audience," *Opportunity,* 8 (February 1930): 42-46;
"Negro Character As Seen by White Authors," *Journal of Negro Education,* 2 (April 1933): 179-203;
"The American Race Problem as Reflected in American Literature," *Journal of Negro Education,* 8 (July 1939): 275-290;
"The Negro Writer and His Publisher," *Quarterly Review of Higher Education Among Negroes,* 9 (July 1941): 7-20;
"Words on a Bus," *South Today,* 7 (Spring 1943): 26-28;
"Spirituals, Blues and Jazz—The Negro in the Lively Arts," *Tricolor,* 3 (April 1945): 62-70;
"Negro Folk Expression," *Phylon,* 11 (Autumn 1950): 318-327;

"Negro Folk Expressions: Spirituals, Seculars, Ballads, and Work Songs," *Phylon,* 14 (Winter 1953): 45-61;

"A Century of Negro Portraiture in American Literature," *Massachusetts Review,* 7 (Winter 1966): 73-96;

"A Son's Return: 'Oh Didn't He Ramble,' " *Kujichaqulia* (November 1973): 4-6.

The importance of Sterling A. Brown in Afro-American literature and culture rests on his position as an innovative poet, a folklorist, and a pioneer critic. He was among the first to identify the foundations of the black aesthetic tradition and, in so doing, saw folk culture as central to the originality and imagination in Afro-American writing. His extensive exploration of folk forms, such as the blues, worksongs, and ballads, led him to experiment in the late 1920s and 1930s with these forms in his own poetry. Aware of the vibrant qualities of folk speech, he rescued black dialect from the

Sterling Brown (courtesy of the Prints and Photographs Collection, Moorland-Spingarn Research Center, Howard University)

wastebins of minstrelsy and successfully demonstrated that it could be used to express more than the proverbial two stops of pathos and humor disparaged by James Weldon Johnson.

Brown was an innovative poet as well as a ground-breaking critic of writing by and about blacks. In a series of pioneering studies which appeared in the 1930s, he gave an insider's view of how social attitudes can affect and often distort the way a group is portrayed. He outrightly rejected the stereotypes and clichés that had come to represent black life and character on the American scene. With the publication of *The Negro in American Fiction* (1937), Brown brought into the liturgy of Afro-American criticism the singular truth that the treatment of an oppressed group in literature parallels its treatment in life, and the greater the incidence of oppression, the greater the degree of misrepresentation and exploitation in literature. In *Negro Poetry and Drama* (1937), Brown moved criticism to a new level of maturity as he demanded of the poet and the playwright that their work bear the full weight of the black aesthetic tradition.

Above all Brown's critical approach has been characterized by the synthesis of European and American literary and folk traditions. As his life nearly coincides with the development of modern Afro-American literature, his creative method and aesthetic philosophy have reached back in time and into the future to make meaningful the complex set of values, sensibilities, and forces that define the black cultural experience. Cognizant of the vagaries of American society in which, for any number of racial and ethnic groups, one culture is learned and the other lived, Brown has synthesized what he could of American and European cultures, has explored his own indigenous culture, and has rejected the negativism that certain segments of the society have attached to blackness.

Brown's gift for bringing together and reconciling diverse social, cultural, and intellectual elements marked his personal and professional life. Born into the black middle class of Washington, D.C., he did not accept its narrow interpretations of privilege and cultivation. Frequently, he was amused at the "dicty air" of some of his upper-class black acquaintances and, in his lighter moments, could effect rather good impersonations of them at their pompous best. Though a man of very fair complexion, Brown recognized the divisiveness of color consciousness. While some of his generation who were as fair as he chose to "pass," he did not consider this option. Ironically, at the height of the black power movement at Howard University, students who thought Brown and his wife were white barred them from a celebration given in his honor. This incident served to convince him more that "any glorification of black that brings about cruelty is bad."

Brown also resisted the pull of class consciousness. Educated at Williams College and Harvard University, he claimed that he received his finest education from the semiliterate farmers and migrant workers of the rural South. It is significant also that, though he was the son of a Howard University dean of religion, he did not confine his referents to the boundaries of a preacher's home; he was as at home with the blues and the jazz sounds of the barrel house as he was with the hymns of the congregational church. He counted among his friends musicians Jelly Roll Morton and Leadbelly, as well as writer Arna Bontemps and American diplomat Ralph Bunche.

Born on 1 May 1901 in a house at Sixth and Fairmount Streets in Washington, D.C., Sterling Allen Brown was the last of six children and the only son born to Adelaide Allen Brown and the Reverend Sterling Nelson Brown. He was raised on the campus of Howard University where his father had taught in the School of Religion since 1892. The year Brown was born his father became the pastor of Lincoln Temple Congregational Church. Brown grew up with accounts of his father's early years in Tennessee, his struggle for an education, and his friendship with noted leaders such as Frederick Douglass, former Congressman John M. Langston, former Senator B. K. Bruce, and Booker T. Washington. Although Brown was impressed by his father's vision and his involvement in the civil rights struggle, he admired another, more personal side of his father which he captured in the poem "After Winter." In these poetic reminiscences of leisure days with him on a farm near Laurel, Maryland, Brown portrayed his father as hopeful, loving, and unmistakably earthy.

For the young boy growing up at Howard University, there were many outstanding figures whom he could emulate. University dean and social historian Kelly Miller; cultural philosopher and critic Alain Locke, whom Brown recalled as "a very slight man with a very big brain"; Montgomery Gregory, director of the Howard Players; and sociologist and activist W. E. B. Du Bois were among them. However, the person who most encouraged Brown's admiration for literature and the cultural heritage of black people was his mother. Adelaide Allen was born and raised in Tennessee and graduated as valedictorian from Fisk University. She

was a skillful reader of poetry and introduced her son to the poems of Henry Wadsworth Longfellow, Robert Burns, and Paul Laurence Dunbar, among others. Brown recalled in a 1973 interview with Steven Jones, "We lived on Eleventh Street then above Lincoln Temple Church, and I remember even now her stopping her sweeping . . . now standing over that broom and reading poetry to me, and she was a good reader, great sense of rhythm."

Receiving his entire elementary education in the public schools of Washington, D.C., Brown attended Dunbar High School, then noted for its distinguished teachers and its tradition of graduating the nation's outstanding black leaders and professionals. Among Brown's teachers, Angelina Weld Grimké and Jessie Redmon Fauset, creative artists in their own right, taught him a strict sense of academic discipline. In history, Brown was taught by Haley Douglass, the grandson of Frederick Douglass, and by Neville Thomas, president of the Washington branch of the NAACP.

Several of Brown's classmates, who called him "Dutch" in those days, achieved distinction later in life: anthropologist W. Montague Cobb; Judge William H. Hastie; Charles Drew, who gained a national reputation for his research in blood plasma; and distinguished linguist Mercer Cook. His experiences at Dunbar were sources of pride that indelibly marked Brown's identity and outlook.

Brown entered the ivy league Williams College at the age of seventeen, one of a handful of blacks who attended on an academic scholarship. Students were segregated at Williams, and Brown's activities revolved around a nucleus of black students. Brown occupied the time that was not spent with his studies serving as an alternate on the debating team, waiting tables in Berkshire Hall, and playing tennis for the Common Club Tennis Team. Brown and Allison Davis (who later became the distinguished John Dewey Professor at the University of Chicago) teamed up for an imposing doubles combination that won national competitions.

At Williams Brown learned to think critically about literature. George Dutton, whom Brown described in "A Son's Return" (*Kujichaqulia*, November 1973) as "a sarcastic, sharp witted man who didn't suffer fools gladly," was the teacher who most influenced him and inspired in him an interest in critical realism and modern fiction. Through Dutton, Brown was introduced to the work of Feodor Dostoyevski, Leo Tolstoy, Gustave Flaubert, Thomas Hardy, Joseph Conrad, and Sinclair Lewis. It was also at Williams that Brown began to write poetry.

In 1922 Brown graduated Phi Beta Kappa from Williams and entered Harvard University. As a graduate student there, he studied with scholars Bliss Perry and F. O. Matthiessen. There also he discovered a book that opened new vistas in his understanding and appreciation of poetry. *Modern American Poetry* (1921), edited by Louis Unter-meyer, introduced him to the work of the imagists, who were committed to the use of clear, crisp images, brevity, and freedom from timeworn forms; in its pages he read Edwin Arlington Robinson and Robert Frost, both of whom greatly influenced Brown's developing literary outlook. Robinson's sympathetic portraits of the tragic, ironic, and pathetic lives of people in Tilbury Town and Frost's faithful recording of the language, customs, and temperament of the people in New Hampshire intrigued Brown. Frost and Robinson impressed the young poet with their democratic vision, their love of regionalism, and their deep respect for the frank, often brutal truths of realism. As a poet, Brown later identified himself with Robinson for his dramatic technique of creating a series of personalities which he called "portraitures." Brown's vision, like Robinson's, was essentially tragic. Like Frost, Brown rooted his portraits in realism. Not a photographic realist, however, Brown preferred to show the essential truth of life, in Frost's words "to strip it to form." He also shared with both authors their belief in the poetic potential of the American idiom, their interest in the common man, and their freedom in handling new material. In fact, the writers who most appealed to Brown during this period when he was crystallizing his poetic approach were those who used freedom as their banner: freedom to experiment, freedom from stilted, florid diction, freedom to choose new forms and subject matter. Consequently, during his stay at Harvard, Brown incorporated into his own approach to writing many of the literary attitudes and poetic techniques that were characteristic of the works of Robinson and Frost, as well as of Carl Sandburg, Edgar Lee Masters, and Vachel Lindsay.

After earning a master's degree in 1923 from Harvard, Brown was convinced that he wanted to teach. Although he was discouraged by several friends who thought he could put his talents to better use, he was so certain of the importance of teaching that he influenced other Williams men to go into the profession. At the suggestion of his father and of historian Carter G. Woodson, Brown went to Virginia Seminary in Lynchburg, where he taught English for the next three years. There Brown directed much of his energy to writing. "For

the first time," he said in a 1972 interview, "I found something to write about. I found a world of great interest, and it was a world of people, and the poetry of the time—the poetry that I was reading—was a people's poetry."

The black people of the rural communities surrounding Lynchburg were steeped in the tradition of spirituals, the blues, aphorisms, old lies, and superstitions, and they taught the young professor something of their humor, irony, fortitude, and shrewdness. Among these people Brown met while at Virginia Seminary were Mrs. Bibby, the mother of one of Brown's students, and itinerant musician Calvin "Big Boy" Davis, both of whom Brown wrote about in his later poetry. Mrs. Bibby typified in many ways the tough-mindedness and spiritual strength Brown admired, and he portrayed her in the companion pieces, "Virginia Portrait" and "Sister Lou," which appeared in *Southern Road* in 1932. Davis also inspired at least three poems in *Southern Road*. A wandering guitar player whom Brown's students brought to class to play his spirituals and "gut bucket" blues, Big Boy Davis became a friend of Brown's. In the poem "When de Saints Go Ma'ching Home," Brown reconstructed one of Big Boy's memorable performances, and in the poems "Odyssey of Big Boy" and "Long Gone," Brown invokes the lore of the roustabout or wanderer, black men like Big Boy who, by compulsion and necessity, spend most of their lives wandering from town to town and from one menial job to another.

In Brown's subsequent teaching posts at Lincoln University in Missouri (1926-1928) and at Fisk University (1928-1929), his fascination with the folk continued. He spent long hours listening to the hilarious tales told by a Jefferson City waiter called "Slim," who later appears as the master yarn-spinner in Brown's Slim Greer series. On the back roads in Missouri, Brown talked with Revelations, a self-appointed prophet of doom, and on the fringes of the Fisk University campus in Gillie Barber Shop, he met the proprietor whom he described as "the best liar I ever ran across."

In these rural people Brown found a tragic sense of life that he later explored in his poetry. He also found in them an unbeatable spirit that enabled them to accept and endure hardship; their stoicism became a part of his outlook.

Brown met his future wife, Daisy Turnbull, on one of his tennis trips to Roanoke, Virginia; they were married in September 1927. Daisy Brown shared with her husband an enthusiasm for people, an infectious sense of humor, and a rejection of

2464 6th St. N.W.,
Washington, D. C.
November 13, 1934.

My dear Mr. Spingarn:

I am requesting, very belatedly, the assistance you offered this summer. When your letter came I was out in the country, and I was not sure then that I would continue the proposed biographical sketch of Albery Whitman. I find now that I am still to do it, and I am therefore anxious to get the material you spoke of. The information was new to me; I am afraid I have not been very thorough in my research.

I expect to come to New York this week-end. If it is at all convenient I should like to call to see you, and see the note by Whitman, as well as the collection you have told me of. I am to make the article on Whitman critical as well as biographical, and I should like to skim through the book you mentioned, at least.

Letter to Arthur B. Spingarn requesting information about nineteenth-century poet Albery A. Whitman (courtesy of the Arthur B. Spingarn Collection, Moorland-Spingarn Research Center, Howard University)

On my arrival in New York I shall try to get your telephone number from Walter White; I asked him for it once before, but the one he gave me turned out to be your brother's.

I want to apologize for my long delay in acknowledging the graciousness of your offer. I am very sorry. That I believe myself to be the most procrastinating and unbusiness-like person in the wide world does not make me any the less sorry.

Sincerely yours,
Sterling A. Brown

bourgeois pretension. Her own deep poetic sense made her at once his sharpest critic and most devoted admirer. She inspired several of Brown's early poems, including "Long Track Blues" and "Against That Day."

In 1927 Brown received his first attention as a poet with the publication of "When de Saints Go Ma'ching Home," which won first prize in an *Opportunity* writing contest. From 1926 to 1929 several of the poems that would later be published in *Southern Road* in 1932 were printed in such magazines as the *Crisis, Opportunity, Contempo*, and *Ebony and Topaz*. His early efforts as a poet must be seen in the critical context of the unprecedented outpouring of writing known as the New Negro Renaissance. Though often not included in the group of writers usually mentioned in connection with the New Negro Renaissance—Claude McKay, Countee Cullen, Jean Toomer, and Langston Hughes—Brown shared with them a concern for a deeper and franker self-revelation than had been possible in the waning years of conciliation and racial apology from the 1890s to the 1910s.

The New Negro spirit of liberation and innovation reached Brown on the college campuses of the South. While at Virginia Seminary, Brown read McKay's *Harlem Shadows* (1922). McKay's poetry impressed Brown with its militancy as well as its sensitive and sympathetic images of Harlem life. For Brown, Jean Toomer's *Cane* (1923) embodied innovation in language, form, and feeling. *Cane*'s portraits of southern characters—the mystical Fern and the lovers of the tragic triangle in "Blood Burning Moon"—intrigued him. However, Hughes had the greatest appeal for Brown. When Brown read *The Weary Blues* (1926), he realized that Hughes and he were fellow travelers: they both valued the inexhaustible resources to be mined from folk music and speech, and they sought to transform the musical forms of the blues, worksongs, ballads, and spirituals into new forms of poetry. In response to Hughes's work as an urban poet, Brown, as a poet of rural life, said, "I knew that what I had laid out as a path was not a blind alley."

In 1929 Brown returned to Washington to teach at Howard University. His father, who was ill, did not live long enough to see his son become a member of the faculty. During Brown's early years there, Howard, under the leadership of Mordecai W. Johnson, was becoming "the capstone of Negro education." It attracted a host of brilliant minds, including several men Brown had admired as a boy: Alain Locke, the first black American Rhodes Scholar and the intellectual leader of the

New Negro Renaissance, was a professor of philosophy; Ernest Everett Just, an internationally-known scientist, taught biology; and Kelly Miller was a professor of sociology. Brown joined the English Department while Charles Eaton Burch was the chairman and Benjamin Brawley was the most widely known critic on its faculty.

Brown was an active member of the University's committees and for many years directed the Howard University Players theater group. Although he was at the center of academic life, Brown was an outsider in his own department. He believed that several of his English department colleagues did not understand or appreciate what he was attempting to do in his poetry. His interest in the blues and jazz appeared to them unacademic at best. Brown felt a greater affinity with men like Ralph Bunche in political science, E. Franklin Frazier in sociology, Abram L. Harris in economics, Charles H. Thompson in education, and Rayford W. Logan in history, all of whom joined the faculty in the 1930s. In this circle of scholars, Brown cultivated a view of literature that issued from an understanding of the historical, sociological, economic, and political dimensions of American society. In the anthology *The Negro Caravan* (1941), he credits these scholars with shedding light on the reality of the black American experience: "No reader with an open mind could review the work of these scholars and retain the stereotyped concepts of Negro life and character."

Seven years after coming to Howard, Brown turned his attention to the Works Progress Administration (WPA) Federal Writers' Project. From 1936 to 1940 he held the position of Editor of Negro Affairs, one of the few significant positions given to blacks under the New Deal. Brown's appointment was the result of the insistence of several black leaders, such as Bunche, Walter White, and John P. Davis, "that a Black person knowledgeable in literary criticism and history be appointed at the national level to look out for Black Affairs."

With a small editorial staff, Brown coordinated all the Federal Writers' Project studies by and about blacks. He reviewed copy prepared for inclusion in state guides, and he suggested revisions. Beginning in 1934 he supervised the collection of extensive ex-slave narratives. Believing the history of the American black to be essentially "a story untold," Brown encouraged studies in black history and folklore in several states. Of the special projects initiated at his suggestion, *The Negro in Virginia* (1940) became the model for other studies of its kind. However, Brown made his single, most enduring contribution to the Writers' Project with the writing of the massive guidebook, *Washington, City and Capital* (1937). To this volume he contributed the essay "The Negro in Washington," a master stroke of social criticism, which was at once an assessment and indictment of the plight of blacks in the nation's seat of justice.

In his efforts as national editor of Negro affairs, Brown recognized the sociohistorical forces that affected the way in which blacks were portrayed in guidebooks and other government publications. Although he was not able to alter the blatant neglect of black subjects in the early guidebooks and was aware that some writers would continue to cast blacks in stereotypes, he insisted on the validity of the black cultural heritage, and he used the Writers' Project to unearth the little-known story of black Americans.

In 1945 Brown was offered a teaching position in the English department at Vassar College. The offer of an appointment to the faculty of the all-white university made national headlines. Brown had taught at Vassar for three terms prior to his appointment and had already received national recognition as an author and editor, and as a Guggenheim Fellow (1937-1938), a Julius Rosenwald Fellow (1942), a member of the Carnegie-Myrdal Study, a member of the committee on Negro studies of the American Council of Learned Societies, and as an editor for the *Encyclopaedia Brittannica*. With the announcement of the offer from Vassar, Brown was viewed by some of his colleagues at Howard as having reached an appropriate plateau.

Brown decided to remain at Howard. Though he spent several summers away from Washington—at the University of Minnesota, 1945; New York University, 1949 and 1950; University of Illinois (Circle Campus), 1967 and 1968—Brown continued to teach at Howard until his retirement in 1969. Some years later he explained his decision: "I am devoted to Howard. These are my people, and if I had anything to give, they would need it more."

Reflecting on his long career as a teacher, Brown said, "My legacy is my students." In a career that spanned more than forty years, Brown naturally had an impact on thousands of students, yet his influence can be seen dramatically in the life's work of his most outstanding students. Among them was Ulysses Lee, who worked with Brown on the editorial staff of Negro affairs in the Federal Writers' Project and who also coedited *The Negro Caravan* (1941) with Brown and Arthur P. Davis.

Amiri Baraka (LeRoi Jones) attributed much of his understanding of black music to Brown, noting that Brown's vast knowledge and enviable collection of blues and jazz recordings made black music "historical." Kenneth Clark, noted psychologist and author of *Dark Ghetto* (1965), said that Brown opened his eyes to "the awe, the wonder, the fascination of human creativity." For actor Ossie Davis, Brown "was doing a black thing from a black point of view when it wasn't stylish." Davis said, "We have a tradition, a heritage, a straight line of thought, and Sterling is one of the progenitors—still unable to count his children."

Brown's first fifteen years at Howard, from 1929 to 1945, were his most productive years as a writer. During this period he contributed poetry, reviews, and essays to *Opportunity, New Republic, Nation, Journal of Negro Education, Phylon, Crisis,* and other publications. His essays covered a wide range of topics including the American theater, folk expressions, music, athletics, oral history, and social customs. Brown's most influential essay of this period was "Negro Characters As Seen by White Authors" published in the *Journal of Negro Education* in 1933, in which he first brought attention to the misrepresentation of black character and life in American literature.

In a span of nine years, Brown published the four books that established his reputation as an important poet and critic: *Southern Road* (1932), *The Negro in American Fiction* (1937), *Negro Poetry and Drama* (1937), and *The Negro Caravan* (1941). Shortly after the publication of *Southern Road,* Locke hailed Sterling Brown as "The New Negro Folk Poet" and claimed that the book ushered in "a new era in Negro folk expression" and brought "a new dimension in Negro folk portraiture." Locke called Brown a folk-poet because he registered the people's sentiment in their terms.

In *Southern Road,* Brown dares "to give quiet but bold expressions" to their private thoughts and speech. His poetry achieves a rich folk expressiveness because it is immersed in the cadences, the tone, and the nuances of folk speech. The force of his language, which goes beyond simple recorded orthographic differences in dialects, can be attributed to Brown's saturation with the blues of W. C. Handy, Ma Rainey, and Bessie Smith, and with the jazz of Duke Ellington and Fletcher Henderson.

Southern Road is also a corridor to the personal histories of black folk. The road that Brown embarks upon leads into a world analogous to Spoon River, Tilbury Town, or Yoknapatawpha County. It is no wonder that in Brown's title poem the road is transformed into human drama. In "Southern Road," the poet dramatizes the poignant story of a "po' los' boy," who faces the rest of his life on a chain gang. Using the worksong, a form traditionally intended to convey the communalism of hard work, the poet particularizes the experiences of his personal tragedy. The convict's grunts serve to punctuate the heaviness of his lot: a life sentence, a street-walker daughter, a wayward son, a pregnant wife, a father who died cursing him, and a mother grown old with misery. Nevertheless, his response to existence is charged with a realistic acceptance of his circumstances and a toughness of spirit that leave no room for self-pity.

> Chain gang nevah—hunh—
> Let me go;
> Chain gang nevah—hunh—
> Let me go;
> Po' los' boy, bebby,
> Evahmo'

Ordinary people live alongside the imaginary road in Brown's collection. Some are based on real personalities: Ma Rainey, Revelations, Big Boy Davis, and Mrs. Bibby. Other characters, such as Maumee Ruth, Sporting Beasley, Deacon Zachary, and Sam Smiley, achieve a reality as Brown attributes to them the mind, the vernacular, and the concerns of real people who express their stoicism, humor, fatalism, toughness, profaneness, reverence, and ethnic spirit. The folk preoccupation with elegant heroes, their drive for survival and resistance, and their reach for the universal in human experience through the particular experience are major concerns in Brown's poetry. He also wished to communicate with a wider audience in a language that combined folk authenticity with the craftsmanship of a self-conscious writer. Like Alain Locke, he was aware of the resources of collective folk widsom and explored what Locke called "the real treasure-trove of the Negro poet." Indeed, the black folk tradition highlighted in *Southern Road* became the single most important influence in Brown's entire literary career.

Brown, however, went beyond merely retrieving characters and themes from folk materials; he forged new forms from them. In the poem "Old Lem," Brown focuses upon the subtle and complex sensibility of an old man grown weary of mob violence. With stark simplicity devoid of false sentimentality, Old Lem tells the story of his buddy, "Six foot of man/Muscled up perfect/Game to the heart," who defied the tradition of caste and "spoke

out of turn at the commissary." For his insolence he is murdered. Yet much of the effectiveness of the poem emanates from Brown's successful recycling of the folktale "Old Sis Goose," in which a common goose seeks justice in a court of foxes and ends up having her bones "picked." Lem says:

> Their fists stay closed
> Their eyes look straight
>> Our hands stay open
>> Our eyes must fall
>>> *They don't come by ones*
>> They got the manhood
>> They got the courage
>>> *They don't come by twos*
> We got to slink around
> Hangtailed hounds
> They burn us when we dogs
> They burn us when we men
>> *They come by tens.*

The effective incremental repetition, strongly stressed verbs, terse lines, and lucid reportage in this poem also characterize "Strong Men," the poem that best lays claim to being Brown's signature poem. Taking its central theme from Carl Sandburg's line "The strong men keep comin on," Brown celebrates the indomitable spirit of black people in the face of racism and economic and political exploitation. Much of the force of the poem results from the poet's re-creation of a sense of stoicism in a syntax of heavily stressed verbs preceded by contrasting pronouns "they" or "you." The cadence of the poem suggests the rhythm of a martial approach which quickens as the poem reaches its conclusion.

> What, from the slums
> Where they have hemmed you
> What, from the tiny huts
> They could not keep from you
> What reaches them
> Making them ill at ease, fearful?
> Today they shout prohibition at you
> "Thou shalt not this"
> "Thou shalt not that"
> "Reserved for white only"
> You laugh.
> One thing they cannot prohibit—
>> The strong men . . . coming on
>> The strong men gittin' stronger.
> Strong men. . . .
> Stronger. . . .

There is in the assertive tone of the poem an awareness that the race has been able to resist hostile forces and endure despite adversity.

In Brown's poetry the language of black people—the dialect, the idioms, the style—retains its richness and verve. Brown brought the use of dialect in poetry to new respectable heights, despite the lively debate on its value as a literary medium. James Weldon Johnson, who had earlier called for "a form that will express the racial spirit by symbols from within rather than by symbols from without," congratulated Brown in 1932 for infusing "his poetry with genuine characteristic flavor." Brown's inventive blues ballad "Ma Rainey" is an excellent example of his ability to reproduce faithfully the people's speech. "I talked to a fellow, an' the fellow say,/'She jes' catch hold of us, somekindaway.'" With its compressed phrasing and its elimination of unnecessary tense and adverbial constructions, the speech that Brown creates is what people say to each other when they are most natural.

Brown also embraces the musical forms of Afro-American folk culture. Poems like "Ma Rainey," "Memphis Blues," and "New St. Louis Blues," recreate the blues ethos; "Crossing," "When de Saints Go Ma'ching Home," "Virginia Portrait," and "Sister Lou" capture the dignity and solemnity of the spirituals; and, with varying notes of tragedy, humor, and bravado, narratives such as "Slim Greer," "An Old Woman Remembers," and "Crispus Attucks McKoy" achieve a virtuosity which rivals that of the anonymous folktales and ballads.

In other poems in *Southern Road*, especially those in the "Vestiges" section, Brown gives rare glimpses of a more subjective, more personal self. The poems in this section are dedicated to Brown's wife Daisy, whom he calls Rose Anne. Memories of their courtship and their love provide the basis for most of the poems. In "Thoughts of Death" and "Against That Day," Daisy Brown's presence is deeply felt. Even though Brown wrote these poems almost fifty years before his wife's death in 1979, the thought of losing her induced in him a great poignancy. In the last poem in this section, "Mill Mountain," the poet addresses the issue of how to master pain. The message of the poem appears to be that attempts to evade the unpleasant reality of life are futile. In a larger sense the poem contains a kernel of Brown's philosophical approach to the value of poetry. For Brown, poetry, to be of value, must reflect reality and reveal truth. Though his poetry may sound notes of pessimism, it just as often conveys a sense of acceptance, encouragement, and hope. For ultimately, according to his experience, peace and beauty come from an acceptance of truth, however frank and harsh.

After the publication of *Southern Road*, which established him as a promising poet, Brown emerged as a mature critic of Afro-American literature. Beginning in 1931 he wrote a monthly series of critical reviews in *Opportunity* called "The Literary Scene: Chronicle and Comment." For almost ten years this series provided Brown with a forum for his comments on the modern development in American literature. Among the concerns that came to comprise his critical platform were the need for a literary audience interested in the genuine development of black writers, the validity of portrayals of black life and character, and the achievement of a high level of craftsmanship.

Addressing these concerns, Brown wrote several important, pioneer studies. In "The Blues as Folk Poetry" (1930), Brown gave the earliest, serious treatment to the structure, imagery, sound, and meaning of the blues. Three years later, he published "Negro Character As Seen by White Authors" (1933) in which he discussed the significant influence of white writers in portraying black characters, ranging from the blatant stereotypes of Thomas Nelson Page to the sympathetic, realistic portraits of Erskine Caldwell. In 1937 he published *The Negro in American Fiction* and *Negro Poetry and Drama* which surveyed the development of black literature in America from its earliest stirrings in the 1700s to the tumultuous decade of the 1930s. In these book-length studies, he argued that the majority of books about black character merely repeat a handful of timeworn stereotypes. According to Brown stereotypes such as The Contented Slave, The Brute Nigger, The Comic Negro, The Tragic Mulatto, and The Exotic Primitive attached themselves so firmly to American literature that, in time, they assumed a life of their own. He makes it clear that he does not consider everything a stereotype that shows up the weakness of black character. However, whether the stereotyping desecrates black character or flatters it, any gross overgeneralization is fatal to the development of a great and convincing literature.

In 1941 Brown wrote "The Negro Writer and His Publisher" in which he discusses the role of the critic in influencing the theme, content, and form of black writing. To those critics who level charges of "selling the race down the river" against authors who veer from a standard way of portraying black life, he recommends instead that they keep to the job of pointing out untruthfulness and maintaining the independence and integrity of the critical at-

Arna Bontemps, Melvin B. Tolson, Jacob Reddix, Owen Dodson, Robert Hayden, Sterling Brown, Zora Neale Hurston, Margaret Walker, and Langston Hughes in October 1952 at the Festival of Negro Poets in Jackson, Mississippi (by permission of the Tolson family)

titude. He further asserts that unwarranted praise and critical philanthropy, no matter how well meant, are totally inimical to the development of a high level of creative expression.

Brown, along with Ulysses Lee and Arthur P. Davis, edited *The Negro Caravan* (1941), a now classic collection of essays, poetry, fiction, and folklore. In this work he warns against "a double standard of judgment which is dangerous to the future of Negro writers." He argues that black writers have been influenced by the same literary traditions that have influenced all American writers: "Puritan didacticism, sentimental humanitarianism, local color, regionalism, realism, naturalism, and experimentalism." Therefore, he advances the theory that the bonds of literary tradition appear to be stronger than race. Applying this thesis to his appraisal of the New Negro Renaissance, Brown sees the American literary renaissance and the New Negro movement as coinciding in their mutual reaction against sentimentality, didacticism, optimism, and romantic escape. However, Brown believes

that the Harlem phase of the New Negro Movement failed directly in proportion to the attempt by publishers, promoters, and literary patrons to exploit it for its differences by claiming a prurient and perverse primitivism. Though highly critical of those who "trooped off to join Van Vechten's band," Brown applauded the brilliant experimentation of such writers as Hughes and Toomer. "At their best," he said, "they belonged with the renascent American poets who in the tones of ordinary speech rediscovered the strength, the dignity, the vital core of the common place."

Throughout his career as a critic, Brown has challenged black writers to choose their subject matter, style, and form without regard for external pressures. He has challenged them to avoid committing the costly error of timidity at being black and urged them to "look into their hearts and write." The error of "timidity" is more costly, Brown cautions, when it results in the self-imposed alienation that comes from a writer's desire "to be considered a poet and not a Negro poet," and from a miseducation that has taught contempt for anything "peculiarly Negro." The "final interpretation of Negro life must come from within," Brown said in "More Odds" (*Opportunity*, 1932). He believes that alienation stalls the writer's acceptance of responsibility for the role of his culture's interpreter.

Finally, through his sane judgments, his breadth of knowledge, and his finely controlled ironic language Brown has, in his criticism, successfully interpreted the influence of social attitudes of class and caste on fixed ideas about black character and life. Just as the power in his poetry is rooted deeply in an understanding of the folkways of his people and a mastery of the craft, his effectiveness as a critic is rooted in his awareness of the events and needs of his time. Part of Brown's contribution to Afro-American literature is his ability to discern American society and his keen awareness of the discrepancies and distortions as well as the ironies and realities of life. In other words, Brown's criticism reflects the truth of Harry Levin's statement, "Literature is not only the effect of social causes; it is also the cause of social effects."

As a pioneer in black criticism, as an innovator in poetry using folk songs and folk speech as referents, and as a respected authority on black culture, Brown has made a significant impact on the development of black American literature for half a century. Darwin T. Turner, a critic of Afro-American literature, said, "No other Black has inspired as much admiration and respect from his students and successors in the field. In every stream of creative Black literature, Sterling Brown is the source to which critics return."

By virtue of his position as mentor and pioneer, Brown can rightfully be called a forerunner of the black poetry movement of the 1960s and 1970s. Identifying Brown with Margaret Walker, Gwendolyn Brooks, Lance Jeffers, Arna Bontemps, Langston Hughes, Owen Dodson, and Dudley Randall, critic Addison Gayle in the introduction to *The Forerunners* (1975) said that these poets did not take the easy route of using stereotypes. Instead, as Brown had, they looked closely at the dimensions of a people's lives, noted their strengths and weaknesses, created new images, metaphors, and symbols from their history, and discovered truer paradigms for black life and character. In this respect, they and Brown shared with such younger poets as Amiri Baraka, Askia M. Touré, Haki Madhubuti, Sonia Sanchez, Larry Neal, Mari Evans, and others the belief that those who would be free must accept the responsibility of defining themselves in their own terms.

As a forerunner, Brown prepared the way for the resurgence of interest in black literature and studies witnessed during the last two decades. Before many scholars recognized black studies as an academic discipline, Brown taught courses in black literature and culture. He read his poetry and lectured on folklore to college and literary audiences all over the country. His keen knowledge of his subject and his skillful reading of his own poetry attracted a large following.

Brown's influence also reached beyond the boundaries of the United States. Leopold Sedar Senghor, one of the architects of Negritude, called Brown "an original militant of Negritude, a precursor of the movement." Senghor, who became aware of Brown's poetry and criticism in the 1920s and 1930s through the pages of *Opportunity*, attributes to Brown, McKay, Cullen, Hughes, and other writers of the New Negro Renaissance the inspiration for the cultural movement whose concepts fostered identity with blacks in Africa and in the diaspora.

Brown retired in 1969 after a forty-year career as a teacher at Howard University. It was only in the late 1960s that Brown even began to read his poems regularly at Howard, though he had read at many colleges and universities throughout the country during his career. This neglect may be explained to some degree by a reluctance on the part of some conservative faculty members to appreciate a professor who knew the blues and jazz and guitar-playing roustabouts. As historian Michael Winston states, "Nonconformity cost him more than he realized." For most of his life, Brown had been highly critical of superficial respectability; this criticism carried over into academia where he saw the doctorate symbolizing, in some cases, intellectual snobbishness instead of intellectual competence. Brown, whose temperament was not well-suited for the isolation and myopia often required of the researcher, never took a doctoral degree. Widely known as a raconteur par excellence, he was most comfortable telling vintage stories whose characters came alive with each of his elaborate gestures and subtle witticism.

The five years before his retirement were troubled for Brown. He began to exhibit the stress caused by what he perceived to be years of critical and professional neglect and unachieved personal goals. Inclined to periods of deep depression for which he was occasionally hospitalized, Brown craved attention. Sterling Stuckey, who introduced the second edition of *Southern Road*, said that this need was satisfied to some degree by his audiences at poetry readings. Each time Brown had a successful reading, his spirits were buoyed. Though, as Stuckey pointed out, he had "great gifts as a poet," he wondered how the younger generation would receive his poetry and "he was troubled by a not inconsiderable lack of recognition."

Nineteen sixty-eight and 1969 finally brought him greater recognition from the students. According to critic Stephen Henderson, "Howard students said that they wanted a Black university, and they wanted it named after Sterling A. Brown." In 1971 Howard University awarded him an honorary doctorate, one of several he would eventually receive from the University of Massachusetts, Northwestern University, Williams College, Boston University, Brown University, Lewis and Clark College, Lincoln University (Pennsylvania), and the University of Pennsylvania.

Although Brown produced a relatively small number of books, his achievement and influence in the field of American literature and culture are significant. Brown has affirmed the continuity of the black creative experience in America, making the necessary connections between oral folk culture and self-conscious literature, identifying in his own poetry and in the writings of others their debt to the folk, and bringing together the particular racial experience and the universal human experience.

Bibliography:

Robert G. O'Meally, "An Annotated Bibliography of the Works of Sterling A. Brown," in *The Collected Poems of Sterling A. Brown*, edited by Michael S. Harper (New York: Harper & Row, 1980), pp. 243-255.

References:

Houston A. Baker, *Long Black Song: Essays in Black American Literature and Culture* (Charlottesville: University of Virginia Press, 1972);

Kimberly W. Benston, "Sterling Brown's After Song: 'When De Saints Go Ma'ching Home' and the Performance of Afro-American Voice," *Callaloo*, nos. 14 & 15 (February-May 1982): 37;

Black History Museum Committee, *Sterling A. Brown: A UMUM Tribute* (Philadelphia: Black

History Museum, 1976);

Arthur P. Davis, *From the Dark Tower: Afro-American Writers, 1900-1960* (Washington, D.C.: Howard University Press, 1974);

Genevieve Ekaete, "Sterling Brown: A Living Legend," *New Directions: The Howard University Magazine*, 1 (Winter 1974): 5-11;

Addison Gayle, Jr., ed., *Black Expression: Essays By and About Black Americans in the Creative Arts* (New York: Weybright & Talley, 1969);

Stephen Henderson, "Sterling Brown," *Ebony* (October 1976): 130;

Eugene Clay Holmes, "Sterling Brown: American Peoples' Poet," *International Literature*, 8 (June 1934): 117-122;

George E. Kent, *Blackness and the Adventure of Western Culture* (Chicago: Third World Press, 1971);

Alain Locke, *Negro Art: Past and Present* (Washington, D.C.: Associates in Negro Folk Education, 1936);

Locke, ed., *The New Negro* (New York: Boni, 1925);

Jerre Mangione, *The Dream and the Deal: The Federal Writers' Project, 1935-1943* (Boston: Little, Brown, 1972);

Robert G. O'Meally, "Reconsideration," *New Republic* (11 February 1978): 35;

Dudley Randall, "Black Aesthetic in the Thirties, Forties, and Fifties," *Modern Black Poets*, edited by Donald Gibson (Englewood Cliffs, N.J.: Prentice-Hall, 1973);

J. Saunders Redding, *To Make a Poet Black* (Chapel Hill: University of North Carolina Press, 1959);

Charles H. Rowell, "Sterling A. Brown and the Afro-American Folk Tradition," *Studies in the Literary Imagination*, 7 (Fall 1974): 131-152;

Jean Wagner, *Black Poets of the United States: From Paul Laurence Dunbar to Langston Hughes*, translated by Kenneth Douglas (Urbana: University of Illinois Press, 1973);

Hollie West, "The Teacher . . . Sterling Brown, the Mentor of Thousands," *Washington Post*, 16 November 1969, pp. F1-F3.

Countee Cullen

Alan Shucard
University of Wisconsin-Parkside

See also the Cullen entries in *DLB 4, American Writers in Paris, 1920-1939* and *DLB 48, American Poets, 1880-1945, Second Series.*

BIRTH: Probably Louisville, Kentucky, 30 May 1903, to Elizabeth Lucas.

EDUCATION: B.A., New York University, 1925; M.A., Harvard University, 1926.

MARRIAGES: 9 April 1928 to Nina Yolande Du Bois (divorced, 1930). 27 September 1940 to Ida Mae Roberson.

AWARDS AND HONORS: Witter Bynner Poetry Contest Prizes: 1923, 1924, 1925; John Reed Memorial Prize (*Poetry* magazine), 1925; *Crisis* Magazine Spingarn award, 1925; Harmon Foundation Literary Award, 1927; Guggenheim Fellowship, 1928.

DEATH: New York, New York, 9 January 1946.

BOOKS: *Color* (New York & London: Harper, 1925);
The Ballad of the Brown Girl: An Old Ballad Retold (New York & London: Harper, 1927);
Copper Sun (New York & London: Harper, 1927);
The Black Christ and Other Poems (New York & London: Harper, 1929);
One Way to Heaven (New York & London: Harper, 1932);
The Medea and Some Poems (New York & London: Harper, 1935);
The Lost Zoo (A Rhyme for the Young, But Not Too Young) (New York & London: Harper, 1940);
My Lives and How I Lost Them (New York & London: Harper, 1942);
On These I Stand: An Anthology of the Best Poems of Countee Cullen (New York: Harper, 1947).

PLAY PRODUCTION: *St. Louis Woman,* by Cullen and Arna Bontemps, New York, Martin Beck Theatre, 30 March 1946.

Countee Cullen

OTHER: *Caroling Dusk: An Anthology of Verse by Negro Poets,* edited, with contributions, by Cullen (New York & London: Harper, 1927);
Frank Ankenbrand and Isaac Benjamin, *The House of Vanity,* Introduction by Cullen (Philadelphia: Leibman, 1928);
St. Louis Woman, by Cullen and Arna Bontemps, in *Black Theatre,* edited by Lindsay Patterson (New York: Dodd, Mead, 1971).

PERIODICAL PUBLICATIONS: "Poet on Poet— *The Weary Blues,*" *Opportunity,* 4 (February 1926): 73;
"The Dark Tower," *Opportunity,* 4 (December 1926): 388; 5 (February 1927): 53-54; 5 (March 1927): 86-87; 5 (April 1927): 118-119;

5 (May 1927): 149-150; 5 (June 1927): 180-181; 5 (July 1927): 210-211; 5 (August 1927): 240-241; 5 (November 1927): 336-337; 5 (December 1927): 373-374; 6 (January 1928): 20-21; 6 (February 1928): 52-53; 6 (March 1928): 90; 6 (April 1928): 120; 6 (July 1928): 210; 6 (September 1928): 271-273;

"Countee Cullen to His Friends," *Crisis,* 36 (April 1929): 119;

"Countee Cullen on Miscegenation," *Crisis,* 36 (November 1929): 373;

"The Development of Creative Expression," *High Points,* 25 (September 1943): 26-32;

The Third Fourth of July, by Cullen and Owen Dodson, *Theatre Arts,* 30 (August 1946): 488-493.

If any single writer can be said to represent the New Negro Renaissance, that extraordinary flowering of Afro-American arts centered in Harlem in the 1920s, that writer is almost certainly Countee Cullen. Paradoxically, he was urbane but at the same time naive, somewhat cynical, but also—and perhaps above all—romantic. A protester against violations of black dignity and rights and a questor after both African roots and racial reconciliation in America through art, Cullen manifested the yearnings and frustrations that pervaded the Harlem Renaissance in general. His work embodied the diverse qualities forged in the furnace of American racial attitudes and articulated by such intellectual leaders of the New Negro movement as W. E. B. Du Bois, Alain Locke, and James Weldon Johnson. No one can be said to have more clearly reflected in literature the ideas of those men than Countee Cullen.

Early biographical information about Cullen is sketchy. Although New York is frequently given as his place of birth and Baltimore is listed as another possibility, he was probably born in Louisville, Kentucky, on 30 May 1903. His mother, Elizabeth Lucas, named him Countee LeRoy. She apparently turned the rearing of the young Cullen over to Elizabeth Porter, who may have been his paternal grandmother and who cared for him until her death in New York in 1918. The Reverend Frederick Asbury Cullen and Carolyn Mitchell Cullen of the Salem Methodist Episcopal Church in Harlem took the fifteen-year-old Countee Porter into their home and unofficially adopted him.

Cullen attended public schools in New York, where his creative skills were early made manifest. In elementary school he had begun writing poetry, and at the predominantly white De Witt Clinton High School, he distinguished himself in a variety

of ways. He served as vice-president of the senior class and treasurer of the Inter-High School Poetry Society, winning second prize for "In Memory of Lincoln" in a contest sponsored by the Society. He also served as chairman of the senior publications committee and editor of the school's literary magazine, *The Magpie,* which published his "I Have a Rendezvous with Life" in its January 1921 issue. The poem was very well received, and it earned for Cullen a prize in a contest sponsored by the Federation of Women's Clubs. Cullen matched his artistic successes with scholastic achievements by winning election to Arista, Clinton's scholastic honor society. It is no wonder then that the young man was well prepared to enter college when he graduated from Clinton on 26 January 1922.

Young Countee's adoption by the Cullens was propitious for the creation of a poetic sensibility that blossomed in high school and that would be in tune with the Harlem Renaissance. The World War I era migration of black Americans to urban centers such as New York, to run the war machinery and fill in for white workers serving in the military, produced the first real black urban consciousness in America. The awareness that accompanied the sociopolitical tensions of the day fueled the arts of the New Negro. The sensitivity of Afro-Americans to white American condescension was heightened by the social abuse received by returning black soldiers, whose heroism and sacrifice during the war did little to ameliorate the racial climate. Reverend Cullen's rectory at the Salem Methodist Episcopal Church, with Harlem's largest congregation, was the place to take the measure of Afro-American feeling in the United States. Cullen could scarcely have avoided being aware of the charged issues that were discussed by his new father's congregation. Indeed Reverend Cullen took an active role in addressing the problems of Afro-Americans in the early twentieth century. In 1919 he called on President Woodrow Wilson with a delegation of black community leaders to persuade the president to stop further hangings of black soldiers in Texas after thirteen had been executed for discharging firearms in Houston. Later Reverend Cullen was elected president of the Harlem chapter of the NAACP, and he was one of the supporters of a movement to send Du Bois to Geneva to represent Afro-Americans at the League of Nations.

While these political issues might have been engaging for the young Cullen, he was less attracted to the religion practiced in the home. The Cullens were fundamentalists whose fastidious interpretation of the Bible may have caused their adopted son some discomfort. These early conflicts would serve as the basis for Cullen's ambivalence toward religion later in his life.

If Countee Cullen's home life in Harlem gave him access to one of the richest political and religious environments of black America, his education provided him firm intellectual footing in the white world. From the largely white De Witt Clinton High School in the Bronx, he went to the University Heights campus of New York University, where, in his sophomore year in 1923, he won second prize in the national Witter Bynner Poetry Contest for "The Ballad of the Brown Girl," a piece that later received extravagant praise from Irving Babbit at Harvard. The poem essentially instituted the racial theme that would become so central to Cullen's poetry. The poem is adapted from an old ballad. Originally the term "brown girl" meant primarily a peasant girl, and the poem delineated a triangle involving a nobleman and two maids, a "brown girl" and one higher born. In the Cullen adaptation, the nobleman marries the brown girl, but when Fair London, the "lily-white maid," speaks out against miscegenation, she is stabbed by the brown girl. The husband, who has refused to defend his wife against insult, avenges the white girl's death by strangling his wife with her own hair. Apart from the overt racial suggestions of the plot, Cullen associates emotional wealth, energy, and passion with the brown girl, who comes from royal African lineage; emotional poverty and passionlessness are the attributes of Fair London. Significantly, in the end, when all are dead and buried, "The Brown Girl sleeps at her true lord's feet/Fair London by his side."

Cullen's insistence that the brown girl descend from black kings reflects what Arthur P. Davis would later call "the alien-and-exile theme" that was pervasive in Cullen's work and in the literature of the Harlem Renaissance generally. This reaching back from the oppression of the Afro-American experience to the supposed happier times in the native Africa of long ago marks the note of romanticism that runs through Cullen's work.

In 1924 Cullen continued his success in the Witter Bynner Poetry Contest by winning first honorable mention for "Spirit Birth." He won first prize in the Witter Bynner contest in 1925 and, in that same year, he won second prize in the *Opportunity* literary contest for "One Who Said Me Nay."

The accolades continued to be heaped on Cullen in 1925. He was elected to Phi Beta Kappa (one of eleven graduates so honored), won *Poetry* mag-

Countee Cullen (courtesy of the Schomburg Center for Research in Black Culture, the New York Public Library, Astor, Lenox and Tilden Foundations)

azine's John Reed Memorial Prize for "Threnody for a Brown Girl" and *Crisis* magazine's Spingarn contest for "Two Moods of Love," and he took second prize in the poetry contests of *Palms* and *Opportunity*. In 1925 he also graduated from New York University and published *Color,* his first volume of poems.

The seventy-three poems in *Color* are divided into three sections: "Color," "Epitaphs," and "Varia," with the "Color" section including those for which Cullen is most well known by contemporary readers, especially "Yet Do I Marvel," "A Brown Girl Dead," "To A Brown Girl," "Simon the Cyrenian Speaks," "Incident," and "Heritage." "Epitaphs" includes poems on Keats and Paul Laurence Dunbar, and the "Varia" section, less thematically unified, includes, among others, "She of the Dancing Feet Sings" and "To John Keats, Poet. At Springtime," both frequently anthologized.

Cullen begins, in this volume, to articulate some of the problems of racial identity that would plague him through the years. His desire to be known as a poet, not as a *black* poet, is central to "Yet Do I Marvel." The persona does not doubt God's goodness or His willingness to explain curious phenomena, such as why moles are blind or why Tantalus and Sisyphus must suffer their fates, but he has finally been pushed to the limit of Christian credibility. He finds the status of the black poet the most shocking: "Yet do I marvel at this curious thing:/To make a poet black, and bid him sing!" The poem laments an incongruity between blackness and creativity, one belied by Cullen's own creative genius but one that tortured him nonetheless.

In "Simon the Cyrenian Speaks," Cullen depicts the bearer of Christ's cross as a black man who has been singled out because of his color; however, the speaker transcends the impulse to consider Christ racist and joins in his "dream," becoming in the process more powerful than those who have persecuted Christ:

> At first I said, "I will not bear
>   His cross upon my back;
> He only seeks to place it there
>   Because my skin is black."
>
> But He was dying for a dream,
>   And He was very meek,
> And in His eyes there shone a gleam
>   Men journey far to seek.
>
> It was Himself my pity bought;
>   I did for Christ alone
> What all of Rome could not have wrought
>   With bruise of lash or stone.

In identifying blacks with Simon, Cullen gives them a central role in Christian myth and absolves them of any guilt associated with the crucifixion.

Another frequently anthologized poem from the volume, "Incident" is graphic in its depiction of the effect of racial prejudice upon impressionable children. An eight-year-old black visitor to Baltimore has his vacation spoiled when he is called a "nigger": "I saw the whole of Baltimore/From May until December;/Of all the things that happened there/That's all that I remember." The poem could also serve as a metaphor for Cullen's plight, for the black poet who preferred not to have labels assigned to his creativity.

Cullen continued his racial theme in several other poems in the volume. In "Atlantic City Waiter," he speaks of the menial who must swallow his pride and act subserviently and conceal the natural elegance that is his patrimony, the grace of "Ten thousand years on jungle clues." "Fruit of the Flower" also resounds with allusions to racial memory, and "A Song of Praise" expresses the desirability of the narrator's own dark love, whose walk is like a primitive African dance, over the reader's "fair" love. Of all of Cullen's poems in *Color* and elsewhere that search out the meaning of the lost Africa, the best-known "Heritage" is his longest and most reflective treatment of the subject. In answer to his own challenge "What is Africa to me," the poet proceeds to offer a mixture of romantic and realistic, Christian and pagan images, some gleaned from readings and others concocted from an active imagination. The speaker becomes passionate at the thought of his ancestral homeland but comes to understand that he must suppress his feelings; the ancient Africa is unreachable from America, and to harbor false hope can only lead to madness. The speaker knows that he must contain himself or he will be destroyed:

> *All day long and all night through,*
> *One thing only must I do:*
> *Quench my pride and cool my blood,*
> *Lest I perish in the flood.*
> *Lest a hidden ember set*
> *Timber that I thought was wet*
> *Burning like the dryest flax,*
> *Melting like the merest wax,*
> *Lest the grave restore its dead.*
> *Not yet has my heart or head*
> *In the least way realized*
> *They and I are civilized.*

His meditation on Africa leaves the poet unsated. His impulse to reach back to mother Africa was shared by many of his fellow New Negro artists and black artists from other countries. This Pan-Africanism came to be known as the "Negritude" movement in the arts. Poems such as "Heritage" also gave powerful literary expression to Marcus Garvey's Universal Negro Improvement Association, which, for all of its comic-opera trappings, was a serious expression of discontent in America and longing for Africa. If poems that reveal atavistic stirrings seem a little out of place in the work of the extremely correct Countee Cullen, they serve to show the extent of his romanticism and the strength of the hunger for roots evidenced in the New Negro Renaissance.

Most of Cullen's racial poems—and, therefore, a preponderance of his work—are direct expressions of outrage or sorrow at the plight of

Afro-Americans. Since he despised unfairness wherever he perceived it, he railed at other injustices, as well—the Sacco and Vanzetti decision, for example—but since injustice to him and the black community was what stung most immediately, that is what he usually cried out against. Although his protest was more muted than that of such of his contemporaries as Claude McKay and Langston Hughes, Cullen was, by nature and training, a gentleman and a gentle man with his own voice.

The success of *Color* presaged great times for the twenty-two-year-old Cullen. His star shone so brightly that only a brilliant future was predicted for him. His letters from Harvard, which he entered in 1925, to his close friend Harold Jackman (to whom he had dedicated "Heritage") suggest that Cullen was a cocky young man, an attitude that is entirely understandable in view of his early success. He finished his education at Harvard in 1926, when he graduated with his master's degree. Also in 1926 he became assistant editor to Charles S. Johnson at *Opportunity* magazine.

The following year, 1927, would again be a banner year for Cullen. He received the Harmon Foundation Literary Award for that year. He also published his prizewinning poem "The Ballad of the Brown Girl" as a separate volume, and *Copper Sun,* his second collection of poetry, also appeared in 1927. It contains the memorable "From the Dark Tower," as well as other favorites such as "Threnody for a Brown Girl." "From the Dark Tower," dedicated to Charles S. Johnson, depicts black people as the planters of the American civilization from which others have gathered the bounty. Although he anticipates some vague future time when that situation might change, the poet can only caution endurance in the meantime: "So in the dark we hide the heart that bleeds,/And wait, and tend our agonizing seeds." The volume also contains some of the love poems, many of them expressing ambivalent attitudes, that Cullen would return to again and again in his career. Eternal love is distinctly Christian, never Dionysian, for love, Cullen insists in "If Love Be Staunch," endures as "water stays in a sieve." In "The Love Tree," the speaker wants his beloved to water their unhappy love with her tears and with bloody hands keep it free of weeds. The lovers are crucified so future couples will know that " 'Twas break of heart that made the Love Tree grow."

Cullen's success continued in 1927 with his editing of *Caroling Dusk: An Anthology of Verse by Negro Poets,* a volume that enabled him to articulate in specific terms his philosophy of poetry writing and publishing. He intended his poetry to be a bridge between the races; therefore, he had modeled his own work after poets A. E. Housman and especially John Keats, but his choice of models did not reflect a pandering to white approval. There was no black or white art for Cullen, only art. He thus declared in the foreword to *Caroling Dusk:*

> This country's Negro writers may here and there turn some singular facet to the literary sun, but in the main, since theirs is also the heritage of English language, their work will not present any serious aberration from poetic tendencies of their times. . . . As heretical as it may sound, there is the probability that Negro poets, dependent as they are on the English Language, may have more to gain from the rich background of English and American poetry than from any nebulous atavistic yearnings toward an African inheritance.

Caroling Dusk contains contributions by most of the young writers of the Harlem Renaissance, thus making it an invaluable reference source today.

In December of 1926, shortly before the appearance of *Caroling Dusk,* Cullen strengthened his role as assistant editor at *Opportunity* by developing a column for that journal. Called "The Dark Tower," the column would run until September of 1928. Cullen used the column as another way of perpetuating his philosophy of creativity. He advocated a kind of self-censorship on the part of Afro-American writers in order that they not make the racial bridge too difficult for whites to cross. He advised Langston Hughes, for example, in his review of *The Weary Blues* (1926), not to become a "racial artist" but to work for a more "quiet way of communing" that would be "more spiritual for the God-seeking heart." "Negroes should be concerned with making good impressions," he was to assert in another "Dark Tower" column, in order to promote themselves to a position from which they could compete for power and property in America. Art should not distort truth, he argued, but "there are some things, some truths of Negro life and thought, of Negro inhibitions, that all Negroes know, but take no pride in." Those should not be "broadcast . . . to the world," for to do so, Cullen feared, would "strengthen the bitterness of our enemies, and in some instances turn away the interest of our friends. Every phase of Negro life should not be the white man's concern."

Such admonitions were, however, only one element of Cullen's sense of race in America. In

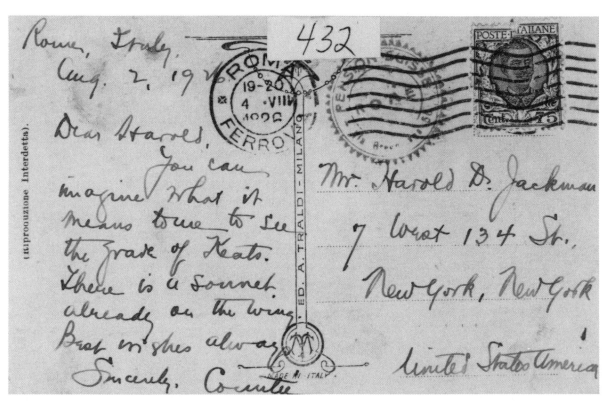

Postcard to Cullen's lifelong friend (by permission of James R. Rhone, the Estate of Countee Cullen; courtesy of the Schomburg Center for Research in Black Culture, the New York Public Library, Astor, Lenox and Tilden Foundations)

the very columns in which he called for caution, he lost no chance to celebrate Afro-American art. He decried, for example, the failure of white critics to understand a black character in *Stigma* (1927), a play by Dorothy Manley and Donald Huff. He often praised quite strident racial motifs in black writing, discovering, for instance, that the "clearest notes" in Amy Spingarn's *Pride and Humility* (1927) were "those poems which have a racial framework." On at least one occasion, he even attempted to further the career of a young poet whom Cullen mistakenly took to be "of our pigmentary persuasion." While Cullen was able to appreciate the work of both black and white poets, his taste in verse ran to the romantic and traditional, and he was liable to criticize more radical work, regardless of the author's color. Amy Lowell, for example, Cullen declared in his review of her posthumous *Ballads for Sale* (1927), "actually wrote very few real poems. There is a legerdemain of style.... But for the hungry heart to feed upon [,] for the emotions to kindle and flame by, there is little." In a way that was entirely consistent with his conception of art as a unifier rather than a divider of peoples, he tried to be racially evenhanded in his criticism. Paradoxically, his fairness is precisely what made Cullen, more than anything else, a racial poet.

Cullen planned for his study tour funded by the Guggenheim Fellowship to begin in 1928. Just before his departure on 10 April 1928, he married Nina Yolande Du Bois, daughter of W. E. B. Du Bois. Highly touted as the affair of the year in the Harlem community, the wedding was widely attended. The marriage, however, did not last long; the couple was divorced in Paris in 1930, after receiving a series of letters in which Du Bois had tried to bring about some kind of reconciliation.

In 1929 Cullen published *The Black Christ and Other Poems*, another volume focusing frequently upon racial themes and conflicts. In "To Certain Critics," he felt obliged to defend himself against voices that argued that he should be more shrill in his protest. Pain knows no color, he responded in effect; but he really needed no defense, for when his inner voice compelled him to sing, more often than not the voice sang a song of protest, sometimes of controlled rage. In "Song of Praise," he converts the rage into an assertion of the superiority of black passion, as he had in *The Ballad of the Brown Girl*. In "The Black Christ," Cullen tries to find peace in his often troubled religious response to the world. He had declared about himself in *Caroling Dusk:* "Countee Cullen's chief problem has been that of reconciling a Christian upbringing with a

pagan inclination. His life so far has not convinced him that the problem is insoluble."

By the time he published *The Black Christ and Other Poems* in 1929, he had made his choice for the loving comfort that Christianity could bring him. In the long narrative title poem, the narrator begins with a celebration of his coming to God despite earthly obstacles—"my country's shame." As the result of a pure relationship with a white woman, the narrator's brother has been beaten to death by a white mob, transfigured with a saintly luminescence as he dies. The narrator questions the worthiness of the white Christ who would permit such a cruel, ungodly act to occur, but his angelic mother's exhortation to faith and the appearance of the now-resurrected brother combine to win the doubting narrator back to the fold. The speaker's conversion signals the advent of a sort of terrestrial paradise for the family, which now has a bounteous harvest from field and bough, while "Job's dark sister," the pious mother, knits and prays.

The Black Christ and Other Poems also focuses on Cullen's recurring theme of love and the ambivalence he had toward it. David Levering Lewis, in his study of the Harlem Renaissance, *When Harlem Was in Vogue* (1981), links Cullen's ambivalence to the possibility that he was homosexual, an idea rumored during Cullen's lifetime. Lewis's speculation is based on interviews that he had with some of Cullen's Harlem associates. At all events, sexual ambivalence in the form of mistrust of women and the love of them comes through in his love poetry. His repeated association of love with death comes through in *The Black Christ* and takes the form of the potential effects death may have on a love relationship, as a means of escape from a ruinous love affair or as a menace to a more satisfactory one, as in such poems as "At a Parting," "Ghosts," and "There Must be Words." There is a frailty, a feverishness about Cullen's lovers—especially the male ones—that is impossible to miss. The narrator-lover is almost always conscious of the approach of the end of the affair, perhaps because of the fickleness of his partner, perhaps because of death's imminence; in nearly every kiss, there is a sigh of despair.

After *The Black Christ and Other Poems,* Cullen's poetic output slowed. Indeed, by the end of the 1920s, Cullen had published all of the poems for which he is remembered.

In 1932 Cullen's publisher, Harper, accepted and published his only novel, *One Way to Heaven,* a work with some notable virtues but a damaging structural defect that generally kept critical reception cool. One of the novel's two plots involves the relationship between Mattie Johnson, a straitlaced Harlem maid, and Sam Lucas, a one-armed Texas gambler and con man, a trickster of the type familiar to Afro-American lore. Drawing upon his experiences at his father's church for background, Cullen draws a convincing picture of Sam's feigned conversion in church on Christmas Eve, as a result of which Mattie both undergoes her own genuine conversion, after years of refusal, and falls in love with Sam Lucas. As the plot descends into melodrama, Sam marries Mattie but takes a lover. Mattie has a baby who dies only hours after it is born. Sam, on his deathbed, does the only decent thing that he has ever done. Having overheard Mattie express her fear that Sam will be damned, Sam—this time to spare Mattie—claims to undergo a second conversion, this one the consequence of a fake epiphany.

Probably the best elements of the novel are the satirical characters involved in the secondary plot, centered in the salon of Constancia Brandon, Harlem's popular hostess, wife of a physician and oil magnate. Constancia plays ringmaster to a menagerie of Harlem's most superficial intellectuals, a crowd drawn from Cullen's impressions of the partygoers whom he had observed in the 1920s when he was one of Harlem's intellectual idols. The types that he had seen at A'Lelia Walker and Carl Van Vechten's social gatherings are all in the novel: Garveyites, white liberals, an array of New Negro artists, and assorted grotesques. Most memorable, perhaps, except for the irrepressible Constancia herself, is a white southern intellectual bigot, a professor who has spewed out a tract called *The Menace of the Negro to Our American Civilization*. Only Constancia Brandon in all the world could get her guests to sit through the professor's lecture of racial poison and actually applaud politely at its conclusion.

The main problem with the novel, as critics were quick to notice, is that its two plots have little bearing on one another. Although Mattie is Constancia's maid and Constancia helps Sam with his job hunting and arranges for Mattie and Sam's wedding at one of her home circuses, there is little else to unify Cullen's tale of two classes. When *One Way to Heaven* appeared, Rudolph Fisher, author of another Harlem novel that examined class differences, *The Walls of Jericho* (1928), astutely stated its deficiency. Cullen, he said, was "exhibiting a lovely pastel and cartoon on the same frame." One newspaper reviewer said that "a superb short novel

has been sacrificed to convention or . . . Mr. Cullen has been unwilling to regard Sam and Mattie as important enough to justify devoting all his novel to them." Cullen had written a novel in which he probably came closer to the folk than he ever did in his poetry, particularly through his characterizations of folk types like the trickster and the solid old aunty. He succeeded in making Constancia both a broadly comic and yet sympathetic character, whose goal of bringing disparate people together to live in a civilized American society was not fundamentally different from Cullen's own ultimate aim. But the novel was, nonetheless, flawed, and Cullen's hope for a career as a novelist was stymied.

Always fond of the theater, Cullen, who would publish his version of *Medea* in 1935, now used his novel to try to make his mark as a dramatist. With a collaborator, Harry Hamilton, he prepared a stage adaptation of *One Way to Heaven*, which, although never produced commercially, demonstrates that Cullen had a fair dramatic faculty. In the end, there is more tediousness and contrivance in the play than in the novel, but Cullen and Hamilton did tinker enough with the plot and characters to telescope time effectively and to achieve a good measure of theatrical force, largely through inventing a sexual relationship between Constancia and Sam that is absent in the novel. The stage version does not suffer from the disunity of the novel itself.

Also in the early 1930s, Cullen decided to work with young people, to make his contribution to the racial struggle as a teacher. In 1934 he became a teacher at Frederick Douglass Junior High School in New York, where he taught French and English. Cullen's publication of poetry continued to slow down from the pace he had kept in the 1920s. In 1935 he published his treatment of the classical *Medea*, along with a selection of new poems. In this volume, he extends his persistent motif of the danger and perfidy of female lovers. "Medusa" and "The Cat" are typical. To Cullen the blinding consequence of looking on Medusa is not brought on by her ugliness but, on the contrary, by her magnificent beauty, to which the sensitive male is destined to succumb. In "The Cat," even as the narrator sits stroking the animal, he intuits in it "A woman with thine eyes, satanic beast/Profound and cold as scythes to mow me down." Cullen also returns to the theme of death that he had found so attractive in earlier works. Not surprisingly he sometimes greeted death as surcease from the pain of racial oppression. For example, in

"Only the Polished Skeleton," the speaker stresses the racially leveling quality of death. Stripped of the flesh that triggered suffering, the raceless skeleton can calmly rest and measure "the worth of it all it so despised."

While he was teaching, Cullen began to write children's stories that would promulgate his belief in the values of decency and equality among the young. Two collections of these stories were published, *The Lost Zoo* (1940) and *My Lives and How I Lost Them* (1942).

In 1939 Cullen tried his hand at playwriting again. He saw strong dramatic possibilities in Arna Bontemps's first novel, *God Sends Sunday* (1931). Bontemps agreed, and, with the nagging question in the background of whether Cullen should remain in New York teaching his junior-high-school students or accept a chair at Fisk University, Cullen threw himself into the writing of the play that he and Bontemps called *St. Louis Woman.* He interrupted his work on 27 September 1940 to marry Ida Mae Roberson, sister of singer Orlando Roberson.

In 1945 Cullen and Bontemps seemed to have a chance for both a Broadway production of *St. Louis Woman,* which had taken the form of a musical, and a Hollywood treatment of it that would feature Lena Horne in the starring role. A number of Cullen's friends, including Walter White of the NAACP, pressured him to abandon the project because, they argued—although White's own daughter was to appear in *Strange Fruit* (1944) as a young black woman who has an illicit relationship with a white youth in the fields—*St. Louis Woman* was degrading to the black community. Cullen was outraged and dejected. Few besides the close companion of his last years, his second wife, Ida, would take a public stand in his defense, not even his bosom friend Harold Jackman. There were delays, postponements, squabbles with an impatient Bontemps, and then Lena Horne backed away from the commitment. Shortly thereafter, on 9 January 1946, Cullen died of uremic poisoning in New York City's Sydenham Hospital.

St. Louis Woman, in fact, debases blacks no more than, say, Richard Wright's *Native Son* (1940) does or Tennessee Williams's plays demean whites. It is a human drama set in the Targee Street ghetto of St. Louis. There are bars and racetrack denizens, crime and rapacity, but there is love, too, and punishment, courage, and loyalty. Strongly reminiscent of George Gershwin's *Porgy and Bess* (1927), it is built around a triangle involving Della Greene, an internally soft, externally tough beauty, who is the undisputed property of Bigelow Brown, bully, gambler, and saloonkeeper, until L'il Augie, a self-assured little jockey, proves to have more nerve and more sensitivity than Brown. Augie takes Della from Brown, and, in the violence that follows, Della, Augie, and various minor characters show themselves to be far more virtuous than they are seedy. When the play was finally produced at the Martin Beck Theatre in New York on 30 March 1946, with score and lyrics by Harold Arlen and Johnny Mercer and featuring Pearl Bailey as bar girl Butterfly, reviews were mixed.

Cullen had worked on a few scripts in addition to *St. Louis Woman.* He collaborated with Owen Dodson on a one-act play, *The Third Fourth of July,* which appeared in the August 1946 issue of *Theatre Arts.* He never succeeded, however, in making a name for himself as a playwright.

Cullen's reputation, as he knew that it would be, was left to rest on the poems that he had published in the years of the Harlem Renaissance. He died prepared for that. The poet who had invented the story of his origins also gathered the pieces that he wanted for his memorial in the manuscript of *On These I Stand: An Anthology of the Best Poems of Countee Cullen,* which appeared in 1947.

The volume contains selections from *Color, Copper Sun, The Black Christ,* and *The Medea and Some Poems.* It also includes six previously unpublished poems, *The Ballad of the Brown Girl,* and two selections from *The Lost Zoo.* One of the unpublished poems, "Christus Natus Est," dated Christmas 1943, in the midst of World War II, confirms that Cullen's spiritual journey ended in acceptance of Christian faith. The carol acknowledges human suffering but strongly maintains Christian hope. "The manger still/Outshines the throne," Cullen insists; "Christ must and will/Come to his own."

Not until Houston A. Baker, Jr.'s short book on Cullen's work, *A Many-Colored Coat of Dreams: The Poetry of Countee Cullen* (1974), was there really a sustained and sound study of the body of Cullen's poetry. In the 1920s black and white critics alike had tended to heap uncritical praise on him for racial reasons, though there had been a growing admission, as his collections came out over time, that he was not growing as a poet. Harvey Curtis Webster commented astutely in his review of *On These I Stand,* in *Poetry,* July 1947: "One of Cullen's great misfortunes must have been that he was usually commended by both Negroes and whites for extra-poetic reasons. He was praised by Negroes because he was a Negro of distinction, by whites because they feared dispraise might be called prej-

440

Song In Spite of Myself.

Never love with all your heart,
    It only ends in aching,
And bit by bit to the smallest part,
    That organ will be breaking.

Never love with all your mind,
    It only ends in fretting;
In musing on sweet joys behind,
    Too poignant for forgetting.

Never love with all your soul;
    For such there is no ending,
Though a mind that frets may find control,
    And a shattered heart find mending.

Give but a grain of the heart's rich seed,
    Confine some under cover,
And when Love goes bid him Godspeed,
    And find another lover.

Countee Cullen

udice. Consequently Cullen's poetry was never severely and sympathetically criticized while he was alive to benefit by it." But Cullen did have moments of self-insight and of self-doubt, despite the reticence of critics to evaluate his work objectively. By the end of the 1920s, Cullen, in "Self Criticism" (*The Black Christ and Other Poems*), demanded of himself to know whether he would always sing a "pallid" and "wan" song, the "failing note" stuck in "the throat of the stricken swan." Better not to sing, the poem concluded, than never to move beyond the message "That the fittest song of Earth is a dirge,/And only fools trust Providence."

If the critics were too gentle with Cullen for nonpoetic reasons, for nonpoetic reasons, too, the Afro-American critics of the 1960s were too harsh with him. Creating the militant new black aesthetic of the 1960s, and conditioned by it, Don Lee (Haki Madhubuti) and others overlooked the exploration of the racial theme in Cullen, overlooked the protest and the pain. Not hearing him because their ears were attuned to notes of protest only on their frequency, they condemned Cullen as a sort of Uncle Tom. Lee even referred to him as "a well-known poet of the Harlem Renaissance period [who] refused to acknowledge that he was a 'negro' or Black poet." The Afro-American critics, looking backward through the fervor of the 1960s, were inclined to forget that Cullen maintained an integrity that others, understandably, compromised in the pressures of the 1920s. After he had published the brilliant *Cane* (1923), Jean Toomer, for example, was said to have melted into the white world, and Langston Hughes, who was to live long enough to change with the changing racial values and was a model to 1960s black critics, had accepted help from the white Vachel Lindsay to get his first volume of poems published. Yet when Carl Van Vechten had offered to help Cullen into print, Cullen had insisted on finding his own way to win the white-dominated publishing game. He did not for a moment forget or permit others to forget that he was black, but his foremost compulsion was to demand the complete and necessary liberty of the human artist, without any limitation of blackness or whiteness.

The difficulties with the corpus of Cullen's poetry rest with the fact that he tended to write derivative poetry, to produce a kind of Keatsian poetry that had already been done a hundred years before—and by poets who could do it better. He knew about modernist poetry, the work of Ezra Pound, Amy Lowell, and T. S. Eliot, and the imagists, but their work had little meaning for him.

Cullen's world view was a product of the Harlem Renaissance, during which period, as Nathan Irvin Huggins has remarked, "enslavement to white forms and values had been most pronounced in that art which was to have been the real evidence of the Negro's coming of age." The movement was delighted with itself, as it had every reason to be, for its varied achievements. Later writers would build on the achievement of people like Cullen, who had stood shoulder to shoulder with W. E. B. Du Bois and James Weldon Johnson and other shapers of the vision that saw blacks eventually building with whites an America where race did not matter. "In a time when it is the vogue to make much of the Negro's aptitude for clownishness or to depict him objectively as a serio-comic figure," Du Bois declared, "it is a fine and praiseworthy act for Mr. Cullen to show through the interpretation of his own subjectivity the inner workings of the Negro soul and mind." Cullen was content with his point of view, if not with his aesthetic progress. He was what Du Bois proclaimed the New Negro Renaissance to be all about; Harlem was carrying him around on its shoulders as the exemplar of Du Bois's Talented Tenth. By any reasonable definition, Cullen was a racial poet, but he reserved the right not to be categorized, to be circumscribed by the label or its implications, and for that position, Johnson happily said of him: "Cullen himself has declared that, in the sense of wishing for consideration or allowances on account of race or recognizing for himself any limitation of 'racial' themes, he has no desire or intention of being a Negro poet. In this, he is not only within his right; he is right." If later critics were to assail him for being the Harlem Renaissance poet, Cullen left a message for them in *On These I Stand*, in "To Certain Critics." "No racial option narrows grief," Cullen observed, and if there are those who cannot understand what he tried to accomplish through his writing, "I'll bear your censure as your praise,/For never shall the clan/Confine my singing to its ways/Beyond the ways of man."

References:

Houston A. Baker, Jr., *A Many-Colored Coat of Dreams: The Poetry of Countee Cullen* (Detroit: Broadside Press, 1974);

Stephen H. Bronz, *Roots of Racial Consciousness: The 1920's: Three Harlem Renaissance Authors* (New York: Libra Publishers, 1964);

Arthur P. Davis, "The Alien-and-Exile Theme in Countee Cullen's Racial Poems," *Phylon*, 14 (Fourth Quarter 1953): 390-400;

Davis, *From the Dark Tower: Afro-American Writers 1900-1960* (Washington, D.C.: Howard University Press, 1974);

David F. Dorsey, "Countee Cullen's Use of Greek Mythology," *College Language Association Journal*, 13 (1970): 68-77;

Nathan Irvin Huggins, *Harlem Renaissance* (London, Oxford & New York: Oxford University Press, 1971);

James Weldon Johnson, *Black Manhattan* (New York: Knopf, 1930);

David Levering Lewis, *When Harlem Was in Vogue* (New York: Knopf, 1981);

David Littlejohn, *Black on White: A Critical Survey of Writing by American Negroes* (New York: Viking, 1966);

Alain Locke, *Four Negro Poets* (New York: A. & C. Boni, 1925);

Edward Margolies, *Native Sons: A Critical Study of Twentieth-Century Negro American Authors* (Philadelphia & New York: Lippincott, 1968);

J. Saunders Redding, *To Make a Poet Black* (Chapel Hill: University of North Carolina Press, 1939);

Roger Rosenblatt, *Black Fiction* (Cambridge, Mass.: Harvard University Press, 1974);

Alan R. Shucard, *Countee Cullen* (Boston: Twayne, 1984);

Amritjit Singh, *The Novels of the Harlem Renaissance: Twelve Black Writers 1923-1933* (University Park & London: Pennsylvania State University Press, 1976);

Jean Wagner, *Black Poets of the United States: From Paul Laurence Dunbar to Langston Hughes*, translated by Kenneth Douglas (Urbana, Chicago & London: University of Illinois Press, 1973);

Harvey Curtis Webster, "A Difficult Career," review of *On These I Stand, Poetry*, 70 (July 1947): 224-225.

Papers:
Cullen's papers are at the libraries of Atlanta University and the University of California, Berkeley, and in the James Weldon Johnson Collection at the Beinecke Library, Yale University.

William Waring Cuney
(6 May 1906-30 June 1976)

Lucy Kelly Hayden
Winston-Salem State University

BOOKS: *Puzzles*, edited by Paul Breman (Utrecht, Holland: DeRoos, 1960);
Storefront Church (London: Breman, 1973).

OTHER: Langston Hughes, ed., *Four Lincoln University Poets*, includes poetry by Cuney (Lincoln University, Pa.: Lincoln University, 1930);
Lincoln University Poets; Centennial Anthology, 1854-1954, edited by Cuney, Langston Hughes, and Bruce McM. Wright (New York: Fine Editions, 1954).

One of the "second echelon" transitional poets of the Harlem Renaissance, William Waring Cuney, along with writers Frank S. Horne, Georgia Douglas Johnson, Donald Jeffrey Hayes, Helene Johnson, Gwendolyn Bennett, Arna Bontemps, and Anne Spencer, is often critically overlooked, although he made substantial contributions to the New Negro movement. Best known for his minor masterpiece "No Images," which won first prize out of 1,276 entries in the *Opportunity* poetry contest in 1926, Cuney used his musical and literary talents to depict the black experience in a career that spanned half a century. Cuney's obscure biography and unusual publication history make it difficult to arrange his work chronologically. Furthermore, since his poetry is not particularly autobiographical, critics have not been able to date events in his life from Cuney's work.

William Waring and his twin brother, Norris Wright, were born to Madge Louise Baker and Norris Cuney II, in Washington, D.C., on 6 May

1906. Although there is little detail about Cuney's early life, he was a descendant of two prominent, racially mixed families whose ancestors include: a Swiss family (Cuneys) that immigrated to America before 1803; Captain William Waring, a Scotchman who settled in Virginia as early as 1750; two slave matriarchs, Hester Neale Stuart (a Cuney), who was descended herself from Potomac Indian, Negro, and Caucasian blood, and the racially mixed Mother Vessels (a Waring). Among Cuney's modern relatives, many of whom are prominent, was folklorist and musicologist Maud Cuney Hare, who was an active minor figure behind the scenes of the Harlem Renaissance arts movement. Cuney's brother became a teacher of linotype and a printer who brought out the last work of poet Georgia Douglas Johnson.

Cuney received a public school education in Washington and attended Howard University briefly. He then matriculated at Lincoln University in Pennsylvania, and he is sometimes referred to as one of the Lincoln University poets, along with Langston Hughes, William Allyn Hill, and Edward Silvera. In 1954 Cuney, Hughes, and Bruce McM. Wright edited *Lincoln University Poets; Centennial Anthology, 1854-1954*. At Lincoln, Cuney decided to follow a career in singing, and he was an active member of the school's glee club and a quartet. Subsequently he studied at the New England Conservatory of Music in Boston and in Rome. Cuney, like his brother who had studied for a career in piano, never performed professionally. Some of his lyrics were used by other performers, most notably Josh White, who recorded some of Cuney's protest songs in the Depression-era album *Southern Exposure* (for which Richard Wright wrote the introductory text). When it became clear to Cuney that he would not be a professional singer, he turned his attention to more literary pursuits.

Among his contemporaries, including Bontemps, Hughes, Bernard Bell, Sterling A. Brown, Blyden Jackson, and Rosey Pool, Cuney was a favorite minor poet. His poems were frequently published in anthologies such as Countee Cullen's *Caroling Dusk: An Anthology of Verse by Negro Poets* (1927), and in magazines such as the ill-fated *Fire!!* (November 1926). His career was interrupted during World War II, when he served in the South Pacific as a technical sergeant in the army. His tour of duty lasted three and a half years and earned him the Asiatic Pacific Theater Ribbon and three Bronze Stars. After the war, Cuney picked up his career as a poet, this time in the Bronx, New York. He returned to his study of music as a "special"

William Waring Cuney (courtesy of the Prints and Photographs Collection, Moorland-Spingarn Research Center, Howard University)

The clarity of these early gemlike poems is a pronounced feature of "No Images," the most frequently anthologized of Cuney's work and the penultimate piece in *Puzzles*. It was written when he was eighteen; two years later, in 1926, while Cuney was still a student at Lincoln University, it won an *Opportunity* magazine contest and was published in the magazine's June contest issue.

In this poem that is prototypical of the concerns of the Harlem Renaissance, Cuney sounds the themes of the desirability, strength, and vulnerability of black worth, pride, and creativity in a society whose values are inimical to blacks. The ironically titled "No Images" takes, as its central double image, the modern Afro-American woman and her counterpart in an older civilization:

> She does not know
> Her beauty,
> She thinks her brown body
> Has no glory.
>
> If she could dance
> Naked
> Under palm trees
> And see her image in the river,
> She would know.
>
> But there are no palm trees
> On the street,
> And dish water gives back no images.

The poet knows that the brown girl has beauty and glory, but acculturation into a white society and economic poverty have caused her not only to lose awareness of her merit but to denigrate herself. If she were in Africa or the Caribbean, where women like her set the standards for beauty, she would have a different, clearer "image" of herself reflected back by society. She is not unlike Claude McKay's dancer in a Harlem nightclub who "seemed a proudly-swaying palm/Grown lovelier for passing through a storm," but whose social and economic status has also conspired to prevent her from knowing her own worth. The closing image of dishwater emblematizes, according to critic Eugene Redmond, "a kind of death—a spiritual and moral death/death—for Cuney," which embodies the stultifying "decadence of Western civilization." The theme of the effects of Western civilization on the black American becomes more particularized in poems that chronicle the landmark events of the twentieth century. In the undated "The Neighbors Stood on the Corner," in *Puzzles*, Cuney addresses the effects of World War II on the Afro-American.

The piece is a moving narrative about a suicide whose wife had left him: Cuney implies that the suicide's problems ran deeper than the dissolution of his marriage: " 'He was overseas—/Colored, and in the army—/You know what that did to our boys.' " Contemplating the tragic event, one neighbor humorously reflects, "Me, I'll stay here with troubles,/What's new about worry?" If Western civilization brought oppression and cultural dissolution to the black American, it also brought him a source of faith and inspiration, Cuney seems to feel. In the gospel poem "Darkness Hides His Throne," collected in *Puzzles and Storefront Church,* Cuney takes the first six lines almost verbatim from a popular gospel song:

> My God is so high,
> you can not get over Him.
>
> My God is so low,
> you can not get under Him.
>
> My God is so wide,
> you can not get around Him.

Cuney provides a summary in the seventh line, "He can not be measured," and, in the final lines, an explanation, "Darkness covers His pavilion,/darkness hides His throne." Other poems merge the two dominant themes of music and religion in a more theoretical way. In the short "Three Secrets," Cuney advises readers to maintain "three secrets" to achieve wholeness in life: "The way of prayer,/The voice of faith,/The mystery of song."

Like William Wordsworth, Cuney frequently chooses his subjects from the ranks of the common man and depicts them in the language of the common man. This "rustic" approach, however, frequently dissolves before the context of modern experience. The violence and despair in "Derelict" are a far cry from Wordsworth's English countryside:

> He came home and found his wife
> And children dead
> From a boiler explosion
> At times he comes up-town
> From the bowery for a day or two.
> You see him on the street for a while,
> Then he goes away again
> You do not see him for a long time.

But Cuney, being a comprehensive poet, portrays characters from the middle and wealthy

1906. Although there is little detail about Cuney's early life, he was a descendant of two prominent, racially mixed families whose ancestors include: a Swiss family (Cuneys) that immigrated to America before 1803; Captain William Waring, a Scotchman who settled in Virginia as early as 1750; two slave matriarchs, Hester Neale Stuart (a Cuney), who was descended herself from Potomac Indian, Negro, and Caucasian blood, and the racially mixed Mother Vessels (a Waring). Among Cuney's modern relatives, many of whom are prominent, was folklorist and musicologist Maud Cuney Hare, who was an active minor figure behind the scenes of the Harlem Renaissance arts movement. Cuney's brother became a teacher of linotype and a printer who brought out the last work of poet Georgia Douglas Johnson.

Cuney received a public school education in Washington and attended Howard University briefly. He then matriculated at Lincoln University in Pennsylvania, and he is sometimes referred to as one of the Lincoln University poets, along with Langston Hughes, William Allyn Hill, and Edward Silvera. In 1954 Cuney, Hughes, and Bruce McM. Wright edited *Lincoln University Poets; Centennial Anthology, 1854-1954*. At Lincoln, Cuney decided to follow a career in singing, and he was an active member of the school's glee club and a quartet. Subsequently he studied at the New England Conservatory of Music in Boston and in Rome. Cuney, like his brother who had studied for a career in piano, never performed professionally. Some of his lyrics were used by other performers, most notably Josh White, who recorded some of Cuney's protest songs in the Depression-era album *Southern Exposure* (for which Richard Wright wrote the introductory text). When it became clear to Cuney that he would not be a professional singer, he turned his attention to more literary pursuits.

Among his contemporaries, including Bontemps, Hughes, Bernard Bell, Sterling A. Brown, Blyden Jackson, and Rosey Pool, Cuney was a favorite minor poet. His poems were frequently published in anthologies such as Countee Cullen's *Caroling Dusk: An Anthology of Verse by Negro Poets* (1927), and in magazines such as the ill-fated *Fire!!* (November 1926). His career was interrupted during World War II, when he served in the South Pacific as a technical sergeant in the army. His tour of duty lasted three and a half years and earned him the Asiatic Pacific Theater Ribbon and three Bronze Stars. After the war, Cuney picked up his career as a poet, this time in the Bronx, New York. He returned to his study of music as a "special"

William Waring Cuney (courtesy of the Prints and Photographs Collection, Moorland-Spingarn Research Center, Howard University)

student at Columbia University. In 1950 his poetry, along with Hughes's, was translated and introduced to the German reading public by Eva Hesse O'Donnell in the newspaper *Die Neue Zeitung*. In 1953 she and Paridam von dem Knesebeck published *Meine dunklen Hände* ("My Dark Hands"), a collection of translated modern Afro-American lyrics, containing several of Cuney's poems. In 1958 Rosey Pool and Paul Breman edited an anthology of Afro-American poetry titled *Ik Zag Hoe Zwart Ik Was* (*I Saw How Black I Was*), in which the poems, including two by Cuney, were given in English and Dutch.

Sometime subsequent to the war, probably in the 1950s, Cuney had several broadsides published, including *The Alley Cat Brushed His Whiskers, Two Poems: Darkness Hides His Throne [and] "We Make Supplication"* (printed by N. Wright Cuney), and *Women and Kitchens*.

Although his poems had gained a certain popularity, it was not until 1960 that his first collection, *Puzzles*, was compiled by Breman and published by a bibliophile society in Holland on the virtual eve of America's new black aesthetic renaissance of the 1960s and 1970s. After 1962 Cuney became reclusive and cut himself off from the black literary community. However, a critical comment made by John O. Killens in his *Black World* article, "Another Time When Black Was Beautiful" (November 1970), caused the poet to break his long, self-imposed silence. Speaking of the "Conception" section of Cuney's brief trilogy "My Jesus," Killens called the piece "humorous, irreverent, and idiomatic." "Conception" is succinct:

Jesus' mother never had no man.
God came to her one day an' said
"Mary, chile, kiss ma han'."

Cuney's brief reply to Killens was published in *Black World* (March 1971). In part it read: "During the Harlem Renaissance, James Weldon Johnson selected three of my poems—'Conception,' 'Crucifixion,' and 'Po' Jesus'—for his anthology titled *Book of American Negro Poetry*. A quick reading of these poems will show that the poems are idiomatic, not humorous, and not irreverent."

In 1973 Breman compiled a second volume of Cuney's poetry. *Storefront Church* contains eighteen poems, many of which were early pieces. "Darkness Hides His Throne," "No Images," and "Guitar Music" had all appeared in *Puzzles*. A modest number of Cuney's poems, which have been anthologized and recorded, have never been col-

lected. Although anthologist Rosey Pool erroneously calls Cuney a "prolific writer," she correctly identifies the focus of his work: "for Waring Cuney there's poetry in every facet of human, and especially of Negro, struggle and achievement."

Cuney's poems are frequently universal in scope. He is a poet whose perception is first and foremost that of a human being; but, as a black poet, he reflects racial concerns and often employs folk speech and rhythms. Black music, both sacred and secular, plays an integral role in his work, and he is particularly noted for incorporating the blues into his writing. Religion is a frequent theme in much of his writing, and, naturally, it dominates *Storefront Church*. However, Cuney's métier is human relationship, no detail of which is too trivial for him to examine and describe. His subjects are frequently ordinary people represented in brief, vivid character sketches and verbally economic portraits.

His technique was consistent throughout his career. He adopted and retained the use of free verse, frequently identified with the most gifted of the Harlem Renaissance poets, in both his standard English poems and in the many idiomatic, folk-oriented poems. Cuney effectively uses the poetic anecdote, which in his hands is sometimes moralistic, sometimes humorous, sometimes both. He makes a conscious effort to cultivate simplicity, clarity, and truth in his work; and, although some pieces may seem to be too prosaic, he often achieves a purity of vision. The popularity of "The Death Bed," for example (first published in *Fire!!*, 1926), rests on this unity and simplicity of vision reminiscent in theoretic approach to the works of Emily Dickinson and in humor to that of Robert Browning. The persona of this piece is an old dying man whose family insists upon praying for his soul, despite his insistence that they do not. He sends them from the room but can still hear distant prayers as he tries to sound his own note "on a song he knew." But all the while he is worried "That they were in there praying,/And all the time he wondered/What it was they could be saying." The well-anthologized poem "Finis" also captures Cuney at a moment of clarity and simplicity. Two people are no longer lovers and the speaker, having established that their "Love has drifted/To a quiet close,/Leaving the empty ache that follows when beauty goes," cautions his recent mistress not to make the mistake, next time she falls in love, of loving too much. Clearly this fault has been the speaker's own, and the poignant little poem closes on a subtextual note of regret.

1122 TINTON AVE
BRONX 56, NY
FEBRUARY 18, 1954

DEAR MR. SPINGARN,

I TALKED WITH MRS. SPEYER ON THE PHONE YESTERDAY. I CALLED TO TELL HER THAT LINCOLN WILL PUBLISH THE LINCOLN POETS MANUSCRIPT WHICH YOU ARE NOW READING. I'M SO GLAD THAT SHE GAVE IT TO YOU TO LOOK AT AHEAD OF TIME." A FEW DAYS AGO DOWN AT LANGSTON'S I READ OVER YOUR LIST OF BOOKS IN THE CRISIS FOR '53. AT SOME FUTURE TIME I WOULD LIKE TO HAVE A TALK WITH YOU AFTER YOU RETURN THE MANUSCRIPT TO MRS. SPEYER. WITH BEST WISHES AND KIND REGARDS I AM.

SINCERELY YOURS,
WARING CUNEY

Letter to Arthur B. Spingarn (courtesy of the Arthur B. Spingarn Collection, Moorland-Spingarn Research Center, Howard University)

The clarity of these early gemlike poems is a pronounced feature of "No Images," the most frequently anthologized of Cuney's work and the penultimate piece in *Puzzles*. It was written when he was eighteen; two years later, in 1926, while Cuney was still a student at Lincoln University, it won an *Opportunity* magazine contest and was published in the magazine's June contest issue.

In this poem that is prototypical of the concerns of the Harlem Renaissance, Cuney sounds the themes of the desirability, strength, and vulnerability of black worth, pride, and creativity in a society whose values are inimical to blacks. The ironically titled "No Images" takes, as its central double image, the modern Afro-American woman and her counterpart in an older civilization:

> She does not know
> Her beauty,
> She thinks her brown body
> Has no glory.
>
> If she could dance
> Naked
> Under palm trees
> And see her image in the river,
> She would know.
>
> But there are no palm trees
> On the street,
> And dish water gives back no images.

The poet knows that the brown girl has beauty and glory, but acculturation into a white society and economic poverty have caused her not only to lose awareness of her merit but to denigrate herself. If she were in Africa or the Caribbean, where women like her set the standards for beauty, she would have a different, clearer "image" of herself reflected back by society. She is not unlike Claude McKay's dancer in a Harlem nightclub who "seemed a proudly-swaying palm/Grown lovelier for passing through a storm," but whose social and economic status has also conspired to prevent her from knowing her own worth. The closing image of dishwater emblematizes, according to critic Eugene Redmond, "a kind of death—a spiritual and moral death/death—for Cuney," which embodies the stultifying "decadence of Western civilization." The theme of the effects of Western civilization on the black American becomes more particularized in poems that chronicle the landmark events of the twentieth century. In the undated "The Neighbors Stood on the Corner," in *Puzzles*, Cuney addresses the effects of World War II on the Afro-American.

The piece is a moving narrative about a suicide whose wife had left him: Cuney implies that the suicide's problems ran deeper than the dissolution of his marriage: " 'He was overseas—/Colored, and in the army—/You know what that did to our boys.' " Contemplating the tragic event, one neighbor humorously reflects, "Me, I'll stay here with troubles,/What's new about worry?" If Western civilization brought oppression and cultural dissolution to the black American, it also brought him a source of faith and inspiration, Cuney seems to feel. In the gospel poem "Darkness Hides His Throne," collected in *Puzzles and Storefront Church*, Cuney takes the first six lines almost verbatim from a popular gospel song:

> My God is so high,
> you can not get over Him.
>
> My God is so low,
> you can not get under Him.
>
> My God is so wide,
> you can not get around Him.

Cuney provides a summary in the seventh line, "He can not be measured," and, in the final lines, an explanation, "Darkness covers His pavilion,/darkness hides His throne." Other poems merge the two dominant themes of music and religion in a more theoretical way. In the short "Three Secrets," Cuney advises readers to maintain "three secrets" to achieve wholeness in life: "The way of prayer,/The voice of faith,/The mystery of song."

Like William Wordsworth, Cuney frequently chooses his subjects from the ranks of the common man and depicts them in the language of the common man. This "rustic" approach, however, frequently dissolves before the context of modern experience. The violence and despair in "Derelict" are a far cry from Wordsworth's English countryside:

> He came home and found his wife
> And children dead
> From a boiler explosion
> At times he comes up-town
> From the bowery for a day or two.
> You see him on the street for a while,
> Then he goes away again
> You do not see him for a long time.

But Cuney, being a comprehensive poet, portrays characters from the middle and wealthy

Waring Cuney

PUZZLES

Selected and introduced by Paul Breman - With 8 two-color woodcuts by Ru van Rossem

De Roos Utrecht 1960

For my mother

With Love

Waring

January 25, 1961

Cover and dedication page for the first collection of Cuney's poetry (courtesy of the Oberlin College Library)

classes as well as those from the working class and other walks of life. On his crowded canvas one sees, for example, in "Old Saying," a church deacon who is having an affair with a choir singer two years older than his younger daughter; a wealthy married woman who runs away with a man without a cent; and a successful but unscrupulous divorce lawyer who becomes an alcoholic; in "Bobby-sox girl," a young girl who is posing for her graduation picture "In a V-neck sweater"; and in "Girl from Oklahoma," a woman who has the three B's, beauty, brains, and bucks," but sees "a psychiatrist/ Three hours a week,/Because she's lonely."

In *Black Poetry in America*, Blyden Jackson criticizes Cuney's depiction of black experience on the grounds that he may have needed less ingenuity to portray a "deprived" brown girl, as in "No Images," than was needed to dramatize the "beauty . . . and racial worth of some of the middle-class brown girls who were Cuney's blood kin or close associates." But Jackson's attack seems unfounded in the face

of the range of Cuney's subjects. He depicts the "privileged" brown girl as well as the "deprived."

Cuney enlivens several poems about the human condition in *Puzzles* and elsewhere with a touch of humor. In "Women and Kitchens," he asserts, "No kitchen/Is big enough/For two women." "They can be sisters," friends, in-laws, or strangers; but, one kitchen is too small for any two of them even if it is "a city block long."

In the fable poem "An Alley-Cat Brushed His Whiskers," Cuney presents an amusing personification of a cat watching its antagonist, a dog, being caught and driven away in an automobile by a dog-catcher:

The alley-cat
Brushed his whiskers,
Blinked a cat-blink
Smiled a cat-smile,
And laughed a cat-laugh.

The title poem of *Puzzles* attests to Cuney's romantic concern with human relationship. It is a soft word-picture of a woman's hair, eyes, and voice. Presumably, the "puzzles" of the title relate to the unfathomability of beauty and the persona's amazement at being the woman's love object. But Cuney is not naive; in "Love" he warns that "Love is one thing at one time,/Something else at another time." If readers will not "Take my word for it," Cuney says, they can "Wait until you find out for yourself."

Finally, the last poem in *Puzzles* and the third to be collected in *Storefront Church* as well, "Guitar Music" is a meditation on the combined efforts of craftsman and singer in bringing to life the spirit of musical creativity. The poem underscores the equal importance of "The heart of the guitar-maker" who brings the "plane, a chisel/Sandpaper, varnish" to the creation and "The singing heart/ Of the singer of songs."

Cuney's strong use of music for form and theme is especially clear in *Storefront Church*. Here

Cover for the 1973 collection of Cuney's poetry

music is melded with religion. The book is dedicated "for Adeline," perhaps Adeline [or Adelina] Dowdie Cuney, an early family member who was a soprano singer. The collection's title piece is a preacher's sermon aimed at getting "sinners" to accept Christ. Less a poem than an artifact of oral black tradition in America, it nonetheless functions as the book's organizing principle. The heart of the community, the heart of faith is represented here for Cuney by the plaintive folk music forms of the storefront church, so ubiquitous in black America. The collection begins with "Darkness Hides His Throne," followed by the gospel poem "Roll, Jordan, Roll," in which the title serves twice as a refrain to the persona's uncertainty about whether he will be remembered after death and whether his soul will "freeze" in the chilly river. Like the storefront church itself, Cuney's gospel and blues poems recognize the stern realities of life, but also maintain, while facing those realities, an indomitable fortitude and sense of unity. His blues poems include "Hard-time Blues," in which Cuney implies the importance of the rural, economically poor South in the development of the blues and the importance of the blues in the lives of the folk community:

Went down home 'bout a year ago
things so bad, Lord, my heart was sore.
Folks had nothing was a sin and shame
every-body said hard time was the blame.
        Great-God-a-mighty folks feeling bad
        lost every thing they ever had.

Cuney experiments with forms in his poems, and in very few of his blues pieces does he use the classic three-phrase form; although in "Let Me Tell You Blues Singers Something," a one-stanza poem, he twice repeats the phrase "Let me tell you blues singers something, one thing maybe that you do not know." Then he offers a final aphorism with the moral authority of a preacher:

The songs of the Lord will take you down any
kind of lonely old road you have to go.

In another blues piece Cuney pays homage to "the empress of the blues." The four-line poem is titled "Bessie Smith":

Oh, Tennessee road,
late at night—
where do you die
if your face ain't white?

The poet alludes to Bessie Smith's tragic automobile accident in 1937. At about three o'clock in the morning, she was riding from an engagement in Memphis, Tennessee, to Clarksdale, Mississippi. Ten miles from her destination, the accident occurred. Although reports conflict as to what happened, clearly Cuney subscribes to the version in which the forty-three-year-old singer was first taken to a white hospital where personnel refused to administer treatment or admit her. She was taken to the poorly equipped Negro hospital, where she died the next morning. Cuney, who was thirty-one at the time of Smith's death, conveys his grief as well as his indignation that she was a victim of southern segregation.

Cuney is so conversant with black musical forms that he is able to imitate different types of music in his poems. He uses ragtime syncopation in his tribute to two ragtime pianists in "Jelly Roll and Lucky." The lines replicate the meter of stride piano, a strong rhythmic accompaniment of the left hand:

When
Ferdinand Morton
plays
Twelfth Street Rag
. . . .
When
Luckeyeth Roberts
plays
Railroad Blues[.]

In similar fashion, a jazz poem (collected in Pool's anthology *Beyond the Blues*), "Charles Parker, 1925-1955," uses a trochaic foot to imitate the bebop rhythm associated with the alto saxophonist:

Listen,
This here
Is what
Charlie
Did
To the Blues.

Bernard Bell, commenting on this poem, observes, "Cuney obviously knows how to scat with the best of them":

This here
bid-dle-dee-dee
bid-dle-dee-dee[.]

And later in the poem, he executes an improvisation on "Baa Baa Black Sheep":

Bopsheep
have you any cool?
bahdada
one horn full.

Later in the poem Cuney laments—

Charlie's
Dead,
Charlie's
Gone,
But
John Burkes
Carried on.

("John Burkes" is a reference to John Birks "Dizzy" Gillespie.)

"Prayer for a Visitor" in *Storefront Church* is the only poem by Cuney that alludes to the civil-rights movements of the 1960s and 1970s. The persona, probably a preacher, asks God that the visitor, a white man, may "see the light." He continues:

Lord—
this white man
here in our church—
if he is a policeman
come to listen about
the sit-ins, and the sit-downs,
the meetings, and the picket lines—
Lord,
You tell him
that we have just begun.

Like "Prayer for a Visitor," many of Cuney's other poems are simple vignettes, sketches, or opinions written in a straightforward language that makes them seem like artifacts of folk life in urban black America. These more prosaic pieces in his canon are, in their way, as representative of the modern movement in black literature as "No Images" is representative of the Harlem Renaissance, since they open to scrutiny a unique perspective of Afro-American life.

References:

Bernard W. Bell, "Contemporary Afro-American Poetry as Folk Art," *Black World*, 20, no. 5 (1973): 16-26, 74-78;

Arna Bontemps, *The Harlem Renaissance Remembered* (New York: Dodd, Mead, 1972);

Bontemps, "The Negro Contribution to American Letters," in *The American Negro Reference Book*, edited by John P. Davis (Englewood Cliffs, N.J.: Prentice-Hall, 1966);

C. G. Woodson, "The Cuney Family," *Negro History Bulletin* (March 1948): 123-125, 143;

Woodson, "The Waring Family," *Negro History Bulletin* (February 1948): 99-107.

Raymond Garfield Dandridge

(1882-24 February 1930)

Joanne V. Gabbin
James Madison University

BOOKS: *Penciled Poems* (Cincinnati: Powell & White, 1917);

The Poet and Other Poems (Cincinnati: Powell & White, 1920);

Zalka Peetruza and Other Poems (Cincinnati: Mc-Donald, 1928).

OTHER: Robert T. Kerlin, *Negro Poets and Their Poems,* includes poetry by Dandridge (Washington, D.C.: Associated, 1923), pp. 54, 169-172, 221-222;

Newman Ivey White and Walter Clinton Jackson, eds., *An Anthology of Verse by American Negroes,* includes poetry by Dandridge (Durham, N.C.: Trinity College Press, 1924);

James Weldon Johnson, ed., *The Book of American Negro Poetry,* expanded edition, includes poetry by Dandridge (New York: Harcourt, Brace, 1931), pp. 190-194.

Raymond Garfield Dandridge, called by one critic "the adopted son of the lyric muse," wrote most of his poems from an invalid's bed in Cincinnati. In his short and poignant career as a writer, which began in 1912 and ended with his death in 1930, he revealed himself to be a modestly talented poet with a sensibility that was sincere and reflective. Although Dandridge was not a great poet, it is useful to view him as a gauge of the literary temperament of one of the most tumultuous and stimulating periods in American history. In his work, Dandridge responded to the persistent and strong appeal of the traditional dialect poetry of the Dunbar school and the equally strong pull of the literary and cultural forces of the New Negro Renaissance. His poems, with varying degrees of skill and depth, mirror a man reading clearly the vicissitudes of his audience and the concerns, crusades, and newly kindled aspirations of his race.

Raymond Garfield Dandridge was born in 1882 and reared in Price Hill, a suburb of Cincinnati. He attended the city's public schools and worked at various jobs while attending the Hughes Night High School. Excelling in athletics, he was

Ray Garfield Dandridge

an outstanding runner and swimmer for his school. After graduation Dandridge began a career as a house painter and decorator, realizing a talent he had exhibited earlier in art classes at the local Young Men's Christian Association.

In 1911 he was stricken with fever which resulted in an illness that kept him in bed for nearly a year. When he had begun to think that his long bout with illness was over, he suffered a partial paralysis that left him without the use of his legs and his right arm. Lying on his back, he taught himself to write with his left hand and began to compose verse. His poetry was born out of a quiet and courageous spirit that prompted him to give his ideas and feelings the shape and movement his body had been denied. Basing most of his reflections on the earlier, active part of his life, he remained aware of the world outside through reading, correspondence, and interaction with a large circle of friends.

Dandridge never married. Though there is vague reference to a sweetheart throughout his poetry, her identity remains as shadowy as many other aspects of his personal life. His mother, Ellen C. Dandridge, to whom he dedicated his first work, was his devoted nurse and companion during his illness and was often the subject of his verse. He had a sister and two brothers. Though some autobiographical insights may be gleaned from several of his poems, "Price Hill" most directly chronicles his early life: his growing up on the "Hill," his leaving his home and sweetheart "huntin' fo' de busy whirl," and his returning when his health and strength had given out.

> I find honey in de breeze,
>   On de Hill.
> Find rail 'holesome rest an' ease
>   On de Hill,
> Dar is somethin' I cain't tell,
> Gibs me hopes ob gettin' well
> Mebbe it's de home lak smell,
>   On de Hill.

There he stayed with his mother for the next nineteen years. With the gift of a telephone from a friend, he supplied their only means of support by soliciting orders for coal for Roger Kemper Rogan's coal company. Rogan and his wife, along with Calvin D. Wilson, helped Dandridge publish his last book, *Zalka Peetruza and Other Poems* (1928).

During his confinement from July 1912 until his death at the age of forty-eight on 24 February 1930, he published three books of poems: *Penciled Poems* (1917), *The Poet and Other Poems* (1920), and *Zalka Peetruza and Other Poems*. His verse appeared in magazines and newspapers, and for a time he was literary editor on the *Cincinnati Journal*. Known locally as "The Paul Laurence Dunbar of Cincinnati," he received a considerable amount of support from patrons and friends in selling and distributing his books. His work was represented in several anthologies, including *Negro Poets and Their Poems* (1923) by Robert T. Kerlin; *The Book of American Negro Poetry* (expanded edition, 1931), edited by James Weldon Johnson, and *An Anthology of Verse by American Negroes* (1924), edited by Newman Ivey White and Walter Clinton Jackson. Jean Wagner, author of *Black Poets of the United States* (1973), only briefly mentions Dandridge's work. He said, "were it not for the excessive generosity of some anthologists," his name (along with the names of several other emulators of Dunbar) "would be forgotten." More than likely in Dandridge's case, the generosity that Wagner attributes to the anthologists had much to do with the empathy they felt for the invalid who turned to writing as an outlet for his emotional and intellectual energy. Winston Morrow, who wrote the foreword for Dandridge's second book, *The Poet and Other Poems*, explains: "Even the most casual perusal of these pages will impress the reader with the wide range of thought dis-

played by the author. Only an inkling, however, is given of his 'unconquerable spirit.' Shut in within four walls by a strange decree of nature for many long years, racked at times by the most excruciating pains, denied free intercourse among his fellowmen and handicapped in a thousand other ways, he has overcome all these and composed these spritely lines." Here the reviewer's compassion replaces a clear-eyed critical judgment of the poet's work, and Dandridge, like so many other black writers during the early twentieth century, becomes the victim of high praise and a double standard of criticism because of issues extraneous to the quality of his writing. However, whether one dismisses his work or lavishes it with praise, his poetry provides clear evidence of dominant developments in black American literature that energized the talents of major and minor poets alike.

Approximately half of his poems, and many of his most successful ones, are in the dialect tradition. Paul Laurence Dunbar, who masterfully expressed the nuances of folk speech and life in dialect, provided Dandridge with his consummate model. Like Dunbar, Daniel Webster Davis, James Edwin Campbell, J. Mord Allen, James David Corrothers, and John W. Holloway, Dandridge was drawn to the temperament of humble folk, their charm, humor, and spontaneity, their pastoral scenes and situations, and mostly the lilt, rhythms, and music of their speech. "Tracin' Tales" is a good example of Dandridge's melding of the natural sound of folk speech and humor made effective by his familiarity with folk wit and verbal extravagance. As the speaker seeks to explain why he and "Maffew Pleasen' view" had such a "tremendous fuss," the reader gets caught up in "tracin' " the tale:

> Den I goes straight to Ismah, an'
>   Iss sen's me to Jack,
> An' Jack sed his wife got it frum
>   Ann Marildah Black.
> Right on to Ann Marildah's
>   I ambles on mah way.
> To fine dat she had bin enformed
>   by Belledonah Grey.
>
> Boun' dat I'd had de truf fo' long,
>   I tuk out once mo';
> An' soon Ise stan' 'in, hat in han',
>   et Belledonah's do';
> An' w'en I broached her 'bout it, she sed,
>   ob co'se twas true,
> Caze it cum confidensul frum
>   Maffew Pleasen' view.

In " 'Ittle Touzle Head" Dandridge recalls the warmth and affection of Dunbar's "Little Brown Baby." In fact he makes a close study of much of the subject matter that Dunbar exploited: musicians and singers, the antics of social scoundrels, courting and unrequited love, hearth and home, animal lore, nostalgia for bygone times, celebration of good food and good times, homely advice and moral platitudes, "gettin' religion," and superstition are among the subjects that attracted Dandridge's attention.

Some of his dialect poems—"The Prodigal," "De Drum Majah," and "Sprin' Fevah"—give evidence that Dandridge benefited from a good musical ear and a talent for creating rhythms that capture the lilt and cadence of folk speech. He also displays a genuine folk humor in his dialect pieces. For example, in a romance blighted by a lazy good-for-nothing husband in "A Recalled Prayer," Dandridge comically exploits the naive narrator who falls prey to "Hahd Cidah," and with fun-loving sympathy he ridicules the foolishness of a big-mouth innocent in "Close Mouf." Dandridge's good-natured approach to life in these poems and his calculated avoidance of the harsher sides of human nature are probably responsible for the popularity of this school of poetry.

However, Dandridge's dialect poetry, with rare and welcomed exceptions, is imitative and mediocre. Sterling A. Brown in *Negro Poetry and Drama* (1937) writes, "Although here and there he turns off an interesting observation, his dialect poetry is conventional and crude, and his concern for misspelling is too great." Brown's criticism is rooted in his belief that dialect need not be dismissed "as capable of only two stops, humor and pathos" but as "capable of expressing whatever the people are." Dialect poetry can capture the wit and beauty of folk parlance and the shrewdness and stoicism of the folk personality and transcend what Brown calls the "pat phrases," "stock illustrations," and "misspellings" of conventional dialect poetry. Citing gratuitous and unwarranted tampering with the language, Brown says that "for dialect's sake [Dandridge] writes *ruff, fashun, taik, campane* and forces into dialect words that are uncomfortably out of place." Though the examples are plentiful, the first stanza in "Fifty-fifty" shows Dandridge's uneven and erratic use of language.

> I 'ten'ed a campane speakin'
>   Et de Town Hall uddah night,
> Heard de canadate fo' office,

> Flail his 'ponett lef' an' right.
> He called him a lo'down scoundrel,
>   Heartless graftah, fraud an' bum;
> Tole us ef he gets elected
>   Sho' nuff hard times boun' to cum.

Dandridge's poetry evidences his confusion about the purpose and intent of dialect. He does not appear to be certain whether the dialect should fit the mold expected by good-humored, condescending readers who found pleasure in far-out linguistic excursions into misspelling and predictable sentiments or whether the dialect should attempt to approximate the sound and sense of a language that was self-affirming and self-defining.

Consequently Dandridge does not exhibit the depth or, for that matter, the ambivalence of his major model. While Dunbar was often tormented by the knowledge that the literary world had overlooked his serious standard English poems "to praise a jingle in a broken tongue," Dandridge was merely content to imitate, oblivious to the tensions that prompted Dunbar to write "The Poet," in which the speaker laments the unpopularity of the poet's "lays" of life and love. In his own poem of that title, Dandridge addresses the problems of subsistence and unrewarded toil that poets have wrestled with for ages.

> He dare not live by wage of pen,
> Most poorly paid of poor-paid men;
> With shoes 'er run, and threadbare clothes,
> And editors among the foes
> Who mock his song, deny him bread
> Then sing his praise when he is dead.

For all of his identification with Dunbar, however, Dandridge remained a mere artisan.

As the popularity of the dialect tradition made Dandridge a convert, the dramatic changes in attitude and philosophy of those who created the New Negro Renaissance of the 1920s captured his imagination, and he wrote some of his most reflective and stirring lines. The oratory and polemics of Marcus Garvey, the cultural philosophies of Alain Locke and W. E. B. Du Bois, and the writings of Claude McKay, Jean Toomer, Countee Cullen, James Weldon Johnson, and Anne Spencer all reached Dandridge in Cincinnati. His vision broadened, Dandridge found he was in tune with the voices of protest. Reminiscent of Claude McKay's now classical call to arms in "If We Must Die," Dandridge challenges his black brothers in "Time to Die":

RAYMOND G. DANDRIDGE
814 CHATEAU STREET
PRICE HILL
CINCINNATI, OHIO

Mar. 4, 1927.

Mr. A. B. Spingarn
29 East 9th St.
New York, N. Y.

My dear Mr. Spingarn;

On receiving your letter, I mailed to you, under separate cover "The Poet and Other Poems." The price is $1.25. Thanking you for your patronage and hoping you may find something in my little book of amusement or interest, I am gratefully yours,

Ray. G. Dandridge

Letter to Arthur B. Spingarn (courtesy of the Arthur B. Spingarn Collection, Moorland-Spingarn Research Center, Howard University)

Black Brothers, think you life so sweet
That you would live at any price?
Does mere existence balance with
The weight of your great sacrifice?
Enough to live and die a slave?

Newman Ivey White and Walter Clinton Jackson in *An Anthology of Verse by American Negroes* see this poem, along with "Supplication, Brother Mine" and "Color Blind," "showing a vigorous and somewhat militant racial feeling." In "My Grievance" the shift from a pleading, bended-knee posture is clear.

Yes, I admit a grievance
I also boldly challenge you—
Come stand where I once stood and fell!
I dare say you will do as well.

Dandridge creates the persona of a more self-assured black man who not only challenges the oppressor but dares to shine a searching light on his own race. In "To An Unchanged Judas," he scorns the race traitor, the "cannibalistic vulture/Grown fat upon your brother's blood." Another poem, "Awake and Forward," appears to be directly inspired by Marcus Garvey's rhetoric and the pomp and circumstance so characteristic of his followers in the Universal Negro Improvement Association. Garvey's "Back to Africa" movement caused thousands of blacks to turn their eyes toward Africa in longing and anticipation.

Awake, my sleeping Ethiopia;
Proclaim inheritance thine own!
Into quick'ning flame, to rid the dross
And purify thy better self.

In keeping with the New Negro's search for his historical and cultural roots in Africa and the diaspora, he also sought images of inspiration and pride in a pantheon of heroes. Booker T. Washington, Abraham Lincoln, and Toussaint L'Ouverture are singled out in Dandridge's poems. The Haitian hero is elegantly described:

Fearless, black, unlettered slave
From nowhere, sprang in time to save
The freedom of a fault'ring band
A tremble 'neath a tyrant's hand.

In a poem entitled "Emancipators," Dandridge calls the roll of Americans who gave significantly in the struggle for the abolition of slavery. John Brown, Frederick Douglass, William Lloyd Garrison, Harriet Beecher Stowe, and others are brought to the attention of the race as liberators.

Black America! In Fame's Hall go place
This group; where naught can e'er erase
A single noble character, or dim one glorious deed;
For they were sowers of the seed—

Much of Dandridge's poetry is optimistic and democratic. As Alain Locke in *The New Negro* (1925) saw the "radicalism of the Negro" as "no limitation or reservation with respect to American life" but as "a constructive effort to build the obstructions in the stream of his progress into an efficient dam of social energy and power," Dandridge saw the existence of racialism as providing the opportunity for understanding. Though he does not argue vehemently, as Du Bois did, for the participation of black soldiers in World War I, he does express the hope that their "spilt blood" not fall "short of Freedom's aim."

Democracy means more than empty letters
And Liberty far more than partly free;
Yet, both are void as long as men, in fetters,
Are at eclipse with Opportunity.

Of the characteristic concerns of the New Negro Renaissance writers, the desire to reveal the self more deeply and with greater honesty appears to have been the touchstone that generated Dandridge's one exceptional poem. "Zalka Peetruza" is the portrait of a woman "who was christened by Lucy Jane."

She danced, near nude, to tom-tom beat
With swaying arms and flying feet,
'Mid swirling spangles, gauze and lace,
Her all was dancing—save her face.

James Weldon Johnson suggests that the poem warrants a comparison with McKay's "The Harlem Dancer." In both poems there is a woman whose lovely, swaying body captures the passionate gazes of those she entertains. The women in both poems, for all their sensual realness, have distanced themselves from the onlookers as though their souls were in some faraway place. Only through the woman's "falsely-smiling face," in McKay's poem, and the woman's "eyes obsessed with vacant stare," in Dandridge's, do the readers, like the onlookers, realize her great indifference to them.

Twas thus, amid force driven grace,
We found the lost look on her face;
And then, to us, did it occur
That, though we saw—we saw not her.

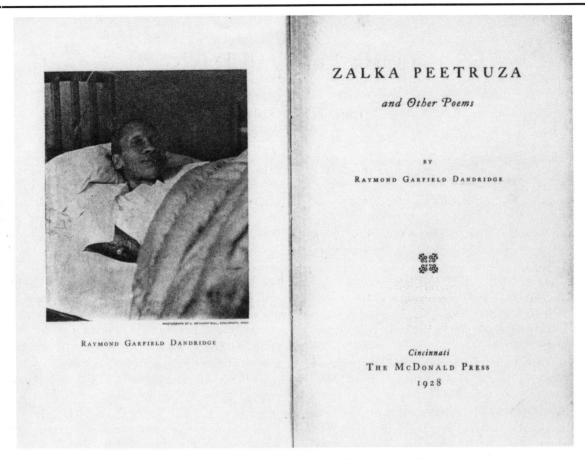

Frontispiece and title page for Dandridge's last collection of poems

Though Dandridge often struggled with poetic meter and left standing some rather clumsy efforts in versification, in "Zalka Peetruza" his meter is true. The language is consistent and controlled, and in some cases it is strikingly original.

The Harlem vogue, and the exoticism that it conjured up for joy seekers in the 1920s, is represented well in the poem. The very name Zalka Peetruza taken on by this simple girl clothes her in a robe of exotic primitivism. Fortunately Dandridge, like McKay and Sterling Brown in "Cabaret," demands a tougher, more complex portrait than the stereotype would imply. However, Dandridge does not accomplish Brown's searing satirical tone as he portrays rich "grandees" who fantasize about dark southern beauties. Nor does he avoid, as McKay did, the pitfall of moralistic sounding off. Still, with all considered, "Zalka Peetruza" remains one of his finest pieces.

Perhaps Dandridge best serves as a gauge for the period because of his intense desire to create himself anew through his writing. He shares with all the black writers of the 1920s an excitement that comes with discovery and self-affirmation. He also shared with them an unmistakable faith in the race's potential. Despite the racial handicaps—the misunderstanding, the violence, the economical and political disenfranchisement—black writers wrote of militancy, achievement, opportunity, and pride. Therefore, it is his spirit that unites Dandridge most with his contemporaries.

References:

William Coyle, ed., *Ohio Authors and Their Books: 1796-1950* (Cleveland: World, 1962), p. 152;

Robert B. Eleazer, *Singers in the Dawn: A Brief Anthology of American Negro Poetry* (Atlanta: Conference on Education and Race Relations, 1934);

Jean Wagner, *Black Poets of the United States: From Paul Laurence Dunbar to Langston Hughes*, translated by Kenneth Douglas (Urbana: University of Illinois Press, 1973), p. 179.

Frank Marshall Davis

(31 December 1905-   )

John Edgar Tidwell
University of Kentucky

BOOKS: *Black Man's Verse* (Chicago: Black Cat Press, 1935);

I Am the American Negro (Chicago: Black Cat Press, 1937);

Through Sepia Eyes (Chicago: Black Cat Press, 1938);

47th Street; Poems (Prairie City, Ill.: Decker Press, 1948).

OTHER: Sterling A. Brown, Arthur P. Davis, and Ulysses Lee, eds., *The Negro Caravan*, includes poems by Davis (New York: Dryden Press, 1942);

Robert Hayden, ed., *Kaleidoscope: Poems by American Negro Poets*, includes poems by Davis (Harcourt, Brace & World, 1967);

Abraham Chapman, ed., *Black Voices: An Anthology of Afro-American Literature*, includes poems by Davis (New York: New American Library, 1968);

Langston Hughes and Arna Bontemps, eds., *The Poetry of the Negro, 1746-1970*, includes poems by Davis (Garden City: Anchor/Doubleday, 1970);

Nick Aaron Ford, ed., *Black Insights*, includes poems by Davis (Waltham, Mass.: Ginn, 1971);

Stephen Henderson, ed., *Understanding the New Black Poetry*, includes poems by Davis (New York: Morrow, 1973);

Michael W. Peplow and Arthur P. Davis, eds., *The New Negro Renaissance: An Anthology*, includes poems by Davis (New York: Holt, Rinehart & Winston, 1975).

Frank Marshall Davis nearly faded from the pages of American literary history when he left the United States mainland in 1948. Once hailed as a "Newer Negro," Davis wrote poetry that demonstrated a talent for "realistic portraiture," irony, and knowledge of black life and seemed to fulfill the unfinished promise of the New Negro Renaissance poets. Then Davis abandoned a promising career as journalist and poet for the comparative quiescence of Hawaii. Except for a few poems pub-

lished in 1950, he was virtually silent until 1973, when he was "rediscovered" by literary critic Stephen Henderson and poet-publisher Dudley Randall, who dubbed Davis the "mystery poet," since little had been heard of him for twenty-five years. Mystery or not, on a 1973 tour of black colleges arranged by Henderson, Davis was enthusiastically greeted by students as "the long lost father of modern Black poetry" who had been "twenty years ahead of his time." Demystifying the man and his poetry reveals a certain truth to their praise. Somewhat like the writing of the black arts movement, Davis's poetry is characterized by robust statements of urban themes, a fierce social consciousness, a strong declamatory voice, and an almost rabid race pride.

Life in early-twentieth-century south-central Kansas, especially Arkansas City, shaped Davis's attitudes and values. Born 31 December 1905 to parents who divorced the next year, he learned very early that "Ark City" was not the haven suggested by its Biblical reference. When he was five years old, for example, some white third-graders who had heard an account of lynching experimented with the practice themselves, nearly hanging Davis. His early lessons about racism inculcated in Davis an inferiority complex that made him shy and extremely self-conscious; it also nurtured a consuming hatred of white people. Graduating from high school afforded him an opportunity to "escape" to Wichita, Kansas, in 1923.

"Giles Johnson, Ph.D.," from Davis's first collection, *Black Man's Verse* (1935), sardonically presents a dilemma confronted by most blacks who wished to pursue a higher education in the early decades of this century: viable employment. Johnson, who earns four college degrees and speaks Greek and Latin, nevertheless dies of starvation because "he wouldn't teach/and he couldn't porter." Davis, however, did not share Johnson's fate. Formal courses at Friends University and informal ones as busboy at the Wichita Club prepared him for enrollment into the School of Journalism at Kansas State Agricultural College in Manhattan in

60

1924, where Davis's career as a poet had its auspicious, if not accidental, beginning.

A class assignment to write either an essay or a poem led to Davis's discovery of free verse in a magazine of "experimental" poetry. His own verse experiments earned approval not only from his instructor but also from the Ur Rune Chapter of the American College Quill Club, a national creative writing organization that later accepted him as a member. Davis's initiation into their society firmly established his reputation as the "poet who looks like a prize-fighter," an epithet that described him physically and that captured the characteristic voice in his poetry.

Most of Davis's verse has been considered protest poetry. It is often strident, vitriolic, and polemical. Thus literary critics, focusing in the main on Davis's use of poetry as a vehicle for his politically leftist social criticism, have been divided about his work. In a representative although especially vituperative statement, Jean Wagner ob-

Frank Marshall Davis (courtesy of the Prints and Photographs Collection, Moorland-Spingarn Research Center, Howard University)

serves that journalism intrudes upon Davis's sensibilities as creative writer. His description of Davis's "principal defect," poetic propaganda, as "a sort of bad taste which his journalistic activities did nothing to mitigate" is unwarranted or at least exaggerated. Davis regards news writing and poetry as two different forms of expression: journalism is "objective" writing and poetry "subjective." To address everyday reality subjectively has been Davis's motivation for writing poetry. But lynching, urban blight, and world war are subjects that resist pure lyricism. Against these social ills, he has been an untiring polemicist, and therefore concerned with protest and propaganda. Free verse, a mode that lends itself to persuasion and rhetorical turns, provides him a medium to comment subjectively on social problems. Nonetheless, if Nick Aaron Ford's comments can be taken as typical, a common complaint among critics is that Davis's poetry "is so blunt and militant that it has little chance of winning sympathetic consideration. In addition, much of it offends good taste." Davis assumes all poetry is propaganda; therefore, a poet writing from the "ivory tower" about the world is no less propagandistic than a social realist. This view of the artist as having a responsibility to society ignores questions of taste. If poetry is defined as densely textured, metaphoric language, then much of Davis's poetry will be found wanting, since it often relies on making statement rather than suggesting idea. But much Depression literature was written in that realistic vein, and Davis was thoroughly one with his age.

In 1927 Davis left Kansas State after two and a half years of study. He moved to Chicago which became his symbol of "raw, savage strength." Although the city had an intellectual community that was making tentative efforts to establish a black literary movement, it offered little sustenance to Davis's initial growth as a poet. Little interaction occurred between Chicago's black and white writers, and he was virtually on his own, starving in more ways than one. Motivated to write "for bread and beans," he hacked out articles and short stories for *National* magazine and the *Light and Heebie Jeebies.* Eventually he found employment with a succession of black newspapers: the *Chicago Evening Bulletin,* the *Whip,* and the *Gary American.* His Chicago experiences led him to feel a kinship with the poetry of midwestern white poets Carl Sandburg, Edgar Lee Masters, and Vachel Lindsay. Although he was well acquainted with the works of New Negro Renaissance writers Countee Cullen, Rudolph Fisher, Langston Hughes, and Jean Toomer, and although he could have gone to New York himself, Davis felt he could do for Chicago what they did for Harlem. Sandburg's influence is readily discernible in a poem such as "Chicago's Congo (Sonata for an Orchestra)." A reply to Sandburg's celebration of hog butchers, toolmakers, stackers of wheat, and freight handlers in "Chicago" (1914), "Chicago's Congo" reminds us that "Chicago's blood is kaleidoscopic" and that "the artist who paints this town must use a checkered canvas."

Davis returned to Kansas State in the fall of 1929, but his stay was brief because it was apparent to him that he was to become a casualty of the Depression. In 1930 he was recruited to Atlanta by W. A. Scott to upgrade the semiweekly *Atlanta World* to a triweekly paper. Under Davis's editorship, it became the *Atlanta Daily World,* America's first successful black daily newspaper. "Chicago's Congo," in the meantime, had attracted the attention of Frances Norton Manning, a sophisticated white woman who had a bohemian life-style. She energized Davis intellectually and emotionally, encouraging him to return to Chicago in 1934. She introduced him to Norman Forgue, former sailor and welterweight boxer, who had a passion for publishing beautiful books. His Black Cat Press brought out *Black Man's Verse* on a royalty basis in the summer of 1935.

Black Man's Verse is experimental, cacophonous, yet sometimes harmonious. The collection presents a variety of black experiences in lyrical moods that range from the tragic to the comic. Refusing to request a promotional and interpretative introduction to his verse, Davis stands behind it all and announces assertively that his "chief delight has been to experiment with free verse," which he greatly prefers "to the usual run of rhyme." The main imperatives of free verse, as Paul Fussell observes, are to establish texture without metrical regularity and to eschew rhyme. Davis indeed experimented with free verse, but his craft seldom evinced the polish that comes with the struggle to resist metrical regularity. His best poems use parallelism and some repetition to achieve the effects of oratory. The third verse paragraph of "Chicago's Congo" exemplifies his practice:

> Sing to me of a warrior moon victorious in a Congo sky . . . show me a round dollar moon in the ragged blue purse of Chicago's heavens . . . tell me of a hundred spoil laden blacks tramping home from the raid . . . point me out a hundred brown men riding

the elevated home on payday . . . pick me the winners . . . in Chicago? . . . in the Congo?

Parallel syntactic units establish, on one hand, the structure of the paragraph. Structure, however, relates to content in that it compares blacks' experiences from two different worlds. While each locale seems guided by its own exigencies, parallelism suggests black commonality, not difference. The "warrior moon" and "dollar moon" and the "spoil laden blacks" and "hundred brown men" lead to the rhetorical question of who wins. Instead of determining a winner, however, the question inevitably concludes that both groups labor under similar necessities.

Davis is comparatively more successful in his experimentation with black music, especially jazz. In subject matter, theme, technique, or style, music figures prominently in more than seventeen poems in *Black Man's Verse.* Jazz represents for Davis a rebellion against the Western tradition in music, just as free verse symbolized a break with regular rhythm and rhyme in poetry. Davis often combines the spirit of protest in jazz and free verse with his objections to racial oppression, producing a poetry that loudly declaims against injustice. His efforts, however, do not always smoothly blend subject, mood, and music. In a poem like "Lynched (Symphonic Interlude for Twenty-one Selected Instruments)," for example, the relationship of lynching to a symphony is not readily apparent. But other, less declamatory ones are exceptional: "Mojo Mike's Beer Garden" is "an unscored symphony/ of colors and sounds." And "Cabaret," which Harriet Monroe of *Poetry* said was "the best built and most successful of the longer pieces [in this volume]," asks: "Where do blues leave off and hymns begin?" It continues:

> Grotesque gyrations
> Rhythmic contortions
> Ambulatory mammals
> Unconscious aesthetes
> Irrefragably urged
> (These the dancing dozens)
> By importuning inhibitions
> The jazz band conjures[.]

Echoing in the background of many of his jazz pieces is the technical influence of Vachel Lindsay, without Lindsay's racial myopia.

A section of *Black Man's Verse* that has generally had a wide appeal is "Ebony Under Granite," for which Davis is indebted to Edgar Lee Masters's

Spoon River Anthology (1915). Black sleepers under these headstones, like their white counterparts buried on the hill near Spoon River, represent a variety of portraits, faults, ironies, and strengths. Rev. Joseph Williams preserves the pursuit of truth in the Second Baptist Church by satisfying the women church members sexually. Unlike her sisters who trade virginity for comfort, marriage rights, and respectability, Goldie Blackwell collects two dollars and independence and keeps respectability to herself. Gambler Acey White loses the final pot to the "Big Dealer." The financially successful Robert Whitmore dies of apoplexy when he is mistaken for a waiter from Georgia. Arthur Ridgewood, unable to decide between poetry and medicine for a vocation, dies "from a nervous breakdown/caused by worry/from rejection slips/and final notices from the finance company." George Brown, who for forty years watched powerlessly as white Mississippi voters cheated at the polls, was sentenced to life in the Illinois state penitentiary when he voted more than once in a Congressional election. The plight of many black writers is captured in Roosevelt Smith's bout with literary critics, whose sensibilities he could never please. As a result he "traded conscience/and critics for the leather pouch and bunions/of a mail carrier."

Book reviewers, sensing a charting of new territory by a black writer, were almost unanimous in their praise of *Black Man's Verse*. Their statements, however, reveal personal proclivity as much as analysis. From white reviewers such as William Rose Benét came the excited welcome that "there is not a trace of whining or maundering in this book. There is a natural dignity in the utterance, and intelligence." In a similar statement, a *Nation* reviewer wrote: "With little of the melancholy of his race, little influenced by the mood or style of the spiritual, Mr. Davis accepts the raw vigor of his environment and responds to its casual aspects of beauty in a free-running verse that has something of the hard brightness of Sandburg." Black reviewers such as Alain Locke greeted Davis as a bearer of "fresh talent and creative imagination." Sterling Brown stated that Davis "is at times a mystic escapist, but at his best he is bitterly realistic." Benjamin Brawley, however, called him an "obstreperous" poet who has "such assurance as could hardly be equalled in this world or in the world to come." For this collection Davis was awarded a grant from the Julius Rosenwald Foundation in 1937.

I Am the American Negro (1937) rapidly followed the publication of *Black Man's Verse*. It voices strident criticism of racial discrimination and dia-

tribe against civilization and progress, and it promotes black history, as his earlier volume had done. Except for the appearance of several love poems—including "Flowers of Darkness," "To One Who Would Leave Me," "Awakening," and "Come to Me"—the dominant mood is cynical and pessimistic. The reader is forewarned that "Fairy words . . . a Pollyanna mind/Do not roam these pages." Instead the reader is treated to "coarse victuals" and a "couch of rough boards." The title piece, a "docudrama" in free verse and prose, inveighs against the "stones that formed the temple of America's Social System," Davis's metaphor for the complex of "Jim Crow" laws that systematically exclude blacks from history texts and society. "Modern Man—The Superman," curiously subtitled "A Song of Praise for Hearst, Hitler, Mussolini and the Munitions Makers," recalls Dostoyevski's Underground Man who observes that civilization has become more vilely loathsome. Davis's marginal notations, while probably not intended for actual performance, underscore the experimental nature of this poem. For example, the first such notation for "Modern Man—The Superman" reads: "Eight airplane motors, each keyed to a different pitch, are turned on and off to furnish musical accompaniment within the range of an octave." " 'Mancipation Day," "Onward Christian Soldiers," and "Christ is a Dixie Nigger" sarcastically portray the meaning that Christianity and freedom have for blacks. An appropriate coda for these concerns might be the last line of "Note Left by a Suicide": "I am too brave to live."

Like the earlier collection, *I Am the American Negro* contains a section entitled "Ebony Under Granite." Here we find Moses Mitchell, whose distinguished service cross saves his life from a sheriff's bullet; he is later hanged by judicial decree. Sam Jackson, nearly dead from starvation, is shot to death by a police officer who sees him breaking into the Dew Drop Inn Cafe. Unpromising writer Jonathan Wood receives a rejection slip from life. Neither Cleo Greeley, who earlier lived a promiscuous life and later married respectably, nor her sister Sarah, whose sexual inexperience causes her husband to seek pleasure from other women, is remembered by anyone. Benjamin Blakey, prominent Odd Fellow, church deacon, husband, and father, dies without learning from which of his six "kept" women he contracted his fatal social disease. Nicodemus Perry, contemplating the sexual liberties white men took with his mother and sisters, is mortally wounded by several loiterers for "assaulting" a white woman whom he accidentally bumped.

Frank Marshall Davis, 1984 (photo by Dennis Oda)

The snobbish, extremely color-conscious Mrs. Clifton Townsend dies of shame when she bears a "penny-brown" son. Editor Ralph Williamson, who for twenty years waged unending warfare against racial discrimination, dies after dreaming "Of a perfect nation/Without prejudice or segregation." And as if anticipating the criticism of being bitter and cynical, Davis in "Frank Marshall Davis: Writer" writes what might prove his fitting epitaph:

I was a weaver of jagged words
A warbler of garbled tunes
A singer of savage songs
I was bitter
Yes
Bitter and sorely sad
For when I wrote
I dipped my pen
In the crazy heart
Of mad America
. . . .
But
I did not die
of diabetes . . .[.]

I Am the American Negro did not attract as much attention from reviewers as *Black Man's Verse*. It

was generally well received, but a recurring complaint was that it was a continuation of Davis's previous book. Alain Locke commended Davis for writing the "outstanding verse effort" of 1937. Yet he lamented that *I Am the American Negro* "has too many echoes of the author's first volume . . . it is not a crescendo in the light of the achievement and promise of the author's initial volume."

Through Sepia Eyes was a limited edition Christmas remembrance published in 1938. For Locke, it was further confirmation of Davis's social protest orientation. Describing the volume as the product of a "twangy lyre," he nevertheless hailed its longest poem, "Chicago Skyscrapers," as the "master poem of the year." "To Those Who Sing America" is a tapestry of lines from the national anthem and contradictions in American race relations. "Life is a Woman" is an elaborate conceit. "Coincidence" traces the irony of one instance of southern interracial genealogy in Donald Woods, white, and Booker Scott, colored, who are born on the same day, experience similar growing pains, and die at the same moment. The speaker inquires: "Would it be better understood/Why the lives of both/Traveled parallel/. . . Were it generally known/That the father of Donald/Under cover the same day/Had likewise sired Booker?" All of these poems were later included in *47th Street* (1948).

From 1935 to 1947 Davis worked as executive editor for the Associated Negro Press in Chicago, the news-gathering agency serving black newspapers. In addition he found time to start a photography club, work for political parties, participate in the Allied Arts Guild and League of American Writers, and interact with black writers of the Southside Chicago Writers Group. The League of American Writers provided Davis his first opportunity to work closely with white writers. Having rid himself of his feelings of inferiority by reading the black history written by W. E. B. Du Bois, Carter G. Woodson, and J. A. Rodgers, Davis developed a healthy self-concept and a wider view of social problems. With encouragement from Richard Wright, Margaret Walker, Margaret Taylor Goss Burroughs, and others, Davis wrote *47th Street*, whose title piece he describes as a "word picture of the main thoroughfare of Chicago's Congo during wartime."

47th Street is the culmination of Davis's thought and poetic development. Many of his earlier poems were characterized by an almost black nationalist political sensibility. This volume, however, registers a shift to a more proletarian belief. As he explains in a foreword to this collection, the concept of race inadequately describes groups of people because it bases race distinctions primarily on skin color and political necessity. The concept of culture, however, with its basis in "customs" and language, more accurately categorizes people since it emphasizes milieu. Davis is nevertheless a "realist." He finds that he is prevented from being anything except Negro when he writes. That is, living in America means for him living a racially proscribed life which "produces certain distinct ways of thinking." Although many of his themes concern the effects of discrimination on him, Davis considers himself one of the common people, subjected to domination by the world's economic rulers. Thus *47th Street*, while filled with portraits of black life, must be seen as an expression of class, not racial consciousness. It is dedicated to his second wife, who was white.

The first section of *47th Street* varies considerably in theme and subject from Davis's earlier work. Unlike his previous descriptions of Southside Chicago as exclusively black, the title poem, "47th Street," presents a "rainbow race" of people: "In them the bold black pride of Africa/The restless upward surge of Europe/The moody mystery of America's Indians/Now wedded/By the constant catalyst of copulation." The idea of progress and civilization found in "Pattern for Conquest," "Egotistic Runt," and "Chicago Skyscrapers" ironically contrasts with the urban destitution in "Tenement Room." Mojo Mike's Cafe in "Black Weariness" provides temporary surcease from the battle to make America live up to its ideals. "Snapshots of the Cotton South" is both indictment and challenge; it condemns prevailing racist institutions and social behavior, but it also exhorts starving black and white southern sharecroppers to unite against a common economic oppressor. The next section contains antiwar poems, including "Peace Quiz for America," "For All Common People," "War Zone," "Nothing Can Stop the People," and "Peace is a Fragile Cup." Together they question the meaning of democracy and urge the rise of the common man. Section three contains love poems, and the last section is like the earlier "Ebony Under Granite" poems. From this last group, "Self-Portrait" especially reveals Davis's motivation for being a socially conscious writer whose pen is like a weapon: "I would be/A painter with words/Creating sharp portraits/On the wide canvas of your mind/Images of those things/Shaped through my eyes/That interest me;/But being a Tenth American/In this democracy/I sometimes sketch a miniature/Though I contract for a mural."

One discomfited reviewer said the collection seemed to result in propaganda, not poetry. He was left with the uncomfortable feeling of "having shared almost too painfully the author's sense of injustice." The House Un-American Activities Committee, the Senate's Eastland Committee, and the Federal Bureau of Investigation were also uneasy about Davis's work. What they saw was politically subversive material. During this era of McCarthyism, many libraries and schools removed Davis's books from their shelves. Ironically, several poems were being translated in European countries while they were being banned in the United States.

In the meantime, a planned vacation to Hawaii in December 1948 evolved into a permanent change of address. Davis's departure signaled to some his defection from the black struggle for racial equality in America, but Hawaii, at that time, was also beset with many problems among the Japanese, whites, Chinese, Koreans, Filipinos, Puerto Ricans, Hawaiians, Samoans, and Tongans. Davis's move to Hawaii was not an abrogation of social responsibility, but a change of venue. In between rearing five children and operating a small wholesale paper business, he wrote a regular weekly column for the *Honolulu Record*. Many of these experiences and his views of ethnicity in Hawaii are detailed in an unpublished manuscript entitled "That Incredible Waikiki Jungle."

Frank Marshall Davis's work not only questioned social ills in his own time but also inspired blacks in the politically charged 1960s. Davis's poetry is generally that of an advocate urging social change. Despite his continued experimentation with verse, he did not achieve the technical success found, for example, in Robert Hayden's modernism or Sterling Brown's sensitive adaptation of southern black folk forms. Too often the necessity to expose social ills limits the metaphoric range of Davis's language. What he does not achieve in technique, he makes up for in vivid, realistic images of urban life that rival, and often surpass, his predecessors Sandburg and Lindsay. Davis is perhaps at his best in the "Ebony Under Granite" poems. His use of wit, irony, and understatement reveal him to be remarkably perceptive of human frailty and strength and able to provide insight into human nature. Langston Hughes best summed up Davis's weakness and his strength when he wrote of Davis's work: "When his poems are poetry, they are powerful."

Interviews:

Dudley Randall, "An Interview With Frank Marshall Davis," *Black World,* 23, no. 3 (1974): 37-48;

John Edgar Tidwell, "An Interview With Frank Marshall Davis," *Black American Literature Forum,* 19 (Fall 1985): 105-108.

References:

Nick Aaron Ford, "A Blueprint for Negro Authors," *Phylon,* 11, no. 4 (1950): 374-377;

Paul Fussell, *Poetic Meter and Poetic Form,* revised edition (New York: Random House, 1979);

Helena Kloder, "The Film and Canvas of Frank Marshall Davis," *CLA Journal,* 15, no. 1 (1971): 59-63;

Carol Oukrop, " 'Diplomat' Discovered in Hawaii," *Alliance: An Ethnic Newspaper at Kansas State University* (November 1984): 1-2;

Jean Wagner, *Black Poets of the United States,* translated by Kenneth Douglas (Urbana, Chicago & London: University of Illinois Press, 1973), pp. 187-190.

S. Randolph Edmonds

(30 April 1900-28 March 1983)

Allen Williams
Grambling State University

BOOKS: *Shades and Shadows* (Boston: Meador, 1930);

Six Plays for a Negro Theatre (Boston: Baker, 1934);

The Land of Cotton and Other Plays (Washington, D.C.: Associated Publishers, 1942).

PLAY PRODUCTIONS: *Rocky Roads,* Oberlin, Ohio, Oberlin High School, 15 May 1926;

Job Hunting, Baltimore, Morgan College, 18 February 1928;

Shades and Shadows, Baltimore, Douglass High School, 24 April 1931;

Bad Man, New York, February 1932;

Nat Turner, New Orleans, Dillard University Theatre, 17 January 1936;

The High Court of Historia, New Orleans, Dillard University Workshop Theatre, February 1939;

The Land of Cotton, New Orleans, Longshoreman's Hall, 20 March 1941;

Simon In Cyrene, New Orleans, Dillard University Little Theatre, 11 February 1943;

Earth and Stars, New Orleans, Dillard University Little Theatre, 13 February 1946;

Whatever the Battle Be, Tallahassee, Lee Auditorium, 3 November 1950.

OTHER: *Nat Turner,* in *Negro History in Thirteen Plays,* edited by Willis Richardson and May Miller (New York: Associated Publishers, 1935);

Black Man, in *The Negro Caravan,* edited by Sterling A. Brown, Arthur P. Davis, and Ulysses Lee (New York: Dryden, 1941), pp. 507-520;

"Black Drama in the American Theatre, 1700-1970," in *The American Theatre, A Sum of Its Parts,* edited by Henry B. Williams (New York: French, 1971), pp. 379-424;

Earth and Stars, revised, in *Black Drama in America,* edited by Darwin T. Turner (Greenwich: Fawcett, 1971).

PERIODICAL PUBLICATIONS: "Not Many of Your People Come Here," *Messenger* (May 1928);

"Some Whys and Wherefores of College Dramatics," *Crisis* (1929);

"Some Reflections on the Negro in American Drama," *Opportunity,* 8 (April 1930): 303-305;

"The South—A New Mecca of Art and Literature," *Arts Quarterly* (April-June 1937);

"Of Poets and Poetry," *Arts Quarterly* (July-September 1937);

"Rag Tag," *Arts Quarterly* (October-December 1937);

S. Randolph Edmonds

"Education in Self-Contempt," *Crisis* (August 1938);

"The Diary of a Dramatist in Eire," *Arts Quarterly* (March 1939);

"Negro Drama in the South," *University of North Carolina Playbook* (December 1940);

"Some Stereotypes and Themes in Negro Literature," *Florida A & M University Bulletin* (Spring 1949);

"Who's Wrong: The NAACP or Negro Artists?," *Pittsburgh Courier*, 3 November 1951, p. 9.

In an essay entitled "A Criticism of the Negro Drama" (1928), Eulalie Spence named Paul Robeson, Rose McClendon, Florence Mills, and others as performers who had reached an undeniable place of prominence in the theater. She could name no black dramatists of comparable status. Garland Anderson and Willis Richardson had appeared briefly on the scene in the early 1920s, but neither had established himself as a professional playwright. If black playwrights were to emerge and provide plays for blacks to perform, Spence suggested, they must "portray the life of their people, their foibles, their sorrows, ambitions, and defeats; that these portrayals be told with tenderness and skill and a knowledge of the theatre and the technique of the times." Even as she offered her challenge, S. Randolph Edmonds was making his first excursions into playwriting.

Edmonds, considered the dean of black educational theater in America, contributed more than any other individual to the development of interest in theater and in dramatic organizations in black colleges. His forty-eight plays and numerous articles and essays address the concerns most prominent in the lives of black Americans. Edmonds organized the first speech and drama department in a black university in the United States at Dillard University in 1935. Under his direction, the drama group at Florida A & M University made several overseas USO tours and served as official ambassadors for the United States while touring seven African countries. Edmonds's prolific playwriting, recognized leadership, and pioneering efforts in black academic dramatics have established a central place for him in the annals of the American theater.

Sheppard Randolph Edmonds was born on 30 April 1900 to George Washington and Frances Fisherman Edmonds in Lawrenceville, Virginia. His paternal grandparents, Toab and Betty Edmonds, and their eighteen children had been slaves on what is now known as the Jackson Plantation. Upon learning of General Lee's surrender at Appomattox, Toab hitched a pair of mules to a double wagon, into which he packed his wife and all the children he could find and headed down the road. When Betty counted the children, she found two missing; one of them was Randolph's father. Toab reluctantly turned the mules around and went back to the old Jackson farm, where both he and his wife remained until their deaths. They are now buried in the old slave burying ground in a corner of the farm.

Edmonds's father, George Washington Edmonds, born in 1858, grew up on the Jackson farm and married Frances Fisherman from a neighboring plantation. She had been born in 1861 in New Orleans, where her mother had been taken by her owners so that the family might get away from the Civil War battles around Petersburg, Virginia, the location of their plantation. Thus, both of Edmonds's parents were children when emancipation came. Edmonds had four sisters and four brothers. According to his own account, he was a quiet and easygoing boy, and, though he grew rapidly, he was weak. He was beaten regularly by his peers until he reached the age of twelve or thirteen. Edmonds recalled in an interview that "one very small boy, every recess, would throw me down and sit on top of me so I never saw anything except the sky during that whole year. . . ."

Edmonds's school year during his early education consisted of only about five months because black children had to work on the plantations. He attended high school at Saint Paul's Normal and Industrial School (now St. Paul's College), in Lawrenceville. He graduated as valedictorian of his class in 1921, and he took prizes in English and history.

In rural Lawrenceville, where theaters were only available for those whites who had time to enjoy such luxury, Edmonds did not even see a motion picture until he was fifteen years old. The only plays he saw were those presented at the elementary and high schools in the county. But during the summer months of 1918 to 1920, Edmonds worked in New York City to earn money for his tuition and expenses, and while there he went to the theater for the first time. After that, most of his summer earnings as a waiter were used for tickets to see New York shows.

After high school, Edmonds was encouraged by J. Alvin Russell, then the director of academics at St. Paul's and the son of the school's founder, to attend Oberlin College, Russell's alma mater. Ed-

monds received a scholarship and entered Oberlin. He never received financial assistance from his family; his father—widowed from the time Edmonds was twelve—was a debtor, tenant farmer, and sharecropper for a plantation owner. Edmonds helped maintain himself in school by scrubbing floors, doing odd jobs, waiting tables, barbering, and painting and decorating. After going through a difficult financial period, Edmonds was forced to stay out of school for a year, but he graduated from Oberlin in 1926 with a B.A. degree in English literature.

Edmonds began writing plays as part of his work at Oberlin. He and other black students organized the Dunbar Forum, a group whose main purpose was to stage discussions, debates, dramatic readings, original creative literature, and plays. Initially Edmonds had concentrated on learning to write poetry, short stories, and essays, but after reading plays by Henrik Ibsen and other playwrights he decided to try his skills in that genre. During Edmonds's senior year the Dunbar Players staged his first full-length play, *Rocky Roads* (1926), and a year later, three of his short plays. The success of these plays aroused in him deep interest in college dramatics. He was also influenced by reading about the successful playwriting programs of George Pierce Baker, who ran drama workshops at Harvard University; Thomas Wood Stevens at Carnegie School of Technology; and especially Frederick H. Koch at the University of North Carolina at Chapel Hill, who, with his distinguished student-playwright Paul Green, had the greatest influence on him. Koch's philosophy of writing plays based on the experiences of the regional people who were to see them made a deep and lasting impression on Edmonds. Moreover, Green's highly successful folk plays seemed easier to emulate to a beginning student than trying to follow what Edmonds calls "the jack-o-lantern gleam" to Broadway. His main thrust in the early years after college was toward the folk play and toward building a college and regional audience for drama, especially in the South and in black colleges and universities.

In 1926 Edmonds accepted a position as instructor in English and Drama at Morgan State College in Baltimore, Maryland. He organized the Morgan Dramatic Club, which became widely known through its productions, and in 1930 he formed the Negro Intercollegiate Drama Association, the first organization of its kind for black colleges and universities. He did not limit his activities to the campus. On 10 May 1929 the group appeared in the Seventh Annual Little Theatre Tour-

FORUM OFFICERS

President.............................Mr. Clarence Gresham
Vice-President.........................Miss Floy Debnam
Secretary.............................Miss Maggie Winstead
Treasurer.............................Mr. T. A. Bows
Chairman of Program Committee....Mr. Randolph Edmonds
Chairman of Ways and Means Committee..Miss Susie E. Bailey
Pianist...............................Mr. T. Nelson Baker

MUSICAL NUMBERS

Prelude—Piano Selections..........Miss Carrie Mae Booker

Between First and Second Acts

Solo ....Mr. Pankey

Act Two, Scene Three

Orginial Waltz Song—"Ruby"............................
...................By Messrs. H. Baker and R. Edmonds

Between Second and Third Acts

Violin Selection..........................Miss Ruby Harris

NOTE

The next meeting of the Dunbar Forum will be on May 23rd, at the Mt. Zion Baptist Church, on South Pleasant Street. This is our annual original production day. Original stories, poems, essays, songs and music will be given. Everybody welcome.

The Dunbar Forum Presents

Rocky Roads

An Original Negro Comedy Drama in Three Acts

Written and Directed
by
Randolph Edmonds

High School Auditorium
Saturday Evening, May 15, 1926, at 7:30 P. M.

Covers for the playbill for Edmonds's first produced play

nament sponsored by Walter Hartwig on Broadway, presenting *The Man Who Died at Twelve O'Clock* by Paul Green. Although they did not win a prize, the Morgan Players were rated by New York critics as fourth out of twenty contestants. The group returned to New York in February 1932, becoming the first black college players to perform there. During this visit they also performed Edmonds's folk play *Bad Man* in a 26 February broadcast on NBC radio.

Edmonds continued his academic training at Columbia University in the summers from 1927 to 1930 and received the M.A. degree in 1921. Although he majored in Shakespearean drama at Columbia, he studied playwriting under Minor Sathans and play production under Milton Smith.

In 1931 Edmonds married the great-granddaughter of abolitionist orator Henry Highland Garnett, Irene Colbert, whom he had met in Baltimore. They had two children, Henriette Highland Garnett and S. Randolph, Jr. Irene Edmonds died in 1968.

While at Morgan, Edmonds was granted a sabbatical leave from 1934 to 1935 to study drama

at Yale University under a fellowship from the Rockefeller Foundation. After he returned to Morgan College he was invited to organize and head the speech and theater department at Dillard University in New Orleans. Although he left Morgan in the fall of 1935, several of his students were able to carry on the program Edmonds had organized there in the first department of drama in any black school.

During the twelve years that Edmonds spent at Dillard University he saw more clearly the tremendous possibilities for the national growth of educational theater. In 1936 he organized black colleges in the South and the Southwest into the Southern Association of Dramatic and Speech Arts (SADSA) and served as its president for seven years. Later the Association was renamed The National Association of Dramatic and Speech Arts (NADSA). Edmonds also organized Louisiana high school drama groups into a developing, progressive, interscholastic theater organization. It became an active part of the Louisiana Interscholastic Athletic and Literary Association (LIALA). His productions and tours with the Dillard University Players met with increasing success.

In 1942 Edmonds and James E. Gayle organized the Crescent Concerts Company in New Orleans. It is the first concert company known to have been owned and controlled by blacks. Paul Robeson, Phillipa Duke Schuyler, Marian Anderson, and Anne Brown were among the artists who appeared in concerts arranged by Edmonds's company. Unfortunately the company had a short life because the officers had difficulty in clearing and booking entertainers through the officials who had to approve all entertainment for the city of New Orleans. It ceased operation in 1943.

The effect of all of Edmonds's experiences in the theater brought him to a realization of three fundamental problems facing the black American theater: the need for playwrights, the need for trained, talented leadership, and the need for audience development. He began to address those needs first by assembling the plays he had written in courses at Oberlin. He published this first anthology in 1930; *Shades and Shadows* contained six imaginative plays of fantasy in dramatic form: *The Devil's Price, Hewers of Wood, Shades and Shadows, Everyman's Land, The Tribal Chief,* and *The Phantom Treasure.* Edmonds stated in the foreword that his "plays" were to be read aloud and were not intended to be acted on the stage. In fact, in only two of the plays, *The Devil's Price* and *Shades and Shadows,* was there any attempt to introduce action, motivation, and other requisites of good drama. Edmonds had not yet developed his command of dramatic technique; however, the *Pittsburgh Post Gazette* review of 2 May 1931 said: "Mr. Edmonds' talent lies in a blend of the natural Negro superstition with a literary style sufficient to carry the author's purpose. Somewhat amateurish in dialogue, it is expected that with further experience he will be able to make important contributions to the literature of his race."

When Edmonds published his second anthology, *Six Plays for a Negro Theatre* (1934), his writing skill had clearly improved. The plays in this volume—*Bad Man, Old Man Pete, Nat Turner, Breeders, Bleeding Hearts,* and *The New Window*—in contrast to those in *Shades and Shadows,* were meant to be performed. In the preface Edmonds explained that his plays were intended for "Negro Little Theatres, where there has been for many years a great need for plays of Negro life written by Negroes." Nonetheless, he also expressed the hope that they "contain some universal elements that will rise above the narrow confines of the nation or race of characters."

Many of Edmonds's plays, and all the plays in his second collection, are written in dialect, which was the fashion of the times, exemplified by such popular plays as *The Green Pastures* (1929), *In Abraham's Bosom* (1927), and *Porgy* (1927). During his career, he defended his use of dialect against such commentators as James Weldon Johnson, who, in his preface to *God's Trombones* (1927), says he had stopped using dialect himself because it has "but two complete stops, pathos and humor." Edmonds believed that dialect could be used in authentic tragedy to evoke as much emotion as did plays written in standard English. Edmonds felt the popularity of his plays did not, however, depend on dialect but on worthwhile themes, sharply drawn conflicts, positive characters, and melodramatic plots. As late as 1970, *Breeders,* one of his one-act dialect plays, won first place in a high school drama tournament held at Florida A & M University in Tallahassee, Florida.

Six Plays for a Negro Theatre showcases the "folk play," which, as defined by Frederick Koch, is "concerned with folk subject matter: with the legends, superstitions, customs, environmental differences, and the vernacular of the common people. For the most part they are realistic and human; sometimes they are imaginative and poetic." Koch articulates the goal of the folk dramatist as a depiction of "man's desperate struggle for existence and . . . his enjoyment of the world of nature. The term 'folk' with us applies to that form of drama which is earth-rooted in the life of our common humanity."

The first play in the collection is *Bad Man,* a one-act play set in a lumber camp where life is sad and the workers represent an odd mixture of righteousness and evil. As the play begins, Maybelle's father has just left her to visit the logging camp, where her brother, Tom, and her love interest, Ted, are working. Early in the play, Edmonds also introduces the character of Thea Dugger, "a bad man in many ways all right. . . . He ain't scared o' de debbil."

During the course of the play the news comes that a group of angry white men are intent on lynching a black man to avenge the murder of an old white man. At the crisis of the drama, the white men threaten to burn the shack but agree to be pacified if the guilty person will surrender. Though the blacks within the shack are innocent, the mob must be satisfied. Thea volunteers to be the victim because he wants to show himself as a brave and decent man in the presence of Maybelle who told

Advertisement for Edmonds's concert-booking company, the first such business run by black entrepreneurs

him earlier in the play that he had "a good streak" in him even though he had killed six men. He walks out of the shack, leaving everybody stunned. Voices indicate that he is seized by the mob and burned. Ted, upset by the proceedings, wants to rush out in the defense of Thea but is stopped by Tom. Ted's final speech reflects the helplessness of the black man in facing the evils in the society: "Yuh is right, dead right. We ain't nothin' but sawmill hands. All we is s'posed tuh do is to cut logs, saw lumber, live in dingy shanties, cut, fight, and kill each other. We ain't s'posed tuh pay no 'tention tuh a burnin' man . . . but ef de people wid larnin' can't do nothin' 'bout hit, 'tain't nothin' we can do. 'Tain't nothing we can do."

The plot is melodramatic; the obvious conflict between good and evil is given dignified treatment through the theme of the brutalizing effects of white supremacy and the efforts of black people to survive in spite of it. The love element lifts the play spiritually and gives an added dimension to the rugged sawmill setting and strong folk atmosphere.

The second play in the collection is *Old Man Pete*, a one-act play set in a Harlem apartment of a prominent black family. It is primarily a statement on the adjustment problem of the southern black man who migrated to the North in the first quarter of the twentieth century. Two married sons and a daughter have brought their parents from Virginia to live with them in New York. Soon the children grow ashamed of their parents' dialect, their countrified ways, and their outspoken criticism of city morals. A meeting is called to discuss the problem.

The parents, Mandy and Pete, realize that they do not fit into their children's way of life and decide to leave for the train station. At the close of the play the two old people freeze to death while sitting on a bench. The children are strivers and their interests have become superficial; they are easily taken in by new fads and are afraid of not being accepted in the community because of their parents. They do not wish to be connected with their southern background in any fashion. The plot is weakened because Edmonds does not provide the old people sufficient motivation to walk out to their death. The characterization of Pete and Mandy and their children, however, is lively and interesting enough to make the melodramatic ending unnecessary.

The third play in the collection, *Nat Turner*, is a character study of the slave who fomented the armed revolt of slaves on a plantation in Virginia in 1831. Turner is shown as a religious visionary, whose mysticism was the outgrowth of a genuine humanitarian impulse. He assembles a group of slaves in preparation for a revolt, but his group is soon defeated. Turner escapes and, disappointed by his early defeats, wonders about his future and about whether he erred in attempting to gain freedom through bloodshed. He says, "Hark is captured, and dere ain't no army. Whut is ah gwine tuh do now, Lawd? What can ah do? Ah knows whut ah'll do. Ah'll go hide under dat pile fence rails 'till ah can git another army. . . . Was ah wrong, Lawd, tuh fight dat black men mount be free? Whut is ah gwine tuh do now? Show me a vision, Lawd, lak yuh did when de sperits was fightin' in the air. Talk tuh me, Holy Ghost, lak yuh did when yuh told me tuh seek de kingdom of heaven. . . ." The play has rhythmic dialogue which is effective for folk speech, and it has colorful images.

The fourth play in the collection is *Breeders*. Ruth, a slave, disobeys the overseer's command that she marry Salem, a rough farmhand. She loves David, but the overseer does not consider David a good prospective "breeder." The overseer takes Ruth by the hand to the bedroom, but David tries to prevent Salem from molesting Ruth. He takes out his razor and swings at Salem, but the larger and stronger Salem grabs his wrist and with the other arm encircles David's neck in a strangling hug. Once Salem releases him, David falls accidentally on the razor and cuts his own throat. Salem goes to get help from other field hands. He returns to take Ruth as his wife but discovers she has taken poison in a final act of defiance.

Breeders is full of melodrama and sentimentality, but the characters are clearly drawn. The resolution in this play is atypical for melodrama but not uncommon for the treatment of black characters in folk plays written during this period.

Bleeding Hearts, the fifth play in the collection, is a vivid commentary on the state of the impoverished black farmer who is only slightly better off with his new freedom than he was as a slave. The play makes a strong statement on the harshness of overseers during the days of slavery. Miranda, the wife of a black farmer, dies of pneumonia because of a lack of adequate medical treatment from white doctors. The play is melodramatic, and the conflict is sharply drawn.

The sixth and last play in the collection, *The New Window*, takes place in a home in the backwoods of Virginia. Bullock Williams, a bootlegger, is a tough wife-beater, a bully, and a killer. He will kill any of his associates whom he suspects of being disloyal, especially with respect to his bootlegging.

The play depicts the revolt of Bullock's wife and stepdaughter against his brutality. Ultimately, Bullock is killed by the brother of one of his victims.

In 1942 Edmonds published his third anthology, *The Land of Cotton and Other Plays*. In addition to the title play, the collection included *Gangsters over Harlem, Yellow Death, Silas Brown,* and *The High Court of Historia*. There does not seem to be a thematic organizational principle to *The Land of Cotton and Other Plays,* and the plays collected in this volume are perhaps better understood in the context of other of Edmonds's works, rather than as a whole. *The High Court of Historia,* anomalous to the rest of the collection, carries over Edmonds's preoccupation with the fantastic which he had first treated in *Shades and Shadows*. It has more in common with a number of later plays.

In 1938 Edmonds's interest in "fantasy plays" was revived when he received a Rosenwald Fellowship to study at Dublin University and in the London School of Speech and Dramatic Arts.

While attending a conference at the University of London, Edmonds had met Lord Dunsany, author of supernatural and fantastic drama and literature. Edmonds heard lectures by Dunsany and had several personal interviews with him. He also saw the world premiere of Dunsany's *Alexander* (1938) at the Malvern Festival, and, with new insights derived from these experiences, Edmonds decided to write plays which dealt with universal problems that could be treated through the fantastic.

The result of Edmonds's experiences with Dunsany can be seen in *The High Court of Historia,* originally produced by the Dillard Players' Guild during its Black History week in the Workshop Theatre on the campus at Dillard University in February 1939. The play attacks the apathetic point of view held at that time by most black historians toward the teaching of black history. Afriopus, a black historian, is on trial and found guilty because he has neglected to teach the history of his own race and has failed to write and study the contributions of the black man. After the historian has been sentenced, he pleads with the king:

AFRIOPUS: I Call on thee, O High King, because I realize my mistake. If you will give me another chance, I will reform. I will do as all other historians do. I will look at life from the standpoint of my own people. I will join the association for The Study of Negro Life and History. I will buy all the books of Woodson, Wesley and Du Bois and teach my children pride of race as well as of nation. Give me another chance!

HIGH KING: I will give thee one more chance if thou seest that thy people will not only know their own history but be proud of it. Woe be unto thee if thou failest this time, however; for no matter where thou goest thou cannot escape the wrath of the High King. . . .

Much of Edmonds's philosophy is found in this play: clearly, he was concerned about the teaching of black history during the 1920s and 1930s, well before the radical education movement endorsed teaching black history during the 1960s and 1970s.

In addition to *The High Court of Historia,* Edmonds wrote four other fantasies: *Simon in Cyrene* (produced in 1943), in four acts; *The Shape of Wars to Come* (1943), in one act; *Shadow Across the Path* (1943), in one act; and "Prometheus and the Atom"(1955), in three acts.

Simon in Cyrene, a religious drama in four acts, depicts the life of Simon, the African who helped Christ bear his cross. After his association with the Master, Simon returns to his native country with a determination to become the first Apostle. Upon his arrival, he finds that his sweetheart, Cuesto, is about to be sacrificed to bring rain to the country. Simon shows his resentment by speaking out in the temple; he must then flee to a neighboring country. There he learns that, through God, he has the power to bring a dead child back to life as Peter and the disciples had done. This power enables him to secure an army, return to his homeland, and rescue his sweetheart by force; however, during the rescue mission he is fatally wounded, but he calls down rain from heaven before he dies. His final act goes unnoticed, and, after his death, his sweetheart is still sacrificed to the idol god, Odunga.

Another fantasy, "Prometheus and the Atom" (written in 1955), is a three-act play about man's misuse of power and the development of the atom bomb. Prometheus stole fire from heaven, gave it to man, and for doing this he was tried and sentenced by Zeus to centuries of horrendous sufferings. Man's misuse of power is illustrated in two actions: the Cythians declared war on the Colchains and burned their cities; the United States dropped the atom bomb on the Japanese and destroyed their cities. The implication is clear; man has learned little in the thousands of years since Prometheus.

A group of Edmonds's plays can be classified as social problem plays. In one, *Earth and Stars*

Dr. James H. Butler, professor of drama at the University of Southern California, presenting Edmonds with a special award from the American Theatre Association, August 1972 (photo by Cal Visuals)

(1946), Edmonds creates the story of protagonist Rev. Joshua H. Judson, who has left Ohio to come to a southern city and to initiate into his pastorate a program of "social action" following that outlined in his book, "The Modern Church." He believes that "the modern minister must be interested in the problems of the people here on earth as well as in that heavenly kingdom beyond the stars," and he sets out to minister to the physical and recreational needs of his congregation as well as to their spiritual needs.

The Land of Cotton is a full-length social drama in four acts about the southern sharecropper. Begun while the author was a student at Yale University and finished in Dublin, Ireland, while he was abroad in 1938, the play won first prize in a nationwide contest sponsored by the Foundation of Expressive Arts in Baltimore and was produced at a community theater in New Orleans. The plot centers around the system of tenant farming in the South. Gurry Lambert, a tenant farmer, and Caleb Macklin, a sharecropper, and others attempt to organize the farmers into a union to combat injustice. The farmers have difficulty in organizing their union because of the presence of the Ku Klux Klan.

Earth and Stars and *The Land of Cotton* are the best examples of Edmonds's social problem plays, although he wrote others of this type: "The Man of God" (written in 1931), "A Merchant in Dixie" (written in 1923), "A Virginia Politician" (written in 1927), "One Side of Harlem" (written in 1928), "For Fatherland" (written in 1934), and "Yellow Death" (1935). The first four of these were destroyed when Edmonds's house was flooded. "For Fatherland," a one-act play dealing with love of country, takes place in Germany. Rose's father and husband had both been soldiers, and now her son Fritz, a member of the military, has been accused of treason. He is arrested, but he escapes and goes home where the soldiers find him hiding in a closet. Though Rose pleads for Fritz's life, he is taken outside and shot by the guards. "Yellow Death" is a one-act historical play about Sid Thomas, a soldier in the Spanish-American War. The play takes place in a basement room in Sibany, Cuba, in July 1898. Yellow fever is killing many of the soldiers, and though Sid has fought bravely on the battlefield with his regiment, he is in terror of contracting the disease. Although Sid talks about leaving, he remains there to the end without getting the fever.

The three-act plays *Illicit Love* and "Wives and Blues" combine social problems with other enduring themes. The first of these is a variation on the Romeo and Juliet story. The second is a dramatization of a newspaper story by Ralph Matthews concerning the roles three wives play in a man's life. Edmonds also wrote three farce-comedy dramas, as he called them: *Rocky Roads* deals with the escapades of a young medical student at Howard University; "Sirlock Bones" is a comedy that features a detective in blackface; and *Down in the Everglades* is about two lost black men who are discovered by an Indian girl.

In his efforts to develop black educational theater, Edmonds seized every available opportunity to write essays to enlighten the public and to solicit its support for the theater in general. Many of the essays were published in the *Crisis, Opportunity*, the *Arts Quarterly, Phylon*, and the *Messenger*, journals to which most black writers of the day contributed. Edmonds saw these periodicals as a great opportunity to promote his ideas on educational theater and community drama.

Edmonds retired in 1970 with forty-eight plays to his credit that are still produced widely in black colleges and are discussed in black and white universities. Much of that criticism centers on Edmonds's use of dialect and his treatment of tragic characters. Literary concerns aside, the significance of Edmonds's plays rests upon their depiction of the struggle of the black man as he tries to gain his rights and freedom in the southern United States. He shows that the old ways of treating the black man can no longer be accepted. Edmonds's popular status with the American public is clearly reflected in the list of honors and awards that have been presented to him. He was awarded a Doctorate of Letters from Bethune-Cookman College, named a Fellow by the American Educational Theatre Association, presented a special citation by the American Theatre Association, honored with a special

festival of his plays by the National Association of Dramatic and Speech Arts, and commemorated by the Randolph Edmonds Players Guild at St. Paul's College. No one has contributed more to black educational theater than has Edmonds in his pioneering efforts to open the black theater movement and to inspire others to participate in it. Edmonds's characters are quite human and often have heroic qualities. He achieved his purpose in finding dramatic qualities in the daily lives of blacks, and because the black audiences identified with the characters and were familiar with the scenes and actions, the plays became very popular with them.

References:

Doris Abramson, *Negro Playwrights in the American Theatre, 1925-1959* (New York: Columbia University Press, 1969);

Fannin S. Belcher, Jr., "The Place of the Negro in the Evolution of the American Theatre, 1768-1940," Ph.D dissertation, Yale University, 1945;

J. C. Bledsoe, "Has the Negro a Place in the Theatre?," *Opportunity* (July 1928);

Frederick Bond, *The Negro and The Drama* (Washington, D.C.: Associated, 1940);

William Brasmer, Dominick Consolo, and Darwin T. Turner, eds., *Black Drama: An Anthology* (Columbus: Merrill, 1970);

Benjamin Brawley, *The Negro Genius* (New York: Dodd, Mead, 1937);

Marilyn Janice Gayle, "S. Randolph Edmonds: Pioneer in Negro Educational Theatre," M.A. thesis, Indiana University, 1960;

William Halstead, "National Theatre Organizations and Theatre Education," in *The History of Speech Education in America*, edited by Karl R. Wallace (New York: Appleton-Century, 1954);

James V. Hatch, *Black Image on the American Stage: A Bibliography of Plays and Musicals 1770-1970* (New York: DBS, 1970);

Fannie E. F. Hincklin, "The American Negro Playwright, 1920-1964," Ph.D. dissertation, University of Wisconsin, 1965;

Edith J. R. Isaacs, *The Negro in the American Theatre* (New York: McGrath, 1947);

Frederich N. Koch, "Drama in the South," *Carolina Playbook* (June 1940): 1-14;

Press Book of Florida Agricultural and Mechanical University: 1958 (Tallahassee, Fla.: Office of Public Relations, Florida Agricultural and Mechanical University, 1958);

William Reardon and Thomas Pawley, *The Black Teacher and The Dramatic Arts: A Dialogue, Bibliography, and Anthology* (Westport, Conn.: Negro University Press, 1970);

Floyd L. Sandle, *The Negro in the American Educa-tional Theatre* (Ann Arbor: Edwards Brothers, 1964);

Walter White, "The Negro on the American Stage," *English Journal*, 24 (March 1935): 181-182.

Jessie Redmon Fauset

Carolyn Wedin Sylvander
University of Wisconsin-Whitewater

BIRTH: Camden County, New Jersey, 27 April 1882 to Redmon and Annie Seamon Fauset.

EDUCATION: B.A., Cornell University, 1904; Sorbonne (France), circa 1925; M.A., University of Pennsylvania, 1919.

MARRIAGE: 1929 to Herbert Harris.

DEATH: Philadelphia, Pennsylvania, 30 April 1961.

BOOKS: *There is Confusion* (New York: Boni & Liveright, 1924; London: Chapman & Hall, 1924);

Plum Bun (New York: Stokes, 1929; London: Elkin Mathews & Marrot, 1929);

The Chinaberry Tree; A Novel of American Life (New York: Stokes, 1931; London: Elkin Mathews & Marrot, 1932);

Comedy, American Style (New York: Stokes, 1933).

OTHER: "The Gift of Laughter," in *The New Negro*, edited by Alain Locke (New York: Boni, 1925).

PERIODICAL PUBLICATIONS:
FICTION
'Emmy," *Crisis*, 5 (December 1912): 79-87; 5 (January 1913): 134-142;

"My House and a Glimpse of My Life Therein," *Crisis*, 8 (July 1914): 143-145;

" 'There Was One Time,' A Story of Spring," *Crisis*, 13 (April 1917): 272-277; 14 (May 1917): 11-15;

"The Sleeper Wakes," *Crisis*, 20 (August 1920): 168-173; 20 (September 1920): 226-229; 20 (October 1920): 267-274;

"When Christmas Comes," *Crisis*, 25 (December 1922): 61-63;

"Double Trouble," *Crisis*, 26 (August 1923): 155-159; 26 (September 1923): 205-209.

POETRY
"Rondeau," *Crisis*, 3 (April 1912): 252;

"Again It Is September," *Crisis*, 14 (September 1917);

"The Return," *Crisis*, 27 (January 1919): 118;

"Mary Elizabeth," *Crisis*, 19 (December 1919): 51-56;

"Oriflamme," *Crisis*, 19 (January 1920): 128;

"La Vie C'est La Vie," *Crisis*, 24 (July 1922): 124;

"Dilworth Road Revisited," *Crisis*, 24 (August 1922): 167;

"Song for a Lost Comrade," *Crisis*, 25 (November 1922): 22;

"Rencontre," *Crisis*, 27 (January 1924): 122;

"Here's April!," *Crisis*, 27 (April 1924): 277;

"Rain Fugue," *Crisis*, 28 (August 1924): 155;

"Stars in Alabama," *Crisis*, 35 (January 1928): 14;

" 'Courage!' He Said," *Crisis*, 36 (November 1929): 378.

NONFICTION
"New Literature on the Negro," *Crisis*, 20 (June 1920): 78-83;

"Impressions of the Second Pan-African Congress," *Crisis*, 22 (November 1921): 12-18;

"What Europe Thought of the Pan African Congress," *Crisis*, 22 (December 1921): 60-69.

A minor, though pivotal, figure of the Harlem Renaissance, Jessie Redmon Fauset was the author of four novels and numerous short stories, essays,

Jessie Redmon Fauset (courtesy of the Schomburg Center for Research in Black Culture, the New York Public Library, Astor, Lenox and Tilden Foundations)

the United States and an understanding of the unique situation of the American black woman. Though her novels are rife with romantic and entertaining plots, largely revolving around the black middle class, she is nevertheless, thorough in confronting race and sex stereotyping.

Jessie Redmon Fauset, as she was listed in the family Bible, seventh child of an outspoken and assertive African Methodist Episcopal minister, was born in Camden County, New Jersey, a suburb of Philadelphia, Pennsylvania. After the death of Annie Seamon Fauset, Redmon Fauset married a widow with three children and fathered three more offspring. Fauset's family was poor, but cultured. She attended the Philadelphia public schools and graduated from the High School for Girls in 1900, probably as the only black student in the school. An honor graduate, Fauset sought admission to Bryn Mawr College, but apparently the school avoided the issue of having to accept a black student by initiating support for her to receive a scholarship to Cornell University. Fauset graduated from Cornell in 1905, possibly the first black woman to be elected to Phi Beta Kappa. Returning to Philadelphia, she was denied employment in the segregated schools there, and she spent one year teaching in Baltimore before beginning, in 1906, a fourteen-year tenure teaching French at the M Street High School (later renamed the Dunbar school) in Washington, D.C. From 1918 to 1919 Fauset completed a Master of Arts degree at the University of Pennsylvania and was, by this time, working with W. E. B. Du Bois and the *Crisis*. In 1919 she moved to New York as literary editor of that publication, beginning her years of most intensive writing and most extensive support of other black authors.

Jessie Fauset's first novel, *There is Confusion* (1924), was inspired, she said, by the publication of T. S. Stribling's *Birthright* (1922), "the most significant novel on the Negro written by a white American." "Let us who are better qualified to present [the truth of Negro life] than any white writer, try to do so," she said in an interview with Marion Starkey published in *Southern Workman* in May 1932. *There is Confusion* was published by Boni and Liveright, who also published Jean Toomer's *Cane* (1923) as well as the work of T. S. Eliot, William Faulkner and other notable authors. The novel presents the parallel stories of two families united through the marriage of Joanna Marshall and Peter Bye. Tracing the lives of the main characters from childhood on, and including detailed information about the ancestry of both families and about friends of the main characters as well, Fauset cre-

poems, and articles written between 1910 and 1933. From 1919 to 1926 she was the literary editor of the *Crisis* magazine of the National Association for the Advancement of Colored People. After 1926 she became a contributing editor. In 1920 and 1921 she edited and wrote *The Brownies' Book,* a children's magazine that was a project of W. E. B. Du Bois. In "discovering" and encouraging major black writers of the Harlem Renaissance, both formally and informally, her work is unsurpassed: she promoted the work of George Schuyler, Jean Toomer, Countee Cullen, Langston Hughes, and Claude McKay. In her own writing, particularly in her essays and novels, Fauset demonstrates an awareness of the far-reaching implications of the black struggle in

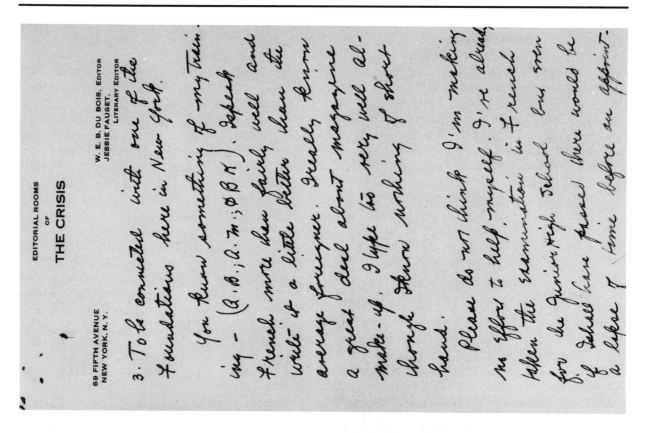

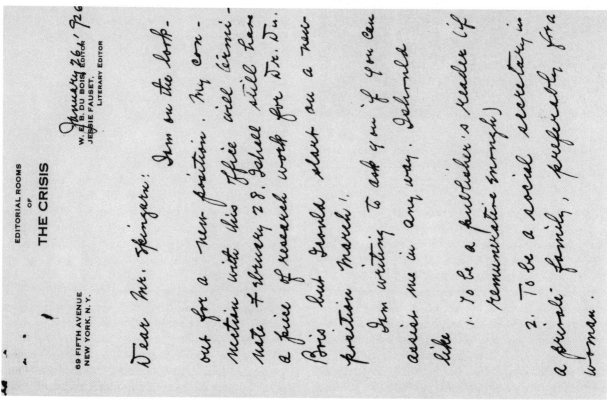

Letter to Joel Spingarn (courtesy of the Schomburg Center for Research in Black Culture, the New York Public Library, Astor, Lenox and Tilden Foundations)

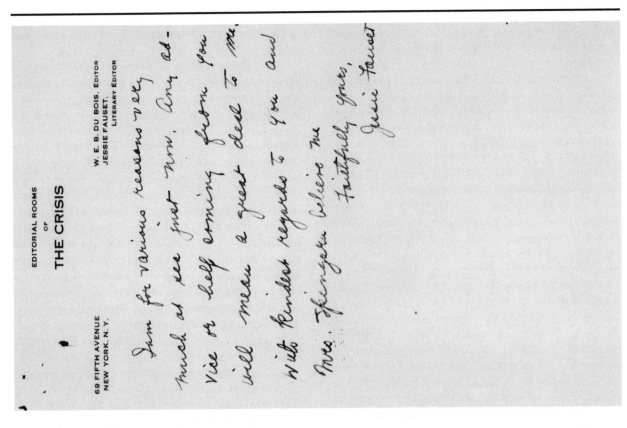

ates confusing text with undeveloped, often ineffective characters, descriptions, dialogue, and leaps in time.

Despite its formal weaknesses, *There is Confusion* is worth reading for the ideas and themes Fauset articulates. The book explores the limited vocational alternatives available to women, especially black women, and also shows women breaking out of these limits without being excessively punished. The novel explores the racial discrimination and sociocultural inheritance faced by the northern urban black, and it depicts a wide range of characters and actions against a backdrop of American slave history and racially mixed heredity. Fauset subtly explores alternatives to society's sometimes limiting norms. She looks upon religion in the black church, for example, as a social institution capable of giving support to people with a variety of problems, rather than as a received body of supernatural truth. Similarly, biblical motifs are used for their historical significance, not their religious significance. Black folk material as the basis for individuality in black art is demonstrated in Joanna's use of a black children's dance-game as her entree into the theatrical world. If one theme could be said to dominate *There is Confusion,* it is that surviving the hardships engendered by discrimination places the black person and the race in a position of superiority. As the character Brian says:

> The complex of color. . . . every colored man feels it sooner or later. It gets in the way of his dreams, of his education, of his marriage, of the rearing of his children. The time comes when he thinks, 'I might just as well fall back; there's no use pushing on. A colored man just can't make any headway in this awful country.' Of course, it's a fallacy. And if a fellow sticks it out he finally gets past it, but not before it has worked considerable confusion in his life. To have the ordinary job of living is bad enough, but to add to it all the thousand and one difficulties which follow simply in the train of being colored— well, all I've got to say, Sylvia, is we're some wonderful people to live through it all and keep our sanity.

There is Confusion received generally favorable reviews. A *New York Times* book review pointed to the novelty of its having been written by a college-educated Negro woman, and the December 1924 *London Times Literary Supplement* found the novel an "able and unusual story" which charmed the English reader by its "apt allusions to circumstances of Negro life."

Critical readings of *There is Confusion* since its first publication have concentrated narrowly and often erroneously on Fauset's depiction of black middle-class characters. Arthur P. Davis, for example, in his 1974 book, *From the Dark Tower: Afro-American Writers 1900-1960* (1974), calls Fauset the "most prolific, and in many ways the most representative, of [the] glorifiers of the Negro middle class," and calls *There is Confusion* her "fullest and most representative novel" because it renders "more of the typical attitudes and shibboleths held by the New Negro middle class of the 1920's than any of her others." Davis concludes, "She is really trying to make a very small group of Negroes represent all Negroes." While Fauset sympathizes with the black bourgeoisie, Lee R. Edwards and Arlyn Diamond point out in their note accompanying an excerpt of Fauset's second novel, *Plum Bun* (1929), collected in *American Voices, American Women* (1973), that Fauset also "realizes the potential sterility and destructiveness of their overwhelming concern with whiteness and respectability."

Many formal devices in *Plum Bun* make it, in many ways, her best work. She corrects the glaring structural weaknesses of her first novel by concentrating in the second one on a major character, Angela Murray, from whose point of view the story is told. Time spans and time transitions in *Plum Bun* are shorter and smoother than they were in *There is Confusion.* The external world is described in more detail and is used to complement Angela's changing perceptions as she goes from an ambitious and attractive young mulatto who passes for white to a mature and sensitive artist claiming her black heritage.

The Murray family is not as wealthy as the Marshalls of *There is Confusion,* and the theme of importance of family, of roots, of enduring and honest relationships is made separate from the social and economic class of the characters. Fauset continues to treat racial discrimination in her second novel but concentrates on the peculiar ironies of discrimination against the "black" who is, by all appearances, white. The focus, again, is not simply on the discrimination, but on the various ways characters develop from having to deal with historical, biological, psychological and economic realities. Angela Murray's psychology—her decision to pass and her subsequent decision to reclaim her racial heritage—is fully explored. In centering on Angela, Fauset is able to explore fully the limitations of gender roles, as well as women's attempts to break free of some of those roles.

Fauset's title is taken from the second stanza of a nursery rhyme, which also provides the book's epigraph: "To market, to market/To buy a Plum Bun;/Home again, Home again,/Market is done." The first section of the novel, "Home," describes the Murray family life on Opal Street in Philadelphia, the death of Angela's parents, the differences between the dark sister, Virginia, and Angela, who decides to go to New York and pass for white. The seven chapters of the second section, "Market," open with Angela's arrival in New York and end with Virginia's arrival there. The third section, "Plum Bun," is devoted to Angela's affair with the rich, white Roger Fielding. "Home Again," the fourth and longest section, is spent exploring Angela's attempts to establish meaningful and lasting relationships with carefully chosen men and women in her life. In the short final section, "Market is Done," Angela, a painter, is awarded a trip to France, but reveals her racial identity in response to reporters' badgering of a black woman, Miss Powell. For her honesty, Angela is ultimately rewarded with a Paris reunion with her true love, Anthony Cross, who has lingered in the background in triple disguise as a poor black who looks white.

Plum Bun is a frequently misunderstood, but carefully constructed black American Bildungsroman in which racial difference is the societal barrier perceived by the growing central character first as an absolute and, finally, as a false distinction of value to be overcome, ignored, and replaced. In American society, where class does not loom as the unalterable state "reasonably" imposed upon a character, unchangeable skin color becomes the social tool for discrimination. *Plum Bun* is an American romance which satirizes traditional romantic assumptions, particularly in regard to race and sex. Black blood is customarily a "bar sinister" to American romance. Angela sees it in just that way at the beginning of the novel; her romantic ideals of adventure and love point directly toward being white, and marrying white as well as rich. While she believes in the American fairy-tale romance, marriage with her white prince, Roger Fielding, eludes her. It is only when Angela has come to a new understanding of skin color, money, and marriage that Roger arrives at her door with his marriage offer; he is, of course, no longer a prince to Angela, for he represents none of her new and true ideals.

Early reviews of *Plum Bun* and more recent criticism have, for the most part, failed to penetrate the formal nursery rhyme and fairy-tale disguise Fauset made use of to appeal to the unsophisticated reader. In a 10 April 1929 review in the *New Republic*, for example, the subject matter and the convincing character of Angela were praised, while the "melodramatic, unreal" storyline was deplored. David Littlejohn's *Black on White* (1966) dismisses all Fauset's "vapidly genteel lace-curtain romances" as not rising "above the stuffy, tiny-minded circulating-library norm," and Robert Bone's *The Negro Novel in America* (1966) finds that "in spite of an admirable persistence, her novels are uniformly sophomoric, trivial, and dull."

Jessie Fauset's last two novels contain some departures from the content and form of her first two. *The Chinaberry Tree* (1931) and *Comedy, American Style* (1933) are more significant in showing Fauset's intentions rather than her accomplishments, for the last two novels are in many ways a weakening and scattering of the formal strengths of *Plum Bun* and a return to some of the stylistic flaws of *There is Confusion*. Fauset herself, according to her half-brother, Arthur Huff Fauset, preferred her first two novels.

The plot of *The Chinaberry Tree* is based on a story Fauset had heard when she was fifteen, and which she had written as a short story, "Double Trouble." She wrote the novel in the summer of 1931, while she was taking a French class at Columbia University. During the academic year, Fauset was teaching at De Witt Clinton High School in New York City.

In *The Chinaberry Tree*, Fauset explores "the homelife of the colored American who is not being pressed too hard by the Furies of Prejudice, Ignorance, and Economic Injustice." The Frederick A. Stokes Company, which had published *Plum Bun*, balked a bit at *The Chinaberry Tree*, agreeing to publish it only after Fauset succeeded in getting Zona Gale to write an introduction. Readers at Stokes, Fauset wrote to Gale on 20 October 1931, "declare plainly that there ain't no such colored people as these, who speak decent English, are self-supporting and have a few ideals."

A small New Jersey community named Red Brook provides the setting for the exploration of values in *The Chinaberry Tree*. White townspeople appear in only one scene in the book, as onlookers at a community skating party. It is black Red Brook society which has over the years ostracized mulatto Aunt Sal Strange, lover of the deceased Colonel Halloway, for bearing Laurentine out of wedlock. The beautiful Laurentine has grown up oversensitive to what an unwitting small playmate once

*Jessie Fauset, Langston Hughes, and Zora Neale Hurston at
Tuskegee Institute in 1927*

called her "bad blood," and she seeks to overcome the past by marriage to a respectable man.

Melissa Paul has come from Philadelphia to live with her aunt and cousin, not knowing that her mother, Judy Strange, had left Red Brook after a much talked-about affair with her best friend's husband, Sylvester Forten. Part of young Melissa's confidence of bearing and attitude of superiority to Aunt Sal and Laurentine comes from her mistaken assurance of her legitimacy. Malory Forten, sent away to school after his father's affair with Judy Strange, returns to Red Brook and conducts a secret courtship with Melissa Paul. Their conventional ideas match exactly, making of them the perfect pair upon which Fauset can spring her most unconventional surprise: just before their marriage they discover they are half-brother and sister.

Laurentine, Melissa, and Malory represent the longing for respectability, decency, and normalcy, while three other characters, Aunt Sal, Dr. Stephen Denleigh, and Asshur Lane, embody less conventional definitions of these terms. Aunt Sal's view of her love match with the colonel is not the

community's view. Dr. Denleigh, whom she eventually marries, scolds Laurentine, when she confesses her "illegitimacy" to him: "What bosh to talk to a physician! Biology transcends society! . . . The facts of life, birth and death are more important than the rules of living, marriage, law, the sanction of church or man." Asshur Lane, who eventually marries Melissa, is the youngest and most saintly of these revisionist philosophers. He finally provides the theme of the book: "Life, Death, and Essential Honor were the only matters which greatly concerned him in his simple code. Life was for enjoyment; Death was to be met,—with great dignity,—only when it could be no longer avoided; Honor consisted in downing no man and in refusing to consider oneself downed." The theme of *The Chinaberry Tree* is not, as Nick Aaron Ford says in *Black Insights* (1971), "the middle class Negro's abhorrence of miscegenation without the benefit of matrimony," but the opposite: true values of life and death and human relationships as opposed to the limited and limiting false values of society's rules.

Theatrical elements are implicit in *The Chinaberry Tree*. Fauset showed great interest in drama in the 1920s in her New York City social life and in her *Crisis* literary editing. In her 1932 interview with Marion Starkey, she named theater-going as her favorite recreation. "The boast of her life," Starkey writes, "is that she once appeared on the Broadway stage with the French actress, Cecile Sorel. 'You may have noticed me; I was part of the mob in the guillotine scene in DuBarry.' " Fauset's theatrical interest did not, however, lead to the writing of plays. In 1922 Fauset replied to an invitation to write drama that she had no experience in playwriting and did not dare attempt it. Rather, her expertise and interest in drama appears to have found its way into her final novels. Fauset uses suggestions of Greek tragedy extensively to lend impact to her narration, although the underlying philosophical and religious assumptions of tragedy are not adopted. Neither does Fauset intend to say that life is like a Greek tragedy; rather, she is always pointing out distinctions between convention and virtue, between fate and choice, and between inevitability and responsibility. To enhance the dramatic impact of the novel, Fauset employs descriptions of costumes, festive seasonal events, moonlight scenes where reality and dream merge, and a natural setting dominated by the chinaberry tree.

Nonetheless, the achievement of Fauset's third novel falls short of that of her second. The novel's flaws include poor treatment of its parallel story lines, which take place in 1890 and 1930 respectively, and intrusive, unincorporated incidents which are only explained partly by its method of composition. She wrote the novel "in a straightforward manner, almost without revision," Fauset said in her interview with Marion Starkey, but she made "certain interpolations that I put into the original story. For instance, the incident that happened to Dr. Denleigh and Laurentine at the restaurant in Pelham happened, almost exactly as it is described, to my husband and me last summer while I was writing my novel." There seems to be no function for this incident in which an immigrant waiter is rude to the black customers. It raises many questions which Fauset may not have consciously intended to introduce into the novel.

Some of the weaknesses of *The Chinaberry Tree* may have resulted from Fauset's poor judgment about subject matter. When Fauset was writing *The Chinaberry Tree* the height of the Harlem Renaissance was over, and the Depression was on. Black writers were experiencing a decline in popularity and decline in income and were finding it ever more difficult to publish. Fauset may have tried to pick popular subjects to engage audience support.

Fauset, who wished to be able to support herself by her writing, looked "wistfully to the day" when she would be able to devote a year or two to a novel, "just to see what I really could do if I had my full time and energy to devote to my work." In 1932 she "confesses" to studying issues of the *Saturday Evening Post* "in a candid effort to analyze and isolate the germs of popular writing." Nonetheless, her work failed to garner financial success, and she had to continue teaching to support herself.

Despite the demands of her teaching career on her time, Fauset wrote one more novel, published in 1933, when she was fifty-one years old. *Comedy, American Style* focuses on the ironies of American black life with more directness and less sentimentality than any of her previous novels, and it includes more characters who do not succeed in attaining true understanding. Fauset's depiction of Olivia Cary, the mother in this novel, has been called "the most penetrating study of color mania in American fiction" by Hugh Gloster in *Negro Voices in American Fiction* (1948).

All of Olivia Cary's actions stem from her hatred of being black and her desire to be white. Fauset is not totally convincing in explaining the motivation for this color mania, although she does provide some insight into this character when she reveals that Janet Blanchard, Olivia's mother, is strongly class conscious, and that the young Olivia takes pleasure at being mistaken for a little Italian girl. The reader also learns that Olivia is incapable of loving. If the explanation of Olivia's "mania," her self-hatred, is weak, the depiction of the negative power she wields over the lives of her husband and children is not. She marries a doctor, Christopher Cary, who, while light enough to pass for white, never exercises that option. Their first two children, Christopher and Teresa, are raised, through the intervention of their father's teaching, relatively free of their mother's dominating concern. The third child, Olivia predicts, will be "the handsomest and most attractive of us all. And I'll name him after myself." Olivia has a long convalescence from the third birth and does not see the baby until he is a month old. He is just as she predicted: the handsomest and most attractive of them all, and named Oliver after her. He is also, like Olivia's father, obviously Negro. "That's not my baby!" she cries.

Three of the Cary family are destroyed by Olivia's color mania. Oliver becomes a young suicide. Teresa, forced to marry a man she does not love, dies emotionally. Olivia lives on in eventual isolation and poverty. Only the father and young Christopher overcome and survive, through much pain and difficulty, the damage Olivia causes. Showing alternatives to Olivia Cary's response to American racism, Fauset locates her primary positive character outside the family. Phebe Grant is a blond and blue-eyed black woman of the lowest social class who plays no games with her racial inheritance. "I belong to the black or Negro race," she responds to a teacher at a young age. When she is older, and having risen from a seamstress with a white family to a shop-owning modiste, Phebe refuses to marry a rich white man on false pretenses. Finally, after a mature and responsible marriage to the young Christopher Cary, she remains absolutely loyal through intense temptation.

For these struggling characters—the elder and younger Christophers, and Phebe—there is a kind of happy ending, at least a temporary victory over their trials and an increased strength from having endured. There is no easy way of dealing successfully with life or race in America, Fauset reminds her readers, but there are alternatives to Olivia Cary's imitation white life. Phebe Grant's alternative is acceptance of her inheritance, hard work, unswerving loyalty and honesty.

Fauset demonstrates most clearly, in *Comedy, American Style*, than in her three other novels, the great difficulty of obtaining happiness and full, honest human relationships, for there are central characters in this book who do not succeed in reaching these goals. It is not true, however, that most of the characters "are ultimately frustrated, ill-adjusted and doomed, . . . victims of their own desire to deny their race, and of the cruelty, prejudice and lack of understanding by which they are surrounded," as an early review in the *New York Times* stated 19 November 1933. Fauset merely concludes her long novel with a realistic assessment of black life in America.

Fauset experimented with dramatic forms in her final novel, as she had in *The Chinaberry Tree.* The six subtitles of the novel are elements of a play: "The Plot"; "The Characters"; "Teresa's Act"; "Oliver's Act"; "Phebe's Act"; and "Curtain." While these terms create ironic ambiguity in the novel, they do not sufficiently offset Fauset's inability or unwillingness to manipulate language with the imagination or skill required to create out of her plan a truly great novel. In Teresa's, Phebe's, and Oliver's "Acts," for instance, Fauset fails to use language suited to the perceptions of each character respectively. Fauset's lack of linguistic inventiveness is particularly noticeable in "Oliver's Act." The central character here is an intelligent, sensitive child whose perspicacity, nevertheless, cannot penetrate the mystery of his mother's disaffection for him. Fauset writes about his perceptions in a stilted, precise, intellectual prose; for example, she writes, "because of his mother's indifference, he had known, before he was six years old, three widely different homes. In his childish way he had made contrasts and had long since decided which home—by which at that time he meant environment—he truly preferred."

The final section of this bitter comedy of American life, "Curtain," finds Olivia Cary in Paris, trying to maintain a pretense of being white, rich, loved by her family. She is last seen looking out into the "thin watery sunshine" of the "tangled garden" outside the window of her cheap rented room. Outside, a mother and son sit reading and laughing together. "He was a slender, rather tall lad, but young," Fauset writes in the concluding lines of the novel. "About the age of Oliver in the days when he used to come running up to his mother's room to confide in her about his algebra." Olivia is finally passing as white; no person and no situation can endanger that new status because she has destroyed her ties to her family and heritage. Fauset's unsympathetic protagonist reinforces the author's theme, which dominates in all four of her novels: racial

Portrait of Jessie Fauset (courtesy of the Schomburg Center for Research in Black Culture, the New York Public Library, Astor, Lenox and Tilden Foundations)

and sexual barriers abound, but what really counts for happiness and for fulfillment are human relationships.

Jessie Fauset's work for the *Crisis,* both in her own writing and her editing, and for the shortlived children's magazine, the *Brownies' Book,* for which she did both the editing and much of the writing, contributed to the proliferation of black arts during the Negro Renaissance. Fauset's poetry, simple and lucid, is unremarkable, though certain poems are rather frequently anthologized, as are some of her translations of the work of Haitian poets. Her short stories contain many of the themes and characters she developed more fully in her later novels. They are of interest primarily for the insight they supply into her composition and revision techniques. In her book reviews and articles there is evidence of her wide-ranging interests in literature, travel and other areas of knowledge. She reported on the Second Pan-African Congress held in Europe in 1921 and wrote of her experiences at the Sorbonne and while traveling in France and Algeria from 1925 to 1926. Her articles range from such topics as Egyptian nationalism to Brazilian emancipation.

Jessie Fauset's intelligence, precise language usage, and intense sensitivity seem better suited to her essays than to her fiction. "Tracing Shadows," for example, from the September 1915 issue of the *Crisis*, reveals her skill with the travel essay. In relating the experience of being a student in Paris during the outbreak of World War I in August 1914, Fauset shows an awareness of the differing experiences of others and an ability to find relevant universal significance in her personal observations. Her incisive essays of the 1920s, particularly the five which deal with her experiences in France and Algeria in 1925 and 1926, are especially noteworthy for their focus on women's problems.

Of Jessie Fauset's stature as an editor during the Harlem Renaissance, Langston Hughes wrote in his autobiography, *The Big Sea*, "Jessie Fauset at the *Crisis*, Charles Johnson at *Opportunity*, and Alain Locke in Washington were the three people who mid-wifed the so-called New Negro literature into being. Kind and critical—but not too critical for the young—they nursed us along until our books were born." More than discovering or encouraging authors like Hughes, Countee Cullen, Jean Toomer, and Claude McKay, Fauset included in the *Crisis* many articles dealing with literary movements of the day. She published a large number of women writers, black and white, whose stories, poems, and essays articulated views ranging from conservative to radical on racial and sexual issues. There is evidence that Du Bois had a difficult time dealing with authors and their writing after Fauset left the *Crisis* in 1926; certainly, the literary quality of the publication diminished after that date.

For the *Brownies' Book,* published in twenty-four issues from January 1920 to December 1921, it is Fauset rather than Du Bois who should have received major credit. Fauset wrote the dedication: "To children, who with eager look/Scanned vainly library shelf, and nook,/For History or Song or Story/That told of Colored People's glory,—/We dedicate the *Brownies' Book*." For this publication, Fauset wrote hundreds of signed and unsigned poems, stories, dialogues, biographies, articles; she edited manuscripts and correspondence with other contributors as well. As Elinor Sinnette wrote in a 1965 *Freedomways* article, "The Brownies' Book," "as a teacher . . . [Fauset] saw daily the need for children and young people to have insight into their past and hope and pride in their future." The periodical is a delightful publication that expands the impression of Fauset as an efficient editor, a friend to young writers, and a creative writer in her own right.

Jessie Fauset married Herbert Harris in 1929, and for several years the couple made their home with her sister, Helen Fauset Lanning, on Seventh Avenue in Harlem. In the early 1940s, after Helen Lanning's death, the Harrises moved to Montclair, New Jersey, where they lived until Herbert Harris's death in 1958. While these years appear to have been happy, they were not as productive for writing as Fauset had wished. In a 1946 article in the *Delta Journal*, a sorority quarterly, Fauset is described as working on a fifth novel. It was never published. After her husband's death, Fauset moved to Philadelphia to live with her stepbrother Earl Huff. By this time she suffered from arteriosclerosis, which led to her death in 1961 from hypertensive heart disease.

Jessie Fauset's influence on black art in the period of the Harlem Renaissance was extensive. Nevertheless, her work has been dismissed frequently by critics who have erroneously assumed her novels reflect her easy early life and who believe she is simply promoting the black middle class. More accurately Fauset's work reflects the growth of a struggling, self-made, sophisticated, widely read and deliberate literary artist, whose thematic concerns and formal experiments are worth critical investigation. In comparison with another well-known female novelist of the period, Nella Larsen, Fauset has a wider scope of interests, a more inclusive range of themes and concerns, but correspondingly a less intense presentation.

Fauset's essays reveal her curiosity and sympathy, but the novels, too, leave an impression of strength gained through difficulties overcome. Far from promoting a limited notion of respectability, Fauset emphasizes recognition of a morality which is at variance with society's codes. Fauset's strength may lie in her unobtrusive presentation of alternatives for defining the black American woman: more exploratory than dogmatic, more searching than protesting.

References:

Addison Gayle, *The Way of the New World: The Black Novel in America* (Garden City: Anchor/Doubleday, 1976);

Abby Arthur Johnson, "Literary Midwife: Jessie Redmon Fauset and the Harlem Renaissance," *Phylon* (June 1978): 143-153;

Marion Starkey, "Jessie Fauset," *Southern Workman* (May 1932): 217-220;

Carolyn Wedin Sylvander, *Jessie Redmon Fauset, Black American Writer* (Troy, N.Y.: Whitston, 1981);

Jean Fagan Yellin, "An Index of Literary Materials in *The Crisis*, 1910-1934: Articles, Belles-

Lettres, and Book Reviews," *CLA Journal*, 14 (1971): 197-234, 452-465.

Rudolph Fisher

(9 May 1897-26 December 1934)

Eleanor Q. Tignor
LaGuardia Community College, CUNY

BOOKS: *The Walls of Jericho* (New York & London: Knopf, 1928);
The Conjure-Man Dies: A Mystery Tale of Dark Harlem (New York: Covici-Friede, 1932).

PLAY PRODUCTION: *Conjur' Man Dies*, New York, Lafayette Theatre, 11 March 1936, adapted by Fisher from his novel.

PERIODICAL PUBLICATIONS: "The City of Refuge," *Atlantic Monthly*, 135 (February 1925): 178-187;
"South Lingers On," *Survey Graphic*, 6 (March 1925): 644-647;
"Ringtail," *Atlantic Monthly*, 135 (May 1925): 652-660;
"High Yaller," Part I, *Crisis*, 30 (October 1925): 281-286; Part II, *Crisis*, 31 (November 1925): 33-38;
"The Promised Land," *Atlantic Monthly*, 139 (January 1927): 37-45;
"The Backslider," *McClure's* (August 1927): 16-17, 101-104;
"Blades of Steel," *Atlantic Monthly*, 140 (August 1927): 183-192;
"The Caucasian Storms Harlem," *American Mercury*, 11 (August 1927): 393-398;
"Fire by Night," *McClure's* (December 1927): 64-67, 98-102;
"Common Meter," Part I, *New York News*, 8 February 1930; Part II, 15 February 1930;
"Dust," *Opportunity*, 9 (February 1931): 46-47;
"Ezekiel," *Junior Red Cross News* (March 1932): 151-153;
"Ezekiel Learns," *Junior Red Cross News* (February 1933): 123-125;
"Guardian of the Law," *Opportunity*, 11 (March 1933): 82-85, 90;

"Miss Cynthie," *Story*, 3 (June 1933): 3-15;
"John Archer's Nose," *Metropolitan, A Monthly Review* (January 1935).

With the 1925 publication of medical intern Rudolph Fisher's short story "The City of Refuge" in the *Atlantic Monthly*, the consensus among the black literati of the New Negro cultural movement of the 1920s was that a new member to the circle had arrived. In a 1959 letter Arna Bontemps wrote that through Countee Cullen he had heard of "a young new writer from Washington who had just sold two stories to the *Atlantic*. This news has gone around literary circles in Harlem, because up to that time none of the young writers of the New Negro Movement had been able to break into that magazine. So the stage was set, and 'City of Refuge' created something of a sensation." Langston Hughes described Fisher as "the wittiest" of the Harlem Renaissance group, "whose tongue was flavored with the sharpest and saltiest humor. He and Alain Locke together were great for intellectual wise-cracking. I used to wish I could talk like Rudolph Fisher." Locke himself, in *The New Negro: An Interpretation* (1925), referred to Fisher as one of the "new generation not because of years only, but because of a new aesthetic and a new philosophy of life."

Rudolph John Chauncey Fisher was born in Washington, D.C., on 9 May 1897 to clergyman John Wesley Fisher and Glendora Williamson Fisher. One of three children, Fisher grew up and attended school in New York and Providence, Rhode Island, where he graduated from Classical High School in 1915 with honors. At Brown University, as a James Manning and Francis Wayland Scholar, he majored first in English and then in biology, graduating with department honors in the

Rudolph Fisher (courtesy of the Schomburg Center for Research in Black Culture, the New York Public Library, Astor, Lenox and Tilden Foundations)

latter discipline. In addition to his overall academic achievement, his gift for science, and his skill in public speaking, he won first Caesar Misch Premium (in German) during his freshman year, first prize in the Carpenter Prize Speaking Contest his sophomore year, and the Dunn Premium his junior year. In 1917 he represented Brown in an intercollegiate public speaking contest at Harvard University, winning first prize. In the Class Day Program, 1919, Fisher is listed as Class Orator, and the Brown University Commencement Program that year shows that he delivered one of three orations, his entitled "The Emancipation of Science." The 1919 *Liber Brunensis* described Fisher as "orator and biologist." With one more year of study at Brown, during which he was also a graduate

assistant in biology, Fisher earned the M.A. degree. Speaking of his education, Fisher called Brown University "a most generous institution, [that] gave me a great many prizes and scholarships . . . and all of the keys, Phi Beta Kappa, Delta Sigma Rho, and Sigma Xi. There was undoubtedly an oversupply that year!" At the Howard University Medical School from 1920 to 1924, he was an outstanding student and served as an instructor in embryology. On 6 June 1924 he graduated with highest honors. Classmates recall him as a brilliant, intellectual, witty, sophisticated gentleman. He interned at Washington's Freedman's Hospital, and on 22 September Fisher married Jane Ryder, a Washington, D.C., teacher. The Fishers had one son, Hugh.

In 1925, the year Fisher's stories "The City of Refuge," "South Lingers On," "Ringtail," and "High Yaller" were published, he moved to New York to become a fellow of the National Research Council at Columbia University's College of Physicians and Surgeons. He trained there in bacteriology, pathology, and roentgenology for two years before he opened a practice in New York. Even before he moved to New York, Fisher was feeling conflict about his two careers, which he recorded in his correspondence in 1925 and 1926 with Carl Van Vechten, well-known white patron of Afro-American literature who took a particular interest in Harlem and the New Negro writers. In a letter dated 13 August 1925 he wrote about the demands of his medical career and closed the letter metaphorically: "I am Moses on the mount, gazing hopelessly into the promised land."

In *McClure's* magazine (August 1927) he would write of his dual interests: "An A.B. degree . . . in '19 urged me into art and an A.M. degree in '20 urged me into science; and so I studied medicine to heal my fractured ambition. An M.D. in '24 saved my life by permitting me to write both fiction and articles for literary journals and research reports for the scientific journals."

From the publication of his first work in 1925 until his untimely death in December 1934, Fisher wrote two novels, including the first black American detective novel, a play that was produced, more than a score of short stories, and a small number of juvenile tales.

Fisher's earliest story, written while he was in medical school, addresses the experience of the southerner transplanted into Harlem. He would polish his treatment of this theme in subsequent tales. The central character of "City of Refuge," ironically named King Solomon Gillis, is a poor

672 St. Nicholas Ave.,
New York N.Y.
20·X·25

Dear Alain Locke,

Many thanks for your notelet, whose ~~typography~~ may have looked like code but was nevertheless largely intelligible.

My understanding is that you missed nothing by failing (to hear) either) Bledsoe or to see Appearances. Noone has praised either to me.

I've not really begun to get down to business at the laboratory, where I seem to. be quite my own lord and master. Only one significant thing at all has happened to me since I've arrived, and it had nothing to do with the research work: I learn I am to have a place in "Best Short Stories of 1925" (Small Maynard) "The City of Refuge" again. It is getting its share of attention isn't it?

Received a letter from Cosmopolitan asking to "see some" of my "work". The quotation marks are mine.

Letter to Alain Locke (courtesy of the Alain Locke Papers, Moorland-Spingarn Research Center, Howard University)

- 2 -

Saw Jessie Fauset Sunday and quite captivated her by playing dance-music. This is not for publication. I've forgotten just what I said afterwards but it brought forth the insistence that I explain in person and private. (Singular)

As for plans, I too am unsettled, but Mrs. Bud is clamoring so for a personal hearing that I think she'd better come up next month. I shall take an apartment somewhere — Pearl is going to join me when she arrives — and no doubt by the time you get here we'll all be out in the street, so that you can rescue us.

Let me know when you get here. Aud. 4312. Apt 4F. But don't expect me to go anywhere except calling. I've barely carfare till the first check.

Hopefully
Rudolph

man who kills a white man in North Carolina and flees to Harlem. Gillis envisions Harlem as a place of justice and wealth for Negroes. One of Fisher's naive rural southern migrants who is perfect prey for a city racketeer, Gillis finds corruption instead of justice as he is duped by a fellow black southerner, Mouse Uggams, into becoming involved in a dope-peddling operation. If it is not a perfect haven, "the city of refuge" still can offer Gillis moments of reprieve, if not joy. "The City of Refuge" was reprinted in Edward J. O'Brien's *Best Short Stories of 1925.*

Fisher's five-part story "South Lingers On" was published in March in *Survey Graphic* and reprinted in *The New Negro* as "Vestiges, Harlem Sketches." Actually five individual tales on a single theme, "South Lingers On" is a continuation of Fisher's examination of the influence of southern folkways on new arrivals to the Harlem scene. The first sketch, which Locke subtitled "Shepherd, Lead Us" when he included it in *The New Negro,* makes use of an old faithful black preacher who became one of Fisher's most popular character types. The Reverend Ezekiel Taylor is set against the hypocritical Harlem gambler turned preacher, the Reverend Shackleton Ealey, who preys upon the southern migrants as they attempt to hold on to their religious past.

Jake Crimshaw, former Virginia farmer lacking in city skills, is the major character in the second sketch. He does not find employment, despite the fact that he goes job hunting in his best Sunday overalls; and, although a city cynic has told him that to be successful, one must be dishonest, Jake remains caught up in his long-held dream of Harlem as heaven. The third piece in "South Lingers On" introduces the theme of conflict between generations. Of the two major characters, Grammie is a product of the South and the remnants of slavery who sees Harlem as a place of sin and corruption. She is the first in a line of "grandmother-as-guardian" characters Fisher created in his fiction. Her granddaughter Majutah, the other main character, has spent most of her life in Harlem and sees it as a place of pleasure. Majutah lies to her grandmother about going to the cabaret, which the older woman views as an iniquitous meeting place. Majutah's cabaret, however, is a place for music and dancing, not for vice, and Fisher's exposition of the women's differing perspectives forms the focus of the piece.

The fourth sketch, which Locke subtitled "Learnin'," addresses the subject of higher education in an economically lower class Negro family.

Anna, a Harlem teenager with a college scholarship, and her mother have difficulty convincing her father of the merits of a college education. The final sketch, "Revival," has as its central character a minister's son, Lucky, who, like some of Fisher's other young characters, desires to renounce his religious and moral ties with his southern heritage. Lucky cannot, however, ignore his inward response of faith to a fire-and-brimstone sermon at a revival meeting in Harlem.

"Ringtail," published in the *Atlantic Monthly's* May 1925 issue, is Fisher's only short story in which a West Indian is the protagonist. It illustrates intraracial conflict between black Americans and British West Indians. Cyril Sebastian Best, a proud, revengeful Trinidad native who acts coldly superior to American Negroes, and his antagonist, Harlem resident Punch, vie for the love of a Bermuda woman, Hilda Vogel. Fisher uses the love story to examine divergent views of Marcus Garvey's Back-to-Africa Movement of the 1920s by having each of the characters voice a different opinion.

"High Yaller," so titled because of the commonly used phrase to describe fair-skinned Negroes, is also a story of intraracial prejudice. Evelyn Brown, the protagonist, rejected by most of her darker-skinned peers, including dark rival Mayme Jackson, is pressured into passing for white. Jay Martin, who has a dark complexion, sympathizes with Evelyn and tries to help her cope with the difficulties of being mulatto. Jay and Evelyn date and are often taken for a racially mixed couple. Evelyn disappears and Jay is detained for his involvement with a "white" woman. Interracial prejudice is a secondary theme in this story which won for Fisher first prize in the 1925 Amy Spingarn fiction contest in *Crisis* magazine. Fisher's publication record from 1927, the year he set up his medical practice, attests to the continued duality of his interests. He published four short stories, "The Promised Land" and "Blades of Steel" in the *Atlantic Monthly* and "The Backslider" and "Fire by Night" in *McClure's*; one essay in a literary journal, "The Caucasian Storms Harlem" in the *American Mercury,* and an article in a scientific journal, "The Resistance of Different Concentrations of a Bacteriophage to Ultraviolet Rays" in the *Journal of Infectious Diseases.*

In December (*McClure's* magazine) Fisher wrote facetiously of himself: "A distinguished literary journal made the error of accepting my first short story—just because I graduated from medical school. You can see what that did to my future. Now every time I begin to think my profession has claimed me for its own, some journal comes along and accepts another story. It's a hard life, really. The most uplifting thing I've ever written is a prescription for grippe. I've gone in for x-ray now— seeking greater penetration."

"The Promised Land," much like its precursor "City of Refuge," focuses on the corruptive nature of life in Harlem. "Mammy" and her two adult grandsons, Sam and Wesley, closely knit cousins from rural Virginia, migrate to Harlem where economic opportunity and social circumstances taint their friendship. A mutual love interest, Ellie, an aloof, materialistic city girl, plays a key role in the tragic outcome to their relationship. The title ironically suggests the empty "promise" of Harlem as a refuge for blacks. As Mammy says, "All hit do is promise."

Fisher's stories are rife with realistic details of life in Harlem. "The Promised Land," for example, highlights a rent party, so popular in the 1920s, and in "The Backslider" the scene of conflict is a storefront church. His tales are filled with deceitful characters, including hypocritical preachers, bootleggers, and gamblers who con the ingenuous and turn innocents into thieves. His scientific background works its way into his stories as well. For example, in "Blades of Steel," a story about deceit, violence, and revenge, Fisher incorporates his knowledge of genetics and his conclusions about negative environmental influences into his delineation of the antagonist, Dirty Yaller Cozzens, a street character whose name connotes his evil nature.

In his nonfiction essay "The Caucasian Storms Harlem" (*American Mercury*, 1927), Fisher explores how the black Harlem of the 1920s had become a center for white entertainment and exploitation. Apart from any literary interest the essay may hold, this exposition of the era reflects the exuberance and exhibitionism of the time. Speaking of a quiet, elegant Chinese restaurant on 136th Street, first known as Hayne's Cafe and later as the Oriental, he narrates: "Here we gathered: Fritz Pollard, All-American half-back, selling Negro stock to prosperous Negro physicians; Henry Creamer and Turner Layton, who had written 'After You're Gone' and a dozen more songs, and were going to write 'Strut, Miss Lizzie'; Paul Robeson, All-American end, on the point of tackling law, quite unaware that the stage would intervene; Preacher Harry Bragg, Harvard Jimmie MacLendon and half a dozen others." There he and his friends met the actor Bert Williams, who dined there every

night and sometimes joined them in the singing of songs.

At the Edmonds', at Fifth Avenue and 130th Street, Fisher and his crowd heard the blues singer Ethel Waters (billed just as Ethel), who soon became a vaudeville star. They made the rounds at Connor's, the Garden of Joy, and other nightclubs. Fisher hypothesizes at one point that the new "color" of Harlem's cabarets might be "a reaction to the Negro invasion of Broadway." He could not understand whites' negative evaluations of such black Broadway shows as *Put and Take* (1921), *Liza* (1922), *Strut Miss Lizzie* (1922), and *Runnin' Wild* (1923); but he was pleased that the Florence Mills Broadway revues were successful. He admired her magnetic personality, her ability to triumph over obstacles, her modest attitude, and her concern for the race. In the essay, he goes on to observe that some black performers had attained greater recognition and acceptance in England than at home and that they were all models of respectability off stage. This respectability, he believed, was in part responsible for their success.

Fisher's first novel, *The Walls of Jericho*, published in 1928, was well received. It was compared with two other depictions of Harlem life, *Home to Harlem* (1928) by the Jamaica-born Harlem Renaissance author Claude McKay and *Nigger Heaven* (1926) by Carl Van Vechten. Both books had been offensive to many black critics because of their emphasis on exoticism, sex, and the low life of the black community. Fisher's novel was the "clean" Harlem novel that many felt needed to be written. The book was also applauded for its realism, its skillful construction, its good-natured humor, its light satire and irony, and its witty language (though not as witty as the author's own conversation, according to Langston Hughes). Fisher's insider's view of Harlem and of the race, his detached, sophisticated treatment of his subject, and his inclusion of a glossary of Harlemese for those who did not understand it opened up the black life of New York to the uninitiated. The book was praised by many of Fisher's peers, including Eric Walrond, with whom Fisher would be caricatured in *Infants of the Spring* (1932). Alice Dunbar Nelson recommended Fisher's work as "a pleasant antidote for a lot of psychopathic slime masquerading under the name of novels." The *New York Times* reviewer commended Fisher for "an undoubted literary knack." Critical reaction to his overall character delineation was divided. One black reviewer objected to a truck driver as hero, while many critics lauded his skill in portraying the stage-type, Harlemese-speaking Bubber Brown and Jinx Jenkins. The *Crisis* reviewer, however, asked why Rudolph Fisher had not ventured "to write of himself and his own people; of Negroes like his mother, his sister, his wife," the respectable Negro middle class.

Fisher wrote *The Walls of Jericho* on a bet. One of his friends had challenged him to try his hand at blending all of Harlem society into a single story. Representing the black working class are Joshua "Shine" Jones, Jinx Jenkins, Bubber Brown, and Linda Young, a K.M. ("Kitchen Mechanic" or maid), whose desire for upward mobility bridges the gap between the "rats" (lower class) and the "dickties" (middle and upper class, usually lighter skinned and educated); Fred Merrit, a mulatto lawyer who could almost pass for white, is the prime example of the dicktie category.

Fisher uses his plot to show two kinds of gathering places and social activity within the urban black community. One is the bar/pool hall setting, Patmore's Pool Parlor, in which Shine and his buddies "hang out." Conversations in Patmore's provide background about the animosity between Patmore and Fred Merrit, who has prosecuted Patmore for running down a pedestrian and insisted upon his paying a ten-thousand-dollar fine if he were not confined to prison. It is also here that Jinx and Bubber serve the dramatic function, through another conversation, of informing the audience of how Shine, a "hard" man, has been all but ruined by falling in love with Linda.

Fisher's other gathering site is a local dance, at which dickties and rats rub elbows without one being overly antagonistic toward the other. Still, there are distinctions to be made; the rats occupy the lower floor of the dance hall, sitting at tables there rather than in the theaterlike box seats on the second level from which the dickties and their white guests get their fill of Harlem nightlife. Those in the boxes come down to dance, then retire to their vantage points.

Fisher uses the perspective of the box seat to give a slice of Harlem Renaissance politics and racial interactions. He gives us a glimpse of Agatha Cramp, the misguided white liberal, in her stereotypical and uninformed reaction to the crowd; she is even more convinced that they need uplifting than she was when she broached the subject with Linda, her maid. By allowing Miss Cramp to believe that Fred Merrit is white, Fisher devises the perfect scheme to undercut her liberalism.

The disparate groups further come together in revealing ways when Fred Merrit buys a house in Miss Cramp's neighborhood, and when Shine, Jinx, and Bubber move his furniture in. Miss Cramp becomes alarmed at the thought of living next door to a black man, who woos Linda away by offering her more money. Shine is convinced that Merrit has designs on Linda and goes to confront him, only to discover that Merrit's house has been burned down and that he sits moaning the loss of the only picture he had of his mother. Shine, thought to be "hard," becomes sympathetic toward Merrit, a feeling that increases when it is revealed that Patmore was the one who burned Merrit's house. Shine and the other working-class blacks play a central role in bringing about the punishment of Patmore; through seeing Merrit's suffering, they reach new understandings of humanity that are not based on complexion and social status.

After the publication of *The Walls of Jericho* Fisher became superintendent of the International Hospital on Seventh Avenue, a position he held from 1929 to 1932. Concomitantly he worked as a roentgenologist for the New York City Health Department from 1930 to 1934, and he was a first lieutenant in the medical division of the 369th Infantry from 1931 to 1934. A Harlem community leader, he served on the literature committee of the 135th Street YMCA and as lecturer at the 135th Street Branch of the New York Public Library, a major black cultural center during the Harlem Renaissance.

In addition to his literary, medical, civil, and military activities, Fisher continued writing short stories and worked on a novel manuscript that was published in 1932. *The Conjure-Man Dies: A Mystery Tale of Dark Harlem* is recognized as the first black detective novel. Jinx Jenkins and Bubber Brown from *The Walls of Jericho* reappear in this tale of murder and intrigue in Harlem. When Jinx seeks advice from a conjure man, his adviser is murdered during the interview. Jinx is interrogated along with the other people who have been waiting to see the conjure man. The question of murder almost becomes moot when the body disappears and the man believed to be dead is suddenly alive and well. The tangled web of events into which Jinx and Bubber have stumbled leaves Jinx framed for the crime and Bubber trying to use his newly discovered detective skills to free him. The case would perhaps be lost from the beginning if it were not for two other significant characters. John Archer, the doctor who has been called to examine the man believed to be the conjure man, turns out to be better at detective work than the police themselves. His helper, a humanistically oriented detective

Langston Hughes, Charles S. Johnson, E. Franklin Frazier, Rudolph Fisher, and Herbert Delaney (courtesy of the Schomburg Center for Research in Black Culture, the New York Public Library, Astor, Lenox and Tilden Foundations)

named Perry Dart, exists as much to assist in solving the crime as he does to give Archer a chance to show how talented he is. The circumstances surrounding the conjure man's death are complicated indeed; yet through these men and their work, Fisher succeeds in unraveling the intriguing puzzle and maintaining audience interest in its solution.

Archer and Dart, Fisher maintained in an interview on a New York radio station "Meet the Author" program, were to stand in relationship of a bowman (archer) and his arrow (dart): "the vision of the former gives direction and aim to the action of the latter." In fact, John Archer, who knows more about detective work than any physician on record, is clearly a persona for Fisher. By making his fictional doctor not only far advanced in the knowledge of his own profession but surprising enough in solving mysteries to earn the respect of a veteran detective, Fisher is able to combine the literary and medical worlds to which he was equally strongly attracted. Further, as a foil for Dart, whom Fisher also clearly respects, Archer enables the au-

thor to engage in lengthy philosophical and scientific discussions under the guise of solving a murder. There is pleasure in observing two obviously talented men working through their various theories concerning the murder; Fisher also injects humor.

Love of conversation and preference for philosophical musings are also apparent in the conversations Dr. Archer has with N'Gana Frimbo, the resurrected conjure man. Frimbo shares with Archer a venturing out from his profession, for this man who wears the guise of a charlatan is well versed in European philosophy, African mysticism, medical science, psychology, and various other disciplines.

The novel begins with the death of the conjure man. Then, through a series of flashbacks, Fisher reveals what has led up to his death. As the past is unraveled Fisher slowly reveals who the characters are, what their relationships to each other are, and the nature of the problems plaguing each that might have warranted an attack on

Frimbo. The return to the present and the effort to discover the missing body serve to heighten the novel's intrigue, as well as to provide an exploration of the mazelike house whose very architecture has figured in the murder. In Bubber's efforts to free Jinx, Fisher also provides opportunities to view Harlem street and club life, including a few scenes in Patmore's Pool Parlor, the same establishment that appears in *The Walls of Jericho*. In addition to adhering to the conventions of the detective novel, therefore, Fisher also provides enough local color to ensure the distinctively Afro-American flavor of his novel.

As critics have pointed out, the novel is important not only because it is well-written and engaging but because it is a rarity for its genre among Afro-American writers. Arthur P. Davis offered special praise for Fisher's choice of the conjure man character, N'Gana Frimbo, who is Harvard-educated; he envisioned Fisher's unique perspective as presaging a new direction for Afro-American literature. Black writers before Fisher had not attempted to make their mark in detective fiction.

Fisher had planned to continue his doctor and detective stories into a Dart-Archer series with at least two more novels, one of which he had already begun and tentatively titled "Thus Spake the Prophet." He considered the Harlem setting and its people mysterious to outsiders and therefore appropriate for the mystery genre. He pointed out that Negro characters, prior to his all-Negro novel, had played only minor roles in detective fiction by whites, and he claimed that he would be "very happy" to become known as "Harlem's interpreter."

After *The Conjure-Man Dies*, Fisher wrote two children's stories that treat some of the same themes that appear in his more mature fiction. Both stories are about twelve-year-old Ezekiel, who has migrated from Georgia to Harlem; they show a rural child's adjustment to an unfamiliar urban environment. "Ezekiel" was published in the *Junior Red Cross News* in March 1932 and "Ezekiel Learns" in the same journal in February 1933. Fisher was working on another story in the Ezekiel series just prior to his death.

In 1933 Fisher returned to the subject of grandmother-as-guardian in two tales, "Guardian of the Law" and "Miss Cynthie." Both Harlem stories feature wise, witty, protective grandmothers. Using justifiable trickery, Grammie of "Guardian of the Law" acts in the best interest of her rookie policeman grandson Sam. With the grandmother at the center of the story, Fisher devised a humor-

ous tale of foul play in Harlem. "Miss Cynthie," the best of Fisher's grandmother stories and his final one, focuses on a spry, seventy-year-old lady who comes from the Deep South to New York to be with her grandson. The epitome of the black matriarch, she headed her family during slavery, kept the generations intact afterwards, and, after coming north, "unawed and still with her ancient dignity," watched over her children in the strange world of the city. For this story, Fisher won a place in Edward J. O'Brien's *Best Short Stories* for 1934.

In addition to his published work, four undated manuscript stories are housed at Brown University: "Across the Airshaft," "The Lost Love Blues," "The Man Who Passed" (also called "False Face" and an indecipherable title), and "The Lindy Hop." These stories, worthy of publication, add to Fisher's Harlem panorama. "Across the Airshaft" depicts the practice of the highjacking of rent col-

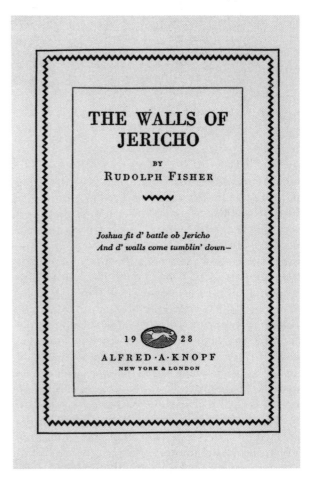

Title page for Fisher's first novel, which includes an "Introduction to Contemporary Harlemese" for uninitiated white readers

lectors in Harlem. It also touches upon prostitution. A moral young black woman, Betty Green, rejects the advances of a white man. She is befriended by the protagonist, Ripley Halliday, and the story ends happily with overtones of romance between the two. "Lost Love Blues" is a continuation of Fisher's exploration of the theme of the southerner coping with the "promise" of Harlem. The central characters are a hopeful young couple, Cinnamon and Jed, who are beset by urban employment problems, bootleggers, city slickers, and conjurers. Despite these negative forces, deep love wins at the end. "The Man Who Passed" treats the problem of prejudice with a unique twist; a white reporter, Perryn Joel, attempts to pass for black in Harlem in order to get an inside story of life there. Dope peddling, gambling, race riots, and white stereotyping of Negroes are daily realities of Harlem that Fisher features in this piece. In "The Lindy Hop" Fisher repeated his theme of the conflict of generations, with a grandmother and granddaughter very similar to the pair in his 1925 "Majutah" sketch. Tillie and her protective Grammie disagree on the younger woman's decision to be a dance-hall hostess. Through trickery the determined grandmother triumphs.

When Fisher became ill, about six months before his death in December 1934, he was working on a dramatization of *The Conjure-Man Dies*. It is a three-act play following basically the same plot as the novel. On 11 March 1936 it opened at the Lafayette Theatre in Harlem as a production of the Negro Unit of the Federal Theatre Project. A popular play, *Conjur' Man Dies* was seen by 83,000 people in Harlem until its closing on 4 July 1936. It was also produced by the WPA traveling outdoor players in some of the New York parks. Later it was produced by the Karamu Players of Cleveland, Ohio, as part of that city's WPA Federal Theatre Project.

The drama critics' reviews of the Lafayette Theatre production were mixed. The reviewer for the *New York Amsterdam News* recommended the play for its entertainment value but said that some cutting of street scenes and dialogue would have made for a better performance. Whites, he said, missed much of the humor of the Afro-American idiom. That certainly seemed to have been the experience of Brooks Atkinson, who called the play "Harlem mumbo-jumbo." The humor was better understood by Burns Mantle of the *Daily News*, who saw it as "salable entertainment." Doris Abramson, who wrote about *Conjur' Man Dies* in the 1960s, concluded that Rudolph Fisher could not be held

accountable for its flaws: "With more experience in the theatre, this brilliant young man who wrote such dramatic stories might have written a good play, but he died before he had a chance to do so." According to Pearl Fisher, her brother wrote two other plays during the days of his failing health, both unpublished and never produced, "The Vici Kid" and "Golden Slippers."

The January 1935 issue of the *Metropolitan*—the only issue ever published—containing Rudolph Fisher's novelette "John Archer's Nose" was on sale at newsstands at the time that newspaper accounts of his death were published. A sequel to *The Conjure-Man Dies*, again set in Harlem, the story features detective Perry Dart, unofficially assisted by the meticulous and erudite Dr. John Archer. The theme, again, is superstition, although Mother Dewey replaces Fisher's earlier conjure man. The woman's rudimentary conjuring leads to a murder in her household, which consists of the mother, two sons, Sonny and Ben, a daughter named Petal, and Ben's wife, Letty. The exposition is carefully plotted following the established rules of detective fiction, but this shorter mystery lacks the suspense, the force, and the structural complexity of Fisher's earlier novel.

In spite of Fisher's pioneering work in detective fiction and his popularity during his lifetime, his works were all but forgotten until 1959, when Sterling A. Brown, then teaching at Howard University, urged one of his master's students to complete a two-part work on Fisher: a study of his prose fiction and the preparation of an edition of his stories. The prose study was completed in 1961; the other work is yet to appear. It will take the completion of such critical studies, several of which are in process, to heighten interest in Fisher's work. His significant contributions to the Harlem Renaissance certainly warrant more attention than they have received.

References:

Doris E. Abramson, *Negro Playwrights in the American Theatre, 1925-1959* (New York: Columbia University Press, 1969);

Sterling A. Brown, *The Negro in American Fiction* (Washington, D.C.: Associates in Negro Folk Education, 1937);

Hugh M. Gloster, *Negro Voices in American Fiction* (Chapel Hill: University of North Carolina Press, 1948);

Eleanor C. Queen, "A Study of Rudolph Fisher's Prose Fiction," M.A. thesis, Howard University, 1961.

Papers:
Four unpublished stories and a modified version of a published story are in the Brown University Archives, Providence, Rhode Island. Letters writ-ten to Carl Van Vechten are at Yale University's Beinecke Rare Book and Manuscript Library, New Haven, Connecticut.

George Wylie Henderson
(14 June 1904-   )

Emmanuel S. Nelson
University of Tennessee

BOOKS: *Ollie Miss* (New York: Stokes, 1935; London: Secker, 1935);
Jule (New York: Creative Age, 1946; London: Allen, 1946).

PERIODICAL PUBLICATION: "Harlem Calling," *Redbook* (April 1934).

George Wylie Henderson commands an important position in the history of Black American writing because his novels provide a vital literary link between the writers of the Harlem school and those in the school of Richard Wright. His first novel, *Ollie Miss* (1935), relies upon a distinctly black tradition as the basis for his art; it also reflects his commitment to the concept of cultural dualism so strongly advocated by the proponents of the Harlem school. A work remarkable for its aesthetic and technical properties, *Ollie Miss* expresses a sensibility clearly shaped by the Harlem Renaissance of the 1920s. A skillful interpretation of rural life in the Deep South during the first quarter of the twentieth century, it unfolds a turbulent human drama in the midst of pastoral serenity. Henderson's second novel, *Jule* (1946), marks a philosophical shift toward racial protest, and it is, therefore, clearly akin to the novels of Richard Wright and those influenced by him. In *Jule* Henderson draws from his racial and cultural heritage for artistic raw material, and he also relies on his newly intensified social consciousness to create a microcosm of the great migration of rural southern blacks to the elusive promised land of the industrial North. *Jule* alludes to the shaping of the American urban nightmare, which to many articulate, postwar,

black writers became a basis for angry social dissent. Although the novels of Henderson have not received the critical attention they deserve, they are important for the link they provide in the continuum of modern Afro-American literature.

Grandson of a farmer and son of a Protestant minister, Henderson was born in Warrior's Stand, Alabama. He spent his childhood in this tiny hamlet in the Deep South. As a teenager he attended Tuskegee Institute, where he learned printing. Armed with that technical skill, he went to New York in search of a better life during the uncertain years of the Depression. After several months of unemployment and disillusionment, he became an apprentice in the printing offices of the *New York Daily News*. While still an apprentice, he published many short stories in the *Daily News* and *Redbook*.

The now nearly forgotten *Ollie Miss* is clearly Henderson's finest achievement; much of its power grows out of the author's characterization. The straightforward novel is the record of a crucial phase in the life of its heroine. Eighteen-year-old Ollie arrives out of nowhere at Uncle Alex's farm in a small southern town. She asks for a job, and Uncle Alex hires her as a farmhand. Her antecedents remain a mystery throughout the novel, thus underscoring her alienated condition in life. The opening chapter provides a glimpse of Ollie's uneventful life on the farm, and the reader learns of her decision to visit Jule in spite of her guardian's disapproval of him. A lengthy flashback then familiarizes the reader with the protagonist, an apparently simple, illiterate, rural woman who is physically strong, has an enormous appetite, and works very hard. Left to fend for herself, she has become self-reliant and demonstrates an unarticulated streak of feminism. Working alongside the men on the farm, she refuses any chivalrous special treatment. Dignified, strong-willed, and assertive, she confronts life, makes clear choices, and faces the consequences. When others on the farm fabricate tales about her past life and make insinuations about her conduct, Ollie feels no obligation to explain herself to anyone. Despite the appalling condition of her life, she does not seek the abstruse consolations of Christianity or passively resign herself to a capricious fate. She ably handles the staggering odds of being black and female in the southern rural folk culture. With dignity and grace, she transcends life's frustrations and anguish. She survives.

After the flashback the action returns to the novel's present time. Ollie walks several miles to reach Jule's cabin, but finds it empty. She learns that he has gone to a camp meeting in a nearby hamlet; she finds him and spends a night with him, but Jule leaves her in the morning, rejecting her love and any prospects of sharing his life with her. Confused, Ollie persistently follows him to the campground and discovers he has taken a new lover. In a confrontation with the other woman Ollie is badly slashed with a knife. Bedridden, she discovers that she is carrying Jule's baby. The new life within her strengthens her will; she rejects the now contrite Jule who has offered to stay with her. She decides to shape the course of her life independently.

Despite the narrow canvas of the novel's simple plot, Henderson creates a work of pastoral elegance. The realism of the rural setting is achieved through a sustained use of nature imagery and through the author's authentic, confident use of black dialect. He captures the rhythms and nuances of black speech with remarkable precision. Consider Nan's explosive explanation for why Ollie Miss is not "fit" to stay at Alex's house: "dat hussy was up to Lucy West's house Saddy night. Up dere dancin' and friskin' herself right in front o' dat low class o' niggers from Hannon yonder. Prancin' an' twistin' herself wid dem mens lookin' right smack at her! . . . And den dey gits to fightin' and carryin' on—wanting to cut one 'nuther throats ovah dat gal. I could see'm. I was settin' right dere on my porch, watching." His characters emerge as rec-

ognizable folk, not as unimaginative caricatures. Drawing upon his experience of rural black life, he captures the essence of human experience without having to resort to sociological explanations, philosophical justifications, or extraliterary concerns. He is interested primarily in interpreting black culture, not in demanding racial equality and social justice. Like Harlem Renaissance writers Jean Toomer, Langston Hughes, and Countee Cullen, Henderson blends his artistic vision with cultural consciousness and carefully eliminates social protest. In fact Henderson avoids racial conflict and social tension by keeping white characters largely out of the fictional world of *Ollie Miss*. The only white character, who makes a very brief appearance in the novel, does not speak.

Critical reaction to *Ollie Miss* was positive. Even those reviewers who were generally unsympathetic to Henderson were impressed by his eye for detail, his ability to interpret folk life, and his skill at characterization. The novel was soon forgotten, however. Critical histories of black fiction discuss it only cursorily or in the context of discussion of other works.

Jule, published in 1946, is a sequel to *Ollie Miss*. Autobiographical in nature, it lacks the intensity and power of Henderson's first novel, but it has a more complicated plot and makes a bold social statement. The story is about growing up black and male in America during the first half of the twentieth century. It is a record of the protagonist's movement from innocence to experience, and the theme of initiation is central to the novel. The protagonist is the illegitimate son of Ollie and the elder Jule. Set in Hannon, Alabama, the first few chapters relate Jule's childhood, his friendship with Rollo, a white boy, and Jule's love for Bertha Mae, a lovely sixteen-year-old black girl. It is his love for Bertha that leads to violence and the novel's first racial conflict. Boykin Keye, an illiterate and brutal white man in sexual pursuit of Bertha, finds her with Jule and attacks his young competitor. Jule easily overpowers his middle-aged assailant and leaves him hurt and helpless, but his innocence and sense of order and security have been shattered. Fearing reprisal from whites, Jule hurriedly bids goodbye to his mother and runs away to New York. Hungry and penniless, he roams the streets, progressively losing more and more of his innocence as he is initiated into the mysteries of liquor and sex. He is transformed from an adolescent into a young adult. Henderson captures the terror, anguish, and alienation of his lost, young, rural protagonist in the teeming me-

Pages from a letter that Henderson wrote to Jesse E. Moorland after the publication of W. E. B. Du Bois's The Souls of Black Folk *(courtesy of the Jesse E. Moorland Collection, Moorland-Spingarn Research Center, Howard University)*

no doors closed to us in the mansion of life, any more than to other races.

Whether we have the ability to enter all of them or not, cannot be known until we have had the opportunity to try.

But now I have a matter of business to lay before you. Have you heard of the proposed Congress of Colored Congregational churches and schools? I inclose circulars which are self-explanatory. We have set the date at Sept. 19–23. The prospect is that Atlanta will be the place.

Proctor and Sims of Memphis were both speakers at our Commencement, when we sketched our program. We have put you down to conduct a Sunny Riples meeting, with Rev. C. S. Haynes. This will be at 7 P.M. Sunday the 20th. You will have a pretty broad field. Unlike last year's Congress, this will not interfere with your vacation.

We expect a great meeting. The churches and schools are responding heartily.

We have Scanton down for an address.

Write me soon as I wish to print the program.

We shall not go north this summer. I am too busy in this Convention affair.

tropolis. Soon Jule finds a job, works hard, makes new friends, meets girls, and even hobnobs with black professionals, but he experiences racial conflicts along the way: a southern white woman delights in calling him "nigger"; Old Douglass refuses to admit Jule into the printers' union purely on racial grounds. Jule discovers the North is as racist as the South that he so desperately fled. But Jule is Ollie's son: he knows how to survive. With the help of Bob, a decent and cultured young white friend, Jule breaks the color barrier and becomes a full-fledged member of the printers' union. The novel concludes with his temporary return to the South to attend his mother's funeral and to make plans to marry his old flame, Bertha Mae, and he then returns to New York.

In *Jule* Henderson effectively handles social and racial protest, concerns so conspicuously absent in his first work. Protest, however, is held rigidly under control, and there are no emotional explosions. The white characters are somewhat naively and simplistically divided into "good" whites and "bad" whites. Boykin Keye's inhumanity is "balanced" by Rollo's recognition of the unconditional equality of all human beings. If Old Douglass is arrogantly racist, another white character—Bob—is firmly committed to racial justice. It is precisely this lack of realistic complexity in the characters that makes *Jule* a disappointing novel. The skill with which Henderson delineated the character of Ollie Mae is largely absent in *Jule*. The ineffectiveness stems primarily from the author's indifference to the psychology of his characters, his failure to deal with their complex internal states.

Jule was generally received negatively by reviewers, many of whom were disappointed that Henderson, so promising in *Ollie Miss,* had failed to prove his potential in his second novel. Hubert Creekmore, writing in the *New York Times Book Review,* commented that Henderson had "used a kind of writing that may be best called primer style. Almost every sentence is simple, declarative, and short. The dialogue is similar and has much the same rhythm and cadence no matter who speaks, white or Negro. It may have been his intention to project some of the naivete of Jule in his prose, but the results are often monotony, exasperation and unnecessary explanation." In a contemporary review of the work, J. Lee Greene, writing in *The History of Southern Literature* (1985), shares the evaluation of Henderson's lessening of artistic control

in *Jule*. He calls the plot "forced and hackneyed" and asserts that Henderson, in using the "well-worn formula of the Southern black migration novel," brings little to *Jule* "that is fresh, innovative, or aesthetically pleasing," comparing it to the much better *Ollie Miss* for his final assessment:

> The richness of character creation and setting that distinguishes *Ollie Miss* gives way in *Jule* to wooden and static character portrayal; the expert handling of familiar folk types and themes in *Ollie Miss* becomes a faulty portrayal of outworn stereotypes; the economy of style and vividness of imagery becomes trite prose, empty dialogue, and scattered purple passages. Artistically, *Jule* is certainly one of the glaring failures among novels about black life published during [the 1940s].

Possibly due to the commercial and critical failure of *Jule,* Henderson never wrote another novel.

A writer in a minor key, George Wylie Henderson, nevertheless, created in *Ollie Miss* an unforgettable and enduring portrait of black womanhood and, in *Jule,* helped set the stage for postwar black writers to launch their indictment of America. Henderson's vision in both of his novels is a vigorous affirmation of life. His works are a celebration of the dignity and humanity of the poor, the ordinary, and the forgotten, and it is his broad and uncompromising humanism—his recognition of the intrinsic value of every human life—that makes his vision, if not his art, powerful and enduring.

References:

Robert Bone, *The Negro Novel in America* (New Haven: Yale University Press, 1965);

Patricia Kane and Doris Wilkinson, "Survival Strategies: Black Women in *Ollie Miss* and *Cotton Comes to Harlem,*" *Critique,* 16, no. 1 (1974): 101-109;

Noel Schraufnagel, *From Apology to Protest: The Black American Novel* (De Land, Fla.: Everett/Edwards, 1973);

Darwin Turner, "The Negro Novelist and the South," *Southern Humanities Review,* 1 (1967): 21-29;

Waters Turpin, "Evaluating the Work of Contemporary Negro Novelists," *Negro History Bulletin,* 11 (December 1947): 59-60.

Leslie Pinckney Hill
(14 May 1880-15 February 1960)

Patsy B. Perry
North Carolina Central University

BOOKS: *The Wings of Oppression* (Boston: Stratford, 1921);
Toussaint L'Ouverture: A Dramatic History (Boston: Christopher, 1928).

OTHER: James Weldon Johnson, ed., *The Book of American Negro Poetry,* includes poetry by Hill (New York: Harcourt, Brace, 1922);
Robert T. Kerlin, *Negro Poets and Their Poems,* includes poetry by Hill (Washington, D.C.: Associated Publishers, 1923);
"So Quietly," "Tuskegee," "The Heart of a Woman," in *The Negro Caravan,* edited by Sterling A. Brown, Arthur P. Davis, and Ulysses Lee (New York: Dryden, 1941), pp. 338-339;
"What the Negro Wants and How to Get It: The Inward Power of the Masses," in *What the Negro Wants,* edited by Rayford W. Logan (Chapel Hill: University of North Carolina Press, 1944);
"The Teacher," "Tuskegee," in *The Poetry of the Negro,* edited by Langston Hughes and Arna Bontemps (Garden City: Doubleday, 1949), p. 46.

In the January 1939 issue of *Opportunity,* editor Elmer A. Carter praised poet, dramatist, essayist, and lecturer Leslie Pinckney Hill for having given twenty-five years of "brilliant educational leadership" to the Cheyney Training School for Teachers *and* for having given "to the Negro of his community and of his country the benefit of a cultured mind, a dauntless spirit, far vision and lofty and unchanging faith in his future in America." This early assessment was even more appropriate in 1951 when Hill retired from an active career in scholarship and educational administration. He loved America and labored unceasingly in encouraging his fellow Americans to live up to the highest principles of freedom and equal justice.

Leslie Pinckney Hill was born in Lynchburg, Virginia, on 14 May 1880 to Samuel H. and Sarah E. Brown Hill. According to the Campbell County

Leslie Pinckney Hill (courtesy of the Prints and Photographs Collection, Moorland-Spingarn Research Center, Howard University)

census of June 1880, Samuel Hill worked as a stationary engine operator and Sarah Hill was a laundress. In addition to Leslie Pinckney, the census lists three other Hill children: Susan, age nine; Samuel, age seven; and Ann, age five. Educated in a Lynchburg elementary school, he moved with his family to East Orange, New Jersey, where he attended high school. At Harvard University he worked as a waiter to supplement his scholarship while he earned an A.B. degree in 1903 and an A.M. degree in 1904. Hill, justifiably proud of his achievements at Harvard, "sought to inspire others by displaying on his vest his Phi Beta Kappa Key, America's highest symbol of distinguished scholarship." Accepting his first professional assignment at Tuskegee Institute, Hill taught English and education under Booker T. Washington from 1904 to 1907, the period during which the W. E. B. Du Bois-Washington controversy was at its height. In fact Hill was initiated into that historical debate concerning education and race relations which continued throughout his lifetime. From 1907 to 1913 Hill was principal of the Manassas Industrial Institute in Manassas, Virginia. This administrative position prepared him for his later work in education. In 1913 he became head of the small, private Institute for Colored Youth in Cheyney, Pennsylvania, a school which he guided toward full recognition and state support by 1920. During Hill's administration from 1913 to 1951, the institute became Cheyney Training School for Teachers (1914), State Normal School (1920), and Cheyney State Teachers College (1951).

Although Hill was a writer, he was quintessentially an educator, a role reflected in the foreword to each of his books. In his 1921 volume of poetry, *The Wings of Oppression*, he announced his hope that some poems would exhibit the "indestructible spiritual quality of my race." Similarly, he stated that his blank verse drama, *Toussaint L'Ouverture: A Dramatic History* (1928), together with other creative literature of Negro America, "must correct and counter-balance this falsehood" that the black race has made no substantial contributions. Whether offering "corrections" on behalf of black Americans or lyrics of universal appeal, Hill was always the schoolmaster whose lesson extended beyond the spiritual quality of his race to encompass all of humanity.

The Wings of Oppression is comprised of sixty-nine poems. The title poem is followed by five sections: Poems of my People, Poems of the Times, Poems of Appreciation, Songs, and Poems of the Spirit. Each section contains anywhere from four to twenty-four poems. Written in rhyming couplets, tercets, blank verse, and sonnet forms, these poems are clearly aligned with the genteel traditions of nineteenth-century English poetry. Hill makes excellent use of the central image of wings as instruments for ascending and for sustaining flight. On the "wings of oppression" the downtrodden and sorrowful may "mount beyond a world of care/On visions bright beyond compare/Of better things tomorrow." Specifically, Hill characterizes oppressed groups as those especially chosen by God to endure pain and suffering. Through

them, Hill maintains, God will eventually establish universal brotherhood.

Hill's philosophy contrasts with that of other writers who gained prominence during the Harlem Renaissance, that period characterized by protest, racial pride, and creativity. In Alain Locke's 1925 essay "Enter the New Negro," widely acclaimed as the definitive statement of creative and social goals of the period, three philosophical positions are presented as those with which the "thinking Negro" faced America. Locke labels as extreme attitudes Claude McKay's defiant, ironic challenge and James Weldon Johnson's filial appeal and counsel. Between defiance and appeal, however, Locke sees as representative of black America's prevailing mood the central challenge expressed in Johnson's "To America":

How would you have us, as we are?
Or sinking 'neath the load we bear,
Our eyes fixed forward on a star,
Or gazing empty at despair?

On this middle ground and, of course, on any position of defiance, it is clear that Hill is worlds away from most of his contemporaries in outlook. It is interesting to note, however, that Johnson included several of Hill's poems in *The Book of American Negro Poetry* (1922) just one year after Hill's *The Wings of Oppression* appeared, while not one of Hill's poems appeared in *The New Negro*, the 1925 interpretation of the Harlem Renaissance movement edited by Alain Locke. Hill enjoyed intellectual and social relationships not only with Johnson and Locke but with Jessie Redmon Fauset, W. E. B. Du Bois, Robert R. Moton, and other participants in the renaissance. These thinkers rejected his portrayal of the gentle, supine sufferer as a too easy moral solution of past ages.

Though he was at odds with many of his fellow writers, Hill explores three subjects he considers important: a "one-world conscience for all men," small victories achieved toward that goal, and blind discrimination. In "Jim Crow," "Cora," and "To a Caged Canary in a Negro Restaurant," Hill describes the denial of public accommodations to blacks. He also defines these practices in "Jim Crow" as the "relic of old sterile customs past." Using the image of the caged canary, who nonetheless sings a happy song, he compares its bondage to his own and prays, "So let my will, albeit hedged about/By creed and caste, feed on the light within." He continues, "So let my people bide their time and place,/A hindered but a sunny-hearted race."

Despite discrimination, then, Hill's black Americans have an attitude of calm acceptance. He explores this position further in "Self-Determination," in which he develops four points in what he calls "The Philosophy of the American Negro." This philosophy promises that "We will not hate.... We will not cease to laugh and multiply.... We will not use the ancient carnal tools.... We will not waver in our loyalty."

To sustain these noble promises Hill offers whatever hope he can, reasoning that even a small victory is better than nothing. As turbulent as the racial climate was in the South during and following World War I, for instance, Hill saw the black soldiers' valiant participation in that war as a step toward attaining the full rights of citizenship. In "The Black Man's Bit," he pictures black soldiers returning to an enlightened Southland "To be as men among their fellow-men." He predicts that their Dixie homeland "will be proud of them.... Will welcome them and show it." Though Hill's prediction of racial harmony was not borne out, his suggestion that black soldiers would return as proud, self-respecting men was accurate. In fact the patience and calm endurance which Hill advocates in several poems does not signal a complete lack of understanding or feeling on his part. He deplored the existence of Jim Crow in the armed services and the racist violence among civilians. After reading a *New York Times* news item on the lynching of a black man at Smithville, Georgia, on 21 December 1919, he wrote "So Quietly," an emotion-packed sonnet which promises that "Stern truth" will reveal America's corruptions. This poem, published in many anthologies, is clearly one of Hill's best.

In the poet's vision of a world free of corruption, the weak, humble, despised men are the bearers of truth, the counselors of peace, and the designers of a new social structure. Charged with searching spiritual depths, the oppressed are appointed to bring light into a dark world. Hill summarizes their position and their mission in these lines from his blank verse poem "Armageddon": "So viewing all my brothers in distress,/Hindered and cursed and aliens, I have wept/.../That they might know themselves a chosen folk,/.../New arbiters of social destiny,/New health veins in the body politic,/A high-commissioned people, mingled through/With all the bloods of man...."

Whether the view expressed in this poem has ever been held by large numbers of black Americans is questionable. However, readers would almost certainly agree with Hill's statement in *The*

Wings of Oppression stressing the significance of "that dark civilization which the colored man has built up in the midst of a white society organized against it." That black Americans advanced despite great opposition must be due, in large measure, to "a certain elevation of spirit" with which Hill credits them in his poetry. Hill's poems were widely published in anthologies and in such leading periodicals of the day as *Crisis, Life, Opportunity, Outlook, Phylon,* and the *Teacher-Education Journal.*

Characterized by James Weldon Johnson as "the most ambitious single poem attempted by any present-day Negro poet," *Toussaint L'Ouverture: A Dramatic History* (1928) is Hill's blank verse drama portrait of Toussaint L'Ouverture as a preeminent figure advocating peace, brotherhood, and freedom for all. Based on the life of the Haitian leader who had been a slave until he was forty-five, this five-part drama is divided into thirty-five scenes. Hill's specific goal in the piece is the presentation of "something more than a decade of Negro achievement under the leadership of Negro Genius." It is not surprising, therefore, that he places great emphasis on the traits which made Toussaint L'Ouverture a great leader. In the first scene of part one, a character identified simply as Old Man advises two revolutionary leaders to listen to Toussaint L'Ouverture who has "a prophet's head and God ... in his heart." This characterization of Toussaint L'Ouverture as an astute, God-fearing strategist informs all of his actions and remains central to subsequent descriptions of him. Toussaint L'Ouverture resolves "to be God's instrument" in making all men free. Having been "raised by God to know [his] calling," Toussaint L'Ouverture is successful in convincing other Haitian leaders that massacre of the usurping white populace is wrong. He emphatically states: "I mean we must not only let him live,/But overcome his evil with our good." It appears that Toussaint L'Ouverture, had he not been thwarted by deceptive French officers, might have established a peaceful state, the goal for which he fought and died. In his drama about Toussaint L'Ouverture, Hill enacted much of his own philosophy.

Hill's movement toward a world vision of one race under God in *Toussaint L'Ouverture* and in the earlier volume, *The Wings of Oppression*, was again the focus of his 1944 essay "What the Negro Wants and How to Get It," which appeared in *What the Negro Wants*, edited by Rayford W. Logan. Hill concludes his essay by affirming the American Negro's intense desire for "Full citizen status in our American democracy," an objective to be reached by the

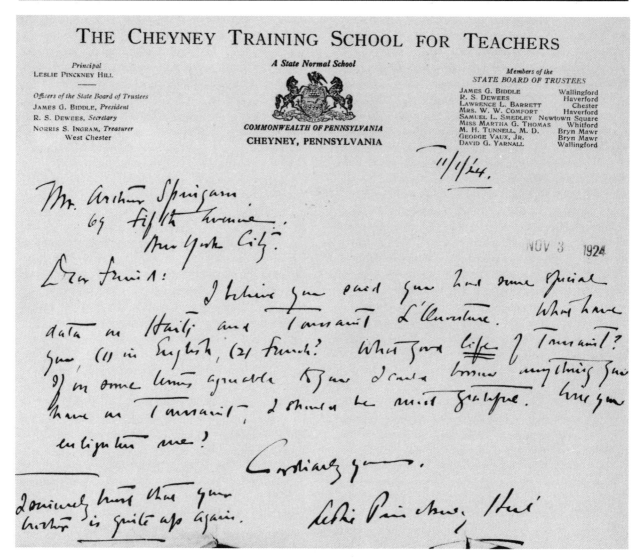

Letter requesting information about the liberator of Haiti, the subject of Hill's 1928 blank-verse drama (courtesy of the Arthur B. Spingarn Collection, Moorland-Spingarn Research Center, Howard University)

masses under "a leadership motivated by a world-encompassing philosophy which is rooted in the will of God. . . ." Classifying Hill as one of fourteen contributors who had "devoted many years of study to America's most difficult and intricate minority problem," Logan respected both Hill's concept of the "problem" and his blueprint for a possible solution.

Not all of Hill's works, however, are about race relations. He wrote numerous articles and lectured frequently on his experiences which grew out of his leadership of Cheyney State Teachers College. Some of his poems, as well, are pure lyric expressions having no racial overtones. One of Hill's best-known pieces is "The Teacher," in which

he summarizes three timeless tasks of instructors: imparting knowledge, urging industry, and encouraging love for all creatures of the earth. Written as a prayer for God's guidance, "The Teacher" is a universal plea. In fact, all the poems in *The Wings of Oppression*, except the title poem and thirteen additional ones grouped under Poems of my People, have broad applications. A reader has only to examine such titles as "Lines Written in the Alps Above Chamonix," "To William James," "To a Nobly-gifted Singer," and "Katerina Breshkovskaya" to be convinced of Hill's range and depth of ideas. Under the heading Poems of the Times, he issues "A Call to Poets," challenging them to "Rise up from dalliance with little things," and "To

All Leaders of Men," he advises traveling "through the ways where labor stalks/Portentous with its load." He pays homage to the French patriot in "Clemenceau," to the Irish martyr Lord Mayor MacSwiney in "Brixton Prison," and to the memory of William Penn in "The Founder." In short, Hill's poetic expressions are marked by solemnity, appeals for universal brotherhood, and emphases on what he himself outlined in "Values" as "things . . . of matchless worth:/Health and a task, the dreams of youth,/Beauty and law, and love, and truth."

Civic-minded as well as creative, Hill made contributions as a public figure which are nearly as outstanding as his work in poetry, scholarship, and administration. He translated his poet's vision and spiritual ideals into active programs, serving while in Virginia as president of the board of trustees of Manassas Industrial School and as secretary-treasurer of the Association of Negro Secondary and Industrial Schools. After establishing himself in Cheyney, Pennsylvania, he continued providing leadership in organizations for the benefit of his fellowman. He was founder and president of the West Chester Community Center and of the Pennsylvania State Negro Council; he was a member of the Interracial Committee of Philadelphia, the Peace Section of the American Friends Service Committee, the Committee of National Council of Student Christian Associations, and the N.E.A. Committee on the Defense of Democracy through Education; and he participated in many other civic committee and board activities. He was awarded honorary degrees by Lincoln University, Morgan State College, Haverford College, and the Rhode Island College of Education. Hill died on 15 February 1960 at Mercy-Douglass Hospital in Philadelphia, Pennsylvania.

References:

Benjamin Brawley, *The Negro Genius* (New York: Dodd, Mead, 1937);

Milton M. James, "Leslie Pinckney Hill," *Negro History Bulletin,* 24 (March 1961): 135-138;

Benjamin E. Mays, *The Negro's God* (New York: Atheneum, 1969).

Frank S. Horne
(18 August 1899-7 September 1974)

Sarah M. Washington
South Carolina State College

BOOK: *Haverstraw* (London: Breman, 1963).

OTHER: "On Seeing Two Brown Boys in a Catholic Church," "To a Persistent Phantom," and "Letters Found Near a Suicide," in *Caroling Dusk: An Anthology of Verse by Negro Poets,* edited by Countee Cullen (New York: Harper, 1927);
"On Seeing Two Brown Boys in a Catholic Church," "Kid Stuff," "Toast," and "Letters Found Near a Suicide," in *The Poetry of the Negro 1746-1949,* edited by Langston Hughes and Arna Bontemps (Garden City: Anchor/ Doubleday, 1949);
"Kid Stuff," "Notes Found Near a Suicide," "To a Persistent Phantom," and "Symphony," in *American Negro Poetry,* edited by Bontemps (New York: Hill & Wang, 1963).

PERIODICAL PUBLICATIONS: "Black Verse," *Opportunity,* 2 (November 1924): 330-332;
"Letters Found Near a Suicide," *Crisis,* 31 (November 1925): 12-13;
"I Am Initiated Into the Negro Race," *Opportunity,* 6 (May 1928): 136-137;
"Harlem," *Crisis,* 35 (June 1928): 196;
"The Man Who Wanted to be Red: A Story," *Crisis,* 35 (July 1928): 225-226, 242-243;
"The Epic of Fort Valley," *Crisis,* 36 (June 1929): 190, 206-207;
"More Letters Found Near a Suicide," *Crisis,* 36 (December 1929): 413;
"Henry A. Hunt: Sixteenth Spingarn Medallist," *Crisis,* 37 (August 1930): 261;
"Running Fools: Athletics in a Colored School," *Crisis,* 37 (November 1930): 375-376;
"Concerning White People," *Opportunity,* 11 (March 1934): 77;
"The Industrial School of the South," *Opportunity,* 13 (May 1935): 136-139; (June 1935): 178-181;
"Dog House Education," *Journal of Negro Education,* 5 (July 1936): 339;

Frank Horne

"Providing New Housing for Negroes," *Opportunity,* 18 (October 1940): 305-308;
" 'Balm in Gilead': A Christmas Jingle," *Crisis,* 72 (December 1965): 646-647;
" 'Mamma!,' " *Crisis,* 73 (April 1966): 213;
"He Won't Stay Put: A Carol for All Seasons," *Crisis,* 77 (December 1970): 403-404.

Frank S. Horne is an important minor voice of the Harlem Renaissance whose reputation rests primarily upon a group of award-winning poems he published in the *Crisis* in 1925. His success during this period links him to New Negro Renaissance poets, but his poems are generally more personal and traditional in concern than many of those of the other young writers of the 1920s. While several of these younger artists wrote of the New Negro, his atavistic connections to the deep South and to Africa, Horne focused on death, illness, and a crisis of faith shared by many white writers of the early twentieth century. A northerner who went against the pattern of migration by going to live in the South, Horne wrote poetry early in his life before becoming a physician and an administrator with the United States Housing Authority in Washington, D.C., and later in New York.

Horne was born in Brooklyn, New York, and grew up in that area. He attended undergraduate school at the City College of the City University of New York, where he received his bachelor's degree in 1921. He was an outstanding track star at City College, gaining experience that would serve him in good stead during his teaching career in the late 1920s. He earned a master's degree from the University of Southern California and a Doctor of Optometry degree from Northern Illinois College of Ophthalmology and Otology in 1923. While he was able to practice ophthalmology in Chicago and New York for a few years, his medical profession was cut short by what he called a "mean illness," which forced him to seek a warmer climate. Although information about Horne's life is skimpy, it may be assumed that the illness resulted in some loss of the use of his legs. Many of his later poems use images of failing to walk, of the legs being strapped into cumbersome contraptions, and of the pain associated with "reluctant" legs.

Though he developed an early interest in writing, Horne acknowledged that Charles S. Johnson, editor of *Opportunity,* and Gwendolyn Bennett, one of the younger poets, urged him to publish his work. His first prose was published while he was still a physician; "Black Verse," a review of *Anthology of Verse by American Negroes,* edited by Newman Ivey White and Walter Clinton Jackson, appeared in the November 1924 issue of *Opportunity.* Horne praised the editors for their effort to mark the achievements of Afro-American poets but criticized them for their stereotypical expectations of poetry purely of a racial bent. He singled out the inclusion of work by Countee Cullen for special praise and encouraged other young poets to sound distinct notes in their creativity.

Although Horne wanted to write good prose, he was more successful as a poet. He reached his height of success in 1925, when he received second prize in the poetry category in the Amy Spingarn Contest in Literature and Art sponsored by the *Crisis* magazine. He submitted his winning entry, "Letters Found Near a Suicide," under the pseudonym of Xavier I; the poems were published in the November 1925 issue of the journal. There were eleven letters in the prizewinning version of the poem; by 1930 Horne had added an additional seven poems to "Letters," all of which would be published as the first section of *Haverstraw,* his collection brought out by Breman in 1963.

"Letters Found Near a Suicide" is characteristic of the variety of somber issues Horne treats; he describes the setting of a man's preparation for death, during which the persona directs several short poems to individuals who have had significant roles in his life. "To All of You," the first letter in the series, sets the stage for the poetic flirting with suicide; the persona is curious about "the bosom of this deep, dark pool/Of oblivion" and is destined to explore "those far shores/That knew me not." "To Mother," the third letter in the series, bemoans the fact that living is a painful existence beyond man's control. The speaker wonders how anybody can care, particularly his mother, whom he has caused much agony, but he knows the power of a black mother's love. If he dies she will grieve and want him back, because to her suicide is not the answer.

In "To Chick," the tenth and longest letter in the series, the speaker recalls his childhood friend and their football-playing days. Together they had been awesome, charging across lines to score, universally recognized as "The Terrible Two." To offset the possibility that Chick might view his suicide as less than sporting, less than manly, the speaker couches his death in the familiar terms of the football skirmish. He has essentially "scored" in killing himself, moved on to another level of victory that Chick can at least envision vicariously. He urges Chick to remember that they had been great warriors, thereby suggesting that he view this final act from the positive perspective of fighting and winning.

When you gaze at me here
Let that same light
Of faith and admiration
Shine in your eyes
For I have battered the stark stonewall
....
I have kept faith with you
And now
I have called my signal,

Found my opening
And slipped through
Fighting and squirming
Over the line
To victory . . .

"To Chick" is perhaps the most celebratory of the poems, for others, such as "To Jean," "To Catalina," "To Mariette," and "To Wanda," show the speaker's disappointment in love and his inability to understand his place in the world.

In 1927 illness forced Horne to move from New York to Georgia, where he began a teaching and administrative career at Fort Valley High and Industrial School (later Fort Valley State College). Although he was light enough to pass for white, he did not choose to do so. His coming south, therefore, gave him a perspective comparable to that of Charles Chesnutt. He was especially sensitive to the changes in accommodation and treatment as he

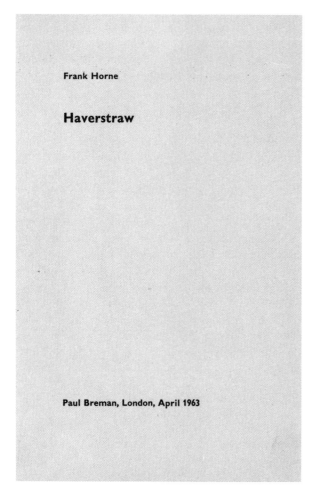

Frank Horne

Haverstraw

Paul Breman, London, April 1963

Title page for Horne's only published poetry collection, the second half of which he called "Lyrics for the halt"

journeyed into the South. In "I Am Initiated Into the Negro Race," published in *Opportunity* in 1928, he detailed the transition from privilege and comfort to the physical absence of these luxuries, connecting them to actual travel from points north to those in the South. His initial negative impressions, however, did not prevent him from doing useful work or from supporting the industrial school concept.

He continued his creative efforts in 1928 by publishing "Harlem," a poem, and "The Man Who Wanted to be Red," a short story, in the *Crisis* magazine. "Harlem" most approximates the work of other young writers of the period, especially Langston Hughes. Horne uses the background of a saxophonist's performance to conjure up images of what Harlem means. In its experimental stanzaic form and its attempt to imitate jazz rhythms, it is reminiscent of many of the folk-based poems Hughes wrote:

". . . Oh say it, brother
Say it . . ."
Pullman porters, shipping clerks an'
          monkey chasers
Actors, lawyers, Black Jews an' fairies
Ofays, pimps, low-downs an' dicties
Cabarets, gin an' number tickets
All mixed in
With gangs o' churches—
Sugar-foot misters an' sun-dodgin' sisters
Don't get up
Till other folks long in bed . . .
. . . Hey! . . . Hey!
"Say it, brother
Say it . . ."

"The Man Who Wanted to be Red" is called "a fairy tale for children of the earth." The story is an allegory of the slave trade and the animosity between blacks and whites in the United States. Horne depicts the "Reds," a predatory race who enslave the "Greens," bringing them to the Kingdom of Ur to work for them. Eventually, some of the Red men notice the beautiful Green women and have children by them. These children become the "Whites," a degraded outcast group. Juda, the protagonist of the story, is a "White." From experiments initially begun by his Red father, he perfects a technique for turning Greeners into Reds. He abandons his plan, however, when he witnesses a group of Reds abusing a Green; he does not want the people with whom he identifies through his mother to turn into such brutes. As a story for children, the piece is engaging through its emphasis upon unusual colors to show how absurd racial prejudices can be.

As trainer of the track team at Fort Valley High, Horne led his runners to several championships in the late 1920s and early 1930s. In "Running Fools: Athletics in a Colored School," published in the *Crisis* in 1930, he discussed the exploits of some of his famous stars (male and female) and introduced the larger world to life in an industrial school. He extended this introduction in "The Industrial School of the South," the two-part series published in *Opportunity* in 1935; he shared the philosophy of training espoused by Booker T. Washington at Tuskegee and was greatly inspired by his example.

Most of Horne's poems first published in the *Crisis* were almost immediately reprinted in anthologies. In 1927 Countee Cullen published "Letters Found Near a Suicide" in the critically acclaimed *Caroling Dusk.* He also included "On Seeing Two Brown Boys in a Catholic Church" and "To a Persistent Phantom" in that volume. "On Seeing Two Brown Boys in a Catholic Church" touches on the religious theme that Horne would return to in his poetry. For him, it is initially ironic to see the black boys in a traditionally "white" church, but when he contemplates the matter further, he concludes that their presence is appropriate, for the crucifix upon which they gaze epitomizes their lives. Their existence as black human beings will be equivalent to a cross of suffering associated with their blackness.

Others of his poems from this period are political as well as didactic. For instance, in "Nigger, A Chant for Children," Horne teaches history by listing names of eminent, famous black people such as Hannibal, Othello, and Crispus Attucks. He feels that the world should know these "Niggers," and black children should not be hurt by name calling but be proud of the great ones of the race.

The use of the word "nigger" in the title is a deliberate effort to transcend the negative connotations of that word. It is also a declamation against injustice. In this seven-stanza poem, Horne repeats "nigger" for dramatic emphasis and creates ironic contrasts through the juxtaposition of children's songs and the shouts of the bigot. In spite of persecution and prejudice, he was able to say to Afro-American children that blacks historically have had a great deal to be proud of, and no race-baiting epithets need cause them to lose sight of this fact.

In 1929 Horne published "More Letters Found Near a Suicide" in the *Crisis* magazine. The seven new poems included "To the Poets," "To

Frank Horne (courtesy of the Prints and Photographs Collection, Moorland-Spingarn Research Center, Howard University)

Henry," "To One Who Called Me 'Nigger,' " "To Caroline," "To Alfred," "To You," and "To James," which has perhaps become Horne's most widely read piece of "Letters Found Near a Suicide." In "To James," he shows that competition in racing is similar to competition in life. The speaker believes that one must give his best and live his fullest at every moment, and he envies those who are able to do that. The speaker himself feels, as Horne must have felt physically or emotionally, since he was unable to give his best in life due to the "mean illness" to which he often referred.

> Live
> as I have taught you
> to run, Boy—
> it's a short dash.
> Dig your starting holes
> deep and firm
> lurch out of them
> into the straightaway
> with all the power
> that is in you
> look straight ahead
> to the finish line

think only of the goal
run straight
run high
run hard
save nothing
and finish
with an ecstatic burst
that carries you
hurtling
through the tape
to victory . . .

The tone of the advice suggests a father speaking to his son, an imaginative role comparable to the one Horne played with his track students. The reference to victory also harks back to "To Chick" and suggests a pattern of living as well as a code for dying.

During the nine years he worked at Fort Valley High and Industrial School, Horne moved from teaching to serving as dean and acting president. He also occasionally completed prose pieces for journals. In 1930 he wrote the essay for *Crisis* in which Henry A. Hunt, the former principal of Fort Valley High and Industrial School, was recognized for receiving the Spingarn medal. In 1936 he moved out of education and into work with various housing agencies. By 1940 he was acting special assistant to the administrator of the U.S. Housing Authority, and he had turned his attention to writing about problems connected with public housing; his article "Providing New Housing for Negroes" appeared in the October 1940 issue of *Opportunity*. His life of public service eclipsed his poetry writing, and it was not until 1963, when the Englishman Paul Breman brought out a collection of his poems, that Horne's poetry became readily accessible to a larger audience.

Haverstraw, Horne's collected poetry, is a thin volume consisting of an expanded eighteen poems in "Letters Found Near a Suicide," which comprises the first section, and eight poems in the second section, entitled "Haverstraw." The suicide poems are listed with the notation "(1920-1930)," indicating that their composition extended beyond the original *Crisis* publication in 1925; a section from the last poem, "To James," had appeared as the epigraph for the "Running Fools" essay in 1930 as well as in the *Crisis* "More Letters Found Near a Suicide" in 1929. The "Haverstraw" poems are listed with the notation "(1960)," suggesting that Horne had perhaps had long intervals during which he had not written poems. Except for moving "To Mother" to the second position in the series

and "To . . ." from the eighth position to the sixth, the ordering of the original poems is the same.

In "To the Poets" Horne comments on the traditional view of the sentimental poet by describing him as singing "raptures to the grave." Perhaps the grave is the only place the poet's singing may be appreciated. In "To Henry," he suggests that only in the regions of forgetfulness will he find the answers to perplexing problems of being.

The complexities of Horne's own existence are summed up in the sixteenth letter in the collection, "To You." Addressing Christ, the persona recounts that he was always taught that by kneeling in church "And eating of your body/And drinking of your blood" he could be born again and saved. However, one night he "offered up/The sacrifice of body/Upon the altar/Of her breast." The speaker upon whom the world weighs heavily queries:

You
Who were conceived
Without ecstasy
Or pain
Can you understand
That I knelt last night
In your house
And ate of your body
And drank of your blood
. . . . and thought only of her?

Through the ambiguous symbol of the woman—a lover, or Mary, or even human nature itself, the poet articulates the problem of having his soul saved by one who was conceived without human feelings—ecstasy or pain. Horne's Catholic background obviously informs the poem.

The "Haverstraw" section of the volume is more personal in orientation, as the dedication reflects: "Lyrics for the halt/To Dr. Seymour Bluestone and his competent staff in token of their interest and compassion." The eight poems make recurring references to physical and spiritual illness, perhaps chronicling Horne's emotional journey through pain and suffering. In "Walk," he stresses the need to walk again in spite of falling: "I know that I will walk again/into your healing/outstretched arms/in answer/to your tender command. . . ./I have been lost/and fallen/in the dark underbrush/but I will arise and walk/and find the path/at your soft command." In "Mamma!" he imitates the role of the child in looking for some source beyond himself to reach out and assist "this faltering leg/and this unconscious arm."

In "Patience" he symbolically chides those who offer such counsel by describing his pent-up emotions and his desire to have immediate release. He asks if patience will enable him to do routine things such as climb up a stair or pick up a spoon. How can he be patient when he does "not have a hundred years/nor forty/nor ten"? He beseeches the god who measures time in a different way ("To whom a thousand years/are but the wink of a languid eye") to grant him a similar ability to deal with the time that weighs so heavily upon his hands.

Religious references are also the center of "Hubbard Tank," in which the ill body immersed in water is compared to "the baptismal fount/of John the Baptist," and "Communion," in which the poet questions whether death is the only way to be reunited with God, whom circumstances had taught him to live without.

The volume ends with "Symphony," in which the persona pictures the dancing sunlight shining into his sick room upon his "legs strapped in leather" as a variation of the rhythms of the universe.

> Are prancing light
> and faltering crutch
> variations of the dance
> of suns
> and moons
> and pain
> and glory
> point and counterpoint
> to the baton
> of the maestro
> to whom
> all rhythms
> and periods
> are the stuff
> of the symphony
> of life . . . ?

The volume is more subdued than joyful, more painful than celebratory. Yet it pictures a poet grappling with some of the central issues of life and being.

After the publication of *Haverstraw*, Horne published poems occasionally in the *Crisis*, including " 'Balm in Gilead': A Christmas Jingle" in 1965, the reprinting of " 'Mamma!' " from *Haverstraw* in 1966, and "He Won't Stay Put: A Carol for All Seasons" in 1970. In " 'Balm in Gilead' " he likens the treatment of blacks during the 1960s, especially the deaths of the five black girls bombed in the church in Birmingham, Alabama, and the assassination of Malcolm X, to the martyrdom of Christ. In "He Won't Stay Put" Horne illustrates his ability to change with the times, to use the speech patterns and stanzaic forms typical of the black arts movement; his subject, however, is still the question of the place of religion in the world. "I ain't got me/no piney tree/ain't got no sparkling balls to hang/no golden cord/ain't got no silver strands/to glint delight," he asserts in suggesting that Christmas decoration and Santa Claus are foreign ideas to him. Why look to special seasons for hanging things on trees, he then asks, for every day someone has been nailed on trees, beginning with Christ and extending to Martin Luther King, Malcolm X, Medgar Evers, and others. None of them have "stayed put," which may mean that religion is just as fanciful as Santa Claus or just as likely to fail.

Haverstraw and Horne's sporadically published poems are a testament to the fact that, in spite of the pressures of illness and public service, he cared enough about creativity to leave a little monument for posterity. When he died in 1974, he was far from being a famous poet, but those who had consistently anthologized his work over the years recognized that his poems were worthy of continued reading and discussion.

References:

Sterling Brown, *Negro Poetry and Drama* (Washington, D.C.: Associates in Negro Folk Education, 1937);

Ronald Primeau, "Frank Horne and the Second Echelon Poets of the Harlem Renaissance," in *The Harlem Renaissance Remembered*, edited by Arna Bontemps (New York: Dodd, Mead, 1972), pp. 247-267.

Langston Hughes

R. Baxter Miller
The Langston Hughes Society

See also the Hughes entries in *DLB 7: Twentieth-Century American Dramatists* and *DLB 48: American Poets, 1880-1945, Second Series.*

BIRTH: Joplin, Missouri, 1 February 1902, to James Nathaniel and Carrie Mercer Langston Hughes.

EDUCATION: Columbia University, 1921-1922; B.A., Lincoln University (Pennsylvania), 1929.

AWARDS AND HONORS: *Opportunity* magazine poetry prize, 1925; Amy Spingarn Contest (*Crisis* magazine) poetry and essay prizes, 1925; Harmon Gold Medal for *Not Without Laughter*, 1931; Rosenwald Fellowships, 1931, 1941; Guggenheim Fellowship, 1935; Litt.D., Lincoln University (Pennsylvania), 1943; National Institute and American Academy of Arts and Letters Award in Literature, 1946; Anisfield-Wolf Award, 1953; Spingarn Medal, 1960; Litt.D., Howard University, 1963; Litt.D., Western Reserve University, 1964.

DEATH: New York, New York, 22 May 1967.

BOOKS: *The Weary Blues* (New York: Knopf, 1926; London: Knopf, 1926);
Fine Clothes to the Jew (New York: Knopf, 1927; London: Knopf, 1927);
Not Without Laughter (New York & London: Knopf, 1930; London: Allen & Unwin, 1930);
Dear Lovely Death (Amenia, N.Y.: Privately printed at Troutbeck Press, 1931);
The Negro Mother and Other Dramatic Recitations (New York: Golden Stair Press, 1931);
The Dream Keeper and Other Poems (New York: Knopf, 1932);
Scottsboro Limited: Four Poems and a Play in Verse (New York: Golden Stair Press, 1932);
Popo and Fifina: Children of Haiti, by Hughes and Arna Bontemps (New York: Macmillan, 1932);
A Negro Looks at Soviet Central Asia (Moscow & Leningrad: Co-operative Publishing Society of Foreign Workers in the U.S.S.R., 1934);

Langston Hughes (Morgan and Marvin Smith photo; courtesy of the Schomburg Center for Research in Black Culture, the New York Public Library, Astor, Lenox and Tilden Foundations)

The Ways of White Folks (New York: Knopf, 1934; London: Allen & Unwin, 1934);
A New Song (New York: International Workers Order, 1938);
The Big Sea: An Autobiography (New York & London: Knopf, 1940; London: Hutchinson, 1940);
Shakespeare in Harlem (New York: Knopf, 1942);
Freedom's Plow (New York: Musette Publishers, 1943);
Jim Crow's Last Stand (Atlanta: Negro Publication Society of America, 1943);
Lament for Dark Peoples and Other Poems (N.p., 1944);

Fields of Wonder (New York: Knopf, 1947);

One-Way Ticket (New York: Knopf, 1949);

Troubled Island [opera], libretto by Hughes, music by William Grant Still (New York: Leeds Music, 1949);

Simple Speaks His Mind (New York: Simon & Schuster, 1950; London: Gollancz, 1951);

Montage of a Dream Deferred (New York: Holt, 1951);

Laughing to Keep from Crying (New York: Holt, 1952);

The First Book of Negroes (New York: Franklin Watts, 1952; London: Bailey & Swinfen, 1956);

Simple Takes a Wife (New York: Simon & Schuster, 1953; London: Gollancz, 1954);

The Glory Round His Head, libretto by Hughes, music by Jan Meyerowitz (New York: Broude Brothers, 1953);

Famous American Negroes (New York: Dodd, Mead, 1954);

The First Book of Rhythms (New York: Franklin Watts, 1954; London: Bailey & Swinfen, 1956);

The First Book of Jazz (New York: Franklin Watts, 1955; London: Bailey & Swinfen, 1957);

Famous Negro Music Makers (New York: Dodd, Mead, 1955);

The Sweet Flypaper of Life, text by Hughes and photographs by Roy DeCarava (New York: Simon & Schuster, 1955);

The First Book of the West Indies (New York: Franklin Watts, 1956; London: Bailey & Swinfen, 1956); republished as *The First Book of the Caribbean* (London: Edmund Ward, 1965);

I Wonder As I Wander: An Autobiographical Journey (New York & Toronto: Rinehart, 1956);

A Pictorial History of the Negro in America, by Hughes and Milton Meltzer (New York: Crown, 1956; revised, 1963; revised again, 1968); revised again as *A Pictorial History of Black Americans*, by Hughes, Meltzer, and C. Eric Lincoln (New York: Crown, 1973);

Simple Stakes a Claim (New York & Toronto: Rinehart, 1957; London: Gollancz, 1958);

The Langston Hughes Reader (New York: Braziller, 1958);

Famous Negro Heroes of America (New York: Dodd, Mead, 1958);

Tambourines to Glory (New York: John Day, 1958; London: Gollancz, 1959);

Selected Poems of Langston Hughes (New York: Knopf, 1959);

Simply Heavenly, book and lyrics by Hughes, music by David Martin (New York: Dramatists Play Service, 1959);

The First Book of Africa (New York: Franklin Watts, 1960; London: Mayflower, 1961; revised edition, New York: Franklin Watts, 1964);

The Best of Simple (New York: Hill & Wang, 1961);

Ask Your Mama: 12 Moods for Jazz (New York: Knopf, 1961);

The Ballad of the Brown King, libretto by Hughes, music by Margaret Bonds (New York: Sam Fox, 1961);

Fight for Freedom: The Story of the NAACP (New York: Norton, 1962);

Something in Common and Other Stories (New York: Hill & Wang, 1963);

Five Plays by Langston Hughes, edited by Webster Smalley (Bloomington: Indiana University Press, 1963);

Simple's Uncle Sam (New York: Hill & Wang, 1965);

The Panther & The Lash (New York: Knopf, 1967);

Black Magic: A Pictorial History of the Negro in American Entertainment, by Hughes and Meltzer (Englewood Cliffs, N.J.: Prentice-Hall, 1967);

Black Misery (New York: Knopf, 1969);

Good Morning Revolution: Uncollected Social Protest Writings by Langston Hughes, edited by Faith Berry (New York & Westport, Conn.: Lawrence Hill, 1973).

PLAY PRODUCTIONS: *Mulatto*, New York, Vanderbilt Theatre, 24 October 1935;

Little Ham, Cleveland, Karamu House, March 1936;

When the Jack Hollers, by Hughes and Arna Bontemps, Cleveland, Karamu House, April 1936;

Troubled Island, Cleveland, Karamu House, December 1936; opera version, libretto by Hughes, music by William Grant Still, New York, New York City Center, 31 March 1949;

Joy to My Soul, Cleveland, Karamu House, March 1937;

Soul Gone Home, Cleveland, Cleveland Federal Theatre, 1937;

Don't You Want to Be Free?, New York, Harlem Suitcase Theatre, 21 April 1938;

Front Porch, Cleveland, Karamu House, November 1938;

The Organizer, libretto by Hughes, music by James P. Johnson, New York, Harlem Suitcase Theatre, March 1939;

The Sun Do Move, Chicago, Good Shepherd Community House, Spring 1942;

Street Scene, by Elmer Rice, music by Kurt Weill, lyrics by Hughes, New York, Adelphi Theatre, 9 January 1947;

The Barrier, libretto by Hughes, music by Jan Meyerowitz, New York, Columbia University, January 1950; New York, Broadhurst Theatre, 2 November 1950;

Just Around the Corner, by Amy Mann and Bernard Drew, lyrics by Hughes, Ogunguit, Maine, Ogunguit Playhouse, Summer 1951;

Esther, libretto by Hughes, music by Jan Meyerowitz, Urbana, University of Illinois, March 1957;

Simply Heavenly, New York, Eighty-fifth Street Playhouse, 20 October 1957;

The Ballad of the Brown King, libretto by Hughes, music by Margaret Bonds, New York, Clark Auditorium, New York City YMCA, 11 December 1960;

Black Nativity, New York, Forty-first Street Theatre, 11 December 1961;

Gospel Glow, Brooklyn, New York, Washington Temple, October 1962;

Tambourines to Glory, New York, Little Theatre, 2 November 1963;

Let Us Remember Him, libretto by Hughes, music by David Amram, San Francisco, War Memorial Opera House, 15 November 1963;

Jerico-Jim Crow, New York, Village Presbyterian Church and Brotherhood Synagogue, 28 December 1964;

The Prodigal Son, New York, Greenwich Mews Theatre, 20 May 1965.

OTHER: Alain Locke, ed., *The New Negro,* includes nine poems by Hughes (New York: A. & C. Boni, 1925);

Four Negro Poets, includes twenty-one poems by Hughes (New York: Simon & Schuster, 1927);

Four Lincoln University Poets, includes six poems by Hughes (Lincoln University, Pa.: Lincoln University Herald, 1930);

Elmer Rice and Kurt Weill, *Street Scene,* lyrics by Hughes (New York: Chappell, 1948);

The Poetry of the Negro, 1746-1949, edited by Hughes and Arna Bontemps (Garden City: Doubleday, 1949);

Lincoln University Poets, edited by Hughes, Waring Cuney, and Bruce McM. Wright (New York: Fine Editions Press, 1954);

The Book of Negro Folklore, edited by Hughes and Bontemps (New York: Dodd, Mead, 1958);

An African Treasury: Articles/Essays/Stories/Poems by Black Americans, selected, with an introduc-

tion, by Hughes (New York: Crown, 1960; London: Gollancz, 1961);

Poems from Black Africa, edited by Hughes (Bloomington: Indiana University Press, 1963);

New Negro Poets: U.S.A., edited by Hughes (Bloomington: Indiana University Press, 1964);

The Book of Negro Humor, edited by Hughes (New York: Dodd, Mead, 1966);

The Best Short Stories by Negro Writers, edited, with an introduction, by Hughes (Boston & Toronto: Little, Brown, 1967).

TRANSLATIONS: Federico García Lorca, *San Gabriel* (N.p., 1938);

Jacques Roumain, "When the Tom-Tom Bears" and "Guinea"; Refino Pedroso, "Opinions of the New Chinese Student," in *Anthology of Contemporary Latin-American Poetry,* edited by Dudley Fitts (Norfolk, Conn.: New Directions, 1942), pp. 191-193, 247-249;

Roumain, *Masters of the Dew,* translated by Hughes and Mercer Cook (New York: Reynal & Hitchcock, 1947);

Nicolas Guillén, *Cuba Libre,* translated by Hughes and Ben Frederic Carruthers (Los Angeles: Ward Richie Press, 1948);

Leon Damas, "Really I Know," "Trite Without Doubt," and "She Left Herself One Evening," in *The Poetry of the Negro, 1746-1949,* edited by Hughes and Arna Bontemps (Garden City: Doubleday, 1949), pp. 371-372;

García Lorca, *Gypsy Ballads,* Beloit Poetry Chapbook, no. 1 (Beloit, Wis.: Beloit Poetry Journal, 1951);

Gabriela Mistral (Lucila Godoy Alcayaga), *Selected Poems* (Bloomington: Indiana University Press, 1957);

Jean-Joseph Rabearivelo, "Flute Players"; David Diop, "Those Who Lost Everything" and "Suffer, Poor Negro," in *Poems from Black Africa,* edited by Hughes (Bloomington: Indiana University Press, 1963), pp. 131-132, 143-145.

Few writers become household names, yet such is the case of Langston Hughes, who was perhaps the most significant black American writer in the twentieth century. His poems, novels, short stories, dramas, translations, and anthologies of the works of others span the period from the early days of the Harlem Renaissance in the 1920s to the black arts movement in the late 1960s. His early work was influenced by his contact with contemporary creative figures such as Countee Cullen, Aaron

Douglas, and Josephine Baker. In his late twenties and early thirties, he helped to inspire writers Margaret Walker and Gwendolyn Brooks. Later he encouraged writers of a third generation, including Ted Joans, Alice Walker, and Mari Evans.

Between 1921 and 1967 Hughes became both famous and loved. Even before he had helped young blacks gain entry to the major periodicals and presses of the day, his innovations in literary blues and jazz were acclaimed. As he worked to free American literature from the plantation tradition, he introduced new forms that reflected confidence and racial pride. He displayed social awareness in his fictional characters and technical mastery in his works.

James Mercer Langston Hughes was born to Carrie Langston Hughes and James Nathaniel Hughes on 1 February 1902 in Joplin, Missouri. Carrie's father, Charles Howard Langston, moved to Kansas in search of greater racial and financial freedom. His penchant for the literary and his desire to transcend the farm and the grocery store in Lawrence, Kansas, were passed on to Hughes. Charles's brother, John Mercer Langston, the poet's great-uncle, contributed to the family's literary efforts by penning an autobiography, *From the Virginia Plantation to the National Capital* (1894). The financially secure John Mercer Langston willed to his descendants a big house as well as stocks and bonds.

Hughes's mother, Carrie Langston, had briefly attended college, and she demonstrated a dramatic imagination through writing poetry and delivering monologues in costume. James Nathaniel Hughes, the poet's father, studied law by correspondence course, but when he was denied permission by the all-white examining board to take the Oklahoma Territory bar examination, he moved to Joplin with his wife in 1899. There, after four years of marriage and the death of his first child (in 1900), angered by unremitting poverty and faced with supporting an eighteen-month-old child, James Hughes left the United States in October 1903 for Mexico, where he eventually prospered and thus was able to contribute to the support of his son. Carrie Hughes refused to accompany him, and, unable to get even menial jobs in Joplin, she moved constantly from city to city looking for work, occasionally taking the young Langston with her. For most of the next nine years, however, the poet lived in Lawrence with his maternal grandmother, Mary Leary Langston, although he visited his mother briefly in Topeka,

stayed with her in Colorado, and traveled with her to Mexico in 1908 to see his father.

As a youngster, Hughes was acutely aware of the luxury in which his cousins lived in Washington in contrast to the poverty in which he and his grandmother lived, but she never wrote to them for help. He learned early that bills do not always get paid but that resourcefulness was essential to survival. Unlike most other black women in Lawrence, Kansas, his grandmother did not earn money by domestic service. She rented rooms to college students from the University of Kansas, and sometimes she would even live with a friend and rent out her entire house for ten or twelve dollars a month.

In 1907 Langston's mother took him with her to a library in Topeka, where he fell in love with books, in part because he was impressed that the library did not have to pay rent. Through the double perspective of boy and man, he recalled: "even before I was six books began to happen to me, so that after a while there came a time when I believed in books more than in people—which, of course, was wrong."

Hughes's grandmother influenced his life and imagination deeply. She was a gentle and proud woman of Indian and black blood. He remembered that she once took him to Oswatomie. There, she shared the platform as an honored guest of Teddy Roosevelt because she was the last surviving widow of the 1859 John Brown raid. Following her death in April 1915, Hughes lived briefly with his mother who had by then (possibly in the previous year) married Homer Clark. When Clark left town to seek a job elsewhere, Carrie Hughes left Langston with his grandmother's friend Auntie Reed and her husband, who owned a house a block from the river and near the railroad station. Devout Christians, they constantly urged Hughes to join the church. In a revival meeting, Hughes saw his friend bow to adult pressure and confess to having seen Jesus. The boy was immediately saved, or at least his elders thought so. Feeling guilty for keeping the elders up late, Hughes feigned a religious conversion, but that night he could not stop crying alone in bed. The Reeds thought he was pleased with the change in his life, but Hughes marked the incident as the beginning of his disbelief because Jesus had not intervened to save him.

In the seventh grade, Hughes secured his first regular job—cleaning the lobby and toilets in an old hotel near school—which would later inspire "Brass Spittoons," a poem he published in *Fine Clothes to the Jew* (1927). Late in the summer of 1915,

notes

Monday 1927

Not "Lincoln, Pa.," but,—
Lincoln University, Pa.

Dear Alain,

It was good to hear from you and to hear how busy you are. I hate to be "snowed-under" all by myself! I've got so much to do and so many letters to answer that I've stopped doing anything, and have been playing somebody's banjo all evening till I thought about writing to you..... "Fine Clothes" is still getting grand reviews,— all the way from "He's a great poet" to "He's a low-down hound." How they do vary! Did you see Alice Dunbar's in the Washington Eagle this week? .... Has yours come out? .... If you do see any you can clipp for me, do so, as my clipping bureau is missing everything but the pictures. I think they see only the tabloids, or else they don't know how to read. .... There have been some grand letters, too, from all points of the compass. Even from folks who haven't seen me for 20 years

A 1927 letter to Alain Locke, written after the publication of Hughes's second book (courtesy of the Alain Locke Papers, Moorland-Spingarn Research Center, Howard University)

yet knew me at once from the *Opportunity* picture,—which proves the genius of Reiss.... The American Legion is trying to put poor Kerlin's Liberal Club out of West Chester. .... Woodson was to come out to speak for us Sunday but fell ill of a cold.... I've got one, too,... When will our phamplet come out? I'm sure it'll be fine and am anxious to see it.... The *Messenger* took my stories and are using one in the April number with illustrations.... Camden was great. You must meet Mrs. Livery and Vernon Rich when you go there. They're both at Walt's house. You might make a Tues. evening talk or something there. Camden papers give great publicity.... I went to a Med. clinic at Penn and saw Dr. Deaver remove kidneys, appendices, hernias, and uteruses. I didn't know Billy could furnish anything quite so intense. Even students fainted,— but not I. It was much less grewsome than a bull fight..... I want to see you, (because I've decided to go South) but New York is impossible at the moment. You see I'm even reduced to tablet paper for my letters. As Clara says "City fro' me!" It's a hard world.... I'll have to order a "Weary Blues" for Newman. Haven't even one of those. (I've got to find a 1st edition copy for my self somewhere.)

Bien a toi,   Langston

Langston Hughes at Lincoln University, 1928 (courtesy of the Schomburg Center for Research in Black Culture, the New York Public Library, Astor, Lenox and Tilden Foundations)

Hughes rejoined his mother, stepfather, and Clark's son Gwyn. They lived in Lincoln, Illinois, for a year and in 1916 Homer Clark moved the family to Cleveland. Hughes entered Central High School that autumn and had a successful four years there. He wrote poems for the *Belfry Owl*, the student magazine, helped win the city championships in track, was on the monthly honor roll, and edited the school yearbook. Among the teachers, many of whom he found inspirational, was Latin teacher Helen Chesnutt, daughter of well-known novelist Charles W. Chesnutt.

From 1916 to 1920 Hughes had many Jewish friends, because he found the children of foreign-born parents to be more democratic than those of other white Americans. He escorted a Jewish girl when he first attended a symphony-orchestra concert. Fellow students introduced Hughes to socialist ideas; they lent him Ethel Boole Voynich's *The Gadfly* (1891), copies of the *Liberator* and the *Socialist Call,* and took him to hear Eugene Debs, a socialist leader. Though Hughes never became an extreme leftist, his early years shaped his commitment to the poor and led him to read Arthur Schopenhauer, Friedrich Nietzsche, Edna Ferber, and Guy de Maupassant, whom he found fascinating.

Hughes spent the summer of 1919 with his father in Mexico. Unfortunately Hughes found he disliked his father's materialistic outlook. Depressed most of the time, Hughes contemplated but rejected the idea of committing suicide.

Back in the United States, Hughes dated a seventeen-year-old black woman, who was newly arrived from the South. They had met at a dance in a school gym and she inspired the lyric "When Sue Wears Red," the first of many poems in which Hughes would celebrate the beauty of black women.

When Susanna Jones wears red
Her face is like an ancient cameo
Turned brown by the ages.

Come with a blast of trumpets,
Jesus!

In July 1920 on the train to visit his father in Mexico, crossing the Mississippi River to St. Louis, Hughes wrote the short lyric, "The Negro Speaks of Rivers." Through the images of water and pyramid, the verse suggests the endurance of human spirituality from the time of ancient Egypt to the nineteenth and twentieth centuries. The muddy Mississippi made Hughes think of the roles in human history played by the Congo, the Niger, and the Nile, down whose water the early slaves were once sold. And he thought of Abraham Lincoln, who was moved to end slavery after he took a raft trip down the Mississippi. The draft he first wrote on the back of an envelope in fifteen minutes has become Hughes's most anthologized poem:

I've known rivers;
    I've known rivers ancient as the world and
        older than the flow of human blood in human
        veins.

My soul has grown deep like the rivers.

I bathed in the Euphrates when dawns were young.
I built my hut near the Congo and it lulled me to
    sleep.
I looked upon the Nile and raised the pyramids above
    it.
I heard the singing of the Mississippi when Abe Lin-
    coln went down to New Orleans, and I've seen
    its muddy bosom turn all golden in the sunset.

I've known rivers:
    Ancient, dusky rivers.

My soul has grown deep like the rivers.

Hughes lived with his father in Mexico until September 1921 agonizing over his father's desire for him to attend a European university and his own preference for attending Columbia University in New York. As an escape he went to bullfights in Mexico City almost every weekend. He was unsuccessful in writing about them, but he did write articles about Toluca and the Virgin of Guadalupe. The *Brownies' Book*, a magazine just begun by W. E. B. Du Bois's staff at the *Crisis*, published two poems by Hughes in the January 1921 issue and *The Gold Piece*, his one-act play for children, in the July 1921 issue. Jessie Fauset, the literary editor, also accepted one of his articles and the poem "The Negro Speaks of Rivers" for the June 1921 issue of *Crisis*.

In the fall of 1921, with his father's permission, Hughes enrolled at Columbia University. His dream quickly turned into grim reality: the cold weather was depressing, the buildings were like factories, and the program and students were not to his liking. He abandoned school in favor of attending Broadway shows and lectures at the Rand School; he read what he wanted. In the spring he missed an important exam to attend the funeral for the black performer, Bert Williams, and each night he went to see *Shuffle Along*, where he sat in the gallery and adored Florence Mills. After finals, Hughes dropped out of Columbia and worked at various odd jobs while he gave his undivided attention to the milieu and the people who would shape the Harlem Renaissance.

During the winter of 1923 Hughes wrote the poem that would give the title to his first volume of poetry. "The Weary Blues," about a piano player in Harlem, captures the flavor of the night life, people, and folk forms that would become characteristic of the experimental writing of the renaissance. The piano player uses his instrument to create the "call and response" pattern essential to the blues. He is alone and lonely: "Ain't got nobody in all this world,/Ain't got nobody but ma self./I's gwine to quit ma frownin'/And put ma troubles on the shelf," but his piano "talks" back to him. Through the process of playing the piano and singing about his troubles, the man is able to exorcise his feelings and arrive at a state of peace:

And far into the night he crooned that tune.
The stars went out and so did the moon.
The singer stopped playing and went to bed
While the Weary Blues echoed through his head.
He slept like a rock or a man that's dead.

In structure and subject matter the poem varies from traditional forms. Although there are rhymes and onomatopoeic effects ("Thump, thump, thump, went his foot on the floor"), there are also unusual lines, such as

    Sweet Blues!
Coming from a black man's soul.
    O Blues!

Such lines serve to move the poem beyond its traditional components and to locate the ethos in Afro-American culture. A frequently anthologized poem, "The Weary Blues" treats blues as theme and structure and was a fitting choice as the title of a volume designed to focus on the masses of black people rather than the elite.

Alain Locke, Professor of Philosophy at Howard University, wrote to commend Hughes on the poems which had appeared in *Crisis*. But when Locke, a former Rhodes scholar, asked to visit Hughes, the young poet declined fearfully because he did not think he was prepared for such distinguished company.

In the spring of 1923 Hughes left Harlem for sea travel; he secured work as a cabin boy on a freighter to Africa. Off the point of Sandy Hook, New Jersey, he threw into the sea a box of books that reminded him of hardships of his past: attics and basements in Cleveland, lonely nights in Toluca, dormitories at Columbia, and furnished rooms in Harlem. He wrote, in *The Big Sea* (1940), of his first reaction to seeing Africa: "My Africa," he says, "Motherland of the Negro Peoples! And me a Negro! Africa! The real thing."

Hughes returned to the United States late in 1923 but was in Paris by the spring of 1924. Locke visited him there to solicit poems for a special issue of the *Survey Graphic*, an issue which was the basis for the book, *The New Negro* (1925).

181 West 135th Street,
New York, N. Y.
October 13, 1931.

Mr. William Pickens
N. A. A. C. P.
69 Fifth Avenue
New York City

My dear Mr. Pickens:

I have had the feeling for sometime that the modern
Negro Art Movement in America has been largely over the heads,
and out of reach, of the masses of the Negro peoples. It's
appeal within the race has been mainly to a small group of
"intellectuals", and as for books, most colored folks have
not been able to pay two dollars or more for volumes of
novels or poems. In many cases the context, too, of Negro
books has been uninteresting or displeasing to a large part
of the race. They have not cared for jazz poetry or low-
down novels—and one can't blame them much—since they
usually know such things all too well in life.

In recent Negro poetry, I have felt that there has been
a distinct lack of rhymed poems dramatizing current racial
interests in simple, understandable verse, pleasing to the
ear, and suitable for reading aloud, or for recitation in
schools, churches, lodges, etc. I have felt that much of
our poetry has been aimed at the heads of the high-brows,
rather than at the hearts of the people. And we all know
that most Negro books published by white publishers are advertised and sold largely to white readers, and little or no
effort is made to reach the great masses of the colored
people.

I have written "THE NEGRO MOTHER" with the hope that my
own people will like it, and will buy it. If they do, I shall
write other booklets of both verse and prose in this unpretentious fashion, to sell for as reasonable a price. I am
sending you this personal letter, not for publication, (please),
but merely to inform you of the raison d'etre behind this
little booklet. I would appreciate your comments on its
merit.

Sincerely yours,

Langston
Langston Hughes

Letter explaining Hughes's reasons for writing his 1931 booklet of poems. The twenty-page volume was so popular, Hughes told Carl Van Vechten in 1932, that in Birmingham, Alabama, it "sold like reefers on 131st Street." (By permission of the Estate of Langston Hughes; courtesy of the William Pickens Papers, the Schomburg Center for Research in Black Culture, the New York Public Library, Astor, Lenox and Tilden Foundations)

Locke, who invited Hughes to Venice and gave him a personally guided tour, knew who the architects of the stately old buildings were and where Wilhelm Wagner, the nineteenth-century German composer, had died. Hughes was not impressed; in less than a week, he was bored with palaces, churches, and paintings, as well as English tourists. He confirmed that Venice, too, had back alleys and poor people. He left for New York, where he took a few poems to Countee Cullen, whom he had already met and whose work he admired. With Cullen he attended an NAACP benefit party, where he met Carl Van Vechten.

In 1924 Hughes met Arna Bontemps, a crossing of paths that would have happy consequences for the two writers throughout their lives. They formed a mutual fan club, with Hughes greatly admiring Bontemps's ability to create in the midst of a demanding domestic life and Bontemps perhaps admiring Hughes's freedom and ability to write in spite of constant movement. The two writers complemented each other and worked well on a number of projects that extended for decades, including collaboration on children's books and a plethora of anthologies. Hughes, the faster writer of the two, sometimes had to wait for the slower Bontemps to complete his share of a promised work, but the delays did not harm their friendship or the quality of the work. When Bontemps became librarian at Fisk, he kept in touch with Hughes as he traveled to various parts of the world; indeed, perhaps Bontemps formed one of the centers around which Hughes would revolve for the remainder of his life.

The winter of 1925 found Hughes working in Washington, D.C., with Carter G. Woodson at the Association of Negro Life and History. This employment turned out to be brief because the paperwork hurt his eyes. He quit the "position" to take a "job" as a busboy at the Wardman Park hotel, where he met poet Vachel Lindsay. One afternoon Hughes put copies of his poems, "Jazzonia," "Negro Dancer," and "The Weary Blues," beside Lindsay's dinner plate and went away. On his way to work the next day, Hughes read in the headlines that Lindsay had discovered a Negro busboy poet. Lindsay advised Hughes to continue writing and to seek publication for his poems.

In 1925 Hughes won his first poetry prize in a contest sponsored by *Opportunity*, the official magazine of the Urban League, and Casper Holstein, a wealthy West Indian numbers banker. At the gathering at which prizes were awarded, Hughes met Mary White Ovington and James Weldon

Johnson and renewed his acquaintance with Carl Van Vechten, who asked Hughes if he had sufficient poems for a book. Hughes sent a manuscript to him, and Van Vechten liked the verses well enough to forward the volume to Alfred A. Knopf, his publisher. Blanche Knopf informed Hughes of her intention to publish the book.

Through Van Vechten Hughes met Arthur Spingarn, a prominent lawyer. Earlier that day he had accepted a long-standing invitation to tea from Spingarn's sister-in-law, Amy Spingarn. In Faith Berry's words: "emotional ties were formed between Hughes and the Spingarn family that lasted for the rest of their lives. As Hughes's attorney and personal friend for more than forty years, Arthur Spingarn made the poet's personal concerns his own and was unstinting in his public praise and admiration for Hughes." Amy Spingarn became a secret benefactor of the poet and provided him continual encouragement. She even offered to finance his education.

Hughes's poetry during this period is youthfully romantic. In the elevated lyric, "Fantasy in Purple," the African drum of tragedy and death becomes a metaphor for humanism and survival. "As I Grew Older" blends reflection and nostalgia as the speaker, framed by light and shadow, seeks

Langston Hughes, 1933 (courtesy of the Schomburg Center for Research in Black Culture, the New York Public Library, Astor, Lenox and Tilden Foundations)

to rediscover his dream. In "Mexican Market Woman," Hughes's narrator uses simile to create a dark mood of weariness and pain. And through the persona in "Troubled Woman," the narrator portrays humanity similarly bowed but unbroken. With blues irony the voice modifies implicitly the pessimistic side of the spirituals ("nobody knows de trouble I seen") into the more optimistic side ("I know trouble don't last always"). "Mother to Son," a dramatic monologue, shows how dialect can be used with dignity. The image of the stair as a beacon of success inspires hope in both the son and the reader. All of the poems appeared in *The Weary Blues,* which was published in January 1926.

Critical response to *The Weary Blues* was mixed. Reviews in the *New York Times, Washington Post, Boston Transcript, New Orleans Times-Picayune, New Republic,* and elsewhere were laudatory; the only derogatory review in a white publication was in the *Times Literary Supplement,* which called Hughes a "cabaret poet." Reviewing the book in the February 1926 issue of *Opportunity,* however, Cullen found some of the poems "scornful in subject matter . . . and rhythmical treatment of whatever obstructions time and tradition . . . placed before him" and called Hughes one of those "racial artists instead of artists pure and simple." In the *Crisis* Fauset praised Hughes's liberation from established literary forms. No other poet, she said, would ever write "as tenderly, understandingly, and humorously about life in Harlem." Admiring the book for the cleanness and simplicity, Locke viewed Hughes, in *Palms,* as the spokesman for the black masses.

After a brief visit to Lincoln, Illinois, in February 1926, Hughes enrolled at Lincoln University in Pennsylvania. When classes were over for the summer, he moved to New York and into a rooming house on 137th Street, where novelist Wallace Thurman also lived. Thurman, managing editor of the *Messenger,* joined with Hughes, John P. Davis, Bruce Nugent, Zora Neale Hurston, Aaron Douglas, and Gwendolyn Bennett to sponsor *Fire!!,* a progressive and innovative periodical. Its first and only issue earned indignation from Du Bois and dismissal from Rean Graves, a critic for the *Baltimore Afro-American:* "I have just tossed the first issue of *Fire* into the fire. . . . Langston Hughes displays his usual ability to say nothing in many words."

Hughes attended lively parties sponsored by hair-straightener heiress A'Lelia Walker and Van Vechten. Many of the same people usually attended the gatherings of the two sponsors, though more writers typically visited Van Vechten's. There

Hughes met Somerset Maugham, Hugh Walpole, and Zora Neale Hurston's one-time employer Fannie Hurst, as well as William Seabrook and Louis Untermeyer.

In New York that summer Hughes wrote and rewrote the poem, "Mulatto," which would appear in *Saturday Review of Literature* and in the collection *Fine Clothes to the Jew* (1927). When he read the poem one evening at James Weldon Johnson's, Clarence Darrow called it the most moving poem he had heard. While Hughes himself said the verse was about "white fathers and Negro mothers in the South," the craft transcends the autobiographical paraphrase. Through the view of one son, a victim of miscegenation, the speaker judges the father's contemptuous indifference and illustrates the callousness of white America in particular and humanity in general. Finally, he shows the hatred of the legitimate son for the bastard speaker, for the former signifies the inner collapse of the human family through racism.

"Mulatto" reinforces the techniques used in the ballad "Cross," published earlier but also collected in *Fine Clothes to the Jew.* In the poems Hughes enlarged the basic inequality among blacks into social and symbolic meaning, the "problem of mixed blood . . . one parent in the pale of the black ghetto and the other able to take advantage of all the opportunities of American democracy." He also emphasized the peculiar plight of the mulatto. "Cross" proclaims:

My old man died in a fine big house.
My ma died in a shack.
I wonder where I'm gonna die,
Being neither white nor black?

Critics in the black middle class objected to *Fine Clothes to the Jew* on ideological grounds. Their philosophical differences with Hughes went back to 1922, for he had decided then to serve the black masses and to avoid middle-class affectation. Black academicians had insisted, on the contrary, on a social image which would still promote racial integration. When it became apparent that Hughes had not complied, a headline in the *Pittsburgh Courier* read "Langston Hughes's Book of Trash," and another appeared in the *New York Amsterdam News:* "Langston Hughes, the Sewer Dweller."

During his ensuing years of study at Lincoln, Hughes met Charlotte Mason (who liked to be known as "Godmother") on a weekend trip to New York in 1927. A friend had introduced him to the elderly white lady, who delighted Hughes immediately and who, despite her age, was modern in her ideas about books, Harlem theater, and current events. She became his literary patron, a title both disliked. With her support Hughes began work on his first novel, *Not Without Laughter* (1930), which he envisioned as a portrait of a typical black family in Kansas. His personal background could not serve as a resource since his grandmother never worked in domestic service and rarely attended church: his mother had been a newspaperwoman and stenographer. Hughes began writing furiously, tacking short biographical sketches of characters to the walls in his room. At first he wrote a chapter or two a day and revised them, but the revisions were so unsatisfactory that he decided to write the book straight through. After the completion of the first draft in about six weeks, he went to Provincetown for a vacation before classes started. In the summer and fall of 1929, his senior year at Lincoln, Hughes revised the novel, continuing the process after graduation and through the summer. What had seemed acceptable to him before he went to Canada seemed to have diminished in quality upon his return. Yet the novel was accepted for publication and appeared in 1930.

In *Not Without Laughter* Hughes chose fidelity to the folk spirit instead of abandoning it for the middle-class trappings of his Lincoln education. The novel relates the growth of Sandy Williams, who lives with and is greatly influenced by Hagar, his religious grandmother. Sandy's mother Anjee spends most of her time working as a domestic and waiting restlessly for Jimboy, her guitar-playing, rambling husband, to make one of his trips home. Hagar's oldest daughter, Tempy, has separated herself from the family by assimilating middle class culture and adopting values alien to her upbringing; Harriett, the youngest daughter, is the vibrant lover of life who defies her mother by attending parties and seeking to become a blues singer. At Hagar's death, it is the unlikely Harriett who carries on her values and encourages Sandy to continue his education.

Family and home unify the novel, with Hughes combining fiction and history in his depiction of social setting and character. In his portrayal of the Williams family's disintegration and reunification, he draws upon his familiarity with the barbershop in Kansas City and his experience with a wandering stepfather. He includes songs from childhood and has Sandy go to Chicago as he once did. The book is successful in capturing the folk flavor so vital to Hughes.

In the early winter of 1930 Hughes broke irreparably with Mason. He had loved her kindness and generosity, including her sincere support for black advancement and liberal causes. He had admired her awareness of then-budding stars Duke Ellington and Marian Anderson, and he had appreciated the humility which had made her remain his anonymous patron. In providing excellent supplies for his creative work, she had broadened his cultural life through visits to the Metropolitan Museum of Art, to concerts at Carnegie Hall, and to the musicals of the day. Yet they had disagreed on political philosophy and race. Mason believed that blacks linked American whites to the primitive life and should only concern themselves with building on their cultural foundations. Hughes rejected such a simplistic view of the role of blacks in the modern world. Although he did not openly criticize Mason, he became psychosomatically ill following his final meeting with her.

Hughes also broke with Hurston that winter. After one of her many trips to the Deep South, Hurston and Hughes began to work on the folk comedy "Mule Bone," a play based on an amusing

Amy Spingarn's portrait of Hughes (courtesy of the Schomburg Center for Research in Black Culture, the New York Public Library, Astor, Lenox and Tilden Foundations)

tale she had collected, one which portrayed a quarrel between two church factions. Apparently Hughes outlined the plot while Hurston embellished the dialogue and strengthened the humor. Before she returned south, the two were supposed to complete a first draft from which Hughes was to write the final revision. Back in Cleveland to live with his mother, Hughes attended a performance by the Gilpin Players, after which he learned from Rowena Jelliffe, the director, that she had just received an excellent Negro folk comedy from Hurston. Though a group in New York had turned down the play, an agent had given Jelliffe permission to try it out in Cleveland. Unable to reach Hurston by phone, Hughes wired her unsuccessfully, and, after three unanswered letters, Hurston replied finally from New York. She admitted sending the play to her agent and speculated angrily that Hughes would only have spent his half of the royalties on some girl she disliked. She went to Cleveland later to close the deal, but then she recanted because "the girl she did not like had been in." The incident led to a rift that was never mended and has become one of the classic breakups in Afro-American literary history.

Now almost thirty, Hughes was determined to make a living from writing. He set out with Zell Ingram, a student at the Cleveland School of Art, to tour the South by car. In Daytona Beach he met Mary McLeod Bethune, who suggested that Hughes do readings throughout the region since his achievements could be inspiring in the prevailing climate of racial restriction. Hughes considered the advice but did not act upon it until his trip was over. He and Ingram spent the summer in Haiti. Although he did not use the letters of introduction from Walter White, William Seabrook, Arthur Spingarn, and James Weldon Johnson to upper-class Haitians, he did meet Jacques Roumain, a cultured Haitian who appreciated indigenous folklore. Later, with approximately four dollars between them, Hughes and Ingram arrived back in Miami. When they returned to Daytona Beach, Bethune cashed a thirty-dollar check for them and asked to share the ride back to New York.

Hughes received a grant for $1,000 from the Rosenwald Fund to tour black colleges in the South. He purchased a Ford and then, having no license, he struck a deal with Lucas Radcliffe, a fellow alumnus of Lincoln. Radcliffe would drive and manage accounts while he would read poetry. Both men would share the profits.

The trip, starting in the fall of 1931, deepened Hughes's commitments to racial justice and literary expression. When the nine Scottsboro boys were accused unjustly of raping two white prostitutes, he observed unhappily that black colleges were silent. "Christ in Alabama," a poem comparing the silence of the black colleges to that of the bystanders at the Crucifixion, caused a sensation in Chapel Hill, North Carolina, where playwright Paul Green and sociologist Guy B. Johnson had invited Hughes to read in November. About a week before the scheduled arrival, Hughes received a note from a white student, Anthony Buttita, who invited him to share a room. Buttita and his roommate, Milton Abernethy, had printed two of Hughes's publications, "Christ in Alabama" and an article, in *Contempo*, an unofficial student magazine. The poem had included lines such as:

> Christ is a Nigger
> Beaten and black—
> *O, bare your back.*
> . . . .
> Most holy bastard
> Of the bleeding mouth:
> *Nigger Christ*
> *On the cross of the South.*

The subsequent appearance by Hughes nearly caused a riot, but his rescue from the angry crowd that attended the reading did not deter his challenge to racial segregation. He ate with the editors in a southern restaurant and thereby helped to set a new tone for race relations in Chapel Hill.

At various stops in other towns, the poet's audiences overflowed. Blacks admired the young poet who had "walked into a lion's den, and come out, like Daniel, unscathed." Bethune praised the same heroism in Hughes's poetry. For her and others he read "The Negro Mother," which projects spiritual inspiration and endurance through images of fertility. In the remembrance of suffering, the speaker urges her children to transform the dark past into a lighted future. When Hughes completed the reading, Bethune embraced and consoled him: "My son, my son."

Communal love and history informed the poet's life and work. Following a program in New Orleans, he took an hour to encourage the then-adolescent poet Margaret Walker. In preparing for a reading at Tuskegee Institute in February, he thought about educator Booker T. Washington, who had founded the institution in 1881. Often at odds with the more militant Du Bois, a Hughes mentor during the renaissance, Washington had at

*Dust jacket for the Liberty Book Club edition of Hughes's
1947 translation*

least won partial approval from Sandy in *Not Without Laughter.*

As a youngster in Lawrence, Hughes had
been taken to hear Washington speak at Topeka.
Later, Hughes had read *Up From Slavery* (1901),
Washington's well-known autobiography. At Tuskegee, Hughes met the current president, Robert
Moten, as well as the famous scientist, George
Washington Carver. His talks with many English
classes continued to be a source for his literary
imagination, as did his whole trip.

The 1932 trip, which ended in San Francisco
(at the home of Noel Sullivan, who would later be
helpful to Hughes) after stops in Arkansas and
other places, encouraged the literary relationships
which shaped Hughes's imaginative life and made
him speculate on both the nature and the obligation
of art. This heightened awareness framed his journey to Russia that year as part of a film company.
When Hughes met Arthur Koestler, the Hungar-

ian-born British writer in Ashkhabad, the two explored Soviet Asia together. Koestler provided the
opportunity for Hughes to reflect on emotion and
creativity: "There are many emotional hypochon-
driacs on earth, unhappy when not happy, sad
when not expounding on their sadness. Yet I have
always been drawn to such personalities because I
often feel sad inside myself, too, though not inclined to show it. Koestler wore his sadness on his
sleeve." Schooled in Western individualism,
Hughes defended the artist's autonomy against the
political directives of bureaucrats. Koestler re-
torted that the simultaneous expression of politics
and individuality were difficult, especially when
politicians lacked appreciation for creativity. At
certain moments, Koestler argued, social aims transcended personal desires, though the Russian
writer had begun to see Stalinist repression and to
turn against communism. Grateful for the discussions with Koestler, Hughes probably thought his
own ideas unchanged, but the encounter had renewed his leftist inclinations.

Hughes's meeting with Marie Seton furthered
his leftist leanings. When he moved into a Moscow
hotel, she lent him a copy of D. H. Lawrence's short
stories. *The Lovely Lady* (1933). He liked "The Rock-
ing Horse Winner" particularly because the pos-
sessive, terrifying, and elderly woman reminded
him of Charlotte Mason. In attempting futilely to
write an article about Tashkent, he began to remember a story told once by Loren Miller, a young
lawyer in California. In a small Kansas town, a very
pretty black woman attracted the attention of the
only black doctor, undertaker, and minister. While
all three enjoyed her favors, she became pregnant,
but the father was unknown. When the doctor performed an abortion, the girl died. The undertaker
took charge of her body, and the minister preached
at her funeral. Hughes reworked the tale into an
interracial story which would appear in *The Ways
of White Folks* (1934). The black "girl" became a
white middle-class youngster, Jessie Studevant,
whose parents did not want her to have a relationship with a Greek boy, Willie Matsoulos, an immigrant whose father ran an ice-cream stand.
When the girl's mother forced her to have an abortion, Jessie died. Hughes revised his source satiri-
cally to picture the deep pathos and hypocrisy in
American society.

Yet the craft of the story transcended any social message. Through the setting of Melton, a
small town in Iowa, the shrewd narrator clarifies
misplaced values. He sets Cora's daughter, the
black Josephine, against Mrs. Art's white Jessie.

Hughes with a group of students in South Carolina, where he had gone to attend an auction benefiting the Association for the Study of Negro Life and History (courtesy of the Schomburg Center for Research in Black Culture, the New York Public Library, Astor, Lenox and Tilden Foundations)

Whereas the first dies from unavoidable neglect, the second dies through willful decisions. Indeed even the name "Art" allegorizes coldness in Western creativity. Through the omniscient, ironic narrator, Hughes reflects on aborted life while he implies the need for human sympathy.

In 1933 the stories "Home" (*Esquire,* 1934) and "Blues I'm Playing" (*Scribner's,* May 1934) were accepted for publication. "Home" juxtaposes the artist's quest for beauty and truth with the lyncher's self-indulgent animalism. Roy Williams, a violinist by day and jazz player by night, returns from Europe to Hopkinsville, Missouri, where he provokes envy in the local whites. When he bows to Mrs. Reese, a benevolent white music teacher, he is killed by the whites who are jealous of his talent, clothing,

and education. The story shows that music can neither transform such mobs nor protect the artist from vicious attack. Despite the apparent defeat, the humane greeting of the two musicians survives spiritually.

In "The Blues I'm Playing," Hughes reworks the disturbing break with Mason into a plot involving a black pianist, Oceola Jones, who abandons the Western classics. Though her patron Dora Ellsworth, a childless widow, believes in art alone, Jones believes in both art and life (Mason actually preferred "primitive folk art" to the classics), but a more complex psychology informs the story. To accept the innovative ideas of Oceola would mean to admit the misdirection of Ellsworth's own life and to transcend Western dualism. When Ellsworth refuses to do so, the two women represent a theoretical and ideological struggle over aesthetics. In the story, Oceola's wildly syncopated jazz is contrasted with both the classical music and the slow-singing blues. In the onomatopoeic climax of Oceola's final song, music becomes both a personal and cultural liberation. Oceola has the last word, as through her the writer transmutes the personal life into the symbolic quest for self.

In Russia Hughes had learned well the relationship between writing and mythmaking. The representative of a leading American newspaper had intentionally printed a story in New York that the film company with which Hughes was traveling was stranded and starving in Moscow. When the filmmakers showed the reporter the clippings, he merely grinned. But Hughes, to provide a clearer picture, praised the many positive changes which Americans ignored in revolutionized Russia, particularly the open housing and reduced persecution of Jews. Yet Hughes turned away from Russia eventually because he refused to live without jazz, which the communists banned, for they limited artistic freedom generally.

Determined to confront worldwide fascism and racism, Hughes returned to San Francisco by way of the Orient in 1933. His trip home demonstrates his headstrong personality. Though Westerners in Shanghai had warned him that the watermelons were tainted and potentially fatal there, he ate well, enjoyed the fruit, and lived to write the story. Warned to avoid the Chinese districts, he visited those areas and found the danger illusory. In Tokyo the police interrogated, detained, and finally expelled him. In the Japanese press's inflated stories of Korean crimes, he read the pattern of racism so familiar in the States. Aware that victims become victimizers in turn, he understood the Japanese debasement of the Chinese, and, on the way back to the United States, he warned that Japan was a fascist country.

Between 1933 and 1934 Hughes retired temporarily from world politics. In Carmel, at Sullivan's home "Ennesfree," he completed a series of short stories which were later included in *The Ways of White Folks.* He also wrote articles, including one on the liberation of women from the harems of Soviet Asia. Grateful to Noel Sullivan for the time to write, Hughes worked from ten to twelve hours a day, producing at least one story or article every week and earning more money than he ever had. He sent most of his earnings to his mother, who was ill at the time. Having broken with his father in 1922, Hughes learned, too late to attend the

funeral, that his father had died in Mexico on 22 October 1934. Hughes traveled to Mexico and remained there from January to April of 1935, during which time he read Cervantes's *Don Quixote.* From Cervantes he derived a masterful blend of tragedy and comedy to complement the appreciation of natural beauty he had learned from Maupassant and the complexity of literary psychology he had learned from Lawrence.

He needed the humor for the Broadway production of *Mulatto,* the dramatic rewrite of the short story, "Father and Son." Hughes was amazed at the changes proposed. The character played by Sally Williams, sister of the protagonist Bert, should have gone away to school; instead, she remained at home to provoke sexual sensationalism by getting raped. The play was banned in Philadelphia and nearly prohibited from playing in Chicago. But on Broadway it had a long run. *Mulatto* played there for a year, from 1935 to 1936, and it was on the road for two more seasons.

As a correspondent in 1937 for the *Baltimore Afro-American* during the Spanish Civil War, Hughes was deeply impressed by Pastora Pavón, the famous flamenco singer known as La Niña de los Peines, whose bluesy art resisted both war and death. When Hughes heard that she had refused to leave besieged Madrid, he traveled there to see her. Her midmorning appearance among hand-clapping, heel-tapping guitarists was striking. She sat in a chair and dominated the performance as she half-spoke and half-sang a *solea.* To Hughes her voice was wild, hard, harsh, lonely, and bittersweet, reminding him of black Southern blues because, despite the heartbreak implied, it signified the triumph of a people.

Hughes stayed on the top floor of the Alianza de Intelectuales in 1937; his room faced the fascist guns directly. Yet he stayed and met with the white American writers visiting Spain, including Ernest Hemingway, Martha Gelhorn, Lillian Hellman, and critic Malcolm Cowley. Nancy Cunard and Stephen Spender turned up as well, as did non-English-speaking writers such as the French novelist André Malraux and Pablo Neruda, the leftist poet from Chile. Of these writers, Hemingway influenced Hughes most deeply. Hemingway had won a fight with an Englishman over some misunderstanding concerning the man's wife. When the squabble resurfaced as a short story, Hemingway described the incident so pointedly that few people in Madrid at the time could mistake the source, though he had exaggerated the other man's slightness and the woman's stockiness. He portrayed the man as hiding under a table as shots rang out, thereby leaving his wife unprotected. Actual witnesses, however, claimed that the Englishman took cover only after assurances that his wife was safe.

Hughes appreciated the writer's imaginative revision of the event but hoped to disguise better the autobiographical sources for his own fiction. Still, Hemingway had melded history and autobiography successfully into imaginative writing.

In December 1937 Hughes went to Paris for the holidays, where he saw Nancy Cunard, Bricktop, and the Roumains. Louis Aragon introduced him to George Adam, who translated short stories into French, and Pierre Seghers, who would become Hughes's publisher. Hughes had heard from Russian intellectuals that Spain was to be considered only a training ground for Hitler's and Mussolini's armies. It was a country for bombing practice by fascist pilots, and the impending World

THE SWEET
FLYPAPER
OF LIFE

Roy DeCarava and Langston Hughes

When the bicycle of the Lord bearing His messenger with a telegram for Sister Mary Bradley saying "Come home" arrived at 113 West 134th Street, New York City, Sister Bradley said, "Boy, take that wire right on back to St. Peter because I am not prepared to go. I might be a little sick, but as yet I ain't no ways tired." And she would not even sign for the message —since she had read it first, while claiming she could not find

(continued on page 3)

Cover for first paperback edition of the book that combines DeCarava's photographs and Hughes's text to present a positive view of Harlem life

War II would be everywhere. When Jacques Roumain claimed the world would end, Hughes quipped, "I doubt it . . . and if it does, I intend to live to see what happens."

Hughes's work continued to earn public recognition from 1938 to 1967, the year of his death. The poems in *A New Song* (1938) are politically sensitive and direct, yet replete with social irony and personal determination. "Let America Be America Again" shows the loss of an ideal, yet invokes the reappearance of it. Through the images of eye sores, the satirical poem, "Justice," emphasizes social blindness.

After founding the New Negro Theater in Los Angeles during 1939, Hughes wrote a script for the hollywood film, *Way Down South*. From May through September he completed *The Big Sea,* the first segment of his autobiography, and when the book came out the next year (1940), he received a Rosenwald fellowship to write historical plays. In 1941 he founded the Skyloft Players, who produced his musical *The Sun Do Move* in Chicago in 1942. Whatever his claims for poetry, his imprint on Afro-American drama was certain.

Shakespeare in Harlem (1942), his next book of poems, was well crafted. In the blues monologue, "Southern Mammy Sings," a poor black narrator opposes a white socialite. In biblical overtones the speaker criticizes present and past war as well as the failure of interracial democracy. "Ballad of the Fortune Teller" presents humorously and colloquially the situational irony of a woman who allegedly foretells the future of others but fails to prophesy her lover's desertion of her. In the deceptively simple "Black Maria," an enthusiastic urbanite focuses, almost allegorically, upon the music playing in a tenement upstairs instead of on a hearse passing in the street below.

Such meanings escaped most of the critics. Saying that *Shakespeare in Harlem* was a "careless surface job," and that Hughes was "backing into the future looking at the past," Owen Dodson was unduly harsh. Alfred Kreymborg, however, was reminded of such "master singers of Vaudeville as Bert Williams and Eddie Leonard . . . a subtle blending of tragedy and comedy, which is a rare, difficult, and exquisite art." Edna Lou Walton, overlooking the poet's new growth in complexity and symbolic depth, wrote: "Hughes only writes as he always has. His poems, close to folk songs, indicate no awareness of the changed war world . . . Easily listened to, they do not invoke sufficient thought."

Langston Hughes (courtesy of the Schomburg Center for Research in Black Culture, the New York Public Library, Astor, Lenox and Tilden Foundations)

When *Shakespeare in Harlem* had been published, Hughes returned to New York. For a while he shared a three-room apartment with Emerson and Toy Harper, two old family friends, and he wrote verses and slogans to help sell U.S. Defense Bonds. In a weekly column for the *Chicago Defender*, a black newspaper, he began to publish the tales of Jesse B. Semple—later called Jesse B. Simple—a folk philosopher who would capture the hearts of thousands of readers. In 1946 he won a medal and prize of $1,000 from the American Academy of Arts and Letters. In the early months of 1947 he served as Visiting Professor of Creative Writing at Atlanta University. For a few weeks in 1949 he was poet in residence at the Laboratory School of the University of Chicago.

In *One-Way Ticket* (1949) Hughes infused humorous realism with satire and biblical irony. His well-known persona, Alberta K. Johnson, became the hilarious folk counterpart in poetry to his comic character Jesse B. Simple in prose. In one poem,

Madam asserts her independence from the phone company as well as from a lover:

> You say I O.K.ed
> LONG DISTANCE?
> O.K.ed it when?
> My goodness, Central,
> That was *then!*
>
> I'm mad and disgusted
> With that Negro now.
> I don't pay no REVERSED
> CHARGES nohow.

Madam blames society for her misfortunes in life and love while she directs the criticism inward to her own character. Her self-image is sometimes overblown and superstitious. Possibly happiness has eluded her because she doubts her worthiness to be loved.

The critical reception to *One-Way Ticket* was mixed. G. Lewis Chandler observed the humor, irony, and tragedy, as well as the folksiness, subtlety, puckishness, and hope. The communal "I" reminded him of Walt Whitman, and he praised the poet's ability to deepen racial material into universal experience. Rolfe Humphries, who acknowledged Hughes's forbearance, praised the basic restraint of vocabulary, the simple rhymes, the short lines, the absent violence, and the missing hyperbole. Hughes needed, he thought, to be more elaborate, involved, and complex; to exploit more fully education, travel, reading, and music other than the blues.

However modern he was, Langston Hughes would never abandon black folk life for Western imagism. In *Montage of a Dream Deferred* (1951), his first book-length poem, dramatic and colloquial effects challenged his lyricism. Numerous projects in the writing of history and short fiction, such as *The First Book of Negroes* (1952) and *Simple Takes a Wife* (1953), drained his poetic energies. His style became more sophisticated. Through monologue and

A 1965 Christmas card that Hughes created and sent to friends (courtesy of the Schomburg Center for Research in Black Culture, the New York Public Library, Astor, Lenox and Tilden Foundations)

free verse, he stressed dramatic situations and mastered the apostrophe. In blending content with form, he fused narrative with sound effects.

The critics overlooked such skill. Rolfe Humphries, who commented that the poems in *Montage of a Dream Deferred* confused him, as work by Hughes often did, saw an irreconcilable split between Hughes the spokesman and the individual. The statement, he said, was oversimplified and theatrical. Babette Deutsch believed that the verses, which invited approval, "lapsed into a sentimentality that stifles real feeling." Conscious about the limitations of folk art, she asserted that Hughes should resemble more his French contemporaries. Saunders Redding said Hughes offered nothing new; he called his idiom constant and his rhythms more be-bop than jazz. Despite a sophisticated ear, according to Redding, Hughes was too concerned with personal reputation and innovation.

After testifying in 1953 before the Senate subcommittee chaired by Joseph McCarthy investigating the purchase of books by subversive writers for American libraries abroad, Hughes received fewer offers to read poems over the next several years but enhanced the craft of his fiction. When *The Best of Simple* (1961) appeared he had developed a comic veneer and lightness which concealed complex symbolism artfully. Through urban dialect he had juxtaposed the seriousness of the Great Migration in Simple's past with the humorous tone of the moment. Simple's folk imagination struck a balance with the polished reason of Boyd, his bar buddy.

In "Feet Live Their Own Life," Simple's comic discourse suggests an awareness of the present and the past. Through the caricatured figure of the former Virginian, Hughes helps the reader to laugh at himself and at American society. In "There Ought to be a Law," Simple calls for a game preserve for "Negroes." Another tale, "They Come and They Go," is a narration about Simple's eighteen-year-old second cousin, Franklin D. Roosevelt Brown, coming North. The youngster's stepfather has whipped him, and the mother has predicted the same failure for the youth as that which beset his "no-good" father. But Hughes's narrator manages a sympathetic warmth for all involved.

In 1960 Hughes visited Paris for the first time in twenty-two years, and he would from then on make many trips on cultural grants from the state department—an irony indeed, since until 1959 he was on the "security index" of the FBI's New York office. He would visit Africa a number of times, and revisit Europe. The year 1961 saw the publication of Hughes's crowning achievement. *Ask Your*

Since the publication of *The Weary Blues* in 1926, Langston Hughes has been the leading interpreter in poetry of the life of the Negro in the United States. Today his poems are born of the racial dilemma that has rocked this country in the last decade; he writes of freedom marches, sit-ins, speeches, prayers, violence, and nonviolence, from Alabama to Harlem; he tells of a tragedy in Birmingham and a death in Yorkville. Forty-four of these poems are new, and the remaining twenty-six, which are drawn from previous books, take on new significance in this collection.

LANGSTON HUGHES

THE PANTHER AND THE LASH

POEMS OF OUR TIMES

$1.95

Covers for the last volume of Hughes's poetry to be published in his lifetime

Mama is as much Juvenalian as Horatian in its satiric response to the rising anger of the 1960s. Fusing poetry with jazz, Hughes interweaves myth and history. He moves now into the child's mind and then into the man's; he reverses himself and begins afresh. Through fantasy, travesty, allusion, and irony, he depicts singers, actors, writers, politicians, and musicians. With a deepened imagination, he draws upon the rich themes of his entire career, such as humanism, free speech, transitoriness, and assimilation; nationalism, racism, integration, and poverty. He speculates about Pan-Africanism and personal integrity. Praising Hughes's commitment to universal freedom, Rudi Blesh called *Ask Your Mama* "a half angry and half derisive retort to the bigoted, smug, stupid, selfish, and blind." Dudley Fitts, who compared it to Vachel Lindsay's *Congo* (1914), drew parallels between Hughes and the Cuban poet Guillén, as well as between Hughes and the Puerto Rican Luis Matos.

Though many white Americans believed blacks had moved too fast, Hughes complained about slowness and regression. The last poem he is said to have submitted for publication before his death in New York City's Polyclinic Hospital on 22 May 1967 was "Backlash Blues." Yet other poems are more optimistic. In "Frederick Douglass" his narrator anticipates the return of good, despite a period of regression, like that which began in 1895, the year of Douglass's death, with Booker T. Washington's Atlanta Compromise speech in which he spoke of the races as being "separate as the five fingers." Douglass is one of the many complex heroes whom Hughes had portrayed, including such memorable figures as Roy Williams, Oceola Jones, or Bert Norwood (all in *The Ways of White Folks*). Creative and good people reinforce one another in human history, and they come again.

Following Hughes's death critical commentary was respectful. Reviewing *The Panther & The*

Lash (1967), Bill Katz praised the writer's commitment to diverge from both liberal and reactionary views of race. Lamine Diakhaté called Hughes a "pilgrim who affirmed the identity of man in the face of the absurd ... showed the problems of blacks in a democratic society, restored the rhythmical language of Africa introduced by jazz in America, and demonstrated inextinguishable hope." Francois Dodat noted Hughes's humanistic faith. Most celebrators mention the writer's great generosity.

While Hughes's reputation today is even more secure, his life and times still merit serious scholarship. Early on he engaged the serious interest of scholars such as Arthur Davis, Darwin Turner, and James Emanuel. More recently the writings have received the scrutiny of Charles H. Nichols, Faith Berry, Richard K. Barksdale, and Arnold Rampersad. Indeed, Hughes's creative work has inspired significant studies in imagery, structure, and myth. His technical and spiritual contributions to black American literature will endure.

Letters:

Arna Bontemps-Langston Hughes Letters, 1925-1967, edited by Charles H. Nichols (New York: Dodd, Mead, 1980).

Bibliographies:

Donald C. Dickinson, *A Bio-Bibliography of Langston Hughes, 1902-1967* (Hamden, Conn.: Shoe String Press, 1967);

R. Baxter Miller, *Langston Hughes and Gwendolyn Brooks: A Reference Guide* (Boston: G. K. Hall, 1978).

Biographies:

Faith Berry, *Langston Hughes: Before and Beyond Harlem* (Westport, Conn.: Lawrence Hill, 1983);

Arnold Rampersad, *The Life of Langston Hughes; Volume 1: 1902-1941. I, Too, Sing America* (New York: Oxford University Press, 1986).

References:

Richard K. Barksdale, "Langston Hughes: His Times and His Humanistic Techniques," in *Black American Literature and Humanism,* edited by R. Baxter Miller (Lexington: University Press of Kentucky, 1981), pp. 11-26;

Barksdale, *Langston Hughes: The Poet and His Critics* (Chicago: American Library Association, 1977);

George Houston Bass, "Five Stories about a Man Named Hughes: A Critical Reflection," *Langston Hughes Review,* 1 (Spring 1982): 1-12;

Black American Literature Forum, special Hughes issue, edited by R. Baxter Miller, 15 (Fall 1981);

Lloyd W. Brown, "The Portrait of the Artist as a Black American in the Poetry of Langston Hughes," *Studies in Black Literature,* 5 (Winter 1974): 24-27;

Arthur P. Davis, "Langston Hughes: Cool Poet," *CLA Journal,* 11 (June 1968): 280-296;

Davis, "The Tragic Mulatto Theme in Six Works by Langston Hughes," *Phylon,* 16 (Winter 1955): 195-204; republished in *Five Black Writers,* edited by Donald B. Gibson (New York: New York University Press, 1970), pp. 167-177;

W. E. B. Du Bois and Alain Locke, "The Younger Literary Movement," *Crisis,* 27 (February 1927): 161-163;

James Emanuel, *Langston Hughes* (New York: Twayne, 1967);

Emanuel, "The Literary Experiments of Langston Hughes," *CLA Journal,* 11 (June 1967): 335-344;

Nathan Huggins, *Harlem Renaissance* (New York: Oxford University Press, 1971);

Blyden Jackson, "A Word About Simple," *CLA Journal,* 11 (June 1968): 310-318;

David Levering Lewis, *When Harlem Was in Vogue* (New York: Knopf, 1981);

Peter Mandelik and Stanley Schatt, *Concordance to Langston Hughes* (Detroit: Gale Research, 1975);

R. Baxter Miller, " 'For a Moment I Wondered': Theory and Form in the Autobiographies of Langston Hughes," *Langston Hughes Review,* 3 (Fall 1984): 1-6;

Therman B. O'Daniel, ed., *Langston Hughes: Black Genius* (New York: Morrow, 1971);

Stanley Schatt, "Langston Hughes: The Minstrel as Artificer," *Journal of Modern Literature,* 4 (September 1974): 115-120;

Darwin T. Turner, "Langston Hughes as Playwright," *CLA Journal* (June 1968): 297-309;

Jean Wagner, "Langston Hughes," in *Black Poets of the United States,* translated by Kenneth Douglas (Urbana: University of Illinois Press, 1973), pp. 385-474.

Papers:

The James Weldon Johnson Memorial Collection, Beinecke Library, Yale University, includes letters, manuscripts and typescripts of published and unpublished work, lecture notes, and various magazine and newspaper clippings and pamphlets. Additional materials are in the Schomburg Collec- tion of the New York Public Library, the library of Lincoln University in Pennsylvania, and the Fisk University library.

Zora Neale Hurston

Wright State University

BIRTH: Eatonville, Florida, 7 January 1891, to Lucy Ann Potts and John Hurston.

EDUCATION: Howard University, 1919-1924; B.A., Barnard College, 1928; Columbia University, 1934-1935.

MARRIAGES: 19 May 1927 to Herbert Sheen (divorced); 27 June 1939 to Albert Price III (divorced).

AWARDS AND HONORS: Guggenheim Fellowships, 1936 and 1938; Litt.D., Morgan State College, 1939; Anisfield-Wolf Award for *Dust Tracks on a Road*, 1942.

DEATH: Fort Pierce, Florida, 28 January 1960.

BOOKS: *Jonah's Gourd Vine* (Philadelphia & London: Lippincott, 1934);
Mules and Men (Philadelphia & London: Lippincott, 1935);
Their Eyes Were Watching God (Philadelphia & London: Lippincott, 1937);
Tell My Horse (Philadelphia: Lippincott, 1938); republished as *Voodoo Gods* (London: Dent, 1939);
Moses, Man of the Mountain (Philadelphia: Lippincott, 1939); republished as *The Man of the Mountain* (London: Dent, 1941);
Dust Tracks on a Road (Philadelphia: Lippincott, 1942; London: Hutchinson, 1944);
Seraph on the Suwanee (New York: Scribners, 1948);
I Love Myself When I Am Laughing . . . & Then Again When I Am Looking Mean & Impressive, edited by Alice Walker (Old Westbury, N.Y.: Feminist Press, 1979);
Spunk, The Selected Stories of Zora Neale Hurston (Berkeley: Turtle Island Foundation, 1985).

PERIODICAL PUBLICATIONS: "Spunk," *Opportunity* (June 1925);
"Color Struck," *Fire!!*, no. 1 (1926): 7-13;
"How It Feels to be Colored Me," *World Tomorrow*, 11 (May 1928);
"What White Publishers Won't Print," *Negro Digest*, 7 (April 1950): 85-89.

From the 1930s through the 1960s, Zora Neale Hurston was the most prolific and accomplished black woman writer in America. During that thirty-year period she published seven books, numerous short stories, magazine articles, and plays, and she also gained a reputation as an outstanding folklorist and novelist. She called attention to herself because she insisted upon being herself when blacks were being urged to assimilate in an effort to promote better relations between the races. Hurston, however, saw nothing wrong with being black: "I do not belong to that sobbing school of Negrohood who hold that nature somehow has given them a lowdown dirty deal." Indeed she felt there was something so special about her blackness that others could benefit just by being around her. Her works, then, may be seen as manifestos of selfhood, as affirmations of blackness and the positive sides of black life. For many of her readers, black and white, they reveal life's possibilities. She had gotten glimpses of those possibilities back in her native Eatonville.

Zora Neale Hurston (courtesy of the Prints and Photographs Collection, Moorland-Spingarn Research Center, Howard University)

She was born on 7 January in Eatonville, Florida, to John Hurston and Lucy Ann Potts Hurston. She kept the exact year of her birth such a secret that it was only recently that a conclusive date, 1891, was uncovered. In her autobiography, *Dust Tracks on a Road* (1942), she claims that one morning, she "just rushed out herself," the umbilical cord being cut by a passerby. She was the fifth of eight children. Her mother was a former country schoolteacher, her father a wayfaring carpenter, Baptist preacher, mulatto from "over the creek" in Alabama. The all-black, incorporated, self-governing town of Eatonville fostered and nurtured the strong, unshakable sense of self that was later to inform Hurston's fiction and govern her life. Lucy Ann Hurston died when Zora was thirteen, and it is this fact more than any other that disrupted Hurston's schooling and her life. She was passed around from relative to relative, rejected by her father and his new wife, and forced to fend for herself. She took a number of odd jobs to make ends meet and attended school only intermittently. In June 1918 she graduated from Morgan Academy, the high school division of what is now Mor-

gan State University. In the fall of 1918 she entered Howard University, attending Howard's college preparatory program in 1918-1919 and taking university courses intermittently until 1924. At Howard she met and studied under poet Georgia Douglas Johnson and the young philosophy professor Alain Locke. She also met Herbert Sheen, who, on 19 May 1927, became her first husband. As Sheen later told Hurston's biographer, Robert Hemenway, the marriage was doomed "to an early, amicable divorce" because Hurston's career was her first priority.

Hurston had been extremely imaginative and curious as a child; these qualities inform her fiction. She records in her autobiography that as a child "I used to climb to the top of one of the huge chinaberry trees which guarded our front gate and look out over the world. The most interesting thing that I saw was the horizon. . . . It grew upon me that I ought to walk out to the horizon and see what the end of the world was like." This tendency toward the picaresque colors her work. Her main characters are dreamers who long for experience and spiritual freedom and want to break with the fixity of things. Hurston's first short story, "John Redding Goes to Sea" (May 1921), was written in this picaresque tradition and was published in *Stylus,* the official magazine of the literary club at Howard University. The protagonist of "John Redding Goes to Sea" cannot "stifle that longing for the open road, rolling seas, for peoples and countries I have never seen." The story brought the young author to the attention of sociologist Charles S. Johnson, and by January 1925 Hurston was in New York City with "$1.50, no job, no friends, and a lot of hope."

She could not have arrived in New York at a more opportune time. The Harlem Renaissance, the black literary and cultural movement of the 1920s, was already under way. Countee Cullen, James Weldon Johnson, and W. E. B. Du Bois were already in New York. Other black writers from all over—Claude McKay from Jamaica, Eric Walrond from Barbados, Langston Hughes from Kansas, Wallace Thurman from Salt Lake City, Jean Toomer and Sterling Brown from Washington, D.C., Rudolph Fisher from Rhode Island—were flocking to New York, as Hughes so aptly put it, to "express their individual dark-skinned selves." Charles S. Johnson was just founding *Opportunity: A Journal of Negro Life,* and he was interested in material that exemplified New Negro (the phrase coined by Alain Locke) philosophy. Hurston's works celebrated blackness, and she became an enthusiastic contributor to the New Negro Renaissance literary movement. The short story "Spunk" was published in *Opportunity* in June 1925 and in Locke's landmark publication *The New Negro* (1925). Hurston's play *Color Struck* was later reworked and published in the one-issue periodical *Fire!!* (1926). Hurston had made a propitious beginning, but many frustrating years were to pass before she would publish a full-length work.

At an awards dinner sponsored by *Opportunity,* Hurston's works won second prizes, but, more important, Hurston herself was introduced to two people: novelist Fannie Hurst (*Imitation of Life,* 1933), who gave Hurston a job, and Annie Nathan Meyer, who arranged for her to receive a scholarship to Barnard College. Between 1925 and 1933 Hurston saw several of her works published, including "John Redding" and the tale "Muttsy," which appeared in *Opportunity; The First One,* a play collected in Charles Johnson's *Ebony and Topaz: A Collectanea* (1927); and "The Gilded Six-Bits" in *Story* (1933).

Near the end of her studies at Barnard, Hurston came to the attention of anthropologist Franz Boas, who was then teaching at Columbia. Impressed by a term paper Hurston had written, Boas decided to make an anthropologist of her. Under Boas's tutelage, Hurston learned the value of the material she had already incorporated into her fiction. She learned to view the good old lies and racy, sidesplitting anecdotes that were being passed around among black folk every day in her native Eatonville as invaluable folklore, creative material that continued the African oral tradition and reflected the ebb and flow of a people. Encouraged by Boas and a $1,400 fellowship from the Carter G. Woodson Foundation, Hurston decided to collect some of this Afro-American lore, to record songs, customs, tales, superstitions, lies, jokes, dances, and games.

Unfortunately her southern, country subjects balked at her "Barnard" accent, and her mission failed. As she says in her autobiography: "When I went about asking, in carefully-accented Barnardese, 'Pardon me, do you know any folktales or folk-songs?' the men and women who had whole treasuries of material seeping through their pores looked at me and shook their heads. No, they had never heard of anything like that around here. Maybe it was over in the next county. Why didn't I try over there?" As a result, Hurston was not able to collect enough material "to make a flea a waltzing jacket." She was not to make the attempt again until

she accepted the patronage of Charlotte Osgood Mason.

Mason was a wealthy, white Park Avenue matron who supported Indian and Afro-American arts and any other endeavors which she felt exemplified "primitivisms." Hurston was probably introduced to Mason by Alain Locke, who seems to have functioned as Mason's emissary to black artists. When Hurston met Mason in September 1927, Mason was already the patron of Langston Hughes, Miquel Covarrubias, Louise Thompson, and Richmond Barthe. To them and to Hurston, Mason became a beneficent godmother and a surrogate parent, wielding her strong wand over them, prescribing and proscribing the courses of their lives. She was impressed by Hurston's credentials, and on 1 December 1927 she drew up a formal contract which would allow Hurston to return to the South to collect folklore. The contract promised a monthly stipend of $200, a moving picture camera, and one Ford automobile. Hurston was "faithfully" to perform her task: and "to return to Mason all of said information, data, transcripts of music, etc., which she shall have obtained." Though this opportunity was what Hurston needed, its accompanying restrictions were not. Hurston felt like a child laboring under a difficult taskmaster.

Though between 1927 and 1931 Hurston collected mounds of material from small communities in Alabama and Florida, for several years she was unable to get any of it published. With Mason's approval, she was able to feature some of it in musical revues. The bulk of it, however, remained unpublished, even after the 1931 severing of the Mason-Hurston contract (Mason continued to offer intermittent support even after the contract ended).

Hurston had gone to New York expecting to fulfill her dreams. As the correspondence between Hurston and Mason in the Alain Locke Collection at Howard University shows, however, Hurston's dreams were bitterly deferred. She was desperately trying to prove herself to Mason and to herself, and she was beginning to doubt her abilities as a writer. Feeling herself an albatross around Mason's neck, she began to consider other sources of livelihood. In one letter, she proposed opening a chicken specialty business as a way of easing the financial burden she had become to Mason. In another, she wrote: "I want to remain in your love, but I shall take nothing further from you in a material way. I shall feel that perhaps someone with a greater gift deserves your help more than I. . . . I feel justified in accepting from you only if you

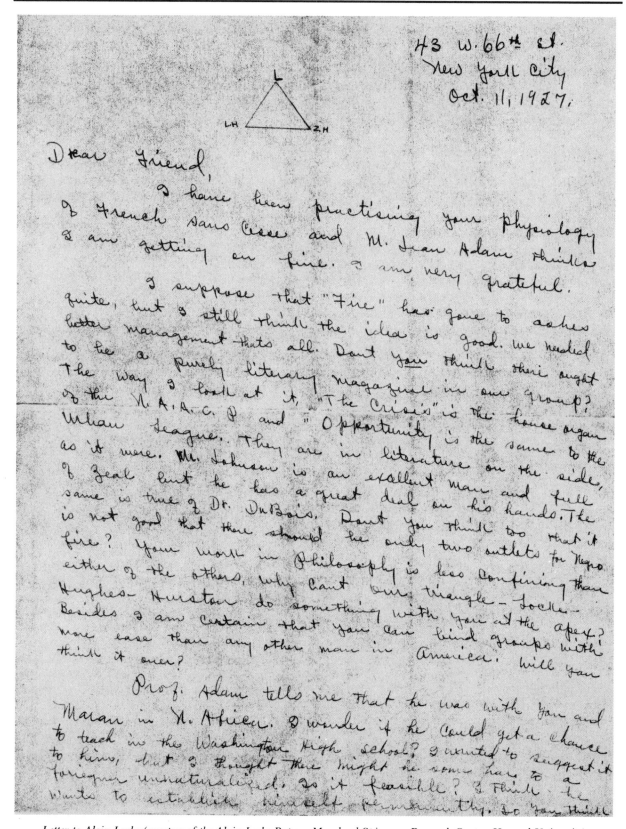

Letter to Alain Locke (courtesy of the Alain Locke Papers, Moorland-Spingarn Research Center, Howard University)

are fostering ability. If I am convinced that I have nothing the world wants then you are too high for my mediocrity to weigh down."

Fortunately Hurston's musical revues received good notices; unfortunately, they generated little money. Still, there was one flattering response to one of these revues, *The Great Day:* "George Antheil, the French composer, paid me the compliment of saying I would be the most stolen-from Negro in the world for the next ten years at least. He said that this sort of thievery is unavoidable. Unpleasant, of course, but at the bottom a tribute to one's originality." *The Great Day,* which was first performed at the John Golden Theatre on 10 January 1932, was, like her other musical revues (staged between 1931 and 1935), Hurston's attempt to bring pure black folk culture to both northern and southern audiences. What she had not yet been able to publish, she was able to present on stage with authentic folk characters. Much of the basis for the script of *The Great Day* may be found in Hurston's *Mules and Men* (1935).

By 6 January 1932 Hurston was working with the Creative Literature Department of Rollins College at Winter Park, Florida, in an effort to produce a concert program of Negro art. Though she produced a successful program, her personal problems only increased. She was intermittently ill, plagued by a painful stomach ailment which was to trouble her until her death. She wrote to Mason that she had "little food, no toothpaste, no stockings, needed shoes badly, no soap." Apparently little had changed for Hurston since her penurious arrival in New York seven years earlier.

She returned to New York only to have Locke, in his role as Mason's emissary, suggest that she return south to find work. She returned to Eatonville where the pastoral atmosphere worked wonders, and Hurston was soon feeling "renewed like the eagle." She found time to compose a play, "Mule Bone," with Langston Hughes, but a rift developed after Hurston tried to have the comedy staged before Hughes had completed his work on it. Meantime, Hurston's contact with George Antheil was paying off. In the fall of 1931 Antheil, now acting as the amanuensis of Nancy Cunard, asked Hurston to contribute some folklore essays for Cunard's *Negro: An Anthology—1931-1933* (1934). Hurston complied with six essays: "Characteristics of Negro Expression," "Conversions and Visions," "The Sermon," "Mother Catherine," "Uncle Monday," and "Spirituals and Neo-Spirituals." All six were subsequently published in the anthology.

Hurston was happy about these publications, but she still had not published a book. She had submitted her "story book"—her cache from her folklore-collecting days—to various publishers but none had been interested enough to publish it. She had to publish a short story, "The Gilded Six-Bits," and her first novel, *Jonah's Gourd Vine* (1934), before the "story book" would get a serious reading.

"The Gilded Six-Bits" is the best short story in the Hurston canon and it is the one most frequently anthologized today. It has more depth than the other stories, its characters are more developed, and its dialect has much of the texture apparent in the novels. Like most of Hurston's works, it explores the marriage relationship and its attendant difficulties. The marriage between Missie and Joe Banks epitomizes the pastoral and all that is right with a simple, country, edenic existence. It is threatened, however, by a city slicker who seems to have realized everyone's dreams and who snares Missie Banks with his "gold." The Bankses survive this invasion of their small paradise and reconcile themselves to their humble surroundings. They now know that the promises of the city and of the open road are often gilded and that, for the fulfillment of their dreams, they must fall back upon themselves.

When "The Gilded Six-Bits" appeared in *Story* in 1933, Hurston's fate was already decided. Bertram Lippincott of Lippincott publishers had read the story in manuscript and had written to know if Hurston was writing a novel. She was not but said that she was, moved from Eatonville to Sanford, Florida, and sat down to write "Big Nigger," published as *Jonah's Gourd Vine* (1934). Hurston claims in *Dust Tracks* that the notion for *Jonah's Gourd Vine* had been in her head since 1929 but "the idea of attempting a book seemed so big, that I gazed at it in the quiet of the night, but hid it away from even myself in daylight." For one of the few times in her life, she was afraid to strike out on her own. She wanted to tell a story about "a man," but "Negroes were supposed to write about the Race Problem." Fortunately, she wrote her story, and the novel was published the first week of May 1934. Lippincott was pleased with the novel and wrote to Carl Van Vechten, a mutual friend, that he felt the book "a really important contribution to the literature on the American Negro." The novel sold well and was even recommended by the Book-of-the-Month Club for May. Reviewers were impressed by the novel's rich language, "its compelling beauty and deep passion." Many of the reviewers, however, missed the essence of the story.

Hurston in the late 1930s

Jonah's Gourd Vine is an impressive first novel. Set in various parts of Florida, the novel centers around John Buddy Pearson, a likable but exasperating character, modeled in part after Hurston's own father. Though a Baptist minister, John all too frequently feels the temptations of life tugging at his sleeves. He spends his Sundays in the pulpit as a holy man, but he spends Mondays through Saturdays living the adulterous life of an ordinary one. Hurston wrote to James Weldon Johnson on 16 April 1934: "I see a preacher as a man outside of his pulpit and so far as I am concerned he should be free to follow his bent as other men. He becomes the voice of the spirit when he ascends the rostrum." The plot turns on Pearson's attempts to live this double life in a community where ministers are supposed to be above the common man and thus above reproach.

John does not understand the objections of his parishioners and refuses to live the life they prescribe for him. Through careful characterization, Hurston makes a strong case for Pearson. He

is obviously the product of a philosophy which recognizes no difference between the material and spiritual realms. Larry Neal explained it best in his introduction to the 1971 reprint of the novel. What Hurston gives us in *Jonah's Gourd Vine*, says Neal, are "two distinctly different cultural attitudes toward the concept of spirituality. The one springs from a formerly enslaved communal society, non-Christian in background where there is really no clear dichotomy between the world of spirit and the world of flesh. The other attitude is clearly more rigid, being a blend of Puritan concepts and the fire-and-brimstone imagery of the white evangelical tradition." John's problems, then, are caused by his inability to reconcile himself to the society in which he must live. The real tragedy, notes Nick Aaron Ford (*The Contemporary Negro Novel*, 1936), is that John never really discovers "the cultural dilemma that created his frustration. His rise to religious prominence and financial ease is but a millstone around his neck. He is held back by some unseen cord which seems to be tethered to his racial heritage. Life crushes him almost to death, but he comes out of the mills with no greater insight into the deep mysteries which surround him."

Other critics have focused upon the inconsistent imagery of Jonah's gourd vine in the novel and Hurston's failure to produce a work whose parts all work together to produce a unified whole. In spite of these problems, however, the novel's theme is universal, its handling of it impressive. As Robert Hemenway remarks, "Although the sum may be less than the parts, the parts are remarkable indeed."

After *Jonah's Gourd Vine,* the "story book," called *Mules and Men,* appeared. Bertram Lippincott liked *Mules and Men* but thought it too short for publication. He wanted a $3.50 book, 180 pages more than the 65,000 words Hurston had submitted. To lengthen the book, Hurston added the "between stories conversation and business" and a condensed article on hoodoo she had written in 1931 for the *Journal of American Folklore.* The book was finally published in 1935.

As folklore, *Mules and Men* offers invaluable insight into a people and a way of life. As Boas explains in his foreword to the volume, "To the student of cultural history the material is valuable not only by giving the Negro's reaction to every day events, to his emotional life, his humor and passions, but it throws into relief also the peculiar amalgamation of African and European tradition which is so important for understanding historically the character of American Negro life, with its strong African background in the West Indies, the importance of which diminishes with increasing distance from the south."

The last third of the book, in essence, the hoodoo article, has drawn considerable attention to Hurston. Here Hurston chronicles her many experiences with the hoodoo culture in New Orleans. In some cases she apprenticed herself to local hoodoo doctors and was able to learn a number of "spells" with which she later threatened her second husband. According to *Mules and Men* Hurston found the practice of hoodoo to be widespread, "burning with a flame in America with all the intensity of a suppressed religion."

Despite its undeniable value *Mules and Men* was not favorably reviewed by a number of critics, most of them black. Sterling Brown found the picture it presented "too pastoral, with only a bit of grumbling about hard work, or a few slave anecdotes that turn the tables on old marster. . . . *Mules and Men* should be more bitter, it would be nearer the total truth." Harold Preece, a white radical,

attacked Hurston, saying, "When a Negro author describes her race with such a servile term as 'Mules and Men' critical members of the race must necessarily evaluate the author as a literary climber." Hurston certainly wanted to succeed, but that she omitted the bitter tone of her black subjects from *Mules and Men* for this reason is by no means clear. It is probably nearer the truth to say that Hurston sought to capture the sometimes happy, affirmative side of black life, to show that the picture of blacks being "saturated with our sorrows" was a partial, if not a false one. As she explained in *Twentieth Century Authors,* "We talk about the race problem a great deal, but go on living and laughing and striving like everyone else."

Between novels Hurston traveled the country with her musical revues. She presented *From Sun to Sun* to audiences in Florida, *The Great Day* and *Singing Steel* to audiences in Chicago. After one of the performances in Chicago she was approached by representatives of the Julius Rosenwald Foundation who offered her a fellowship to pursue a doctorate in anthropology and folklore at Columbia University. Hurston initially accepted the fellowship but soon objected to the rigorous, partly "irrelevant" schedule she was required to follow. She bristled under the restrictions and soon took off for more congenial parts.

In the fall of 1935 she joined the WPA Federal Theater Project. While working with the Project, she was awarded a Guggenheim Fellowship to collect folklore in the West Indies. By 14 April 1936 she was in the Caribbean, collecting material for her second book of folklore, *Tell My Horse* (1938). She stopped in Haiti and Kingston, Jamaica, proposing to make an exhaustive study of Obeah (magic) practices. She did much more than study magic, however, for the romantic atmosphere of the islands triggered emotions that had been "dammed up in" her since she had left the United States. Back in America she had been romantically involved with a twenty-three-year-old college student who had been a member of the cast for *The Great Day.* As usual the callings of Hurston's career were stronger than those of her heart, and she had left the young man to continue to pursue what she considered her mission in life. Fortunately, she was able to transpose her emotions into great literature, releasing on paper, in just seven weeks, what was to become her best novel, *Their Eyes Were Watching God.* Lippincott liked the story, and the book was published on 18 September 1937.

Their Eyes Were Watching God has been called "a classic of black literature, one of the best novels of the period." It is that and much more. It is a tribute to self-assertion and black womanhood, the story of a young black woman in search of self and genuine happiness, of people rather than things, the story of a woman with her eyes on the horizon. The heroine, Janie Crawford, against her better judgment, lives conventionally for much of her life. When she finds no real satisfaction in that life, she strikes out, like Huckleberry Finn, and like Hurston herself, for the territory and the possibility of a better life beyond the horizon.

Janie Crawford wants "marriage lak when you sit under a pear tree and think." The limited, noncommunicative alliances that she makes, however, desecrate this image. She sees herself as a pear tree in bloom, but she is around forty years old before she finds the right "dust-bearing bee." Before that, she marries two men who represent her grandmother's and society's ideas of success. Both husbands own or acquire property, are much older than Janie, and are conventional in their thinking, the second husband even going so far as to group women with "chilluns, and chickens, and cows," all helpless beings who need a man to think and do for them. The first marriage had been arranged by the well-meaning grandmother to provide some "protection" for Janie; the second had been Janie's own doing. Janie survives these marriages by retreating into herself. She discovers that "she had an inside and an outside and how not to mix them."

Janie realizes her "pear tree" dreams with the man who becomes her third husband. Although Vergible "Tea Cake" Woods is several years Janie's junior, he is more mature and wiser in the ways that count. Whereas Janie's other husbands had wanted to restrict Janie's participation in life, Tea Cake, a hedonist, encourages her to enjoy it to the fullest. There are no forbidden areas. The two give and take equally and, for Janie, arriving at the horizon seems imminent.

To Janie, Tea Cake is "a glance from God," the embodiment of the best life has to offer. She eagerly embraces her life with him, throwing off the shackles of womanhood and society. Though their marriage is shortened by Tea Cake's untimely death—Hurston, for reasons readers have yet to appreciate, has Janie shoot him after he is bitten by a rabid dog—Janie has lived a full life during the year and a half of the marriage. As she tells her best friend, Phoeby: "Ah been a delegate to de big 'ssociation of life. Yessuh! De Grand Lodge, de big convention of livin' is just where Ah been dis year and a half y'all ain't seen me." As she settles down to live through her memories, she has no regrets. She has seen the light—"If yuh kin see de light at daybreak, you don't keer if you die at dusk. It's so many people never seen de light at all. Ah wuz fumblin' round and God opened de door."

The novel is a powerful affirmation of life, of physical and spiritual fulfillment. Its power is in its language, its vividly emotional, folksy, often heart-rending descriptions of the day-to-day yearnings of a woman who wanted more than a house and "respectability."

Their Eyes Were Watching God was followed by the publication of *Tell My Horse* (1938), the book based on Hurston's findings in the West Indies. For various reasons, it did not sell well. Less interesting than *Mules and Men*, it tried unsuccessfully to analyze the politics of the West Indies. It was not really the book Hurston had wanted to write. Frightened by some of the rituals she had observed, she had felt it wiser to write a book that would be "safe and acceptable" rather than honest.

Beginning in fall 1939, Hurston worked for a time as a drama instructor at North Carolina College for Negroes at Durham. While there, she met Paul Green, who was working in the drama department at Chapel Hill. The two discussed the possibility of writing a play together, but they never got beyond the discussion stage. Hurston was nevertheless hard at work. Not only had she found time to marry Albert Price III, a man at least fifteen years her junior, but she had also found time to write her third novel. *Moses, Man of the Mountain* was published in November 1939.

Moses, Man of the Mountain is an ambitious amalgam of fiction, folklore, religion, and comedy, all provocatively combined. Darwin Turner calls it Hurston's "most accomplished achievement in fiction," Robert Bone, a "brilliant allegory" in the picaresque tradition, and Robert Hemenway, "one of Hurston's two masterpieces ot the late thirties," "one of the more interesting minor works in American literary history."

The book is a bold, problem-ridden reworking of the Moses legend. Hurston's Israelites appear to be American blacks, and Moses is a hoodoo man. The abundant humor these changes generate frequently clashes with the solemnity of the novel's subject. Hemenway was prompted to call the book a "noble failure," Locke, to call it "caricature instead of portraiture," and Ralph Ellison, to say that "for Negro fiction it did nothing." Hurston, writing to Edwin Grover, to whom she dedicated the book, admitted: "I have the feeling of disappointment about it. I don't think that I achieved all that I set out to do. I thought that in this book I would achieve my ideal, but it seems that I have not yet reached it. . . . It still doesn't say all that I want it to say." In spite of its problems, however, the novel is often compelling and deserves serious critical attention.

The winter of 1940-1941 found Hurston in New York contemplating what to write next. When her publisher suggested an autobiography, she at first balked at the idea—"it is too hard to reveal one's inner self, and still there is no use in writing that kind of book unless you do"—but soon settled in California with a rich friend, Katharine Mershon, to begin the book. From October 1941 to January 1942 she also found time to work as a story consultant at Paramount Studios. She revised the manuscript back in Florida, and *Dust Tracks on a Road* was published in late November 1942.

Unlike *Moses, Man of the Mountain*, the autobiography sold well and won the Anisfield-Wolf Award for its contribution to better race relations. Critics, however, found much to attack about the volume. Arna Bontemps concluded that "Miss Hurston deals very simply with the more serious aspects of Negro life in America—she ignores them," while others felt it perhaps the "best fiction she ever wrote."

Still, the book pleased many readers, for Hurston was deluged with requests for magazine articles. Soon her political views were appearing in *American Mercury, Saturday Evening Post, Negro Digest, World Telegram,* and *Reader's Digest.* Many of these essays, because of their controversial sentiments, caused friction within the black community. In the *World Telegram* article (1 February 1943), for instance, Hurston claimed that "the Jim Crow system works." Two years later, in a December 1945 *Negro Digest* article, she was "all for the repeal of every Jim Crow law in the nation here and now." Her black readers were understandably suspicious and confused. Hurston was able to repair some of the damage with the explanation she offered through an interview with the *New York Amsterdam News:* "A writer's material is controlled by publishers who think of the Negro as picturesque. . . . There is an over-simplification of the Negro. He is either pictured by the conservatives as happy, picking his banjo, or by the so-called liberals as low, miserable, and crying. The Negro's life is neither of these. Rather, it is in-between and above and below these pictures."

When World War II began, Hurston was living in Saint Augustine, Florida, teaching part-time at Florida Norman, the local black college. Later she moved to Daytona Beach where she purchased

Wanago, a houseboat, which allowed her to take scenic tours up and down the Halifax and Indian rivers. She read Marjorie Rawlings's *Cross Creek* (1942), which impressed her, and struck up a correspondence with the novelist. This relationship would later help to further Hurston's career.

Though Hurston continued to write novels, they were all rejected because they lacked the quality of her published works. No doubt the quality of these works suffered because she was "burning to write" another one, a story about "the 3000 years struggle of the Jewish Peoples for democracy and the rights of man." She eventually wrote this story under the title of "Herod the Great." The manuscript remains unpublished, however, a depressing part of the Hurston papers at the University of Florida, Gainesville.

Hurston's friendship with Rawlings resulted in Rawlings's publisher, Scribners, taking an interest in Hurston's work. By May 1947 Hurston had sold Scribners the option on a new novel, later called *Seraph on the Suwanee,* and had taken off for Honduras to write. The novel was published on 11 October 1948. Hurston's readers were in for a surprise: *Seraph on the Suwanee* was about white folks.

Set in various parts of Florida, *Seraph on the Suwanee* explores the psyche of Arvay Henson, a poor, neurotic white woman who feels that nothing good is ever going to happen to her because she does not deserve it. She must grow and learn to appreciate herself. The battle is an exasperatingly long one, for Arvay and for the reader, but Arvay emerges whole and with a positive sense of self. Hurston wrote to her editor that it was "very much by design" that the novel's characters are white and to Carl Van Vechten that "I have hopes of breaking that old silly rule about Negroes not writing about white people." She had always felt that people were people, all of whom reacted pretty much the same to the same stimuli. *Seraph on the Suwanee* was her proof of that hypothesis.

Critics have found the novel confusing and have speculated that perhaps Hurston was joining the ranks of a new group of assimilationist writers—Willard Motley, Chester Himes, and Ann Petry. Since Hurston never published another novel, it is difficult to say where her interests were tending (although the manuscript for "Herod the Great" seems to indicate her subject matter was undergoing a broadening treatment). *Seraph on the Suwanee* sold well and good things seemed to be in the offing. Those things were not to be, however; the nadir of Hurston's life was just around the corner.

Page from the manuscript for Jonah's Gourd Vine, *on the back of which Hurston drafted a letter to Bertram Lippincott (by permission of the Estate of Zora Neale Hurston; courtesy of the Schomburg Center for Research in Black Culture, the New York Public Library, Astor, Lenox and Tilden Foundations)*

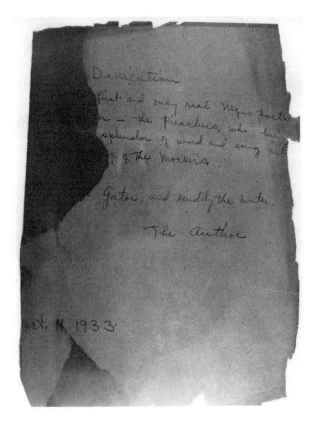

Title page and dedication page from the manuscript for Jonah's Gourd Vine, *published in 1934 (by permission of the Estate of Zora Neale Hurston; courtesy of the Schomburg Center for Research in Black Culture, the New York Public Library, Astor, Lenox and Tilden Foundations)*

On 13 September 1948 Hurston, then living in New York, was arrested and charged with committing an immoral act with a ten-year-old, the son of a woman from whom Hurston had rented a room during the winter of 1946-1947. Though Hurston was able to prove that she had been out of the country at the time of the alleged crime and the charges were subsequently dropped, the story was leaked to the press and sensational, humiliating news headlines followed. Hurston was devastated. She wrote to her friend Van Vechten that, "I care nothing for anything anymore. . . . My race has seen fit to destroy me without reason, and with the vilest tools conceived of by man so far. . . . All that I have ever tried to do has proved useless. All that I have believed in has failed me. I have resolved to die. . . . I feel hurled down a filthy privy hole." Fortunately, she did not die, though the incident took its toll. Although she continued to publish in national magazines and sold an option on another novel to Scribners, she left New York and refused to communicate with her friends.

In March 1950 she was discovered working as a maid in Rivo Alto, Florida. She claimed to be resting her mind and collecting material firsthand for a piece she intended to write about domestics; it is more probable that she needed the money.

In the winter of 1950-1951, at the invitation of friends, she moved to Belle Glade, Florida. In the spring she wrote to her literary agent that she was penniless, "just inching along like a stepped-on worm from day to day. Borrowing a little here and there." It was becoming embarrassing, however, "having to avoid folks who have made me loans so that I could eat and sleep. The humiliation is getting to be much too much for my self-respect, to look and look at the magnificent sweep of the Everglades, birds included, and keep a smile on my face." The infrequent sale of a magazine article brought temporary relief, but over the next ten years Hurston worked at odd jobs. She lived in a one-room cabin she had purchased in Eau Gallie, her stomach ailments and money problems making this period less than idyllic.

In 1952 Hurston was hired by the *Pittsburgh Courier* to cover the Ruby McCollum case; in 1956 she found work as a librarian at Patrick Air Force Base but was fired in 1957, ostensibly for having too much education for the job; in December 1957 she became a reporter for the *Fort Pierce Chronicle*, the local black weekly; and in 1958 she did some substitute teaching at Lincoln Park Academy, the black public school of Fort Pierce. These frequently humiliating jobs did not daunt Hurston's spirit. In

Zora Neale Hurston (photo by Carl Van Vechten, by permission of Joseph Solomon, the Estate of Carl Van Vechten)

1955, in a letter to the *Orlando Sentinel,* she expressed her outrage about the 1954 Supreme Court Desegregation Decision. According to Hurston it all centered around "the self-respect of my people. How much satisfaction can I get from a court order for somebody to associate with me who does not wish me near them. . . . It is a contradiction in terms to scream race pride and equality while at the same time spurning Negro teachers and self-association."

On 29 October 1959, after suffering a stroke, Hurston was forced to enter the Saint Lucie County Welfare Home. She died there on 28 January 1960 and was buried in an unmarked grave in Fort Pierce's segregated cemetery, the Garden of the Heavenly Rest. She had died in poverty, and a collection had to be taken up to pay for her funeral. As the minister said at her funeral, however, Zora Hurston had lived a rich life: "Zora Neale went about and didn't care too much how she looked. Or what she said. Maybe people didn't think so much of that. But Zora Neale, every time she went about, had something to offer. She didn't come to you empty. They said she couldn't become a writer recognized by the world. But she did it. The Miami paper said she died poor. But she died rich. She did something."

Hurston would have agreed with the minister. She had lived the good life. She had risen from obscurity, after all, to become a member of the American Folklore Society, the American Anthropological Society, American Ethnological Society, New York Academy of Sciences, the American Association for the Advancement of Science; and she was listed in the 1937 edition of *Who's Who in America*. She had been courted by political figures and, most important, she had published an exceptional body of literature. Like Janie of *Their Eyes Were Watching God,* she had seen the "light," and no amount of dusk could dim its glow. As she wrote in 1941 while working on her autobiography:

> While I am still below the allotted span of time, and notwithstanding, I feel that I have lived. I have had the joy and pain of strong friendships. I have served and been served. I have made enemies of which I am not ashamed. I have been faithless, and then I have been faithful and steadfast until the blood ran down into my shoes. I have loved unselfishly with all the ardor of a strong heart, and I have hated with all the power of my soul. What waits for me in the future? I do not know. I can't even imagine, and I am glad for that. But already, I have touched the four corners of the horizon, for from hard searching it seems to me that tears and laughter, love and hate make up the sum of life.

Interest in Hurston had diminished long before her death. Her works had been long out of print, and the literary world was being dominated by such male giants as Richard Wright, Ralph Ellison, and James Baldwin. Fortunately, however, a few readers were beginning to discover Hurston, and in the 1970s this interest mushroomed into a coterie of Hurston followers. Robert Hemenway published his valuable work, *Zora Neale Hurston: A*

Literary Biography, in 1977; Alice Walker edited *I Love Myself When I Am Laughing . . .* , a collection of Hurston's most impressive works, published in 1979; Lillie P. Howard published *Zora Neale Hurston* (1980) in the Twayne U.S. Authors series; a number of articles on Hurston appeared in literary journals; and various publishers reprinted *Their Eyes Were Watching God, Mules and Men, Jonah's Gourd Vine,* and *Dust Tracks on a Road.* The University of Florida set up a Zora Neale Hurston Fellowship in Anthropology; the City of Orlando, Florida, acknowledged Hurston's accomplishments by naming a city building after her. Today, the Hurston renaissance is in full swing. All of her published works have been or soon will be reprinted; some of the unpublished works and a collection of her letters may be available soon; several dissertations and books on Hurston are being written, including one that links her work with Alice Walker's. Hurston continues to live in her works and in the hearts and minds of those who have read them. Though her shortcomings as a writer will continue to bother those who have never written novels themselves, her honesty and power as a storyteller will one day earn her the place she deserves in the history of the American novel.

Biography:
Robert Hemenway, *Zora Neale Hurston: A Literary Biography* (Chicago: University of Illinois Press, 1977).

References:
Nick Aaron Ford, *The Contemporary Negro Novel* (Boston: Meador, 1936);
Lillie P. Howard, *Zora Neale Hurston* (Boston: Twayne, 1980);
Darwin T. Turner, *In A Minor Chord* (Carbondale: Southern Illinois University Press, 1971).

Papers:
Hurston's papers are in the James Weldon Johnson Collection, Beinecke Library, Yale University; in the Alain Locke Collection, Howard University Library, Washington, D.C.; at the University of Florida, Gainesville; and at Fisk University, Nashville, Tennessee.

Charles Spurgeon Johnson

(24 July 1893-27 October 1956)

Kathleen A. Hauke
Morris Brown College

SELECTED BOOKS: *The Negro in American Civilization* (New York: Holt, 1930);

Negro Housing: Report, President's Conference on Home Building and Home Ownership, edited by John M. Gries and James Ford (Washington, D.C.: President's Conference on Home Building and Home Ownership, 1932);

The Economic Status of Negroes (Nashville: Fisk University Press, 1933);

Shadow of the Plantation (Chicago: University of Chicago Press, 1934);

Race Relations: Adjustment of Whites and Negroes in the United States, by Johnson and Willis D. Weatherford (Boston & New York: Heath, 1934);

The Collapse of Cotton Tenancy, by Johnson, Edwin R. Embree, and W. W. Alexander (Chapel Hill: University of North Carolina Press, 1935);

A Preface to Racial Understanding (New York: Friendship Press, 1936);

The Negro College Graduate (Chapel Hill: University of North Carolina Press, 1938);

Growing Up in the Black Belt: Negro Youth in the Rural South (Washington, D.C.: American Council on Education, 1941);

Statistical Atlas of Southern Counties (Chapel Hill: University of North Carolina Press, 1941);

Patterns of Negro Segregation (New York & London: Harper, 1943; London: Gollancz, 1944);

To Stem This Tide: A Survey of Racial Tension Areas in the United States, by Johnson and others (Boston & Chicago: Pilgrim Press, 1943);

Into the Main Stream: A Survey of Best Practices in Race Relations in the South (Chapel Hill: University of North Carolina Press, 1947);

People Vs. Property: Race Restrictive Covenants in Housing, by Johnson and Herman Hodge Long (Nashville: Fisk University Press, 1947);

Education and the Cultural Crisis (New York: Macmillan, 1951).

OTHER: *Ebony and Topaz, A Collectanea*, edited by Johnson (New York: National Urban League, 1927);

"Recent Improvements in Race Relations," in *Recent Gains in American Civilization*, edited by Kirby Page (New York: Harcourt, Brace, 1928).

PERIODICAL PUBLICATION: "A Southern Negro's View of the South," *New York Times Magazine*, 25 September 1956, pp. 15, 64, 66, 67.

Charles Spurgeon Johnson (photo © by Fabian Bachrach; courtesy of the Schomburg Center for Research in Black Culture, the New York Public Library, Astor, Lenox and Tilden Foundations)

Charles Spurgeon Johnson, literary entrepreneur, sociologist, and president of Fisk University for a decade, "single-handedly propelled" the Harlem Renaissance into being, according to Langston Hughes. Hughes's evaluation of the man who founded and edited the National Urban League's *Opportunity* magazine and sponsored literary contests and celebratory dinners for the young writers and artists of the early 1920s attests to Johnson's role in shaping one of the most impressive cultural movements in American history. As the chief black American sociologist of his period, Johnson also wrote the scholarly books that documented the causes of race riots, the effects of racism on the personalities of black youth, and the need for blacks to become a part of the mainstream of American life. As president of Fisk University from 1947 to 1956, Johnson joined in the administrative effort to make Fisk "the Harvard of Negro colleges," thereby sculpting the school into such a bastion of middle-class black behavior that such later well-known Fisk students as Julius Lester and Nikki Giovanni could not find a comfortable place in it.

Johnson was born on 24 July 1893 to Winifred Branch and the Reverend Charles Henry Johnson of Bristol, Virginia. His diminutive preacher father, through force of personality and the Bible, had once so shamed a lynch mob that lynching ceased in Bristol. Reverend Johnson, born a slave, had been tutored by his master in Latin, Greek, Hebrew, and English and American literature. The young Charles read the books in his father's library; this liberal exposure to literature may have been responsible for sparking the interest that spurred his involvement with the writers of the 1920s.

He was also early influenced toward his career in sociology by the people in the barbershop where he swept the floor. Observing how the black barbers and white customers talked and behaved toward each other—their codes and patterns—Johnson was "neither pleased nor angered, just curious," his friend Edwin Embree writes, and from that time "he made a business of being curious." Edgar A. Toppin asserts that "he developed habits of seeking to understand rather than condemn," habits that served him in good stead in his sociological studies.

Johnson attended Wayland Academy between 1909 and 1913 and received a B.A. from Virginia Union University in Richmond in 1916. At the University of Chicago, where he pursued a doctorate and studied under famed sociologist Robert E. Park, adopting his theory of race relations, Johnson also formulated the philosophy that would inspire his nurturing of the Harlem Renais-

Charles Spurgeon Johnson

sance. He came to believe with Park that the races would eventually be assimilated, that interracial friendships were the solvent that would finally "cut across and eventually undermine all barriers of racial segregation and caste." His engineering of ways for blacks and whites to come together during the Renaissance was a literal carrying out of his philosophy.

Returning from Europe, where he had served as a sergeant-major in the army during World War I, Johnson was caught in 1919 in the crossfire of the Chicago race riot. This incident served as the direct catalyst for his two-pronged effort to improve the American racial climate. The first prong involved employing scholarly, scientific methods in gathering information about the black community. Such empirical, sociological research—done in an objective spirit—would educate the public and suggest to decision makers appropriate courses for social action. The second prong entailed inducing attitudinal changes through the arts. Blacks had been excluded from almost every phase of American life except the arts, making it a "small crack in the wall of racism" that would become for Johnson "a fissure worth trying to widen."

Johnson joined the Urban League in Chicago and openly pursued change through his scholarly work. More covertly, he planned to encroach upon the cultural field by founding *Opportunity*, a monthly magazine and official organ of the Urban League, in 1923. Arna Bontemps recollected that Johnson's "subtle sort of scheming mind had arrived at the feeling that literature was a soft spot . . . in the armour of the nation, and he set out to exploit it." *Opportunity* was designed to "encourage the reading of literature both by Negro authors and about Negro life, . . . to foster a market for Negro writers . . . to bring these writers into contact with the general world of letters to which they have been . . . timid and inarticulate strangers; to stimulate and foster a type of writing . . . which shakes itself free of deliberate propaganda and protest." Johnson viewed the journal as providing an alternative to the *Crisis,* which, though it published literature, was much more oriented toward social protest.

During this busy time, Johnson was also becoming a family man. He had married Marie Antoinette Burgette on 6 November 1920, and their sons, Charles Jr. and Robert, had been born in 1921 and 1922. A third son, Jeh Vincent, was born about the time *Opportunity* was launched, and a daughter, Patricia Marie, was born in 1924.

Johnson's launching of *Opportunity*, which included the alerting of white editors and publishers to black artists and the funding of prizes for the best poetry, fiction, and visual art submitted annually, was one of the primary contributing catalysts in the creation of the Harlem Renaissance. Johnson asked his secretary, Ethel Nance, to make dossiers on black creative folk, to identify the people of promise and then entice them to come to Harlem where they could spur one another on. Sensitive to the artistic temperament and the importance of editorial reassurance, Johnson responded to submissions to *Opportunity* with utmost tact, so that even rejections encouraged. He turned down an overly long story from Angelina Grimké, after he had become "unwrapt from its fascination," telling her, "You have achieved a rare thing: that tragedy of life which escapes the melodra-

matic; characters which are real, unpretentious and lovable; [and] . . . good sound humor, no special pleading—all these with a delightfully competent touch."

Johnson also enlisted the aid of other prominent people in the encouragement and preservation of black arts. He recognized a kindred spirit in Arthur Schomburg, the Puerto Rican-born bank messenger who collected books and artifacts by black people. Schomburg assisted Johnson in planning the first *Opportunity* awards banquet, at which Jessie Fauset's *There is Confusion* (1924) formed the focus of celebration. Many of the aspiring young writers, such as Gwendolyn Bennett, Langston Hughes, and Countee Cullen, attended that banquet and, later, others like it. There they met many of the blacks and whites who could assist them in furthering their careers.

Johnson also succeeded in getting Caspar Holstein, a well-known and wealthy numbers banker, to put up the money for the *Opportunity* prizes. In 1926, when Arna Bontemps won *Opportunity*'s Alexander Pushkin Prize for poetry, Holstein had given $1,000 for prizes. Johnson was able, therefore, to reach the publishers, editors, writers, and less directly literary personages in his pursuit of changing minds through cultural achievements.

The first *Opportunity* prizes were perhaps the most successful. In subsequent years there were more contestants, but the submissions were of a lesser quality, causing Johnson's enthusiasm to wane. In 1927, the year before he left the Urban League, Johnson gathered what he judged to be the best of the work published in *Opportunity* and collected it in *Ebony and Topaz, A Collectanea.* The volume contains poetry (including some from undergraduates around the country), short fiction, drama, essays, translations, paintings, drawings, and facsimiles. Most of the familiar artists and writers had work in the volume, including Gwendolyn Bennett, Arna Bontemps, Sterling A. Brown, Countee Cullen, Aaron Douglas, Langston Hughes, Zora Neale Hurston, and Helene Johnson. Special features included essays by E. Franklin Frazier on "racial self-expression," Guy B. Johnson on John Henry, Alain Locke on the "New Negro Renaissance," Julia Peterkin on Gullah culture, Dorothy Scarborough on black folk song, and Arthur Schomburg on Juan Latino. It also included a long poem by Elizabeth Barrett Browning and a short play by Paul Green. The volume is a diverse sampling of Johnson's conception of Afro-American artistic pursuits in the 1920s and of works from nonblacks writing on topics about blacks.

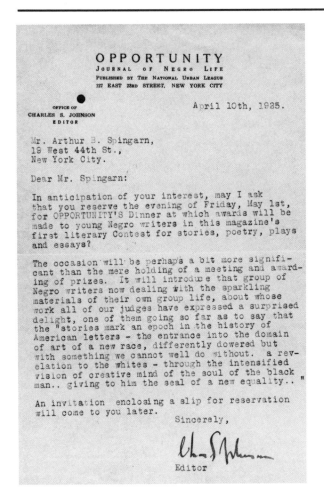

Opportunity's first contest-awards dinner was a landmark event at which both new and established black writers were introduced for the first time (courtesy of the Arthur B. Spingarn Collection, Moorland-Spingarn Research Center, Howard University)

Johnson left the Urban League in 1928 and went to Nashville, Tennessee, to direct Fisk University's Sociology Department. There he pursued his sociological research and set up a "Fisk machine" comparable to that which Booker T. Washington had set in motion at Tuskegee at the turn of the century. He sat on practically every board that considered black applications for fellowships or grants. U.S. Presidents Hoover, Roosevelt, Truman, and Eisenhower enlisted him for service on many commissions. He produced several volumes of reports, many of them praised for the quality of the research as well as the facility in writing.

Harlem Renaissance writers Hughes and Bontemps, the latter librarian at Fisk during Johnson's tenure, joked back and forth about Johnson's vanity and power. Bontemps noted in late 1948, "CSJ rolled out in a new 1949 Lincoln . . . the biggest and best of the brand!" Later, Hughes wrote Bontemps, "Ask Charles S. Johnson if he has an ivory tower for me there at Fisk. I think I eventually would like to retire from both public and private life." In 1955 when many black artists were being

Charles Spurgeon Johnson (courtesy of the Rose McClendon Memorial Collection of Photographs of Celebrated Negroes by Carl Van Vechten, Moorland-Spingarn Research Center, Howard University)

sent overseas by the U.S. State Department on "cultural missions," remuneration at "all expenses and 700 bucks per month!," Hughes teased Bontemps, "Why don't you get Charles S. to get you such a trip? You look cultural." The joking did not connote disrespect; later, when Hughes was traveling in the Caribbean in 1959, he wrote Bontemps that the thinkers of Trinidad "give Charles S. Johnson's lectures there credit for bringing to power the current crop of political intellectuals."

Yet Johnson's power and his scholarly reputation did not transcend his blackness in the United States, and he suffered acutely from the usual racial insults accorded blacks. Attending a convention of the American Sociological Association once, he was told to use the back entrance. Deputized by the League of Nations to investigate reports of sales of Liberian boys to Portuguese planters on the island of Fernando Po, in 1930, he had to travel third class. No shipping line would sell him better accommodations because of objections by white passengers. St. Clair Drake spoke of the severe migraine headaches Johnson suffered when he attended countless conferences on interracial cooperation. Joe Richardson, Fisk historian, said that "a different reality intruded as soon as the black professor left the campus library and boarded the back of the bus to go downtown."

Nevertheless Johnson persisted with his research, proving that black people were not simply "victims," but "many-sided people," struggling at times but also possessing "resiliency, endurance, cultural strength, and a sense of community." His contributions have certainly outlived his discomfiture.

The awards he received are also a testament to the esteem in which he was held. He received an honorary doctorate from Virginia Union University in 1928 and the William E. Harmon gold medal "for Distinguished Achievement among Negroes in Science" in 1930. He won the Wolf-Anisfield Award for *The Negro College Graduate* in 1938 and a second honorary doctorate from Howard University in 1941. The University of Glasgow, Scotland, awarded him a Doctor of Laws in 1951 and Columbia University awarded him a Doctor of Letters. He was also the Second Distinguished American named to the Ebony Hall of Fame in 1957.

Johnson moved from the chairmanship of the sociology department to the presidency of Fisk University in 1947 and stayed there until his sudden death nine years later. He died of a heart attack in the Louisville, Kentucky, train station when he was

Johnson being installed as President of Fisk University by L. Hollingsworth Wood, Vice-Chairman of the school's Board of Trustees. The sixth president of the all-black university, Johnson was the first black man to hold that position (courtesy of the Schomburg Center for Research in Black Culture, the New York Public Library, Astor, Lenox and Tilden Foundations).

on his way to a Fisk board of trustees meeting in New York.

Although Johnson never resumed the central literary role he played during the Harlem Renaissance, his place in black literary history as father of the renaissance is secure. His literary voice stood for excellence, thoroughness, clarity, and nurturance. Without his quietly aggressive assistance, many of the voices who shaped the Afro-American literary canon beyond the renaissance would not have come into prominence. His philosophy of using art to improve race relations paved the way for the more militant position of using art for the social, moral, and political purposes that characterized the writers of the 1960s.

Bibliography:

George L. Gardner, *Bibliography of Charles S. Johnson's Published Writings* (Nashville: Fisk University Library, 1960).

References:

Jervis Anderson, *This Was Harlem: A Cultural Portrait, 1900-1950* (New York: Farrar, Straus & Giroux, 1981);

Ernest W. Burgess, "Charles S. Johnson: Social Scientist and Race Relations," *Phylon* (Fourth Quarter 1956): 317;

Edwin R. Embree, "A Scholar and a Gentleman," in *Thirteen Against the Odds* (New York: Viking, 1945), pp. 47-70;

Patrick J. Gilpin, "Charles S. Johnson: Entrepreneur of the Harlem Renaissance," in *Harlem*

Renaissance Remembered, edited by Arna Bontemps (New York: Dodd, Mead, 1972), pp. 215-246;

Nathan I. Huggins, *Harlem Renaissance* (New York: Oxford University Press, 1971), pp. 4-5, 27-29;

John O. Killens, "Another Time When Black Was Beautiful," *Black World,* 20 (November 1970);

David Levering Lewis, "Dr. Johnson's Friends: Civil Rights By Copyright," *Massachusetts Review,* 20 (Autumn 1979): 501-519;

Lewis, *When Harlem Was In Vogue* (New York: Knopf, 1981);

Ethel Ray Nance, "The New York Arts Renaissance, 1924-1926," *Negro History Bulletin,* 31 (April 1968);

Ralph L. Pearson, "Charles S. Johnson: The Urban League Years, a Study of Race Leadership," Ph.D. dissertation, Johns Hopkins University, 1970;

Joe M. Richardson, *A History of Fisk University, 1865-1946* (University: University of Alabama Press, 1980);

Richard Robbins, "Charles S. Johnson," in *Black Sociologists: Historical and Contemporary Perspectives,* edited by James E. Blackwell and Morris Janowitz (Chicago: University of Chicago Press, 1974);

Nancy Joan Weiss, " 'Not Alms, But Opportunity': A History of the National Urban League, 1910-1940," Ph.D. dissertation, Harvard University, 1969.

Papers:
There are collections of Johnson's papers in the Special Collections Department at Fisk University Library, the Armistead Research Center at Dillard University, New Orleans, and the Schomburg Center for Research in Black Culture, New York Public Library. The Library of Congress is the official depository of the National Urban League papers, among which are materials relating to Johnson.

Georgia Douglas Johnson

(10 September 1886-May 1966)

Winona Fletcher
Indiana University

BOOKS: *The Heart of a Woman and Other Poems* (Boston: Cornhill, 1918);

Bronze: A Book of Verse (Boston: Brimmer, 1922);

Plumes: A Play in One Act (New York & London: French, 1927);

An Autumn Love Cycle (New York: Vinal, 1928);

Share My World: A Book of Poems (N.p., 1962).

PLAY PRODUCTIONS: *Blue Blood*, New York, 1927;

Plumes, Brooklyn, Central YMCA, 28 February 1928;

Frederick Douglass Leaves For Freedom, Los Angeles, New Negro Theatre, 1940.

OTHER: Robert T. Kerlin, *The Voice of the Negro, 1919,* includes poems by Johnson (New York: Dutton, 1921);

Frederick Douglass and *William and Ellen Craft,* in *Negro History in Thirteen Plays,* edited by Willis Richardson and May Miller (Washington, D.C.: Associated, 1935);

Introduction to *Second Movement,* by Robert E. Fennell (Hawkins, Tex.: Privately printed, 1962);

A Sunday Morning in the South, in *Black Theatre, U.S.A.: Forty-five Plays by Black American Playwrights, 1847-1974,* edited by James V. Hatch and Ted Shine (New York: Free Press, 1974).

PERIODICAL PUBLICATIONS: "Omnipresence," *Voice of the Negro,* 2 (June 1905): 387; "A Song of Courage," *Liberator,* 7 (September 1924): 23.

Georgia Douglas Johnson

After a period of nearly sixty years, the judgment of knowledgeable critics has coalesced to grant Georgia Douglas Camp Johnson, poet, playwright, and composer, a place among the best writers of the early twentieth century. Omitted from most popular anthologies and textbooks, even when her black contemporaries gained admission, she was labeled "minor" primarily because as a black woman of the genteel school she was overshadowed by what J. Saunders Redding calls the "masculine literature of the 'New Negro.'" In another sense, Johnson lived in the shadow of genteel poet Sara Teasdale, with whom she was most frequently compared at the beginning of her career. Both poets wrote romantic, conventional verse, usually designated "small poems" because of their length (four to eight lines with occasional poems of up to fourteen lines); both wrote lyrics that were drawn from simple introspection and instinct; neither concerned herself with religion or metaphysics. However, Johnson's uniqueness lies in her essence and development as a black poet whose writing reveals an awareness of the sociocultural and racial conditions of her own life that affected her creativity. Today Johnson's poetry is often variously assessed as "exquisite utterance," "lyric sensibility," "sincere simplicity," "sharply chiselled," "passionate and plaintive," and "delicate and clear."

As one of the first modern black female poets to gain recognition, Johnson, whose collections of verse were published between 1918 and 1930, is an important link in the chain of American black female lyric poets. Johnson's life, like that of her better-known contemporary Langston Hughes, spanned most of the literary movements of this century, and her Washington, D.C., home was the popular gathering place of early Harlem Renaissance figures such as Hughes, Countee Cullen, Alain Locke, Jessie Fauset, S. Randolph Edmonds, and Willis Richardson. Johnson was a prolific writer; over 200 of her poems were published in her four collections; other poems and several dramas have appeared in journals and books primarily edited by blacks. Cedric Dover, in a 1952 *Crisis* essay of tribute to Johnson, says "her universal values, her influence on people far removed from her environment, arise from a sensitive response to her own scene. . . . she knows . . . she has heard their voices and because she has heard we were helped to hear. . . . She has given us something of her own poetry and courage—a great achievement which the passing years and the 'new poetry' must not be allowed to obscure."

Johnson was born to George and Laura Jackson Camp in Atlanta, Georgia, on 10 September 1886. She was educated in the public schools of the city and at Atlanta University, and she went on to attend Howard University in Washington, D.C., and Oberlin Conservatory of Music in Ohio. Her marriage to Henry Lincoln Johnson, a distinguished Washington lawyer and politician, produced two sons: Henry Lincoln, Jr., and Peter Douglas. Before Henry Johnson, Sr.'s death in 1925, his appointment as Recorder of Deeds under President Taft brought the Johnsons to Washington as active pioneers in the city's social and political life. Johnson was a leader and energetic participant in most of the groups and organizations in the Washington area committed to concerns of women and minorities. She combined her literary career with several types of government jobs. At the time of the publication of her third book, for instance, she was working in the Department of Labor as Commissioner of Conciliation under Calvin Coolidge.

Johnson wrote few self-revelations; she does, however, imply the autobiographical basis of her writing. For instance, in "The Poet Speaks" she says:

How much living have you done?
From it the patterns that you weave
Are imaged;
Your own life is your totem pole.
Your yard of cloth
Your living.

Many of the real day-to-day details of Georgia Douglas Johnson's life remain private. Until the recovery of her papers, which all her peers agreed literally overflowed from her home, brief sketches guardedly told by close friends or students provide the bulk of information available to researchers. From these sketches Johnson's dynamic, if idiosyncratic, personality emerges. Rosey Pool, who interviewed Johnson at her home in preparation for her 1962 book, *Beyond the Blues*, wrote of the then seventy-five-year-old Johnson: she "lives in Washington amidst the most chaotic amassment of usable and broken-down typewriters, television sets, radios, furniture and piles of books and papers, among which she finds any single one with unerring instinct. Her gait and talk make one think of an ancient Greek oracle, and the poems written during the renaissance thirty years or more ago are still very much herself: 'Consider me a malady that served its simple time,/or but the residue of fire that settles in the urn.' " Poet May Miller described how she would draw a favorite little stool from amid the mass of tangible objects and live creatures (stray cats and dogs) in Johnson's home to sit attentively at her peer's feet while she watched in amazement as Johnson selected papers effortlessly and with unfailing accuracy from her unique filing system: notes stuck along the panes of her French doors. A story that appeared in the *Pittsburgh Courier* on 7 July 1928, when Johnson was forty-one, under the headline "Georgia Douglas Johnson Fears She Won't Have Time to Complete All of The Work She Has Planned," reveals the abundant and kaleidoscopic nature of Johnson's creativity. She had, she said, five books "that could, on short notice, be prepared for the publishers, if she had time to do it: 'The Torch,' inspirational bits written by famous authors, culled from a lifetime of reading. . . . The work now reposes in thirty different scrapbooks . . . 'The Life and Times of Henry Lincoln Johnson' . . . the third embryonic volume is 'Rainbow Silhouettes,' short stories of mixed bloods. . . . The fourth is 'The Autumn Love Cycle,' a complete story told in poetry; the fifth will be a volume composed of prose sketches written in the colored press under the heading, 'Homely Philosophy.' " Only *An Autumn Love Cycle* has been published.

On the occasion of accepting the *Opportunity* first prize for her 1927 play, *Plumes,* Johnson offered an explanation for the multidirectional nature of her literary work: "I write because I love to write. . . . Long years ago when the world was new for me, I dreamed of being a composer—wrote songs, many of them. The words took fire and the music smouldered and so, following the lead of friends and critics, I turned my face toward poetry and put my songs away for a while. Then came drama. I was persuaded to try it and found it a living avenue—and yet—the thing left most unfinished, less exploited, first relinquished, is still nearest my heart and most dear."

In an introduction to her poems which Countee Cullen selected for his 1927 anthology, *Caroling Dusk,* Johnson narrates the early experiences that led her to a literary career:

> Many years ago a little yellow girl in Atlanta, Georgia, came across a poem in a current paper that told of a rose struggling to bloom in a window in New York City. A child tended this flower and her whole life was wrapt [sic] up in its fate. This poem was written by William Stanley Braithwaite, years before the world knew how marvelous was his mind. Some one told the reader of these lines that the writer was colored and straightway [sic] she began to walk upward toward him.

Johnson goes on to relate how "Dean Kelly Miller at Howard University saw some of her poetic efforts and. . . . directed her to send something" to his friend Braithwaite in Boston. She did so and received approbation from him for her writing. Jessie Redmon Fauset, who was then teaching in Washington, Johnson further narrates, helped her collect her work for her first book, *The Heart of a Woman;* Braithwaite wrote the introduction.

While Johnson's poetry had been published at least as early as 1905 ("Omnipresence" in the *Voice of the Negro,* June 1905), and in the *Crisis* as early as 1916, *The Heart of a Woman and Other Poems* was her formal introduction to the reading public as one of the first black feminist poets. Braithwaite described the collection as "intensely feminine," which, he said, "means more than anything else that they are deeply human."

The sixty-two short poems collected in *The Heart of a Woman* are barely organized by content. In a conventional approach to emotion, Johnson focuses each lyric on a single feeling, as in such poems as "Sympathy," "Contemplation," "Isolation," "Retrospect," and "Fantasy." The predominant tone of the collection is serious, if not somber, and Johnson explores her subjects through metaphorical language that is sometimes clichéd—"cry of the heart," "silent tomb," "phantom happiness," "trembling lip"—and sometimes original—"dead leaves in the heart." As in the poems of Braithwaite, there is no hint of race, and no reflection of the turmoil going on in the world; Johnson's ferment is subjective.

The title poem of the volume is also the first poem in it, suggesting that it was intended to set a particular tone for the collection. Johnson depicts "the heart of a woman" as a roaming figure, alien to its environment, which finds its place about the "turrets and vales" of life; disappointed with exploration, it returns to a reclusive existence ("enters some alien cage") and "breaks, breaks, breaks on the sheltering bars." The heart of a woman, therefore, is presented as a pathetic creature unable to secure for itself a place in the world; it is attracted to withdrawing from that harsh, unnurturing environment.

"The Heart of a Woman" does coincide with the flights of imagination characteristic of the poems Johnson has composed. They abound with dreams; nature (its beauty and its changes); love or pain too acute for expression; wordless kisses; loneliness, seclusion, and isolation; the transitoriness of existence; lack of fulfillment; and brief moments of bliss. In many instances an unidentified speaker expresses a sentiment that is too vague or incomplete to be focused on for long. "Where?," for example, suggests that the speaker's love is unrequited and that she has refused to accept that condition, or that the lover has died and she will not accept his demise.

> I called you through the silent night
> Across the brooding deep,
> I sought you in the shadowland
> From out the world—asleep.
> ....
> Though voiceless, you will hear my call,
>   Your soul will heed my cry,
> Will rise, and mock the prison where
>   Your bones recumbent lie.

In "Foredoom" the woman's situation is even less specific—"Her life was dwarfed, and wed to blight,/ Her very days were shades of night." Beyond the general conclusions that wrong choices for living have been made or that some exterior constriction has been forced upon the woman, the poem remains suggestive rather than specific.

With titles such as "Query," "Pent," "Despair," "Recompense," and "Illusions," the poems depict a poet whose concerns, though they may be genuine, are distanced, through the use of abstractions, from the reader. For example, in "Query," the question "Is she the sage who will not sip/The cup love presses to her lip?" is less about a particular plight of a particular individual than it is about an abstract approach to the effects of love. "Good-bye to the hopes that were never fulfilled,/Good-bye to the fond dreams that failed" ("Despair") and "Who has not built his castles in the free and open air?" ("Illusions") are again less the representations of specific plights than they are reflections of what the poet perceives to be proper poetic pursuits. The majority of the poems focus on general virtues or basic human conditions; even though there may be a legitimacy about them, they fail to engage the reader beyond first readings. There is little to encourage a return to the poems for further meditation and contemplation. For William Stanley Braithwaite to have called the poems "intensely feminine" is at best a misnomer and at worst a condescending conception of "the heart of a woman."

"Poetry," a poem near the end of the collection, may account for the approaches to the sentiments expressed in the volume. It asserts: "Behold! the living thrilling lines/That course the blood like madd'ning wines." If indeed poetry is an almost uncontainable expression that leaps "with scintillating spray/Across the guards of ecstasy," then perhaps it is impossible for the poet ever to reduce those sentiments to the specificity of graphic reality; the power of the "artesian well" that "entwines the fragments of a heart" keeps the poet at what she envisions to be a higher plane of thought and conceptualization than clarity would warrant. The metaphor also coincides with the heart of a woman folding up its "little dreams" and retreating from the realities of the world.

Robert T. Kerlin suggested in 1923 that there was a "tragic mystery" underlying Johnson's writing. The poignancy of her poetry, which is elsewhere called "autumnal" and tragic, Kerlin views as witness to Johnson's bruised spirit. Poems such as "Smothered Fires"—"A woman with a burning flame/Deep covered through the years/With ashes—ah! she hid it deep,/And smothered it with tears"—cause Kerlin to view *The Heart of a Woman* as "the saddest book produced by her race." He further insists that "the lyric cry has not been more piercing in anything written on American soil, piercing all the more for the perfect restraint, the sure artistry. It was a heart surcharged with sorrow in which these pearls of poesy took shape from secret wounds. The heart of one woman speaks in them for thousands in America, else inarticulate."

By the time Johnson's second volume of poetry, *Bronze* (1922), appeared, she had joined the circle of black American thinkers who were bridging the genteel age and the age of the New Negro: W. E. B. Du Bois, Countee Cullen, Sterling Brown, Benjamin Brawley, Angelina Grimké, Zora Neale Hurston, Langston Hughes, James Weldon Johnson, Claude McKay, and others. While she remained intensely concerned with the status of the heart of a woman, that organ had become for her "the heart of a colored woman aware of her social problems and the potentiality of the so-called hybrid." In "Black Woman," for example, the speaker warns: "Don't knock on my door, little child, . . . / I must not give you birth!" In *Bronze* Johnson also reached out to the people who had blazed the trail from slavery through Reconstruction to the modern world of segregation and racism.

The three poems in "Exhortation," the first section of the volume, clearly establish Johnson's place among the racially conscious poets of the 1920s. The first poem, "Sonnet to the Mantled," stands in dramatic contrast to the prevailing images in *The Heart of a Woman*. She pictures a group casting its shackles aside, "Erect and strong and visioned, in the day/That rings the knell of Curfew o'er the sway/Of prejudice—." She encourages the "children of night" in "Sonnet to Those Who See But Darkly" and urges togetherness in "Brotherhood."

The changed tone continues throughout the volume, but especially in the third and fourth sections, "Shadow" and "Motherhood." In "Shadow," titles such as "Sorrow Singers," "Prejudice," "The Passing of the Ex-Slave," and "The Octoroon" clearly indicate Johnson's focus upon black history. In "Hegira," she explores the then-current issue of blacks migrating from the South to the North by posing a series of questions in the first stanza and answering them in the remainder of the poem.

Oh, black man, why do you northward roam, and leave

1461 - S. St. N.W.
Wash. D.C. Aug. Sept. 2 - 17.

Dear Mr. Schomberg,

At last I am getting this poem to you. I have been trying to get my book under way — it is almost launched but not quite. In fact I am very much like the girl who was to be married she said — having her various pieces of furniture, in fact all save the blessed man. Do you know what represents the man. Guess that & you have the story.

The card from Atlantic was a pleasure. I remember Dr. Jackson very distinctly.

Let me know if this en closure suits you. Mr. Braithwaite is in publishing the book, under the title of "The Heart of a Woman & Other Poems." How is that title?

Mrs. Jackson the sculptures, is in N. Y. Mrs. Hunter is at her summer home — the "Hermitage." You would like a trip out there. She is an idealist.

Very Sincerely yours,
Georgia Douglas Johnson.

Letter to Arthur Schomburg (courtesy of the Schomburg Center for Research in Black Culture, the New York Public Library, Astor, Lenox and Tilden Foundations)

all the farm lands bare?
Is your house not warm, tightly thatched from storm,
    and a larder replete your share?
....
I have toiled in your cornfields, and parched in the
    sun,
    I have bowed 'neath your load of care,
I have patiently garnered your bright golden grain,
    in
        season of storm and fair,
....
And so I'm away, where the sky-line of day sets the
    arch of its rainbow afar,
To the land of the north, where the symbol of worth
    sets the broad gates of combat ajar!

Of all of Johnson's poems, the ones in the "Motherhood" section have perhaps earned the most praise. "The Mother" depicts a slave mother who must soothe "her mantled child" and cover up the misery and woe that "only God will ever know." In her portrayal of black mothers refusing to give birth during slavery ("Black Woman"—"Be still, be still, my precious child,/I must not give you birth!") or lamenting the fact that their newly born children will grow up to be slaves ("Shall I Say, 'My Son, You're Branded' "), Johnson brings an angle of vision to slavery that was perhaps shared only by Frances E. W. Harper among the early poets. There are also other sentiments expressed in the "Motherhood" poems, as in "Benediction," in which the speaker encourages her son to venture out alone:

I may not, if I would,
Retrace the way with you,
My pilgrimage is through,
But life is calling you!
Fare high and far, my son,
A new day has begun,
Thy star-ways must be won!

In "Credo" Johnson expresses her belief that black people will one day have their place in the sun: "I believe in the ultimate justice of Fate;/That the race of men front the sun in their turn"; and in "We Face the Future," she further suggests that black people who have waited through long trials will be rewarded: "And we, with sable faces pent, move with the vanguard line,/Shod with a faith that Springtime keeps, and all the stars opine."

She ends the volume in a celebratory way, offering poems in "Appreciations" to blacks and whites who have had a hand in furthering the progress of black people. She includes John Brown,

Abraham Lincoln, William Stanley Braithwaite, W. E. B. Du Bois, and Mary Church Terrell, among others. She selects "To Atlanta University" to end the volume in a celebration of the educational opportunities available to black people, a possibility for the future that mitigates some of the harshness and stifling history pervading the volume.

Du Bois's forthright foreword to the collection praises and mildly condemns Johnson's work:

> Those who know what it means to be a colored woman in 1922 and know it so much in fact as in feeling, apprehension, unrest, and delicate, yet stern thought—must read ... *Bronze*. ... none can fail to be caught here and there by a word—a phrase—a period that tells a life history or even paints the history of a generation. ... Her word is simple, sometimes trite, but it is singularly sincere and true, and as a revelation of the soul struggle of the women of a race it is invaluable.

Apparently *Bronze* was widely read, for there followed numerous reviews and critiques of it by readers "touched—even captured by the strange force of its burning enthusiasm." Zona Gale, commenting on Johnson's verse in *Literary Digest International Book Review*, called it "both passionate and plaintive.... She speaks for the ... 'children of sorrow, dethroned by a hue,' those, in fine, 'who walk unfree, though cradled in the hold of liberty.' ... Never have they who are 'the fretted fabric of a dual dynasty,' made by the mingling of dark and light, found a voice at once more delicate and clear."

This second volume gives evidence of a new strength in Johnson's feelings of protest against injustice and racism. The impact that Alain Locke and others of the New Negro movement were having on her life and writings was clear in her "deeper, more mellow note," as Benjamin Brawley described the change in her writing.

In 1925 Johnson's husband died following a third stroke. Both sons were attending Dartmouth College, and Johnson was forced to assume new pragmatic responsibilities. She did not, however, relinquish what May Miller calls the "Saturday Soirees," the literary gatherings at the Johnson home. In fact the ranks of New Negro figures attending Johnson's informal salon were expanding to include writers like Miller and Jean Toomer. The New Negro Renaissance had reached its zenith and the country was moving rapidly toward the end of what Cedric Dover calls the "effulgence of the 20's" and toward the financial crash of 1929, circumstances which may have affected Johnson's third volume of poetry, *An Autumn Love Cycle* (1928). It reflected more of the earlier, romantic poet and less of the voice of social protest than *Bronze* had prepared the world to expect. An unidentified reviewer assessed *Bronze* as an "interlude [by an] author [who] is not primarily a racial poet. With the present volume she returns to the universal theme, the heart of a woman."

Alain Locke, who wrote an introduction to the collection, concludes that Johnson "has dug patiently in the veins of her own subjective experience . . . with a candor that shows that she brings to the poetic field what it lacks most—the gift of the elemental touch."

An Autumn Love Cycle focuses upon the various states of love, from enraptured initial engagement to disillusionment with the loss of love. It is divided into "The Cycle," "Contemplation," "Intermezzi," "Penseroso," and "Cadence." Although all the sections focus on love, "The Cycle" provides the complete circle of emotional response to it. In the first poem, "I Closed My Shutters Fast Last Night," the speaker despairs that love will ever find her. This mood continues in "Footsteps," where she waits to hear those steps she knows and begins to change in "Oh Night of Love" and "Autumn," where references to "rapt ecstatic hours" and movement from a "prison door" to "blinding sunlight" suggest that some change has occurred. "You are the very sun, the moon,/The starlight of my soul," she then declares in "Proving," and the emotional highs and lows continue until "Delusion," "Sunset," and "Finis," in which the poet essentially ends up where she had begun, recognizing that she had been blind in love, barring the chambers of her heart, and offering death her hand in a repudiation of "the portals of desire."

Though longer than most of the poems in *The Heart of a Woman*, those in *An Autumn Love Cycle* frequently return to the kinds of sentiments expressed there—vague references to feelings and experiences without specific grounding for them. "One Day," in the "Contemplation" section, is typical: "There's nothing certain, nothing sure/Save sorrow. Fragile happiness/Was never fashioned to endure."

The "Intermezzi" section contains "I Want to Die While You Love Me," the poem that has perhaps become Johnson's trademark. Favoring death to the end of love, the poet declares: "I want to die while you love me/Oh, who would care to live,/'Til

love has nothing more to ask/And nothing more to give." The volume ends with "Afterglow," a reflective poem in which the speaker reviews her various escapades in love and concludes that all of them were worth the pain and the beauty: "And I would give a thousand world/To live it all again!"

Shortly after the publication of Johnson's third book, the country was hit by the Great Depression. Johnson had already tried her hand at dramatic writing in the 1920s, and she had won first place in *Opportunity*'s drama contest in 1927 for her one-act play *Plumes*. She had also worked with the Krigwa players and seen them produce her drama *Blue Blood* with May Miller and Frank S. Horne, and had recognized the impact that drama could have as a weapon of social protest when she wrote *A Sunday Morning in the South*, her first drama in support of the antilynching campaign following World War I. Discouraged by publishers' lack of interest in another volume of her poetry and encouraged by friends to try writing plays, Johnson was receptive to the United States government's 1935 effort to inaugurate a nationwide, federally sponsored theater as a part of President Roosevelt's New Deal and Works Progress Administration. Hallie Flanagan, Federal Theatre Project National Director, in a much-publicized address to launch the project, had declared that "the theatre must grow [and] become conscious of the implication of the changing order, or the changing order [would] ignore, and rightly so, the implications of the theatre." Convinced that the FTP would be a haven for fledgling playwrights and that experimental productions not likely to get produced elsewhere would be mounted, as would plays of social protest, Johnson submitted at least five plays to the Federal Theatre between 1935 and 1939, when the project closed. None were accepted in any of the producing units of FTP. Three of the plays submitted are specifically on the themes of lynching and rape; two are historical sketches based on the desperation of slaves to escape from servitude to freedom. The reasons the FTP play readers gave for refusing Johnson's plays demonstrate how black playwrights, in general, failed in the American theater of the 1930s.

In the one-act drama "Blue-eyed Black Boy," Jack Walter, a twenty-one-year-old black man on his way home from work, innocently brushes against a white woman. He is charged with an attempted attack, arrested, and jailed. He becomes the intended victim of a lynch mob. Jack's mother, hearing the mob moving toward the jail to get her son, retrieves, in desperation, a small ring from a

Georgia Douglas Johnson

secret hiding place. She then sends the black doctor, who is soon to marry her daughter, in haste to the governor with a message from "Pauline who gave birth to a son 21 years ago." She adds with emphasis: "Just give him the ring and say, 'Pauline sent this, she says they goin' to lynch her son born 21 years ago,' mind you say 'twenty-one years ago'—then say—listen close—'look into his eyes and you'll save him.'" The ring and the message are delivered, the governor remembers his liaison with Pauline, the militia is called out, the lynching is stopped, and Jack is sent home safely to his mother.

Like many social protest plays of the 1930s, "Blue-eyed Black Boy" is a tightly structured drama with compressed action; the entire playing time of the script is less than twenty minutes. Johnson, having already exhibited technical aptitude of high quality in her writing, handles exposition well through inference and understatement, plants a note of suspense, and concentrates on protesting the plight of black women and their mulatto sons. The dialogue distinguishes between the simple dialect of the uneducated, older characters and the more polished speech of the young, educated characters. The audience never sees the blue-eyed boy and, while this contributes to the suspense, the omission might have contributed to the play being attacked as an "incomplete drama." FTP readers dismissed the work as a pointless piece of melodrama; one reader added, "it is obviously designed to discourage lynchers and to show that proud governors have slack moments."

"Safe," a play which Johnson apparently submitted along with "Blue-eyed Black Boy," is set in a three-room cottage of a simple black family in a southern town in 1893. A young wife awaits the imminent birth of her child as a crazed lynch mob passes by dragging their sobbing black victim. The young boy's agonizing pleas for his mother shatter the expectant mother's composure. Almost before the laughter of the crowd and the cries of the victim die down, she goes into labor and delivers her child. The healthy cry of the newborn is heard from the adjoining room and shortly thereafter the doctor emerges to announce the birth of a fine son. The doctor relates the mother's reaction:

She asked me right away, "Is it a girl?" . . . And I said, "no child, it's a fine boy," and then I turned my back a minute to wash my hands in the basin. When I looked around again she had her hands about the baby's throat choking it. I tried to stop her, but its little tongue was already hanging from its mouth—it was dead! Then she began, she kept muttering over and over again "Now he's safe—safe from the lynchers! Safe!"

The three readers who evaluated "Safe" were more impressed by it than were the readers who responded to "Blue-eyed Black Boy"; however, they were all aghast at the notion that a lynching could take place for no obvious "good reason" and impugned the playwright for suggesting this in her drama. One reader's criticism is typical of all others: "An extremely dramatic, tragic piece. But the glaring weakness of utter exaggeration is too bright—and it fails not because the idea is not dramatic, but because it follows from an absurdity— that they lynch Negro boys 'Down South' for defending themselves from thieves. In fact, the crime that produces lynching is vastly fouler." Despite facts to the contrary, the readers fell victim to the myth that "only rape produced lynching down South" and expected the playwright to protect the myth by ignoring the truth. One reviewer felt it was a "truly nice piece of work for a little theatre" and admonished the playwright for not showing more suffering and anxiety; she was advised to rewrite the piece. Johnson's use of economy in the writing of "Safe" did not necessarily diminish the degree of "suffering and anxiety" of her characters. The conclusion is explosive. "Safe" was lost until it was recovered in 1974 and placed in the George Mason University Special Collections and Archives.

"A Sunday Morning in the South" is also preserved in the Archives at George Mason; one copy includes music. Two versions of the script provide an opportunity to see Johnson, the playwright, at work.

The second version has been compressed from "a one-act play in two scenes" to "a one-act play in one scene." A new character is added to facilitate the action of going after "the good white man"—in this instance a woman who will save the innocent victim. In this version, the dialogue is truer to the dialect and rhythm pattern of the characters' black speech, and the exposition and didacticism of the author are less intrusive than in the first version. The second play loses some dramatic impact by having the news of the lynching reported by a third party rather than having the protagonist receive the information firsthand.

"A Sunday Morning in the South" takes place in 1924; the setting is still a humble cottage occupied by a grandmother, Sue Jones, and her two young grandsons, nineteen-year-old Tom and seven-year-old Bossie. Sunday morning church music is heard from nearby as the play opens. A neighbor on her way to church reports that a white woman has claimed "rape by a young black man." They all suspect that the rape charge is untrue, and, knowing it will fan more racial hatred, they shudder at the thought of what will happen if the young man is found. Almost immediately two white officers come with the girl who vaguely identifies Tom as the man who raped her. Despite the grandmother's pleas and assurance that Tom was at home asleep all night, the boy is arrested and supposedly taken to jail. Sue (in the second version) sends for help from "Miss Vilet, the good, white woman," but learns that Tom is lynched before anybody can save him. The shock of the news kills Sue.

Of Johnson's three plays specifically addressing lynching, this one was the only play that met with the approval of all the readers. Nonetheless the play was never produced. The reports read from a rather terse: "Very simple and inexpensive; for labor, Negro, liberal, radical audiences," to an enthusiastic "Here is the first piece I have read about lynching that truthfully shows the futility of resisting the insane minds of a lynching mob with gentility. . . . Johnson handles the theme, one of the many causes of mob madness [sic] and with deftness gives dramatic emphasis to this evil. Her characters appear as if from life. It has Tenseness [sic] and reality. It is not offensive to either group. It is a sermon against this national shame. I recommend for Little Theatre." The clue to why "A Sunday Morning in the South" was approved may be found in the reader's phrase "it is not offensive to either group." The dilemma of which audience to address persisted for Johnson as for all black writers. Audience sympathy for the characters seems to make people transcend the need to take sides and makes the play more acceptable. Subtextual statements on the hypocrisy of Christianity may also have touched sensitive chords in the readers' consciences. Although never produced by the Federal Theatre Project, the play has become the best known of Johnson's plays since its publication in *Black Theatre U.S.A.: Forty-five Plays by Black American Playwrights, 1847-1974* (1974) fifty years after it was written.

The Child.

That dusky child upon your knee,
Is breath of God's eternity;
Direct his vision to the height,
Let naught obscure his royal right.

Altho the vistas of renown
Glow iron-barred, thru fortune's frown,
'Tis his to mould the master-key,
That wields the lock of Destiny!

                              G. Douglas Johnson.

Fair copy (courtesy of the Schomburg Center for Research in Black Culture, the New York Public Library, Astor, Lenox and Tilden Foundations)

Johnson's other two scripts submitted to FTP are not social protest dramas per se. Both *Frederick Douglass* and *William and Ellen Craft* are set in the days of slavery and concern the efforts of slaves to escape to the North and freedom. In the first play, Frederick tells Anne, his "sweetheart freewoman," "I'm a-workin' for freedom an' you," and saves every penny he can to get to "that great big free country up North." His plans change, however, when he learns that his old master has arrived in town with intentions to send him back to the plantation where he cannot buy his freedom. He must escape immediately. In *William and Ellen Craft,* a beautiful octoroon slave, whose "pretty white face is [her] curse," is trying to avoid exploitation by her master by escaping with her "brown slave fiance" via the Underground Railroad. When news comes that "De white folks done found all about de underground," Ellen agrees to cut off her long hair and don Marse Charles's suit, which Aunt Mandy is mending. She becomes the "spittin' image of her daddy, ole Marse Charles," and boards the real train to Philadelphia, accompanied by her "slave William."

Even during the era when Johnson's major focus was on drama, she remained a poet. She continued to publish her poems in journals, primarily in *Opportunity.* With the coming of World War II, she joined others who wrote in support of America and her allies. Many of her earlier published poems had been inspired by another world war, though they still applied to the world situation.

By the mid 1940s, and until her death in 1966, Johnson's poetry was appearing frequently in journals such as *Phylon* and the *Journal of Negro History* and in anthologies and collections by black editors who had again come into favor with national publishers. She was still active in the social and political life of Washington and campaigned for Thomas Dewey in the 1944 presidential election.

Johnson, who had always seemed eccentric to some acquaintances, sometimes found herself in direct conflict with other members of the Washington inner city life. She refused to give up her home on S Street and stood up to the young street blacks whom she considered "a disgrace to the race." According to playwright Ted Shine, she became known as "the old woman with the headband and the tablet around her neck." Shine cannot ever recall seeing Johnson without the large yellow pencil and blue notepad tied on a ribbon around her neck, just in case an idea came to her and she needed to jot it down quickly. She continued to write and publish her work until she died at the age of seventy-nine. In the introduction to her final volume of poetry, *Share My World* (1962), she wrote "*Share My World* may never have become a reality if it had not been for the encouraging help of . . . my private printer. For several years through the courtesy of N. Wright Cuney [twin brother of poet Waring Cuney], a photographer and printer, I have been able to send a poem each year to my friends and acquaintances. With his suggestion and his offer to print some of these poems in book form, I am able to share my world with you." One of the poems of this last volume, "One Lives Too Long," captures Johnson's feelings as she neared her eightieth birthday: "I'd live forever if I could/But now I know the gift of death/Is merciful and understood." In 1965 Johnson returned to Atlanta University "to receive the honorary degree of Doctor of Literature, which she accepted modestly but with much pride."

When death came for Georgia Douglas Johnson, May Miller sat by her bedside stroking her hand and repeating quietly over and over, "Poet Georgia Douglas Johnson." Owen Dodson, one of her many literary sons, read, "I Want To Die While You Love Me" at her funeral. Miller recalls urging Henry Lincoln, Jr., as she and Owen Dodson rode back in the car from the funeral, to please preserve the barrels of papers that his mother kept at home. Her most poignant memory, however, of the last day is that of Henry Lincoln Johnson placing on his mother's coffin a small bouquet of roses which he had picked from her "French Riviera"—a fence beside the house along which Johnson had planted running roses and jokingly called her "French Riviera" because she had always wanted to get to the real place and never did. It was a son's final gesture of love for his mother. It reiterated the message sung throughout all of Johnson's writing: "May the saving grace of the mother-heart save humanity." It was a fitting tribute to a lyric soul whose artistry remains to "gem the archives of a better day."

References:

Cedric Dover, "The Importance of Georgia Douglas Johnson," *Crisis,* 59 (December 1952): 633-636, 674;

Winona L. Fletcher, "From Genteel Poet to Revolutionary Playwright: Georgia Douglas Johnson as A Symbol of Black Success, Failure, and Fortitude," *Theatre Annual,* 40 (February 1985): 40-64;

J. Saunders Redding, *To Make a Poet Black* (College Park, Md.: McGrath, 1939), p. 96.

Papers:
Manuscripts of plays by Johnson are in the Federal Theatre Project Collection at George Mason University.

Helene Johnson

(7 July 1907-   )

Raymond R. Patterson
City College of the City University of New York

WORKS: "What Do I Care for Morning," "Sonnet to a Negro in Harlem," "Summer Matures," "Poem," "Fulfillment," "The Road," "Bottled," and "Magalu," in *Caroling Dusk: An Anthology of Verse by Negro Poets,* edited by Countee Cullen (New York: Harper & Row, 1927), pp. 216-223;
"Poem," "The Road," "Sonnet To A Negro In Harlem," "Remember Not," and "Invocation," in *The Book of American Negro Poetry,* revised edition, edited by James Weldon Johnson (New York: Harcourt, Brace, 1931), pp. 279-282;
"Summer Matures," "Fulfillment," "Magalu," "Remember Not," "Invocation," and "The Road," in *The Poetry of the Negro 1746-1970,* edited by Langston Hughes and Arna Bontemps (Garden City: Anchor/Doubleday, 1970), pp. 261-266.

One of the youngest and brightest of the Harlem Renaissance poets (she was five years younger than Langston Hughes and twenty-one years younger than Georgia Douglas Johnson), Helene Johnson is remembered today for perhaps a half dozen poems that capture the concerns and convey the promise and excitement associated with the Harlem literary scene of the mid 1920s. For a brief period beginning in 1925, when her work began appearing regularly in the National Urban League's *Opportunity: A Journal of Negro Life,* as well as in several important anthologies and, on one occasion, in *Vanity Fair* magazine, she, along with Langston Hughes, Countee Cullen, Arna Bontemps, and Sterling Brown, was repeatedly hailed as representing the best of the younger generation of poets who were part of the New Negro movement. Ultimately, however, she did not fulfill her brilliant promise and in retrospect can only be considered a minor poet of the period.

Very little has been recorded about Johnson's life. The few details that are available must be gleaned from the pages of magazines and anthologies where her poems appeared. William Stanley Braithwaite's *Anthology of Magazine Verse for 1926* provides the most informative note available, probably drawn from a questionnaire sent to the nineteen-year-old Boston poet. Helene V. Johnson reported that she was a product of Boston schools; unmarried; fond of the theater, tennis, dancing, hiking, and rowing; and considered Walt Whitman, Alfred Lord Tennyson, Percy Bysshe Shelley, and Carl Sandburg her favorite poets. In addition she was a member of the Saturday Evening Quill Club of Boston. During the preceding year she had won first prize in a short story contest sponsored by the *Boston Chronicle* and had her first poem published in *Opportunity.* The poem "Trees at Night," a series of dark, vivid images in free verse, had won eighth honorable mention in *Opportunity*'s first literary contest.

Opportunity, edited by Charles S. Johnson, along with the NAACP's official periodical, the *Crisis,* and the *Messenger,* provided encouragement to young black writers who were routinely excluded from white publications. In the year Johnson received her first honorable mention, the winner of first prize in poetry had been Langston Hughes, for "The Weary Blues." Countee Cullen had been awarded second prize, and both Hughes and Cullen had tied for third. Clement Wood, Witter Bynner, John Farrar, and James Weldon Johnson had served as judges.

In the July 1925 issue of *Opportunity,* another Helene Johnson poem, "My Race," appeared with a note that "Helen [*sic*] Johnson is a young poet, living in Brookline, Mass." The poem, a direct, simple statement structured on a paradox, expresses wonder at the unrealized potential the poet saw in black life, a theme popular among the younger writers who felt they were at the beginning of a new era of racial achievement. "My Race" was followed by a third poem, "Metamorphism," in the March 1926 issue of *Opportunity*. "My Race" and "Metamorphism," a meditation on the changeable nature of the sea, establish themes which are the focus of much of Johnson's poetry: the sensuous beauty of the natural world and the problems of racial oppression and personal freedom.

The panel of judges for *Opportunity*'s second literary contest, among them William Rose Benét, Alain Locke, Vachel Lindsay, and Robert Frost, awarded honorable mention to three Helene Johnson poems, "Fulfillment," "Magalu," and "The Road." First prize had been divided between Waring Cuney for "No Images" and Lucy Ariel Williams for "Northboun'." The Alexander Pushkin Poetry Prize had gone to Bontemps for "Golgotha Is a Mountain." The prize money, totaling $1,000, was donated by Caspar Holstein, a black man, a wealthy numbers banker and resident of Harlem known for his philanthropic support of cultural affairs.

"Fulfillment" is a Whitmanesque celebration of life and its varied experiences, ranging from climbing "a hill that hungers for the sky" to riding a crowded trolley car, "Squeezed next to a patent-leather Negro dreaming/Of a wrinkled river and a minnow net." Yet like many of her poems, "Fulfillment," perhaps influenced by her interest in Shelley and romanticism, is based on a paradox that is given focus in the concluding lines: "Ah, Life, let your stabbing beauty pierce me . . . ," and the poet is left "to die bleeding—consummate with Life."

Eugene B. Redmond in *Drumvoices: The Mission of Afro-American Poetry* (1976) does not treat these anti-Victorian strains in Helene Johnson's poetry but does focus on the theme of identity, which he calls "cultural (African) reclamation." "Magalu," with its rejection of Christianity, "a creed that will not let you dance," Redmond places beside Cullen's "Heritage," in which the poet (actually the adopted son of a minister) laments the unresolved conflict that he felt between his instincts, derived from his African ancestry, and Christianity. Johnson's "The Road" ("brown as my race is brown") carries forward the theme of racial identity given validity through association with aspects of the natural

world—a theme developed more directly in later poems.

In September 1926 Johnson again published in the pages of *Opportunity*, and in the October issue, poet and artist Gwendolyn Bennett informed readers of her column, "The Ebony Flute," that Helene Johnson and Dorothy West (the author of the 1948 novel *The Living Is Easy*) were cousins and both members of the Saturday Evening Quill Club of Boston. The two writers, the column went on to say, were extremely modest and reluctant to discuss their work at meetings. Despite this modesty, the young Boston poet did attract the attention of William Stanley Braithwaite, who reprinted two of her poems in his influential annual, *Anthology of Magazine Verse*.

In October and November of 1926 Johnson published poems in the *Messenger* and in the first and only issue of *Fire!!*, the magazine edited by Wallace Thurman, along with Langston Hughes, Richard Bruce Nugent, and others. That same winter, apparently encouraged by her publishing success, Johnson and West journeyed to New York City to study journalism at the Extension Division of Columbia University; her teacher was the novelist John Erskine. Some months after arriving in New York, she sold a poem to *Vanity Fair* magazine and immediately became a Harlem literary celebrity. The poem was entitled "Bottled" and appeared in the May 1927 issue. In an ingenious, colloquial style that might owe some allegiance to Sandburg, the poet compares a bottle of Sahara Desert sand on a Harlem library shelf with a Seventh Avenue "darky dressed fit to kill" and comes to the realization that, like the sand, the black man has been "bottled" by Western civilization, an idea that Jean Wagner in *Black Poets of the United States* (1973) points out is echoed in Waring Cuney's "No Images" and in the work of Hughes and Claude McKay.

When *Opportunity*'s third literary contest was held, Johnson was awarded second prize in the Holstein Poetry Section for her poem "Summer Matures," a surprisingly erotic evocation of the summer's fullness and the legend of Sappho's unconsummated love for Phaon. Fourth prize in poetry went to her "Sonnet To a Negro In Harlem," with its memorable characterization of a young Harlemite: disdainful, magnificent, bold, "You are too splendid for this city street!" First prize went to Sterling A. Brown, the Pushkin Prize to Bontemps. The judges were Braithwaite, Cullen, Sandburg, Joseph Auslander, Maxwell Bodenheim, and Ridgely Torrence.

Harlem in 1927, even for a reportedly shy Helene Johnson, must have been an exciting place to be if one were a promising young poet. There were her studies at Columbia, literary parties to attend, Park Avenue patrons to meet and astound, and there were the streets and the people of Harlem. Nevertheless, little is recorded of this period in her life except that she became a member of The Fellowship for Reconciliation, an international organization working for justice, interracial good will, and for passive resistance to war and violence. We do, however, get a fictional glimpse of Johnson and West in Wallace Thurman's satiric novel of the Harlem Renaissance, *Infants of the Spring* (1932). They appear briefly, in the company of a character that might suggest Zora Neale Hurston, and are described as "two young girls, recently emigrated from Boston. They were the latest to be hailed as incipient immortals. Their names were Doris Westmore and Hazel Jamison. Doris wrote stories. Hazel wrote poetry. Both had become known through a literary contest fostered by one of the leading Negro magazines. Raymond liked them more than he did most of the younger recruits to the movement. For one thing, they were characterized by a freshness and naivete which he and his cronies had lost. And, surprisingly enough for Negro prodigies, they actually gave promise of possessing literary talent."

The year before, Cullen had included a poem by Johnson in the all-Negro issue of *Palms* which he had been asked to guest edit. When his *Caroling Dusk: An Anthology of Verse by Negro Poets* (1927) was issued, it contained eight poems by her. It is these poems, discussed in Redmond's *Drumvoices*, upon which Helene Johnson's reputation rests as a Harlem Renaissance poet. In Cullen's introduction to the collection, Johnson's more colloquial verse is cited as representing an aspect of the diversity found in American Negro poetry, and Cullen compares her work favorably with the popular verse in American slang written by John V. A. Weaver.

Between November 1928, when "A Missionary Brings a Young Native to America" appeared in *Harlem* magazine, and the publication of James Weldon Johnson's revised edition of his 1922 anthology, *The Book of American Negro Poetry* (1931), five poems by Helene Johnson appeared in the *Saturday Evening Quill*, the annual publication of the Quill Club of Boston. In the preface to *The Book of American Negro Poetry*, James Weldon Johnson comments, "It is interesting to note how Countee Cullen, Langston Hughes, Sterling A. Brown, Helene Johnson, Arna Bontemps, Frank Horne, Waring

Cuney, Gwendolyn Bennett, and others of the group react to this matter of 'race.' While they have not written exclusively poetry rising out of race-consciousness, it is manifest that their best efforts spring from that source." In introducing Helene Johnson's poetry, James Weldon Johnson tells us that her "earliest work bore the stamp of a genuine poet. She is one of the younger group who has taken, so to speak, the 'racial' bull by the horns. She has taken the very qualities and circumstances that have long called for apology or defense and extolled them in an unaffected manner. A number of her best poems are done in colloquial style—a style which numberless poets of this new age have assumed to be easy; she realizes the hard fact that an effective poem in colloquial style demands as much work and workmanship as a well-wrought sonnet. Miss Johnson also possesses true lyric talent."

Sometime after 1929 Helene Johnson returned to Boston. Exactly when and for what reason is not known, but the move signaled the end of her prominence as a poet, just as the stock market crash in 1929 announced the ending of the Harlem Renaissance. "It was the crash of the stock market on Wall Street in 1929," Bontemps recalled many years later. "It took from 1929 to 1931 to reach uptown to Harlem. You heard a lot of things but it was not until 1931 that you could tell that anything had happened on Wall Street. That is what ended it; it was a blow to publishing. Recovery didn't come until the New Deal. By then the black writers of Harlem were all scattered." By 1930 Langston Hughes had broken with his patron and moved to Cleveland. The following year Arna Bontemps was living in Alabama.

In 1934 when Dorothy West released the first issue of *Challenge: A Literary Quarterly*, editing it from Boston, it included a poem by Johnson, along with stories by Hughes and Bontemps and an article on the spirituals by Harry T. Burleigh. James Weldon Johnson wrote the foreword. A note in the magazine said that Helene Johnson was "perhaps the most highly rated of the women poets. We would like to see more of her in print." The September 1934 issue published a letter to the editor, received "In Langston Hughes' round handwriting," stating, "You've done a grand job. I hope you'll have lots of readers. And it's swell to see Helene (Johnson) in print again."

The third issue of *Challenge* appeared in May 1935. Harold Jackman, to whom Cullen had dedicated his poem "Heritage," was associate editor. "Let Me Sing My Song," a poem by Johnson, appeared in this issue along with a note about the author: "Helene Johnson is so retiring that some people believe her name to be a pseudonym. But she is married and unmatronly, and still has a fine talent that should be burning more brightly." (It was not until 1970, when the Hughes-Bontemps anthology *The Poetry of the Negro 1746-1970* was published, that Helene Johnson's married name, Hubbell, was made public.)

The fourth issue of *Challenge* appeared in January 1936, and it contained a letter from a Memphis subscriber complaining of "the most inept effusions" of the poets in the previous issue. The writer went on to say, "Most disappointing are those who, young once, showed promise surpassing even our latest young'uns. I'm thinking of Waring Cuney's 'Song of a Song,' Mae V. Cowdery's two 'poems' in your third issue, and Helene Johnson's 'Let Me Sing My Song.' Look at *Fire* (remember it?) and you'll see the same poetry but refreshing then in that they were new and showed promise."

When the second volume of the magazine appeared in the fall of 1937, its name had been changed to *New Challenge*. Richard Wright was associate editor, and the list of contributors included Hughes, Sterling Brown, Frank Marshall Davis, Margaret Walker, Owen Dodson, Alain Locke, Ralph Ellison, and Robert Hayden. *New Challenge* announced an era of social consciousness among black writers that, for reasons as yet unknown, failed to inspire the pen of Helene Johnson.

Although she is still living, Helene Johnson has carefully maintained her privacy, even more so than when she was a teenager venturing upon a literary career in the Harlem of the late 1920s. She cannot today be considered a poet on the level of Hughes, Cullen, or Brown. Between 1925 and 1935 she published scarcely more than two dozen poems, and all but a few are flawed by excesses that can rightly be ascribed to her youth. But her best work reveals a freshness and a zest for life and announces a racial awareness that distinguishes her as an indispensable voice of the New Negro movement that anticipated black poetry of the 1960s in its transformation of negative stereotypes into images of pride.

References:

Gloria T. Hull, "Black Women Poets from Wheatley to Walker," in *Sturdy Black Bridges*, edited by Roseann P. Bell, Bettye J. Parker, and Beverly Guy-Sheftall (Garden City: Anchor/Doubleday, 1979), pp. 69-86;

Eugene B. Redmond, *Drumvoices: The Mission of Afro-American Poetry* (Garden City: Anchor/Doubleday, 1976), pp. 207-209, 331-332, 363;

Jean Wagner, *Black Poets of the United States* (Urbana: University of Illinois Press, 1973), p. 184.

James Weldon Johnson

Keneth Kinnamon
University of Arkansas

BIRTH: Jacksonville, Florida, 17 June 1871, to James and Helen Louise Dillet Johnson.

EDUCATION: A.B., Atlanta University, 1894; Columbia University, 1903-1906.

MARRIAGE: 10 February 1910 to Grace Nail.

AWARDS AND HONORS: Honorary A.M., Atlanta University, 1904; Litt.D., Talladega College, 1917; Litt.D., Howard University, 1923; Spingarn Medal, 1925; Rosenwald Grant, 1929; W. E. B. Du Bois Prize for Negro Literature, 1933; Lewis Carroll Shelf Award for "Lift Every Voice and Sing," 1971.

DEATH: Wiscasset, Maine, 26 June 1938.

SELECTED BOOKS: *The Autobiography of an Ex-Colored Man* (Boston: Sherman, French, 1912); republished as *The Autobiography of an Ex-Coloured Man* (New York & London: Knopf, 1927);
Fifty Years and Other Poems (Boston: Cornhill, 1917);
God's Trombones; Seven Negro Sermons in Verse (New York: Viking, 1927);
Black Manhattan (New York: Knopf, 1930);
Saint Peter Relates an Incident of the Resurrection Day (New York: Privately printed, 1930);
Along This Way; The Autobiography of James Weldon Johnson (New York: Viking, 1933; Harmondsworth, U.K. & New York: Penguin, 1941);
Negro Americans, What Now? (New York: Viking, 1934);
Saint Peter Relates an Incident: Selected Poems (New York: Viking, 1935).

OTHER: *The Book of American Negro Poetry,* edited by Johnson (New York: Harcourt, Brace, 1922; enlarged, 1931);
The Book of American Negro Spirituals, edited by Johnson (New York: Viking, 1925);
The Second Book of American Negro Spirituals, edited by Johnson (New York: Viking, 1926); republished with *The Book of American Negro Spirituals* in *The Books of American Negro Spirituals* (1940).

PERIODICAL PUBLICATIONS: "Self-Determining Haiti," *Nation,* 111 (August 1920): 236-238, 265-267, 295-297, 345-347;
"Lynching: America's National Disgrace," *Current History,* 19 (January 1924): 596-601;
"Making of Harlem," *Survey Graphic,* 6 (March 1925): 635-639;
"Romance and Tragedy in Harlem," *Opportunity,* 4 (October 1926): 316-317, 330;
"The Dilemma of the Negro Author," *American Mercury,* 15 (December 1928): 477-481;
"Race Prejudice and the Negro Artist," *Harper's,* 157 (November 1928): 769-776;
"Negro Authors and White Publishers," *Crisis,* 36 (July 1929): 228-229;
"Communism and the Negro," *New York Herald Tribune Magazine,* 21 July 1935, pp. 2, 25, 27.

Versatility is the most salient characteristic of the life and career of James Weldon Johnson. Equipped with restless intelligence, abundant energy, and "an abhorrence of spare time," he crowded almost a dozen occupations into a busy lifetime, excelling in most of them: teacher, school principal, journalist, lawyer, songwriter, diplomat, novelist, poet, civil rights crusader, anthologist, professor. Throughout his various activities three concerns persisted. First, he was usually involved in education in one way or another, viewing it both as a route to individual achievement and as a means of racial advancement. Second, he devoted his considerable talents mainly to the service of his race, notably during his decade and a half as a major leader of the National Association for the Advancement of Colored People (1916-1930), and in other ways at other times of his life. Third, through his belletristic writing and his anthologies he was both contributor to and preserver of the Afro-American literary tradition, linking the nineteenth century to the Harlem Renaissance.

Johnson's family background encouraged achievement and cultural pursuits. His father,

James Weldon Johnson (courtesy of the Prints and Photographs Collection, Moorland-Spingarn Research Center, Howard University)

James Johnson, was a self-educated man who, as a waiter in New York and a headwaiter in Nassau and then in Jacksonville, Florida, achieved economic security and adopted middle-class values. While in New York he met and courted Helen Louise Dillet, a young woman of African-French-English ancestry, a native of Nassau who had grown up in New York, received a good education, and developed her musical talent. When Dillet returned with her mother to her native island in 1861, James Johnson followed her and secured a position in a large hotel. They were married in 1864 and prospered initially, but an economic recession forced the couple and their infant daughter to move to Jacksonville, a rapidly expanding city becoming an important tourist center. Here were born James William (changed in 1913 to Weldon) Johnson and, two years later, John Rosamond Johnson.

Growing up in an increasingly secure middle-class home with books and a piano, young James was inculcated with strict notions of integrity by his father and with intellectual and artistic interests by his mother. The first black woman public school teacher in Florida, Helen Johnson encouraged a love of learning in her sons, whom she taught at home before they attained school age and again in the classroom at Stanton School. From her they learned to read and to play the piano. A precocious child, James was quickly reading Charles Dickens, Sir Walter Scott, John Bunyan, and Jacob and Wilhelm Grimm. Formal education at Stanton School extended only through the eighth grade, from which James graduated in 1887, but travel and friends had a broadening effect. While still a small child he accompanied his family on a visit to Nassau, and in 1884 he spent a summer in New York with his grandmother and her sister. He took a Whitmanesque pleasure in the bustling movement and noise of the great city: "I loved the ferryboats—the rushing crowds, the stamping teams and yelling teamsters, the tooting whistles, the rattling windlasses and clanging chains when we left and entered the ship." As he further recalled in his autobiography, *Along This Way* (1933), "I was born to be a New Yorker." This cosmopolitan sense of self was reinforced by his friendships with Ricardo Rodriguez Ponce, a Cuban youth from whom he learned Spanish; Judson Douglass Wetmore (the "D—" of *Along This Way*), the near-white prototype for the protagonist of *The Autobiography of an Ex-Colored Man* (1912); and, somewhat later, a cultured and widely traveled white physician named Dr. Thomas Osmond Summers, for whom he worked as an assistant and with whom he traveled to Washington on a professional trip. Reading literary erotica and religious agnosticism in Dr. Summers's library, young Johnson expanded his interests in additional directions.

His development continued at Atlanta University, where he matriculated in the preparatory division after graduation from Stanton. In 1894 he received the A.B. degree from the collegiate division. At least as important as the rather rigorous academic curriculum, he received an education in racial issues from which he had been somewhat sheltered in Jacksonville. This other education included, he remembered forty years later, "preparation to meet the tasks and exigencies of life as a Negro, a realization of the peculiar responsibilities due to my own racial group, and a comprehension of the application of American democracy to Negro citizens." Not only was race a constant topic of discussion and debate among the undergraduates, but Johnson spent two summers teaching in a black rural school near Hampton, Georgia, an invaluable experience with a mode of black life new to him. In the summer before his senior year he traveled to Chicago to work in the great Columbian Exposition. Here on "Colored People's Day" he heard the aged Frederick Douglass speak and the young Paul Laurence Dunbar read from his poetry. With Dunbar, who was not yet famous, he quickly initiated a friendship and literary relation that would continue for many years thereafter.

Upon graduation and not yet twenty-three years of age, Johnson left Atlanta University as a member of a singing quartet touring New England to raise money for the institution. Back in Jacksonville in the fall as principal of Stanton, now perhaps the largest public school in the state, he was thoroughly prepared by education, travel, and experience to assume his self-defined role as "leader and helper to my race." In addition to improving Stanton by adding ninth and tenth-grade courses, he attempted to educate the city's adult black community by starting a newspaper, the *Daily American*, which was published for eight months in 1895 and 1896. In his editorials Johnson promoted racial self-help while defending civil rights for the race against the resurgence of white supremacy. The financial failure of the newspaper was disappointing, but he hoped other avenues to racial leadership could be opened. Although not a single black person had ever been admitted to the Florida bar, Johnson began to read law in the office of a friendly white attorney. After a year and a half he passed a rigorous bar examination despite the obvious racial hostility of the examiners. As a lawyer, however, he found routine paper work tedious, and his continuing duties at Stanton occupied much of his time. Johnson was growing restless in Jacksonville, too small an arena to contain either his talents or his ambitions. Furthermore, racial restrictions were tightening as the new century began.

The pattern of Johnson's career alternated between administrative and artistic roles. He had written poetry in college and even before, and the postgraduation concert tour had revived his earlier interest in music. When his brother John returned to Jacksonville in 1897, after successfully having studied at the New England Conservatory of Music and after having completed a tour with a black variety show, James was about ready to resume creative activity. Together the brothers wrote "Tolosa, or The Royal Document," which was "a comic opera satirizing the new American imperialism" in a Gilbert-and-Sullivan mode. James supplied the story and lyrics while his brother composed the music. A trip to New York in the summer of 1899

did not lead to the production of the work, as the brothers had hoped, but it did introduce them to some of the key figures of the musical stage, including Oscar Hammerstein. Among the celebrated black theatrical personalities they met were the comedians Bert Williams, George Walker, and Ernest Hogan and the musicians Bob Cole, Will Marion Cook, and Harry T. Burleigh. Cook had collaborated on the operetta *Clorindy, or the Origin of the Cakewalk* (1898) with Paul Laurence Dunbar, who, now famous, renewed his friendship with Johnson. The life of black bohemia in New York fascinated the schoolmaster; Jacksonville certainly had nothing comparable. "I now began to grope toward a realization of the importance of the American Negro's cultural background and his creative folk art," he was to write in *Along This Way*, "and to speculate on the superstructure of conscious art that might be reared on them."

The creative side of Johnson's personality was now in the ascendancy. While still in New York, he wrote with his brother and Bob Cole the song "Louisiana Lize," selling it to a popular white singer. Returning to Jacksonville, he wrote one of his best dialect poems, the plaintive love lyric "Sence You Went Away," which was published in *Century* in 1900, the first time the author appeared in print in a national magazine. With his brother he shortly afterward wrote "Lift Every Voice and Sing," which was to become known as the "Negro National Anthem." Back in New York the following summer (and the summer thereafter), the brothers formed a songwriting partnership with Bob Cole. Almost immediately successful in bringing out hit songs, the team nevertheless worked at a disadvantage with the Johnsons in Florida most of the year. After a fire destroyed a large area of Jacksonville, including the Stanton School, and after an ugly and dangerous personal encounter with state militiamen brought in to keep order, Johnson's hometown seemed even less attractive than before. The school was rebuilt, shoddily, and he returned to work as principal. A romance with a teacher from Tampa briefly competed with the allure of Tin Pan Alley, but in the fall of 1902 he resigned from Stanton, moved to New York, and devoted himself to the team of Cole and Johnson Brothers.

The trio produced dozens of songs, including such hits as "Under the Bamboo Tree," "The Congo Love Song," "My Castle on the Nile," "I Ain't Gwinter Work No Mo'," "The Maiden with the Dreamy Eyes," "Nobody's Lookin' But de Owl and de Moon," "I've Got Troubles of My Own," "Tell Me, Dusky Maiden," "Mandy, Won't You Let

James Weldon Johnson

Me Be Your Beau," "The Old Flag Never Touched the Ground," and "Oh, Didn't He Ramble." The income these songs brought was welcome, and the life was glamorous, on Broadway and on tours across the United States and in Europe; however, Johnson had serious reservations about such ephemeral work as genuine artistic expression. Reading Walt Whitman's *Leaves of Grass* (1855) in 1900, he became aware of the limitations of the dialect poetry he had been writing, depending as it did on white stereotypes of black life. Similarly, the vogue of coon songs on the musical stage catered to racist attitudes. To achieve their popularity, Cole and Johnson Brothers had to work in this medium and to meet its expectations. Johnson managed to avoid the worst crudities of the genre, but in so doing he universalized his subjects by appealing to the bland sentimentalities of popular taste in love songs. At any rate, he had begun formulating plans for more serious literary work. In

his spare time, he began a course of graduate study at Columbia University, especially under the well-known critic Brander Matthews, who both respected his work in the popular theater and encouraged his more ambitious ventures.

Through the good offices of a political friend, Charles W. Anderson, Johnson's career now took another turn, leading far away from New York. As the most influential black Republican in the city and a close friend of Booker T. Washington, Anderson exerted the leverage needed to secure Johnson a minor diplomatic post, that traditional sinecure for literary types. At the end of May 1906 Johnson arrived in Puerto Cabello, Venezuela, on the Caribbean, as United States Consul. Here he did indeed find time for his writing, producing numerous poems and making good progress on a novel. His next consular position, a slightly more desirable one in Corinto, Nicaragua, kept him busier dealing with business affairs, political unrest, and then revolution (1909-1912). But in 1910 he took a furlough to marry Grace Nail, the cultivated daughter of a prosperous New York tavern owner and real estate dealer, and he also found time to complete the novel *The Autobiography of an Ex-Colored Man* and to see it through the press. It was published anonymously by a small Boston house in 1912 while the author was still in Nicaragua.

The Autobiography of an Ex-Colored Man tells the story of a light-skinned black man who finally crosses the color line and passes as white. Born in Georgia, the son of a prominent white man and his well-kept mistress, whose "skin was almost brown," he is moved, while still a small child, with his mother to Connecticut, where they are established in a comfortable cottage. The monthly checks sent from Georgia are supplemented by the mother's work as a seamstress, making possible a genteel upbringing with a piano and books available in the home. But neither his quick mind nor his musical talent can shelter the boy from trauma when he discovers his racial identity through a humiliating episode at school. His father visits their house when the boy is twelve, but decreases his contact with his illicit family afterwards, not even responding several years later when the mother appeals to him in her last illness. She dies soon after her son's graduation from high school, leaving him quite alone in the world.

The protagonist's adult life drifts rather aimlessly. Returning to Georgia to matriculate at Atlanta University, he has his savings stolen on his second day in the city. Moving on to Jacksonville, he goes to work in a cigar factory and prepares to settle down and marry a schoolteacher. Instead, he is laid off and decides to go to New York, where he falls into the sporting life, becoming adept at gambling and playing ragtime music. Catching the fancy of a wealthy white man, he accompanies him to Europe, living first in Paris, then in Amsterdam and Berlin. In the latter he finally forms a goal for his existence: he would "voice all the joys and sorrows, the hopes and ambitions, of the American Negro, in classic musical form." Returning to the States, he disembarks in Boston, and, after sampling the life of the black middle class there, he travels south to Washington, Richmond, and Nashville. With Macon as a point of departure, he moves out into the Georgia hinterlands absorbing rural life, folk culture and its musical expression. Witnessing a lynching overwhelms him with racial shame, however, and he decides to return north and pass for white. Thoroughly emulating white values, he attends business college, gets a job, saves assiduously, and then speculates successfully in New York real estate. Marrying a white woman completes his transformation into "an ex-colored man," but at the end of the novel he realizes that he has "sold [his] birthright for a mess of pottage."

The Autobiography of an Ex-Colored Man is a novel, not an autobiography, but by issuing it anonymously Johnson hoped that it would be read as a true life story, giving it greater authenticity and impact than a work perceived as a mere piece of fiction. Certainly the protagonist is not Johnson himself, who could not pass and would not have wanted to. Nevertheless, the sources of the novel lie largely in Johnson's own experiences and friendships. His boyhood friend Judson Douglass Wetmore eventually passed and married two white women, the second a southerner. Like the protagonist of the novel, too, Wetmore became wealthy. On the other hand, many of the episodes parallel events in Johnson's own life. *The Pilgrim's Progress* and the Grimms' fairy tales were read by the novelist and his fictional character at a comparable age. Like his creator, the protagonist was disappointed in the drab backwardness of Atlanta, with its unpaved streets and lack of other urban amenities. Life in the Tenderloin district of New York attracted the protagonist as it had Johnson, who records his response in *Along This Way:* "an alluring world, a tempting world, world of greatly lessened restraints, a world of fascinating perils; but, above all, a world of tremendous artistic potentialities." In Paris the fictional character stays with his patron at the Hotel Continental and frequents a large café, where he improves his French by speaking with

James Weldon Johnson (courtesy of the Schomburg Center for Research in Black Culture, the New York Public Library, Astor, Lenox and Tilden Foundations)

attractive young women. The author with his brother and Bob Cole stayed at the same hotel and worked on his French in the same way. Author and character responded to London as well as Paris in similar ways. Returning to the United States and traveling south, the protagonist encounters revival meetings like those Johnson attended as a child with his grandmother, even including an actual singing leader, "Singing Johnson," whom the writer was later to describe in his preface to *The Book of American Negro Spirituals* (1925). Most importantly, both Johnson and his fictional character were attracted to the riches of black folk expression and wished to make it available to a larger audience by rendering it in more artistic form.

Utilizing such biographical sources in *The Autobiography of an Ex-Colored Man,* Johnson presents a complex, psychological self-portrait of a weak, confused, vacillating, self-indulgent man, who is yet capable of noble impulses and actions. Victimized by the circumstances of his birth as a "tragic mulatto," alienated from both races, he is victimized even more by the racist values which permeate American society and to which he finally yields. The first-person narration which Johnson employs allows the reader to observe closely the self-serving—often self-deceptive—habit of mind which the protagonist brings to all his experience. At the same time the point of view engages the reader's concern and even compassion, for the character surely has deep problems that admit of no easy solution. His first problem is the basic question of identity. As a child the protagonist assumes that he is white, absorbing the racism of his schoolmates. When he uses a racial epithet in a conversation with his mother, she reprimands him but does not tell him the truth. He does not learn he is black until he is required to sit down in his classroom after the principal asks the white students to stand. Humiliated, he confronts his mother. She equivocates, admitting that she is not white, but insisting that his "father is one of the greatest men in the country" and has imparted to their son "the best blood of the South." Shielded by his doting mother, herself an adorer of white values, he is ill-equipped to manage the forced transition (his first "passing") from white to black. Never really gregarious, he now becomes solitary, spending most of his time with books and music. When his mother dies, his alienation is complete. Seeing large groups of black people for the first time when he travels to Atlanta to attend college, he is revolted by "the unkempt appearance, the shambling, slouching gait and loud talk and laughter of these people." He is able to enter "the freemasonry of the race" only by way of "the best class of coloured people" he later meets through music teaching and church attendance in Jacksonville. In outlining the tripartite class division of southern blacks, the protagonist identifies with the black bourgeoisie, who as "the advanced element of the coloured race . . . are the ones . . . who carry the entire weight of the race question; it worries the others very little." Fortunately, social exclusivity is a compensation for the burden, for where their numbers permit, these "advanced" members of the race have created a "society possessing discriminating tendencies which become rules as fast as actual conditions allow." But his identification with this group, as with all others, is tenuous, for he also socializes with his coworkers at the cigar factory, and he slips easily into black bohemia when he goes to New York. When he goes to Europe, rescued by the wealthy white man "who was the means by which I escaped from this lower world," he lives as a white man, for, as his friend

tells him, he is one "by blood, by appearance, by education, and by tastes." Finally he decides to pass back into black life, committing himself to his music. In the South again, his response to black life more aesthetic than spontaneous, his commitment cannot survive the shock of the lynching he witnesses. Having passed from white to black, from black back to white, and from white to black again, he decides to pass permanently into the white world. In a last gesture toward racial loyalty he reveals his race to his white fiancée, who at last overcomes the shock and accepts him in marriage, bearing a dark-haired daughter and a fair son ("a little golden-headed god") before dying young.

Obviously ambivalent about racial identity and corresponding cultural values, the protagonist also seems sexually ambiguous. Pampered by his mother, raised without a father, shy with girls, emotionally volatile, he develops a close friendship with an older dull-witted but devoted boy. Of much briefer duration is his unspoken puppy love for an older girl. Even briefer is the account of falling in love with a young woman in Jacksonville, an episode dismissed in two sentences, but the story of his close attachment to his rich, white, male friend is related at length. "A clean-cut, slender, but athletic-looking man" with a "tinge of grey about his temples," the cultured gentleman first appears at the black night club where the protagonist plays ragtime. Sitting "languidly puffing cigarettes," he is so pleased by the playing and the person of the narrator that he sends him five dollars. Soon he is the main source of income for the protagonist, who plays for his parties and his private pleasure, often for hours at a time. The relationship grows "familiar and warm," the narrator noting that "he had a decided personal liking for me." When a wealthy white woman with a black lover later invites the protagonist to drink champagne with her at the club, the lover appears and shoots the woman. Badly shaken by this outcome of interracial heterosexual love, the protagonist walks the streets until he is picked up by his millionaire friend, who takes him home to spend the night and then to Europe the following day. Johnson carefully refrains from making the homosexual theme explicit, but when the protagonist resolves to return to the South and its music, the point seems obvious: "I dreaded the ordeal of breaking with my millionaire. Between this peculiar man and me there had grown a very strong bond of affection," so strong, indeed, that reminiscences of their relationship "could easily fill several chapters."

Confused about his racial and sexual identities, the protagonist, like Ralph Ellison's invisible man, lacks even a name, making his grasp of who he is even more tenuous. As Robert Stepto has shown in *From Behind the Veil* (1979), the protagonist symbolically violates his heritage, even as a child in Georgia, when he digs up colored glass bottles in the flower bed of his house, an African survival intended to signify the "flash of the spirit." Much later, as a man in New York, he notes on the walls of the night club the photographs of Frederick Douglass and other notables but comments only that because they are autographed they are "a really valuable collection," the value imputed to them more monetary than cultural. Above all, even his music, by which he intends to embrace black culture and perpetuate it, is actually a betrayal of it. To give "classic form" to ragtime or spirituals is to impose an alien white structure inimical to the essence of the music. Even when he wishes to, the protagonist cannot divest himself of white values. As a piano player, his finest achievement is a ragtime version of Mendelsohn's "Wedding March." Then he is inspired by a German who "had taken rag-time and made it classic" to bastardize music in a similar way. He himself recognizes that his motives are mixed. His selfish desire for eminence in an unexploited musical field is as important as his sincere desire to bring black music as racial expression to a wider audience.

When in the final chapter the ex-colored man avows "white man's success"—money—as his new goal, he is only fulfilling a paternal prophecy: on his evening visits to the house in Georgia, his father had given the child shiny coins to be saved, the final one a ten-dollar gold piece drilled through the middle and tied around the boy's neck, where it stayed for most of his life. Materialism of the gilded age, not racial values or even artistic expression, wins the struggle for the ex-colored man's soul, but to his credit he does not rest easy in its triumph. In contrast to leaders of the race struggling for justice, he realizes at the end of the novel, he has only "a vanished dream, a dead ambition, a sacrificed talent." Too weak to achieve tragic stature, the ex-colored man at least deserves our pity. Cut off from the sustaining force of black culture, he is exposed to the destructive forces of white racism and materialism. Denied a coherent identity, he must inhabit a marginal psychological as well as social territory. The final irony of a novel whose mode is ironic is that his white success is his black—and human—failure.

The Autobiography of an Ex-Colored Man achieves more psychological depth and complexity of characterization than any previous Afro-American novel or autobiography, but like that of its predecessors its literary artistry is compromised by long expository digressions on the American racial situation for the edification of the white reader. In these passages it is often difficult to tell whether the narrative voice is that of character or author, a difficulty which blurs rather than enhances the characterization. When Johnson attempts to dramatize this exposition, as in the long, contrived smoking-car debate on racial matters in chapter ten, the effect is an impeded narrative. Despite this failure to resolve artistic and didactic aims, a perennial problem in Afro-American literature, Johnson's novel is a significant achievement for its time, giving memorable expression to an important theme and preparing the way for the mature fictional art that was to come later in the century.

The Autobiography of an Ex-Colored Man was little noticed, receiving only a handful of reviews, but "Fifty Years," an occasional poem celebrating racial progress since the Emancipation Proclamation, won much praise after its appearance in the *New York Times* on 1 January 1913. By this time Johnson had returned from Nicaragua on leave to handle his father's estate. Blocked in his efforts to secure a more desirable consular post, he resigned from the diplomatic service in September. After a year in Jacksonville, he returned to New York and began journalistic work for the *New York Age*, agreeing to provide "conservative and constructive" editorials on a variety of topics, mainly concerning the race. Actually, he was unequivocal, even somewhat militant, in pressing for equal rights and racial cooperation, if rather conservative on nonracial issues. Moreover, he resumed his political activity, attacking Woodrow Wilson and supporting Charles Evans Hughes in the presidential election campaign of 1916. All the while he was writing poetry and preparing the collection *Fifty Years and Other Poems*, which was published by the Cornhill Company of Boston late in 1917.

Of the sixty-five poems in the volume, only ten had been previously published in periodicals (*Century*, the *Scroll*, the *Independent*, the *Crisis*, and the *New York Times*). Like his friend and sometime model, Paul Laurence Dunbar, Johnson wrote both standard English verse and dialect poetry. As Dunbar had separated the dialect poems in *Majors and Minors* (1896), Johnson relegated the dialect poems in his book to a section called "Jingles and Croons," containing sixteen poems, five on love and the oth-

Bob Cole, James Weldon Johnson, and Rosamond Johnson formed a vaudeville partnership at the turn of the century

ers on a variety of topics conventionally associated with the black rural South. In his preface to *The Book of American Negro Poetry*, published only a few years after *Fifty Years and Other Poems*, Johnson complained: "The Negro in the United States has achieved or been placed in a certain artistic niche. When he is thought of artistically, it is as a happy-go-lucky, singing, shuffling, banjo-picking being or as a more or less pathetic figure." Dialect poetry, he concluded, "is an instrument with but two full stops, humor and pathos." He could have been describing his own dialect poetry, which generally tended to confirm the stereotype, but one wonders why Johnson accepted such limitations. Were white expectations so dominant that he had to eschew the religious and protest themes of black folk songs and folk poetry? Instead of more significant themes, "Jingles and Croons" contains poems about stealing poultry ("Answer to Prayer" and "An Explanation"), eating watermelons and opossums ("The Seasons," "Possum Song," and "July in Georgy"), and playing the banjo ("A Banjo Song").

Some of the jingles are humorous enough ("The Rivals," "Tunk"), and some of the croons achieve genuine pathos ("Sence You Went Away," "De Little Pickaninny's Gone to Sleep"). Furthermore, Johnson's versification is fluent and facile. Consider these stanzas from "Sence You Went Away":

> Seems lak to me de stars don't shine so bright,
> Seems lak to me de sun done loss his light,
> Seems lak to me der's nothin' goin' right,
>   Sence you went away.
>
> Seems lak to me de sky ain't half so blue,
> Seems lak to me dat ev'ything wants you,
> Seems lak to me I don't know what to do,
>   Sence you went away.

Nevertheless, his dialect poetry does not rise to Dunbar's standard. "Ma Lady's Lips Am Like de Honey" seems a contrived, overelaborated, and sentimental version of Dunbar's "A Negro Love Song," and "A Plantation Bacchanal" and "A Banjo

175

Song" are feeble efforts, compared to Dunbar's robust "The Party," to depict the festive side of black life.

Dunbar himself disparaged his dialect poetry ("a jingle in a broken tongue"), preferring the medium of conventional English verse. Johnson shared this preference. The first eleven poems in *Fifty Years and Other Poems* treat racial themes: racial progress, the composers of the spirituals, a black educator, black military valor, the mammy, Lincoln, lynching, slavery, interracial sex. The original version of the title poem contained forty-one quatrains reviewing racial history in America from the introduction of the first slaves in 1619 to 1913, concentrating on the fifty years since emancipation and ending, in the last fifteen stanzas, in a despairing view of present impediments to further progress. On reconsideration, the poet decided to delete the final portion, thereby achieving coherence and the uplift required by the occasion at the expense of a more balanced view of racial history. Still, there is some dialogue between despair and hope beginning with stanza eighteen. Perhaps hope wins too easily and the poem lacks complexity, but "Fifty Years" does achieve the confident, resounding tone and the inspirational message Johnson felt to be appropriate to public poetry:

> O brothers mine, today we stand
> > Where half a century sweeps our ken,
> Since God, through Lincoln's ready hand,
> > Struck off our bonds and made us men. . . .

> Courage! Look out, beyond, and see
> > The Far horizon's beckoning span!
> Faith in your God-known destiny!
> > We are a part of some great plan.

> Because the tongues of Garrison
> > And Phillips now are cold in death,
> Think you their work can be undone?
> > Or quenched the fire lit by their breath?

> Think you that John Brown's spirit stops?
> > That Lovejoy was but idly slain?
> Or do you think those precious drops
> > From Lincoln's heart were shed in vain?

> That for which millions prayed and sighed,
> > That for which tens of thousands fought,
> For which so many freely died,
> > God cannot let it come to naught.

More impressive, though, are the sterner poems "To America," "Fragment," and "Brothers." The first two, "Fragment" especially, argue effectively that the national injustice to black people brings divine retribution. "Brothers" conveys a similar message. In lynching a brutalized black criminal, the lynchers are themselves brutalized, making lynchers and lynched brothers in their brutalization. Among the racial poems "The White Witch" is also noteworthy. Its admonition to black men to beware of white women develops a view of the psychosexual dimension of racism remarkably prescient for its time.

Most of the remaining poems in the collection are conventional fin de siècle verse, a bit world-weary, singing for love and idleness, rather facile, not deeply felt. Most are rhymed, but a half-dozen are not. Such a poem as "Deep in the Quiet Wood" certainly does not improve on its model, Whitman. "The Suicide" is more effective, almost achieving colloquial authenticity, and "Girl of Fifteen" is not without a certain psychological interest. All in all, however, *Fifty Years and Other Poems* represents only a modest achievement, neither comparable to nor a precursor of the brilliant *God's Trombones* (1927), published ten years later.

From about the turn of the century Johnson had known the influential ally of Booker T. Washington, Charles W. Anderson, but he had known W. E. B. Du Bois almost as long. In the summer of 1916 upon the invitation of Joel E. Spingarn and at the urging of Du Bois, Johnson attended the important Amenia Conference on racial issues. A few months later he received from Spingarn an offer to become field secretary of the National Association for the Advancement of Colored People, which had been organized in 1910 by whites and blacks to provide a more militant vehicle for racial protest than Washington offered. Accepting the position in December, Johnson was to prove extremely effective in organizing local branches throughout the country, greatly expanding the membership of the organization. He also made an investigative trip to Haiti, exposing the abuses of American occupation of that country in a series of articles for the *Nation* in 1920. Later in the same year he became general secretary (the chief executive position) of the NAACP. Throughout the 1920s he provided effective leadership, aided by such subordinates as Walter White and William Pickens. Emphasizing legal action, publicity, and political pressure, Johnson coordinated the most effective movement against racism of its time. Even when he failed to win an immediate goal, as in the defeat of the Dyer Anti-Lynching Bill, he called the country's attention to the issue of racial injustice.

"I got immense satisfaction out of the work which was the main purpose of the National Association for the Advancement of Colored People," Johnson recalled in *Along This Way*: "at the same time, I struggled constantly not to permit that part of me which was artist to become entirely submerged." Official duties, including much travel and public speaking, occupied most of his time, but he managed to compile three important anthologies in the 1920s. The first of these, *The Book of American Negro Poetry* (1922), has pioneering importance as the first such collection ever made. In it Johnson includes thirty-one poets, all of whom lived well into the twentieth century. Earlier poets are not included, but Johnson discusses Phillis Wheatley, Jupiter Hammon, George Moses Horton, Francis Watkins Harper, James Madison Bell, and Albery A. Whitman in his long preface sketching the development of Afro-American poetry. This preface also examines some of the poems represented in the anthology, giving special praise to William Stanley Braithwaite and Claude McKay, and expounds on some of Johnson's favorite themes: the distinctive contribution of blacks to American cultural expressions (folk tales, spirituals, cakewalk, ragtime), the importance of literature and art as proof

of equality and the measure of a people's greatness, and the limitations of the dialect tradition (nevertheless copiously represented in the collection). *The Book of American Negro Poetry* appeared a bit too early to include the important younger poets of the Harlem Renaissance—Langston Hughes, Countee Cullen, Arna Bontemps—but it helped to foster a favorable climate for that literary movement by earning respect for black poetry and expanding its audience. When a revised and enlarged edition of the anthology appeared in 1931, Johnson did give a generous sampling of the work of the new poets.

The other two anthologies, *The Book of American Negro Spirituals* (1925) and *The Second Book of American Negro Spirituals* (1926), likewise increased respect for black creativity. With musical arrangements by John Rosamond Johnson and Lawrence Brown, the two books offered a rich collection of 122 songs with a long preface to the first volume and a shorter one to the second. These prefaces combine a historical account with aesthetic and linguistic analyses. Johnson explains that blacks had come to take pride in the spirituals, once thought crude and backward, and that whites were increasingly recognizing them as valuable contributions to the national culture. The publication of the volumes greatly accelerated this process of appreciation. Almost all the reviews were favorable, including those by such black critics as W. E. B. Du Bois and Walter White and by white critics such as H. L. Mencken, Mark Van Doren, and Carl Van Vechten.

It is ironic that Johnson, an avowed agnostic, contributed so significantly to increased respect for the soulful richness of black Christianity. Before collecting spirituals, he had paid tribute in "O Black and Unknown Bards" to their creators. Religious themes appear elsewhere in his poetry, as in "Prayer at Sunrise" and in the untitled envoi to *Fifty Years and Other Poems*. But these are overshadowed by the superb achievement of *God's Trombones: Seven Negro Sermons in Verse*. The individual titles are "Listen, Lord—A Prayer," "The Creation," "The Prodigal Son," "Go Down Death—A Funeral Sermon," "Noah Built the Ark," "The Crucifixion," "Let My People Go," and "The Judgment Day." Two of the best of these, "The Creation" and "Go Down Death—A Funeral Sermon," had previously appeared in periodicals, the former in the *Freeman* in 1920. Johnson began work on "The Creation" after hearing a black preacher in Kansas City in 1918, but his interest in the poetic potential of the material preceded this occasion: "I had long been planning that at some time I should take the primi-

Grace Nail Johnson

tive stuff of the old-time Negro sermon and, through art-governed expression, make it into poetry. I felt that this primitive stuff could be used in a way similar to that in which a composer makes use of a folk theme in writing a major composition. I believed that the characteristic qualities: imagery, color, abandon, sonorous diction, syncopated rhythms, and native idioms, could be preserved and, at the same time, the composition as a whole be enlarged beyond the circumference of mere race and given universality."

This plan was fully realized in "The Creation," in particular, and in *God's Trombones*, as a whole. The analogy to the plan of the protagonist of *The Autobiography of an Ex-Colored Man* is clear, but the form and language of Johnson's poems are far more faithful to their folk sources. Eschewing regularities of meter, rhyme, or length of line, *God's Trombones* relies on speech rhythms—especially syncopation—and the Biblical narratives to give structure to the poems. Instead of the often-stilted diction of his verse in formal English or the contrived cuteness of the dialect of "Jingles and Croons," the language of the collection is easy, colloquial, sinewy, yet capable of a vast range of emotion, as illustrated by the following lines from "Go Down Death—A Funeral Sermon":

Weep not, weep not,
She is not dead;
She's resting in the bosom of Jesus.
Heart-broken husband—weep no more;
Grief-stricken son—weep no more;
Left-lonesome daughter—weep no more;
She's only just gone home.

Day before yesterday morning,
God was looking down from his great, high heaven,
Looking down on all his children,
And his eye fell on Sister Caroline,
Tossing on her bed of pain.
And God's big heart was touched with pity,
With the everlasting pity.

And God sat back on his throne,
And he commanded that tall, bright angel standing at
    his right hand:
Call me Death!
And that tall, bright angel cried in a voice
That broke like a clap of thunder:
Call Death!—Call Death!
And the echo sounded down the streets of heaven
Till it reached away back to that shadowy place,
Where death waits with his pale, white horses.

In this volume, rather than conventional melancholy or plantation stereotypes, Johnson expresses the dignity and depth of the racial religious experience in its own idiom, but in a way that does indeed appeal finally to the universal hunger for spiritual consolation. Ranging from cosmic grandeur of awesome proportions to fiery denunciation of sinners to the most tender solicitude for bereavement, the themes of *God's Trombones* receive expression that has the inevitability, resonance, and emotional authority of great art. Johnson's finest literary achievement, the book was favorably reviewed by such fellow luminaries of the Harlem Renaissance as Du Bois, White, Countee Cullen, and Alain Locke, as well as by white poets and critics like Joseph Auslander, Arthur Guiterman, Harriet Monroe, and Harry Alan Potamkin.

Unfortunately, Johnson wrote very little new poetry in the last eleven years of his life. *Harper's* published a love poem entitled "Futility" in 1929. *Saint Peter Relates an Incident of the Resurrection Day* was issued privately in 1930 and then included in *Saint Peter Relates an Incident: Selected Poems* (1935) together with thirty-seven poems (some in revised or retitled form) from *Fifty Years and Other Poems* and five poems previously uncollected. The title poem of the last collection is a witty and bitter satire on race prejudice evoked by a news account of a government project to send some white and black mothers of soldiers fallen in World War I to France to visit the graves of their sons. White mothers were to go on a first-class ship, followed by black mothers on a separate and less adequate vessel. The poem itself deals not with this incident, but with St. Peter's account of a future Jim Crow episode. Excavating the tomb of the unknown soldier on the great getting up morning, superpatriotic white groups discover that he is black and wish to re-inter him. Instead, he enters heaven singing "Deep River." Johnson achieves only partial success in this satire, for he does not reconcile the simple faith of the black soldier and the sophisticated skepticism of the narrative voice. Only by putting aside his own agnosticism, as he did in *God's Trombones*, could the poet successfully celebrate the resources of black religion.

During the late 1920s the strain of the hard work of the NAACP combined with his creative activity began to tell on Johnson, then in his mid fifties. When Edwin Embree of the Rosenwald Fund offered him a fellowship in 1929, he eagerly accepted it, taking leave from his organizational duties. As it turned out, Johnson did not resume his position, but resigned at the end of 1930.

Manuscript (by permission of Mrs. O. J. O'Kala and P. Richard Megali, the Estate of James Weldon Johnson)

Shortly thereafter he accepted the Adam K. Spence Chair of Creative Literature at Fisk University. This position allowed the leisure for the literary life that had always competed with activism for Johnson's allegiance.

Johnson's writing of the 1930s is more retrospective and historical than creative, however. Aside from the satirical poem, the major works of this period are *Black Manhattan* (1930), a popular historical treatment of black life in New York, and *Along This Way* (1933), a magisterial autobiography. The first of these two accounts sketches the general history of blacks in New York through the nineteenth century in the first sixty pages; the bulk of the book is devoted to black theatrical, musical, and literary developments in the city and to the rise of Harlem as "the recognized Negro capital" not only of America but the world. *Black Manhattan* emphasizes positive developments and ignores the growth of slum conditions in the 1920s. By the time the book was published the Depression was setting in, quickly making Johnson's optimism seem obsolete.

Much more durable is *Along This Way*, an autobiography that Carl Van Doren correctly called "civilized in temper, ironical, urbane, deft and reflective." Lacking the drama or intensity of other classic black autobiographies such as *Narrative of the Life of Frederick Douglass* (1845), *Black Boy* (1945), and *The Autobiography of Malcolm X* (1965), *Along This Way* complements these with its sophistication and variety of experiences related. Equally valuable for its record of the author's childhood, its account of the important events and personalities of his public life, and its statements of his literary purposes, Johnson's autobiography is less revealing of his private personality. The reserve and detachment characteristic of writers of his generation are always maintained. His wife, Grace Nail, more than fifteen years his junior, is not mentioned a single time in the last hundred pages of the work. Even when he discusses religion or politics, he tends to move toward generalization rather than to probe psychological sources. For our sense of the private man then, we have to rely on the covert hints of his fiction and some of his poetry, but as a record and commentary on his public and literary careers in the full contexts of race and history, *Along This Way* is matched only by the work of his great friend and contemporary, *The Autobiography of W. E. B. Du Bois* (1968).

Along This Way ends with speculations about the future of black people in the United States. These are adumbrated in a short book published the following year, *Negro Americans, What Now?*

James Weldon Johnson (courtesy of the Schomburg Center for Research in Black Culture, the New York Public Library, Astor, Lenox and Tilden Foundations)

(1934). The four chapters of this work outline choices for resolving the racial problem, resources available to black people, techniques and policies needed, and a conclusion with a personal coda. Rejecting emigration, physical force, communism, and separatism, Johnson embraces integration as the only feasible course, naming the NAACP as the most useful organization to coordinate the considerable black power of numbers and institutions into a cohesive force. Actual implementation of integration, Johnson argues, will involve education of whites and blacks, greater involvement in the political process, increased pressure to enter the labor movement and the business community, more cultivation of interracial relations, a combination of conservatism and radicalism in racial leadership, and literary and artistic activity that will demolish old stereotypes. Nothing in this program—essentially the NAACP program—is new, but all of it is argued with the calm, commonsensical manner characteristic of Johnson. A cautious, middle-class thinker on questions of political economy, Johnson predictably gives scant attention to the wide ramifications of the country's severe economic crisis. One might complain, too, that his gradualism is too slow. Still, Johnson's own career as writer and activist offered undeniable proof that progress in racial matters was possible. He had reasons for his optimism.

Johnson's life came to an abrupt end on 26 June 1938, when he was killed in a car-train accident while traveling to his summer home in Maine. The accomplishments of his career, literary and otherwise, constitute a major and imperishable part of the history of Afro-American experience and expression in the early twentieth century.

Biography:

Eugene Levy, *James Weldon Johnson: Black Leader, Black Voice* (Chicago & London: University of Chicago Press, 1973).

References:

Houston A. Baker, "A Forgotten Prototype: *The Autobiography of an Ex-Colored Man* and *Invisible Man*," *Virginia Quarterly Review*, 49 (Summer 1973): 433-449;

Robert A. Bone, *The Negro Novel in America*, revised edition (New Haven & London: Yale University Press, 1965), pp. 45-49;

Arna Bontemps, "The James Weldon Johnson Memorial Collection of Negro Arts and Letters," *Yale University Library Gazette*, 18 (October 1943): 18-26;

Stephen H. Bronz, *Roots of Negro Racial Consciousness, the 1920s: Three Harlem Renaissance Authors* (New York: Libra Publishers, 1964), pp. 18-46;

Richard A. Carroll, "Black Racial Spirit: An Analysis of James Weldon Johnson's Critical Perspective," *Phylon*, 32 (Winter 1971): 344-364;

Eugenia Collier, "The Endless Journey of an Ex-Coloured Man," *Phylon*, 32 (Winter 1971): 365-373;

Collier, "James Weldon Johnson: Mirror of Change," *Phylon*, 21 (Winter 1960): 351-359;

Fisk University, Department of Publicity, *James Weldon Johnson* (Nashville: Fisk University, 1939);

Robert E. Fleming, "Contemporary Themes in Johnson's *Autobiography of an Ex-Coloured Man*," *Negro American Literature Forum*, 4 (Winter 1970): 120-124, 141;

Fleming, "Irony as a Key to Johnson's *The Autobiography of an Ex-Coloured Man*," *American Literature*, 43 (March 1971): 83-96;

Fleming; *James Weldon Johnson and Arna Wendell Bontemps: A Reference Guide* (Boston: G. K. Hall, 1978);

Marvin P. Garrett, "Early Recollections and Structural Irony in *The Autobiography of an Ex-Coloured Man*," *Critique: Studies in Modern Fiction*, 13 (December 1971): 5-14;

Addison Gayle, Jr., *The Way of the New World: The Black Novel in America* (Garden City: Doubleday, 1975), pp. 109-116;

Richard Kostelanetz, "The Politics of Passing: The Fiction of James Weldon Johnson," *Negro American Literature Forum*, 3 (March 1969): 22-24, 29;

Richard A. Long, "A Weapon of My Song: The Poetry of James Weldon Johnson," *Phylon*, 32 (Winter 1971): 374-382;

Brander Matthews, Introduction to *Fifty Years and Other Poems* (Boston: Cornhill, 1917), pp. xi-xiv;

Maurice J. O'Sullivan, Jr., "Of Souls and Pottage: James Weldon Johnson's *The Autobiography of an Ex-Coloured Man*," *CLA Journal*, 23 (September 1979): 60-70;

Ladell Payne, "Themes and Cadences: James Weldon Johnson's Novel," *Southern Literary Journal*, 11 (Spring 1979): 43-55;

Roger Rosenblatt, "*The Autobiography of an Ex-Colored Man*," in his *Black Fiction* (Cambridge: Harvard University Press, 1974), pp. 173-184;

Stephen M. Ross, "Audience and Irony in Johnson's *The Autobiography of an Ex-Coloured Man*," *CLA Journal*, 18 (December 1974): 198-210;

Louis D. Rubin, Jr., "The Search for a Language, 1746-1923," in *Black Poetry in America: Two Essays in Historical Interpretation*, by Rubin and Blyden Jackson (Baton Rouge: Louisiana State University Press, 1974);

Joseph T. Skerrett, Jr., "Irony and Symbolic Action in James Weldon Johnson's *The Autobiography of an Ex-Coloured Man*," *American Quarterly*, 32 (Winter 1980): 540-558;

Robert B. Stepto, *From Behind the Veil: A Study of Afro-American Narrative* (Urbana: University of Illinois Press, 1979), pp. 95-127;

Simone Vauthier, "The Interplay of Narrative Modes in James Weldon Johnson's *The Autobiography of an Ex-Colored Man*," *Jahrbuch für Amerikastudien*, 18 (1973): 173-181;

Jean Wagner, *Black Poets of the United States: From Paul Laurence Dunbar to Langston Hughes*, translated by Kenneth Douglas (Urbana: University of Illinois Press, 1973), pp. 351-384;

Wendell Phillips Whalum, "James Weldon Johnson's Theories and Performance Practices of Afro-American Folksongs," *Phylon*, 32 (Winter 1972): 383-395.

Papers:
Johnson's papers are included in the James Weldon Johnson Collection of Negro Arts and Letters deposited in the Beinecke Library of Yale University.

Nella Larsen
(13 April 1891-30 March 1964)

Thadious M. Davis
University of North Carolina at Chapel Hill

BOOKS: *Quicksand* (New York & London: Knopf, 1928);
Passing (New York & London: Knopf, 1929).

PERIODICAL PUBLICATIONS: "Playtime: Three Scandinavian Games," *The Brownies' Book*, 1 (June 1920): 191-192;
"Playtime: Danish Fun," *The Brownies' Book*, 1 (July 1920): 219;
"Correspondence," *Opportunity*, 4 (September 1926): 295;
"Review of *Black Sadie*," *Opportunity*, 7 (January 1929): 24;
"Sanctuary," *Forum*, 83 (January 1930): 15-18;
"The Author's Explanation," *Forum*, Supplement 4, 83 (April 1930): 41-42.

One of the most promising writers to publish during the Harlem Renaissance, Nella Larsen has earned a reputation as an important Afro-American novelist on the basis of two books, *Quicksand* (1928) and *Passing* (1929). Both novels show a skillful handling of narrative and symbolism, as well as a complexity of vision, that place them among the best fiction produced by New Negro authors in the 1920s.

Biographical data on Larsen has been scanty and often erroneous; however, recent scholarship has uncovered some of the facts of Larsen's biography. Born in Chicago, Illinois, on 13 April 1891, Larsen was the daughter of a Danish mother and, apparently, a West Indian father; she frequently alluded to her "mulatto" status. In an autobiographical sketch written for her publisher in 1926, Larsen says her father died when she was two years

Nella Larsen (courtesy of the Beinecke Rare Book and Manuscript Library, Yale University)

old; "shortly afterward her mother married a man of her own race and nationality." She provided no other information about either her natural father or her mother and stepfather. Implicit in her reticence about her background is some discomfort in being the only black member of her immediate family. She revealed, however, that she had one half-sister with whom she attended a private elementary school in Chicago and grew up among children mainly of Scandinavian and German descent. Nonetheless, throughout most of her public life, Larsen was apparently alienated from her white family members; at the height of her success as a novelist, she observed that she rarely saw her mother or sister, then living in California, because "it might make it awkward for them, particularly my half-sister."

She attended secondary school in Chicago and completed one year (1909-1910) in the high school department of Fisk University in Nashville, Tennessee. Her matriculation at Fisk propelled her into an all-black world with which she was never fully comfortable. Her move to the South also initiated an odyssey that took her to Denmark, where she audited courses at the University of Copenhagen from 1910 to 1912, and to New York City from 1912 to 1915, when she studied nursing at Lincoln Hospital. Except for a brief period (1915-1916) spent as an assistant superintendent of nurses at Tuskegee Institute in Alabama, Larsen resided primarily in the New York area.

When she began writing fiction in 1925, she had already had two careers, one as a nurse and the other as a librarian. After working as a nurse at Lincoln Hospital from 1916 to 1918 and later for the New York City Department of Health (1918-1921), Larsen became a New York Public Library assistant. She received a certificate from its library school in 1923 and was employed as a children's librarian from 1924 to 1926. However, during her years as a nurse and a librarian, she had begun an association with the cultural awakening in Harlem, mainly as the socialite wife of Dr. Elmer S. Imes, a physicist, whom she had married on 3 May 1919. Her job at the 135th Street Branch of the New York Public Library, where the Schomburg Collection of materials on black culture was started, as well as a natural interest in literature, led Larsen to take advantage of her social contacts for writing and publishing. Her first story appeared in print in January 1926, the same month in which she resigned from her position with the library.

Larsen's apprenticeship as a writer was relatively short and included experimentation with the short story. Two of her tales were published in 1926 under a pseudonym. Although her short stories do not have black characters, they present versions of the affluent characters and themes of discontent and concealment that were developed in her novels. Importantly, too, the stories reflect Larsen's penchant for the surprise ending which characterized, and possibly weakened, her longer fiction. In 1926 Larsen began writing her first novel and from that time on considered herself a novelist.

Encouraged by her social acquaintances—Walter F. White, then assistant to James Weldon Johnson at the NAACP and whose second novel, *Flight* (1926), Larsen had attempted to defend in *Opportunity* magazine; and Carl Van Vechten, one of the leading white writers interested in the New Negro awakening and the author of the controversial Harlem novel *Nigger Heaven* (1926)—she completed the first draft of *Quicksand* within a short period of time, "five months in her head and six weeks on the typewriter," as she later told a reporter for the *New York Amsterdam News*. Van Vechten brought the novel to the attention of his publisher, Alfred A. Knopf, who not only accepted it but also asked Larsen for two additional manuscripts.

Quicksand appeared on 20 March 1928 to enthusiastic reviews in the *Amsterdam News, New York Herald Tribune, New York Times, Saturday Review of Literature, Crisis,* and *Opportunity.* Both black and white reviewers recognized Larsen's talents as a new novelist, particularly in the realm of the psychology of characters. W. E. B. Du Bois, in the *Crisis,* hailed the work as "on the whole, the best piece of fiction that Negro America has produced since the heyday of [Charles] Chesnutt." Roark Bradford, in a more qualified appraisal for the *Tribune,* wrote that "in spite of its failure to hold up to the end, the book is good" and praised the "saneness" of Larsen's writing. The *Times Book Review* ran a favorable article that concluded: "This is an articulate, sympathetic first novel, which tells its story and projects its heroine in a lucid, unexaggerated manner. In places, perhaps, it is a little lacking in fire; in vitality one finds it more convincing than moving. But it has a dignity which few first novels have, and a wider outlook upon life than most negro [*sic*] ones." However, it was Alain Locke, one of the major initiators of the Harlem Renaissance, who, in *Opportunity*'s "1928: A Retrospective Review," placed *Quicksand* in its proper perspective: "This study of the cultural conflict of mixed ancestry is truly a social document of importance, and as well, a living, moving picture of a type not often in the foreground of Negro fiction, and here treated for the first time with adequacy. Indeed this whole side of the problem which was once handled exclusively as a grim tragedy of blood and fateful heredity now shows a tendency to shift to another plane of discussion, as the problem of divided social loyalties and the issues of the conflict of cultures."

Quicksand is both cross-cultural and interracial, as the epigraph from Langston Hughes's poem "Cross" suggests: "My old man died in a fine big house./ My ma died in a shack./I wonder where I'm going to die,/Being neither white nor black?" The heroine, Helga Crane, much like Nella Larsen herself, is of Danish and West Indian parentage and is a restless, complex personality who redecorates her external environment or moves whenever she feels entrapped by her narrow, unfulfilling life. Her quest in the novel is for a viable identity as a woman in a modern multifaceted world. The episodic construction follows Helga's search for changes in her emotional and psychological states by moving to different geographic locations: "She began to make plans and to dream delightful dreams of changes, of life somewhere else. Some place where at last she would be permanently satisfied. Her anticipatory thoughts waltzed and eddied about to the sweet silent music of change. With rapture almost, she let herself drop into the blissful sensation of visualizing herself in different, strange places, among approving and admiring people, where she would be appreciated, and understood." No single place measures up to her expectations and needs, and as a result, Helga travels from place to place searching for something in the external world that will bring her inner peace, satisfaction, and happiness.

Initially she leaves a teaching position at Naxos, a small black college in the South that is modeled on Tuskegee Institute. Helga rejects Naxos, its students and teachers, because she feels at odds with the restrictive environment. She sees herself as different, particularly in her appreciation of beauty and color in clothing and furnishings, and she wants the opportunity to live a fuller life than the institution will allow. At the same time, Helga desires approval and recognition of her value and her worth as an individual; however, she is incapable of actually showing it to her colleagues and associates. She is aloof, reticent, and critical of others, though she recognizes that "the feeling of smallness . . . hedged her in." Despite a final interview with the school's principal, Dr. Anderson, who questions Helga's motives, nearly causing Helga to reverse her decision, she departs from the South, which she associates with all the limitations of the school.

Helga travels to Chicago, where she attempts to reclaim her lost childhood by seeking out her

Nella Larsen (courtesy of the Prints and Photographs Collection, Moorland-Spingarn Research Center, Howard University)

maternal uncle, who represents the possibility of financial security. She goes to her Uncle Peter in need of both assistance and direction; however, he is away from home, and his new wife, a white woman, rejects any familial association with a black person and disavows Helga's claim as relative. Unable to find what she considers acceptable work in Chicago, Helga secures a job that takes her to New York and to the center of black life among the upper circles of Harlem in its heyday.

For a short time, Helga's life in New York appears satisfactory, though she recognizes that it is "bounded by Central Park, Fifth Avenue, St. Nicholas Park, and One Hundred and Forty-fifth Street. Not at all a narrow life, as Negroes lived it, as Helga Crane knew it. Everything was there. . . ." She especially enjoys her living arrangements with Anne Grey, a well-to-do, cultured widow, because it provides her with access to Harlem society, which gives Helga "a sense of freedom, a release from the feeling of smallness . . . [experienced] first during her sorry, unchildlike childhood among hostile white folk in Chicago, and later during her uncomfortable sojourn among snobbish black folk in Naxos." Yet she begins to recoil from her new physical space and from the black people surrounding her: "More and more she made lonely excursions to places outside of Harlem." A chance meeting with Dr. Anderson from Naxos reminds her of a "vague feeling of yearning, that longing for sympathy and understanding." Harlem becomes intolerable. A $5,000 check from her Uncle Peter, along with a letter encouraging her to visit her mother's sister in Copenhagen, solves her dilemma. Helga leaves the United States with the intention of settling permanently in Denmark.

Her Aunt Katrina and uncle, Herr Dahl, represent family and kin from a brief, happy interlude in her childhood. Denmark means freedom from the racism of the United States. Nonetheless, once in Copenhagen Helga soon discovers that she is an exotic foreigner, who is attractive ultimately because of her African heritage. Although her aunt and uncle love her, they emphasize her difference and her dependency; in the process, they force Helga to acknowledge the complexity of her situation: that while she yearns to move backward in time and reclaim her youth, she desires to do so as an adult. She realizes that she cannot accomplish her purpose in Denmark among Scandinavians who have no understanding of what it means to be a black person. A proposal by a prominent Danish painter prompts Helga's discovery that she misses the companionship of blacks in her all-white environment. She rejects the proposal and resolves to return to New York.

Helga's reentry into black life in Harlem is even less appealing than her first encounter had been. Failing in an attempt to reach out to Dr. Anderson, whom she recognizes as a potential lover and friend in spite of his recent marriage to Anne Grey, she has a religious experience in a storefront church, marries the preacher who had conducted the service, and returns with him to his native Alabama. Helga starts a new life in the rural black community pastored by her husband, the Reverend Pleasant Green, who represents God and who is a father figure. The simple, conventional Green offers Helga an uncomplicated existence as a minister's wife and as a member of a religion that subordinates human responsibility to God's will. The marriage satisfies her longing to return to childhood: "Secretly she was glad that she had not to worry about herself or anything. It was a relief . . . to put the entire responsibility on someone else." However, the union with the pompous, un-

kempt Green leaves Helga unfulfilled, except in her sexuality, which she had come to accept as a major part of her identity since her conversion: "Emotional, palpitating, amorous, all that was living in her sprang like rank weeds at the tingling thought of night, with a vitality so strong that it devoured all shoots of reason."

Helga's vitality does not last. The poverty and the deprivation of the community are so alien to her that she cannot be happy or "subdue the cleanly scrubbed ugliness of her own surroundings to soft inoffensive beauty." Two pregnancies within twenty months deplete her energy and leave her virtually incapable of caring for her twin boys, her daughter, or herself. With the birth of her fourth child, she becomes too weak to fulfill her roles as wife and mother. Although she convinces herself that she will leave her husband and return to the material comforts of her life in New York, Helga knows that she will not abandon her children, because much of the misery of her own life stemmed from her being rejected by her parents. The desertion by her black father and the "aloofness" of her white mother combine with all her lost opportunities for happiness and create an oppressive sense of emptiness within her, an emptiness which even her children cannot displace. She feels herself engulfed in a "quagmire" of her own making and understands the implications: "It seemed hundreds of years since she had been strong. And she would need strength. For in some ways she was determined to get herself out of this bog into which she had strayed. Or—she would have to die." *Quicksand* ends neither with Helga's escape nor with her death but concludes with her becoming pregnant with a fifth child before she has recovered from the birth of the fourth.

The dramatic ending is graphic realism which may seem too drastic a shift of fortune for the search for self Helga Crane undertakes, but it is thematically and symbolically in keeping with her downward spiral into self-induced despair and destruction. From the beginning, she is a divided person who wants a full, rich life, one marked by achievement and recognition, yet she is also an individual incapable of adhering to any one set path in life, primarily because she does not know what she wants to be or what her potential is. Her own restless nature and her latent sexual desires combine with her conflicting attitudes toward race and gender to cause her downfall. Helga's tragedy is personal but far-reaching in its meaning. The psychological dualism inherent in her obsessive awareness that she is a product of both white and black cultures is intensified by her female perspective. As a mulatto in environments clearly defined by race, Helga has reservations about the world of whites and that of blacks; as a modern woman without the protection of family or money, she has questions about a society with fixed roles for men and women. Unfortunately, she does not have the personal resources and strengths necessary for extricating herself from her dilemma or for formulating a positive definition of herself.

Throughout *Quicksand* Nella Larsen is most effective in her use of symbolism to enhance characterization and to underscore theme. Images of entrapment, suffocation, and asphyxiation become more prominent and integral toward the end of the novel, where they skillfully evoke the heroine's mental and physical condition, but from the outset of the novel, they complement the journey, Larsen's major structural device. The literal journey functions symbolically as well, because *Quicksand* is essentially a Bildungsroman interrelating psychological and social forces in Helga Crane's search for definition and development. Each phase of the spatial journey—Naxos, Chicago, Harlem, Denmark, and Alabama—marks a symbolic stage in her developing consciousness. The narrative structure depends upon the variety of scene changes, yet simultaneously it brings into convergence action and meaning to emphasize Helga's spiritual quest for growth and identity. The novel is both moving and successful, despite Helga's failure, because its messages extend outward from the focus on an individual mulatto heroine and make her restless energy and relentless search endemic to modern identity in general and to female identity in particular. Its suggestive psychological dimensions render *Quicksand* a fresh and fascinating literary work; even though some of the mannered settings and conversations, such as in Naxos and in Harlem of the New Negro Renaissance, now seem dated, they are authentic reflections of the period and retain historical interest for contemporary readers.

From the 1930s to the 1970s, Larsen's first novel was out of print; nonetheless, it continued to receive favorable critical commentary from scholars and students of Afro-American literature. Pioneering critics Sterling Brown, Hugh Gloster, Arthur Davis, and their followers, such as Robert Bone, all praise the strongest elements in *Quicksand* and label Larsen the most gifted novelist among the writers of the Harlem Renaissance. At the same time, early critics also link Larsen to Jessie Fauset, Walter White, and the literature of "passing," be-

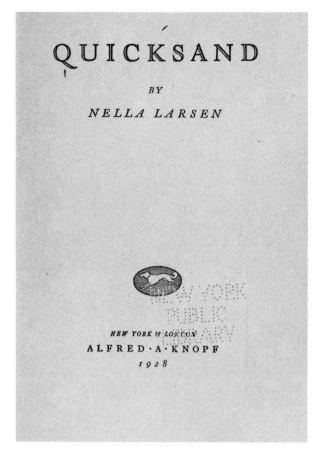

Title page for Larsen's first novel (courtesy of the Schomburg Center for Research in Black Culture, the New York Public Library, Astor, Lenox and Tilden Foundations)

cause of her concern with a heroine of mixed blood. Later critics, particularly those writing in response to the second black renaissance of the 1960s, tend to interpret Larsen's novel in terms of the theme of identity, rather than that of passing. Addison Gayle, for example, calls *Quicksand* "almost modern in its plot and conflicts . . . it seeks to broach the wider question of identity, not the loss of it, but the search for it, and to suggest that this search in a world, race mad, must produce serious psychological problems of the spirit and soul." More recent critics, aware of both the black civil rights movement and the women's movement, applaud Larsen's portrayal of the black female and feminist concerns. Hortense Thornton believes that Helga Crane "can best be understood through considering her sex," while Margaret Perry sees in Larsen "vividness, truth (especially in her revelations of a woman's inner life)." From the publication of the novel to the present, critics have generally praised its complexity, sophistication, and artistry, but not without also calling attention to its weak and not entirely convincing ending.

In 1928 the novice writer dedicated *Quicksand* to her husband; but a year later, when her second novel, *Passing*, appeared, the dedication to popular writer Carl Van Vechten and his wife, actress Fania Marinoff, signaled Larsen's literary arrival. Published 26 April 1929, *Passing* confirmed her promise and her place among New Negro authors. In fact, with the publication of two novels within thirteen months, Nella Larsen at thirty-eight years old had become as prolific as the older Jessie Fauset, who was then considered the major black female novelist and with whom Larsen was frequently compared. Moreover, the epigraph, four lines from the long poem "Heritage" by another leading New Negro writer, Countee Cullen, indicated her connection with the Harlem Renaissance: "One three centuries removed/From the scenes his fathers loved,/Spicy grove, cinnamon tree/What is Africa to me?"

Larsen answered the question posed by "Heritage" in a story that caused considerable interest. *Passing* treats two women from Chicago who had been friends during their childhood. One, Irene Redfield, is from a secure black family and is married to a successful medical doctor in New York City. The mother of two sons, Irene is part of the middle class in Harlem, where she enjoys social prominence and material comforts. The other woman, Clare Kendry, is the daughter of a janitor who drank too much and died in a barroom fight. Raised by her father's white aunts, Clare has escaped a life of drudgery by marrying a wealthy white man, who assumes that she is also white. Much of the narrative is devoted to establishing the difference between the personalities of the two women, the one who "passes" and the one aware of the deception, though the perspective is primarily that of Irene who reacts and responds to the reappearance of her once black friend. Reviews in contemporary white and black publications, such as *Crisis, Opportunity, Bookman, Saturday Review,* the *New York Sun, Herald Tribune,* and *Times Book Review,* all emphasized the exotic theme of passing across the color line and identified the author as "partly of negro [sic] blood," and stressed what the *Sun* reviewer called "that double consciousness which torments the half-caste the world over."

Less skillfully developed than *Quicksand, Passing* is nonetheless a fascinating study in the psychology of a black woman committed to middle-class values and ideals. Irene Redfield, who is light

enough in skin color to pass, recognizes that she wants security more than anything else in her life. She admits that she is unwilling to take risks, either with her own future or that of her sons. Her husband, Brian, is dissatisfied with life in the United States because he longs for freedom from the racism that impinges upon his existence despite his relatively insulated profession and his status in the black community. Irene, however, is unwilling to consider the move to Brazil that Brian desires; she believes that their lives are secure and that they are too well established in Harlem to seek intangible freedoms in a foreign country. Irene feels safe in her life of servants, bridge parties, charity balls, and smart fashions. Change of any sort would be threatening.

Clare Kendry, passing for white as Mrs. John Bellew, enters Irene's life and shows that she has been, and still is, willing to risk anything in order to have whatever she wants. Though seemingly even-tempered and pleasant, she has a "having" nature, as Irene repeatedly observes. What Clare seems to want most is the company of blacks whom she misses in her life with a man who despises them. Although she is the mother of one daughter, she thinks nothing of jeopardizing her marriage by renewing her friendship with Irene, visiting at the Redfields' home, and socializing in Harlem. In fact she seems on the verge of renouncing her position as a wealthy white matron, accepting life as a black person, and possibly taking Irene's husband as a mate.

Much of the tension in the narrative stems from Irene's perception that Clare is a threat to her marriage and to her security. She senses that Brian is attracted to the beautiful, blond, and daring Clare; she fears that he might leave her for the other woman, particularly should she return to her race. Little of Clare's thinking about Brian is central to the narrative; she is somehow as elusive as she is beautiful. Most of what is known about her is filtered through Irene's consciousness, especially her awareness of Clare as having "remained almost what she had always been, an attractive, somewhat lonely child—selfish, wilful [sic], and disturbing." It is Irene who gradually unfolds Clare's character and exposes her own: "a suspicion . . . surprised and shocked her. . . . that in spite of her determined selfishness the woman before her was yet capable of heights and depths of feeling that she, Irene Redfield, had never known." Irene "was aware, too, of a dim premonition of some impending disaster. It was as if Clare Kendry had said to her, for whom safety, security, were all-important:

'Safe! Damn being safe!' and meant it." Irene becomes a woman who is more and more distracted and disturbed as she either discovers or imagines the threat posed by her friend.

Although passing is one of the issues that Larsen treats in the novel, it is not the major theme, despite the suggestiveness of the title. Irene's attitudes toward passing are complex. On the one hand, she resents those individuals, like Clare, who would pass and leave the race, even though she herself casually crosses the color line whenever it is convenient to do so. On the other hand, she admires the nerve that it takes to pass for white and feels obligated to protect the individual who is passing. Irene knows that Clare's reasons for passing are clearly tied to economic pressures, and she finds it difficult to fault her friend's decision to marry into the white race. Clare's feelings about crossing over and her feelings about blacks are, however, never clear. She apparently has great respect for Irene's father and mother, who treated her well when she was a child, and for Irene, who accepted her as a friend despite her poverty, but she does not seem to feel deeply about blacks as a group or about individual blacks whom she meets in the course of the narrative. Certainly she does not appear responsive enough to them to want to leave her present life in order to join them permanently in Harlem; nonetheless, a deep-seated, but indefinable racial attraction seems to draw Clare back to a black world.

In *Passing* Larsen develops the story line of a woman who misses her race enough to risk the detection of her blackness, but she has few options for resolving the tangled plot. Larsen cannot sufficiently motivate Clare to return to her race, yet she cannot logically dismiss Clare's attraction to blacks and to Harlem. At the same time, Larsen cannot wholly approve of Irene's narrow materialism, nor can she punish or condemn her for it. Her solution, unrealistic and somewhat ambivalent, is to have Clare fall, jump, or be pushed from an open window at a Harlem apartment party just as her irate husband appears to denounce her. Irene is made to look suspiciously like a woman who may have committed murder, whether accidentally or intentionally. The narrative concludes with Irene still concerned about appearances and about salvaging as much of her comfortable life as possible, once the threat of Clare has been removed.

Among recent critics *Passing* has received new evaluations that separate it from both the fiction of the tragic mulatto and the literature of passing. Addison Gayle holds the singular view that it is "superior" to *Quicksand* "in terms of character development, organization, and fidelity to language," and that the three-part structure—"Encounter," "Re-encounter," "Finale"—makes for a more well-knit novel. Gayle, however, believes that Larsen "loses both focus and emotional intensity in her attempt to balance Irene Redfield and Clare Kendry against one another." His assessment of the novel's weakness is similar to the objections voiced by Amritjit Singh and earlier critics who observed the fractured focus of the work. Neither critic Sister Mary Ellen Doyle nor Mabel Youman argues with the opinion that *Passing* is flawed, but both point out that its merits may have been obscured by a mistaken critical emphasis on Clare Kendry and the theme of passing, and they insist that the protagonist is actually Irene Redfield, who must be seen as central for an accurate reading of the novel. Their readings have had an impact on other critics; for example, Claudia Tate builds upon Youman and Doyle in attempting to rescue *Passing* from charges of being anachronistic and melodramatic.

Recent estimations agree that the ending is problematic and ambiguous. Margaret Perry, for instance, concludes that "it is entirely possible that [Larsen] wanted this confusion [Clare's death as intentional or accidental suicide or murder] to persist forever in the reader's mind, but this certainly does not give the book any artistic complexity that might intrigue the imagination." Robert Bone suggests that despite "a false and shoddy denouement," *Passing* "is probably the best treatment of the subject in Negro fiction"; not only does Doyle concur but she also observes that because "it is probably the best of the 'passing' novels," it "deserves reassessment." The direction of recent Larsen criticism seems to indicate that the basis of the reassessment will be in terms of her understanding of women characters, or as Perry states, in calling attention to the importance of Larsen's work, a reassessment may well focus upon her "awareness of female sexuality."

Larsen's fiction is indeed concerned with the lives of middle-class women who, though cast in traditional roles, assume responsibility for their own lives. Her heroines are blacks who resemble whites in their skin coloring, as well as in their mannerisms and life-styles. They are modern, urban characters who are far removed from the world of southern blacks and agrarian settings; however, one of Larsen's persistent themes is the relationship of these black characters to their heritage and the legacy of the past. Hers is a sophisticated group enjoying the best that New York has to offer; they attend shows and parties, dress in clothes purchased from smart Fifth Avenue shops, and dine at the best restaurants, but they are not free of the restrictions of racism, a point Larsen is careful to make. Her characters are not free of self-doubt, either, as they search for meaning in their lives; they are vaguely dissatisfied with who and what they are, but they seem basically unable to find a course of action that would allow them to develop fully their potential. Although Larsen's emphasis is on cosmopolitan and fashionable aspects of comfortable existences, she refuses to celebrate the values of the black middle class or to espouse racial "uplift" in propagandistic portraits. While it may be true that her characters do not know and cannot know who they are because of their divided heritages and allegiances, Larsen seems to indicate that their best opportunity for meaningful lives lies with the world of the cultured middle class, who can, to an extent, enjoy the best of both the black and the white worlds. Simultaneously she approves and disapproves of their pretensions and their aping of white manners and mores, but she does not see an alternative to their lives in the folk customs or practices of rural blacks, whose primitivism and poverty offset for Larsen their spiritual and cultural wealth.

Larsen herself valued the material and social benefits of the upper strata in Harlem, and she cultivated the friendship and endorsement of the most prominent blacks and of those whites who supported the New Negro Renaissance. For example, she was twice recommended for the Harlem Award for Distinguished Achievement Among Negroes in the literature category by Lillian Alexander, wife of Dr. E. R. Alexander and one of Harlem's famous hostesses as well as a founder of the National College Women's Organization and chair of the Department of Education at the 137th Street YWCA. She sought out several of the most distinguished blacks and whites in the city for her letters of support: James Weldon Johnson, author and NAACP executive, and Edward Wasserman, wealthy, white banker, for the 1928 awards; and W. E. B. Du Bois, scholar and editor of *Crisis,* and Carl Van Vechten for the 1929 contest. She won the Harmon Foundation's bronze medal for literature in 1928, which placed her second behind Claude McKay who received the gold medal for *Home to Harlem,* but in 1929 Larsen did not receive a Harmon prize. She applied for a Guggenheim Foundation Fellowship in creative writing that year. Her recommendations were from Johnson, Van Vechten, White, Blanche Knopf (wife of publisher Alfred A. Knopf), and Muriel Draper (writer

and interior decorator). She was especially eager to receive a Guggenheim because, as of the 1929 application period, the foundation had not awarded a grant in creative writing to a black woman; she hoped to have the distinction of being the first. Larsen won one of the coveted grants for 1930 on the strength of her past achievement, her recommendations, and her project, which was a novel about the "difference in intellectual and physical freedom for the Negro—the effect on him—between Europe" and the United States.

Although able to garner support for her work from prestigious individuals, Larsen was never one of the more popular authors of the Harlem Renaissance. She remained outside the coterie of writers, yet she knew many of them, such as Johnson, White, Fauset, Rudolph Fisher, and, for a time, Jean Toomer. Unlike the majority of the writers, she did not publish her work in *Opportunity* or *Crisis.* Her associations with literary artists were mainly the result of her social position. Her reserved and standoffish personality seemingly prevented others from gravitating toward her. Her age was another factor contributing to her isolation; nearly thirty-seven years old when her first novel appeared in 1928, she was older than aspiring New Negro authors such as Langston Hughes but younger than those of her social status, Fauset or Johnson for instance. Larsen was, in a sense, a society matron turned novelist, though one who was, as she admitted in 1929, thoroughly modern enough to smoke cigarettes, wear her dresses short, bob her hair, and assume her maiden name for the publication of her novels.

Concerned about appearances, she readily confessed that her mannerisms were acquired and her tastes carefully cultivated. She tried to make her own life as dramatic as that of any of her heroines. For example, she once revealed what she termed "the ritual which the reading of particular books always demands": "a Houbigant scented bath, the donning of my best green crepe de chine pyjamas, fresh flowers on the bedside table, piles of freshly covered pillows and my nicest bed covers." Such ceremony gave Larsen a certain style and allure that others remarked even while they observed her aloofness in social situations. Whereas she enjoyed creating a special aura for herself, she was candid enough to admit that her "greatest weakness" was "dissatisfaction" and that although she was "not quite sure of what she want[ed] to be spiritually," "books, money, and travel would satisfy her materially."

Larsen loved books as much as she did glamour and excitement. Although she was not college-educated, she impressed her associates with her knowledge of books. Walter White was so impressed that he recommended her for a position with the Book League of America, while Charles S. Johnson, editor of *Opportunity* magazine, would write that hers was "a most extraordinarily wide acquaintance with past and current literature." An avid reader and collector, particularly of Knopf's Blue Jade series, Larsen displayed the effects of her reading in her fiction.

She identified Van Vechten and John Galsworthy as her favorite authors; Van Vechten's attention to the details of an "amusing" contemporary scene, particularly in *Peter Whiffle: His Life and Works* (1922), and Galsworthy's to social milieu make their way into both of her novels. James Joyce's *Ulysses*, which she requested in 1927 from a friend traveling in Europe, inspired her experiments with interior monologues in *Passing*. Carlo Goldoni, an eighteenth-century playwright who reformed the Italian theater and wrote for the French, gave impetus to her treatment of social conventions and injustices. Larsen also admired the works of such modern writers as Marmaduke Pickthall, Taylor Gordon, and Rudolph Fisher.

At the height of her popularity in 1930, Larsen prepared for a year in Spain working on her Guggenheim project and enjoying her first trip to Europe. Before her departure, however, she was accused of plagiarism when a reader of *Forum* magazine noticed that "Sanctuary," the only short story she published under her own name, closely resembled "Mrs. Adis," a story by Sheila Kaye-Smith from a 1922 issue of *Century* magazine. Although Larsen wrote an open letter in *Forum* clearing herself of any wrongdoing and had the support of the editors who had seen the story in draft versions, she suffered a loss of her confidence as a creative writer. Thereafter, she not only wrote more painstakingly but also depended upon outside readings of her works in progress. The incident combined with the deterioration of her marriage to make her fellowship year less than productive, though she tried to complete a novel begun before the publication of *Passing*, and she started two new novels during her stay in Spain and France.

Continued success as a published novelist eluded Larsen. Following her return from Europe, she experienced further marital problems, which she attempted to resolve by moving to Nashville, where her husband was teaching at Fisk University. She remained committed to her writing during 1932 and 1933 when she began a fourth novel as well as a fifth in collaboration with Edward Donahoe, a young white writer. None of these projects was published. After her divorce in 1933, Larsen moved to the lower east side of New York, where she associated with writers, artists, and literary people who knew her as a novelist. Greenwich Village rather than Harlem became the center of her social life until the late 1930s when she began to withdraw from her friends and acquaintances there. Between 1937, when she made her first effort to drop out of her social life by pretending to sail for South America, and 1939, when she discontinued all correspondence with her associates in downtown Manhattan, Larsen consciously concealed her activities and whereabouts. For undisclosed reasons, she chose to change her life and to disappear by moving from one apartment building on Second Avenue to another which was just across the street in a smaller building.

Larsen returned to nursing after her former husband's death in 1941, when she lost the alimony that had freed her from holding a job during the

Nella Larsen (photo by Carl Van Vechten, by permission of Joseph Solomon, the Estate of Carl Van Vechten)

1930s. She spent the last twenty years of her life working as a night nurse and supervising nurse at hospitals on the lower east side of Manhattan and living quietly in the same Second Avenue studio apartment. There are no extant records suggesting that she continued to write.

When Larsen was found dead at the age of seventy-two, she was no longer remembered as a major New Negro writer. Ironically her death in 1964 occurred just as a second rebirth in black letters was underway. It was that new black renaissance that fostered a resurgence of interest in the Harlem Renaissance and in Nella Larsen. Much of the effort to restore Larsen to prominence was frustrated by the paucity of information about her life and career; nonetheless, the general consensus of scholars was that she wrote fiction of quality and substance. Arthur P. Davis lamented after his research, "it is unfortunate that Nella Larsen limited herself to two novels," because "she was a sensitive writer, with great skill in narration," so that "it is reasonable to assume, given her intelligence, that she would have improved her fiction techniques if she had written more." His conclusion has been echoed by other researchers. George Kent has speculated that "valuable light on the Renaissance may be shed by a more critical description of her intentions. Certainly one regrets that she did not write more novels and senses that she had a complexity of awareness that might have produced great works."

Nella Larsen's work is today generally considered not only a viable reflection of a black world now past but also a precise delineation of a particular female perspective that has endured. Feminist critics especially have praised her portraits of black women and have seen a paradigm of the woman artist in her promising but truncated career. Mary Helen Washington has asked: "Why didn't she leave us the greater legacy of the mature model, the perceptions of a woman who confronts the pain, alienation, isolation, and grapples with these conundrums until new insight has been forged from the struggle?" Nonetheless, the truth of the vision in Larsen's novels is a tangible legacy. Her intricate explorations of the consciousness and the psychology of female character form a legacy of the voice of a woman writer struggling to be heard, to convey her special messages, and thereby to free herself from the restrictions imposed upon the female by society.

Nevertheless, the fragmentation and duality in Nella Larsen's fiction suggest that it may be more bound by her marginality and her milieu than her "modern" explorations of race, the color line, class, and gender might indicate. Her narratives stop abruptly, present no viable solutions, and remain dominated by dissatisfaction; they reflect an accurate and honest perception of the subject matter, but, despite an adept framing of character and incident, Larsen's narratives do not finally penetrate the meaning of that subject. Yet in the very act of displaying tensions that cannot be resolved or concluded, she reveals an extraordinary grasp of the formal, structural, thematic, and symbolic elements of fiction. Perhaps Larsen was unable to envision conclusions according to the organic, internal logic of her narratives because she understood too well the ambiguities in the unresolved conflicts of her own life as a writer, a wife, and a woman of color.

References:

Robert Bone, *The Negro Novel in America,* revised edition (New Haven: Yale University Press, 1965);

Sterling Brown, *The Negro in American Fiction* (New York: Atheneum, 1965);

William Bedford Clark, "The Letters of Nella Larsen to Carl Van Vechten: A Survey," *Resources for American Literary Study,* 8 (Fall 1978): 193-199;

Arthur P. Davis, *From the Dark Tower: Afro-American Writers, 1900-1960* (Washington, D.C.: Howard University Press, 1974);

Sister Mary Ellen Doyle, "The Heroines of Black Novels," in *Perspectives on Afro-American Women,* edited by Willa Johnson and Thomas Green (Washington, D.C.: ECCA Publishers, 1975), pp. 112-125;

S. P. Fulinwider, *The Mind and Mood of Black America: 20th Century Thought* (Homewood, Ill.: Dorsey Press, 1969);

Hoyt Fuller, Introduction to *Passing,* by Larsen (New York: Collier, 1971), pp. 10-24;

Addison Gayle, Jr., *The Way of the New World: The Black Novel in America* (Garden City: Anchor/Doubleday, 1975);

Adelaide C. Hill, Introduction to *Quicksand,* by Larsen (New York: Collier, 1971), pp. 9-17;

Nathan Huggins, *Harlem Renaissance* (New York: Oxford University Press, 1971);

George Kent, *Blackness and the Adventure of Western Culture* (Chicago: Third World Press, 1972);

Mary M. Lay, "Parallels: Henry James's *The Portrait of a Lady* and Nella Larsen's *Quicksand,*" *CLA Journal,* 20 (June 1977): 475-486;

David Levering Lewis, *When Harlem Was in Vogue* (New York: Knopf, 1981);

Margaret Perry, *Silence to the Drums: A Survey of the Literature of the Harlem Renaissance* (Westport, Conn.: Greenwood Press, 1976);

Hiroko Sato, "Under the Harlem Shadow: A Study of Jessie Fauset and Nella Larsen," in *Harlem Renaissance Remembered,* edited by Arna Bontemps (New York: Dodd, Mead, 1972);

Amritjit Singh, *The Novels of the Harlem Renaissance: Twelve Black Writers, 1923-1933* (University Park: Pennsylvania State University Press, 1976);

Claudia Tate, "Nella Larsen's *Passing*: A Problem of Interpretation," *Black American Literature Forum,* 14 (Winter 1980): 142-146;

Hortense Thornton, "Sexism as Quagmire: Nella Larsen's *Quicksand,*" *CLA Journal,* 16 (March 1973): 285-301;

Edward E. Waldron, *Walter White and the Harlem Renaissance* (Port Washington, N.Y.: Kennikat Press, 1978);

Cheryl Wall, "Nella Larsen," in *American Women Writers,* volume 2, edited by Lina Mainiero (New York: Ungar, 1980), pp. 505-509;

Mary Helen Washington, "Nella Larsen: Mystery Woman of the Harlem Renaissance," *Ms.,* 9 (December 1980): 44-50;

Mary Mabel Youman, "Nella Larsen's *Passing:* A Study in Irony," *CLA Journal,* 18 (December 1974): 235-241.

George Washington Lee

(4 January 1894-1 August 1976)

Edward D. Clark
North Carolina State University at Raleigh

BOOKS: *Beale Street: Where the Blues Began* (New York: Ballou, 1934);

River George (New York: Macaulay, 1937);

Beale Street Sundown (New York: House of Field, 1942).

George Washington Lee is best remembered for both his fictional and factual accounts of black life on Beale Street in Memphis, Tennessee, and his realistic portrayal of black tenant farmers as they related with one another and with the white majority that surrounded them. Lee is also the first black novelist to give detailed treatment to the adventures of a semilegendary racial hero.

Lee was born four miles west of Indianola, Mississippi, to Reverend George and Hattie Lee. Soon after George's birth, his parents separated; when Reverend Lee died, the family had to move into a sharecropper's shack. Determined to raise her family above the level of poor farmers, Hattie Lee managed to enroll George and his brother Abner in the nearest available school. During his early years George Lee worked as cotton planter and picker, grocery boy, houseboy, and dray driver.

With money he earned as a dray driver, Lee satisfied his passion for reading by buying and reading all of the Buffalo Bill and Horatio Alger novels, often identifying with the poor Alger heroes. Following his mother's advice that he continue his formal training, he entered Alcorn Agricultural and Mechanical College in Lorman, Mississippi. To acquire funds to remain in school during the academic year and to help support the family, Lee worked each summer from 1912 to 1917 as a bellhop at Gayoso Hotel in Memphis, Tennessee, an establishment he often alluded to in his writing.

At Alcorn Lee demonstrated an insatiable quest for knowledge, and he greatly impressed his professors with his prodigious reading habits. Especially significant to Lee were the speeches and orations of white abolitionist Wendell Phillips. He particularly appreciated the emphasis on black pride in Phillips's Toussaint L'Ouverture oration: "I attempt to convince you that the Negro blood, instead of standing at the bottom of the list, is entitled if judged either by its great men or its masses, either by its courage, its purpose, or its endurance, to a place as near ours as any other blood known in history." The lines made a permanent impression on young Lee.

Lee took advantage of the opportunity to advance when the War Department in 1917 yielded to the NAACP's demands for Negro commissioned officers by establishing a Negro army officers' training camp at Des Moines, Iowa. Lee was one of twenty-seven Tennesseans selected to attend. After a two-year tour in France, Lieutenant Lee received an honorable discharge on 27 March 1919 and returned to Memphis, where he later became an insurance executive, a fraternal leader, a politician, and a writer.

George Lee's business and political experiences in Memphis between 1919 and 1931 provided excellent training for his writing career. He read regularly the Negro monthlies, the *Crisis* and the *Messenger*. As orator and as respected commentator on the contemporary scene he regularly pointed out that blacks must organize their own businesses and develop black pride. He argued in political speeches that blacks must unite to eradicate the twin evils, poverty and discrimination. Once the Great Depression eliminated much of the prosperity Beale Street had known, Lee decided that he had to write a book that would renew pride and faith in black businesses. Hence, black pride, his business and political theme, also became his major literary theme in his first book, *Beale Street: Where the Blues Began* (1934), a history Lee worked on for three years and four months.

Lee explained in the preface to *Beale Street* that he was giving "a true story of a few of the colorful events that make up the life of Beale Street." He included a foreword by W. C. Handy that gives the story behind "Beale Street Blues" and highly praises the book's content and form. Most accounts in *Beale Street* portray blacks as businessmen who, despite segregation and deprivation, achieve great success. Lee used the accomplishments of Robert R. Church, Sr., to whom the Union Army granted freedom when it came to Memphis in 1862, as a frame for the other narratives. Church created an estate worth millions of dollars and made Beale Street a commercial center for blacks. Most of the other narratives are vignettes of those who have established themselves "solidly in Beale Street's commercial life." Among the vast array of individuals are bankers, ministers, lawyers, realtors, doctors, businesswomen, and insurance executives, all people Lee knew.

To illustrate that Beale Street's successes were not limited to financial rewards, Lee included citizens who particularly exemplified high moral, in-

George Washington Lee

tellectual, and artistic qualities. He described the 1878 yellow fever epidemic during which thousands of white residents escaped Memphis while numerous blacks stayed to help save the city. He praised Mary Church Terrell, the only American delegate to the International Convention of Women in Berlin who addressed the convention in German and in French. Lee lauded Julia A. Hooks, whose integrated music school trained students who later performed with great success in New York and various world capitals. He also praised W. C. Handy, who translated the blues into an art form, for his "distinguished orchestral work, both as composer and leader."

Lee gave further balance to *Beale Street* by including stories of the corrupt and of the poor and uneducated Negroes who also inhabited the area. The reader learns about Dr. G. W. Smith and Ten Dollar Jimmy, drug-ring leader and dope pusher; Dora Smith and Grace Stanley, bordello madams; Percy Simms and Willie Block, pimp and violent lover. Lee presents "twenty-five or thirty colored men and women with rakes, hoes and other digging tools, with buckets and baskets digging around in the garbage and refuse for food." Even at the risk of undercutting his black pride theme, Lee admitted that there were those among Beale Street's intellectual and civic workers who had not employed their talents to improve the living standards of the downtrodden.

Through richly diverse characters, strikingly idiomatic language, highly effective descriptive passages, and a Chaucerian attention to detail—at times overwhelming—Lee successfully captured the tempo of Beale Street.

The book gained wide critical acclaim. It received a favorable review from Clifton Fadiman in the *New Yorker* (July 1934). George S. Schuyler wrote in the *Pittsburgh Courier* (21 July 1934) that Lee "has moved up to the front rank of Negro authors and produced a work of real historical merit." Jonathan Daniels praised *Beale Street* in the July 1934 *Book-of-the-Month Club News*, making Lee the first black to have a book advertised by the Club. The *New York Times*, the *Nation*, and the *New York Sun* expressed varying degrees of approval for the book. Lee's history also enjoyed tremendous financial success, for it gained large black and white reading audiences.

Lee was greatly pleased with the public and critical reception of *Beale Street* and his rising prominence in the Republican party; he had greatly reduced his role in the NAACP and the Urban League. He probably would not have attempted another book had it not been for his learning from Robert Church that Walter White, NAACP executive secretary, and many of the other black intellectuals in the East felt he was not a gifted writer. They argued that *Beale Street* was a success because of the prominence of the street itself, not because of Lee's writing skills. Lee regarded their negative appraisals as a challenge to produce a better book. Three years later, in 1937, after ten drafts and seven rejections, he presented his literary response, the novel *River George*.

The core of the plot for *River George* comes from the third chapter of *Beale Street,* where Lee introduced River George as a Mississippi rouster and notorious community character. Aaron George, the hero of the novel, is a college student at Alcorn A & M who wishes to become a lawyer so he can help to liberate his people "from a bitter bondage which did not end with the signing of the Emancipation Proclamation." Unable to realize his goals because of the death of his father, Aaron George returns home and supports his mother by becoming a sharecropper on Beaver Dam Plantation. But the sense of social responsibility George acquired at Alcorn causes him to reject the ultraconservative attitude of his parents. George dis-

covers he has been cheated by the plantation bookkeeper and later learns that his sweetheart, Ada Green, also belongs to a white man, "Tuh Mister Fred Smith, da Postmaster." He works even harder then to organize the tenant farmers and to get them to question the injustices of the plantation system. George's works further arouse the prejudices of the whites and lead to a tragic confrontation with Fred Smith. During their struggle Smith is killed by a shot from his own pistol after which George flees to Memphis, where he takes refuge on Beale Street with a brothel madam. He then joins the army, becomes a lieutenant, and after serving in France returns to America. Hoping to establish contact with his mother and Ada, George travels to Vicksburg, Mississippi, but is forced to leave because the whites resent his officer's uniform. He is captured in Memphis, but escapes and goes to work as a Mississippi River rouster, later cementing his reputation as a daring and strong man by defeating Black Bill, a worthy antagonist. Still yearning for a closer relationship with his mother and Ada, he returns to Beaver Dam, where he is lynched upon his arrival for the murder of Smith.

Lee effectively used many autobiographical elements that enhance the black pride theme and vivify the difficulties of sharecropping. His attending Alcorn, becoming an army officer and defending his country, and his deep concern for his mother and others are all highly positive attributes that he transferred to his protagonist, Aaron George. After Lee himself had escaped Mississippi tenant farming, he sought ways to fight the corrupt sharecropper system, and he made Aaron George a staunch and powerful opponent of the system. Lee's authentic portrayal of black sharecroppers who labor from morning to night and temporarily find release mainly through Saturday night parties and Sunday religious services is a successful translation of experiences from his early and young adult life into art. And despite the many obstacles they must overcome, Lee's characters, as Lee himself did, bravely face the challenges.

River George received both wide critical approval and adverse reviews. It got a Book-of-the-Month Club recommendation, but the *Brooklyn Eagle* (24 April 1937) concluded that "there are not enough facts to make *River George* good propaganda and there is not enough artistry to make *River George* a good novel." However a *New York Times* reporter (20 June 1937) and a *Washington Tribune* critic (8 May 1937) praised the book for its realistic picture of southern sharecropping. A reviewer for the *Louisville Times* (26 June 1937) wrote:

"Keep writing, books like yours will make you more friends than all the articles on racial questions put together."

Both the praise and the adverse reviews are appropriate. Lee's descriptions of the sharecropper's world and of Beale Street are excellent, but his comments about Harlem are inadequate, and he never discusses Europe despite the fact that Aaron spends over a year there. Regardless, the novel is a compelling exposure of the tenant farmer system and a convincing depiction of a black hero whose work and sturdy bearing often reach epic proportions.

By the end of the 1930s Lee had become so involved in Republican politics and with the E. H. "Boss" Crump political machine that his racial protest leadership was nearly nonexistent. His shift from protest to accommodation is also reflected in his writing, where the major emphasis moved from racial pride to folklore. Lee's last book, *Beale Street Sundown* (1942), fully reflects this thematic change.

Beale Street Sundown is a collection of nine short stories which had appeared as individual works in the *Negro Digest*, the *World's Digest,* and the *Southern Literary Messenger.* Lee fully subscribed to his prefatory comment that "these pieces retail the folkways of Beale Streeters during that gorgeous and melodramatic period when the blues were born." In these short narratives he painted scenes of Beale Street life which are much more works of art than they are social tracts.

The plots reflect great variety. In "Beale Street Anyhow" Matt Johnson and his friends lament the news of a possible street name change and then, through gambling and dancing, conspire to keep the city fathers from changing Beale Street to Beale Avenue. "A Beale Street Treasure Hunt" details an old man's capitalizing on fear and superstition by collecting funds from others to finance a treasure hunt, only to have a ghost appear and frighten all away before the treasure can be unearthed. "The First Blues Singer" is a poignant rendering of the early career conflicts of Alberta Hunter which are brought on by those who wanted her to be a classical singer and her own yearning to be a blues stylist. In "King of the Rousters" Lee describes an encounter between his legendary River George and Bad Sam. "She Made a Preacher Lay His Bible Down" is exactly what Sadie Green, a reformed prostitute, does to Rev. Sylvester Brown when she joins his church choir, wins his love, and causes him to give up the pulpit to marry her. In

"Passing" Myrtle, a black prostitute "passing" in a white whorehouse, falls in love with a black man only to be overwhelmed by ostracism and threats to the extent that she rushes into the river where "a wave of silver mist rolls in and envelops her." "The Beale Street Blues I'm Singing" is a spirited defense for the singing of the blues.

Lee's very interesting and widely popular collection received little national attention, but he derived great satisfaction from the local praise. Harry Martin, an editor from Memphis's *Commercial Appeal,* wrote in the foreword of *Beale Street Sundown* that "his incidents are genuine, his locales authentic, his atmosphere and moods and tempos above challenge." The statement that must have pleased Lee most appeared in a 28 June 1942 *Memphis Press Scimitar* review: "The Boswell of Beale Street has spun the best book of his literary career." The comment is an exaggeration, but Lee's Beale Street mosaic is evidence of tremendous literary growth.

George Lee had no major works published after *Beale Street Sundown.* He continued working for the Republican party and took especially active roles during the Eisenhower presidential years and the Goldwater campaigns for the Republican nomination and the presidency. During the 1960s he became grand commissioner of the Elks and helped raise money for the United Negro College Fund. In May 1968 Lee wrote the lead essay, "Dr. Martin Luther King, Jr.: The Apostle of Non-Violence," for the *Vision,* a journal for the Atlanta Life Insurance Company that he also edited. His other publications consisted mainly of short political and fraternal essays printed in the Elk's Department of Education *Newsletter,* the *Tri State Defender,* the *Memphis Press Scimitar,* and the *Memphis World.*

Lee might have developed into a major author had he not attempted to excel as writer, orator, business executive, politician, and fraternal leader. His three books, however, do make him a significant literary figure, for his history and his fiction artistically present and preserve important segments of early and near mid-twentieth-century black Americana.

References:

Hugh M. Gloster, *Negro Voices in American Fiction* (Chapel Hill: University of North Carolina Press, 1948);

David M. Tucker, *Lieutenant Lee of Beale Street* (Nashville: Vanderbilt University Press, 1971).

John F. Matheus

(10 September 1887-19 February 1983)

Margaret Perry
Valparaiso University

BOOKS: *Ouanga!, Music Drama in Three Acts*, libretto by Matheus and music by Clarence Cameron White (Fort Wayne, Ind.: C. C. White, 1939);

A Collection of Short Stories, edited by Leonard A. Slade, Jr. (Kentucky: Privately printed, 1974).

OTHER: *'Cruiter*, in *Plays of Negro Life: A Sourcebook of Native American Drama*, edited by Alain Locke and Montgomery Gregory (New York: Harper, 1927);

Ti Yette, in *Plays and Pageants from the Life of the Negro* (Washington, D.C.: Associated, 1930);

Dumas' Georges; an Intermediate French Reader, based on Alexandre Dumas's novel, edited, with introduction, notes, and vocabulary, by Matheus and W. Napoleon Rivers (Washington, D.C.: Associated, 1936).

PERIODICAL PUBLICATIONS: "Fog," *Opportunity*, 3 (May 1925);

"Clay," *Opportunity*, 4 (October 1926);

"Swamp Moccasin," *Crisis*, 34 (December 1926);

"The Poetry of Haiti," *Opportunity*, 5 (October 1927);

"Belle Mamselle of Martinique," *Carolina Magazine*, 48 (May 1928);

"Anthropoi," *Opportunity*, 6 (August 1928);

Black Damp, *Carolina Magazine*, 49 (April 1929);

"Coulev' Endormi," *Opportunity*, 7 (December 1929);

"Nomah," *Opportunity*, 9 (July 1931);

"La Brutta," *Opportunity*, 14 (February 1936);

"Sallicolo," *Opportunity*, 15 (August 1937);

"African Footprints in Hispanic-American Literature," *Journal of Negro History*, 23 (July 1938).

John Frederick Matheus was born, one of four sons, in Keyser, West Virginia, to John William and Mary Susan Brown Matheus, on 10 September 1887. His father was a bank messenger who also worked part-time in a tannery. When Matheus was young, his family moved ten miles up the Ohio River to Steubenville, Ohio, where he spent his

John Frederick Matheus

youth. Many of Matheus's twenty-four stories take place in this area at the convergence of West Virginia, Ohio, and Pennsylvania, where, he wrote, "even as the black coal seams run under hills, mountains and deep into the ground, so runs that other black seam of race and color."

Matheus recalls that as a young boy, he enjoyed Harriet Beecher Stowe's *Uncle Tom's Cabin*, which he read to his grandmother—an ex-slave who could neither read nor write. This story had a profound influence on him as a writer and humanist. Matheus also found pleasure and deep interest in Edgar Allan Poe's tales and, later, the experiences of Lafcadio Hearn. The black writers who were best known to him when he was growing up were Phillis Wheatley and Paul Laurence Dunbar. The influence of Dunbar, especially, is apparent in Matheus's works that capture the dialect of poor, illiterate Negroes in the South, such as his play *'Cruiter* (1927).

Matheus attended Western Reserve University, from which he received an A.B. degree in 1910. He had taken a break from his studies to get married to Maud Roberts in 1909. Continuing his education, he received an A.M. degree from Columbia University in 1921 and pursued further study at the Sorbonne in 1925.

For most of his professional career, Matheus was a professor of foreign languages at West Virginia State College (first called West Virginia Collegiate Institute); he was there from 1922 until his retirement in 1958. He also taught languages at Florida A. & M. College, Tallahassee, from 1910 to 1922. He served on a League of Nations commission to investigate slavery in Liberia (1931), spent a year (1945-1946) teaching English in Haiti, and came out of retirement to teach briefly at Kentucky State College and at Hampton Institute. Matheus was an active participant in civic and professional organizations, notably the College Language Association, which he served as treasurer. In a 1980 interview with a reporter from Florida A. & M. University, Matheus, a tireless writer, revealed that he had also been a newspaper reporter. He wrote a column entitled "Pegasus" in a Charleston, West Virginia, newspaper and worked as a spot reporter for the *Cleveland Gazette*.

Matheus's works often treat Christian understanding and reconciliation as methods of dealing with the evils of mankind. He also writes of the meanness and pettiness of whites who were filled with hatred for the Negro in a South unyielding to change. Frequently Matheus's works are based on the folktales and myths he gleaned while studying, traveling, and teaching foreign languages in Europe, Africa, and the Caribbean.

Matheus wrote at least six plays: *'Cruiter, Ouanga!, Tambour, Ti Yette, Black Damp*, and "Guitar." Though he enjoyed some small success in reproducing certain of his plays, Matheus's penchant for genteel, dated, exaggerated language detracted from their appeal. Even Benjamin Brawley, a critic who tended to overpraise writers, observes of a character in *Ti Yette* (the brother of a woman who loves a white man) that he "himself is proud of his

African heritage but has a self-conscious air and uses stilted language...."

Ouanga!, a libretto based upon a story Matheus had written, was put to music by black composer-violinist Clarence Cameron White. This three-act opera tells the story of the man who freed Haiti from French rule and became its president in 1804. Written by 1929, *Ouanga!* was published in 1939 by White. It was aired on a 1948 radio broadcast in New York City and premiered on stage in South Bend, Indiana, in June 1949. It was also performed at the Metropolitan Opera House in May 1956 under the auspices of the Negro Opera Foundation. The *New York Times* praised the piece as "a blend of concert and theatrical styles." White also wrote incidental music for Matheus's unpublished one-act play *Tambour*. This drama, too, is about life in Haiti and was produced in Boston in 1929.

Matheus's desire to treat themes and characters of importance to the black race informs all of his work, particularly his plays which concentrate on the harshness of Negro life and the exploitation and humiliation of Afro-Americans. *Black Damp*, for example, examines the plight of black and white miners trapped in a coal mine disaster. *Ti Yette*, a play flawed by insufficient development of its theme, examines black pride and nationalism through family conflict between a brother and sister.

'Cruiter, a play that was produced in several community playhouses, poignantly tells of the breakup of a poor family in Georgia when the young people go north to better themselves. They must leave behind their beloved grandmother, who cannot adjust to the idea of moving from the South. *'Cruiter* is a more fully realized drama than Matheus's other plays. The language is simple and natural; although the characters are idealized, they speak together with genuine emotional involvement while, at the same time, giving an accurate portrait of the social situation in Georgia prior to World War I. Ruth Miller has noted that "the play is a document of the persistent efforts made by all Blackamerican [sic] writers to challenge the stereotypes of the race that prevailed throughout the era in the North and in the South."

Although Matheus was essentially more interested in playwriting, it was the short story with which he had his greatest literary success. "Fog," his first published story, won first prize in the 1925 *Opportunity* contest for short stories. It was also listed in Edward J. O'Brien's *Best Short Stories of 1925* Honor Roll. Although the story was well re-

Institute, W.Va.
April 16, 1927.

Dear Mr. Locke:

Your letter was a bright ray on a gloomy Easter eve. The check too was quite a surprise as agreeable as unexpected. It is I who am your debtor in the matter of cooperation. I thank you much and heartily.

The success of "The New Negro" has already amply paid me. This check I feel is a bonus.

I am encouraged by your liking "'Cruiter". Sometimes in a dark mood one believes his achievements so fueyile and inadequate that he despairs. Then comes such cheering assurance as yours and the reach that so far exceeds the grasp become heaven and not hell. (Apola gies to Browning).

I am writing my assent in an enclosed letter, that should not contain, perhaps so much of the soul's outpouring. I thank both you and Charles Johnson.

Mrs. Matheus joins me in highest regards, in which, my dear Locke, I shall always subscribe.

Ever sincerely

John F. Matheus.

Letter to Alain Locke in which Matheus grants permission for the publication of his play 'Cruiter in Plays of Negro Life *(1927), edited by Locke and Montgomery Gregory. Matheus's short story "Fog" had been included in Locke's 1925 anthology,* The New Negro *(courtesy of the Alain Locke Papers, Moorland-Spingarn Research Center, Howard University).*

ceived, it displays some structural and stylistic weaknesses, such as an overuse of clichés.

The setting is "on the bridge between Ohio and West Virginia." A group of blacks and whites are in their separate, segregated worlds as they ride a bus wending its way slowly across the bridge. They encounter a fog that becomes more and more impenetrable. The fog symbolizes the clouded minds of some of the people on the bus. A group of white men are on their way to a Klan-like meeting; a young white girl tells her boyfriend, "I don't want to be by those niggers." Their prejudice is counterbalanced by other passengers. While Matheus frequently resorts to clichés to delineate his characters, he still manages to communicate his important theme: ignorance is thick and impenetrable, but, like a fog, it can be replaced by the clear light of understanding. To be sure, the change among the Klan members is immediate if not lasting after the bus nearly plunges with them into a precipice. This brush with death emphasizes the vulnerability of all humans. Even Lafe, the leader of these rough, prejudiced men, asks the old black woman to "Sing us a song, old woman," and then asks the nuns ("I don't believe in Popery," he says) to utter a prayer of thanksgiving for their deliverance from death.

In a 1976 interview Matheus noted: "The story's action is a lateral movement from the particular to the universal: a metaphoric use of the tramcar for the universe, and a grouping together of diverse persons to represent a cross-section of mankind becoming one in a cataclysmic moment. The physical salvation of these people parallels the theme of spiritual redemption. This dangerous moment represents a brief period when inner terror converges with outward commotion to form a bridge of understanding between divergent characters. Redemption through revelation? The author seems to point toward this idea. Thus we see that each person is tested in this moment of near-death. Our attention is focused on types of reaction rather than on individual ones because we do not know any character intimately enough to care for him personally. As readers, we can come away from this story in much the same manner as Crane's correspondent in 'The Open Boat': 'they felt that they could then be interpreters.' Each character in 'Fog,' although seen fleetingly, becomes an interpreter of the event that touches everyone."

In 1926 Matheus published two stories that reflect his artistic interest in the baser side of mankind: "Clay" (*Opportunity*, 1926) and "Swamp Moc-

casin" (*Crisis*, 1926).

The setting for "Clay" is described in terms of bad odors and the oppressive heat of the day; the characters are victims: "Clay was the symbol of their livelihood. . . . Puppets they were all, marionettes of clay. . . ." Like clay, man is malleable by nature, and he will be returned to the earth where "so little difference is there in the grave." Once again death is the equalizer, but the deaths in this story derive from the raw hatred of people intent on maintaining a reprehensible social system.

In "Swamp Moccasin," a story that received first prize in the *Crisis* contest of 1926, the setting is a prison where people are stifled and hate-filled. The system supports inflicting pain and humiliation on blacks. One black man is forced to pick up a swamp moccasin. He has his revenge upon his tormentor: "There he stood a black Laocoon, fascinating the lookers-on. One lightning motion and

John Frederick Matheus

four feet of writhing venom flashed in the air, showing a slick black belly, blotched with old ivory white. Around the neck of the Camp Boss the writhing loops entwined and the cotton-white mouth struck twice in his face." Yet, even as the guard is falling, he shoots the convict in the head.

"Anthropoi" (*Opportunity*, 1928), which illustrates Matheus's social philosophy, contrasts the history of the families of two patriarchs. The antagonists are Bush Winter, "an oversized, swarthy, black-haired mulatto," and Demetrius Pappan, "an undersized, swarthy, black-haired Greek." Pappan prospers in American society because he is white; he even refuses to serve his one-time friend, Bush, when Bush and his family come to the Greek's soda parlor. Both of their sons go to World War I and come home changed; Bush's son becomes impatient with second-class citizenship, and Pappan's son is sensitized to injustice in a racially divided United States. He is nearly killed in a melee brought on by the KKK, and his father suddenly realizes that he and Bush Winter have been closer to one another than he has acknowledged over the years. Their friendship is renewed: "They understood each other, these old, worn fathers, after all."

By the 1930s many of Matheus's stories were based on folktales he had heard during his extensive travels. "Coulev' Endormi" (*Opportunity*, 1929), for example, takes place in Haiti and is an impressionistic sketch that tantalizes the reader with the significance of a mythic figure. But the story fails to bring the legend to life, since too much attention is focused on minor characters.

After the 1930s Matheus's writing pertained closely to his needs as a teacher. He and W. Napoleon Rivers edited a French reader based on Alexandre Dumas's novel *Georges*. Matheus also wrote numerous book reviews and articles. In 1974 he issued a collection of his short stories, privately printed and edited by Leonard A. Slade, Jr.

Matheus's writing of imaginative literature is an example, in many cases, of the early-twentieth-century Afro-American literary artist still using archaic techniques. In his efforts to stress the Negro spirit, its history, and his own belief in and respect for his race, Matheus frequently sacrificed smooth transitions, convincing dialogue, and original expression. This latter weakness led to such expressions as "Madonna eyed Italian mother," "Court house, that citadel of Law and Order" ("Fog"), or "Demetrius Pappan . . . flourished like the green bay tree" ("Anthropoi"). There is a too-generous use of exclamatory phrases and words in uppercase to represent importance or excitement. Much of the writing, then, is dated and overblown. But Matheus contributed to an authentic brand of Afro-American literature. He celebrated the spirit of his own race and railed against ignoble ideas, especially racism and intolerance. At his death Matheus was writing his autobiography; whenever this is edited and published, it will reveal in greater detail the mind and heart of a man committed to an upright life in a world where he lived for a little over ninety-five years.

Reference:
Benjamin Brawley, *The Negro Genius* (New York: Dodd, Mead, 1937), pp. 262-263, 284, 302.

Papers:
Some of Matheus's papers are at Florida A. & M. University in Tallahassee.

Claude McKay

Schavi Mali Ali
Wayne State University

See also the McKay entries in *DLB 4, American Writers in Paris, 1920-1939* and *DLB 45, American Poets, 1880-1945.*

BIRTH: Sunny Ville, Jamaica, 15 September 1889, to Thomas Francis and Ann Elizabeth Edwards McKay.

EDUCATION: Tuskegee Institute, 1912; Kansas State College, 1912-1914.

MARRIAGE: 30 July 1914 to Eulalie Imelda Edwards (divorced).

DEATH: Chicago, Illinois, 22 May 1948.

SELECTED BOOKS: *Songs of Jamaica* (Kingston, Jamaica: Gardner/London: Jamaica Agency, 1912);

Constab Ballads (London: Watts, 1912);

Spring in New Hampshire (London: Richards, 1920);

Harlem Shadows: The Poems of Claude McKay (New York: Harcourt, Brace, 1922);

Home to Harlem (New York & London: Harper, 1928);

Banjo, A Story Without a Plot (New York & London: Harper, 1929);

Gingertown (New York & London: Harper, 1932);

Banana Bottom (New York & London: Harper, 1933);

A Long Way from Home (New York: Furman, 1937);

Harlem: Negro Metropolis (New York: Dutton, 1940);

Selected Poems (New York: Bookman, 1953);

Selected Poems of Claude McKay (New York: Twayne, 1971);

The Passion of Claude McKay: Selected Poetry and Prose, 1912-1948, edited by Wayne F. Cooper (New York: Schocken, 1973).

PERIODICAL PUBLICATIONS: "How Black Sees Green and Red," *Liberator,* 4 (June 1921): 17-21;

"He Who Gets Slapped," *Liberator,* 5 (May 1922): 24-25;

"A Negro to His Critics," *New York Herald Tribune Books,* 6 March 1932, pp. 1, 6;

"Harlem Runs Wild," *Nation,* 140 (3 April 1935): 382-383;

"Lest We Forget," *Jewish Frontier,* 7 (January 1940): 9-11;

"On Becoming a Roman Catholic," *Epistle,* 2 (Spring 1945): 43-45;

"The New Day," *Interracial Review,* 19 (March 1946): 37;

"Why I Became a Catholic," *Ebony,* 1 (March 1946): 32;

"The Middle Ages," *Catholic Worker,* 13 (May 1946): 5;

"Boyhood in Jamaica," *Phylon,* 14 (1953): 134-145.

Festus Claudius McKay was perhaps the most radical of the young black writers who came to prominence during the Harlem Renaissance of the 1920s. Shaped by an attraction to genteel British culture, especially the romantic tradition, derived from his upbringing in Jamaica and shocked into a realization of color prejudices there as well as those he encountered in the United States, McKay struck out in his poetry against confinement from any quarter. Bringing radical sentiments to the sonnet form, he earned a reputation as an uncompromising firebrand. With the publication of the sonnet "If We Must Die" in the *Liberator* in 1919 and the appearance of *Harlem Shadows* in 1922, McKay distinguished himself as a new voice in American and especially black American poetry.

McKay was born in the parish of Clarendon in Sunny Ville, Jamaica, British West Indies, on 15 September 1889 to peasant farmers Thomas Francis McKay and Ann Elizabeth Edwards McKay. He was the youngest of eleven children. His father, a descendant of the Ashanti tribe of West Africa, instilled in the young McKay an appreciation for the purity of black blood. His mother may have been of mixed blood since McKay consistently described her as brown rather than black. Both parents, however, emphasized to McKay the value of pride in racial heritage; his father, in particular, narrated African folktales to McKay and never let him forget his homeland. From tales Thomas McKay told of the enslavement of his own father and his experiences with white men, McKay learned an early distrust for whites. His parents also taught him to be independent, a trait that would be reflected in the philosophies he would espouse.

In spite of the racial pride his family instilled in him, he nonetheless identified with the British empire. His infatuation with British culture shows up in his adolescent poetry. He wrote several pompous verses imitating the English models he had to study in school. "Old England," one of these early efforts, illustrates this infatuation and shows the rhythm and richness of Jamaican vernacular:

> I've a longin' in me debt's of heart dat I can conquer
> not,
> 'Tis a wish dat I've been havin' from since I could
> form a
> t'o't

Claude McKay (photo by Carl Van Vechten, by permission of Joseph Solomon, the Estate of Carl Van Vechten)

> Just to view de homeland England, in de streets of
> London
> walk
> An' to see de famous sights dem' bouten which dere'
> so much
> talk,
> An' to watch de fact'ry chimneys pourin' smoke up to
> de sky,
> An' to see de matches-children, dat I hear 'bout passin'
> by.

McKay would continue this style of writing in his first two volumes of poetry; "Old England" was collected in *Songs of Jamaica* (1912).

Two important influences during McKay's formative years helped to shape his intellectual development: his brother, Uriah Theophilus, who was an elementary school teacher, and Englishman Walter Jekyll, who was on the island to collect Jamaican folklore. McKay had access to their libraries and thus poets like John Milton, Alexander Pope, John Keats, and Percy Bysshe Shelley, all of whose influences can be seen in his poetry. He also read the Victorian authors as well as Dante and Charles Baudelaire.

Uriah Theophilus, who taught in a denominational school and was a lay reader in an Anglican church and a "militant agnostic," strongly influenced McKay's attitudes toward religion. By the time he was ten, therefore, McKay had access to many writers who were considered freethinkers, including Thomas Huxley, William Lecky, and Ernst Haeckel. McKay recalled that when his sister-in-law saw him reading Haeckel's *The Riddle of the Universe* (1900), she called it a "bad book" and tried to prevent him from continuing to read it; his brother intervened.

This atmosphere that encouraged McKay to explore ideas was augmented by contact with Jekyll; he encouraged McKay to read the German philosopher Arthur Schopenhauer, whom he was translating at the time. Jekyll's interest in native island traditions proved even more significant for McKay's intellectual and artistic development. He urged McKay to write poems in the native Jamaican dialect instead of merely imitating poems in English, and he enrolled McKay with the Rationalist Press Association in London.

When McKay was seventeen, he received a scholarship from the Jamaican government to become an apprentice to a cartwright and cabinet-maker in Brown's Town, in the parish of Saint Ann. Perhaps because he did not like the work, or perhaps because the employer was mulatto, McKay left the trade. At nineteen he moved to Kingston, the capital of the island, to become a constable. Here he was exposed to the harsh brutality of race prejudices, with the darker-skinned Jamaicans invariably receiving the worst punishments and with blacks irrevocably locked into the most menial positions in the society, below mulattoes and whites. Blacks were in the majority in his home in the Clarendon mountains, and they occupied chief positions. In Kingston they were relegated to the bottom rungs of society. From his experiences in Kingston, McKay developed an intense hatred for the city, an aversion that would surface as a recurring theme in his work. He left the constable job after ten months, asserting in his preface to *Constab Ballads* (1912) that he had "a most improper sympathy with wrong-doers." Also he had "a fierce hatred of injustice"; recognizing the futility of open rebellion, he returned to the Clarendon mountains.

Now back under the influence of Jekyll, McKay quickly produced his first two volumes of poetry, most of which were written in dialect. Through Jekyll, *Songs of Jamaica* and *Constab Ballads* were published in London in 1912; Jekyll wrote the preface to *Songs of Jamaica*. McKay had captured in the volumes a sense of peasant life in Jamaica. *Songs* responds directly to McKay's childhood and early manhood in the mountains and articulates his clear attachment to land and soil. He included melodies he had composed in the appendix for six of the poems in *Songs* and gave the volume a less sombre tone than *Constab Ballads*.

McKay's dialect-speaking peasants in *Songs of Jamaica* are proud of who they are; their plight comes from the economic system designed to undermine their labors in the soil. In "Quashie to Buccra," for instance, the black man, while cheated out of a fair price for his yams by the white man, nevertheless succeeds in getting the man to appreciate the harvest and the beauty of the land:

De fiel' pretty? It couldn't less 'an dat,
We wuk de bes', an' den de lan' is fat;
We dig de row dem eben in a line,
An' keep it clean—den so it *mus'* look fine.

McKay's love of Jamaica comes through especially in "Clarendon Hills and H.A.H." and "My Native Land, My Home." "Jamaica is de nigger's place,/ No mind whe' some declare:/Although dem call we 'no-land race,'/I know we home is here." A similar sentiment is expressed in "My Mountain Home," in which the poet depicts the lushness of the landscape and vows to return home when he ends his

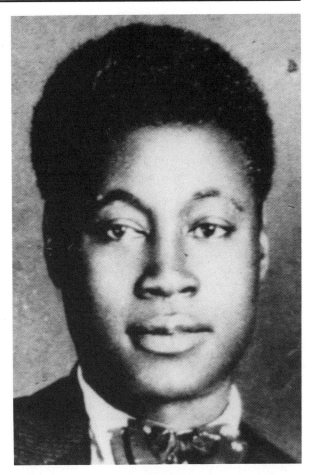

Claude McKay

wanderings. McKay also thinks of the Clarendon mountains as the last resting place of his mother, and in "Mother Dear" he portrays his mother's illness and death. She is depicted as readily accepting death because she is at peace with her environment and with her God.

Although dialect poetry often presents problems to its readers McKay achieves a high level of clarity in this volume. In "Two-an'-Six," for example, a long anticipated market day fails to bring the expected compensation for sugar cane. The light opening "Merry voices chatterin',/Nimble feet dem patterin' " gives way to the reflection: "Cousin Sun is lookin' sad,/As de market is so bad;/'Pon him han' him res' him chin,/Quietly sit do'n thinkin.' "

Constab Ballads addresses the disillusionment of McKay's experiences in Kingston. In "Bumming," the poet comments on the life-style in the city that leads so many people to try to live off others. In "Papine Corner," McKay presents his

203

hatred of the city and of the mulattoes who prefer it. Mulattoes there, McKay says, have created their own caste, and this corner is their gathering place; they are kings and queens of the underworld, with prostitution, crime, and drinking as their distinguishing characteristics. McKay criticizes them for looking down upon other blacks. The "class family," as he derisively calls them, have made themselves foreigners to their own people.

McKay ends the volume with nostalgia for the mountains of home. "Sukee River" becomes a balm with which the poet can soothe his fevered brow and is filled with images of dancing, smiling, and making love with the river. "Love more pure, I ken,/Dan de love o' men,/Knowin' not de fickle mind/Nor de hatred o' my kind;/Purer far, I ken,/Dan de love o' men." As in many of McKay's other poems, the speaker promises to return to Clarendon.

The popularity of the poems in these two volumes led to McKay being awarded (apparently in 1912, though the exact date is unclear) the medal of the Institute of Arts and Sciences in Jamaica in recognition of his achievement; he was the first black islander so rewarded. Ironically he used the stipend attached to his award to leave Jamaica in 1912 for the United States. He landed in Charleston, South Carolina, and went immediately to Tuskegee Institute, Alabama, where he stayed approximately two months. He transferred to Kansas State College with the expectation that agricultural science would be more to his liking. That was not the case, and he left Kansas for New York in 1914. He worked at a series of odd jobs, including several stints in kitchens and as a waiter in Pullman cars.

McKay continued writing poetry during this time, and in December 1917 he published "The Harlem Dancer" and "Invocation" in the *Seven Arts* under the name of Eli Edwards. Frank Harris, Irish-American publisher and critic, printed several of McKay's poems in 1918 in *Pearson's Magazine*, a popular journal of social criticism of the time. It was Harris who launched McKay into the literary world under the name Claude McKay. One of McKay's most militant pieces, "To the White Fiends," was published in *Pearson's* when the *Crisis*, literary organ for the NAACP, refused it. McKay's posture in the poem anticipated the one he would take in "If We Must Die":

Think you I am not fiend and savage too?
Think you I could not arm me with a gun
And shoot down ten of you for every one

Of my black brothers murdered, burnt by you?
Be not deceived, for every deed you do
I could match—out-match: am I not Afric's son,
Black of that black land where black deeds are done?

At this point McKay introduces Christian imagery into the poem that is more functional than biographical:

But the Almighty from the darkness drew
My soul and said: Even thou shalt be light
Awhile to burn on the benighted earth,
Thy dusky face I set among the white
For thee to prove thyself of higher worth;
Before the world is swallowed up in night,
To show thy little lamp: go forth, go forth!

Later in his life, McKay would convert to Catholicism and increase the use of such images in his poetry.

Frank Harris had been impressed with McKay's hard-hitting, critical, daring commentary on race relations. McKay recalled that Harris "had said that the purpose of *Pearson's* was to reach and discover the obscure talents of Americans who were perhaps discouraged, engaged in uncongenial labor when they might be doing creative work. I took his moving message personally, for I was one of those talents." For all of Harris's dedication to the belief that controversial social issues should be expressed by creative writers, his appreciation of McKay's creative talent and knowledge of poetics was largely due to his assumption that people of African descent possessed an inherent primitive natural instinct. He said: "They have plenty of the instinct of the senses, much of which we have lost."

Several months before McKay's poems began appearing in *Pearson's*, he had sent many of them to William Stanley Braithwaite, the highly acclaimed black critic who worked for the Boston *Evening Transcript*. Braithwaite said that McKay's poems were good but that readers could easily tell that the author was black, and this was not advisable since prejudice against everything black was so vast. Consequently he advised McKay to publish poems that did not give away his racial identity. Although McKay made stylistic changes in his new poetry, he was steadfast in his dedication to writing about events that affected blacks and felt that truly creative and socially critical artists necessarily gave away their ethnicity. As he explained in his autobiography, *A Long Way from Home* (1937): "I felt more confidence in my own way because, of all the poets I admire, major and minor, Byron, Shelley, Keats, Blake, Burns, Whitman, Heine, Baudelaire,

Verlaine and Rimbaud and the rest—it seemed to me that when I read them—in their poetry I could feel their race, their class, their roots in the soil, growing into plants, spreading and forming the backgrounds against which they were silhouetted. I could not feel the reality of them without that. So likewise I could not realize myself writing without conviction."

Max Eastman, editor of the *Liberator,* and his sister Crystal became important connections in McKay's life at this time. Eastman began publishing McKay's poetry regularly in 1919, and he also introduced him to Communist sympathizers such as Floyd Dell and John Reed. The most famous of McKay's poems to appear in the *Liberator* was "If We Must Die," which became a kind of symbolic manifesto for the spirit of the Harlem Renaissance. More immediate, however, the poem had been written in response to the racial violence that had occurred throughout America during the summer of 1919. The poem, though not clearly racial in imagery, vividly marked a militant stance in response to racial violence:

> If we must die, let it not be like hogs
> Hunted and penned in an inglorious spot,
> While round us bark the mad and hungry dogs,
> Making their mock at our accursed lot.
> If we must die, O let us nobly die,
> So that our precious blood may not be shed
> In vain; then even the monsters we defy
> Shall be constrained to honor us though dead!
> O kinsmen! We must meet the common foe!
> Though far out-numbered let us show us brave
> And for their thousand blows deal one death blow!
> What though before us lies the open grave?
> Like men we'll face the murderous, cowardly pack,
> Pressed to the wall, dying, but fighting back!

Blacks hailed McKay as an important poet after the publication of the poem. McKay said of his inspiration for the poem: "Our Negro newspapers were morbid, full of details of clashes between colored and white, murderous shootings and hangings. Traveling from city to city and unable to gauge the attitude and temper of each one, we Negro railroad men were nervous . . . we stuck together, some of us armed, going from the railroad station to our quarters. We stayed in our quarters all through the dreary ominous nights, for we never knew what was going to happen. . . . during this time 'If We Must Die' exploded in me."

Critics have considered the poem equal in stature to James Weldon Johnson's "Negro National Anthem," and it has been applied to univer-

sal situations of oppression. Some twenty-five years after its initial publication, "If We Must Die" was reprinted in an English anthology at a time when England, alone and with its back to the wall, was withstanding the onslaught of the Luftwaffe. And the text of the poem was discovered in 1944 on the body of a young white American soldier who had been killed in action. It was also hailed in its immediate context by Sterling Brown, who declared McKay a "poet of the people," maintaining that he had met people who appreciated McKay's poetry in such unlikely places as hotel kitchens in Jefferson City, Missouri, and in barbershops in Nashville.

"If We Must Die," in its far removal from the lyrical Shakespearean sonnet, presaged the major expression McKay's poetry would take: hard-hitting sentiments in recognizable forms. In fact some critics considered McKay's militant expressions in sonnet guise a violation of the basic intent of the form and maintained that he was a poet of hate. Such one-sided criticism clearly did not take into consideration the inspiration for McKay's expression.

After this auspicious literary debut, McKay left the United States for Holland and Belgium in 1919. He also traveled to London, where he lived for a year, working with Sylvia Pankhurst on the *Workers Dreadnought.* Twenty-three of his poems appeared in the Summer 1920 issue of *Cambridge Magazine,* edited by C. K. Ogden. McKay also published *Spring in New Hampshire* in London in 1920, to which the respected critic I. A. Richards contributed a preface. The volume included "Harlem Shadows," which would become the title poem in McKay's collection published two years later. In the poem McKay depicts his recurring dislike for the city by lamenting the plight of young black girls who are drawn into prostitution there. It is the "stern harsh world" that causes the hesitant, "timid little feet of clay" to go "wandering from street to street."

Returning to the United States in 1921, McKay became an associate editor for the *Liberator.* He and Eastman also traveled to Russia together, for this was the period during which McKay supported the revival of the international Communist movement. Wayne Cooper writes in *The Passion of Claude McKay* (1973): "For Claude McKay, revolutionary organization and action seemed clearly preferable to a continuation of the labor and racial strife that marred the American scene after the War. The nation that had vowed in 1917 'to make the world safe for democracy' wound up in 'the

The photograph of McKay speaking at the Kremlin that appeared in the December 1923 issue of the Crisis *(courtesy of the Moorland-Spingarn Research Center, Howard University)*

Red Summer' of 1919 with an orgy of violence and repression at home."

McKay warned white radicals, however, that the racial problems in America would only worsen if they were not faced head-on. McKay felt that blacks needed greater pride, unity, and determination, traits that could not be supplied by whites no matter how sympathetic they were to the plight of blacks. Therefore, along with other noted black socialists of the time, such as W. A. Domingo and Hubert Harrison, McKay worked with Marcus Mosiah Garvey's Universal Negro Improvement Association (UNIA) through the publication of several penetrating articles in *Negro World,* the literary organ of the group. By 1922, after political disagreements with Garvey, McKay abandoned the movement, popularly known as "Back to Africa," whose slogans were "Africa for the Africans: for those at home and those abroad" and "One God, One Aim, One Destiny." McKay never abandoned his belief in the need for black unity, and he continued to advocate for group identity through writing about black themes.

In 1922 Harcourt published McKay's *Harlem Shadows,* the volume that solidified his place in the Harlem Renaissance; McKay said he "steadfastly pursued" the publication of an American book of verse because he "desired to see" "If We Must Die," the sonnet he "had omitted in the London volume, inside of a book." The collection includes the McKay sonnets that are most often anthologized, such as "America," "The White City," "The Harlem Dancer," "Outcast," "The Lynching," "Baptism," and "If We Must Die." It also includes such favorites as "The Tropics in New York," "Flame Heart," "Spring in New Hampshire," and "Harlem Shadows."

The volume captures McKay's struggles with the problems of Western civilization, especially racism in America. In "America" he depicts the peculiar position of black people who are fed the "bread of bitterness" by a country that sinks her "tiger's tooth" into their throats, and he predicts a ghastly future for her unless there is some kind of change. In "The White City," he pictures the hatred that sustains him, and in "Baptism," he asserts that his immersion in the fire of hatred of the United States will make him "a stronger soul within a finer frame." He recognizes his outsider status in Western civilization in "Outcast," in which he maintains that he was born "far from my native clime/ Under the white man's menace, out of time."

McKay focuses upon specific violence done to black people in "The Lynching." A black man accused of some unspecified crime is lynched and burned in a ritual that serves to consolidate whites against blacks and that simultaneously serves to initiate young white boys into their future roles of oppression in the society: "And little lads, lynchers that were to be,/Danced round the dreadful thing in fiendish glee."

"The Harlem Dancer" provides a slightly different focus on interracial relations. In it McKay concentrates on those whites who "slummed" in Harlem during the 1920s looking for exotic excitement that they believed primitive blacks could provide them. In a cabaret scene, a black singer and dancer entertains the crowd in a graceful presentation of art forms that few in her audience are able to appreciate. The speaker pictures her as "a proudly-swaying palm/Grown lovelier for passing through a storm," which is represented by the greedy eyes watching her. Although she receives coins tossed at her, the dancer has transcended the corrupting lot: "But looking at her falsely-smiling face,/I knew her self was not in that strange place."

The poem has been read as an allegory of the prostitution of black art that was common in the 1920s. Blacks were paid to be exotic, to provide the temporary relief that whites came looking for, and many were unscrupulous enough to be accommodating, or they believed that white patronage was essential to their existence. Frequently anthologized, the poem is recognized as one of McKay's best.

Of the poems that were not written in sonnet form, "The Tropics in New York" voices McKay's nostalgia for Jamaica when he comes upon a display of fruit on a New York street. "My eyes grew dim, and I could no more gaze,/A wave of longing through my body swept,/And, hungry for the old, familiar ways,/I turned aside and bowed my head and wept." "Flame Heart" is also a poem of reminiscence, one, in which McKay remembers "The poinsettia's red, blood-red in warm December."

Reviewers of the volume were generally receptive to it. Writing for the *Nation*, W. F. White maintained that McKay's work proved him "to be a craftsman with keen perception of emotions, a lover of the colorful and the dramatic, strongly sensuous yet sensual, and an adept in the handling of phrases to give subtle variations of thought he seeks." He considered McKay a master of the lyric and the sonnet. The reviewer for the *New York*

Times considered portions of the book "mere sentiment," but maintained that McKay succeeded more often than not in portraying "the spirit of the modern Negro." Rex Hunter, in the *New York Tribune*, asserted that, although McKay came "perilously close" to doggerel at his worst, "at his best he produces the sort of instinctive lyricism that is found in folk-songs."

Although *Harlem Shadows* was the last volume of poetry McKay published in his lifetime, he continued to publish poems in the *Liberator* and other magazines. His last poems, in the 1940s, appeared in Catholic outlets as well as in such journals as *Interracial Review*.

In 1923 McKay attended the Fourth Congress of the Communist party in Russia, where he was hailed as a black poet and as a comrade. He gave public readings of his work, and *Pravda* published his May Day poem in translation. McKay felt that a terrific show was being put on for his benefit, and he left the country in June somewhat less supportive of Communist philosophy than he had been earlier.

By the end of 1923 McKay was in Paris, where he earned a living by modeling. Infected lungs, however, caused him to be hospitalized for three months. He recuperated in Midi during the spring of 1924, then returned to Paris. This pattern of movement continued for over ten years. From 1923 to 1934 McKay lived and worked in France, Germany, Spain, and Morocco, following the path of many blacks who traveled outside the United States to study and write during the 1920s. It was in Spain that McKay developed the attraction for Catholicism that would later bring about his conversion. In his years away from America, McKay focused primarily on prose fiction. His three novels, *Home to Harlem* (1928), *Banjo* (1929), and *Banana Bottom* (1933), were written during this period. He also completed a collection of short stories, *Gingertown*, which was published in 1932.

Home to Harlem, originally intended as a short story, is set in Harlem, capital of black life at the time. The protagonist, Jake, represents the simple, down-to-earth, proud black man forced to face poverty and prejudice. Jake goes AWOL from the war and goes "home to Harlem," where he meets Felice, a prostitute who secretly returns the fifty dollars he has paid for her services. Jake searches for her in the hope that they may develop a healthier relationship. McKay uses the quest structure to provide a panoramic view of jazz-age Harlem, showing along the way cabarets, rent parties, poolrooms, gin mills, docks, and dining cars. Episodic

Letter to Alain Locke, the guest editor for the Harlem Number of the Survey Graphic *(March 1925). The issue which served as the nucleus for Locke's 1925 anthology,* The New Negro, *included six poems by McKay, but not "Mulatto" (courtesy of the Alain Locke Papers, Moorland-Spingarn Research Center, Howard University)*

I would not have the Challenge Song published without being accompanied by "mulatto" to strengthen it. The <u>Crisis</u> my dear Locke will be glad to take "Mulatto." Send me back <u>all</u> the things — and I do not care to be mentioned at all — don't want to — in the Special Negro number of the Survey. I am not seeking mere notoriety and publicity. Principles mean something to my life. And if you do publish any of the other poems now and leave out "mulatto" after this protest you may count upon me as an intellectual enemy for life!

I am angry as I say. Certainly Jessie Faucet would show more courage than you have in this case. Damn it Locke — I am surprised — yet not too much. You are a dyed-in-the-wool pussyfooting professor—

Claude—

and impressionistic, the novel serves more to explore Harlem life than to develop more serious themes, though they are implied.

The character Ray provides a contrast in the novel to Jake's epicurean, good-timing philosophy. Jake meets Ray, a young Haitian who would like to become a writer, on, one of his railroad runs. Overly educated, overly westernized, Ray is unable to cast aside the debilitating influence of the white world and return to those parts of Haiti and his culture that most define him. Because he cannot enjoy life as thoroughly as Jake obviously does, he is doomed to mental suffering. The novel ends with Ray rejecting the life to which he has been exposed in the United States and leaving on a ship for Europe. Jake finds Felice and is presumably happy. "By contrasting Jake's happiness with Ray's restless wandering," Robert Bone asserts, "McKay attempts to convey the superiority of instinct over reason. But at bottom, Jake and Ray represent different ways of rebelling against Western civilization. Jake rebels instinctively, while Ray's rebellion occurs on an intellectual plane. Both characters acquire a broader significance only through their negative relationship to contemporary society. McKay's failure to develop this relationship is the failure of the novel."

Home to Harlem was the first novel by a black writer to reach the commercial best-seller lists; it was reprinted five times in two months. Its depiction of the racy life that Carl Van Vechten had presented of Harlem in *Nigger Heaven* (1926) and its ties to the general atmosphere of good-timing made it an instant success. Burton Rascoe, writing for *Bookman*, asserted that the novel was "a book to invoke pity and terror, which is the function of tragedy, and to that extent—that very extent—it is beautiful"; he also applauded the "Negro slang and dialect." The reviewer for the *New York Herald Tribune* complimented the "stark realism" and maintained that the "sordid truths" were presented with simplicity. Others claimed that the book was more valuable as folklore than as fiction, suggesting that it was at times formless.

Banjo (1929) is, in many ways, a sequel to *Home to Harlem*. It deals with the experiences of several black seamen from the West Indies, Africa, and the United States who are together on a beach in Marseilles. The main character here, Lincoln "Banjo" Agrippa, is a black folk hero like Jake in *Home to Harlem*, but, unlike Jake, he is more of a scamp who is well able to use his wit and insight to survive. Banjo meets Ray, an intellectual from Haiti, and this pair illustrates the contrast between the rigidity and mechanism of industrial America and the vitality and naturalness of rural life in the islands. McKay seems to have modeled Ray upon himself. He is a character whose greatest desire is to become a writer, but the problems inherent in the modern urban life force him to become a worker, as Jake had been. Thus McKay illustrates that blacks, no matter what intellectual class they belong to, are part of a single social category. By the novel's end, Banjo decides to sail for America and asks for a salary advance. When he receives it, however, he takes off to another part of Europe, and Ray accompanies him.

One reviewer, focusing on the picture of waterfront life in Marseilles, commented that McKay had achieved an "unforgettable picture" of it. Another critic commented: "If fault is to be found with the author's manner, let it be that he is more loyal to his characters than they are themselves, that his realism is a shade too natural and his naturalism too real. But such considerations need spoil no one's appreciation of a complex task simply and gustily performed." Others complained that the book had "little consciousness of plot or form," but most agreed that the novel was vigorous and engaging, particularly its "racy Negro idiom."

Through his first two novels, Addison Gayle asserts, McKay had been exploring the problem of identity, of the place of the outsider in Western civilization. Since he did not resolve the conflict in either of the first two novels, he tried to do so in the third. In *Banana Bottom* (1933), the protagonist Bita Plant has managed to retain her ties to her people in spite of a British education. Having been brutally raped by a playmate, Bita is rescued by white missionaries Malcolm and Priscilla Craig, who remove her from the black island environment and take her into the white British enclave. Later they send her to Britain to be educated. Instead of depicting Bita falling into the easy trap of reductively viewing white Britain as good and the black island as bad, McKay chronicles her return to the island. The Anglican clergyman and his wife have tried to dominate Bita, but she asserts her independence by returning to Jubilee, the tiny village in Jamaica. She severs her ties with the Craigs and clings to what is healthy in her own background and culture.

Unfortunately most of the reviewers of the book focused more on the scenery and atmosphere than upon theme. Mary Ross, writing for *Books*, strikes the typical view: "The glamour of the tropics is in this book; the extravagant beauty of palm and fern and hibiscus, the violence of hurricane, the brilliance of southern sun. . . . The vividness of the book is due in large part to Mr. McKay's grasp of the special moods, sights and sounds of his country, its festivals, gayety and ideals. . . ." Others commented upon the humor, pathos, and melodrama in the book, but the island scenery remained prominent in the minds of most of the reviewers.

Gingertown (1932), about half of which McKay had written in Paris between 1923 and 1926 and the remainder in Morocco from 1931 to 1932, contains twelve stories that focus primarily on Harlem and Jamaica. The six Harlem stories appear first in the volume; they are "Brownskin Blues," about the exploitation of the black woman; "The Prince of Porto Rico," about a lover who is undone by an unlikely prospect; "Mattie and Her Sweetman," about an aging black woman who keeps a man; "Near-White," about a black woman who passes for a time; "Highball," about a successful black entertainer who never believes he has been fully accepted into the white world; and "Truant," about a West Indian who escapes a boring existence by deserting his wife and child.

Four stories in the volume focus on Jamaica. "The Agricultural Show" depicts a festival. "Crazy Mary" depicts a young mulatto woman's psychological destruction by the sexual repression in her village. "When I Pounded the Pavement" satirizes bureaucracy interfering with folk traditions. "The Strange Burial of Sue," recognized as one of the most successful stories in the volume, centers upon a woman who has strained her husband's tolerance for years by having other lovers with his knowledge. Although she dies under mysterious circumstances, her husband and her lover join forces against the minister who would declare that she has gone to hell.

"Nigger Lover," one of the last two stories in the volume, focuses on a white prostitute in a southern Mediterranean port. Her preference for black men as clients has earned her the title of the story. Her choice arises from an encounter in which a black man was particularly kind to her, paying her more than the expected price. "Little Sheik," set in North Africa, portrays the travels of an insensitive young white woman with classic ugly-American attitudes. Her "little sheik" is a young man she hires as a guide; when he responds to her sexual flirtations, she runs away in panic, only to discover later that the young man is imprisoned for guiding tourists without a license.

McKay's later poetry reflects the many places to which he traveled, including Russia and Spain. Some of these were published in *Selected Poems*

(1953). "St. Isaac's Church, Petrograd" is so impressive that it led McKay to a renewed sense of the presence of God. "Barcelona" celebrates that city as "Tetuan" compliments the mixture of Western and African cultures in that part of Spain. McKay also wrote poems about Morocco.

Shortly after his return to Harlem in the mid 1930s, McKay decided to complete an autobiography that would capture his various travels and experiences. Titled *A Long Way from Home,* the volume appeared in 1937. The autobiography is not a detailed look at Claude McKay the man; rather, it is "an account of McKay's struggle to reconcile his views of art with his concepts of self, blackness, and the proletariat." His disillusionment with Communism was complete by this time, and his depiction of Communists in the volume earned immediate attacks from them.

In 1938 McKay met Ellen Tarry, a Catholic writer of children's books. Tarry, a mulatto, would become a significant person in McKay's life during

Title page for McKay's 1937 autobiography

his last ten years, and it was perhaps a testament to his mellowing perspective that he accepted Catholicism, and friendship with Tarry, one of the "yellow Negroes for whom McKay had a dislike." She invited him to Friendship House, a Catholic welfare and activities center in Harlem. This contact resulted in the publication of *Harlem: Negro Metropolis* (1940), essays on Harlem and its spiritual and religious leaders.

When McKay fell ill late in 1941, having suffered a stroke while working in a federal shipyard, it was Tarry and workers from Friendship House who located him and cared for him. That was the beginning of illnesses from which he would never recover, although he recuperated in a Connecticut cottage during the summer of 1943. His high blood pressure was also a problem but not debilitating enough to prevent him from moving to Chicago in the spring of 1944 to accept a teaching position. On 11 October 1944 McKay was baptized into Catholicism in Chicago.

After he converted to Catholicism, he taught classes at the Catholic Youth Organization in Chicago. In an essay entitled "On Becoming a Roman Catholic," McKay says that he always possessed a religion-oriented mind, but that he never had faith in "revealed" religion. Shortly before his death, he penned the sonnet "Truth," a glowing testimony to his final acceptance of God.

> Lord shall I find it in Thy Holy Church,
> Or must I give it up as something dead,
> Forever lost, no matter where I search,
> Like Dinosaurs within their ancient bed?
> ....
> In this vast world of lies and hate and greed,
> Upon my knees, Oh Lord, for Truth I plead.

The poem reflects a mind still questioning but one sure of the source of the answer he seeks.

Claude McKay, one of the major influences in the search for identity among black Americans, was especially widely read and quoted during the 1960s at the height of the civil rights movement. The most militant organs of political protest joined the passive resistors in considering McKay's works required reading. He epitomized the struggles and contradictions inherent in any oppressed group searching for self-reliance and respect. He remained dedicated throughout his life to the belief that blacks must unify against racism and work

ceaselessly for justice. As Wayne Cooper asserts: "McKay was necessarily preoccupied with the place of the Negro in the modern world. Western Civilization left him no other choice. His very preoccupation, however, made imperative a larger effort on his part to comprehend and relate to the great social and political forces of his age." And Jean Wagner, author of *Black Poets of the United States* (1973), concludes that McKay "remains beyond a doubt the immediate forerunner and one of the leading forces of the Renaissance, the man without whom it could never have achieved what it did."

On 22 May 1948 McKay died of heart failure in a Chicago hospital; he had been at work on a collection of his poems, which appeared posthumously, with a biographical note by Max Eastman, as *Selected Poems* (1953).

Biography:
James R. Giles, *Claude McKay* (Boston: Hall, 1976).

References:
C. W. E. Bigsby, *The Black American Writer, Volume II: Poetry and Drama* (Baltimore: Penguin, 1969);

Sterling A. Brown, Arthur P. Davis, and Ulysses Lee, *The Negro Caravan* (New York: Arno & New York Times, 1970);

Wayne Cooper, ed., *The Passion of Claude McKay* (New York: Schocken, 1973);

Harold Cruse, *The Crisis of the Negro Intellectual* (New York: Morrow, 1967);

James A. Emanuel and Theodore L. Gross, *Dark Symphony: Negro Literature in America* (New York: Free Press, 1968);

Addison Gayle, Jr., *Claude McKay: The Black Poet at War* (Detroit: Broadside, 1972);

Nathan Irvin Huggins, *Harlem Renaissance* (New York: Oxford University Press, 1971);

Carl Milton Hughes, *The Negro Novelist: 1940-1950* (New York: Citadel Press, 1953);

Jean Wagner, *Black Poets of the United States, From Paul Laurence Dunbar to Langston Hughes* (Urbana: University of Illinois Press, 1973).

Papers:
The largest collection of McKay's manuscripts is in the Beinecke Library at Yale University. Some of McKay's letters to Max Eastman are in the Lilly Library at Indiana University, Bloomington, Indiana.

Richard Bruce Nugent

(2 July 1906-   )

Eric Garber

WORKS: "Sadhji," as Bruce Nugent, in *The New Negro*, edited by Alain Locke (New York: Boni, 1925), pp. 113-114;

"Shadows," *Opportunity*, 3 (October 1925): 296;

"Smoke, Lilies, and Jade," as Richard Bruce, *Fire!!*, 1 (November 1926): 405-408;

Countee Cullen, ed., *Caroling Dusk*, includes poems by Nugent, as Bruce (New York: Harper, 1927);

Sadhji, an African Ballet, as Bruce, in *Plays of Negro Life: A Sourcebook of Native American Drama*, edited by Alain Locke and Montgomery Gregory (New York: Harper, 1927), pp. 388-400;

"Narcissus," *Trend*, 1 (January/March 1933): 127;

"Beyond Where the Star Stood Still," *Crisis*, 77 (December 1970): 405-408;

Lighting Fire!! (Metuchen, N.J.: *Fire!!* Press, 1982).

PLAY PRODUCTION: *Sadhji, an African Ballet*, Rochester, New York, Eastman School of Music, 1932.

Richard Bruce Nugent in 1982 (photo by Thomas H. Wirth)

Richard Bruce Nugent was a singular figure during the Harlem Renaissance but his importance was due as much to his unique personal style, sense of humor, and world view as to his modest literary output. He was the ultimate bohemian, thumbing his nose at social, political, and sexual conventions. He knew, and worked with, many of Harlem's artistic luminaries, and his participation in the period's arts and letters added a bold and individual voice to the era's search for Afro-American identity.

Nugent was born to a family of modest means but high social position in Washington, D.C., black society. His parents, Richard Henry Nugent and Pauline Minerva Bruce, were artistically inclined and made sure the arts figured prominently in their sons' education. Gary Lambert Nugent, Richard's younger brother, eventually developed a distinguished career as a jazz dancer. The future writer attended Dunbar High School, but when Richard was thirteen, his father died and the family moved to New York City. There the young man fell in love with the diversity and adventure of

Manhattan. He roamed its streets and neighborhoods for hours, finding excitement everywhere. He worked at numerous odd jobs, from bellhop to errand boy. After several years he decided to become an artist and announced to his mother that he would no longer be seeking employment. Appalled, Mrs. Nugent promptly packed her son's bags and sent him to his grandmother's home in Washington.

Bruce Nugent, as he was by then known, did not stay long. One summer evening in 1925, at one of Georgia Douglas Johnson's famous artistic "at-homes," Nugent met Langston Hughes. Their rapport was immediate and they quickly became friends. Nugent was captivated by the rising young poet's handsome appearance, his worldly experiences, his gentle manner, and his literary success. Hughes opened his new friend's eyes to the possibilities of the emerging New Negro and gave strong support to Nugent's impulse for creative expression. When Hughes returned to New York to attend a Krigwa Theatre dinner in his honor,

Manuscript for an untitled story, written in 1924 or 1925 in Washington, D.C. (by permission of Richard Bruce Nugent; courtesy of Thomas H. Wirth)

dilated ..... Helene --- I whispered --- I approached her --- she drew back ---- the hair on her head seemed to rise --- ruffle --- I approached --- she glided out of my reach --- gracefully ---- as gracefully as a cat --- every movement was feline --- I screamed and rushed to the door ---- she huddled on the couch --- glaring --- that impersonal hate --- I couldn't bare to look at her .... I switched off the light --- and God ---- there flashing glowing in the dark --- I saw --- two slant --- yellow green eyes ---- I saw them --- in the dark --- watching me --- watching watching --- there --- I knew you would laugh --- too much opium you think --- but I know --- I know ---- I saw those eyes --- I saw those eyes ---

4

was lacking that thing --- that something every one has a touch of --- personality --- absolutely devoid of any trace of it --- I kissed her --- loved her --- no response ---- so --- tired --- exasperated I took a drink ---- then --- diabolically --- came a plan ---- I poured the green fluid in a glass --- I poured Creme de minte in mine --- I offered her one --- I held the Creme de minte --- to your health ---- we drank --- I saw her flush .... shudder .... an overwhelming desire to kiss her ---- I took her in my arms --- she lay passive inert --- I kissed her --- face --- throat --- suddenly --- she writhed and snuggled closer and ---- I'll swear she purred ---- actually --- at last --- the marble had come to life --- I playfully ---- lightly bit her ear --- an then --- quick as a flash she had wriggled from my arms .... her hand flashed out --- I felt her nails ---- I nearly said claws tear my neck ---- I fell back ---- startled she crouched in a corner --- near the table ---- and --- her eyes ---- hard --- her eyes ---- were slant as green ---

Nugent came with him. Nugent later remembered this as being the point at which his "period of excitement and happiness and work began."

With Hughes's assistance, Nugent rapidly immersed himself in the exciting Harlem artistic scene. His quick, sometimes cutting, sense of humor, his good looks and intelligence, and his unorthodox mode of living made him a favorite among the loose-knit group of rebellious young artists which Wallace Thurman and Zora Neale Hurston wryly called "The Niggerati." The Niggerati were on the cutting edge of the Renaissance of Afro-American culture and included such artists as Hughes, Thurman, Hurston, Countee Cullen, Harold Jackman, and Aaron Douglas. With his new Niggerati friends Nugent attended dinners sponsored by the NAACP and *Opportunity* magazine, the official monthly of the National Urban League; listened to Jean Toomer's Gurdjieff lectures; socialized at the parties of A'Lelia Walker and the Carl Van Vechtens; and frequented disreputable nightspots along 133rd Street and in Greenwich Village. He was continually without money, relying on his indulgent friends for a place to stay and something to eat. His wardrobe consisted of whatever clothing was around. Many of his poems and drawings were composed on pieces of scrap paper. In his long, first-person narrative "Smoke, Lilies, and Jade," Nugent depicts a young artist named Alex who bears an unmistakable resemblance to the author.

> . . . he wondered why he couldn't find work . . . a job . . . when he had first come to New York he had . . . but he had only been fourteen then was it because he was nineteen now that he felt so idle . . . and contented . . . or because he was an artist . . . he should be ashamed that he didn't work . . . but . . . Alex . . . was content to lay and smoke and meet friends at night . . . to argue and read Wilde . . . Freud . . . Boccaccio and Schnitzler. . . .

Nugent wonders why Alex feels so different from other people and imagines him as "The Tragic Genius."

Nugent enjoyed shocking the prudish with his overtly erotic drawings and poetry and his tales of amorous adventure, many of which were unabashedly homosexual. The notoriety he gathered was sufficient to prompt him to assume the pseudonym "Richard Bruce" to avoid parental disapproval, but his reputation only helped endear him to his new friends. Fellow poet Albert Rice described him as "the bizarre and eccentric young vagabond poet of High Harlem." John P. Davis

later recalled that "Nugent was a true bohemian in every sense of the word. In no ways a *poseur*, he was simply and basically a non-conformist who refused to accept so-called middle class standards of any kind."

One of the most vivid pictures available of Nugent during this period can be found in Wallace Thurman's 1932 novel *Infants of the Spring*. Thurman intended his novel, a satiric roman à clef in which most of the Harlem Renaissance participants appear in thin disguises, to be a serious assessment of the New Negro movement. Nugent appears as Paul Arbian, "a Negro painter whose subjects are bizarre and erotic." Unapologetically bisexual, Arbian is a talented but indolent artist, always quick with his wit and ready to celebrate, but unwilling to work: the quintessential bohemian. "I'm an artist," proclaims Arbian; "I think Oscar Wilde is the greatest man that ever lived. Huysmans' Des Esseintes is the greatest character in literature, and Baudelaire is the greatest poet." A rebel, he refuses to follow the racial aesthetics called for by Dr. A. L. Parkes, Thurman's caricature of Alain Locke. When asked if he has any racial pride at all, Arbian replies coolly, "Fortunately, no. I don't happen to give a good goddam about any nigger except myself." Thurman's Paul Arbian, despite his flippancy and lack of discipline, possesses genuine artistic talent, a trait the author clearly felt Nugent shared.

Nugent's first published poem, "Shadows," actually had to be rescued from the trash can by Langston Hughes before it could be sent to *Opportunity* and, eventually, published. In "Shadows" Nugent voices his feelings of alienation, a situation he finds accentuated by his race.

> A silhouette am I
> On the face of the moon
> Lacking color
> Or vivid brightness
> But defined all the clearer
> Because I am dark,
> Black on the face of the moon.

"Shadows" was reprinted in 1927 in Countee Cullen's poetry anthology *Caroling Dusk*.

Nugent was among the artists and writers asked for contributions by Alain Locke for what was to become his showcase for Afro-American culture and art, *The New Negro* (1925). Locke's anthology contained "Sadhji," Nugent's first published short story. Locke and Nugent had known each other for years, their families being friends, and Locke knew the eccentric youth had

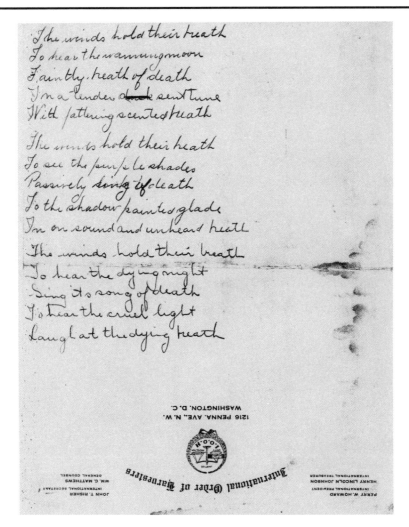

Manuscript for a poem written circa 1925 on the stationery of Henry Lincoln Johnson, husband of Georgia Douglas Johnson, a close friend of Nugent's (by permission of Richard Bruce Nugent; courtesy of Thomas H. Wirth)

talent. Nugent's submission to the project had been a striking black-and-white wash drawing of a young African woman. Locke praised the drawing highly but asked Nugent for a brief written explication to accompany it. Evidently the short, two-page narrative Nugent returned was more useful than his graphic; when *The New Negro* appeared, Nugent's tale was illustrated by Aaron Douglas.

In "Sadhji" Nugent introduces two themes which would recur throughout his work: his reliance on moral, often Biblical, narratives and his fascination with human sexuality, particularly homosexuality. Sadhji is the beautiful wife of an aging African chieftain named Konombjo, whom she deeply loves. She is secretly coveted by Konombjo's son, Mrabo, who patiently awaits his father's death, anticipating his subsequent betrothal to

his stepmother. In turn, Mrabo is loved by Numbo, "a young buck [who] would do anything to make Mrabo happy." To help his lovestruck Mrabo, Numbo murders the elderly chieftain on a hunting expedition, but instead of bringing happiness to Mrabo, the murder brings only misery. When Sadhji learns of her husband's death she throws herself on his funeral pyre. Mrabo is left alone. This simple morality tale is told in a terse, abbreviated fashion, brief sentence fragments punctuated entirely with ellipses. The style is self-conscious but effective.

Locke saw considerable potential in this short African melodrama and continued to encourage Nugent's work on a dramatic version. The resulting one-act play with original musical score by William Grant Sill was published in Locke's and Montgom-

Alien registration form issued to Nugent during his visit to London in 1929 (by permission of Richard Bruce Nugent; courtesy of Thomas H. Wirth)

ery Gregory's *Plays of Negro Life* (1927) and was produced in 1932 at the Eastman School of Music in Rochester, New York.

In the summer of 1926 the "Niggerati" began work on a new literary periodical designed to break with the older black literary establishment and to forge a new Afro-American aesthetic. They called their fledgling quarterly *Fire!!*, after a spiritual Hughes had written with composer Hall Johnson. Thurman, Hughes, and Hurston were designated editors, John P. Davis served as business manager, and Nugent was in charge of distribution. The publication was to be financed by contributions but ultimately had to be subsidized by Thurman. Aaron Douglas designed a stunning black and red cover for the magazine's first edition. Thurman, Hurston, and Gwendolyn Bennett contributed stories. Poetry was submitted by Hughes, Cullen, and Arna Bontemps, and Arthur Huff Fauset wrote an essay condemning the hypocrisy of the intelligentsia. Nugent contributed two brush-and-ink drawings and

his fictionalized self-portrait "Smoke, Lilies, and Jade," which he submitted on a roll of toilet paper. His first version of the story had been accidentally thrown away; written on Nugent's customary paper scraps it had been mistaken for trash.

"Smoke, Lilies, and Jade" (1926) was the first literary work on an explicitly homosexual theme to be published by an Afro-American. The story is intentionally subjective and, like *Sadhji*, punctuated entirely by ellipses. It begins with its autobiographical protagonist, Alex, lost in deep Proustian reverie. He eventually clears his thoughts, rises, and takes to the streets, looking for excitement. At four o'clock one morning, while walking home from a night of merriment, Alex is approached by a sexually attractive stranger. They exchange pleasantries, then Alex invites the man home. " . . . No need for words . . . they had always known each other . . . . as they undressed by the blue dawn . . . Alex knew he had never seen a more perfect being . . . his body was all symmetry and

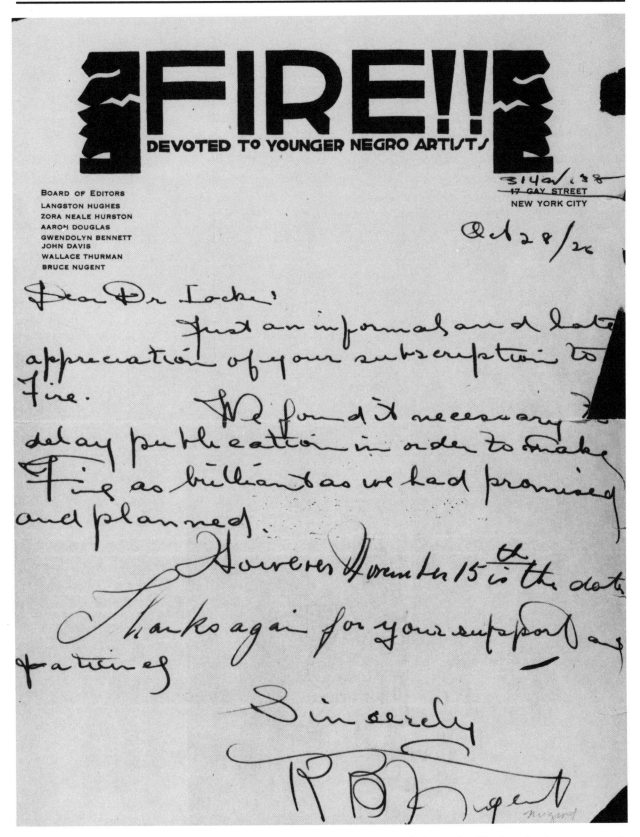

Letter thanking Alain Locke for his patronage of the radical arts magazine Fire!!, *which ceased publication after the appearance of one issue (courtesy of the Alain Locke Papers, Moorland-Spingarn Research Center, Howard University)*

music. . . ." A night of lovemaking leaves Alex in confusion about his sexuality (he is already involved with a woman), but his doubts are quickly resolved. ". . . He loved them both . . . there . . . he had thought it . . . actually dared to think it . . . One *can* love two at the same time . . . one *can* love . . . . . ." Nugent's defense of homosexual love was quite remarkable in its day, and it has lost little of its immediacy through the years.

The editors of *Fire!!* had intended the journal to be controversial, and the inclusion of "Smoke, Lilies, and Jade" insured that. Artists such as Thurman and Nugent were rebelling against the desires of the Afro-American intelligentsia to portray only the uplifting sides of black life. They wanted the freedom to depict all aspects of their experiences as Afro-Americans, from the bourgeois to the bohemian. Thurman decided that in order for *Fire!!* to be truly daring, two particularly sensational pieces were needed: one on homosexuality, the other on prostitution. He and Nugent had flipped a coin to determine who would write what. Thurman's tawdry tale of a sixteen-year-old prostitute, "Cordelia the Crude," was a result of the toss, and it equally outraged middle-class Afro-American sensibilities. The reviewer for the *Baltimore Afro-American* wrote: "I have just tossed the first issue of *Fire!!* into the fire." Alain Locke, in his review of the journal in the *Survey*, noted, "This is left-wing literary modernism with deliberate intent." While he supported the editors' anti-Puritan ef-

forts, he deplored the "effete echoes of contemporary decadence" he found in their pages. In apparent response to the overt homosexuality expressed, Locke counseled that "Back to Whitman would have been a better point of support than a left-wing pivoting on Wilde and Beardsley." The negative reaction was not limited to academic critics. Nugent remembers going to Gregg's Restaurant with Thurman a few days after *Fire!!* was released.

> As we passed through, conversation parted before us like before the prow of a boat and closed after us as we passed by. . . . Not a soul spoke to us. We were in trouble—very deep trouble.

The ostracism did not last long; *Fire!!*'s chief problems were financial. The issue had cost more than anticipated. The printer had never been paid. Nugent, in charge of distribution, had often literally eaten up the profits. As a result, *Fire!!* never published a second issue.

After the demise of *Fire!!*, Nugent spent several years as a cast member of Dubose Heyward's play *Porgy*, touring the United States and Europe. In 1928 he contributed an essay to Wallace Thurman's second periodical effort, *Harlem: A Forum of Negro Life*. Though the contents were solid, featuring articles by Walter White, Langston Hughes, and Theophilus Lewis, *Harlem* proved as ephem-

Receipt from Nugent to Alain Locke acknowledging payment for the play Sadhji *(courtesy of the Alain Locke Papers, Moorland-Spingarn Research Center, Howard University)*

Nugent and his wife Grace in the 1950s (courtesy of Richard Bruce Nugent)

eral as *Fire!!* and survived for only one issue. *Gumby's Book Studio Quarterly,* which was to have published Nugent's "The Tunic With a Thousand Eyes," a stylized version of the Biblical story of Salome, seems never to have made it past the page proof stage. Apparently production of the *Quarterly* halted when its publisher, Alexander Gumby, became gravely ill with tuberculosis in the early 1930s.

The Depression forced some changes in Nugent's life-style, but he continued to work in the creative arts. He worked with the Federal Arts Project and the Federal Theatre. He contributed to the "Negroes of New York" manuscript funded by the Federal Writers' Project. The Harmon Foundation exhibited his artwork during the early 1930s. He

contributed to Dorothy West's *Challenge* and *New Challenge* and to the poetry magazine *Trend.* After World War II, Nugent's creativity was encouraged by his close friend Bernard Kay. It was during this time that Nugent began to write a series of vaguely pornographic homosexual romances. None of these novels has ever been published.

The 1960s was a period of great energy for Nugent. Along with Romare Bearden and several others, Nugent founded the Harlem Cultural Council. He was particularly enthusiastic about the *Dancemobile* and the *Jazzmobile* projects. His Christmas story "Beyond Where the Star Stood Still" was published in the December 1970 issue of the *Crisis.* The story concerns a special gift that Herod's painted young catamite offers to the newborn Jesus. Nugent's elliptical style is missing, but his favored themes of homosexuality and biblical mythology remain.

Recognition has come slowly to Richard Bruce Nugent. The surge of interest in Afro-American history has brought what Nugent describes as a "growing multitude of people who have taped interviews with me in a quest for first-hand impressions of the Negro Renaissance." He has been consulted for works on jazz dance and the Harlem literary scene, for biographies of Langston Hughes, Zora Neale Hurston, Paul Robeson, and A'Lelia Walker. His early defense of homosexuality has been rediscovered by the Gay Rights movement, a cause which Nugent embraces. He appears briefly in the 1984 documentary film about gay history, *Before Stonewall.* He continues to write and draw and charm his visitors in Hoboken, New Jersey.

References:

Robert E. Hemenway, *Zora Neale Hurston: A Literary Biography* (Urbana: University of Illinois Press, 1977);

"Interview with Bruce Nugent," *Artists and Influences: 1982* (New York: Hatch-Billops Collection, 1982), pp. 81-104;

Bruce Kellner, *The Harlem Renaissance: A Historical Dictionary for the Era* (Westport, Conn.: Greenwood Press, 1984);

Wallace Thurman, *Infants of the Spring* (New York: Macaulay, 1932);

Thomas H. Wirth, "Richard Bruce Nugent," *Black American Literature Forum,* 19 (Spring 1985): 16-17.

Marita Bonner Occomy

(16 June 1899-6 December 1971)

Joyce Flynn
Harvard University

BOOK: *Frye Street and Environs: The Collected Works of Marita Bonner Occomy,* edited by Joyce Flynn and Joyce Occomy Stricklin (Boston: Beacon Press, forthcoming 1987).

OTHER: *The Purple Flower,* in *Black Theater USA,* edited by James Hatch and Ted Shine (New York: Free Press, 1974), pp. 202-207.

PERIODICAL PUBLICATIONS: "The Hands— A Story," *Opportunity,* 3 (August 1925): 235-237;

"On Being Young—A Woman—and Colored," *Crisis,* 31 (December 1925): 63-65;

"The Prison-Bound," *Crisis,* 32 (September 1926): 225-226;

"Nothing New," *Crisis,* 33 (November 1926): 17-20;

The Pot-Maker (A Play To Be Read), Opportunity, 5 (February 1927): 43-46;

"One Boy's Story," as Joseph Maree Andrew, *Crisis,* 34 (November 1927): 297-299, 316-320;

"Drab Rambles," *Crisis,* 34 (December 1927): 335-336, 354-356;

The Purple Flower, Crisis, 35 (January 1928);

"The Young Blood Hungers," *Crisis,* 35 (May 1928): 151, 172;

Review of *Autumn Love-Cycle,* by Georgia Douglas Johnson, *Opportunity,* 7 (April 1929): 130;

Exit—An Illusion, Crisis, 36 (October 1929): 335-336, 352;

"A Possible Triad on Black Notes, Part One: There Were Three," *Opportunity,* 11 (July 1933): 205-207;

"A Possible Triad on Black Notes, Part Two: Of Jimmie Harris," *Opportunity,* 11 (August 1933): 242-244;

"A Possible Triad on Black Notes, Part Three: Three Tales of Living: Corner Store," *Opportunity,* 11 (September 1933): 269-271;

"Tin Can," *Opportunity,* 12 (July 1934): 202-205; 12 (August 1934): 236-240;

"A Sealed Pod," *Opportunity,* 14 (March 1936): 88-91;

"Black Fronts," *Opportunity,* 16 (July 1938): 210-214;

"Hate Is Nothing," as Joyce N. Reed, *Crisis,* 45 (December 1938): 388-390, 394, 403-404;

"The Makin's," *Opportunity,* 17 (January 1939): 18-21;

"The Whipping," *Crisis,* 46 (June 1939): 172-174;

"Hongry Fire," *Crisis,* 46 (December 1939): 360-362, 376-377;

"Patch Quilt," *Crisis,* 47 (March 1940): 71, 72, 92;

"One True Love," *Crisis,* 48 (February 1941): 46-47, 58-59.

Marita Bonner Occomy was one of the most versatile twentieth-century black writers. Her contributions to the *Crisis* and *Opportunity* during the two decades after her 1922 graduation from Radcliffe College include essays, reviews, dramas, short stories, and multipart fictional narratives. She lived for substantial periods in three urban centers: Boston, where she was born and educated, Washington, D.C., where she worked for eight years, and Chicago. In Washington she was a member of the S Street salon of black writers formed by the poet and playwright Georgia Douglas Johnson, who became a close friend. Later, Marita Bonner Occomy's innovative fiction of black Chicago set a model for other writers, including Richard Wright, to follow. Occomy's published pieces in the *Crisis* and *Opportunity* were closely studied by aspiring young writers of her period because she so frequently captured the literary prizes offered by both magazines; in the 1933 *Opportunity* fiction award contest, for example, she won first prize and was her own closest competition as runner-up with a second entry.

Marita Bonner was born in Boston in 1899 to Joseph Andrew and Mary Anne (Noel) Bonner. The Bonners had three other children: Bernice, Joseph, and Andrew, who died young. Bonner was educated locally, attending Brookline High School, where she acquired advanced musical training and began to study German, in which she eventually became fluent. In 1918 she entered Radcliffe College and studied English and comparative literature, won admission to Charles T. Copeland's exclusive writing seminar, and continued her studies in musical composition and German literature. Since Bonner was enrolled at Radcliffe during a time when black students were not allowed to live in the dormitories, she lived at home, but she nevertheless managed an active involvement in campus activities, including the Radcliffe song competitions, which she won in 1918 and 1922. During the last phase of her college career, perhaps for financial reasons, Bonner became a teacher at a nearby Cambridge high school. After her graduation in 1922 Bonner continued to teach high school, first in Bluefield, West Virginia, and then in Washington, D.C. Bonner married William Almy Occomy in 1930. She moved to Chicago where she raised three children, William Almy, Jr., Warwick Gale, and Marita Joyce, and eventually taught in the public schools.

Bonner's first published story, "The Hands" (*Opportunity*, 1925), provides insight into the author's methods of coming to grips with experiences different from her own. The short piece is framed by the opening meditation of a narrator who boards a bus and becomes fascinated by the work-

Marita Bonner Occomy, 1922 (courtesy of the Radcliffe College Archives, Harvard University)

roughened hands of an older male rider and who projects a whole imaginary world of work, love, and family served by those hands. Though less technically skilled than Bonner's later work, the story shows the same consciousness of class differences given more personal terms in an autobiographical piece published later in the same year. In "On Being Young—A Woman—and Colored" (*Crisis*, 1925), Bonner expresses the dichotomy she sees between an individual's inner reality and the racial and gender roles forced upon one by society. She conveys her own sense of comparative privilege and her feeling of obligation to identify with the black poor, even when such identification heads toward entanglement "in the seaweed of a Black Ghetto." "The Prison-Bound," published in the *Crisis* the following year, features a heroine, Maggie, who is trapped by bad housing, overweight, listlessness, her husband's white-defined notions of female respectability, and the loss of hope and joie de vivre.

Marita Bonner published her first story of life in Chicago's Black Belt, "Nothing New" (*Crisis*), in 1926, four years before she moved from Washington to Chicago, where she would live for the rest of her life. The story's account of would-be artist Denny Jackson's collision with the society around him touched upon a number of themes that the author would continue to develop: ties between whites and blacks, generational conflicts, and thwarted youthful aspirations. In "Nothing New" Bonner begins to develop her key symbol of the local neighborhood as multiethnic cosmos, an urban universe shared by Irish, Chinese, Russian, Jewish, French, Italian, German, Swedish, and Danish immigrants, as well as the black residents, many themselves recent arrivals from the South. The protagonist Denny encounters the racially unjust society that surrounds the comfortable ethnic cocoon of integrated Frye Street, when he inadvertently strays across an imaginary line into white recreational turf. Perhaps Bonner had in mind the much-publicized 1919 Chicago race riots, which were precipitated by the drowning of young Eugene Williams. While swimming, Williams had drifted south from the unofficially black Twenty-seventh Street beach to the unofficially white Twenty-ninth Street beach, where whites were throwing stones at and threatening black would-be bathers. The coroner's jury concluded that Williams drowned because he feared the stone-throwing whites and kept himself away from the shore.

Bonner would not write fiction set in Chicago again until she moved there. Her stories of the 1930s and 1940s would deal with Chicago as a fallen world in terms of both race relations and the doomed aspirations of the city's black immigrants from the South. Her last two stories published in the 1920s anticipate this development. In the pseudonymously written "One Boy's Story" (*Crisis*, 1927), Bonner examines, through the voice of a naive, youthful narrator, the identity crisis of the illegitimate child of a southern black woman and a white man. In "Drab Rambles" (*Crisis*, 1927), she presents two portraits, one male and one female, of black residents in the final stages of being crushed by the economic slavery and racism they encounter in a northern metropolis. The exact location is unspecified, although there are similarities between Peter Jackson of Sawyer Avenue in "Drab Rambles" and Reuben and Bessie Jackson, the Georgia-born residents of 13 Frye Street and the parents of Denny in "Nothing New."

In Washington, influenced by Georgia Douglas Johnson, Bonner attempted three plays: *The Pot-Maker (A Play To Be Read)* (1927), *The Purple Flower* (1928), and *Exit—An Illusion* (1929). All three plays feature elaborate stage directions and may have been intended for reading rather than performance. Theater historian Addell Austin has recently established that though Bonner was a member of the Krigwa Players in Washington, D.C., writer and fellow Krigwa member Willis Richardson was unaware that Bonner, like himself, was a playwright. Perhaps Bonner had hoped that the group would "discover" her plays as they were published in the *Crisis* and *Opportunity*. *The Pot-Maker*, set in a rural cottage, suggests the naturalistic influence of Johnson; but in *The Pot-Maker*, and in the two plays that followed, Bonner goes beyond naturalism to create a morality play, employing characters who resonate as Everyman and Everywoman. The principal characters undergo a testing situation on an imagined stage whose fourth wall is the territory of death, a force personified as the mysterious lover Exit in Bonner's final play.

Bonner's allegory of the black quest for freedom and happiness in post-Emancipation North America, *The Purple Flower*, inclusively defines the "Us's," the sympathetic group of aspiring protagonists: "They can be as white as the White Devils, as brown as the earth, as black as the center of a poppy. They may look as if they were something or nothing." The "Us's" of all shades are interested in attaining the purple "Flower-of-Life-At-Its-Fullest," blooming on the top of the hill that dominates the stage. Given the timing of *The Purple Flower*'s appearance in the *Crisis* issue of January 1928, it seems probable that the piece resonates with Langston Hughes's *Nation* essay of 23 June 1926, "The Negro Artist and the Racial Mountain." Hughes defined the "racial mountain," an obstacle to black writers, as the "urge within the race toward whiteness, the desire to pour racial individuality into the mold of American standardization. . . ." Knowledge of the Hughes text adds an ironic touch to the play's climax; Bonner's characters, her persistent employment of drumbeats (reminiscent of Hughes's praise of jazz and the "eternal tom-tom beating in the Negro soul"), and her clever two-part stage, divided by a thin "Skin-of-Civilization," demonstrate her determination to create as a "racial" artist and her reservation of the right to critique the civilized and the primitive. Access to the hill on stage is denied to the "Us's" by the White Devils, undersized characters whose forms combine angelic and demonic details. The new plan to obtain the purple flower involves the protagonists' rejection of some past strategies and the new blending of many aspects of the black experience in a cauldron expected to produce magical results. Only near the end of the process do those onstage realize that the success of the concoction requires blood, either black or white, "blood for birth so the New Man can live." *The Purple Flower* deals, on one level, with black aspiration and the relevance of the myth of the American melting pot. On another level, the drama seems to assume the inevitability of violent racial revolution in America. The proclamation of violence sounded in the play echoes again in "The Young Blood Hungers," a short essay published in the *Crisis* four months later.

The brief 1929 drama, *Exit—An Illusion*, gives the reader a feeling of urgency and deals with the problem of acceptance within the black community. Although on the surface a naturalistic drama about a jealous lover's revenge, it ultimately appears to be about Buddy's destruction of Dot through his permanent suspicion and hatred of the white side of her mixed ancestry. It is death, and not a white lover, who hovers near for Dot, but Buddy fails to recognize this until it is too late. Bonner's technical originality is evident in her use of the identical scene to start and end the drama, a scene whose meaning is transformed for the audience by the play's end. In *Exit—An Illusion*, Bonner conveys, through repetition, an almost ritual recognition that all this has happened before.

After her marriage to Rhode Island native and Brown University graduate William Occomy and their move to Chicago in 1930, Marita Bonner Occomy took a short break from writing and then began to write and publish fiction exclusively. Her new subjects included the variety of black Chicago, its class and color demarcations, its interaction with European and, to a lesser extent, Asian immigrants, its effects upon relations between parents and children, and its vulnerability to the crushing economic and social environment of the city. When she resumed publishing in 1933, Occomy noted in the introduction to a story that the piece was part of "A Black Map, a book entirely unwritten." (One might think of an American project paralleling in scope James Joyce's *Dubliners*.) During the 1930s, Occomy made significant changes in her narrative technique to better convey the complexity of her subject matter. The double narrative used in her 1927 prizewinning story "Drab Rambles," described in an author's note as "Two Portraits in Their Proper Frame," set the form for her later work. She composed stories in several separate parts, maximizing the possibilities for the juxtaposition of different characters and of outer and inner impressions of the same character.

The first of the new, multipart narratives of Chicago life was "A Possible Triad on Black Notes," published as three parts in the July, August, and September issues of *Opportunity* (1933). Each part of the triad contains internal juxtaposition of subject matter to supplement the larger juxtapositions of the three pieces. Part One, "There Were Three," introduces a light-skinned family of three and details the events that result in the mother's insanity and "color fixation," while leaving open-ended the abandoned daughter's choice of social streams— black, white, or yellow. The author's foreword speaks of Frye Street as the ultimate ethnic intersection ("All the World is there") and acts as a preface as well to Parts Two and Three, which deal with more respectable working protagonists. In "Of Jimmie Harris," the protagonist, a hardworking and successful immigrant from Virginia, dies of a stroke as his wife Louise sets up his doctor to be her next husband. By the final paragraph, the story's opening line, "Jimmie Harris was dying," has come to mean that the protagonist had been dying for the fifteen years since he had left love and Luray, Virginia, for Chicago's prosperity.

In "Corner Store" Occomy's sole white protagonist, Esther Steinberg, is also acutely aware of a lost world. She recalls her life in the Jewish ghetto of a German town as having more feeling than the overworked and joyless, though increasingly comfortable, life in her husband's grocery store on Frye Street. Esther's husband Anton has long been involved with Ella, a woman of black and Jewish ancestry. He has concealed his relationship by feigning frequent night visits to the *schule*. His daughter, in love with Ella's nephew, now blackmails him. Esther is prostrate and sobbing, at the story's end, and the fabric of the Steinberg family has been so torn that it is impossible to repair.

The two-part story "Tin Can" won the *Opportunity* literary prize for fiction in 1933 and was published in that magazine in July and August 1934. "Tin Can" chronicles the events leading up to inadvertent murder. The similarity of details of the plot to the manuscript and published versions of Richard Wright's masterpiece *Native Son* (1940) suggests the shaping influence of Occomy's urban fiction on Wright, who knew Occomy. The hollow vessel is the dominant image that unifies the two-part narrative, from the tin can and Ma's purse, to the coffin that Jimmy Joe's twisted, electrocuted corpse cannot properly fill, to the speeding, rattling patrol wagon that carries Ma off to the station house instead of the hospital in the final paragraphs. Like *Native Son*, "Tin Can" traces the effects of an environment of poverty, low expectations, and peer pressure on the development of personality.

"A Sealed Pod" features the image of peas situated close together, but not touching. Published in *Opportunity* in 1936, it presents more portrayals of Frye Street families in trouble. It focuses on young Viollette Harris, "warmed with an odd mixture of uncontrolled passions and bloods," until she was murdered by the only man she had ever loved, an Italian immigrant named Joe Tamona. In "A Sealed Pod," as in three 1939 stories, "The Makin's" (*Opportunity*), "The Whipping" (*Crisis*), and "Hongry Fire" (*Crisis*), the negative force of the urban environment seems to destroy children almost before their parents' eyes: Ma Harris comes home from her night cleaning job to find Viollette with her throat cut; David Brown's mother and father in "The Makin's" are too preoccupied with their self-destructive coping mechanisms to do anything but applaud their son's decision to write numbers when he grows up; in "The Whipping," Lizabeth accidentally causes her own son's death when she strikes him for a particularly hurtful lie; and in "Hongry Fire," the domineering mother concerned for her children sees the corrupting urban influence personified by her jaded new daughter-in-law Jule and ultimately poisons Jule and herself as a strategy to save her children from further ruin. Justice in the city is not often so symmetrical: the innocent Ma Harris is left to return mornings to an empty house, and the wrong man is hanged for Viollette's death; nothing happens to the irrespon-

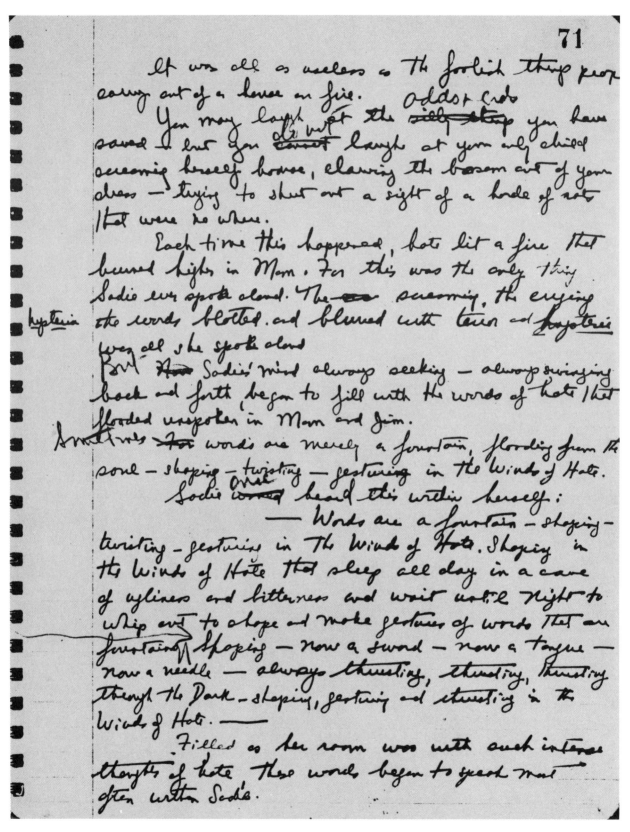

Pages from the journal in which Occomy included writing exercises and fair copies of her stories (by permission of Joyce Occomy Stricklin; courtesy of the Manuscript Collection, Schlesinger Library, Radcliffe College, Harvard University)

"That is to say as it were—" Peter answered.

"Lucy, have you seen a doctor yet?" John asked.

His wife shook her head (there)

"Heh—heh! Lawd!" Dan gave an up from the toes colored laugh. He walked over to his mop and picked it up. "Been to college, too!" he observed to no one.

John's jaw chopped a little. "I'll take my wife to a doctor." he managed to say.

"I'll attend to my daughter's needs," Peter told John.

"Papa! Papa!! You stay out of this!" Lucinda spoke hastily. "You stay out of this now!"

She did not want Peter to pay all the bills.

Had not Margaret hinted to her after that Dan and Mary had money?

"Stay out of man and wife's affairs!" Lucinda repeated.

And nobody laughed, either.

Lucinda rose to her feet and began to adjust her coat.

"My Lord!" Mary said loudly. "My Lord." She said louder. "I got to get back to my scrubbing. Look like to me Lucy aint the first woman what had a body and aint likely to be the last! You 'all worryin 'bout the food and the rent and the clothes and the Lord knows what all and aint nobody said nothing was nothing yet! Seem like to me you puttin your own worry inc where God ought to be. You all liable to be eatin chittlerins——and you liable to be eatin

sible and vicious parents in "The Makin's," and the devoted mother Lizabeth, falsely accused of beating her child to death, cannot as a child of rural Mississippi comprehend enough of the urban bureaucracy even to defend herself. She is imprisoned for life.

Occomy's Chicago portraits do not present middle-class black Chicago as a source of strength or hope. In the pseudonymously written "Hate is Nothing," published in the *Crisis* (December 1938), Occomy, whose own dark skin had occasioned some comments among Chicago's predominantly light-skinned matrons, gives a daughter-in-law victory over a mother-in-law whose notion of respectability is entirely color- rather than behavior-based. Earlier in the same year, in a serial story called "Black Fronts," the most affluent of three women presenting dramatic monologues is the southern-born daughter of a black washerwoman and a white doctor. She is viciously snobbish and color-conscious. Fully drawn examples of middle-class males are rare in Occomy's fiction, although in "Tin Can," years before, both the high school principal and the Reverend Brown are portrayed as hypocrites whose morals are no higher than those of Jimmie Joe's gang.

"Patch Quilt," published in the *Crisis* in 1940, is unusual in Occomy's fiction because it is set entirely in the rural South. Its story of confined lives rendered more confined by a wife's revenge for her husband's adultery may perhaps be seen as Occomy's refusal to romanticize the rural or small-town southern background left behind by many black residents of Chicago. In her last published story, "One True Love" (*Crisis*, 1941), Occomy returned to some of the problems of black female aspiration to which she alluded in "On Being Young—A Woman—and Colored." Her protagonist Nora changes overnight from "just a butter-colored maid with hair on the 'riney' side" to a determined young woman with a dream. Nora's dedication to studying the law is finally unsuccess-

ful. Her failure provides Occomy with an opportunity to show the real obstacles stacked against such a heroine, including scapegoating by other law students and exhausting full-time employment. Nora's superiority is expressed through her refusal to blame others for the failure: "I didn't know enough to pass, that's all." The color line within the color line is less explicitly treated in "One True Love" than in other Occomy stories; but, with the recognition of love between Nora and Sam, "a runty, bow-legged, dark brown janitor's helper," a rapprochement is suggested between light-skinned and dark, between members of the black community with professional or intellectual goals and their working class allies.

After 1941 Occomy continued to write, but devoted more time to raising her children and teaching. At age sixty-eight, she mentioned on a Radcliffe alumna questionnaire that she was currently enrolled in a correspondence course from the Famous Writers' School. Occomy never completed to her satisfaction her planned charting of black Chicago. One reason for this failure may have been her increased intellectual involvement with Christian Science. Occomy gave her new religion generous time and intellectual effort, but may have found in Christian Science's heavy emphasis on individual responsibility and spiritual strength a personal salvation that nevertheless spelled artistic doom. Perhaps she found herself less able to write on some of her favorite themes such as the impact of the urban environment on the individual character; perhaps her own vision looked more often inward.

Papers:

Extant manuscripts and letters of Marita Bonner Occomy are held by the Arthur and Elizabeth Schlesinger Library on the History of Women in America, Radcliffe College, Harvard University, Cambridge, Massachusetts.

Ted Poston
(4 July 1906-11 January 1974)

Kathleen A. Hauke
Morris Brown College

SELECTED WORKS: "Mother's Day Reflections" and "Love," *Blue and the White* (June 1927): 5;

"March on Washington," *New York Amsterdam News,* 10 May 1933;

"A Matter of Record," *New Republic* (26 February 1940): 276;

"You Go South," *New Republic* (9 September 1940): 348-350;

"Law and Order in Norfolk," *New Republic* (7 October 1940): 472-475;

"The Making of Mamma Harris," *New Republic* (4 November 1940): 624-626;

"A Book on Harlem," review of *Harlem: Negro Metropolis,* by Claude McKay, *New Republic* (25 November 1940): 732;

"Harlem and Anti-Semitism" [correspondence between Poston and Claude McKay], *New Republic* (27 January 1941): 118-119;

"The Revolt of the Evil Fairies," *New Republic* (6 April 1942): 458-459;

"My Most Humiliating Jim Crow Experience," *Negro Digest* (April 1944): 55-56;

"Standard Bearer of Negro Education: Dr. Frederick Douglass Patterson," *New York Post Home News,* 7 July 1949;

"Florida's Legal Lynching," *Nation* (24 September 1949): 296-297;

"New York vs. Chicago: Which City is Better Place for Negroes?," by Poston and Roi Ottley, *Ebony* (December 1952): 16-24;

"The 'Simple' World of Langston Hughes," *New York Post,* 24 November 1957, p. M2;

"At Home with the Poet," *New York Post,* 17 June 1962;

"Harlem's Farewell to Langston Hughes," *New York Post,* 26 May 1967.

In 1937 Ted Poston had the distinction of being the third black man hired to work as a general reporter for a major New York City daily newspaper. During his forty-six years as a journalist, Poston covered subjects ranging from social problems to literature, from lynching in Florida to Langston Hughes's poetry. In addition to his journalistic work, Poston wrote several short stories, some depicting childhood and youth and others focusing on problem issues such as color discrimination, labor organizing, and segregation in public facilities. His stories on children—including "The Revolt of the Evil Fairies," which has appeared in a number of textbooks—are being given more attention today when many scholars and teachers are actively pursuing the study of literature about children and adolescents.

Theodore Roosevelt Augustus Major Poston was born in Hopkinsville, Kentucky, on 4 July 1906 to Mollie Cox and Ephraim Poston. He attended the Booker T. Washington Grammar School in Hopkinsville and graduated from Crispus Attucks High School in 1924. At fifteen, Poston ran copy for his family's militant newspaper, the *Hopkinsville Contender,* until it became too controversial for the small town.

He attended Tennessee Agricultural and Industrial College (now Tennessee State University) in Nashville, where he was a forward on the basketball team. After graduation in 1928 the tall, spindly youth followed his two older brothers, Robert and Ulysses, to New York, where they had been officials in Marcus Garvey's Universal Negro Improvement Association. Ulysses Poston got Ted a job at $150 a week writing campaign materials for the Democratic presidential nominee Alfred E. Smith. Poston did not earn that much money again until after World War II.

Poston was a reporter for the *Amsterdam News* when in 1932 the Russian Meschrabpom film company began looking for twenty-two young, black American "actors" who would go to Moscow to make a movie, "Black and White," an exposé of race relations in the United States. Langston Hughes would be the script's editor. For the adventure of it Poston signed on, but once the group was in the Soviet Union, the film endeavor fell through for political reasons. Dorothy West, a Harlem Renaissance writer who was one of the company's actors, explained that the U.S.S.R. needed

229

American engineer Hugh Cooper's expertise in building the Dneprostroi dam, and Cooper said he would not complete the dam if the movie were made. Others say the film was scrapped because America was about to recognize the Soviet Union diplomatically and the U.S.S.R. did not want to thwart the plan by making an untimely anti-American film.

Back in New York, unable to resist taking a risk, Poston and his longtime comrade, Henry Lee Moon, who was to become public-relations director for the National Association for the Advancement of Colored People, led a strike to unionize the *Amsterdam News*. The owners, infuriated after the American Newspaper Guild came in, fired the two at the first legal opportunity.

In 1935 Poston married Miriam Rivers; they were later divorced. In 1941 he married Marie Byrd Jackson, from whom he would also be divorced in 1955.

In these early years of his career, Poston held a number of temporary jobs. He had written for the Federal Works Projects Administration and had waited tables on dining cars on the Pennsylvania Railroad, while writing a weekly column for the *Pittsburgh Courier*. By 1937 he wanted a permanent position, however, so he picked up a telephone book, closed his eyes, and thrust a pin at the listings of New York newspapers. He would later tell friends that the pin hit the *New York Post*. He went to the *Post* and applied for a job. The editors accepted him on the condition that he bring in a

Ted Poston (courtesy of the Schomburg Center for Research in Black Culture, the New York Public Library, Astor, Lenox and Tilden Foundations)

The company for the film "Black and White" en route to the Soviet Union, June 1932. Poston, at far left in the last row, is misidentified as "Ted Postal."

front-page story that day. Poston boarded the Harlem subway, fell asleep, and was awakened several stops later by much commotion outside. He jumped off the car and found a black man threatening a white man in a telephone booth. Poston learned that the white man was a process server seeking to hand a summons to the Harlem religious demagogue Father Divine, and the blacks were some of Divine's "angels" trying to prevent the summons from being served. Poston wrote the story, which ran on the *Post*'s front page the next day. He was hired on a space-rate basis of thirty cents an inch.

When Governor Thomas E. Dewey began to break up the numbers racket in Harlem, Poston, as a Harlem resident, was the *Post* reporter with the most expertise. His illuminating stories soon put him on the newspaper's regular payroll.

Robert C. Weaver described Poston as "a first-class reporter who had a unique ability to extract information from persons of all walks of life." A clear and effective writer, Poston "enjoyed the challenge of tough assignments. He had the courage to face danger and skill to extricate himself in one piece. Of course he did not hesitate to share the details of these perilous exploits with his friends." Henry Lee Moon says, "We called Ted 'the great embellisher': there was always a grain of truth in what he wrote."

Poston liked to regale his friends with the story of the time he covered a press conference called by Mayor William O'Dwyer:

I stayed through the press conference and asked questions here and there but after everyone had left, he told me to wait a minute. He kept me in his office and gave me an exclusive. I looked at him and said, "Mayor, why are you doing this for me? You don't know me." O'Dwyer said that he had looked up during the press conference and seen that I was a black reporter working first string for a daily paper. He said that any Negro working first string for a daily paper must be a hell of a Negro, "so I want to get you in my corner right away."

Humor helped Poston when he went into the deep South to gather civil-rights news. A small-town sheriff asked him if he worked for a white or a colored paper. Poston "ruminated for a minute" and then said, "Well, Sheriff, down here you all have a law that says if a man has one drop of black blood, he's black. I'm the drop of black blood at the *New York Post*, so I guess it's a colored paper."

A good listener and a jovial companion, Poston cultivated journalistic contacts with ease and inspired trust so that his sources were willing to open up to him. His narrative style was fast-moving and conversational.

His penchant for tale-telling extended to literary writing. The most anthologized of his fictional works is his autobiographical short story "The Revolt of the Evil Fairies" (1942). With humor and suspense it tells of the annual colored grammar school play, "Prince Charming and the Sleeping Beauty." A main element in the story is the segregated texture of small-town southern life. Poston relates how the whites "let us" use the opera house, and "even some of the white folks came out" to see the play. He continues, "our leading colored citizens sat right behind them—with an empty row intervening of course." Ironically this racial elitism extended also to the play's black directors. Through his young narrator, Poston recounts,

> Strangely enough, most of the Good Fairies usually turned out to be extremely light in complexion, with straight hair and white folks' features. . . . I made the best grades in my class, I was the leading debater, and the scion of a respected family in the community. But I could never be Prince Charming because I was black.

Acknowledging that some blacks accept the intraracial stigma, Poston has classmate Rat Joiner state, "If you black, you black." The main theme of the story is the insidiousness of prejudice within the black community itself.

"The Revolt of the Evil Fairies," says Ersa Hines Poston, to whom Poston was married on 21 August 1957, "gives an excellent analysis of some of the problems, even in childhood, that haunted and confused Ted." His widow "knew him as a very complex person who harbored many feelings of inferiority. He . . . never felt he had fulfilled his potential."

The earliest extant piece of Poston's writing contrasts two mothers on Mother's Day; one brags about the money or flowers her son gave her, and the other forgoes new shoes for herself because she wants a new dress for her daughter, who is making her first public social appearance. Poston implies that the first mother is full of pride, the second full of love.

During the 1940s Poston published several short stories in the *New Republic*. In the 750-word "A Matter of Record" (1940) Poston combines patches of dialogue, narration, and description to the present life and thought process of a nearly blind, beaten-down black man who had once had a little success in the boxing ring. He now uses an old news story as proof of his past achievement in order to borrow bus fare for him and his sister to get back to Richmond, where they have hope that another relative can find him a job.

"You Go South" (1940) shows a Harlem resident steeling himself for a return to southern Jim Crow rule. Poston clearly and simply presents the black consciousness in a manner that makes it possible for ignorant white liberals of forty years ago to imagine how it feels to be segregated in a filthy train, at a drugstore soda fountain or gas station, or subjected to false charges of "reckless eyeballing."

In "Law and Order in Norfolk" (1940), a "high yaller" man who wants to be a policeman at the time the black Elks are crusading for black cops goes to the Civil Service Office and is taken for "ofay." One of Poston's characters says, "One of them young ofay chicks what clerk down there, she even tries to flirt with him." When the man's race is ascertained, his application is cancelled because "only white males can apply." The NAACP takes the case, which moves into limbo. But Poston closes his story on a note of undaunted hope:

> We ain't tearing our wig. . . . We're just keeping up our poll tax and registration drive. By next year we plan to have 5,000 paid up. And when we reach that number, we'll either get a Negro cop or a new chief of police. Hell, come to mention it, we might get both.

"The Making of Mamma Harris" (1940) is a union story about a woman who is old at forty-nine, having stemmed tobacco for $2.80 a week: "It took me just one day to find out that preachers don't know nothing about hell. They ain't worked in no tobacco factory." Mamma Harris leads tobacco workers in a strike against the factory just when the tobacco harvest is at its height. She brags about how other unions came and helped picket, even "*white* women out here parading for niggers." The union people win but discover that management still finds ways to punish the strikers. Yet Poston ends this story also on a hopeful note, as Mamma Harris doggedly plans another strike.

By 1940 Poston had gone to Washington, D.C., and was trying to integrate Negro workers into defense industries. He was in an effective position for he had already interviewed so many people that he knew everyone of consequence. At that time Poston reviewed Claude McKay's *Harlem: Negro Metropolis* for the *New Republic* (25 November 1940). He found fault with its "bitter indictment of Negro intellectuals": "For McKay, like Garvey and a growing number of prominent Negroes, believes that segregation, voluntary or enforced, is essential to the full development of the Negro minority in America." McKay himself, Poston notes, laments that "The American Negro group is the most advanced in the world ... but sadly lacks a group soul." Poston takes that as proof that separatism will not work. To McKay's claim that the radical trade unionist Sufi Abdul Hamid was not anti-Semitic, only "anti-Jewish," Poston knew from a half-

Roger Smith, William Clark, Ted Poston, and Harriette Easterlin going over copy for the Office of War Information News Bureau, 1943 (courtesy of the Schomburg Center for Research in Black Culture, the New York Public Library, Astor, Lenox and Tilden Foundations)

233

dozen personal interviews with Sufi that the man had tried to get "Nazi financial backing for the creation of a uniformed Black Legion to combat Jews in Harlem," and that in a speech Sufi had urged his followers to "meet a Jew on the street, pull out his tongue and spit down his throat."

But Poston's main disagreement with McKay was McKay's agitating for the acceptance of segregation: Blacks "simply cannot be organized with whites who have a higher standard of wages," said McKay. Poston held out for working in the same unions with whites and pointed to "the benefits Negroes have received in higher wages, shorter hours, trade-union practice, and education."

Poston's "My Most Humiliating Jim Crow Experience" (1944) describes his experiences in Decatur, Alabama, as the only Negro reporter at the third Scottsboro trial. He disguised himself with a ragged overcoat, greasy cap, and well-worn overalls. Using his natural southern accent, he had arrived with mail-order documents made out to him under an assumed name that certified him as an ordained minister. He sat in the "colored" spectators' section of the courthouse. A dozen "slate-faced, agate-eyed traditional cracker" types caught him mailing a report to New York and nearly discovered that he was the "Nawth'n nigger whut's been writin' them lies." The false identification papers saved him from being murdered; the "crackers" made do, Poston claimed, with sending him off with a kick in the pants.

Poston enjoyed playing devil's advocate in print. In *Ebony* magazine he and Roi Ottley argued the respective merits of New York versus Chicago as the more desirable residence for blacks. Poston, for New York, granted Chicago its due: "Although New York boasts some 6,000 Negro-owned and operated business establishments, there is little doubt that Chicago excels it in this field. . . . Chicago businessmen have organized some of the largest and most efficient funeral and burial societies in the world." However, he continued, "That's the real difference. New Yorkers are interested in a more abundant life rather than in a glorious pre-paid death."

In his ability to bring his fictional people to life, Poston resembles Zora Neale Hurston. But while Hurston's fictional world is mainly black, with whites as outsiders, useful only as audience and patrons, Poston's blacks were tricksters who outsmarted the irrational whites on their own turf.

Of the fact that Poston rose so high, Bill Powell of the *Louisville Courier-Journal* has remarked that somebody had failed to get the message across

to "the skinny little black kid in Hopkinsville" in the late 1920s "that he had no chance at all to make it big as a journalist."

C. Gerald Fraser of the *New York Times* feels Poston's significance was that he was a "first": "He worked longer in New York than any other black journalist. . . . I thought it was interesting that he did fiction writing, too; and it was well done. Given half an opportunity he would have done more."

When reporter Joel Dreyfuss went to work at the *Post* in the 1960s, eight white reporters did the legwork. He says that, while Poston, "still the only drop of black blood, wrote the stories, with that flowing, graceful prose. . . . Until late in the 1960s, the usual method of covering black life for most urban papers was for black reporters to do the research and white reporters to do the writing and analysis. Ted Poston's reversal was but another of his casual 'firsts.' " Henry Lee Moon concludes, "He helped to move news about civil rights and black folk from page 79 to page 1."

During his life Poston received a number of awards for his pioneering journalistic and civic work. As early as 1950 he received the Heywood Broun Memorial Award for outstanding reporting from the American Newspaper Guild, CIO, as well as recognition for journalistic contributions to interracial and interfaith understanding from the Irving Geist Foundation and the Newspaper Guild of New York. Also in 1950 he received the George Polk Award for Outstanding National Reporting, given by Long Island University "for coverage of inflamed incidents of racial discrimination in Florida." In 1951 he received the Beta Delta Mu unity award for "efforts to promote interracial brotherhood and amity." He also received a medal for distinguished service from the City of New York and distinguished service plaques from the Boroughs of Brooklyn, Bronx, and Queens. In 1972 he was honored by Black Perspective, an organization of black journalists, for his solitary pioneering efforts and for journalistic excellence.

With the panache of black speech, humor, hyperbole, metaphor, and movement, the fearless and ebullient raconteur Ted Poston elevated journalism to literature and the quest for a story to high drama.

References:
Richard Bardolph, *The Negro Vanguard* (New York: Vintage, 1961), p. 339;
Thomas R. Brooks, *Walls Come Tumbling Down: A History of the Civil Rights Movement, 1940-1970*

(Englewood Cliffs, N.J.: Prentice-Hall, 1974), pp. 96, 108-109, 116;

"Date with a Dish: Barbecued Squab," *Ebony* (August 1955): 96-100;

Joel Dreyfuss, "The Loneliness of Being First," *Washington Post,* 19 January 1974, pp. B1, B3;

Fern Marja Eckman, "Ted Poston—Newspaperman," *New York Post,* 14 April 1972;

Peter Goldman, *The Death and Life of Malcolm X* (Urbana: University of Illinois Press, 1973), p. 31;

Jack Greenburg, *Race Relations in American Law* (New York: Columbia University Press, 1959), p. 349;

Ernie Johnston, Jr., "Pioneering Black Newsman Writes 30 to Brave Career," *Editor and Publisher* (29 April 1972): 34, 40;

Peter Kirss, "Editors Warned on Racial News," *New York Times,* 13 October 1967, p. 28;

David L. Lewis, *When Harlem Was In Vogue* (New York: Knopf, 1981), pp. 288-293;

Henry Lee Moon, "Ted Poston, A Creative Journalist," *Black Perspective* (Spring 1972): 11-40;

Moon, "Ted Poston: A Personal Note," *Crisis* (March 1974);

"Negro Newsmen on White Dailies," *Ebony* (April 1948): 57-60;

"Negroes on White Newspapers," *Ebony* (November 1955): 77-79;

Bill Powell, "Yesteryear with Bill Powell," *Louisville Courier-Journal,* January 1974;

Patricia W. Romero, ed., *In Black America, 1968: The Year of Awakening* (New York: Publishers, 1969), p. 265;

John D. Silvera, *Negro in World War II* (New Orleans: Military Press, 1946), p. 24;

M. L. Stein, *Blacks in Communication* (New York: Messner, 1972), pp. 55-57;

Charles Herbert Stember, *Sexual Racism: The Emotional Barrier to an Integrated Society* (New York: Elsevier, 1976), p. 92;

Doris Willens, "Adventures of a Negro Reporter," *Negro Digest* (December 1949): 13-15.

Willis Richardson
(5 November 1889-8 November 1977)

Patsy B. Perry
North Carolina Central University

BOOK: *The King's Dilemma and Other Plays for Children* (New York: Exposition Press, 1956).

PLAY PRODUCTIONS: *The Deacon's Awakening,* St. Paul, 1921;
The Chip Woman's Fortune, Chicago, 29 January 1923;
Mortgaged, Washington, D.C., Howard University, 29 March 1924;
Compromise, Cleveland, Karamu House, 26 February 1925;
The Broken Banjo, New York, 1 August 1925;
The King's Dilemma, Washington, D.C., May 1926;
The Flight of the Natives, Washington, D.C., 7 May 1927;
The Black Horseman, Baltimore, 12 October 1931;
Miss or Mrs., Washington, D.C., May 1941.

OTHER: *Compromise: A Folk Play,* in *The New Negro: An Interpretation,* edited by Alain Locke (New York: Boni, 1925);
The Black Horseman, The House of Sham, The King's Dilemma, in *Plays and Pageants from the Life of the Negro,* edited by Richardson (Washington, D.C.: Associated Publishers, 1930);
Mortgaged, in *Readings from Negro Authors,* edited by Otelia Cromwell, Eva B. Dykes, and Lorenzo D. Turner (New York: Harcourt, 1931);
Antonio Maceo, Attucks, the Martyr, The Elder Dumas, In Menelik's Court, Near Calvary, in *Negro History in Thirteen Plays,* edited by Richardson and May Miller (Washington, D.C.: Associated Publishers, 1935);
The Flight of the Natives, in *Black Theatre, U.S.A.: Forty-Five Plays by Black Americans 1847-1974,* edited by James V. Hatch with Ted Shine, consultant (New York: Free Press, 1974).

PERIODICAL PUBLICATIONS: "The Hope of a Negro Drama," *Crisis,* 19 (November 1919): 338-339;
The Deacon's Awakening, Crisis, 21 (November 1920): 10-15;

Willis Richardson

"The Negro and the Stage," *Opportunity,* 2 (October 1924): 310;
"The Negro Audience," *Opportunity,* 3 (April 1925): 123;
"Characters," *Opportunity,* 3 (June 1925): 183;
"The Unpleasant Play," *Opportunity,* 3 (September 1925): 282;
The Broken Banjo, Crisis, 31 (February 1926): 167-171; (March 1926): 225-228;
The Idle Head, Carolina, 59 (April 1929): 16-25.

Emerging at the beginning of the New Negro Renaissance, Willis Richardson wrote serious drama portraying the lives of black people. Truly a pioneer, he was the first black to have a Broadway production of a nonmusical, one-act play—*The Chip Woman's Fortune* (produced in 1923)—and the first to compile, edit, and write collections of black plays for young people: *Plays and Pageants from the Life of the Negro* (1930) and, with May Miller, *Negro History in Thirteen Plays* (1935). Richardson wrote three of the twelve dramas in *Plays and Pageants* and five of those in *Negro History in Thirteen Plays.* In addition he encouraged others to write and to produce "Negro plays," and in all of his work, including children's plays and critical essays on contemporary theater, he attempted to interest his readers in high Negro drama which he described as "a mine of pure gold."

Convinced that neither the stereotypical "darkies" of white dramatists nor sterile Negro characters like those of Angelina Grimké's *Rachel* (1920) came close to capturing the richness, diversity, and beauty of his race, Richardson wrote forty-two individual plays that ranged from fairy tales of the future and romanticized actions of famous black leaders to realistic representations of ordinary blacks who suffer from their own weaknesses or society's shortcomings. Richardson acted to prevent the consequences of a challenge posed in 1926 by W. E. B. Du Bois: "Suppose the only Negro who survived some centuries hence was the Negro painted by white Americans in the novels and essays they have written. What would people in a hundred years say of black Americans?" To Richardson's credit, after only fifty years, more or less, his pioneer efforts have resulted in dramatizations of the soul of black people, a soul "truly worth showing."

Willis Richardson was born on 5 November 1889, in Wilmington, North Carolina, the son of Willis Wilder and Agnes Ann Harper Richardson. Summarizing his early years for *Crisis* magazine, Richardson said his family moved to Washington, D.C., following the Wilmington riots of 1898 and that he was "graduated from the M St. [later Dunbar] High School in 1910." While still in high school, he became interested in drama and was encouraged by his English teacher, Mary Burrill, who was writing and staging her own plays. His serious study of the drama was delayed, however, while he established himself as a government employee and began a family.

In 1911 he became a clerk in the U.S. Bureau of Engraving and Printing in Washington, D.C., and on 1 September 1914, he married Mary Ellen Jones. The couple had three children: Jean Paula in 1916; Shirley Antonella in 1918; and Noel Justine in 1920.

According to Richardson, in about 1916 he "saw a performance of Angelina Grimké's 'Rachel' and by that was influenced to study the technique of the Drama." Subsequently from 1916 to 1918 he was enrolled in a correspondence course in poetry, drama, and the novel, after which he "began to write plays." Among the first of these were four one-act children's dramas published in the *Brown-*

ies' Book, a monthly magazine founded by Du Bois and designed especially for "Children of the Sun": *The King's Dilemma* (December 1920), *The Gypsy's Finger Ring* (March 1921), *The Children's Treasure* (June 1921), and *The Dragon's Tooth* (October 1921). In *The Children's Treasure,* Richardson employs realistic details to teach a lesson in charity as five children, including the most selfish one among them, contribute their savings toward the rent of a poor neighbor facing eviction. In the other three plays he focuses on the future and employs the techniques of the fairy tale. In *The King's Dilemma,* Richardson dramatizes the beginning of democracy succeeding rule by kings. *The Gypsy's Finger Ring* is about the age of freedom following the periods of chattel slavery and peonage; *The Dragon's Tooth* projects a future time of love and brotherhood to be realized through children. The plays were in keeping with the major purpose of the *Brownies' Book,* which was to "teach Universal Love and Brotherhood for all little folk—black and brown and yellow and white."

In sharp contrast to the ideal subjects of his children's plays, Richardson's first one-act play for adults, *The Deacon's Awakening,* deals with an immediate, sociopolitical concern, women's efforts to engage in their newly won right to vote. The protagonist, David Jones, a church deacon, abandons his crusade to identify for disciplinary action all aspiring women voters when he discovers that his wife and daughter are organizers and active members of the Voting Society. Although *The Deacon's Awakening* was published in *Crisis* in November 1920 and performed in 1921 by the St. Paul Players of Minnesota, it brought little recognition to its author. Richardson described the stage production as "not much of a success" and himself as still "unheard of" in 1921. In retrospect, however, he should be credited with exploring what was, in 1921, a highly volatile subject in words which are familiar even today. Readers can clearly understand Mrs. Jones's position when she outlines the unfair treatment of girls from birth onward and protests further denial of their opportunities. Classified as a domestic protest drama, *The Deacon's Awakening* is one of a group of plays through which Richardson expresses concern about enfranchisement, equal access to education, and employment opportunities. He skillfully blends these subjects in a scene during which Deacon Jones and Sol threaten to remove their daughters from Howard University as their punishment for having joined the Voting Society. Mrs. Jones intervenes with a convincing argument in favor of women's rights of

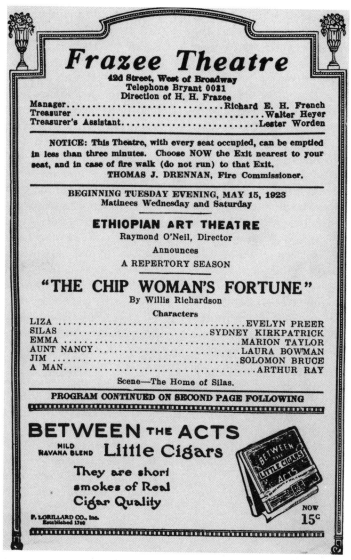

First page of the program for the Broadway production of Richardson's play

citizenship, education, and economic independence.

In 1923 Richardson gained recognition with the production of *The Chip Woman's Fortune* in Chicago, Washington, and New York. In New York it opened at Harlem's Lafayette Theatre on 7 May 1923 and, after eight performances, moved to Broadway, where it premiered at the Frazee Theatre on 15 May 1923. Director Raymond O'Neil's Ethiopian Art Players presented it with Oscar Wilde's *Salome* and a jazz rendition of Shakespeare's *Comedy of Errors*. Recalling the steps which led to Broadway, Richardson stated in a March 1972 interview that: the Ethiopian Art Players originally were organized in Chicago "and they put on Negro plays, but they didn't know any Negro playwrights,

or black playwrights, or whatever you want to call them, so they wrote to *Crisis* and Dr. Du Bois put me in touch. They put on Oscar Wilde's *Salome* and my play *The Chip Woman's Fortune*. They went to New York and played at the Frazier [*sic*] Theater and the reviews were so good that they sold lots of tickets. . . ."

Perhaps it is more accurate to say, however, that the reviews were mixed. On 8 May 1923, *New York Times* drama critic John Corbin wrote: "As a curtain raiser to 'Salome,' . . . 'The Chip Woman's Fortune,' a one-acter by Willis Richardson, was offered. The piece is trifling and at times amusing." On 20 May 1923, Corbin had only praise for Richardson's play, especially for its development of characters: " 'The Chip Woman's Fortune' . . . is an unaffected and wholly convincing transcript of everyday character. No one is glorified or otherwise tricked out to please; no one is blackened to serve as a 'dramatic' contrast. I am referring, of course, to points of essential character, not to that matter of walnut stain. . . . Willis Richardson has limned half a dozen characters candidly, sympathetically, truly." It is futile to make conjectures about the reasons for Corbin's reevaluation of *The Chip Woman's Fortune*. The facts that the play is still anthologized and that it can be read seriously support his second, more detailed assessment of it as a "convincing transcript." Briefly it is the story of Aunt Nancy, who has maintained herself as a member of Silas's household by collecting bits of wood and coal for fuel and by nursing Silas's invalid wife. Faced with the loss of both his job and the prized Victrola for which he has failed to make payments, Silas asks Aunt Nancy's help. She explains, however, that the money which she has saved is for her son, Jim, who is soon to be released from prison. While they are engaged in this discussion, Jim arrives and generously divides Aunt Nancy's fortune with Silas and his family who had taken care of her during his absence. While the play ends on a relatively happy note, there is mild protest in the suggestions that both Jim's imprisonment and Silas's furlough from his job may have been unjust. Describing it as a "miniature folk drama," editor Burns Mantle included *The Chip Woman's Fortune* in *The Best Plays of 1922-23 and The Year Book of the Drama in America*.

Though Richardson was never again to see one of his works on Broadway, he became an influential playwright among theater groups in black high schools, colleges, churches, and communities. As early as 1919 Richardson issued the call for a national Negro theater "able to send a company of Negro Players with Negro Plays across our own continent [and] . . . to the artistic peoples of Europe." While citing the Irish National Theater as an excellent model, he reminded his readers that the Irish possessed no richer resources than did black Americans. He himself used black folk materials and urged the development of a sophisticated theater audience that would respect and sustain the national theater he envisioned. In four essays written for *Opportunity* magazine, he defined and developed his criteria for serious drama. In "The Negro and the Stage" (October 1924), he held that "the theater should always, and seriously, be considered as an educational institution side by side with the school." In "The Negro Audience" (April 1925), he outlined the following points as "things

which should matter . . . if the Negro drama is to prosper and become 'a thing of beauty and a joy forever': whether the characters are well drawn, whether the dialogue is natural, whether the ending is consistent and whether the whole thing is interesting and logical." Focusing on "the peasant class of the Negro group" in "Characters" (June 1925), Richardson described that class as being "different and interesting," important qualities for theater. Finally, in "The Unpleasant Play" (September 1925), he challenged the Negro writer to "make his audience hear the truth, or nothing." Recognized as "the great spirit encouraging the creation of a Negro Theater movement," Richardson supplied original plays for black producers; directed the Little Theater group in Washington, D.C.; and established contacts with professors of drama, chiefly Alain Locke and Montgomery Gregory of Howard University.

On 29 March 1924, the Howard Players produced *Mortgaged*, Richardson's one-act domestic drama exploring the friction between the two Fields brothers. John, a struggling research scientist, is made to feel great indebtedness to Tom, an unscrupulous businessman, who has financed several of John's research projects. When John learns that his chemical formula has been purchased, he offers to underwrite Harvard University expenses for Tom's two children, a somewhat embarrassing offer since Tom had earlier agreed to send John's son to Harvard only if John left his research laboratory for another job. In their anthology *The New Negro Renaissance* (1975) Arthur P. Davis and Michael Peplow included *Mortgaged* under the heading "Best-Foot-Forward Literature," a school of writing which emphasized progressive ideas. Stressing the value of scientific contributions over materialistic interests, *Mortgaged* is a prime example of this tradition based on the talented-tenth philosophy of Du Bois. In May 1925 *Mortgaged* was again performed in a drama tournament by the Dunbar Dramatic Club of Plainfield, N.J. Recalling the event, Richardson made the following evaluation: "The rare thing about this occasion was that out of the eight or ten clubs producing plays, one Negro club produced a Negro play by a Negro author. The play, which I consider one of my poorest, gained fourth place among some of the best American one-acters."

The Broken Banjo, produced by the Krigwa players in New York City on 1 August 1925, is another of Richardson's one-act domestic dramas. The main character, Matt Turner, is obsessed with his banjo to the point of neglecting his wife, Emma.

His meager existence—having been forced to live for a time on Emma's wages and currently reduced to purchasing secondhand shoes for her—affords him little comfort. His only joy is the banjo, which he plays at every opportunity. He is equally zealous in his attempts to rid his household of Sam, his wife's parasitic brother, and Adam, her cousin. During one of their dreaded visits, Sam accidentally breaks Matt's banjo as he tries to take it away from Adam. Sam narrowly escapes Matt's angry assault with the startling announcement that he had witnessed the murder of "old man Shelton." Until this time, Matt had thought that his unintentional but lethal blow to Shelton had gone unobserved. Matt struck out in anger when, in parrying blows, Shelton had shattered his banjo. Now a second time, Matt's beloved banjo is broken. Bereft of music, both literally and figuratively, Matt leaves with a police officer to whom Sam has revealed details of the Shelton murder. In its 30 October 1925 issue, *Crisis* announced that *The Broken Banjo* had won the seventy-five-dollar first prize in the Amy Spingarn Contest in Literature and Art. Eugene O'Neill, who served as one of the contest evaluators, commented: "I am glad to hear that the judges all agreed on 'The Broken Banjo' and that the play was so successfully staged. Willis Richardson should certainly continue working in this field." *Crisis* published this play in its issues for February and March 1926. Following its production in 1934 by the Atlanta University Summer Theatre, the play earned the following comment from Sterling Brown: "the acting of the entire cast had a zest to it that gave dramatic body to a play that in the reading had seemed somewhat thin. There was no question of the play's taking."

In 1925 Richardson finished *Compromise*, another one-act domestic drama. It is the story of two families—the black Lees and the white Carters—and the tragic events which the Lees suffer at the hands of the Carters. Having "accidentally" killed Joe Lee, Ben Carter compromised with Joe's father, Jim Lee, by paying him $100, money with which Jim buys enough strong drink to kill himself. Seven years later, when Alec Lee discovers that Jack Carter has impregnated his sister, he breaks Jack's arm. In this situation, however, no compromise is possible; Ben Carter is "goin' to put the sheriff on" Alec. Though the curtain falls with Alec's mother vowing to save him, *Compromise* makes the point that for southern blacks in the 1920s there was no justice; their very lives were "compromised." *Compromise* was included in Alain Locke's *The New Negro* (1925), and Richardson described the drama as one

in which he had "some confidence." It was first produced by the Gilpin Players at Karamu House, Cleveland, Ohio, on 26 February 1925. Subsequently it was staged by the Krigwa Players in New York, on 3 May 1926, and by the Howard Players, on 8 April 1936.

Richardson's *The Flight of the Natives* and *The Idle Head* are two additional one-act dramas of the 1920s which explore racial dilemmas of past and present times. Produced by the Krigwa Players in Washington, D.C., on 7 May 1927, *The Flight of the Natives* describes the daring escape of six slaves from a South Carolina plantation in 1860. Having suffered lashings, the treachery of slave informers, and threats of being sold down the river, these slaves effect their escape by using their combined strengths. In a concise analysis of this drama, James Hatch cites two important features: Richardson's rejection of the "contented slave" image and his use of the "group protagonist" rather than a central hero whose chances of escape, under the watchful eyes of slavery, would have been slight. Indeed heroes or rebellious slaves paid for their status by being made "examples of" to frighten other slaves into submission. In *The Idle Head* (1929), Richardson continues his exploration of southern peonage. Though the time of this drama is some sixty years following the end of chattel slavery and the setting is the Broadus home rather than a slave cabin, George Broadus is far from being a free man. Admired by his mother for his natural independence, George is denied any demonstration of this manly trait; he is, in fact, blacklisted because he will not grin, bow, or answer to "Sambo." Unable to secure a job and feeling guilty about his inability to aid his mother, George pawns a valuable pin which a white woman had forgotten to remove from a garment sent to be laundered. As the curtain falls, he is carried off to jail—without regard to circumstances—in much the same way that an intractable slave was sold down the river for any similar infraction of his master's law. Whether or not Richardson consciously drew parallels, it is clear that these two dramas make a poignant statement that conditions for southern blacks had not improved much since slavery time. *The Idle Head* was published in April 1929, in the *Carolina* magazine, a literary publication of the University of North Carolina at Chapel Hill.

In 1930, at the request of Carter G. Woodson, founder of the Association for the Study of Negro Life and History, Richardson compiled his first anthology *Plays and Pageants from the Life of the Negro*. In the introduction he cites Woodson as "the real

2023 13th St., N.W.,

Washington, D.C.,

August 9, 1925.

Dear Locke:

I thank you without seeing it for the ending you have added to "Compromise". I am sure whatever you have done is an improvement on the play and your advice is always welcome. I do not know exactly what you want in the biographical sketch, but I shall write a few things here and you may use whatever of them you wish to.

I was born in Wilmington, N.C. Nov. 5, 1889, but my family moved to Washington in August 1899 after the awful riot of the previous November. So I obtained the basis of my education in the high and secondary schools of this city. Whatever literary education I have (and I consider that more important than the other) I gained by years of reading and hard study of three art forms - Poetry, Drama and the Novel. I began to write plays in 1917, but the first of my plays to reach the public in any way was "The Deacon's Awakening" which was published in The Crisis in 1920 and produced in St. Paul during the following year. Then followed four plays for The Brownies' Book, "The King's Dilemma", "The Children's Treasure", "The Gypsy's Finger Ring" and "The Dragon's Tooth". The next to be made visible was "The Chip Woman's Fortune" at Chicago, Washington and New York in 1923, then Mortgaged in 1924 by the Howard Players under you and Gregory, and this year at Plainfield by The Dunbar Dramatic Club. This year "The Broken Banjo", The Crisis prize was produced in New York.

I am reasonably sure that you wont be able to use all this, but I have written it so that you may choose what you need and arrange it the way you wish to.

Ever cordially,

Willis Richardson

Letter to Alain Locke referring to the play by Richardson that Locke included in his 1925 anthology The New Negro *(courtesy of the Alain Locke Papers, Moorland-Spingarn Research Center, Howard University)*

ETHIOPIA AT THE BAR OF JUSTICE

PLAYS AND PAGEANTS
FROM
The LIFE of the NEGRO

Willis Richardson

THE ASSOCIATED PUBLISHERS, INC.
1538 NINTH STREET, N. W. :: WASHINGTON, D. C.

Frontispiece and title page for Richardson's 1930 anthology (courtesy of the Schomburg Center for Research in Black Culture, the New York Public Library, Astor, Lenox and Tilden Foundations)

editor of the pageants" and provides evaluative comments on the contributors, including Thelma Duncan, Maud Cuney-Hare, John Matheus, May Miller, Edward J. McCoo, Inez M. Burke, Dorothy C. Gwinn, and Frances Gunner. Richardson also classifies the works according to theme, temper, and level of difficulty, assuring his audience of having collected "the best material of its kind, . . . plays and pageants suitable for every reasonable need of School, Church, or Little Theater Group." Among the plays Richardson included three of his own that represented his wide range: the children's fairy tale *The King's Dilemma; The House of Sham,* a domestic satire; and *The Black Horseman,* a historical drama. In *The King's Dilemma,* a white prince, having discovered equality in love and friendship, refuses the king's command to give up his black friend; he is

happy when the kingdom is dissolved and the people are given power to govern themselves. First produced in the Washington, D.C., public schools, *The King's Dilemma* won the Public School Prize on 21 May 1926. *The House of Sham,* neatly summarized in its title, satirizes the exploitative practices and shallow strivings of a middle-class black family headed by John Cooper, who admits to having stolen and done "everything else crooked" in his efforts to appear wealthy. In short he is proven to be bankrupt both materially and morally. John Cooper's opposite can be found in *The Black Horseman,* a one-act drama picturing King Massinissa as the embodiment of nobility, bravery, and steadfastness. Ruler of Numidia, Africa, in 204 B.C., King Massinissa resists the treacherous bribes of a Carthaginian prince and saves his nation. This drama was first produced on 12 October 1931 by the Playground Athletic League of Baltimore, Maryland.

In 1935 Richardson published five additional one-act historical dramas in his second anthology, *Negro History in Thirteen Plays,* which he edited with May Miller. In the preface Richardson and Miller state that they "have not attempted to reproduce definitive history, but have sought to create the atmosphere of a time past or the portrait of a memorable figure." Richardson's plays, *Antonio Maceo, Attucks, the Martyr, In Menelik's Court,* and *Near Calvary,* do indeed provide memorable portraits, but, perhaps more important, they epitomize the sterling qualities which Richardson saw as intrinsic in black people. Only in *The Elder Dumas,* Richardson's fifth drama in this collection, does he present a prominent black figure in unflattering terms.

In both *Antonio Maceo* and *Attucks, the Martyr* brave warriors die in the service of their countries. General Maceo, a Cuban freedom fighter, leads a successful rebellion against Spain but is assassinated when his unscrupulous physician betrays him. Crispus Attucks, a fugitive from slavery, leads an attack against British soldiers and is the first to be killed in America's fight for independence from England. Though *In Menelik's Court* and *Near Calvary* do not have clearly focused battlegrounds, they both support Richardson's insistence upon the bravery of black men through explicit comments or through specific actions. For example, in characterizing his people, Menelik II, Emperor of Abyssinia, says, "We do not betray our enemies when they trust us. Our hands are brown and we play a fair game—always above the table." Later, when it is revealed that one of the servants has turned traitor, Menelik contrasts him with the Italian spies and reminds him that nothing was expected from the Italians "but everything was expected of [him], an Abyssinian." In *Near Calvary* Simon bravely carries Jesus' cross, and Laban, when questioned by Caesar's soldiers, admits his belief in Jesus despite the fact that his confession could result in his death. In sum it is Richardson's point that "When men are black and brave they are never traitors."

In *The Elder Dumas,* however, Richardson reveals the unseemly practices of a writer grown careless but, at the same time, overly sensitive to criticism. Alexandre Dumas père, the French mulatto playwright and novelist, is charged with writing hurriedly, representing as his own the ideas of other writers, and sacrificing sound creative achievements for quick financial profits. Perhaps Richardson implies an even greater charge against

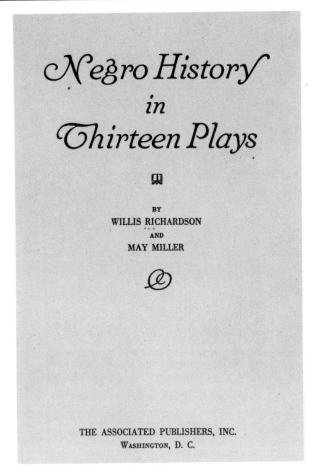

Negro History
in
Thirteen Plays

BY
WILLIS RICHARDSON
AND
MAY MILLER

THE ASSOCIATED PUBLISHERS, INC.
WASHINGTON, D. C.

Title page for the 1935 anthology in which Richardson and his coeditor included plays that, they hoped, would "create the atmosphere of a time past or the portrait of a memorable figure." Many of the plays were commissioned specifically for this collection (courtesy of the Schomburg Center for Research in Black Culture, the New York Public Library, Astor, Lenox and Tilden Foundations).

the elder Dumas, for he presents his character as being more interested in physical retaliation against the critic than in an honest assessment of his criticism.

In 1956, after more than two decades without a major drama publication or production, Richardson issued his third and final collection, *The King's Dilemma and Other Plays for Children.* In this collection he included *The Dragon's Tooth, The Gypsy's Finger Ring, The King's Dilemma,* and the Easter play *Near Calvary.* Emphasizing the importance of love, racial harmony, justice, and equality, these children's dramas bring Richardson back to his original purpose and audience. Perhaps weary of trying to influence mature readers and disappointed that black professional actors and producers had ignored his works, Richardson came to believe that children would be the hope for a world in which a national black drama might flourish.

During the last decade of his life, however, Richardson witnessed a general revival in black drama and a specific interest in his contributions. Between 1969 and 1975, for instance, several of his most popular dramas were republished, including *The Chip Woman's Fortune* in Lindsay Patterson's *Anthology of the American Negro* (1967) and in Darwin Turner's *Black Drama in America* (1971). *The Broken Banjo* was collected in Richard Barksdale and Keneth Kinnamon's *Black Writers of America* (1972); *The Idle Head* and *The Flight of the Natives* appeared in Hatch and Ted Shine's *Black Theater, U.S.A.* (1974); and *Mortgaged* was included in Davis and Peplow's *New Negro Renaissance* (1975). Moreover, as a part of the Oral Black Theatre History Collection of City College, New York, Richardson was interviewed in March 1972 by Hatch and his assistants. And in Wilmington, North Carolina, Richardson's birthplace, a community theater group was established in 1974 as the Willis Richardson Players. Just a few days after Richardson's death, his achievements were cited at AUDELCO's Fifth Annual Theatre Awards program on 21 November 1977 in Harlem, New York. Efforts to reintroduce and recognize more fully Richardson's pioneering contributions signaled the arrival of that sophisticated theater audience which he had envisioned at the start of his career.

References:

Arthur P. Davis and Michael W. Peplow, eds., *The New Negro Renaissance: An Anthology* (New York: Holt, Rinehart & Winston, 1975), pp. xix-xxxi, 70-72;

James V. Hatch and Omarii Abdullah, eds., *Black Playwrights, 1823-1977: An Annotated Bibliography of Plays* (New York: Bowker, 1977), pp. 190-194;

Fannie E. Frazier Hicklin, "The American Negro Playwright, 1920-1964," Ph.D. dissertation, University of Wisconsin, 1965, pp. 149-159;

Bernard L. Peterson, Jr., "An Evaluation—Willis Richardson: Pioneer Playwright," *Black World*, 26 (April 1975): 40-48, 86-88;

Sister Mary Anthony Scally, *Negro Catholic Writers, 1900-1943: A Bio-Bibliography* (Detroit: Romig, 1945), pp. 95-98;

Daniel Walden, ed., *W. E. B. Du Bois, The Crisis Writings* (Greenwich, Conn.: Fawcett, 1972), pp. 275-299.

George Samuel Schuyler

(25 February 1895-31 August 1977)

Norma R. Jones
Alcorn State University

BOOKS: *Racial Intermarriage in the United States* (Girard, Kans.: Haldeman-Julius, 1929);

Black No More; Being an Account of the Strange and Wonderful Workings of Science in the Land of the Free (New York: Macaulay, 1931);

Slaves Today: A Story of Liberia (New York: Brewer, Warren & Putnam, 1931);

The Communist Conspiracy Against the Negro (New York: Catholic Information Society, 1947);

Black and Conservative: The Autobiography of George S. Schuyler (New Rochelle, N.Y.: Arlington House, 1966).

OTHER: "The Negro-Art Hokum," *Nation,* 122 (16 June 1926): 662-663;

"The Van Vechten Revolution," *Phylon* (Fourth Quarter 1950).

George S. Schuyler (Morgan and Marvin Smith photo; courtesy of the Schomburg Center for Research in Black Culture, the New York Public Library, Astor, Lenox and Tilden Foundations)

Satirist and critic, George S. Schuyler made his most important contribution to Afro-American literature during the Harlem Renaissance. His novel *Black No More* (1931) was the first full-length satire on American racism by a black author, while the article "The Negro-Art Hokum" (June 1926) forcefully presented one side of the debate on the "Black Aesthetic." When that debate was renewed during the black arts movement of the 1960s and 1970s, Schuyler's argument still had a contemporary ring. Following the Harlem Renaissance, Schuyler's career as a newsman and editorial opponent of communism claimed all his attention.

George Samuel Schuyler was born in Providence, Rhode Island, on 25 February 1895 to Eliza Jane Fischer and George S. Schuyler. His northern background enabled him to escape many of the worst effects of turn-of-the-century racism. His respectable middle-class upbringing in a racially mixed area of Syracuse, New York, where he attended public schools from 1902 to 1912, provided him with a self-confidence that never deserted him. The occasional taunts of white classmates only encouraged him to stand up for himself. His father, who died when Schuyler was three, was a hotel chef; his stepfather, though poorly educated, was a hard worker, holding a succession of jobs which enabled him to provide a comfortable home for the family. They attended the Episcopal church.

In his autobiography Schuyler frankly recalled the family's boast "of having been free as far back as any of them could or wanted to remember, and they haughtily looked down upon those who had been in servitude." If any of Schuyler's ancestors had been slaves, it would have been before the Revolutionary War (in which a great-grandfather served on the American side). Yet, along with pride in their free Negro heritage, Schuyler's family also inculcated in him a profound respect for the history of black progress following emancipation. This sense of continuity, coupled with his desire for adventure, led him to join the army at age seventeen without graduating from high school.

Schuyler's seven-year stint in the military, which he left as a first lieutenant, was the beginning of a series of experiences which exposed him to many facets of American society. Several of these experiences were later to provide the basis for some of his best descriptive pieces, such as "Woof," about his first sergeant, and "Memoirs of a Pearl Diver," dealing with various jobs as a dishwasher in New York City, which was published in H. L. Mencken's *American Mercury*. During a jobless period he made his home among the hoboes on Manhattan's Bowery. In 1921 he joined the Socialist Party of America, but it is unclear to what extent he accepted their doctrines.

The socialist connection did prove fruitful in that it brought Schuyler together with A. Philip Randolph, who hired him in 1923 to work for the *Messenger*, where he continued as an assistant editor through 1928. In 1924 Schuyler also became the New York correspondent for the *Pittsburgh Courier*, for which he worked in various capacities, including that of associate editor, until 1966. New York City remained Schuyler's home base for the rest of his life, and it was there that he came to know practically all the significant personages in the American black community. His autobiography, *Black and Conservative* (1966), is a mine of information about black artists, intellectuals, and leaders from the 1920s on.

By the end of the 1920s the young journalist was beginning to acquire something of a national reputation, which was not confined to the black press. This was partly due to the influence of Mencken, in whom Schuyler found a real kindred spirit as well as a friend. Characterized by one critic as a "lonely iconoclast," Schuyler seemed to revel in exposing what he deemed fraud and folly, no matter who was responsible. At times this caused fellow blacks to doubt his racial loyalty, even though his attacks on white racism never ceased. Schuyler's willingness to defy prevailing attitudes was evidenced in his 6 January 1928 marriage to an attractive white woman, Josephine Cogdell. The union proved a happy one, lasting until her death in 1969. Their only child, Philippa, was a prodigy who performed her own piano compositions over the radio at the age of four and grew up to some international acclaim as a concert artist. She was also an author and journalist.

George Schuyler's enduring literary reputation rests upon one satirical novel, *Black No More;*

George S. Schuyler, in the 1940s (courtesy of the Schomburg Center for Research in Black Culture, the New York Public Library, Astor, Lenox and Tilden Foundations)

Being an Account of the Strange and Wonderful Workings of Science in the Land of the Free (1931). Most critics consider it far superior to the only other important satire produced during the Harlem Renaissance, Wallace Thurman's *Infants of the Spring* (1932). One evidence of the superiority of Schuyler's book may be the fact that when many out-of-print works by black authors were being reissued during the heightened interest in Afro-American literature in the 1960s and 1970s, *Black No More* was chosen for reprint (1971) while Thurman's book was ignored.

There is something distinctly modern and American about the plot of *Black No More*, involving as it does a scientific process discovered by a brilliant black physician, Dr. Crookman, whereby all Negroes can be changed into whites. Not just their skin color but also African hair and facial features will become irreversibly Caucasian for the fifty-dollar fee charged by one of Crookman's clinics. Crookman thus appears as a representative of the mad scientist stereotype, but he has capitalistic overtones (franchise clinics spring up all over the country).

The plot revolves around the picaresque adventures of black Max Disher who becomes white Matthew Fisher, in which role he becomes the right-hand man of Reverend Givens, leader of the Klan-like white supremacy organization, the Knights of Nordica. Fisher even marries Givens's daughter, who had once refused to dance with him in a Harlem nightclub when he was black.

As the story unfolds, the author manages to satirize many of the leading persons and institutions in black and white America. If the Klan is ridiculed, so also is the NAACP, called the National Social Equality League in the novel. The church is a nest of hypocrites, whether it be the Ethiopian True Faith Wash Foot Methodist Church, whose Bishop Ezekiel Whooper grows wealthy at the expense of his poor parishioners, or the white True Faith Christ Lovers Church of Happy Hill, Mississippi, whose Reverend McPhule (rhymes with fuel) delights in burning "niggers." Poor white workers are shown to be fools, as they are manipulated into placing white supremacy ahead of economic gain. But the ordinary black, too, is a fool, as he pursues the illusion of whiteness through the use of Mme. Sisseretta Blandish's (based on C. J. Walker) hair straighteners and bleaching creams.

Like all good satirists, Schuyler cannot resist attacking any human vice or folly, no matter what the race of the perpetrator. White racism is but one more evidence of human irrationality, ignorance, and greed. The black response to white racism is seldom pure and noble. The ingenious Dr. Crookman has performed a great service for the black race; all the same, he has chosen to wed a white woman.

Schuyler's intention of seeing the racial issue as an instance of pervasive human folly is borne out by the novel's conclusion. Anthropological research produces the discovery that over half of the so-called Caucasians in the U.S. have some Negro ancestry, including the Imperial Grand Wizard of the Knights of Nordica, Matthew Fisher's father-in-law. This news saves the marriage of Fisher, whose wife has just given birth to a beautiful brown baby (she believes the baby's color is inherited from her). The Grand Wizard and the Fisher family flee on an airplane to Mexico, taking with them the Knights' treasury, which will guarantee a comfortable exile. A final irony is the further discovery (by

Dr. Crookman, now U.S. Surgeon General) that the Black-No-More whites are actually several shades whiter than authentic Caucasians. In no time dark skin is all the rage, the whiter whites become the object of discrimination, and Mrs. Sari Blandine (formerly Mme. Blandish) opens a shop for staining skins brown.

Color preference has changed but racism remains, seemingly, because it reveals a deep human need. Schuyler never defines that need, probably because he feels it unnecessary. *Black No More* shows that human beings tend to set themselves in groups apart from their fellows who differ from them in some trivial way; then they do everything possible to exploit and degrade those who are different. The sin of Cain is endlessly repeated.

Despite its serious message, *Black No More* maintains the light tone of Horatian satire, except for one lapse near the end involving a brutal description of a lynching. This shift in tone constitutes

George S. Schuyler (photo by Carl Van Vechten; by permission of Joseph Solomon, the Estate of Carl Van Vechten)

an artistic flaw, but some critics have considered it a necessary proof that the author was aware of racism's real savagery.

The initial critical response from both blacks and whites was quite favorable. Even those who were objects of the novel's ridicule, such as W. E. B. Du Bois, praised it. Several later scholars of Afro-American literature have characterized *Black No More* as an "assimilationist" novel, insisting that it lacks the proper degree of black pride. Perhaps such criticism overemphasizes the novel's purported politics at the expense of analysis of its satirical worth. Nevertheless, critic Arthur P. Davis has called the novel "the best work of prose satire to come from the New Negro Movement." Sadly, Davis's judgment seems not to be shared, despite the novel's many fine qualities: sharp ironies and hilarious double entendres, a plot just believable enough to ensnare the reader's full attention, and a fast enough pace to keep the reader engrossed to the end. Today, despite the 1971 paperback reprint, *Black No More* and its author are largely forgotten, except in one unlikely quarter: the devotees of science fiction claim the book as an early example of the genre's excellence.

Schuyler published only one other novel, *Slaves Today,* which also appeared in 1931. The author had spent almost the first five months of that year as an investigative reporter for the *New York Evening Post*. His mission was to go to Liberia to research charges against that country's government that it was promoting slavery. At some personal risk, the indefatigable reporter traveled through the Liberian countryside, finding the charges all too true. He discovered that by the 1930s, the African nation, which had been founded as a haven for freed slaves from America, was composed of two social classes. On top were the Americo-Liberians who governed the country and controlled its resources at the expense of a native African under class. During the First World War, the corrupt rulers discovered a new source of income by selling forced laborers recruited from among the native Liberians to the Spanish plantation owners of the island of Fernando Po (located off the coast of Nigeria). Rounded up in the bush and sold at fifty dollars a head, the laborers were kept imprisoned, and they endured appalling working conditions, filth, and disease during the term of their contract. Many did not live to return home. In addition, the native inhabitants were sometimes forced to become the personal servants of the rulers and even to submit to sexual abuse.

In a series of syndicated columns which began appearing in June 1931, Schuyler exposed the corruption of the Liberian government and its virtual enslavement of many of its own citizens. He further alleged that the whole system existed with the sanction of Christian missionaries. He also noted that many of the ruling class were educated at mission schools or at denominational colleges in America.

In October 1931 Schuyler published *Slaves Today,* a muckraking novel based on the material covered in his articles. Its tragic main plot is the story of a young native Liberian whose bride is abducted the day after their wedding to become the concubine of a government commissioner. When the young man attempts to rescue his wife, he is captured and sent with a work-gang to Fernando Po. After illness and much hardship, he is finally permitted to return home, still intent on the rescue. But it is too late. The young wife, having contracted a venereal disease from her black master, dies in her husband's arms. He avenges her by assassinating the commissioner, but is himself killed by a guard. Another plot line involves the attempt of some liberal Americo-Liberians to oust the crooked men in power; a rigged election defeats their hopes, and the novel ends with the slave business going on as usual.

Whatever its topical interest, *Slaves Today* has little artistic merit. The plot elements are quite predictable, the characters flat and uninteresting. The only real literary value lies in the satirical portraits of the corrupt Liberians in power and the theme which contrasts those "civilized," western-educated rulers with the decent "savages" whom they oppress.

The newspaper articles and novel got a mixed reaction. Whites were generally favorable. Some blacks, with a greater vested interest in the image of Africa, were confused or hostile. The Harlem Renaissance had seen the apotheosis of Africa; *Slaves Today* raised a challenge to the Garveyite dream and to all other philosophies which promoted the concept of a black-dominated utopia. As in *Black No More,* Schuyler, the fact-oriented journalist, refused to reduce virtue and villainy to a simple matter of race. This same refusal to oversimplify also influenced his reporting when the *Pittsburgh Courier* sent him to Mississippi in 1935 to increase that paper's circulation. In his autobiography Schuyler notes that he frequently checked out "stories of terror and persecution" only to find them untrue.

Schuyler's refusal to accept prevailing views without close examination is also reflected in his

A FOND FAREWELL TO CARLO

He is gone! How strikingly strange it is to contemplate, how sad to ponder, what memories evoked!

He has gone! This unique man as symbolic of this sprawling city of his triumphs as Washington Square, Central Park, Fifth Avenue, Carnegie Hall, and the galleries of the lively arts.

He is gone! And with his leaving there passes yet another of the living memories of the elegance which, despite the onslaughts of modernism for change's sake, still endure.

He is gone! The great philosopher and philanthropist in the finest sense of the word so much abused today; this great benefactor of the arts to whom New York City owes so much of its reputation.

He is gone! And even those who never knew him are nevertheless in his debt; and across the earth they acknowledge it ungrudgingly.

For the greatest philanthropists are those who evoke, enrich, entertain and enlighten the aspirations and ideals of men and women so that civilization and culture bloom and leave lasting impressions.

The greatest benefactors are those who labor and give without desire or prospect of material gain thereby, but for the satisfaction of deeds well done.

And yet how hypocritical it would be to regard the material things as unimportant, as insignificant, as meaningless.

A bouquet, a tidbit, a letter, a fruit, a jar of caviar, a sparkling wine, an illuminated card--these little things are material but not without meaning and importance. These were Carlo's characteristics his friends recall.

He has gone! This man who created a revolution of the spirit, who made such an impact on the arts and letters of his time; who stirred kindred spirits everywhere.

Carlo's gone! He has passed off the stage but through his thoughtfulness and benevolence he gave the que to thousands to step out of the wings.

Here was a gay, errant, kindly, sardonic, humane, unorthodix, sophisticate of the civilized minority, who with Argus eye discerned the treasure of Negro genius and aspiration in the depths of the sea of segregation, and who lifted it out of obscurity to worst Caucasian snobbery astride the highway of progress.

Page from Schuyler's tribute to Carl Van Vechten, dated 23 December 1964, two days after Van Vechten's death

Dust jacket for Schuyler's 1966 book

only important essay in literary criticism, "The Negro-Art Hokum," which appeared in the *Nation*, 16 June 1926. He believes that Negro art—with a past, present, and future—exists in Africa; he does not think that a parallel art exists in black culture in the United States. American black folk art, such as spirituals and the blues, are the expression of "a caste in a certain section of the country. . . . They are no more expressive or characteristic of the Negro race than the music and dancing of the Appalachian highlanders . . . are expressive or characteristic of the Caucasian race." As for the higher art forms of literature, sculpture, and painting, American blacks who are productive show the same influences as their white contemporaries. The effort to show that there exists a separate and different Negro art stems from the same white racist impulse that characterizes blacks as different and therefore inferior.

Schuyler's article is a clear and logical statement of what may be called the "assimilationist" view on the question of a black aesthetic; as such, it still reflects the attitudes of many black writers and critics. The essay itself, however, is considered important because of a more famous essay that was written in response, "The Negro Artist and the Racial Mountain" by Langston Hughes. The Hughes piece has frequently been taken to be a manifesto for a unique, separate, and different black art. Clearly, Hughes refutes the notion that black writers should ignore racial themes and subject matter, but whether he further insists that the Negro writer must always be self-consciously black is another question. Hughes's essay is a compelling plea for artistic freedom and individuality, two qualities dear to Schuyler as well. Certainly, in *Black No More*, Schuyler dealt with black problems and black culture, while showing that these shed light upon the universal human condition.

After *Slaves Today* Schuyler wrote no further fiction. Meanwhile he kept busy as a columnist, reviewer, and editor. The most notable change as he advanced in years was his continuous movement toward extreme conservatism. He had always had some distrust of the Communists, even during his own flirtation with socialism. At the time of the infamous Scottsboro case, he accused the Communists of doing the Negro cause more harm than good by uniting all the whites against blacks. He decried the Communist scheme to establish a separate state for Negroes somewhere in the southern Black Belt as fantastic. Thus, he was a forerunner of numerous black artists and intellectuals, such as Ralph Ellison and Richard Wright, who gradually discovered that the Communist party wished to use the Negro rather than help him.

Schuyler's brand of black conservatism, however, took him much further than a simple rejection of the Communist party and its doctrines. He was an avid McCarthyite during the 1950s and tended to see all forms of black militancy as covert expressions of a red conspiracy. Thus, he vigorously opposed the idea of a march on Washington every time it was suggested. Martin Luther King and the other Civil Rights leaders were, according to Schuyler, so many tools of Moscow. He took violent exception to the awarding of the Nobel Prize to Dr. King, declaring that "the Lenin Prize would have been more appropriate. . . . Dr. King's principal contribution to world peace has been to roam the country like some sable Typhoid Mary, infecting the mentally disturbed with perversions of Christian doctrine, and grabbing fat lecture fees from the shallow-pated."

The tone of the attack on King was so virulent that the *Pittsburgh Courier* refused to publish it; instead, it appeared in the country's leading con-

Allen Morrison, of Ebony *magazine; George Schuyler, representing the* New York Courier; *Aviad Yafeh, of the Israel Office of Information; and George W. Goodman, news director for WLIB, during a broadcast of* The Editors Speak *(courtesy of the Schomburg Center for Research in Black Culture, the New York Public Library, Astor, Lenox and Tilden Foundations)*

servative paper, William Loeb's *Manchester* (N.H.) *Union Leader*. As a result of the King column and similar pieces, Schuyler's relations with the *Courier* became increasingly strained, and he left that paper altogether in 1966, to go to the *Union Leader*. He had joined the John Birch Society in 1961 and from that time contributed to its journal, *American Opinion*. His views were increasingly unpopular in the black community, where he was regarded either as an anachronism or a traitor. In 1965 he was attacked in a *Crisis* editorial as one who could not speak for the black community, whose views could conceivably mislead whites into underestimating "the depth and fury of the Negro's resentment against the restrictions imposed upon him. . . ."

In 1967 Philippa Schuyler was killed in a helicopter accident while covering the Vietnam War

for the *Union Leader;* two years later her mother died. When Schuyler died at New York Hospital on 31 August 1977 he was very much alone. Shortly before his death, he was described by his friend William Loeb as "that brave old gentleman, without loved ones to care [for him] as he watches the world going mad. He lives in that apartment, doing the best he can and not becoming bitter but battling on." He did, however, receive some recognition for his work. In 1968 he received the American Legion Award and a citation from Catholic War Veterans in 1969. The Freedoms Foundation presented him with an award in 1972.

Schuyler's small but secure niche in the history of black American letters is owed to *Black No More*. Its deft satiric wit stands at the source of an important approach assayed by many later writers:

applying to the white oppressor, and to the whole absurdity of the race issue, the lash of laughter.

References:

Arthur P. Davis, "George Schuyler," in *From the Dark Tower* (Washington, D.C.: Howard University Press, 1974), pp. 104-108;

Michael W. Peplow, *George S. Schuyler* (Boston: Twayne, 1980);

Ann Rayson, "George Schuyler: Paradox among 'Assimilationist' Writers," *Black American Literature Forum,* 12 (1978): 102-106;

John M. Reilly, "The Black Anti-Utopia," *Black American Literature Forum,* 12 (1978): 107-109.

Anne Spencer

(6 February 1882-27 July 1975)

J. Lee Greene

University of North Carolina at Chapel Hill

WORKS: "The Poems," in *Time's Unfading Garden: Anne Spencer's Life and Poetry,* by J. Lee Greene (Baton Rouge & London: Louisiana State University Press, 1977), pp. 175-197.

OTHER: "Before the Feast of Shushan," "At the Carnival," "The Wife-Woman," "Translation," and "Dunbar," in *The Book of American Negro Poetry,* edited by James Weldon Johnson (New York: Harcourt, Brace, 1922), pp. 169-173;

"Substitution," "Innocence," "Neighbors," "Questing," "Life-Long, Poor Browning," "I Have a Friend," "Creed," in *Caroling Dusk: An Anthology of Verse by Negro Poets,* edited by Countee Cullen (New York: Harper, 1927), pp. 47-52;

"Letter to My Sister," in *Ebony and Topaz: A Collectanea,* edited by Charles S. Johnson (New York: National Urban League, 1927), p. 94;

"For Jim, Easter Eve," in *The Poetry of the Negro, 1746-1949,* edited by Langston Hughes and Arna Bontemps (Garden City: Doubleday, 1949), p. 65.

PERIODICAL PUBLICATIONS: "Before the Feast at Shushan," *Crisis,* 19 (February 1920): 186;

"Dunbar," *Crisis,* 21 (November 1920): 32;

"White Things," *Crisis,* 25 (March 1923): 204;

"Lady, Lady," *Survey Graphic,* 6 (March 1925): 661;

"Lines to a Nasturtium (A Lover Muses)," *Palms,* 4 (October 1926): 13;

"Rime for the Christmas Baby (At 48 Webster Place, Orange)," *Opportunity: A Journal of Negro Life,* 5 (December 1927): 368;

"Grapes: Still-Life," *Crisis,* 36 (April 1929): 124;

"Requiem," *Lyric* (Spring 1931): 3.

Anne Spencer is not widely known to readers of the present generation, perhaps because she published few of her poems during her life and never published a volume of her poetry or other writings. Nevertheless, the quality of the poetry she

Anne Spencer (courtesy of Chauncey E. Spencer)

252

produced, the cultural and social circumstances under which she wrote, and her association with and influence on writers and others of the Harlem Renaissance period give her an important place in the literary, social, and cultural history of twentieth-century black America.

Anne Spencer was the name under which her poems were published and by which the public knew her after the early 1920s. She was born Annie Bethel Scales Bannister on 6 February 1882 on a farm in Henry County, Virginia. An only child, she spent the first few years of her childhood in Henry County with her parents, Sarah Louise and Joel Cephus Bannister. Sarah and Joel, who had barely escaped chattel slavery, struggled against the restraints of the time and the place to establish the life they desired for themselves and for their daughter. They also struggled against each other. Joel believed that the best way to achieve the life they desired was to acquire material assets by any means available. Sarah, who had grown up in the shadow of Virginia's plantation aristocracy (she was the daughter of a wealthy former slaveholder and his former slave mistress), also yearned for material prosperity, but the life she envisioned was one modeled as closely as possible on the tastes and attitudes of the white aristocracy. To her, form was primary.

Joel and Sarah were optimistic and resourceful. Each was strong-willed, independent, and unbending, characteristics which they passed on to their daughter. Joel demanded, in most instances, that Sarah adhere to the contemporary societal expectations for women and wives; she vehemently objected. Their divergent views and backgrounds and their opposing personalities occasioned frequent arguments. Anne often witnessed these arguments and they had a lasting impact on her. As a child and as an adult she was deeply concerned that while her parents loved each other, they never were friends. Friendship was important in her life and became a major theme of her writings.

The discord between her parents surfaced shortly after their marriage and intensified to the point that they separated about 1887. Sarah and her daughter moved to Bramwell, West Virginia, while Joel remained in Henry County. Anne was placed in the foster care of William Dixie and his wife in Bramwell while Sarah worked as a cook in the restaurant of a local inn. There were very few blacks in Bramwell and no black children in Anne's age group. Consequently, she was alone most of the time. With the exception of the Dixies' children, who were much younger than she, Anne's only

childhood friend during the years she lived in Bramwell was a young white girl who lived in the town. Her relative isolation as a child helped produce and certainly nourished the contemplative side of her character. She was allowed to wander freely about the town and its immediate environs and early developed a love for nature, especially for plant life.

During the first eleven years of her life, Anne's contact with others was almost solely limited to adults, which in part accounts for her childhood and adolescent precociousness. By the time she was seven or eight years old she had acquired a functioning adult vocabulary. She also was pretending to read, initially motivated to imitate Mrs. Dixie, who read often. By the time she was ten years old she could read only the simplest materials, but her interest in learning to read had intensified. At eleven years old she was only marginally literate. Her increasing desire for education surpassed what Sarah (who was barely literate) or what Mrs. Dixie could teach her. Sarah wanted her daughter to be educated, yet she refused to enroll her in a nearby school for blacks whose students were children of coal miners; she did not want her daughter to associate with anyone from a lower social or economic class. Joel, who had kept in touch with Sarah and Anne, insisted that Anne receive a formal education and threatened to take his child to live with him unless Sarah enrolled her in school. In 1893 Sarah enrolled Anne in Virginia Seminary, a boarding school for blacks in Lynchburg, Virginia.

Anne excelled at the seminary. By the end of her first school term her academic standing was among the best for her class, and she had demonstrated exceptional aptitude for courses in the humanities. With a first-rate faculty and highly motivated and intelligent students, the seminary's environment brought quite a positive change to Anne's life, although she never lost the rather reserved and contemplative sides of her character which had been forming since early childhood.

When she entered the seminary she was the youngest student there. This sudden change in her social and intellectual environment created enormous frustrations for her. By then she was almost a teenager, and she needed and longed for peer friendships. Precocious, witty, even aggressive in academic situations with other students, she nevertheless was too shy to interact personally with the students. She began to turn inward to deal with problems typical of her age group, problems exacerbated in her case by the isolation of her childhood. She spent most of her free time alone, contemplating nature and studying. Yet she related well to her teachers and was one of their favorite students. By the beginning of her second year in school she had developed a cordial relationship with Gregory Hayes, the school's president. Hayes was instrumental in teaching her the close affinity between literature and life. Yet her comfortable interaction with adults could not substitute for those peer relationships which would have provided her an outlet for dealing with her more personal concerns.

When she was fourteen years old she turned to writing as a means of coping with the frustrations produced by her adolescence and by the newness of the intellectually stimulating environment. She wrote a poem, "The Skeptic," which concerned the conflicts between her view of life and the views expressed by others. She knew very little about poetry at the time, but from this poem she developed her lifelong habit of writing to express the more private side of her character.

Using writing as an outlet for her emotions allowed her to interact more freely with other students and produced a surge in her academic progress. In 1899 she graduated from Virginia Seminary at the top of her class. She then returned to Bramwell and taught public school in the area for two years. On 15 May 1901 she married her seminary schoolmate Edward Alexander Spencer, and the couple moved to Lynchburg, Edward's home. Three children were born to them during the first decade of their marriage, two daughters and a son. After the birth of her son, Anne Spencer taught for a while at Virginia Seminary in order to supplement the school's teaching staff during a period when the school was having financial problems.

Edward Spencer was economically secure and understood the emotional needs of his wife. Shortly after their marriage, he hired housekeepers and in other ways released her from living the traditional role of housewife and mother. He knew that she

Anne Spencer in her garden (courtesy of Chauncey E. Spencer)

loved nature and that she had an insatiable desire to read and to write. He built her a garden at the back of their house and constructed a one-room cottage at the edge of the garden. In the privacy of the cottage Spencer did most of her reading and writing.

During the first twenty years of her marriage she wrote numerous poems. Her habit during the day was to write down thoughts as they came to her—on paper bags, on scrap paper, in the margins of books, newspapers, and magazines, or on whatever writing surface was immediately available. In the contemplative quiet of the cottage during the evenings she transformed these thoughts into poems. By the time she was thirty-eight, the age at which she first published a poem, she had written hundreds of them. Even her family and friends were unaware of her imaginative writings before her first poem appeared in print.

From the early years of her marriage she was active in community affairs in Lynchburg. In 1918 she was a member of a committee which arranged for the national office of the National Association for the Advancement of Colored People to send a representative to Lynchburg to help establish a local chapter. James Weldon Johnson was the representative and was a houseguest of the Spencers during his stay. Johnson accidentally saw some of her poems and insisted that she allow him to show some of them to his literary friends. Shortly thereafter he began to urge her to publish her poems and offered to help arrange for their publication. She reluctantly agreed, and in 1920 her poem "Before the Feast of Shushan" appeared in the February issue of the *Crisis*.

In 1922 Johnson included five of her poems in his anthology *The Book of American Negro Poetry*. Four of the poems, including "Shushan," thematically focus on the position of women in the larger society and on male-female love bonds. The poems echo the principles and practices of Spencer's life. Without being polemical, the poems assert that women often are the victims of an unsympathetic male-dominated society ("At the Carnival"), that women should not be subordinated to men ("Before the Feast of Shushan"), that a woman should, if she chooses, reject societal proscriptions and be free to determine the nature of her role in a male-female love bond ("The Wife-Woman"), and that friendship is just as important as love in a relationship between two people ("Translation"). In the fifth poem, a quatrain titled "Dunbar," the poet-speaker laments the untimely death of Dunbar, Chatterton, Shelley, and Keats but finds comfort

in the knowledge that while poets are mortal their poems are immortal:

Ah, how poets sing and die!
Make one song and Heaven takes it;
Have one heart and Beauty breaks it;
Chatterton, Shelley, Keats and I—
Ah, how poets sing and die!

Johnson's anthology was well received and reviewers and critics cited Spencer as a fresh and invigorating new voice among black poets. Anthologists and editors began to request her permission to include her poems in their publications. Robert Kerlin (*Negro Poets and Their Poems*) and Louis Untermeyer (*American Poetry Since 1900*) included her in anthologies they published in 1923. Within a few years her poems had appeared in *Crisis, Opportunity, Survey Graphic, Palms,* and other publications. Among those who expressed interest in her writings and in helping her to get published were Alain Locke and H. L. Mencken, both of whom were influential in advancing the publishing careers of poets during the period and thus to some extent in shaping the literary tastes of the time. Locke and Mencken were willing to assist Spencer in becoming more widely published, but only if she were willing to follow their suggestions about the kind of poetry she should write for publication. She was unwilling to conform to their suggestions and thus forfeited their assistance.

One of the poems about which she and editors disagreed was "White Things," a poem which she had written in the late teens. Editors considered the poem too unorthodox in its overt treatment of racial conflict. She refused to revise the poem to conform more to the racial romanticism and subtle treatment of racial themes popular during the period. However, the *Crisis* published "White Things" in March 1923. It was one of the very few "protest" poems she ever wrote and one of her finest poems. In fact, "White Things" belongs with the best poems of racial protest published in twentieth-century America. Although her poetry was widely anthologized and reprinted during the 1920s and after, "White Things" was never reprinted during her life.

White Things

Most things are colorful things—the sky, earth, and
    sea.
        Black men are most men; but the white are
    free!
White things are rare things; so rare, so rare

DUNBAR BRANCH
JONES MEMORIAL LIBRARY
LYNCHBURG, VIRGINIA

Thursday.

No, my dear, I do not feel that 'air', and 'shepherdess' are responsible for throwing the mind away from the central theme, — "idealization, of the commonplace". I used 'air' to indicate bearing, spiritual bearing; the 'shepherdess', sir, hails not from Montana expanses, but from all-souls Arcady. Alas, never to've seen black women with this inside air!

I read your letter slowly, so's my joy in it might be lengthened.

Love,
Anne Spencer

Do not bother to return 'Nasturtium'. I have copy. In that form a burnt and disappointed lover soliloquizes, thanks.

Letter to Alain Locke (courtesy of the Alain Locke Papers, Moorland-Spingarn Research Center, Howard University)

They stole from out a silvered world—somewhere.
Finding earth-plains fair plains, save greenly grassed,
They strewed white feathers of cowardice, as they
    passed;
        The golden stars with lances fine
        The hills all red and darkened pine,
They blanched with their wand of power;
And turned the blood in a ruby rose
To a poor white poppy-flower.

They pyred a race of black, black men,
And burned them to ashes white; then,
Laughing, a young one claimed a skull,
For the skull of a black is white, not dull,
        But a glistening awful thing;
        Made, it seems, for this ghoul to swing
In the face of God with all his might,
And swear by the hell that sired him:
        "Man-maker, make white!"

By 1923 Lynchburg citizens were well aware that a newly published and highly praised poet lived among them. Spencer's outspoken criticism of racial stratification, her stand on other political and social issues, and her blatant defiance of any attempts to restrict her personal freedom had helped estrange her from many of the townspeople during the previous twenty years. The national attention she received as a published poet in the early 1920s somewhat mitigated hostility toward her and allowed her to interact more harmoniously with whites and blacks in the town. Still, on several occasions she was the victim of verbal abuse from whites she encountered in public sectors of the town. Yet Spencer never tempered her stance against racism. After she became known as a published poet, her detractors often dismissed her challenges of the status quo as merely the eccentric behavior of a poet.

Before the 1920s blacks in Lynchburg did not have access to a library, a situation Spencer sought to correct. In December 1923 she applied for a job as librarian with the private, all-white Jones Memorial Library in Lynchburg. Lacking formal training or experience as a librarian, she used her publications and her wide knowledge of books as credentials to recommend her for the job. In January 1924, the board of trustees of Jones hired her to head a branch library to be housed in the all-black Dunbar High School. During the twenty years she remained at Dunbar she had a considerable influence on the intellectual and cultural life of the black community in Lynchburg. She encouraged students and others to read more widely and more critically; she motivated many of Dunbar's students

to continue their education after high school and in general to improve their lot in life.

While working at Dunbar she continued to write and occasionally agreed to submit her poems for publication. In 1927 Countee Cullen's anthology *Caroling Dusk* included the largest collection of Spencer's poems to appear in print during her life. Seven of her ten poems in *Caroling Dusk* had been previously unpublished. The major themes of her pieces in this collection were friendship, human relations, and the personal rights of women. Images of her garden or of nature were predominant. Two of the poems concerned poets and poetry: "Life-Long, Poor Browning" was inspired by the personal and poetic affinity she felt for her favorite poet, Robert Browning; "Substitution" spoke of the function of poetry and of the creative imagination in her own life.

The 1920s was the most active and perhaps the most invigorating decade of her life. She loved her job at Dunbar, tended her garden meticulously, read and wrote constantly, entertained lavishly, traveled frequently, corresponded with leading artists and thinkers, and worked actively to break down racial barriers in Lynchburg. Some of those who resented her personal and open defiance of racial discrimination occasionally circulated rumors (from the 1930s into the 1950s) that her association with persons politically controversial, including artists and entertainers, was proof sufficient that her political sympathies were with Communists or Communist supporters. Ostensibly the rumors were a means of discrediting her, but they neither tempered her activities with civil rights organizations nor caused her to sever ties with persons alleged to have Communist links.

After the 1920s Spencer's acquaintance with nationally known persons was substantial. W. E. B. Du Bois, Paul Robeson, Langston Hughes, and numerous other artists, political activists, entertainers, and other professionals were often guests at the Spencers' home. In turn, she and Edward traveled widely, and their trips to Washington, D.C., and to New York, among other cities where aspiring and established black artists, intellectuals, and socialites gathered, were routine. She had established friendships with Du Bois and Sterling Brown through their association with Virginia Seminary and College. Through Du Bois, Brown, Johnson, Hughes, and Georgia Douglas Johnson she met a variety of people, blacks and whites, in the 1920s and after and thus rapidly expanded her contacts outside her hometown.

Lynchburg was strategically located between the major cities of the Northeast and metropolitan and educational centers of the South. In the early 1920s the Spencers' home assumed an integral place in a network blacks had established years before to compensate for their exclusion from public accommodations when traveling. Middle- and upper-class blacks of various professions who traveled across the Mason-Dixon line used the homes of other well-to-do blacks as convenient places to stop over. A mutual acquaintance usually was all that was necessary to assure that food and lodging would be available to those whose social, economic, or professional status allowed them entrance into this network. The Spencers loved to entertain and their home quickly became popular on the circuit, especially among writers, entertainers, and civil rights advocates. By the mid 1920s Hughes, James Weldon Johnson, Du Bois, and others visited Spencer in order to benefit from an intellectual exchange with her on literary, political, and social issues. Often a writer visited to seek her advice about a particular writing project on which she or he was working. At other times groups of writers gathered at her home to discuss the state of the arts. A consequence of this exchange was that she had a significant impact on the works of several imaginative writers and social critics identified with the Harlem Renaissance.

Anne Spencer attributed the expansion of her intellectual and creative worlds primarily to her association with James Weldon Johnson and thus considered her friendship with him as one of the most important events in her life. Thematically several of her poems about friendship derive from the special nature of her friendship with Johnson. He helped her gain entry into the Harlem Renaissance movement and brought her into contact with minds akin to her own. After his death in an automobile accident in 1938 she allowed only one additional poem of hers to be published during her life, "For Jim, Easter Eve," a poem in tribute to Johnson. Using her garden as the central metaphor, she expressed in the poem the impact Johnson and her garden had had on her life. Within a few years after his death she had withdrawn almost completely from public life.

Spencer's garden was central to her poetry and to her life. In most of her poems images of her garden or of natural scenery suggest an Edenic setting where man is in harmony with his environment. These poems usually begin with a speaker troubled with doubts and uncertainties or with one who feels dejected. Coming into contact with and

Anne Spencer at ninety-one (courtesy of Chauncey E. Spencer)

contemplating the spiritual forces manifested in nature, the speaker soon rejects the doubts and uncertainties and the tone of the poem changes from one of dejection to one of hope and affirmation. In general, this is the case in "Life-Long, Poor Browning" or in "For Jim, Easter Eve," poems in which the garden setting provides solace for the speaker. From her garden Spencer extracted metaphors for human life. She saw in the activities of a bee, a spider, a bird, or another insect or animal metaphors for the fragility and strength of man, metaphors which she incorporated into her poems. When discouraged by the conflicts of her interaction with others, she turned to her garden as a spiritual refuge. The integral place her garden held in her life and in her poetry is expressed in lines from "For Jim, Easter Eve,".

Peace is here and in every season
a quiet beauty.
The sky falling about me
evenly to the compass . . .
What is sorrow but tenderness now
in this earth-close frame of land and sky
falling constantly into horizons
of east and west, north and south;
what is pain but happiness here

amid these green and wordless patterns,—
indefinite texture of blade and leaf.

After her husband died in 1964, the upkeep of her once immaculate garden sharply declined and she became a virtual recluse. She spent her time reading, especially history, and concentrated on writing prose instead of poetry. When she first began to publish her poems in the 1920s, her literary friends urged her to write prose fiction. At one time she did begin a novel, but apparently she never completed it. In the 1930s and 1940s she wrote a series of essays critically examining various American social and political institutions; these essays were intended for publication but never submitted. Her rejuvenated interest in writing prose in the mid 1960s was stimulated by her obsession with reading American history. By about 1969 she had drafted several essays but began to concentrate again on writing poetry. People and events in American history remained her primary subjects during this period and she planned and began to work on a series of poems about persons whom she considered generals, persons such as Hannibal, Douglas MacArthur, John Brown, and LeRoi Jones.

Many years before she had thought about using the abolitionist John Brown as the subject for one of her writings. From 1969 to 1971 she spent an enormous amount of time reading background materials for a long, complex poem which would use Brown as the central figure in the history of man from his beginning to the mid nineteenth century. She wrote intently to complete "A Dream of John Brown," but her health, in general, began to fail and the enormous amount of time she spent reading and writing severely impaired her eyesight. She intended "A Dream of John Brown" to be her greatest poetic achievement and continued to work sporadically on the poem until 1974, when a serious illness forced her to halt her work after having completed several manuscript pages.

From 1971 to 1974 she also revised some of her earlier poems and wrote new ones in preparation for an anticipated collection of her poetry. At ninety years of age she was writing with the explicit intent to have her works published. Prior to this she had taken the initiative only once during her life to have any of her poems published; she always had written for her own enjoyment but had allowed Johnson and others to arrange for the publication of some of her poems. She wrote constantly during the early 1970s, following her lifelong habit of composing her poems in bits and pieces and on scraps of paper scattered here and there in her house. When in 1975 her health deteriorated to the point that she was hospitalized, friends and neighbors visiting her home evidently assumed the countless pieces of paper on which she had written lines of poetry were useless, and they innocently discarded them. Thus, most of the work she had completed during the preceding four or five years was lost. Among the manuscripts not discarded was a short poem written in June 1974 and titled "1975," obviously intended as a final comment on her life and writings:

Turn an earth clod
Peel a shaley rock
In fondness molest a curly worm
Whose *familiar* is everywhere
Kneel
And the curly worm   sentient *now*
Will *light* the word that tells the poet what a poem
    is

Spencer died on 27 July 1975 in Lynchburg, Virginia.

Biographies:
J. Lee Greene, *Time's Unfading Garden: Anne Spencer's Life and Poetry* (Baton Rouge: Louisiana State University Press, 1977);
The Anne Spencer Memorial Foundation, *Echoes from the Garden: The Anne Spencer Story* (a documentary film) (Lynchburg, Va.: Anne Spencer Memorial Foundation/Washington, D.C.: Byron Studios, 1980).

Papers:
The largest collection of Anne Spencer's papers is housed at the Anne Spencer House Historic Landmark in Lynchburg, Virginia. Several of her letters are at the Beinecke Rare Book and Manuscript Library at Yale University.

Wallace Henry Thurman

Phyllis R. Klotman
Indiana University

BIRTH: 16 August 1902, to Beulah and Oscar Thurman.

EDUCATION: University of Utah, 1919; University of Southern California, 1922-1923.

MARRIAGE: 22 August 1928 to Louise Thompson (separated).

DEATH: New York City, 21 December 1934.

BOOKS: *The Negro Life in New York's Harlem* (Girard, Kans.: Haldeman-Julius, 1928);
The Blacker the Berry: A Novel of Negro Life (New York: Macaulay, 1929);
Infants of the Spring (New York: Macaulay, 1932);
The Interne, by Thurman and Abraham L. Furman (New York: Macaulay, 1932).

PLAY PRODUCTION: *Harlem,* by Thurman and William Jourdan Rapp, New York, Apollo Theatre, 20 February 1929.

MOTION PICTURES: *Tomorrow's Children*, Bryan Foy, 1934, screenplay;
High School Girl, Bryan Foy Productions, 1935, screenplay.

PERIODICAL PUBLICATIONS:
POETRY
"The Last Citadel," *Opportunity,* 4 (April 1926): 128;
"Confession," *Messenger,* 8 (June 1926): 167;
"God's Edict," *Opportunity,* 4 (July 1926): 216.
NONFICTION
"Eugene O'Neill's 'All God's Chilluns Got Wings,'" *Outlet,* 1 (October 1924): 19-20;
"Whither Are We Drifting," *Outlet,* 1 (November 1924): 9-11;
"Christmas: Its Origin and Significance," *Outlet,* 1 (December 1924): 11-12;
"In the Name of Purity," *Messenger,* 8 (April 1926): 125;
"Quoth Brigham Young:—This is the Place," *Messenger,* 8 (August 1926): 235-236;

Wallace Thurman (courtesy of the Beinecke Rare Book and Manuscript Library, Yale University)

"Singers at the Crossroads," *Greenwich Village Quill* (March 1927): 14-16;
"Harlem: A Vivid Picture of the World's Greatest Negro City," *American Monthly* (May 1927): 19-20;
"Negro Artists and the Negro," *New Republic,* 52 (31 August 1927): 37-39;
"Nephews of Uncle Remus," *Independent,* 119 (24 September 1927): 296-298;
"Harlem Facets," *World Tomorrow,* 10 (November 1927): 465-467;
"Harlem's Place in the Sun," *Dance Magazine,* 10 (May 1928): 23, 54, 56;
"Negro Poets and Their Poetry," *Bookman,* 67 (July 1928): 555-561;
"Harlem—as Others See It," by Thurman and William Jourdan Rapp, *Negro World* (13 April 1929): 3.

FICTION

"You Never Can Tell," *Outlet,* 1 (September 1924): 6-8;

"You Never Can Tell, Part 2," *Outlet,* 1 (October 1924): 14-15;

"Grist in the Mill," *Messenger,* 8 (June 1926): 165-167;

"Cordelia the Crude," *Fire!!,* 1 (November 1926): 5-7.

From about the end of World War I to the beginning of the Great Depression—the period of the Harlem Renaissance—young black aspiring artists from all over the country were drawn to Harlem. Although most of the young writers came from the South, the East, and the Middle West, the most trenchant critic of the period came from the far West. A brilliant young black writer, he was drawn to the excitement of Harlem where a spiritual and cultural awakening was taking place. It seemed to promise a new beginning, a recognition of black artists by the larger society in a way that had never happened before. In a few years Wallace Thurman became not only a published novelist and successful playwright but also an editor and literary critic, succeeding in a field that had heretofore virtually excluded blacks. Thurman is an especially significant critic because he was both inside and outside the New Negro movement at the same time—a part of the creative spirit of the renaissance as well as a probing intellectual; restlessly seeking perfection in himself and in others, he was never satisfied with measuring artistic achievement in other than literary and aesthetic terms. The most incisive critic of the Harlem Renaissance has not yet been the subject of a full-length published study which would show his life and works to be a significant chapter in Afro-American letters and an integral part of the larger volume of American social and literary history.

Wallace Thurman was born in Salt Lake City long before Afro-Americans were deemed worthy to enter the Mormon priesthood and at a time when the black community was very small indeed. Little is known of his father, Oscar, who apparently moved on to California leaving the child in his mother's care (Thurman alludes to seeing him only one other time—many years later). Thurman's strongest familial attachment, however, was not to Beulah, his mother, who had several subsequent husbands, but to "Ma Jack" (Emma Jackson), his maternal grandmother, to whom he dedicated his first novel, *The Blacker the Berry* (1929).

Thurman was a nervous, sickly child who loved to read and thought of himself as a writer when, at age ten, he wrote his first novel. A devout movie fan, he was impressed by the serials he probably saw at Saturday matinees and tried to write comparable Hollywood scenarios. His interest in film was to be a lasting one. His appetite for reading was never sated, but teachers were unable to influence his eclectic taste. He read the comedies and tragedies of Shakespeare as well as the sonnets; he did not care for George Berkeley, David Hume, or Immanuel Kant, but he did care for Friedrich Nietzsche; he read and reread Gustave Flaubert (*Madame Bovary*), Charles Baudelaire, Charles Saint-Beuve, and Stendahl; he led himself through Herbert Spencer, Henrik Ibsen, Thomas Hardy, Fyodor Dostoyevski, Havelock Ellis, and Sigmund Freud. In high school he dismissed the idea of a literary career but in college changed his mind again.

For a time in 1919 he was a helper at the Hotel Utah Cafe, the same year he enrolled at the University of Utah in Salt Lake City. Transferring to the University of Southern California, he entered a program to prepare for medical school and continued his studies until 1923. From neither of these institutions did he receive a degree. In Los Angeles for the next year and a half, he wrote "Inklings," a column in a black Los Angeles newspaper; worked in the post office (with Arna Bontemps); edited the *Outlet,* a magazine which lasted for six months; and unsuccessfully tried to organize a literary group on the West Coast comparable to those that were developing in the East.

On Labor Day of 1925 he arrived in Harlem. Surviving on odd jobs for a short time, Thurman went to work for Theophilus Lewis, who was then editing his own paper, the *Looking Glass,* as "everything" man—editorial writer, reporter, assistant make-up man, and errand boy—for nothing a week. The Lewises, however, saw to it that he ate regularly. On Lewis's recommendation, he was hired at the *Messenger* as managing editor when George Schuyler went on the road for the *Pittsburgh Courier.* In less than a year, from September of 1925 to mid 1926, he had made the acquaintance of a number of active writers from whom he solicited manuscripts. It was through their contributions that Thurman was able to improve the quality of the *Messenger.* He was responsible for the publication of Langston Hughes's first short stories, for which the *Messenger* paid ten dollars apiece, not because they were good, as he told Hughes, but because the magazine could not find any better.

Front cover and table of contents for the only issue of Thurman's first magazine

During the *Messenger* period Hughes and Thurman roomed at the same house on 137th Street. One of the best descriptions of Thurman, that "strangely brilliant black boy," and his complex personality was later written by Hughes in his autobiography, *The Big Sea* (1940). It was in Thurman's room on 137th Street, however, that the controversial (now famous) magazine *Fire!!* was born. In Washington, D.C., Hughes and young artist Bruce Nugent conceived the idea of a magazine. "Wallie" was their first choice for editor, as well as the unanimous choice of the others who made up the editorial board: Zora Neale Hurston, Aaron Douglas, Gwendolyn Bennett, John Davis. *Fire!!* had a brief but incendiary life. The magazine was to be experimental, Thurman wrote later in an article in the *New Republic* ("Negro Artists and the Negro," 31 August 1927). "It was not interested in sociological problems or propaganda. It was purely artistic in intent and conception." *Fire!!* would be devoted to the work of the young Negro artists who were in effect declaring their literary independence; they would produce their own journal without the blessings of their elders (Du Bois, Locke, and others). *Fire!!* would reflect their own sensibilities; it would weave "vivid, hot designs upon an ebon bordered loom and . . . satisfy pagan thirst for beauty unadorned," the foreword declared.

All members of the editorial board, except John Davis, contributed pieces to the magazine: Hurston, a play and a short story; Thurman, a short story and editorial comment; Hughes, poetry; Bennett, a short story; Aaron Douglas, drawings, incidental art decorations, and cover designs; Bruce Nugent, line drawings and part one of a novel, "Smoke, Lilies, and Jade," perhaps the most "shocking" of the pieces. The only works contributed by nonboard members were an essay by Arthur Huff Fauset and poetry by Countee Cullen, Edward Silvera, Helene Johnson, Waring Cuney, Arna Bontemps, and Lewis Alexander.

Langston Hughes and Wallace Thurman (courtesy of the Trevor Arnett Library, Atlanta University)

Not everyone was as incensed by the magazine as Rean Graves of the *Baltimore Afro-American* when it appeared in November of 1926. ("I have just tossed the first issue of *Fire!!* into the fire.") Many mainstream white critics ignored it, although Robert Kerlin thought it "original in all its aspects," but a number of reactions came from other black critics. Du Bois seemed offended at the mere mention of the magazine, although the *Crisis* carried little more than a brief announcement in the January 1927 issue. Benjamin Brawley thought Thurman's "Cordelia the Crude" should never have been written and that the whole magazine might well be barred from the mails if the U.S. Post Office found out about it. Alain Locke's review was a bit more balanced, although he did fault the magazine for its excesses.

The major problem for the fiery young writers and artists was money. They had difficulty in securing the fifty dollars each had promised in order to help defray expenses. Thurman, who wanted no less than fine quality paper, design, and

layout, was responsible for dealing with the printer, and it was his salary that was ultimately attached to pay the $1,000 debt. Distribution was a challenge never quite met, so numerous copies were never sold or distributed. The irony was that several hundred, if not all, of the remaining copies went up in smoke; they had been stored in the basement of an apartment which caught fire. The first and last issue of *Fire!!* was thus interred.

Most of the young and practically penniless artists and writers associated with the magazine tried to help pay off the debt. Yet Thurman, the only one with a full-time paying job, was left with the major responsibility which plagued him for almost four years. (He had gone from the *Messenger* to the white magazine the *World Tomorrow* as circulation manager; later to the Macaulay Company, a white publishing house, as a reader, and by 1935, as editor in chief.) Undaunted, he launched a new project as editor of *Harlem: a Forum of Negro Life*. This time, however, the financial worries would not be his.

The only issue of *Harlem* was published in November 1928, two months after Thurman's marriage to Louise Thompson, a former schoolteacher. In a letter which Thurman wrote to Locke, soliciting an article for the first edition, he explained that *Harlem* was to be a general magazine (as *Fire!!* was not), which would contain short fiction, poetry, essays, and articles on a variety of subjects both racial and nonracial. He also proclaimed the demise of the *Crisis* and the *Messenger* and the imminent death of *Opportunity*. (In that letter he expressed the hope that Locke had recovered from the "startling news" of his marriage to Louise. The fact was the news shocked most of Thurman's friends, particularly those who knew him as partygoer, partygiver, and self-styled hedonist.) His first (and last) editorial discussed the need for such a journal which would not only eschew the mistakes of the past—shoddy publication methods, editorial astigmatism, narrowness, and intolerance of new points of view—but would also be produced by the artists themselves. Its most significant function would be to offer *intelligent criticism* to the younger writers, as well as to serve as a clearinghouse for the newer Negro literature. The editorial is a calm, considered, almost conciliatory statement of objectives. *Harlem* would not assault the reader's sensibilities, shock, startle, or raise eyebrows (as *Fire!!* was intended to do). Yet its editor had not changed. In Thurman's book review essay, he seemed unable to resist castigating Du Bois for his "narrow and patronizing criticism" of Rudolph

H. K. PARKER PUBLISHING CORPORATION

HARLEM
A FORUM OF NEGRO LIFE

2376 SEVENTH AVENUE

New York City

WALLACE THURMAN, *Editor*
RICHARD BRUCE, *Associate Editor*
AARON DOUGLAS, *Art Editor*
S. PACE ALEXANDER, *Business Manager*

October 3, 1928

Dear Dr. Locke:

I was indeed sorry that I did not know you were in town on last Sunday or I certainly would have looked you up or at least have been present at the Douglases when you were there. I hope that by now you have fully recovered from a hectic time in Europe and the startling news of my marriage to Louise on your return. It was not fair to shock you like that was it?

About Harlem. I suppose Aaron explained about the venture, I am mighty glad of the chance to be able to edit a magazine and let someone else worry about the financial end, in fact, after Fire, that is the only way I would ever venture forth again.

I know you are very busy but that does not keep me from asking you to send me a short article of some kind for our first issue due out during the first week in November. That means that all material must be in our hands no later than the 15th or 20th of October, but surely you can dash off a little something for us by then, on any subject you choose.

Harlem is to be a general magazine, containing verse, fiction, essays, articles on current events and debates on racial and non racial issues. We are not confining ourselves to any group either of age or race. I think that is best. The Crisis and The Messenger are dead. Opportunity is dying. Voila here comes Harlem, independent, fearless and general, trying to appeal to all.

Letter requesting a submission from Alain Locke for Thurman's second magazine, which folded after the appearance of the first issue in November 1928 (courtesy of the Alain Locke Papers, Moorland-Spingarn Research Center, Howard University)

2

Louise and I have an apartment at 90 Edgecombe, apt. 56. Our phone number is
Edgecombe 1979 1979. I hope you call us and visit us when you come to N. Y.
Also let me hear from you as immediately as possible about my request and what
you think in general of the magazine.

No doubt you heard that my novel is due out in a couple of months, and
that I am expecting my play to go into rehearsal almost any day again. And that
I have another play going the rounds and a book of plays scheduled for late winter.
Aside from that I have been quite idle.

Awaiting an early I reply,

With thanks,

Wallace Thurman

Fisher's *The Walls of Jericho,* because Du Bois had faulted Fisher for not using "his genius to paint his own kind." Such criticism set Thurman's "teeth on edge."

Harlem contained short fiction by Hughes, Roy de Coverly, George Schuyler; poetry by Hughes, Alice Dunbar Nelson, Georgia Douglas Johnson, Helene Johnson, Allison Davis, Mae Cowdery; essays by Locke, Walter White, and James Egbert; theater reviews by Theophilus Lewis and Richard Bruce (Nugent); book reviews by Thurman and H. Van Webber; illustrations and sketches by Aaron Douglas, Nugent, and Leon Noyes. It also contained a directory of where to go and what to do in Harlem: churches, restaurants, clubs, "gin mills." Neither the subscriptions, however, nor the advertisements, which were tastefully done, were sufficient to keep the magazine afloat. As it turned out, the public, for whatever reason, was not ready for this brainchild either.

The next Harlem with which Thurman became involved was not a failure. Even as he was inaugurating the short-lived magazine *Harlem,* the play *Harlem,* on which he had collaborated with William Jourdan Rapp, was about to go into rehearsal. Bill Rapp was a white free-lance writer who became associated with Macfadden Publications in 1926, as coeditor of *American Monthly,* then as editor of *True Story.* The two men met when Thurman brought to Rapp's office a card of introduction from a young minister who had known Bill Rapp during his foreign correspondent days. Their collaboration developed into a friendship which lasted until Thurman's death.

According to Burns Mantle, the 1928-1929 New York season was not a good one for the theater. "Talkies" were beginning to seduce audiences away from Broadway, and there was concern that legitimate theater would soon be superannuated. Producers were loathe to invest their money when so few plays made enough to cover the cost of their production (only about six of the first 100 produced that season). Of the top ten chosen by Mantle for inclusion in his annual *Best Plays* publication, only two ran for more than 200 performances, and the Pulitzer Prize winner, *Street Scene,* was not one of these. The critics and the public were clearly out of sync.

What were the possibilities for a dramatic play about Negroes from the rural South trying to survive in Harlem ever getting on the boards? Thurman and Rapp put their play, then entitled *Black Belt,* in the hands of an agent who interested Al Lewis and Crosby Gaige in taking an option on it,

but they insisted that the play would never sell unless the authors wrote a "wow" into the third act. Apparently none of the subsequent revisions wowed Lewis and Crosby, and they eventually bowed out. *Black Belt,* however, came across the desk of Chester Erskine, a young "play doctor" in New York (later a Hollywood film director) just beginning to make a reputation for himself. He told Thurman and Rapp he wanted to arrange for a production which he would direct. Without funds but with indomitable spirit, he set out to raise the money—interesting Edward Blatt, a professional theater company manager, in joining with him—and to revise the play with Thurman. The two worked together putting *Harlem,* changed from *Black Belt* because of its association with Chicago, into shape for production. In the end, according to Erskine, the play was what Thurman wanted it to be, "a realistic melodrama with social overtones." The two also worked together on the casting. They hired a few professional actors, like Inez Clough as the mother and Arthur Hughes (the only white in the show) as the detective, but the cast consisted mainly of students, Pullman porters, professional boxers, teachers, dentists, cigarette girls, cabaret entertainers; Isabell Washington (later the first Mrs. Adam Clayton Powell, Jr.), who starred as Cordelia, came from the chorus line at the Alhambra Theatre. Because of the inexperience of most of the actors, Erskine was able to get approval from Equity for extended rehearsal time—six weeks instead of four.

Harlem, based on Thurman's short story in *Fire!!* which Brawley thought should never have been published, opened at the Apollo Theatre on 20 February 1929 with a cast of sixty. It was a gala evening to which Thurman wore formal dress, borrowed at the last minute in its entirety, including shoes, from Rex Goreleigh, who had a walk-on part in the show. Most of his friends were there, but not his wife, from whom he was becoming rapidly estranged.

The play dramatized the effects of the Great Migration on a southern family: the inability of the southern rural black male to find gainful and secure employment, normal conflict between the generations exacerbated by the tensions of the city, and an attenuation of influence by supportive structures like the church. For southern blacks the dilemma was whether Harlem was the City of Refuge or the City of Sin. The older generation sought solace in their transplanted churches when their dream of a Promised Land refused to become reality; their children, on the other hand, were often

LITTLE BLUE BOOK NO. **494**
Edited by E. Haldeman-Julius

Negro Life in New York's Harlem

A Lively Picture of a Popular and
Interesting Section

Wallace Thurman

*Front cover for Thurman's 1928 booklet about Harlem, which
includes sections on "Night Life in Harlem," "The Amusement
Life of Harlem," and "House Rent Parties, Numbers and
Hot Men"*

eager to ignore the moral and religious preachments of their elders and immerse themselves in the fascinating evils of the city. Pa and Ma Williams have two "good" children who work hard and try to contribute to the support of the family, but they also have one wayward daughter, Cordelia, well on her way to succumbing to the corruption of Harlem. Cordelia is the focal point of their concern and of the play's dramatic conflict. She quickly tires of the decent young West Indian who loves and wants to marry her, easily moving on to Kid Vamp, who provides the murder as well as the gangster connections, and on from him to whomever can offer both money and excitement.

Harlem brought the rent party, along with the Harlem numbers racket, to Broadway. The play was reviewed by all the major New York critics, some expressing wonder if not disbelief at the "strange" custom of raising money to pay the rent.

None of the black reviewers was confused by the rent party, which had become a mechanism for survival in the black community, but some were put off by the emphasis on "low life"—gambling, gin, and gyrations. Most reviewers thought it was worth seeing because it "captured the feel of life" and because it was "remarkably well acted," "exciting," and "constantly entertaining." Negative comments underscored its "vulgarity," its inability to blend white and black elements (gangsters, underworld melodrama, and the Negro experience in Harlem). Arthur Ruhl thought it possible, notwithstanding its defects, that *Harlem* would "hold its own on the liveliness and novelty of its color and as melodrama." *Harlem* did hold its own. It ran for ninety-three performances at the Apollo, longer than 165 other plays which opened that season. It also spawned several road companies, one in Canada, another in the Middle West in Detroit and Chicago, and one on the West Coast. There was also a return engagement on Broadway in October. Thurman followed through on some possible leads for a filmed adaptation in Hollywood. Nineteen twenty-nine was the year both *Hallelujah!* and *Hearts in Dixie* were released. It seemed the propitious moment, but only frustration came of his contacts with Pathé, Universal, M-G-M, and others. While he was out West, in California and on a visit with Ma Jack in Salt Lake City, he worked on a novelized version of *Harlem*, a project in which Virginia Venable, the new Mrs. Rapp, was also engaged.

Although they did not discuss their larger project in public, when they first began to work on *Black Belt* (the title at that time was "Black Mecca") Thurman and Rapp had had in mind a trilogy on black life. The first play would concentrate on the effects of the Great Migration on a southern black family; the second would deal with Marcus Garvey and the Universal Negro Improvement Association; the third would examine the phenomenon of passing and intraracial prejudice, the latter a favorite subject of Thurman's. "Jeremiah the Magnificent," the second play, is in many ways a better work than *Harlem*. In a newspaper interview Thurman once listed his favorite Negro personalities as Frederick Douglass and Marcus Garvey. While he was in Santa Monica, he also wrote an article on Garvey which was never published. Although "Jeremiah the Magnificent" is replete with Thurman's caustic wit, it shows respect for a man Thurman thought something of a genius even though "composed of charlatan, mountebank, saviour and fool."

The play portrays the Garvey character, Jeremiah, as a man with a commanding and charismatic personality; it also shows him to be susceptible to flattery, overly trusting, and easily manipulated. The three-act drama begins with the halcyon days of the "back-to-Africa" movement and ends with a fictional fiasco aboard one of the ships of the "Black Cross" Line. Some of Jeremiah's followers have lost their lives trying to escape the unseaworthy S.S. *Jeremiah;* the others desert him when they hear he has been duped and the organization robbed. It is an ignominious defeat, but Jeremiah is no cunning Brutus Jones, nor does he speak in the "dis" and "dat" dialect Gilpin and Robeson were forced to mouth. Jeremiah is egotistical and ambitious, but his dreams of glory are not for himself alone; he believes in black people and their destiny. His defeat comes about because of his limitations, his inability to choose wise counsel or to recognize perfidy in his own ranks. Jeremiah's gullible followers are satirized as are his most obvious foibles, but the character is not totally undercut. Thurman believed that Garvey did much to awaken "race consciousness among Negroes" and to lay the groundwork for the renaissance. On 30 October 1929, in an article in the *Philadelphia Tribune,* Alvin E. White wrote that "Jeremiah the Magnificent" was in the hands of C. A. Leonard, who announced that he was preparing to produce it and that he was considering Paul Robeson for the role. Perhaps the failure at the box office of another play about Garvey, *Sweet Chariot,* with Frank Wilson and Fredi Washington, deterred Leonard and kept "Jeremiah the Magnificent" from finding a producer. Apparently the play was performed once, sometime after Thurman's death.

"Black Cinderella" (or "Harlem Cinderella"), the third play in the trilogy, which the authors sometimes referred to as the "Color Parade" trilogy, was never completed. A synopsis indicates that it is about J. Seabright Moore, a middle-class lawyer and his wife, who suffer from color prejudice. Their light-skinned daughter, Adelaide, gets all their attention and love while Lavinia, their darker daughter, is made the drudge of the household. Adelaide is betrothed to an upwardly mobile, even lighter-skinned doctor. He refuses to marry her when he finds out that Lavinia is in love with and may marry a man who is not only dark but who does not have a college degree. He will only capitulate if Adelaide agrees to renounce her family and the race. The proud father becomes apoplectic when he hears of Adelaide's desertion and when he finds that the elite (class and caste) real estate

colony he has invested in has gone down in financial ruin. The "happy" ending is reserved for the young "black" couple.

Perhaps the trilogy remained unfinished because the two authors became discouraged. No Hollywood contract was forthcoming for *Harlem* and no producer-director for "Jeremiah." Thurman became involved in a struggle with his estranged wife over a divorce settlement while he was miles away. At least *The Blacker the Berry* (Louise had typed the manuscript) had been completed and published earlier in the year. In fact the copy he inscribed to his friend and collaborator Bill Rapp was dated January 1929. There is no record of what Ma Jack, to whom the book was dedicated, thought of it, although Thurman did report that he had felt pilloried by some of her churchgoing friends who came to pray over him, "beseeching the Almighty to turn my talents into the path of righteousness." (Perhaps they were concerned about

Wallace Thurman (courtesy of the James Weldon Johnson Memorial Collection, Beinecke Rare Book and Manuscript Library, Yale University)

both the play and the novel.) Thurman himself was never satisfied with the novel. The reviews were encouraging but not lyrical. Du Bois in the *Crisis* found Thurman not quite up to the challenge of his subject matter but admitted to some prejudice because of the author's "unpleasant" work in the past. The *Opportunity* reviewer called *The Blacker the Berry* an extended short story and bemoaned the lack of "academic standards in the matter of construction"; V. F. Calverton, in the *New York Herald Tribune,* was negative but sympathetic to the social issue addressed; the *Boston Transcript* was favorable, emphasizing the novel's irony and pathos; the *Chicago Defender* reviewer pointed to the importance of bringing to light the controversial subject of intraracial prejudice.

"The blacker the berry, the sweeter the juice," an old folk saying, applies only ironically to Emma Lou Morgan, a black child born into a "blue-veined" family. In fact her color "shrouds her in" (the quote from Countee Cullen which Thurman uses as a secondary epigraph) until she is finally able, by the end of the novel, to recognize that color consciousness has distorted her life. Emma's negative experiences begin at home; her black father is considered beneath her light-skinned mother and is therefore rejected. Rejection of his child almost unconsciously follows. Emma Lou is unacceptable not only by family standards in Boise but also by the standards of the few Negroes and many whites in town. Nor are things much different when she goes to the University of Southern California. Her restless movements take her eventually to Harlem, where she is sure things will be better. The place where the New Negro movement was in full swing and black-is-beautiful was the slogan of the day, however, was also the place where the most popular shows (including *Shuffle Along*) had "light brown" chorus lines and a famous dark-skinned singer was forced to sing offstage. Harlem is where Emma meets Alva, the man who becomes the immediate cause of her degradation and the catalyst for her eventual self-realization.

Many critics have insisted that in *The Blacker the Berry* Thurman was working out his own feelings of self-hatred, his personal experiences with discrimination both inside and outside the race; the locales almost force the reader to see the novel as autobiography. There was, however, an original for Emma Lou, a woman who grew up in a part of the country with almost as few black people as Utah and Idaho. This friend of Thurman's also resorted to the potent preparations, designed to lighten black skin, that were so deleterious to Emma Lou

Morgan. The magazines of the day were filled with ads for such preparations; George Schuyler's *Black No More* (1931) would soon create a Madame Sisseretta Blandish (read Madame Walker) whose skin lighteners and hair straighteners produced a fortune. It may be more illuminating to see the novel as Thurman's tenuous move to reveal a subject even more taboo than intraracial prejudice. Emma Lou, like many victims of discrimination, takes on the attitudes of those who set the standards, those who determine what beauty is. She looks down on darker-skinned working-class men, believing them to be intellectually inferior as well, and becomes involved with Alva because he is light-skinned and (therefore) handsome. She endures Alva's inhumane treatment of her—his many transgressions, his irresponsible attitude toward his own child—until she observes him in a drunken homosexual embrace. At that point he forces her to recognize what she is seeing. Emma has had numerous opportunities to extricate herself from this degrading relationship; she has been encouraged by the husband of her employer, a Van Vechten type, to pursue her education, to accept herself, but she does not effect any real change in her behavior until this epiphanic moment.

Two major concerns of Thurman the man and the writer emerge in this first novel, neither as yet well realized. Only Bruce Nugent, in his "Smoke, Lilies, and Jade," which was almost designed to offend the public, had dealt with such outré subject matter. James Baldwin was a generation away. Only in so-called bohemian circles was homosexuality or bisexuality not condemned. That bohemian life was portrayed by Thurman in his second novel.

When Thurman returned to New York, he was not in the best of financial circumstances. In spite of the royalties from *The Blacker the Berry* and the various *Harlem* productions, he was in debt. The fact is that he had never been adept at holding on to money. As Theophilus Lewis wrote in his posthumous tribute (*New York Amsterdam News,* 5 January 1935), Thurman was "indifferent toward the rules of life in the material world. Which explains his queer way of handling money. When he had $5 he would go on a spending spree until his money gave out. When he had $500 he would go on a bigger spree until he was broke. He would ignore old debts and spend his money on strays he had never seen before. When he had no money at all he had no qualms about sponging on his friends." That attitude may explain why he wrote a note to Elizabeth Marbury, a wealthy white patron of the arts whom he had met through Dorothy West, asking for money to support the writing of his novel. After having met her only once, he apparently had no qualms about making the request to which she responded positively.

Using the same self-deprecating tone of the novel, Thurman dedicated *Infants of the Spring* to Beulah (his mother), "the goose who laid the not so golden egg." The infants were "actors" in the drama of the "Harlem Renaissance," a script which they had, in the throes of self-delusion, written about themselves. His satire is directed against the poseurs, those who acted the role of artist but produced little in the way of art. One of the epigraphs is from Shakespeare (*Hamlet*), the other from Maxim Gorky, and they reflect the tension in the novel. The first decries the notion that one can count on the future when, although there may be great promise in youth, that promise is often blighted before it has the chance to reach fruition; the second is a tribute to the "possessed," those who are "not quite achieved, who are not very wise," but who are "a little mad." The fictional habitués of "Niggeratti Manor," Iolanthe Sydney's now-famous rooming house in Harlem where Thurman and a number of the young artists and writers lived, were "possessed," but they were not all talented. The story is told from the point of view of Raymond Taylor, a young black writer, who is the author's persona. The major crisis facing him is how to produce serious work when the times seem to be filled with decadence or strident racialism which he sees as restricting to the artist. Thurman writes in *Infants of the Spring*: "He wanted to write but he had made little progress. He wanted to become a Prometheus, to break the chains which held him to a racial rack and carry a blazing beacon to the top of Mount Olympus so that those of Alpine stocks could follow in his wake. . . ." Like Wallace Thurman, Raymond Taylor was not satisfied to be talented; he wanted genius.

A number of the major and minor figures of the renaissance (as well as the renaissance itself) are satirized in the novel; it reads like a "Who's Who of Harlem": Locke, Hughes, Hurston, Cullen, Fisher, Nugent, Eric Walrond, Aaron Douglas, Service Bell, Rex Goreleigh, A'Lelia Walker, even Mrs. Sydney (as Euphoria Blake). Some of the satire is sharp, some gentle. The ingenuous young women from Boston are Dorothy West and her cousin Helene Johnson. There is a good deal of drinking, carousing, and some fairly complex (racially and sexually) mating. Thurman is more candid but not completely explicit about the

homosexuality in this novel. What is most interesting is that Thurman finally puts together all of his philosophical concerns about art and the Negro as artist in a self-conscious movement which he saw rapidly disintegrating. Paul Arbian's final but futile gesture symbolizes that disintegration. Arbian (Bruce Nugent), the most talented of the artists at Niggeratti Manor, commits suicide after he is unceremoniously evicted by Euphoria. Dressed in a crimson mandarin robe, he had climbed into the bathtub, turned on the water, and slashed his wrists with a Chinese dirk, after having spread the penciled manuscript pages of his novel about the floor. Assuming that the novel would be published posthumously with "delightful publicity," he had failed to foresee that the pages would not only be inundated but the writing completely obliterated. The dedication to Joris Huysmans, and Oscar Wilde survives, as does a "distorted, ink black skyscraper, modeled after Niggeratti Manor, and on which were focused an array of blindingly white beams of light. The foundation of the building was composed of crumbling stone. At first glance it could be ascertained that the skyscraper would soon crumple and fall, leaving the dominating white lights in full possession of the sky." The foundation on which the renaissance was built was unsound, Ray and Thurman believed. Ray had already contended that the Negro race could not produce a great writer yet, any more than America could. Jean Toomer was the only Negro he felt had the elements of greatness. "The rest of us are merely journeymen, planting seed for someone else to harvest. We all get sidetracked sooner or later. The older ones become warped by propaganda. We younger ones are mired in decadence. None of us seem able to rise above our environment."

Thurman was vilified by some for heralding the demise of the renaissance; he was congratulated by others for recognizing reality. "Perhaps the new Negro is dead," Fisher wrote in his review, "or perhaps in the warm sunlight of publicity, he stretched himself out and dozed off to sleep. In either case, this novel is no evidence that the brownskinned brother is either roused or revived." The *New York Times* reviewer thought it not "wholly without merit. Some of the discussions are challenging. Some of the scenes . . . are shrewdly observed. . . . It is a more pretentious but less successful book than Mr. Thurman's earlier novel, 'The Blacker the Berry.'" The *National News* reviewer held just the opposite opinion: "Mr. Thurman, being more than a first-rate writer, rises gloriously above the banality of such material. And one cannot help feel-

Title pages for Thurman's novels

ing that *Infants of the Spring* is in every way a much finer novel than *The Blacker the Berry*." The *Opportunity* reviewer felt that the problems considered in the novel were not "thoroughly thought through" by the writer, "and so *Infants of the Spring* has that inevitable underdone taste which flavors the bulk of literary output today." She thought it "not enough to face and attempt to portray stark truth and bitter reality. It is necessary to pass beyond to an affirmed whole-view of them and build upon the strength of that. Only from such inner freedom and power can anything worth-while arise."

Thurman did not again deal in writing with the problems that so concerned him in *Infants of the Spring*, nor with any aspect of black experience. By 1932, when it was published, he had been promoted at Macaulay's and had met his second white collaborator, Abraham L. Furman, there. Together they wrote *The Interne*, which was published by Macaulay that same year. *The Interne* has a strange, muckraking quality; it is in a sense an exposé, like *Tomorrow's Children*, the scenario Thurman was to write for Bryan Foy a few years later. Thurman's interest in medicine dated back to his days at the University of Southern California. He had, in fact, most of his life "enjoyed poor health." Theophilus Lewis wrote (in an article in the *Amsterdam News*, 4 March 1931) that "the man literally luxuriates in being ill. His propensity for making business for doctors and drug stores suggests some interesting statistics. If the pills he has swallowed since he has been in New York were laid end to end they would reach from the Clam House to Frank's place on Seventh Avenue." Whether Thurman's real interest in medicine was from the patient's or the doctor's perspective is difficult to discern. *The Interne* concentrates on the problems of the latter, attempting to examine that important year in the training of young doctors at, as it turned out in an ironic twist of fate, City Hospital on Welfare Island, where Thurman was to breathe his last. What one learns about the bureaucracy of the institution and the unethical behavior of hospital personnel is sufficient to keep any reader as far from these disinfected corridors as possible. Even the dedicated young (white) hero partially succumbs to corruption before coming to his senses and repairing to a decent practice in the country.

The book was panned by the reviewers: it was "squalid" and "tawdry," sensational, little more than an "ineffective narrative." At least the critics who commented on *The Interne* had read it. It is not clear, however, that all those who have commented on *Tomorrow's Children* and *High School Girl*,

the scenarios Thurman wrote, actually saw the films. Neither the scenario nor the film *High School Girl* has surfaced, but *Tomorrow's Children*, the film, is extant.

Bryan Foy, Jr., brought Thurman to the coast in 1934 to write film scripts for his independent production company, reportedly at a salary in excess of $250 a week. Foy, who had been with Warner Bros. for many years, was apparently interested in the social problem film. *Tomorrow's Children*, a low-budget undertaking with few known Hollywood names, was clearly not intended for Oscar competition (1934 was the year of *It Happened One Night*). It is the story of a poor family whose only working member is a seventeen-year-old daughter, dedicated to making life easier for her oft-pregnant mother, drunken out-of-work father, and younger siblings, who are either physically or mentally handicapped. A well-meaning doctor, who has seen the mother through her most recent (stillborn) childbirth, recommends that the "Welfare Society" come to the family's assistance. At that point, two welfare workers descend upon the family insisting that mother, father, *and* daughter be immediately sterilized in order to qualify for assistance.

Although the runner sensationalizes the problem and links sterilization to prevailing Nazi theory (and practice), the film is rather restrained melodrama, and in genre not very different from the Hollywood norm. Nineteen thirty-four was also the year that Universal released the first film adaptation of Fannie Hurst's novel *Imitation of Life*, considered by one black film critic to be the "first important black film" of the 1930s. Hollywood was clearly undergoing a change, but not enough of a change for a major studio to hire a black writer even when it was producing a film with "black" content. *Tomorrow's Children*, on the other hand, has no black characters. The poor family, the Masons, are white. A priest is involved at the end in attempting to persuade Mrs. Mason to save her daughter from sterilization, so the assumption is that they are Catholic. The issue addressed is whether or not the state has the right to decide who shall have children and who shall not (the runner boldly, and correctly, declares that twenty-seven states have sterilization laws on the book). In arguing Alice Mason's case, the doctor reflects some of Thurman's literary and philosophical preferences: "Look at all the great men in the world who may be classified as having been insane or in some other way unfit—Nietzche, Dostoyevski, Edgar Allan Poe. Suppose their parents had been sterilized?" Then the film avoids a resolution by having

Mrs. Mason confess that Alice is not their real child but one she and her husband raised for a woman who left Alice in their care many years before. Nonetheless the film not only explored an issue that was rarely if ever dealt with in Hollywood but also explained in medical terms the surgical procedure for both women and men. In fact the same well-meaning doctor actually uses the term vasectomy! In addition differential justice for rich and poor is emphasized in the courtroom scenes. One accidentally humorous incident involves the son of an affluent family who has a senator argue his case against sterilization, which he easily wins, immediately after the scene in which the son has attempted to strip a nurse of her clothes.

Thurman stayed in Hollywood until May 1934; he later said that being on the set was sheer madness as was the whole Hollywood scene. He drank too much and stayed up too late. When he could no longer cope with ill health, he returned to New York. Although warned by the doctors not to drink, he had one last reunion and celebration with his Harlem cohorts and collapsed in the middle of it. He was taken to City Hospital on Welfare Island, which he and Furman had "memorialized" in *The Interne*. His condition, diagnosed as tuberculosis, gradually worsened until he was too weak to write a response to letters from friends, like Dorothy West, who did not realize how close to the end he was. He died on 21 December 1934 at the age of thirty-two. On Christmas Eve friends who had joined him in so many other gatherings heard the Reverend William Lloyd Imes of St. James Presbyterian Church read the obituary written by Hughes Allison, which ended with this tribute:

> There was one word . . . which Wallace Thurman used to describe a situation or a book or a play or a joke or anything which he thought superior and outstanding— "Priceless."
>
> His life, his work, his success characterize that word—the word and his name are synonymous. Wallace Thurman was Priceless.

Thurman's passing left a real void. As West put it, "he was our leader, and when he died, it all died with him." Theophilus Lewis was distressed that his paper, the *Amsterdam News*, had not done justice to Thurman, and in his article he pointed out

Thurman's value: "As editor, novelist and playwright, he was the most versatile of contemporary Aframerican literary men."

References:
Doris Abramson, *Negro Playwrights in the American Theatre, 1925-1929* (New York: Columbia University Press, 1969);
Faith Berry, *Langston Hughes: Before and Beyond Harlem* (Westport, Conn.: Hill, 1983);
Gerald Haslam, "Wallace Thurman: Western Renaissance Man," *Western American Literature*, 6 (Spring 1971): 53-59;
Robert Hemenway, *Zora Neale Hurston, A Literary Biography* (Urbana: University of Illinois Press, 1977);
Mae Gwendolyn Henderson, "Portrait of Wallace Thurman," in *The Harlem Renaissance Remembered*, edited by Arna Bontemps (New York: Dodd, Mead, 1972);
Nathan Huggins, *Harlem Renaissance* (New York: Oxford University Press, 1971);
Langston Hughes, *The Big Sea, An Autobiography by Langston Hughes* (New York: Knopf, 1940);
Theodore Kornweibel, Jr., *No Crystal Stair: Black Life and the Messenger, 1917-1928* (Westport, Conn.: Greenwood Press, 1975);
David Levering Lewis, *When Harlem Was in Vogue* (New York: Knopf, 1981);
Dorothy Jean Palmer McIver, "Stepchild in Harlem: The Literary Career of Wallace Thurman," Ph.D. dissertation, University of Alabama, 1983;
Huel D. Perkins, "Wallace Thurman, Renaissance 'Renegade'?," *Black World*, 25 (February 1976): 29-35;
George S. Schuyler, *Black and Conservative: The Autobiography of George S. Schuyler* (New Rochelle, N.Y.: Arlington House, 1966);
Dorothy West, "Elephant's Dance, A Memoir of Wallace Thurman," *Black World*, 2 (November 1970): 77-85.

Papers:
The largest collection of Thurman papers is in the James Weldon Johnson Collection at the Beinecke Library, Yale University; some letters are in the Moorland-Spingarn Research Center at Howard University; others are in the William Jourdan Rapp Collection at the University of Oregon Library.

Jean Toomer

Nellie McKay
University of Wisconsin-Madison

See also the Toomer entry in *DLB 45, American Poets, 1880-1945, First Series.*

BIRTH: Washington, D.C., 26 December 1894, to Nathan and Nina Pinchback Toomer.

EDUCATION: University of Wisconsin-Madison, 1914; Massachusetts College of Agriculture, Amherst, 1915; American College of Physical Training, Chicago, 1916; University of Chicago, 1916; New York University, 1917; City College of New York, 1917.

MARRIAGES: 20 October 1931 to Margery Latimer (deceased); child: Margery. 1 September 1934 to Marjorie Content.

DEATH: Doylestown, Pennsylvania, 30 March 1967.

SELECTED BOOKS: *Cane* (New York: Boni & Liveright, 1923);
Essentials (Chicago: Lakeside Press, 1931);
An Interpretation of Friends Worship (Philadelphia: Committee on Religious Education of Friends General Conference, 1947);
The Flavor of Man (Philadelphia: Young Friends Movement of the Philadelphia Yearly Meetings, 1949);
The Wayward and the Seeking: A Collection of Writings by Jean Toomer, edited by Darwin Turner (Washington, D.C.: Howard University Press, 1980).

OTHER: *Balo: A One Act Sketch of Negro Life,* in *Plays of Negro Life,* edited by Alain Locke and Montgomery Gregory (New York & London: Harper, 1927), pp. 269-286;
"Race Problems and Modern Society," in *Problems of Civilization,* edited by Baker Brownell (New York: Van Nostrand, 1929);
"York Beach," in *The New American Caravan,* edited by Alfred Kreymborg, Lewis Mumford, and Paul Rosenfeld (New York: Macaulay, 1929), pp. 12-83;

"Blue Meridian," in *The New Caravan,* edited by Kreymborg, Mumford, and Rosenfeld (New York: Norton, 1936), pp. 633-654;
"Five Vignettes," in *Black American Literature: Poetry,* edited by Darwin Turner (Columbus, Ohio: Merrill, 1969).

PERIODICAL PUBLICATIONS: "Banking Coal," *Crisis,* 24 (June 1922): 65;
"Oxen Cart and Warfare," *Little Review* (Autumn/Winter 1924-1925): 44-48;
"Easter," *Little Review,* 11 (Spring 1925): 3-7;
"Reflections," *Dial,* 86 (1929): 314;
"White Arrow," *Dial,* 86 (July 1929): 596;
"As the Eagle Soars," *Crisis,* 41 (April 1932): 116;
"Brown River, Smile," *Pagany,* 3 (Winter 1932): 29-33;

Jean Toomer (courtesy of the Prints and Photographs Collection, Moorland-Spingarn Research Center, Howard University)

274

"Of a Certain November," *Dubuque Dialogue*, 1 November 1935;

"See The Heart," *Friend's Intelligencer*, 104 (9 August 1947): 423;

"Chapters from *Earth-Being*," *Black Scholar*, 2 (January 1971): 3-14.

When the writers of the early Harlem Renaissance read *Cane* in 1923, in the words of Arna Bontemps, they "went quietly mad." No prior literary description of the Afro-American experience had reached its level of artistic achievement. Jean Toomer, the author of *Cane*, had been mostly associated with progressive white writers of the late 1910s and early 1920s, such as Hart Crane and Sherwood Anderson, but the black avant garde writers claimed him as their own. *Cane* was called the herald of a new day in Afro-American letters, and Toomer was perceived as the most promising Negro writer. It was an auspicious beginning for a new author. Although Toomer continued writing for his whole life, the promise of his masterpiece was not matched again in his published work. By the end of the 1920s Toomer and *Cane* seemed to have disappeared from the world of letters; they remained largely unknown to the reading public for nearly forty years. Then in 1951, *Cane* was republished, and by 1969 it had made a dramatic come back from obscurity. A new generation of thinkers confirmed earlier appraisals of Toomer's book, hailing *Cane* for its critical achievement as well as for its intrinsic worth as the first major book to affirm cultural assumptions of the Harlem Renaissance of the 1920s.

Nathan Eugene Toomer, the son of Nina Pinchback and Georgia planter Nathan Toomer, was born in Washington, D.C., on 26 December 1894. Although known by the surname Pinchback for most of his early life, he used his father's last name as an adult, and when he began to write, he changed Eugene to Jean. He spent his early years in Washington in the home of his maternal grandparents to which his mother had returned after her husband deserted her in 1895. Toomer's grandfather Pinckney Benton Stewart Pinchback had been a powerful politician associated with the Louisiana governor's office in the era of Reconstruction. The Pinchbacks were a racially mixed family. In the autobiographical essay "On Being An American," Toomer described his background as "Scotch, Welsh, German, English, French, Dutch, Spanish, with some dark blood." Although the Pinchbacks were sufficiently fair-skinned to have been considered white, P. B. S. claimed *he* was a

Negro and built his career on that claim. Toomer himself could not readily be identified as black. Until 1906 he lived in his grandparents' home on Bacon Street, in a wealthy white neighborhood which he recalled as being unblighted by prejudice. An assertive child, Toomer found the main source of conflict in his life to be his domineering grandfather. After a devastating illness in 1905 and an eight-month-long convalescence in 1906, Toomer moved to white neighborhoods first in Brooklyn and then to New Rochelle, New York, with Nina Pinchback and her white second husband. He returned to Washington after his mother's unexpected death in 1909.

By 1910, the Pinchbacks had suffered severe financial losses. They had moved into a less affluent, black section of the city. Toomer attended the M Street High School, Washington's secondary school for Negroes. Later Toomer often said that he had an advantage over most other people in knowing the truth about race, for he had lived in both the white and black worlds as a member of each group. In 1914, after having given the matter of his racial identity some thought, he reasoned that he would consider himself an American, neither white nor black. He was convinced that almost all Americans were descended from a number of bloodlines, but that they were just not yet aware of it. He pondered his national identity in his early "The First American." His decision to adopt an American identity had a major impact on his literary career as well as on all other significant events in his subsequent life.

Although he worried about whether his having graduated from a black high school would affect his reception at college, in 1914 he enrolled at the University of Wisconsin, Madison, intending to study agriculture. However, by the end of the year he changed his mind, and he left school shortly after the Christmas vacation. In the four years that followed, Toomer attended as many colleges, and he changed his academic interests just as frequently. In 1915 he entered the Massachusetts College of Agriculture; in 1916 he enrolled at both the American College of Physical Training in Chicago and the University of Chicago; in the 1917 summer session, he entered the City College of New York. He remained at no institution long enough to earn a degree. Each time he began with high hopes, but each time some difficulty arose that he could not overcome, and he left. In 1919 he decided to become a writer.

Jean Toomer's interest in literature began in early childhood, he relates in "Chapters From

Pinckney Benton Stewart Pinchback and Emily Hethorne Pinchback, Toomer's maternal grandparents (courtesy of Marjorie Content Toomer)

Earth-Being: An Unpublished Autobiography" (*Black Scholar,* 1971), when his uncle Bismarck introduced him to the world of books and imagination. Every night Bis would retire after dinner "in bed with a book, cigarettes, and a saucer of sliced peaches prepared . . . in a special way, and read far into the night. Sometimes he would write, trying his hand at fiction." He began to include Toomer in his nightly ritual, introducing him to new ideas and having discussions about them with the boy. When Toomer went to New Rochelle, initially he had difficulty making friends, but he discovered the public library and began to read intensively stories of knights and chivalry: books about King Arthur and the Knights of the Roundtable, Sir Galahad and Sir Lancelot, and the Quest for the Holy Grail. As a child, he loved the outdoors, and was fond of bicycling, baseball, swimming, and tennis. He also learned to sail in New Rochelle and was given a small boat of his own in which he spent much of his time exploring the waters of the Long Island Sound. His first attempts at writing included materials he recalled from these early outdoors experiences. In high school, where his love of reading continued, William Shakespeare and Charles Dickens were his favorite writers.

Although Toomer became aware of the possibilities of a literary life while he was in Wisconsin, he did not give the idea serious consideration until later. At City College in 1917, he began to read George Bernard Shaw and Henrik Ibsen, whose works made him aware of the relationship between literature and society. Soon after, he discovered Walt Whitman's writings and Johann Wolfgang von Goethe's Wilheim Meister novels helped him see how the creative imagination and psychology could be made to serve each other.

Living in New York in 1919, he met many of the up-and-coming young American writers of the day. Among these were Edwin Arlington Robinson, Witter Bynner, Van Wyck Brooks, and Waldo Frank. Frank and Toomer became close friends

*Nina Pinchback, circa 1890 (courtesy of Marjorie
Content Toomer)*

Toomer's life and writings were deeply affected by his search for internal harmony, which was tangentially related to the issue of racial identity. His search for spiritual concord later became synonymous with his search for higher consciousness. He entered into his early adulthood determined to find a system through which he could bring the physical, emotional, and intellectual parts of himself into harmony. His quest for such a system compelled much of his attention through the remainder of his life and, ultimately, was the defining criterion of his happiness, success, shortcomings, and disappointments.

In the summer of 1921 Toomer was living in Washington again, taking care of his ill, aging grandparents, and trying to write, but having no success in this latter endeavor. He met the principal of a small, rural, black school near Sparta, Georgia, who needed someone to take over the management of his institution for a short time. Toomer was invited to take the temporary position, and he welcomed the opportunity as a respite from the drudgery of housekeeping and the frustrations of his unrealized literary efforts. He was also curious about the South and its folk culture. In September he went to Sparta.

Struck by the beauty and power of the people and the land, in spite of racial segregation, poverty, and the unpolished state of the culture, Toomer lived among the rural people with whom he worked. He had a "shack" off by himself, where, he noted, the mud came up through the floor boards when it rained, but which gave him the opportunity to observe the folk while they went about their daily affairs. For the first time he heard the women singing at sunset while they prepared supper and he heard spirituals sung by musically untrained people. He realized the special quality in their emotional responses to these songs. He saw first hand both the brutality, hardships, and social and economic oppression experienced by southern black people, as well as the internal strength and dignity of the black folk culture.

Toomer responded emotionally to this new environment, feeling for the first time in his life a sense of inner balance that enabled him to begin to write in a way that satisfied him. He immersed himself in the spirituality of the experience, and he found his voice. Before he left Georgia in November, he sent a poem to a New York journal, and on the train back to Washington he began to compose the narratives which became the first section of *Cane*. By the end of the year this part of

and were part of Greenwich Village's artistic society. The scope of his reading expanded significantly after he decided to pursue a career in writing. He recalled later that during that time he read the works of Fyodor Dostoyevski, Leo Tolstoy, Gustave Flaubert, Charles Baudelaire, Sinclair Lewis, Theodore Dreiser, Sigmund Freud, Robert Frost, and Sherwood Anderson, with whom he was to have an extended correspondence. He also read books on Buddhist philosophy, Eastern teachings, occultism and theosophy, and the Christian Bible as literature, and magazines, including the *Dial*, the *Liberator*, the *Nation* and the *New Republic*. During this difficult period of apprenticeship, he wrote essays, articles, poems, short stories, and reviews, but nothing he wrote satisfied him, and he linked his ineptness to internal disharmony. He was sure he would not find his literary voice until he solved the problem of his internal disorganization, and he saw no immediate escape from the dilemma this presented to him.

Toomer, circa 1906 (courtesy of Marjorie Content Toomer)

people resisting physical and psychological oppression.

Toomer arranged his pieces in a format intended to unify the rural southern and urban northern black experiences. *Cane*'s focus is circular, moving from black Georgia folk culture to northern city culture, and back to the South, where both experiences merge, if not collide. Even his narrative perspective reinforces the circular thematic structure of the work. The first two sections of the book feature a narrator who is most often a detached observer of the action. It is clear that he is less familiar with Georgia than he is with the cities, for in the first section, he makes several attempts to develop close relationships with the women, but he is unable to do so. They elude him physically, intellectually, and spiritually. He has more success with women in the second section, except in the case of a woman who shares qualities with her country sisters. In the last section of the book, the narrator and central character, Ralph Kabnis, blend into one, rarely becoming distinguishable from each other. Kabnis has both a northern and a southern identity. He moves painfully from resistance to his "other" self, to acknowledgement of the whole history of the self, to expectation of acceptance of his divided self.

The first section, set in Georgia, is made up of twelve poems and six vignettes of the lives of women. Against the background of the grinding and boiling of cane and the stirring of the sweet syrup, black men from the community gather in the night to tell stories around the hot, fragrant, copper cauldron. Toomer's imagery in these sketches is taken mainly from nature, making this section the most lyrical, vivid, mystical, and sensuous part of the book. The initial effect of the imagery can be deceptive, however, for Toomer also weaves dissonance, sarcasm, irony, and harsh realism into the fabric of these vignettes. The lyrical beauty of dusk on the horizon at the beginning of the section metamorphoses into the evil eye of a "blood burning moon" at the finale. The narratives and poems between these two points focus on the conflicts, insecurities, and pressures that beset southern life.

The six women, five black and one white, are symbols of the history of women in the South. The black women are identified with nature, and to varying degrees, they are beautiful, innocent, sensuous, sometimes strong, but always vulnerable, misunderstood, and unpossessable. As nature has always been helpless against the onslaughts of industrialization and the technological advances of

the book was completed; by early spring 1923 the entire book was done.

When Toomer had first begun writing, he had not conceived of a book. He wanted only to set down in prose and poetry his vision of the southern black rural experience. While he was in the South he had been in close correspondence with Waldo Frank, and by the time he had returned to New York early in 1922, Frank advised him to combine his pieces into a book and promised to recommend it to his own publisher, Boni & Liveright.

Taking advantage of the climate of experimentation in language and form that was being fostered by many of the white writers he then knew, Toomer combined prose narratives, poetry, prose poems, and drama to delineate his total experience. The book, an artistic, balanced exploration of the black experience in white America, revolves around the central analogy between the hard and grinding work that takes place before the syrup can come from the cane, and the fortitude of a

Jean Toomer and his Uncle Bismarck, who encouraged Toomer's early interest in literature (courtesy of Marjorie Content Toomer)

the modern age, so, too, are the women desecrated to racial and sexual oppression. The women experience alienation, madness, and death, emblemizing the embattled state of black people and black folk culture. Jean Toomer's women are of the earth because they are sensuous and fecund, but they are not earth mothers. They do not nurture; they, like the land, are ravaged.

The single white woman in the group is as poor and as oppressed by the rigid system of racial segregation as the black women. Toomer understood clearly that black and white people in the South were interdependent in significant ways and that it was impossible to separate the groups' experiences in any comprehensive survey of southern life. Through this character Toomer demonstrates that rigid codes of racial oppression, partly justified by their perpetrators as means of protecting southern white women, can oppress society as well.

The first section of the book ends in a confrontation: a black man is lynched for daring to date the same woman that a white man dates, and the white community has its satisfaction in the

knowledge that the status quo remains intact. The black woman who is left behind is the final victim. Surrounded by chaos and brutality, she sinks into madness.

Cane's second section comprises a kaleidoscope of impressions of the more sophisticated, but narrowing, urban styles of life in Washington, D.C., and Chicago.

Throughout the seven prose pieces and five poems, Toomer's tone and language evoke sensations associated with the vibrations of city life, and the imagery reflects the effects of industrialization and mechanization on human beings in the urban environment. There are only rare images of nature here, no dusky sunsets or golden colors illuminate the landscape, and there is no lyricism. The black people of this section, descendants and survivors of the black southern folk culture, are seeking new homes in the urban North, where man has subdued nature. The migration of people from the South was motivated by hopes of finding a larger life, one outside of southern racism, but the refugees discover only new and different restrictions in the place they had hoped would be the promised land. Yet, there is a crude energy in this section, and it comes from the tension in the people's will to resist and survive the arbitrary restraints of this world.

Toomer's main focus is on the effects on the black spirit of the physical and psychological oppression of northern social and economic institutions. He fastens on the ultimate failure of black people, as a group, to achieve emotional and spiritual wholeness in America. In addition to external restrictions in the North, the newcomers are also in danger of self-imposed psychological restraints. Several of the selections address this issue and show how new value systems replace old ones in the psyche of the recently transplanted urbanites, before they can fully comprehend the meanings of the new. Thus, Toomer suggests that a positive black identity can be attained through an understanding of the past. The burdens of an oppressive history can be used as lessons to shape the future.

Toomer takes the reader back to Georgia, in the third part of the book, where Ralph Kabnis, a black northerner, experiences a nightmare in the canebrake. The earlier focus on mysticism, sensuality, nature, and the elusiveness of women is replaced by a focus on the fear and ambivalence that result from a milieu in which racial oppression is a way of life. In this self-contained drama, Kabnis comes as a school teacher; he is also a poet who dreams that he will become the voice of the South. But Kabnis is the victim of impotency and uncertainty as he searches for his identity in the land of his ancestors. His journey towards that goal incorporates the alienation, ambivalence, and sense of oppressive control that are all part of the black heritage.

Kabnis is aware of the beauty and worth of the waning folk culture, and he wishes to catch its parting song in order to rekindle its spirit to the world. He will do this by bringing together the forces of anger, exploitation, evil, and the will to survive, which have always been elements in black American folk culture. But before he can realize his goal, he must first acknowledge and assimilate the humiliation and pain of the past; he must be disabused of his northern separateness from it.

During his Georgia stay Kabnis learns many things about southern history and the nature of southern white oppression of black people. By the end of the drama he is no longer just Kabnis the northerner whose ancestors came from the South, or an enlightened black man offering gifts of education and art to his backward southern relatives; he is a black man who is beginning to understand the meaning of himself as a northerner and as a southerner, to understand what it is to be a black American.

In a choice between education, politics, and art as ways of comprehending and fusing the various elements of the black American experience into a dignified whole, Toomer chooses art. The northern black political activist, who is present in the drama for a while, leaves before the job is done, and Kabnis gives up teaching just as quickly. It is Kabnis, the poet, who remains to catch the "birthsong" of the new day, and to create *Cane*.

In this book race and sex, city and country, erudition and illiteracy, and beauty and pain are examined as parts of the experience that come together and determine black identity. The folk culture is passing, but its influence is vital among black people. The present is in flux and is itself the search for future direction. Kabnis is the black Everyman on journey in time, to discover a concrete meaning of the American black identity.

The most enduring aspect of *Cane* is that it reveals the intrinsic strength and beauty of black American culture. In 1923 the book represented the distance between the slave heritage and the New Negro of the Harlem Renaissance. The sun and the new day at the end of the book symbolize the triumph of the strength of the folk culture. Without self-glorification or apologies for enduring oppression, *Cane* leaves the reader with a sense of positive individual and group identity.

Between the fall of 1921 and the beginning of 1923 Toomer also worked on other pieces that addressed important Afro-American themes. A short story and two plays—"Withered Skins of Berries," *Balo* and *Natalie Mann*—are his major extant works of the period. *Balo*, a one-act folk drama, was produced by the Howard University Players during its 1923-1924 season, and was anthologized in *Plays of Negro Life* (1927), edited by Alain Locke and Montgomery Gregory. *Natalie Mann* is an expressionist play that has never been staged. Both "Withered Skins of Berries" and *Natalie Mann* were not printed until 1980, when they appeared in *The Wayward and the Seeking*, an anthology of Toomer's writings edited by Darwin Turner.

All of these works have artistic merits. "Withered Skins of Berries" treats the theme of the mulatto passing for convenience. It is set in Washington, D.C., and examines the complexities of the black individual's struggle to rise above race in America. In her economic interests, the mulatto protagonist "passes" and works in an office among whites who are hostile to blacks. The language is as lyrical as the first section of *Cane*, but beyond that, it sheds light on the motivations that propel blacks to move across the color line. *Balo* is a realistic play and is noteworthy because Toomer attempts to experiment with southern black dialect. He presents a positive attitude towards the strength of the black family and community at a time when such an attitude was in decline. Following in the tradition of writers like Leo Tolstoy and Ivan Turgenev Toomer uses the lives of common folk as the subject of art, and he foreshadows black writers like Zora Neale Hurston, Langston Hughes and Sterling Brown, who also use the folk culture as a source of rich artistic inspiration.

Natalie Mann is important in the Toomer canon both for its experimental expressionistic style and its content. Had he been successful in having this play staged, he would have been a pioneer in the field at that time, for when it was written in 1922 only Eugene O'Neill among American dramatists had written and produced works which used similar techniques. Toomer was not only interested in imitating European stage writers who were already using expressionism, but he wanted to demonstrate that language was sufficiently flexible to "objectify mankind's spiritual struggle," and to ridicule those moral and social values which he considered destructive to the human spirit. Through this play Toomer satirizes American business, social, and materialistic ideals. The dialogue is stilted and mechanical, and the actions and expressions of the characters are exaggerated and full of distortions. Stage directions are explicit and detailed, and the players are caricatures rather than realistic characters.

Natalie Mann is the lyrical dramatization of materialism, hypocrisy, and anti-humanistic values versus intellectualism, spirituality, and creativity. It examines negative aspects of black middle-class life in Washington and focuses on one black woman's search for liberation from many of the values of this social group. In their search for social and economic upward mobility, the members of the black middle class imitate the white bourgeoisie, especially its sterile values, at great emotional and spiritual cost to themselves. Above all, they sacrifice inner well-being to a preoccupation with social status. The result is personal alienation and fragmentation in the community.

The protagonist, Natalie Mann, represents "creative revolution" in her search for honest friendships and the chance to love freely and be loved in return. Around her, the community is weak because of social pressures to conform to repressive conventions and to aspire to material gains. There is no intensity of joy or sorrow, of spontaneity and creativity in this environment. The other characters portray conscious denial of all that is natural to the human spirit. Natalie Mann repudiates this denial of life, and ultimately she completely rejects the oppressive conventions of her black middle class up-bringing.

One important aspect of this play is the prominence given to the middle-class black woman. This concern for her dilemma was echoed in other black writers of the later 1920s, especially the women, who found it difficult to escape others' expectations that they would fill traditional roles in spite of their artistic potentials. The novels of Jessie Fauset and Nella Larsen are enlightening for their insights into the conditions which Toomer, preceding them, raises in his play. Toomer was aware that women were particularly victimized in often being denied the opportunity to aspire to careers outside of their roles as wives and mothers. His own mother had been so limited. He saw also that the social attitudes that permitted this kind of oppression were destructive to the entire culture. In restricting women's options to fulfill themselves, men were restricting themselves as well, for the freedom of all depends on the freedom of the individual.

In a larger sphere, Toomer's concern in this and his other works of the early 1920s is that the spiritual heritage of mankind is in jeopardy of strangulation by the antilife forces of the modern world. This perception was central to the thinking of Waldo Frank and the other critical thinkers who were closest to Toomer in that decade. With this group, Toomer wanted to raise American consciousness of the dangers within civilization. Radical in their time, wanting to strip away pretense and emptiness from living and to provide spirituality and deep human feelings, the writers Toomer knew experimented with new forms in language and techniques in efforts to expand literature to accommodate and convey the subjectivism of their views. It was unfortunate for Toomer that *Natalie Mann* was not allowed to reach the public at the time it was written, for it falls in so well with the progressive ideas of his peers.

In spite of his being critically acclaimed as a new leader in black letters, Toomer wanted to be no more than an American writer, and he wanted his work on the black experience to be viewed only as a part of the American experience. Upset and outraged that the book led everyone to see and think of him as a "Negro" writer, he argued publicly that there was no proof of African heritage in his family, and that he was not a Negro. With a good deal of pique, almost immediately after the publication of his book, he turned away from the friends and colleagues who had inspired and encouraged his efforts from 1919 to 1923. He set out, intellectually, to find a new source to restore the internal unity he had enjoyed during the time in which he had been writing the book. He never again wrote of the Afro-American experience in the imaginative mode.

Early in 1924 he encountered the teachings and philosophy of George Ivanovitch Gurdjieff, a Greek and Armenian guru who had traveled extensively in the East studying theology and philosophy. Gurdjieff, viewed by his followers as prophet, priest, and teacher, arrived in the West after the Russian Revolution and World War I precluded the possibility of his opening an institute in Russia. Offering a way to obtain balance between mind, body, and soul, and to achieve full human potential through higher consciousness, he attracted a great deal of attention in the early 1920s. People from diverse backgrounds flocked to the Institute For the Harmonious Development of Man located in Fontainebleau, outside of Paris. The time was right for him, and many Western, middle-class intellectuals, disillusioned with the state of the world and searching for meaning out of the chaos of modern civilization, were willing to adopt his complicated system of psychology, philosophy and dance in the hope of transcending ordinary human capability.

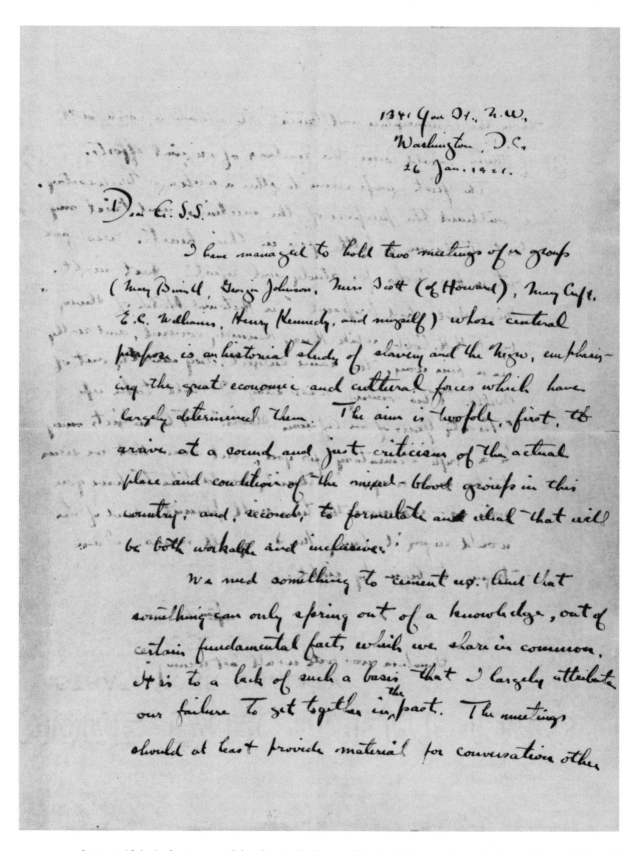

Letter to Alain Locke (courtesy of the Alain Locke Papers, Moorland-Spingarn Research Center, Howard University)

2

—than the commonplace and trivial. As a natural outgrowth
of them should come the reading of original efforts.

The first group came together a week ago Wednesday.
I outlined the purpose of the meetings, and tried my
best to throw a little fire in their hearts. Also gave
out a few books for study and report. Last night,
Miss Scott had prepared "An Historical Sketch of Slavery"
by T. R. R. Cobb, while Henry Kennedy covered, and really
in a fine way, the same subject, dug mostly out of
Wells. This coming Wednesday I shall take up
"Twenty Years of an African Slaver". The subjects may
be a trifle elementary for you; but now that we seem
to be under way, I certainly would like to have you
join us — whenever the time will permit. And if Lee
would enjoy it, bring him, & by all means. I am
trying to begin by eight.

Grandma was with us all last evening —

When Jean Toomer saw a demonstration of the exercises and dances and heard a lecture on the system in 1924, he thought he had found an answer to his quest. He not only joined the movement, but that summer he went to Fontainebleau, and in the fall he became a teacher of the system. By then he had cut almost all his ties with the literary world.

From 1924 to 1932 Toomer worked as a teacher of the Gurdjieff philosophy. Beginning in New York, he tried to establish a group of followers in Harlem. Those who initially turned up to listen to Toomer expound on the attributes of higher consciousness were more interested in him as the author of *Cane* than as the carrier of a new gospel of salvation. The failure of his effort is described in detail in *The Big Sea* (1940), an autobiography by Langston Hughes. Toomer went next to Chicago, where, for several years, he was successful in forming groups among the intellectuals of that city.

Although Toomer rejected the literary world in 1923, he continued to write. In the spring of 1925 a short story, "Easter," appeared in the *Little Review*. "Mr. Costyve Duditch" and "Winter on Earth," two short stories, were published in the *Dial* in 1928, and "York Beach," a novella, in the *New American Caravan* in 1929. His final publication, the long poem "The Blue Meridian," appeared in the *New Caravan* in 1936. None of these works linked him publicly to his earlier literary success.

"Easter" is a work that shows Toomer in transition from the ideas that led from *Cane* to his later writings. While the book embraces a small world, the story has a universal vision. Where *Cane* is lyrical and combines symbolism and realism, "Easter" is surrealistic, and its images are absurd and grotesque. The story largely discredits the Judeo-Christian tradition as the force for the salvation of Western man.

"Mr. Costyve Duditch" was written by a Toomer secure in his mission as a Gurdjieff teacher, for Duditch represents modern man reflected in the light of that philosophy. He is a mechanical man whose life is defined by sterility, the lack of genuine feelings and emotions, and a superficial attitude towards his internal development. Duditch is independently wealthy, and he travels extensively. In his rootlessness and meaningless behavior he is unaware of his potential. Toomer sees this blindness as the universal condition of modern man, and history shows his strong beliefs in the need for a new way to reverse this state of affairs.

"Easter" and "Mr. Costyve Duditch," from a literary point of view, are Toomer's best works be-

tween *Cane* and the end of the 1920s. "Winter on Earth" is mostly philosophical discourse on the need for human beings to strive towards greater individual and collective union with the universe, and "York Beach" is similar. The goal of human life, Toomer is saying, is to develop one's highest potential to achieve higher consciousness. He incorporates ideas on the negative effects of materialism and alienation in the modern world, and stresses the need for more intensive spiritual development. In most of these works, as is also the case in many of the stories in his unpublished manuscripts, the central character is a thinly disguised Jean Toomer, no longer showing the ambivalence of Ralph Kabnis, but exuding confidence in the knowledge that he has found the way to achieve full self-realization.

"The Blue Meridian," his final publication, had its genesis in "The First American," which Toomer composed at the time he pondered his racial identity before he went to college in 1924. The influences of Walt Whitman and Hart Crane are evident in the finished work, and so are those of the Gurdjieff philosophy. Toomer sings his own America, in a poem that pays tribute to all Americans of all races, religions, or creeds. Through the eyes of a Gurdjieffian utopian visionary, "The Blue Meridian" creates a myth of the evolution of a new America. In the poet's new culture, barriers dissolve, and black, white, and red men join to become the blue man, in a synthesis that potentiates spiritual energy.

Much of the language of the poem comes from Gurdjieffian thought. Man, in his ordinary state of being, is asleep, and needs to be awakened. When the union of man and the universe is effected there is awakening. This climax, in Toomer's estimation, is the triumph of man over "not-man," of birth over anti-being. From a past of blindness, mistakes, hate, and greed, men emerge to lose their prejudices and other enslaving attitudes; America can then celebrate as a whole nation.

The symbols of "The Blue Meridian" are drawn from Western and Eastern culture. The symbol of spiritual force in the poem is the Mississippi, whose images frame the work. At the beginning, this powerful river is the "sister" of the Ganges, itself as sacred as the other. At the end of the poem it is called the "main artery of the Western world," and Toomer tells us that it represents the spirit of all our people. The American eagle and the achievement of Charles Lindbergh are as important as the address to the "Radiant Incorporeal," the Absolute of the universe. This

Winold Reiss's portrait of Jean Toomer, published in Alain Locke's 1925 anthology, The New Negro *(courtesy of the Schomburg Center for Research in Black Culture, the New York Public Library, Astor, Lenox and Tilden Foundations)*

combination of elements from ancient and modern worlds, technology and the natural environment underscore Toomer's holistic philosophy through which he could finally see himself as fully integrated into the stream of all human life.

In 1932 Toomer married Margery Latimer, a novelist with New England roots, who had joined a Gurdjieff group he led in Portage, Wisconsin, that summer. Less than a year later she died giving birth to their daughter. In 1934 he married Marjorie Content, a New York woman from an upper-class financial and artistic background. They set up their home on a farm in Doylestown, Pennsylvania, where Toomer lived until his death in 1967.

Toomer's active involvement with the Gurdjieff movement lasted until the time of his first marriage, although he continued to follow many of the tenets of the philosophy for the rest of his life. In 1934 he wrote Gurdjieff and noted that while he still believed in his methods, his responsibilities as a father and husband demanded most of his time and energy, and he could no longer be active in

that work. Many of Toomer's later friends believed that he had had ambitions to set up an institute of his own at Doylestown, a replica of the one at Fontainebleau. However, he was never able to secure the funds to carry out such a project.

Toomer did not find the internal harmony he felt so crucial to his happiness and achievement of full potential in the Gurdjieff movement, although that system appears to have given him the greatest encouragement towards that end. By the middle of the 1930s he was once again searching for a new system. In 1939 he took his family to India, on a trip that lasted nine months. There he conferred with gurus and sages, trying to garner the secrets of inner peace. The trip, however, was only another failure in his search, and two unfinished plays, "Columbo Madras Mail" and "Pilgrims, Did You Say?" are the records of his disappointment over the results of that pilgrimage. He returned to America depressed by the poverty and disease he saw in India, and he noted that such marginal living as he observed there made people greedy for the material things they lacked. It drained their spiritual resources.

Although Toomer had severed connections with the writers who had been his friends and colleagues from 1919 to 1923, he had privately continued to write until the middle of the 1940s. He had made many unsuccessful attempts to have his writings published before he finally gave up in discouragement. Among his unpublished manuscripts are several novels, plays, short stories, poems, and autobiographical fragments.

Publishers had rejected Toomer's post-*Cane* works mainly because the style and content of his writing changed drastically after he became an adherent of the Gurdjieff philosophy, and he had given up the aims of art in literature in exchange for the goals of a proselytizer. One of his lifelong friends, Gorham Munson, in an interview in New York City in 1969, said Toomer gave up the beautiful writing he had done in that "wonderful" book, *Cane,* for something that was not beautiful in writing. His later works were largely didactic, tedious, and dull. Furthermore, many intellectuals thought Gurdjieff was a charlatan and an opportunist, and Toomer did not help his own cause by openly championing such a controversial figure.

The Wayward and the Seeking (1980), selections from Toomer's unpublished works edited by Darwin Turner, includes autobiographical works that are among the most interesting of Toomer's papers. Apart from the factual data they provide, Toomer's autobiographies, many in various stages of incompleteness, are also valuable for the insights into Toomer's psyche they provide. "Earth Being," "A New Identity," "On Being American," "Outline of an Autobiography," and "Why I Joined the Gurdjieff Work," all written between 1928 and the early 1940s, offer Toomer's perceptions of his family and his life between 1894 and the late 1920s. As early as 1929 he submitted one draft for publication, and submissions and rejections of various versions are scattered throughout the history of his career.

In selecting the aspects of his life he wished to explore and reveal through these works, Toomer aimed for a portrait that showed his Gurdjieff involvement as the outcome of his evolution from "waking-sleep" to "self-consciousness." When he looked at his early life, he tended to be indulgent and romantic. His descriptions of the various members of his family and of his childhood in Washington are idealistic. At the same time, his voice is authoritative and independent, even in his portrayals of his father whom he never saw, and whose

name had been banned from mention in his grandfather's house. His most interesting portraits are of his grandfather, and it is clear that Toomer both admired and rebelled against the domineering, charismatic P. B. S. Pinchback.

Toomer's use of women as central characters in his imaginative works becomes understandable through his recollections of the two women who figured most prominently in his early life, his mother and grandmother. His insights into the perceptions of women in works like *Cane* and *Natalie Mann* reflect the sympathy he felt for his own mother whose life was full of unhappiness and disappointments at the hands of her father and her two husbands. She was raised to be a lady, and was never allowed to step outside of that role. Toomer identified with her helplessness and unhappiness, and he often successfully expresses the frustrations of living within such limits through the women in his writings. He also perceived quiet strength in his grandmother, noting that the gentleness of her face was deceptive. While her domain was the management of an orderly and well-organized home for her political husband, her strength was a source of support for him throughout his life.

From Toomer's autobiographies we derive the image of a man who perceived a seriousness in human existence that could not be readily understood through the normal process of everyday living. All things in the universe were connected, he knew, and he wanted to understand and ultimately control that matrix of experiences. His autobiographies are engaging and embody a serious attempt on his part to examine and "name" his experiences.

Toomer's unpublished fiction of the period of the later 1920s until the very early 1940s include four full-length novels—"Transatlantic" (written in 1929) revised as "Eight Day World" (1933 or 1934), "Caromb" (written in 1932), "The Gallonwerps" (first written as a play in 1927 and revised as a novel in 1933), and "The Angel Begoria" in 1943.

"Eight Day World," a 436-page work, was Toomer's longest manuscript. It is the fictionalized account of his shipboard experiences on his first trip to Fontainebleau in 1924. For a long time he was convinced that it was his best work, but no one agreed to publish it. The somber "Caromb," made up of letters from Carmel, California, has its genesis in an unpleasant racial incident that Toomer and his first wife experienced there in 1932. He interweaves the physical beauty of the place with the ugliness and dark underside of attitudes toward race in America. "The Gallonwerps" or "Diked" was a work for teaching with Gurdjieff groups. The theme is the power of human suggestibility, showing that Toomer was not against human manipulation in the right circumstances. The central theme in "The Angel Begoria" is the value of religion as a unifying force between man and God. Written during World War II, he saw that America had an opportunity to lead the world in that direction.

Finally, the Toomer manuscript collection at Fisk University contains, among other items, thirteen poems written between 1936 and 1939 which appear to reconcile his beliefs in the spirit of mankind with the spirit of the universe. All are deeply religious. They are invocations through which the poet seeks ways to come closer to the spirit of the universe which is able to cleanse, enlighten, mend, and blend human beings into his being. As supplicator, he wishes to integrate the inner and outer man to achieve a level of consciousness that will link him to cosmic consciousness.

Toomer's distress over his inability to publish his writings or to find internal harmony was further aggravated by failing health as early as in the 1930s. First, he had feelings of general weakness and a lack of energy. He blamed this condition on his lack of internal harmony. For a man who had exhibited a good deal of athletic prowess in his youth and early manhood, this physical failure was particularly difficult for him to bear. What followed was worse. He had a bout with kidney problems, for which he underwent surgery in the 1940s, and he also had trouble with his eyes. During the final years of his life he was often in a nursing home undergoing intensive treatment for these ailments. These were extremely sad times for him. He was a man who was doubly disappointed in his life, and his mental state hastened his physical deterioration. He died on 30 March 1967; the cause was listed as arteriosclerosis.

Toomer's racial ambivalence and his involvement with the Gurdjieff movement must bear most of the burden of his failure to achieve what might well have been a brilliant literary career. Nevertheless *Cane* is a solid achievement. Those who have been aware of his conscious rejection of his role as a leading black writer believe that in so doing he turned away from the promise of fame. But, he rejected the boundaries of blackness because he wanted nothing less than universal identity.

References:

Donald G. Ackley, "Theme and Vision in Jean Toomer's *Cane*," *Studies in Black Literature*, 1 (Spring 1970): 45-65;

Houston Baker, "Journey Toward Black Art: Jean Toomer's *Cane*," in *Singers of Daybreak: Studies in Black American Literature* (Washington, D.C.: Howard University Press, 1975), pp. 53-80;

Bernard Bell, "Jean Toomer's 'Blue Meridian': The Poet as Prophet of a New Order of Man," *Black American Literature Forum*, 14 (Summer 1980): 77-80;

Bell, "A Key to the Poems in *Cane*," *CLA Journal*, 14 (March 1971): 251-258;

Brian Joseph Benson and Mabel Mayle Dillard, *Jean Toomer* (Boston: Twayne, 1980);

Robert Bone, "Jean Toomer," in his *The Negro Novel in America* (New Haven: Yale University Press, 1958);

Arna Bontemps, *The Harlem Renaissance Remembered* (New York: Dodd, Mead, 1972);

Bontemps, "The Negro Renaissance: Jean Toomer and the Harlem Writers of the 1920's," in *Anger and Beyond: The Negro Writer in the United States,* edited by Herbert Hill (New York: Harper & Row, 1966), pp. 20-36;

Patricia Chase, "The Women in *Cane*," *CLA Journal*, 14 (March 1971): 259-273;

Bowie Duncan, "Jean Toomer's *Cane*: A Modern Black Oracle," *CLA Journal*, 15 (March 1972): 323-333;

Frank Durham, *Studies in Cane* (Columbus, Ohio: Merrill, 1971);

W. Edward Farrison, "Jean Toomer's *Cane* Again," *CLA Journal*, 15 (March 1972): 295-302;

William C. Fischer, "The Aggregate Man in Jean Toomer's *Cane*," *Studies in the Novel*, 3 (Summer 1971): 190-215;

S. P. Fullinwider, "Jean Toomer: Lost Generation or Negro Renaissance?," *Phylon*, 27 (Fourth Quarter 1966): 396-403;

William J. Goede, "Jean Toomer's Ralph Kabnis: Portrait of the Negro Artist As a Young Man," *Phylon*, 30 (Spring 1969): 72-85;

Sister Mary Kathryn Grant, "Images of Celebration in *Cane*," *Negro American Literature Forum*, 5 (1971): 32-34, 36;

Eugene Holmes, "Jean Toomer—Apostle of Beauty," *Opportunity*, 10 (August 1932): 252-254, 260;

Catherine L. Innes, "The Unity of Jean Toomer's *Cane*," *CLA Journal*, 15 (March 1972): 306-322;

James Kraft, "Jean Toomer's *Cane*," *Markham Review*, 2 (October 1970): 61-63;

Michael J. Krasny, "Design in Jean Toomer's 'Balo,'" *Negro American Literature Forum,* 7 (Fall 1973): 103-106;

Todd Lieber, "Design and Movement in *Cane,*" *CLA Journal,* 13 (September 1969): 35-50;

Alain Locke, *Four Negro Poets* (New York: Simon & Schuster, 1927);

Clifford Mason, "Jean Toomer's Authenticity," *Black World,* 20 (January 1971): 70-76;

Nellie McKay, *Jean Toomer: Artist* (Chapel Hill: University of North Carolina Press, 1984);

Gorham Munson, "The Significance of Jean Toomer," *Opportunity,* 3 (1925): 262-263;

C. W. Scruggs, "Mark of Cain and the Redemption of Art: A Study in Theme and Structure of Jean Toomer's *Cane,*" *American Literature,* 44 (May 1972): 276-291;

Marion L. Stein, "The Poet-Observer and 'Fern' in Jean Toomer's *Cane,*" *Markham Review,* 2 (October 1970): 64-65;

Darwin T. Turner, "And Another Passing," *Negro American Literature Forum* (Fall 1967): 3-4;

Turner, "The Failure of a Playwright," *CLA Journal,* 10 (June 1967): 303-318;

Turner, "Jean Toomer: Exile," in his *In A Minor Chord: Three Afro-American Writers and Their Search for Identity* (Carbondale: Southern Illinois University Press, 1971), pp. 1-59;

Turner, "Jean Toomer's *Cane*; Critical Analysis," *Negro Digest,* 18 (January 1969): 54-61;

Jean Wagner, "Jean Toomer," in his *Black Poets of the United States,* translated by Kenneth Douglas (Urbana: University of Illinois Press, 1973).

Papers:

Toomer's manuscript collection, at the Fisk University Archives, includes several novels, plays, a large number of poems and short stories, and a half dozen versions and fragments of autobiographical writings.

Waters Edward Turpin
(9 April 1910-19 November 1968)

Burney Hollis
Morgan State University

BOOKS: *These Low Grounds* (New York & London: Harper, 1937);

O Canaan! (New York: Doubleday, Doran, 1939);

The Rootless (New York: Vantage Press, 1957);

Basic Skills for Better Writing, by Turpin and Nick Aaron Ford (New York: Putnam's, 1959);

Extending Horizons, by Turpin and Ford (New York: Random House, 1969).

PLAY PRODUCTIONS: *Let the Day Perish*, Baltimore, Morgan State College, 21 March 1950;

Saint Michaels Dawn, Baltimore, Little Theatre, Christian Center, Morgan State College, 2 May 1956;

Li'l Joe, Baltimore, Chick Webb Memorial Recreation Center, Dunbar High School, 11 May 1957.

PERIODICAL PUBLICATIONS:

FICTION

"Old Tom," *Morgan State College Bulletin*, 1 (January 1935): 14-22;

"The Homing," *Morgan State College Bulletin*, 1 (June 1935): 11-16.

NONFICTION

"Evaluating the Work of the Contemporary Negro Novelist," *Negro History Bulletin*, 11 (December 1947): 59-60;

"Major Problems of the Negro Writer," *Morgan State College Bulletin*, 15 (March 1949): 6-9;

"The Bedeviled South," review of *The White Band* by Carter Brooke Jones, *Phylon* (Spring 1960): 98-99;

"Elegy, Suburbia North," review of *First Family* by Christopher Davis, *Phylon*, 22 (Fall 1961): 59-60;

"Faulkner's 'Twin Evils,'" review of *Faulkner and the Negro* by Charles H. Nilon, *Phylon*, 24 (1963): 180-181;

"Contemporary American Negro Playwright," *CLA Journal*, 9 (September 1965): 12-24;

"A New and Relevant Mode," review of *The Broken World of Tennessee Williams* by Esther Merle

Waters Edward Turpin

Jackson, *CLA Journal*, 11 (September 1965): 94-97.

POETRY

"Of Nativity," *Morgan State College Bulletin*, 1 (March 1935): 22.

When he was writing his first novel in the mid 1930s, Waters Edward Turpin declared, through one of his major characters, what was to become the central philosophy of the four novels, two plays, and other minor pieces he was to write during the next three decades. The character clearly reflects Turpin's personal convictions when he avers that he wants to

. . . tap the untouched literary material offered by that little-known section of the American scene, the Eastern Shore of Maryland . . . to put into [my] novel form the life of . . . [my] family—all about . . . [my] grandmother and grandfather, and their parents, a sort of Saga of Achievement . . . [to see myself] as just another American . . . [with something] glorious in . . . [my] past and . . . hopeful in . . . [the] future.

Such a statement of purpose suggests accurately for Turpin the roles of historical novelist, regionalist, family chronicler, and mythopoet. It suggests his intention to generate a cultural mythos which brings about a greater appreciation for the achievements of American blacks. When one adds to these observations the role of literary sociologist, which Turpin assumed at the midpoint of his literary career, one concludes that Turpin, perhaps more than any other black writer of the 1930s and 1940s, accepted the challenge to black writers to develop a collective consciousness of racial history and to employ it as the basis for literature. Prior to Alex Haley, Turpin was the most significant black family chronicler.

Turpin was born in 1910 in Oxford, Maryland, a small peninsular town whose economy was based on seasonal work in the fields and in oyster and crab harvesting houses. The town is only a few miles north of Harriet Tubman's home and nearly the same distance south of the plantation on which Frederick Douglass struck his first blow for freedom. Proximity to these two legends gave Turpin an early appreciation for black freedom fighters and even for those among his contemporaries who could rise above the misery and squalor of Oxford and emerge with a semblance of integrity and achievement.

Turpin was inspired by his maternal ancestors and the distinction which they had earned over the years. He was especially proud of his maternal grandfather, Thomas Lambert Waters, who boasted that neither he nor his parents had ever been anybody's slaves and that he had risen over the years to be a successful and enviable farmer, dredge-boat owner, church founder, and community leader, referred to by blacks and whites as "Cap'n Tom." Turpin's grandfather told the boy many tales of Eastern Shore black men who fought and died for their freedom—the stuff of which legends are made. Turpin's mother, Mary Rebecca Henry, who had abandoned her hopes for an ed-

ucation and worked single-handedly to ensure a good one for him, epitomized for him the role played by the black woman in the survival of the family and the race.

Turpin's family moved to New Jersey in 1922. There he encountered the novelist Edna Ferber who influenced his early development as a writer. Turpin's mother began to work in Ferber's Park Avenue penthouse in the 1920s. There she occupied a small apartment, was household manager and cook, and often invited Waters, whom she sent to Morgan Academy in Baltimore for his high school education, to work with her on holidays and some weekends. Ferber adopted Turpin as a literary apprentice, gave him access to her library, and discussed with him her current writing projects. Turpin detected the absence in her writing of black achievers whom he saw as equivalent to the American white frontier pioneers about whom she was writing. His acquaintance with Ferber and the editors, publishers, and writers to whom she introduced him fueled his growing determination to tell the story of black pioneers, no less valiant, adventuresome, or successful than those whom Ferber had immortalized in *So Big*, *Show Boat*, *Cimarron*, and *American Beauty*. Ferber encouraged him to do so.

When Turpin moved to New York City in 1931, following his graduation from Morgan College, he enrolled at Columbia University in pursuit of a master's degree. He was seriously entertaining the idea of a writing career. Living in New York in the wake of the Harlem Renaissance reminded Turpin of the urgent need for young black writers to take up the challenge of carrying on a worthy literary tradition, and, to a certain degree, of compensating for the exhibitionism which was often promoted in that period by such mentors as Carl Van Vechten. Those early New York Depression years, during which Turpin worked for meager wages, motivated him to present candidly the misunderstood and neglected plight of his people. Finally the infamous lynching in Salisbury, Maryland, not far from his place of birth, in December of 1931, put fire under his growing realization that blacks were exploited, mistreated, misunderstood, and unappreciated in American life and literature. The "saga of achievement" over which he had pondered during his Morgan years seemed all the more urgent.

In 1931, after a brief apprenticeship as a short story writer, Turpin began to write his first novel. Between working, attending class, and intermittently writing short sketches and poems about his

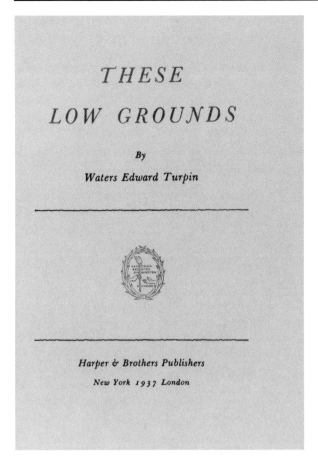

THESE
LOW GROUNDS

By

Waters Edward Turpin

Harper & Brothers Publishers
New York 1937 London

Title page for Turpin's first novel

Harlem experiences and the Maryland lowlands, Turpin worked on the novel. By 1934, having completed his master's degree in English at Columbia and having begun to work for the WPA, he began to search for an audience for his work. He sent three pieces to Morgan College, and they were published and lauded in the *Morgan College Bulletin* in 1935. Encouraged by the Morgan reception, Turpin pressed forward on the novel, but, with inadequate monies coming in from his WPA job as a welfare investigator, he also began to look for a teaching position. In September 1935 he joined the faculty of Storer College in Harper's Ferry, West Virginia, and there was able to complete his novel by the spring of 1936. When Turpin showed the novel to Ferber, she was very pleased and arranged for the manuscript to be sent to Harper. Harper liked the novel and agreed to publish it in the fall of 1937. *These Low Grounds* appeared with an endorsement by Ferber on its jacket: "A fine and important book, dramatic and exciting. Possibly the outstanding negro [*sic*] novel of our day."

These Low Grounds was the first installment on Turpin's "saga of achievement." It is a chronicle of four generations of the family of Martha, a slave whose freedom is secured by the Civil War. Her descendants overcome a few racial and many intraracial obstacles and climb the social ladder from slave to domestic worker to farmer and finally to teacher, between the outbreak of the Civil War and the 1930s. Although the setting shifts to Baltimore, Philadelphia, and New York, the major action of the novel is centered on the Eastern Shore of Maryland, where three generations of the Prince family struggle to build a family. Though "sin and sorrow" are obstacles to their success, the central issue of the novel is the inability of black manhood to prevail over the circumstances which force the black woman into the role of matriarch. At the same time, however, it is an encomium to the perseverance of the black woman as family head and pioneer. In *These Low Grounds* Turpin strives to create epic, legendary figures.

These Low Grounds was enthusiastically received by critics, both black and white, and *Crisis* encouraged sales by offering the novel at a special discount along with an annual subscription to the magazine. Such acceptance by the literary community was welcome, for, by the fall of 1937, Turpin had already made plans for his second novel and the extension of his career as writer. Back in the summer of 1936 he had driven to Chicago to conduct research on the black pioneers who migrated to that city in the second decade of the century. Along with Jean Fisher, whom he had married in 1936, he had interviewed blacks, visited churches and dives, read in old newspapers, consulted with the Urban League, and listened to accounts of the happy migration from small southern towns to the great city which many envisioned as the Canaan of the North. Turpin had sensed that here, too, had been Afro-American pioneers worthy of the saga that he had projected and intimated in *These Low Grounds*. When he returned to Storer College in the fall of 1937, Turpin began to write the novel which he was to call *O Canaan!*

As Turpin worked on *O Canaan!* during the 1937-1938 academic year, he was mindful not only of the praise of his critics but also of their objection to the overly ambitious scope of his first novel—its having attempted to trace rather sketchily four generations of a family in the confines of 350 pages. He therefore limited the scale of *O Canaan!* and concentrated on more detailed limning of characters. Though it was difficult to find adequate time to write while he was teaching and coaching football at Storer, Turpin worked steadily throughout the fall semester and sped up a bit during the spring. By the end of the academic year, he decided to return to Columbia in the fall to work toward an Ed.D. and spent the intervening summer completing his second novel. In the fall he submitted it, this time without Ferber's assistance, to Doubleday, Doran, which agreed to publish the novel in June 1939.

O Canaan! carries the same themes explored in *These Low Grounds.* However, in *O Canaan!* Turpin turns from the blacks on southern farms to those attempting to survive in the sprawling urban metropolis. Its major focus is the great exodus of blacks from places like Three Forks, Mississippi, to the more promising terrain of the north; the prosperity Chicago pioneers experienced as they built up the south side of Chicago; the temporary but debilitating effects of the Depression on their lives; and finally their strong-willed determination to rebound from their economic plight. The Benson and Prince families of *O Canaan!*, like the Princes of *These Low Grounds,* encounter obstacles that only a giant of primordial strength (like Joe Benson) can withstand; and they also witness the ascendance of the black woman as an equal in the struggle for equality and economic sufficiency. The heroes of *O Canaan!* are of mythical and biblical stature, and, more than a family chronicle, the novel is a black odyssey with a hero whose fighting spirit is equal to that of Ulysses.

O Canaan! was also well received by the literary community, though most critics conceded that it did not quite measure up to the quality of *These Low Grounds,* and Turpin was rightfully proclaimed the father of the Afro-American family chronicle.

By the time *O Canaan!* was published, Turpin had conceived of and begun to execute one of the most ambitious and far-reaching plans ever to be conceived by an Afro-American author prior to Alex Haley's *Roots.* It was almost as though he had accepted literally the "New Challenge" that Richard Wright had made as a "Blueprint for Negro Writing" two years earlier. Wright had argued that theme would emerge in Afro-American literature only when black writers were able to feel the "meaning of their history as a race as though they in one lifetime had lived it themselves throughout the long centuries." Actually Turpin had sensed the need to reexamine the Afro-American past before Wright issued his manifesto, but it was not until about 1939 that he began to lay definite plans for writing an extensive family saga of five novels that

would examine Afro-American history by focusing on one single family and tracing it back to its slave roots.

The pentology that Turpin envisioned would consist of his two published novels and three others: "But the Earth Remains," *The Rootless,* and "The Unwanted," to be written in that order. "But the Earth Remains" would focus on the free Maryland black prior to the Emancipation Proclamation, *The Rootless* would dwell on the slave of the Revolutionary period, and "The Unwanted" would be a novel set in the 1930s. Turpin intended to follow his pentology with a series of four plays, and he had hoped that his grand scheme might be initiated by a period of intensive and extensive research in the southern United States, Africa, and the West Indies.

To bring so ambitious a plan to fruition, Turpin needed the opportunity to work at it on a full-time basis, with a steady income to sustain him. During the 1939-1940 year at Columbia he applied for fellowships and research grants, but, none having been awarded him, he accepted another teaching position at Lincoln University in Pennsylvania.

Turpin's nine-year teaching term at Lincoln was to witness the flowering of his career as a writer; unfortunately, it was a flowering that did not receive public recognition. During those years one excellent play and two very good novels (one finished and one left incomplete) were written, but none of them was to be published during the 1940s.

During the winter months of 1940, while awaiting replies from fellowship applications, Turpin worked on a play which he had begun the previous semester at Columbia. The play marked a significant departure from the rather romantic optimism of his first two novels, just as it was a temporary suspension of the work on his pentology. It essentially grew out of his plan to relive the Afro-American experience through literature, but its emphasis was upon frustration, defeat, and failure rather than the achievement underscored in his two novels.

He called the play *Let the Day Perish,* and the parallels between it and the biblical story of Job are crucial and striking. The play, which is a precursor of Hansberry's *A Raisin in the Sun* (1959), dwells on the socioeconomic troubles of a Harlem family during the Depression. Its sharpest focus is on how the black man is emasculated, how the black woman is forced into matriarchy and the role of domestic worker, and how religion and the hard-work ethic fail to sustain the Branson family during times of economic trouble. Although the play ends with the indefatigable resolution to endure, the optimism of the earlier pieces is absent. In this play Turpin turned somewhat from his mythopoetic saga of achievement, and the hero of the play is characterized much like Wright's Bigger Thomas.

In the spring of 1941 Turpin was awarded the Rosenwald Fellowship in creative writing; and, in the summer, having taken leave from Lincoln, he returned to the Eastern Shore of Maryland to do research for the third novel of his pentology. However, his research did not lead to the writing of "But the Earth Remains" (a rather optimistic, pastoral title) as he had planned. Instead, upon his return to Lincoln, he began to compose *The Rootless* (a title more reflective of his feelings during the period), the one novel over which he was to agonize the longest and with the greatest intensity. It is not quite clear when composition of this novel was completed, but evidence confirms that he finished it long before leaving Lincoln in 1949 and suggests strongly that it belongs to the same five- or six-year period when Turpin leaned in the direction of social criticism.

The Rootless traces the Prince family of *These Low Grounds* and *O Canaan!* back to the Annapolis slave ship, where a Coramantee man-child is born during debarkation. The novel follows his growth into manhood and the development of his determination to live a free man or die struggling to become one. More important, however, *The Rootless* follows very closely the gradual deterioration of three generations of Maryland slaveowners and focuses on the lust and power hunger of two of them—Louisa and Mariah Shannon. The novel is Turpin's most strident piece of social criticism, and it debunks, without apology or maudlin sentimentality, the myth of the purity of the southern belle. *The Rootless* is certainly a much more powerful novel than *These Low Grounds* or *O Canaan!*, and it seems to achieve a workable balance between the two impulses—mythmaking and social criticism—which, in the early 1940s, were vying for prominence in Turpin's canon.

The picture is not at all clear as to the extent of Turpin's efforts at getting *The Rootless* published—whether the manuscript was rejected by publishing houses or whether he himself thought it too strong a piece of protest to be considered seriously by white publishers. Whatever the case may have been, without publishing *The Rootless,* Turpin, in the last two or three years of the 1940s, began to write another novel, remarkably different in tone and perspective from *The Rootless;* and he seemed, in writing it, to move back toward the

mythmaking of the earlier works and away from the abrasive social criticism of his more recent pieces.

Instead of completing the pentology he originally projected, Turpin became very interested in the subject of black matriarchy and the black domestic worker, both of which had been strong currents in all of his works. Perhaps because of his reflections on his mother's long tenure as both matriarch and domestic worker before her retirement from Ferber's household in 1948, Turpin came, somewhat reluctantly, to admit that the black woman had been a steadier support for the black family than the man. In a speech before the Association for the Study of Negro Life and History in 1947, Turpin praised the black woman for having "a fibre of integrity and strength" that was responsible for "the magnificent matriarch's role that has been hers in the survival pattern of the American Negro to the present." With the purpose of exploring in detail the ascendancy of the black woman as family head, Turpin put in abeyance his plans for "But the Earth Remains" and "The Unwanted" and began to write a novel which he called, at first, "The Matriarch" and, later, "Long Way Home." By the time that he left Lincoln in 1949, he had completed two sections of the four-part novel.

Although "Long Way Home" was never to be completed, it is a novel with considerable thematic and technical integrity and shows promise of being Turpin's best novel. It focuses, more clearly than any of his other novels, on the life of a single character, Ella Winters, and follows her reluctant and unwilling acceptance of the dual role of head of the family and domestic worker. In many respects, the novel is the portrait of a lady, and it digs deep into the psychology of the black woman, destroying the myth of her happy, almost natural inclination toward motherhood—in her own family and the families of her white employers. Moreover, like Hurston and contemporary female authors, Turpin links the black woman to the theme of the suspended runner so dominant in literature about black men.

Turpin left Lincoln in 1949 to join the faculty of Morgan State College. He was on the brink of becoming an excellent novelist and playwright. In his possession he had a strong, researched, and historically accurate novel about slavery; an exciting play about the Depression years unlike anything written by blacks to that date; an unfinished novel begging for completion; and an incomplete pentology which promised to be the most comprehensive treatment of the Afro-American experience to be witnessed in the history of American belles lettres.

In the course of his nearly two decades at Morgan, Turpin was never able to find the time necessary to finish "Long Way Home." Instead, he either resumed or initiated efforts at gaining exposure for works already written or resigned himself to composing shorter pieces. His academic and creative interests also turned more toward drama than the novel. First he showed *Let the Day Perish* to his colleague and playwright Arthur C. Lamb, and Lamb arranged to perform the play during the spring 1950 semester. Then he gave the manuscript of *The Rootless* to English department chairman Nick Aaron Ford, who wrote an unpublished review of it. Ford's frank, but discouraging, comments on the publishing prospects for the novel were a disappointment for Turpin: however, he remained steadfast in his determination to see the novel in print without compromising its contents.

Whether out of disappointment at Ford's evaluation or enthusiasm over the reception of *Let the Day Perish*, it is not clear, but Turpin then began work on a two-act play on the adolescent years of his fellow Eastern Shoreman Frederick Douglass. The first draft of the play, *Saint Michaels Dawn*, was completed early in 1953, but for the next three

years Turpin worked intermittently at revising it. When the play was finished in 1956, Lamb directed its Morgan premiere. *Saint Michaels Dawn* was apparently written with haste, for it is an unpolished piece. In comparison to *Let the Day Perish*, it was profound in neither theme nor characterization, and it was not at all an improvement over Douglass's own *Narrative*, on which it was based. The characters and actions were stereotypes, the dialogue rather mediocre, and the sequence of action not plausible. Although the play did not show growth for Turpin, it was an echo of the themes prominent in his earlier works. It shared with *The Rootless*, for example, the words and spirit of Sheridan's *The Columbian Orator:* "Hereditary bondsman, know you this: who would be free, themselves must strike the blow!"

By the time that *Saint Michaels Dawn* was finished and performed, Turpin had grown restless about efforts at publishing *The Rootless*. For some time the novel had been with a New York agency in search of a publisher—with no success. By the end of 1956 Turpin decided to publish the book himself. He was hopeful that public reaction to the book would prove the misgivings of publishers wrong. While awaiting the publication of *The Rootless* by Vantage Press, Turpin wrote a libretto called *Li'l Joe*; the music was written by Herman Scwartz

Waters Turpin and Nick Aaron Ford

of the Baltimore Institute of Art. The work was orchestrated by Morgan's R. Hayes Strider. The resulting opera was performed at an area high school in May, and *The Rootless* appeared in June of 1957.

Largely because of circumstances surrounding all vanity publications, *The Rootless* did not generate the strong currents for which Turpin had hoped. Its circulation was greatly limited, and some critics met it with obstinate rejection. Some few, however, like J. Welfred Holmes of Morgan's faculty, recognized the genuine merits of the novel and lamented the social myopia that doomed it to failure before it was published. The refusal of the Enoch Pratt Free Library in Baltimore to put the book in circulation was a microcosm of the cultural prejudice rampant in America in the 1950s.

The failure of *The Rootless* did not quite extinguish Turpin's literary flame. He was still determined to complete his five-novel saga; but somehow his collaborations with Ford, his work in drama, and the demands of his students absorbed so much of his energy and time that his own writing career became secondary. It is ironic and telling that, at the time of his death in 1968, Turpin was working frantically, not on his own novels, but on Jerome Dyson Wright's *Poor, Black and in Real Trouble,* which he was editing and helping Wright to publish.

Turpin's legacy was not so much his accomplishments as a writer; rather it was his vision as an artist and his significant role as progenitor of the Afro-American saga.

References:

Sterling Brown, *The Negro in American Fiction* (Washington, D.C.: Associates in Negro Folk Education, 1937);

Nick Aaron Ford, *Black Insights: Significant Literature by Black Americans—1769 to the Present* (Waltham, Mass.: Ginn, 1971);

Ford, "Tribute to Waters Turpin," *CLA Journal,* 7 (March 1969): 281-282;

Ford, "Waters Turpin As Social Critic," *Middle-Atlantic Writers Association Review,* 41 (Spring 1982): 3-6;

Ford, "Waters Turpin: I Knew Him Well," *CLA Journal,* 21 (September 1977): 1-18;

Hugh M. Gloster, *Negro Voices in American Fiction* (Chapel Hill: University of North Carolina Press, 1948);

Burney J. Hollis, " 'From a Well of Gloom Deep Within': Black Matriarchy in Turpin's *Let the Day Perish* and *Long Way Home,*" in *Swords Upon This Hill: Preserving the Literary Tradition of Black Colleges and Universities,* edited by Hollis (Baltimore: Morgan State University Press, 1984);

Hollis, "A Genesis for the Afro-American Family Saga: The Life and Works of Waters E. Turpin," *Middle-Atlantic Writers Association Review,* 1 (Spring 1982): 1, 7-10;

Hollis, "The Race and the Runner: Female Fugitives in the Novels of Waters Turpin and Sarah Wright," in *Amid Visions and Revisions: Poetry and Essays on Literature and the Arts,* edited by Hollis (Baltimore: Morgan State University Press, 1985);

Hollis, "Waters E. Turpin—Morgan Man of Letters," *Outreach: A Creative Writers Journal,* 1 (Spring 1979): 1-2;

Henry Lee Moon, "*These Low Grounds* by Waters Edward Turpin," *Crisis,* 44 (December 1937): 379-380;

"Negropings," *Time,* 30 (20 September 1937): 71;

Ralph Reckley, "Female Voices in Turpin's *These Low Grounds* and *The Rootless,*" *Middle-Atlantic Writers Association Review,* 1 (Spring 1982): 11-15;

Noel Schraufnagel, *The Black American Novel: From Apology to Protest* (De Land, Fla.: Everett/Edwards, 1973);

Augusta Tucker, "A Distinguished Novel of Negroes in Maryland," *New York Times,* 26 September 1937, p. 6;

Richard Wright, "Introduction: Blueprint for Negro Writing," *New Challenge,* 2 (Fall 1937): 1-3.

Papers:

Turpin's manuscripts, as well as documents gathered from records at Storer College, Lincoln University, Pennsylvania, Morgan State College, the Guggenheim Foundation, and Dr. Jean Fisher Turpin, are collected in the Waters Edward Turpin Collection at Morgan State University.

Eric Walrond
(1898-1966)

Jay R. Berry
University of Iowa

BOOK: *Tropic Death* (New York: Boni & Liveright, 1926).

OTHER: "City Love," in *The American Caravan*, edited by Van Wyck Brooks, et al. (New York: Macaulay, 1927), pp. 485-493.

PERIODICAL PUBLICATIONS:
FICTION
"On Being Black," *New Republic*, 32 (November 1922): 244-246;

"On Being a Domestic," *Opportunity*, 1 (August 1923): 234;

"Miss Kenny's Marriage," *Smart Set*, 72 (September 1923): 73-80;

"The Stone Rebounds," *Opportunity*, 1 (September 1923): 277-278;

"Cynthia Goes to the Prom," *Opportunity*, 1 (November 1923): 342-343;

"Vignettes of the Dusk," *Opportunity*, 2 (January 1924): 19-20;

"A Cholo Romance," *Opportunity*, 2 (June 1924): 177-181;

"The Voodoo's Revenge," *Opportunity*, 3 (July 1925): 209-213.

NONFICTION
"The New Negro Faces America," *Current History*, 17 (February 1923): 786-788;

"The Negro Exodus from the South," *Current History*, 18 (September 1923): 942-944;

"The Black City," *Messenger*, 6 (January 1924): 13-14;

"Imperator Africanus, Marcus Garvey: Menace or Promise?," *Independent*, 114 (January 1925): 8-11.

Eric Walrond was one of the more important literary figures associated with the Harlem Renaissance of the 1920s. A protégé of Charles S. Johnson, the Urban League's national director of research and investigations and editor of *Opportunity* magazine, Walrond made an auspicious literary debut in 1926 with the publication of *Tropic Death*. Indeed the critical reception of this collection of ten stories rivaled that of Jean Toomer's *Cane*. Both works were regarded as examples of avant-garde writing. Even the conservative and socially minded critic W. E. B. Du Bois admitted that *Tropic Death* was "a human document of deep significance and great promise." The stories impressionistically record the cycles of life and death, cultural disorientation, racial conflict, imperialism, and economic hardship in the American tropics. Although Walrond published no other book-length literary works, he did publish short stories and journalistic sketches throughout the early and mid 1920s. But it is for the stories in *Tropic Death*, and his contributions to the Harlem Renaissance, that Eric Walrond should be remembered and studied.

Eric Walrond was born in Georgetown, British Guiana, in 1898, the son of a Barbadian mother and a Guyanese father. He spent the first eight years of his life in Guiana. His parents' marital problems soon led Walrond into an almost nomadic existence. In 1906, after his father deserted them, Walrond and his mother moved to a small village in Barbados to live with her relatives. In Barbados Walrond began his education at St. Stephen's Boys' School, located in Black Rock. Several years later (probably about 1910), Walrond and his mother traveled in search of his father to the Panama Canal Zone, where thousands of West Indians and Guyanese were employed to dig the canal. The attempt at reconciliation proved unsuccessful, and Walrond and his mother settled in Colón. There Walrond completed his public and secondary school education between 1913 and 1916, becoming bilingual and "thoroughly exposed to Spanish culture." This experience served him well when he wrote the stories collected in *Tropic Death*. He was trained as a secretary and stenographer, and he soon acquired a job as a clerk in the Health Department of the Canal Commission at Cristobal. Between 1916 and 1918 Walrond began a journalistic career that he would pursue during his residence in the United States. He worked as a general reporter, court reporter, and sportswriter for the Panama *Star-Her-*

ald, "the most important contemporaneous newspaper in the American tropics."

In 1918, at the age of twenty, Walrond migrated to New York, where he lived for the next decade. He initially attempted to secure employment on the various Harlem newspapers. When these efforts proved unsuccessful he decided to continue his education at the City College of New York. He attended City College for the next three years and Columbia University for one year, where he took creative writing courses. Walrond held a number of jobs during this time to support himself. His clerical and secretarial experience enabled him to secure employment as a stenographer in the British Recruiting Mission as secretary to a local architect and as secretary to the superintendent of the Broad Street Hospital. Walrond's search for secretarial positions brought him sharply into contact with racism and discrimination in America, and these experiences are documented in his early writings.

Until he arrived in the United States, Walrond's experience with racial prejudice and bigotry was very limited. His early stories illustrate his profound disillusionment and disgust with race relations in America. The bitterness of the tone of "On Being Black" (*New Republic,* 1922), his first story published in America, best reflects his disillusionment. The story effectively presents Walrond's personal encounters with racial discrimination in three spheres of activity: consumerism (when he attempts to purchase a pair of goggles to keep dust out of his eyes the shopkeeper assumes he is a chauffeur because he is black), employment (his applications for secretarial jobs are routinely turned down because he is black), and recreation/leisure (he is humiliated by white travel agents when he attempts to book passage on a steamship for a vacation cruise). These experiences heightened his awareness of the need for racial solidarity and may help to explain his later interest in Marcus Garvey's back-to-Africa movement.

Walrond finally acquired a newspaper job in 1921. He became an owner and editor of the *Brooklyn and Long Island Informer* and held the position until 1923, when he became affiliated with Garvey's political and social organization—the Universal Negro Improvement Association. Walrond's bitterness over American racism, coupled with his high but short-lived estimation of Marcus Garvey as a political leader, attracted him to the UNIA. Garvey put Walrond's journalistic talents to good use by making him an associate editor of *Negro World,* the association's weekly newspaper.

In addition to his editorial duties, Walrond wrote articles for various periodicals and journals. All of the articles focus upon aspects of Afro-American life. In "The Negro Exodus from the South" (*Current History,* 1923), he examines the effects of the migration of blacks from the rural South to the urban centers in the North. This article was followed by "The Black City" (*Messenger,* 1924), an essay on Harlem, and "Imperator Africanus, Marcus Garvey: Menace or Promise?" (*Independent,* 1925), an essay that attempts to explain Marcus Garvey's popularity among blacks despite his embarrassing business failures and his political naivete (partially manifested in his affection for pomp and showmanship).

Walrond's most significant article, however, is "The New Negro Faces America" (*Current History,* 1923). In it he critiques three major black leaders and their philosophies and also expresses his opinions of the New Negro movement. Walrond dismisses Booker T. Washington and his followers as representing "old style leadership . . . that believes, like Christ, in 'turning the other cheek.'" He criticizes Du Bois and the NAACP for seeking only "adequate political representation" as the solution to blacks' problems and views Du Bois as having a superiority complex that leaves him alienated from the black masses. Garvey is perceived to possess the greatest leadership potential. He is a man of the people, his UNIA is international in scope, and he has a conscious awareness of Africa. Yet he is also a lover of pomp and theatrics, characteristics that work against him. "The rank and file of Negroes are opposed to Garveyism; dissatisfied with the personal vituperation and morbid satire of Mr. Du Bois; and prone to discount Major Moton's Tuskegee as a monument of respectable reaction." The development of an effective black leadership, Walrond argues, is essential to the survival of the New Negro movement. What are some of the characteristics of the New Negro?

> In the first place he is race conscious. He does not want to be like the white man. He is coming to realize the great possibilities within himself, and his tendency is to develop those possibilities. He is looking toward a broader leadership. . . . The new negro, who does not want to go back to Africa, is fondly cherishing an ideal—and that is, that the time will come when America will look upon the negro not as a savage with an inferior mentality, but as a civilized man. . . . He is pinning everything on the hope, illusion or not, that America will some day find its soul, forget

the Negro's black skin, and recognize him as one of the nation's most loyal sons and defenders.

"The New Negro Faces America" clearly illuminates Walrond's criticisms of the major black leaders, as well as his theoretical position on the role and destiny of the New Negro in American culture.

Essays such as "The New Negro Faces America" illustrate Walrond's growing dissatisfaction with the Garvey program. He soon left the UNIA and *Negro World* for a more active involvement in the New Negro movement, also known as the Harlem Renaissance. Charles S. Johnson, aware of Walrond's journalistic experience, immediately hired him at *Opportunity*, the official publication of the Urban League and very supportive of the Harlem Renaissance. Its most important functions in this regard were providing a forum for young writers and artists and sponsoring literary contests to encourage the production of art.

Walrond's involvement in the Harlem Renaissance also had a literary side. It was during the early 1920s that he began publishing short stories in periodicals as diverse as *Opportunity*, *Smart Set*, and *Vanity Fair*. His serious commitment to short fiction began in 1923 with the publication of four stories: "On Being a Domestic" (*Opportunity*, 1923), "Miss Kenny's Marriage" (*Smart Set*, 1923), "The Stone Rebounds" (*Opportunity*, 1923), and "Cynthia Goes to the Prom" (*Opportunity*, 1923). These stories clearly indicate that Walrond was experimenting with narrative voices, language, and points of view, trying to find an effective and appropriate narrative style.

"On Being a Domestic" is a semidocumentary story that recounts Walrond's experiences as a domestic worker in a large hotel. It effectively juxtaposes his excitement at being in the United States with the realities of racism in America. There are times when he rises above reality to "sip of the atmospheric wine," only to be brought down to earth again by a white woman saying, "I don't want to be alone in the room with you while you're cleaning up," or an impatient woman yelling at Walrond to remove his cleaning bucket from her room: "There it is! Come and get it—you coon!" Walrond reacts to this situation with a bitterness similar to that which permeates "On Being Black."

The first substantial story Walrond published was entitled "Miss Kenny's Marriage." It is a character study of a woman "who invites disaster by marrying a man of twenty-five." Miss Kenny is the middle-aged owner of a hair parlor in Brooklyn,

where she has become fairly wealthy through the sales of Madame Kenny's Tar Hair Grower and Madame Kenny's Glossine. She is a person given to putting on airs of superiority, but when she courts and finally marries a man much younger than herself, she is effectively punished when he withdraws all of the money in her savings account and leaves town. "Miss Kenny's Marriage" bears the marks of an early story. Walrond's style was still maturing and thus the prose seems somewhat awkward and forced. At times the prose is downright florid: "There came a time, however, when fate blew harsh and stormy winds to Miss Kenny's gates." "Miss Kenny's Marriage" is more interesting for its treatment of cultural assimilation than for its rather awkward prose style.

Walrond returned to his concern with racial prejudice in his next story, "The Stone Rebounds." Here he assumes the persona of a white writer who has been ostracized by his colleagues for bringing a black playwright to an all-white literary gathering. Later in the story the black playwright is implicitly and indirectly criticized by his black friends for bringing the white writer into a Harlem cabaret. The theme of racial prejudice also permeates "Cynthia Goes to the Prom." This story focuses upon a young black woman who wants to attend the high school prom. Cynthia, who is quite popular among whites at school, is unwilling to believe that prejudice exists in her social world. Many of her black friends, however, do not share her optimistic outlook; most of them refuse to go to the "white folks' ball." The nameless narrator accompanies Cynthia and several other black couples to the dance, only to receive a quick but thorough introduction to racial prejudice. The hotel orderly at first refuses to direct the couples to the prom; the coat check woman tells the black women that all of the hooks have been taken and that their coats will have to be placed on the floor; the guests treat them as freaks on display; and Cynthia's high school "friends" refuse to acknowledge her presence. Despite the rebuffs Cynthia vows to change the attitudes of her peers. She says, "whenever I get a chance I'm going to these affairs. They've got to get used to us! They must!"

Eric Walrond's earliest stories focused on a realistic presentation of racial situations in New York City. In 1924 his focus shifted to a more impressionistic presentation of life in the American tropics. He would not return to the realistic mode until 1927, when he wrote "City Love," his last story to be published before he left the United States. "Vignettes of the Dusk" (*Opportunity*, 1924) is a pivotal story in this regard. While it is set in New York and its theme is racial prejudice, the style of the five vignettes is decidedly more impressionistic than that of his earlier stories. Indeed certain passages are reminiscent of Jean Toomer's *Cane*. His tendency toward impressionism is carried forward in "A Cholo Romance" (*Opportunity*, 1924) and "The Voodoo's Revenge" (awarded third prize in the short story section of the *Opportunity* literary contest in 1925). Both tales are set in Panama, where Walrond spent much of his youth. His experimentation with style reached its fruition in *Tropic Death* (1926).

Tropic Death is an impressive book of short stories. On the surface the ten stories focus upon dissipation, poverty, famine, and racial prejudice in the American tropics, notably Barbados, Panama, and British Guiana. Underlying these surface concerns, however, are several other themes: the relationship between the natural and human worlds, the relationship between technological development or imperialism and the natural tropical setting, and cultural disorientation and alienation.

Many of the stories in *Tropic Death* emphasize the connection between human activity and the surrounding environment. Events and action in the human world are often mirrored in the natural world. In "The Yellow One," a story about a young Latin couple's journey to Jamaica on a freighter, the intense summer heat creates an atmosphere of claustrophobia and desperation aboard the ship, mirroring the Yellow One's (referring to the young wife's skin color) own desperation as she attempts to procure some hot water for her child. Occasionally images of the natural world foreshadow human activity. After the freighter is tossed about by a stormy and foamy sea, a fight breaks out between two deckhands that results in the Yellow One's death. The connection between human and natural worlds is subtly and deftly handled by Walrond through the manipulation of various images.

Walrond also comments on American imperialism and on the effects of modernization and technological advancement on undeveloped countries. "The Palm Porch" opens with a harsh and ironic critique of technological progress in Panama, replete with traditional American images, such as the new frontier and the virgin land. He equates the construction of the Panama Canal with the continued expansion of the American frontier:

> Below, a rock engine was crushing stone, shooting up rivers of steam and signaling the frontier's rebirth. Opposite, there was proof,

a noisy, swaggering sort of proof, of the gradual death and destruction of the frontier post.

His pessimistic commentary on the fate of the Caribbean landscape is conveyed through powerful images:

> Dark dense thicket; water paving it. Deer, lions, tigers bounding through it. Centuries, perhaps, of such pure, free rule. Then some khaki-clad, red-faced and scrawny-necked whites deserted the Zone and brought saws to the roots of palmetto, spears to the bush cats and jaguars, lysol to the mosquitoes and flies and tar to the burning timber-swamp. . . . After the torch, ashes and ghosts—bare, black stalks, pegless stumps, flakes of charred leaves and half-burnt tree trunks.

Nature's reaction to the intrusion of white men is represented by images of the sea "groaning and vomiting." In other stories in which this theme is explored Walrond's perspective remains consistent.

Racial prejudice and cultural disorientation are common to all of the stories. Often one or both themes act as catalysts to the stories' violent and fatal climaxes. Racial prejudice, for example, is most overt in "Subjection." Here Walrond critiques both prejudice and imperialism when a black canal worker is shot to death by a white marine after he has berated the marine for striking another black worker. Although prejudice is more subtly presented in other stories it is always present.

Walrond uses an impressionistic prose style to elucidate the themes of *Tropic Death*. His sentences are often terse, constructed of short, simple clauses that give the prose a feeling of breathlessness. He is concerned less with developing characters and motivations than with depicting a locale and a cultural situation visually. Like Jean Toomer, Walrond presents his characters and themes in flashes of imagery, in bits of dialogue, and in succinct descriptive clauses. When Rum Coggins is informed that his daughter has died because, in a state of near-starvation, she ingested marl dust, his thoughts are related to the reader in a series of images:

> It came to Coggins in swirls. Autopsy. Noise comes in swirls. Pounding, pounding—dry Indian corn pounding. Ginger. Ginger being pounded in a mortar with a bright, new pes-

tle. Pound, pound. And. Sawing. Butcher shop. Cow foot is sawed that way. Stew—or tough hard steak. Then the drilling—drilling—drilling to a stone cutter's ears! Ox grizzle. Drilling into ox grizzle.

Walrond's description of the often lush tropical locale is similarly impressionistic:

The western sky of Barbados was ablaze. A mixture of fire and gold, it burned, and burned—into the vast sulphrous mass. It burned the houses, the trees, the windowpanes. The burnt glass did amazing somersaults—turned brown and gold and lavender and red. It poured a burning liquid over the gap. It colored the water in the ponds a fierce dull yellowish gold. . . . Sunset over the gap paralyzed. Sunset shot weird amber tints in the eyes of the black peons . . . sent strange poetic dreams through crinkly heads of mule boys tiredly bowed over the reins of some starved-out buckra cart horse.

Finally Walrond's description of human activity, such as the death of a black canal worker, is presented imagistically:

A ram-shackle body, dark in the ungentle spots exposing it, jogged, reeled and fell at the tip of a white bludgeon. Forced a dent in the crisp caked earth. An isolated ear lay limp and juicy, like some exhausted leaf or flower, half joined to the tree whence it sprang. Only the sticky milk flooding it was crimson, crimsoning the dust and earth.

Eric Walrond's imagistic style and his subtle treatment of themes combine to create an experimental and sophisticated work of art. *Tropic Death* did not sell very well, but reviewers such as Du Bois and Langston Hughes held the book in high esteem. Most contemporary critics have tended to ignore Walrond, although Robert Bone in *Down Home* (1975) and David Lewis in *When Harlem Was in Vogue* (1981) have attempted to reassess his work and his stature as a writer.

After the publication of *Tropic Death*, Walrond published very little. He remained on the staff of *Opportunity* until mid 1927, when he left the United States permanently. Until his death in 1966 Walrond traveled extensively in Europe and lived for a considerable time in France. His last days were spent in London, where he was at work on a book about the Panama Canal.

Critical recognition of Eric Walrond is long overdue. His literary accomplishments and his involvement in the Harlem Renaissance have enhanced Afro-American culture; they have also earned him a solid place in the history of Afro-American literature.

References:
Robert Bone, *Down Home* (New York: Putnam's, 1975), pp. 171-203;
Hugh Gloster, *Negro Voices in American Fiction* (Chapel Hill: University of North Carolina Press, 1948), pp. 180-183;
David Levering Lewis, *When Harlem Was in Vogue* (New York: Knopf, 1981).

Walter Francis White
(1 July 1893-21 March 1955)

Walter C. Daniel
University of Missouri, Columbia

BOOKS: *The Fire in the Flint* (New York: Knopf, 1924; London: Williams & Norgate, 1925);
Flight (New York & London: Knopf, 1926);
The American Negro and His Problems (Girard, Kans.: Haldeman-Julius, 1927);
The Negro's Contribution to American Culture (Girard, Kans.: Haldeman-Julius, 1927);
Rope and Faggot: A Biography of Judge Lynch (New York & London: Knopf, 1929);
What Caused the Detroit Riot?, by White and Thurgood Marshall (New York: NAACP, 1943);
A Rising Wind: A Report on the Negro Soldier in the European Theatre of War (Garden City: Doubleday, Doran, 1945);
A Man Called White: The Autobiography of Walter White (New York: Viking, 1948);
How Far the Promised Land? (New York: Viking, 1955).

Walter White (courtesy of the Schomburg Center for Research in Black Culture, the New York Public Library, Astor, Lenox and Tilden Foundations)

Although his two novels—*The Fire in the Flint* (1924) and *Flight* (1926)—are his sole contributions to fictive literature, Walter White was a significant figure in the Harlem Renaissance period. From the time he began working for the National Association for the Advancement of Colored People in 1918, until he became executive secretary of that organization in 1931, and until his death in 1955, White was an unceasing advocate for equality and democracy in the United States.

Fair-skinned, blond, blue-eyed, and with Anglo features, White was born in Atlanta, Georgia, on 1 July 1893 to George and Madeline White. During the race riot of 1906 in Atlanta, he stood beside his father, armed with a rifle, ready to defend the family home against possible attack by the white mob foraging the neighborhood. He grew up and went to public school in the Atlanta area and attended Atlanta University for his secondary education and his bachelor's degree, which he received in 1916.

After graduation White worked for a few years in the home office of the Atlanta Life Insurance Company and became a vociferous supporter and guiding force of the Atlanta Branch of the NAACP. White attracted the attention of James Weldon Johnson, secretary of the then-fledgling NAACP, during one of Johnson's visits to the Atlanta branch. As a result of their association, White went to New York in 1918 as assistant secretary to the NAACP, thereby becoming Johnson's assistant.

Because he could pass for white, Walter White became the NAACP's secret weapon against lynching. He was able to report eye-witness accounts of racial disturbances in a series of essays he wrote for the organization. Once, while working on an assignment in Arkansas, he was sworn in as a deputy sheriff and told he had the legal authority to shoot Negroes. With his ability to move freely within the power structure of whites in communities torn by racial strife and lynchings, White was able to gain the confidence of individuals who told him openly their plans and was then able to warn black citizens of the dangers that awaited them. White used these experiences to present in his novels a unique view of America's racial confrontations during the first decades of the twentieth century.

Along with James Weldon Johnson, Charles S. Johnson, Alain Locke, Jessie Fauset, and W. E. B. Du Bois, White inspired many of the younger writers of the Harlem Renaissance, including Countee Cullen, Claude McKay, Langston Hughes, Rudolph Fisher, and Zora Neale Hurston. White was a strong supporter of the "New Negro" metaphor, which was made a household phrase by Alain Locke's *The New Negro* (1925). Further he had joined Locke in seeking to establish a Negro Foreign Fellowship Fund that would provide opportunities for young black writers to live and work in the reasonably free social and artistic atmosphere of Europe. Through his NAACP contacts, White could bring the attention of the most prominent editors and publishers to aspiring black writers. Like his mentor, James Weldon Johnson, White believed that creative writing, in particular, had its own place in the movement for racial uplift. He once commented on the function of art in American society: "It has long been my feeling that the greatest aid towards solution of problems of race and color is to be gained through the art approach, and by the very excellence of each race's and each individual's gifts will come lessening of hatred and distrust and cruelty of race to race. Harry Burleigh, Roland Hayes, Paul Robeson, Countee Cullen, Dr. Du Bois and other artists in their various fields are, I feel, tearing down barriers of all sorts."

While White did not side with the literary figures who advocated the "best foot forward" approach to writing or with those who advocated treatment of the masses, including the "low life" elements, he did reject the use of stereotyped characters in fiction and drama. In attacking the race problem in America, he believed Afro-American writing should not leave out racial and interracial conflict, even if the writers were accused of being propagandistic. His first novel emerged from a challenge to depict black life more accurately than white writers had done.

James Weldon Johnson invited White to accompany him to an appointment with H. L. Mencken, then editor of the *Smart Set*. Not long after their meeting, White received a note in which Mencken asked what he thought about *Birthright*

(1922), T. S. Stribling's novel about Negroes. White responded with what he later recalled as a "lengthy and painfully erudite criticism," pointing out that Stribling was writing from outside the Negro's experience. He especially disagreed with Stribling's portrayal of educated Negroes. Mencken, in his characteristic manner, replied, "Why don't you do the right kind of novel? You could do it, and it would create a sensation." White had never thought of writing fiction, but after talking over the idea with Johnson and others, he agreed to take advantage of Mary White Ovington's offer of her cottage at Great Barrington, Massachusetts. He and his wife, the former Gladys Powell, whom he had married on 15 February 1922, packed up and went to New England for two weeks, during which time White wrote *The Fire in the Flint* (1924).

The years immediately following the close of World War I are the focus of the novel, which is set in Central City, Georgia. It depicts the sociocultural strangulation experienced by Kenneth Harper, a young, black, idealistic doctor who has been educated in Europe. Harper returns to his hometown, confident that he can improve the life of his friends and neighbors, both black and white. Unfortunately Central City remains gripped in prewar attitudes; few changes have come to it. No matter how well Harper might be prepared to live a full and contributing life among his own people, the hostile social fabric will not allow him to move above the place the South has determined for blacks, a fact that merges history and fiction in the book.

Not surprisingly Harper incurs the envy of the white townspeople who would prefer that he be like other blacks. When a black man in Central City is murdered, Harper must acknowledge that the customs he has told himself no longer apply in Central City indeed hold sway; the black man was murdered by the local sheriff's brother. Replacing his idealistic isolation and Puritan ethic with commitment to social change, Harper seeks to redress the plight of his fellow blacks in the community. Together with the Reverend Ezekiel Wilson, pastor of the local Mt. Zion Baptist Church, Harper emblemizes the New Negro in Central City. He helps black farmers organize a cooperative to purchase foodstuff and other necessities to avoid indebtedness to the white landowners. Ironically Harper has been in Atlanta seeking help from liberal whites for his cooperative when he returns home to find that his sister has been raped by young white men. His younger brother, who has killed some of the

Madeline and George White

violators, has committed suicide rather than be captured by a lynch mob.

Despite tensions that follow the Harper family's conflict with the white mob, Harper agrees to answer a call to visit a local white girl whose life he has saved through an operation; but the call to her home is a trap. A mob is in wait for him and kills him.

Ezekiel Wilson is also an important character. He has been educated; yet, in order to make himself acceptable to his congregation and to the white people in the town, he wears the mask of ignorance. He speaks in dialect, and his sermons are uninspiring. He simply goes through the motions of living out his life in the town. When Harper approaches him and enlists his aid for the black farmers, Wilson's mask drops away and reveals a highly intelligent, motivated professional black man. Wilson, in concert with Harper, believes in the possibilities for the town until the mob takes over and dashes the hopes of the black citizens.

Charles S. Johnson pointed out in a review of the novel that White could have documented the facts of the plot from many materials in the NAACP files. The novel reflects them accurately

and dramatically. More than that, however, it illustrates the tragedy of the black professional person in southern, racist settings. Robert Bone, in *The Negro Novel in America*, called White's novel "an antilynching tract of melodramatic proportions" that is essentially a series of essays, "strung on an unconvincing plot, involving the misfortunes of a colored doctor and his family in a small Southern town." Bone does not consider the historical motivations that brought Afro-American literature into existence. Johnson comes closer to the point, however, when he notes that the South's literature, up to the 1920s, had been "limited to a petulant defense literature." White's novel, Johnson wrote, breaks new ground because it deals with "the natural and unrelieved tragedy of the Negro in his new consciousness in the South." Other contemporary critics claimed that the novel was little more than propaganda and that it did not give a realistic picture of race relations.

The Fire in the Flint went through three printings, and it was published in England in 1925, but copies did not sell well there. In the years immediately following its American release, the novel was translated into French, Norwegian, German,

Russian, and Japanese. Its popularity may well have surpassed that of any other work of fiction created by an Afro-American. It was serialized in the *Pittsburgh Courier* in 1926. Several attempts were made to render a dramatic production of it. Eugene O'Neill was the first person to suggest that the dramatic qualities of the plot could be effectively reworked into a stage play. A version by White and George Widder was rejected when it was submitted to Edwin Knopf and Horace Liveright. As late as 1932 some interest in making the plot into a play was still being discussed. Cecil B. DeMille considered buying film rights, but decided on *Porgy* as a better depiction of black life in the United States.

Before the first novel was completed, White had begun work on a second. He seemed to enjoy the role of author and, particularly, the interest he had engendered among influential literary and business figures. He used his contacts wisely, always aware that his creative writing would lie in the arena of race relations in the United States. He wrote to James Weldon Johnson that he had shared the outline of his new novel with Carl Van Vechten, who liked it. He promised the new work would be less dramatic than the first, but it would go deeper beneath the surface of race relations in America.

It would explore the spiritual foundation in which black Americans were anchored, and it would not preach so much as it would tell a story. Fully aware of the strong criticism that had been directed against his first novel, White was nonetheless heartened by the commotion the book had created. He wrote in his autobiography that this reception motivated him to write *Flight* (1926). In his choice of subject matter for the plot he was working at ameliorating the view of the "tragic mulatto" in southern American fiction established by writers such as Thomas Nelson Page and Thomas Dixon. Through their fiction, these white writers argued that mixed blood among blacks embodied the worst qualities of both races and hence created people who were a menace to society. White's attack on such a distorted perspective of blacks, who found themselves in an ambiguous category of heritage in their native land through no fault of their own, was compatible with his commitment to racial equality.

Flight explores the problem of passing as white in the North, but it also probes the motivations and values of the black bourgeoisie in Atlanta. Carl Hunter, the quixotic son of a black Atlanta family, seduces Mimi, a newcomer from New Or-

Jane, Walter, Walter Jr., and Gladys White (Morgan and Marvin Smith photo; courtesy of the Schomburg Center for Research in Black Culture, the New York Public Library, Astor, Lenox and Tilden Foundations)

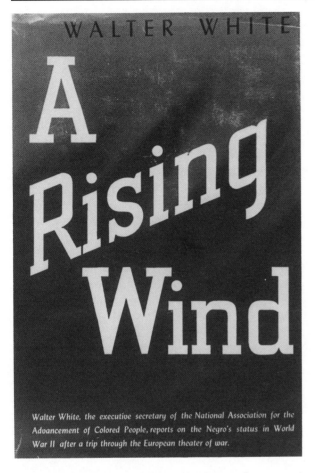

WALTER WHITE

A Rising Wind

Walter White, the executive secretary of the National Association for the Advancement of Colored People, reports on the Negro's status in World War II after a trip through the European theater of war.

Dust jacket for White's 1945 book. The title comes from a speech in which Eleanor Roosevelt, quoting Thomas Wolfe, said, "a wind is rising throughout the world of free men everywhere, and they will not be kept in bondage."

leans. She becomes pregnant. Enraged by Hunter's suggestion that she should have an abortion, Mimi goes to Philadelphia to give birth to her son. Subsequently she places him in an orphanage in Baltimore. Feeling that she has freed herself from the responsibility for the child, Mimi settles in Harlem where she lives reasonably comfortably until she feels forced by the vicious gossip of a visitor from Atlanta to cross the color line. Passing for white, she can obtain employment that was unavailable to her as a black woman. She secures a job at Francine's, a high-class shop on Fifth Avenue. She progresses rapidly, eventually becoming an executive in the establishment, and she moves into a preferred social circle. There she meets and marries Jimmy Forrester, a white banker, but Mimi secretly makes forays into Harlem from time to time. Psychologically unable to straddle both cultures at once, Mimi, hearing a Negro artist sing spirituals

at a Carnegie Hall concert, decides she will return to her own people to find happiness. The major line of action in the novel follows the pattern of the tragic mulatto in a new key. It is the black woman who is brought, unwittingly, to an affirmation of the identity that she has been forced, by her own people, to disown.

Quite aside from the social problem of "passing" and the duplicity it represents—on the part of whites who sired mixed-blood children—the novel explores with penetration the elitest posture of Atlanta's black society. The black bourgeoisie values, according to White, light complexions and the acquisition of wealth. In showing their disdain for Catholics, Jews, and dark-skinned Negroes, these southern blacks show themselves, ironically, to be as bigoted as whites. He made clear, however, his contention that skin color and material wealth had become the highest values for these black Americans primarily because they were secure in imitating the whites among them. Like Fauset, White makes the strong point that universal and eternal values among human beings lay in the deprived Negroes, not in their elite brothers. For those who were mistreated, by whites and blacks among whom they lived and worked, could sing, laugh, maintain faith in themselves, and survive in an industrial society. White's celebration of this element of black Americans is expressed in Mimi's trips to Harlem and in her appreciation of the spirituals.

Although *Flight* treats some subjects not previously discussed in black literature, such as the unwed mother, it won both praise and criticism. As one critic put it, Mimi would not compromise in her soul even if it meant loss of comfort and social reputation. The same critic complains, though, that White was so concerned with the thesis of the novel at this point that he created "one of the most manipulated heroines in literature." There are also structural problems in the novel, including its avoidance of difficult exposition. While black readers may have understood Mimi's reason for "passing," less perceptive critics raised the question of how a truly proud person could reject her people to cross the color line. White knew the reality informing Mimi's decision and wanted his readers to know that the ultimate tragedy lies not so much in passing as it does in the inability to achieve optimum success with the disadvantage of color.

Modern criticism of *Flight* has made the point that in it White probably sought to "execute a conception beyond his capacity." That criticism seems valid, especially inasmuch as White never consid-

Arthur Spingarn, Walter White, and an unidentified woman (Morgan and Marvin Smith photo, courtesy of the Schomburg Center for Research in Black Culture, the New York Public Library, Astor, Lenox and Tilden Foundations)

ered himself a professional novelist. In more skill-ful hands, *Flight* might have explained the Babbittry of Atlanta black "blue-vein" society and the way its heartless pursuits of white America's standards of excellence robbed the race of a sense of humanity. In writing about this problem that he knew at first-hand, White anticipated some aspects of E. Franklin Frazier's concept of the black bourgeoisie and its distance from the mainstream of black American culture.

In 1926 White received a Guggenheim Fel-lowship Grant for creative writing which he could apply to a foreign country of his choice. The sti-pend of $2,500 was hardly adequate for him and his family to live on, but they decided to spend the time in France. Several of White's acquaintances, including Rebecca West, G. B. Stern, and Carl and Fania Van Vechten, encouraged him to take ad-vantage of the new opportunity and helped him to make arrangements for housing in the south of France. The fellowship was given to make it pos-sible for him to write a novel about three genera-tions of blacks. His benefactors believed that, removed from the daily work of the NAACP and

its relentless struggle against lynching and injustice in the United States, White could produce a valu-able contribution to American prose fiction. Nei-ther he nor his supporters seemed concerned that any work White would write would be largely so-ciological. Instead of writing a novel, he found him-self writing a study of what he considered the economic, political, social, religious, and sexual in-fluences of lynching in the United States. This anat-omy of lynching, *Rope and Faggot: A Biography of Judge Lynch* (1929), was cordially received by re-viewers in the North and the South. It was recog-nized as the first formal attempt to analyze the causative factors of lynchings. White wrote later that he was "immensely pleased that a number of colleges, universities and high schools included the book in their required reading or reference lists."

Although his literary works were limited to two novels, White published scores of articles and reports in a variety of American periodicals. He wrote a weekly column for the *Chicago Defender* and occasionally for the *New York Herald-Tribune*. At one point during World War II, he served as a corre-spondent for the *New York Post,* reporting on activities of Negro servicemen in the European and Pacific theaters of war. In 1949 White divorced his first wife, and, on 6 July of that year, he married Poppy Cannon, a white woman, who, after his death in 1955, published a biography of him.

During his long career as a civil rights champion and as executive director of the NAACP, White was accorded several honors. Among them are the Spingarn Medal (1937), the Haitian Order of Merit, the Sir James Jeans Award, the Star of Ethiopia, and an Honorary Doctor of Laws degree from Howard University.

Biography:

Poppy Cannon, *A Gentle Knight, My Husband Walter White* (New York & Toronto: Rinehart, 1956).

References:

Robert A. Bone, *The Negro Novel in America* (New Haven & London: Yale University Press, 1965), pp. 98-100;

Poppy Cannon, "The Lover That Never Died," *Ebony*, 12 (January 1957): 17-20+;

Charles F. Cooney, "Walter White and the Harlem Renaissance," *Journal of Negro History*, 57 (July 1972): 231-240;

Charles W. Scruggs, "Alain Locke and Walter White: Their Struggle for Control of the Harlem Renaissance," *Black American Literature Forum*, 14 (Fall 1980): 91-99;

Edward E. Waldron, "Walter White and the Harlem Renaissance: Letters from 1924-1927," *College Language Association Journal*, 16 (June 1973): 438-457;

"Walter White," Editorial, *Crisis*, 62 (April 1955): 229-232;

"Walter White," Editorial, *Crisis*, 85 (March 1978): 77-78.

Papers:

Letters and significant documents relating to the life and work of Walter White are in the National Association for the Advancement of Colored People Papers in the Manuscript Division of the Library of Congress.

Appendix

Two Influential Figures:
Alain Locke
and
Carl Van Vechten

Editor's Note

Though neither qualifies for inclusion in this volume on the key figures of the Harlem Renaissance, Alain Locke and Carl Van Vechten played influential roles in identifying, nurturing, publishing, and publicizing the writers who changed the shape of American black literature. Alain Locke's concept of the New Negro provided black thinkers and writers a positive self-image, a fresh direction for their creative energies, and an aesthetic standard based on the Afro-American experience. Carl Van Vechten's enthusiasm for black culture, expressed in his writings, photography, and promotional activities, helped introduce the writers and artists of the Harlem Renaissance to wider white audience appreciation. Although diametrically opposed in their political and aesthetic views, they, along with such key figures as Charles S. Johnson and the Spingarn family, recognized early on the necessity for catalyzing black creativity.

Alain Locke
(13 September 1886-10 June 1954)

Ernest D. Mason
North Carolina Central University

BOOKS: *A Decade of Negro Self-Expression* (Charlottesville, Va., 1928);

The Negro in America (Chicago: American Library Association, 1933);

The Negro and His Music (Washington, D.C.: Associates in Negro Folk Education, 1936);

Negro Art: Past and Present (Washington, D.C.: Associates in Negro Folk Education, 1936).

OTHER: *The New Negro: An Interpretation,* edited, with contributions, by Locke (New York: A. & C. Boni, 1925);

Four Negro Poets, edited by Locke (New York: Simon & Schuster, 1927);

Plays of Negro Life: A Source-Book of Native American Drama, edited by Locke and Montgomery Gregory (New York & London: Harper, 1927);

The Negro in Art: A Pictorial Record of the Negro Artist and of the Negro Theme in Art, edited, with annotations, by Locke (Washington, D.C.: Associates in Negro Folk Education, 1940);

When People Meet: A Study in Race and Culture Contacts, edited by Locke and Bernhard J. Stern (New York: Committee on Workshops, Progressive Education Association, 1942).

The distinguishing feature of Harlem Renaissance culture is that one cannot really separate the formal, social, ethical, political, and thematic dimensions without violating the intent and spirit of the work. The art of the Harlem Renaissance, part of a broader project of artistic social rebellion, was characterized from its creation to its reception by passion and intensity. Most Harlem Renaissance artists not only wanted to develop Afro-American literature into high art but desired to transform American social life and race relations as well. As a result much of the creative work of the period was guided by the ideal of a New Negro which signified a range of ethical ideals that often emphasized and intensified a higher sense of group and social cohesiveness. Harlem Renaissance art was, accordingly, infused with a sense of mission

and a sense of the artist's calling. The writers took their work seriously and sought to transform both themselves and their audiences in their activity. Many literally expected liberation—and often salvation—from their work and were perhaps the first group of Afro-American writers to believe that art could radically transform the artist and attitudes of other human beings. The major theoretician of this new cultural and aesthetic vision during the Harlem Renaissance was Alain Locke.

Alain Leroy Locke was born on 13 September 1886 and died on 10 June 1954. He was, therefore, a child of the Emancipation Proclamation and a witness to the Supreme Court's historical desegregation decision. He grew up in Philadelphia, which he characterizes in "Self-Portrait": "with her birthright of provincialism flavored by urbanity and her petty bourgeois psyche with the Tory slant." Such a background he confesses, "at the start set the key of paradox," and, he continues, "verily paradox has followed me the rest of my days." After attending Central High School and the Philadelphia School of Pedagogy, Locke entered Harvard University in 1904 where he studied under William James and other classic American philosophers, "clinging" he says, "to the genteel tradition of Palmer, Royce and Munsterberg, yet attracted by the disillusion of Santayana and the radical protest of James." After graduating from Harvard in 1907 with a highly distinguished academic record, he studied at Oxford University in England from 1907 to 1910 as the first black Rhodes scholar and earned a bachelor of literature degree. From Oxford he went to the University of Berlin for another year of advanced work in philosophy, immersing himself in the writings of Franz Brentano, Alexius von Meinong, and Christian von Ehrenfels. His association with Howard University started in 1912 with his appointment as an assistant professor of English and philosophy. In 1916 he returned to Harvard to work under the idealist philosopher, Josiah Royce, but, after Royce's death, took his doctorate in value theory under Ralph Barton Perry. Two years later he returned to Howard University as professor of philosophy and remained there until his retirement in 1952.

In addition to his celebrated anthology, *The New Negro* (1925), Locke wrote a number of social, philosophical, and aesthetic essays and books which continued to give a decisive impetus to the atmosphere of cultural and social experimentation. The New Negro movement suggested a self-consciousness about art, literature, music, and life among Afro-Americans that the previous generation had not felt to the same degree. As Locke says in *The New Negro:*

> With this renewed self-respect and self-dependence, the life of the Negro community is bound to enter a new dynamic phase, the buoyancy from within compensating for whatever pressure there may be of conditions from without. The migrant masses, shifting from countryside to city, hurdle several generations of experience at a leap, but

Alain Locke (courtesy of the Schomburg Center for Research in Black Culture, the New York Public Library, Astor, Lenox and Tilden Foundations)

more important, the same thing happens spiritually in the life-attitudes and self-expression of the Young Negro, in his poetry, his art, his education and his new outlook, with the additional advantage, of course, of the poise and greater certainty of knowing what it is all about. From this comes the promise and warrant of new leadership. As one of them has discerningly put it:

> We have tomorrow
> Bright before us
> Like a flame.
>
> Yesterday a night-gone thing
> A sun-down name
>
> And dawn today
> Broad arch above the road we came.
> We march!

In one of the first articles to document Locke's role as mentor during the Harlem Renaissance, Richard A. Long, discussing Locke's colleagues and the publication of *The New Negro,* notes that behind his "editorial achievement lay the literary and artistic activity of the *Crisis,* edited by W. E. B. Du Bois, and of *Opportunity,* edited by Charles S. Johnson. Jessie Fauset was Du Bois's assistant at the *Crisis* for literature, while Alain Locke himself from the founding of *Opportunity* by the Urban League in 1923, had contributed largely to its development both directly and indirectly." Since *The New Negro* grew out of a special Harlem number of *Survey Graphic,* for which Locke was guest editor, the question of who actually gave Paul Kellog, editor of the magazine, the idea for the issue remains an interesting one. Du Bois claimed the credit for his own staff, while Johnson said he was the first to offer to share some of Locke's essays with Kellog. Whichever is true, it is quite clear that Locke's own role in the development and final outcome of this classic account of black art and thought during the 1920s is a significant and secure one.

Locke's associations ranged from his professional involvement with Edith Isaacs of the *Theatre Arts Monthly* to his active support of the Players at Howard University, from his devotion to the singer Roland Hayes to his acquaintance with such Afro-French intellectuals as René Maron, Paulette Nardal, and Jean Price-Mars. Locke actively encouraged young black writers, artists, and scholars wherever he found them. It is, accordingly, asserts Long, "no exaggeration to say that the Harlem Renaissance as we know it is marked strongly by the presence of Alain Locke, and would have been something rather different without him and the role of mentor which he filled with modesty and elegance." The significance of Locke's role during the Harlem Renaissance has been acknowledged even by those contemporaries such as Du Bois who did not particularly like Locke or agree with his ideas. This fact alone testifies to the force of Locke's thought and the impact of his character.

Locke's *The New Negro* contained the first really thoroughgoing examination of the psychology of the New Negro movement. In documenting the younger American black generation's social and cultural innovations, he compared the movement with similar shifts in folk expression and self-determination taking place in India, China, Egypt, Ireland, Russia, Czechoslovakia, Yugoslavia, Russia, Bohemia, Palestine, and Mexico. His cultural pluralism was similar to, though not identical with, the optimism and idealism of such American progressive reformers as Waldo Frank, V. F. Calverton, Randolph Bourne, and Van Wyck Brooks. According to Locke, many of the conditions that were molding a new American attitude were also molding a New Negro. The objectives of the New Negro's "outer" life were, he said, "none other than the ideals of American institutions and democracy." His "inner" objectives, on the other hand, were aimed at repairing a damaged group psychology and reshaping a warped social perspective. In this new group psychology, Locke noted the "lapse of sentimental appeal, then the development of a more positive self-respect and self-reliance; the repudiation of social dependence, . . . and finally the rise from social disillusionment to race pride. . . . He resents being spoken of as a social ward or minor, even by his own, and to being regarded a chronic patient for the sociological clinic, the sick man of American Democracy." Speaking again of the New Negro in "Negro Youth Speaks," Locke discussed literary pioneers Du Bois, Charles W. Chesnutt, Angelina Grimké, Paul Laurence Dunbar, Anne Spencer, Georgia Douglas Johnson, James Weldon Johnson, and others, pointing out that they had spoken for the Negro in an effort to interpret the race for others. The New Negroes, in contrast, "have now stopped speaking for the Negro—they speak as Negroes. Where formerly they spoke to others and tried to interpret, they now speak to their own and try to express." Jessie Fauset, Claude McKay, Willis Richardson, Jean Toomer, Eric Walrond, Rudolph Fisher, Langston Hughes, and Countee Cullen were among the most familiar of these newer black artists. Among them,

Toomer, Cullen, Hughes, and Fisher received special encouragement from Locke.

Locke had much admiration for this younger generation of black writers, not merely because they had natural talent but because many of them sought to convey in their works a sense of loyalty to the black masses and folk. S. P. Fullinwider's statement that Locke "reflected the inability of the middle class truly to empathize with the city masses" during the Harlem Renaissance is, thus, not readily understandable. "Much derision," Fullinwider continues, "was directed at Locke by Renaissance poets and writers—as often as not he was set up as a symbol of what the writers were in revolt against. . . . He did not try to hide the polish usually associated with a Rhodes Scholar and Harvard Ph.D. In short, he was easily stigmatized as—'dicty'—he stood apart from the masses—by those writers who were in a great lather to escape from the category themselves."

It is true that Locke, like Du Bois, was a strong advocate of a "talented tenth" and felt little could be expected, politically, from the economically deprived masses alone. Thus, in his writings, there are such expressions as "exceptional few," "nationally representative classes," "leaderless masses," and "vulgar crowd." For example, in "The High Cost of Prejudice" (*Forum*, December 1927), he wrote: "Both as an American and as a Negro, I would much rather see the black masses going gradually forward under the leadership of a recognized and representative and responsible elite than see a frustrated group of malcontents later hurl these masses at society in doubtful but desperate strife." In no way, however, do such statements demonstrate that Locke had contempt for the black masses or that he deliberately sought to distance himself from them. On the contrary, Locke's "elitism" and advocacy of the "talented tenth" represented a devotion to the causes of the masses, and he esteemed elitism only insofar as it furthered political, economic, and cultural net gains:

> By recognizing the talent and the representative types among Negroes, an easing and vindicating satisfaction can be carried down into the Negro masses, as well as the most quickening and stimulating sort of inspiration that could be given them. Their elite would then become symbols in advance of expected justice and of a peaceful eventual solution. They would be literally an investment in democracy. . . . Not only great satisfaction, but great social incentive can be

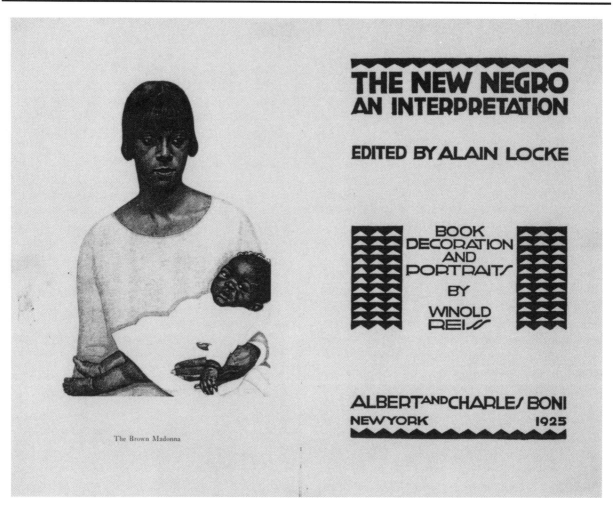

Frontispiece and title page for Locke's landmark anthology

created for the masses in the recognition of the outstanding few,—as a group representative, however, and not with the reservations to which Negro talent of a previous generation had to submit, namely, of being regarded as a prodigy, a biological sport.

The clear inference here is that to bridge the gap, to bring the level of the masses' sense of appreciation and understanding closer to the consensus of the best-qualified opinion, to stop claims of black inferiority, and to eventually stop racism were Locke's only intentions in advocating a black elitism. The education of the masses in artistic appreciation and understanding was for Locke especially essential. On the dialectic of production and consumption he wrote in "The Ethics of Culture" (*Howard University Record,* January 1923):

> As a race group we are at the critical stage where we are releasing creative artistic

talent in excess of our group ability to understand and support it. Those of us who have been concerned about our progress in the things of culture have now begun to fear as the greatest handicap the discouraging, stultifying effect upon our artistic talent of lack of appreciation from the group which it represents.... Here is our present dilemma. If the standard of cultural tastes is not rapidly raised in the generation which you represent, the natural affinities of appreciation and response will drain off, like cream, the richest products of the group, and leave the masses without the enriching quality of its finest ingredients. This is already happening: I need not cite the painful individual instances. The only remedy is the more rapid development and diffusion of culture among us.

It was, then, Locke's understanding of the nature of art, culture, and human society—rather than his "middle-class sensibility"—that led him to take the position he did on the black masses during the Harlem Renaissance. The participation of the masses in the movement was considered by Locke to be fundamental. In his own words, "It is the rank and file who are leading, and the leaders who are following. A transformed and transforming psychology permeates the masses."

Intrinsically related to Locke's defense of the masses during the Harlem Renaissance, and equally crucial for an understanding of his aesthetic and cultural leadership, is Locke's philosophy of community. While the philosophical pluralism of Locke's teacher at Harvard, William James, greatly influenced Locke's approach to the various conflicting "ideological communities" of the world and nation, Locke could never fully appreciate James's individualism, or James's concern for individuals and particulars, as opposed to universals and wholes. Rather, the individual, in Locke's thinking on community, was always submerged in some group or some larger culture and, therefore, received very little positive attention. Although greatly influenced by the pragmatism of James, Locke remained an objective idealist throughout his life. He remained an idealist, not only in the presence of James and his influence but also despite the influence of his teacher, dissertation adviser, and philosophic realist, Ralph Barton Perry. His ability to escape the individualism of both can be attributed in part to his attachment to the philosophy of Royce. But one has also to consider Locke's temperament, for had he been a different sort of person his approach to the idea of community may have been more like that of his colleague and frequent rival, W. E. B. Du Bois.

Of the many disagreements Locke and Du Bois had, the role of the individual in community and group life was, perhaps, one of the more crucial ones. Not only had William James been Du Bois's teacher and dissertation adviser, he was, according to Du Bois himself, his close friend, and the influence of James's personality and individualism on Du Bois is very pronounced. One often neglected feature of Du Bois's thought is that the community—world, national, or racial—is merely a means toward individual freedom. Throughout his writings he consistently uses such expressions as "self-realization," "self-consciousness," "self-respect," and "self-examination." He was in many ways an individualist in the existential sense, as the

goal for him was always to be real manhood and real womanhood, the individual freedom to think, to love, and to aspire. The means toward this type of individuality and freedom was to be racial solidarity and community action. But the end product was to be not so much group freedom as individual, personal freedom.

Locke was totally opposed to Du Bois on this point, maintaining that the emphasis must always be on the group. The distinction here is, admittedly, a very subtle one, but it is also very basic for understanding Locke's race loyalty during and after the Harlem Renaissance. The Harvard philosopher who had the greatest theoretical influence on Locke's thinking about the black community was Josiah Royce, whose work emphasized group memory and group hope. Certain features of Royce's philosophy of community were taken over almost entirely by Locke and incorporated into his thinking. According to Royce, a community is established when each of its members accepts as part of his own individual life the same past events that each of his fellow-members accept. This Royce calls a community of memory. Another type of community is established when each member expects the same future events. This phenomenon Royce calls a community of hope. The perfect community is a complete fusion of these two elements—the community of memory and the community of hope. Accordingly, the first condition upon which the existence of a community depends is the power of an individual to extend his life so as to include past and future events. The idea of community was thus a very practical conception for Royce. It involved the idea of deeds performed and ends sought—deeds and ends common to all individuals who constitute the community, which means that all individuals must identify with the cooperative action performed by them.

Locke took over these ideas almost entirely and incorporated them into his views on Africa and the general community of black America. In his article "Apropos of Africa" (*Opportunity*, February 1924), Locke, speaking of what he called the "homing instinct," pointed out that virtually all cultural groups exhibit a tendency to "turn back physically or mentally, hopefully and helpfully, to the land of their origin. And we American Negroes in this respect cannot, will not, be an exception." So strong were the vestiges of slavery in the minds of Harlem Renaissance intellectuals that even those who did show an interest in Africa focused almost exclusively on the West Coast. But, as Locke went on to point out in his article, the black people of America represent all the racial stocks of Africa and are "culturally the heirs of the entire continent." Continuing, Locke noted that "if the Negro is interested in Africa, . . . if he is to link himself up again with his past and kin, he must link himself up with all of the African peoples. As the physical composite of eighty-five per cent at least of the African stocks, the American Negro is in a real sense the true Pan-African, and . . . should be the leader in constructive Pan-African thought and endeavor." Locke found it both strange and disconcerting that, in terms of Pan-Africanism, the masses had more of a sense of community and, hence, were more ready and ripe for action than the leaders and educated few: "The Garvey movement has demonstrated that conclusively. Perhaps in the perspective of time, that will appear to have been its chief service and mission, to have stirred the race mind to the depths with the idea of large-scale cooperation between the variously separated branches of the Negro peoples. This is without a doubt the great constructive idea in the race life during the last decade, and must become the center of constructive endeavor for this and the next generation." Again in opposition to Du Bois, Locke was thus not convinced that the Garvey movement had failed completely, although he did take cognizance of its shortcomings.

Locke expounded his philosophy of community once again in an address delivered to the 1925 graduating class at Hampton Institute (now Hampton University), published as "The Command of the Spirit" in *Southern Workman* (July 1925): "To the extent . . . that I have the privilege of telling you what I think about the attitude in which you should confront life, let me say, sincerely and simply: Take up your life work in a spirit of service but not in a spirit of sacrifice. Accept this situation with a sober sense of social responsibility. . . . Find your larger self in some group project and realize the philosophy of a fine African proverb that says, 'Through others I am somebody.' Learn to merge ambition and self-realization with the common good and with the ideals of race realization." He concludes that the "highest education . . . has the greatest social coefficient; the lowest that which has the largest personal coefficient, certainly if that be purchased at the sacrifice of the former."

It is in the context of this type of thinking on community and racial life that frequent debates erupted between Locke and some of the Harlem Renaissance writers. Locke's thinking during the Harlem Renaissance clearly gave way to a kind of

monistic order. He expected only one loyalty, a loyalty to the folk spirit of the larger black community, and most of the writers failed to meet that demand. As Richard Long has pointed out, only Langston Hughes met this criterion fully, and although Sterling Brown expresses a similar loyalty, "his work is grounded rather exclusively in the folk tradition without that larger world reference which Alain Locke wished to see expressed. Jean Toomer had, of course, anticipated this concern in *Cane*, but his voice was scarcely heard after *The New Negro* consecrated his position." Claude McKay could also have fulfilled Locke's vision if, wrote Locke, in "Spiritual Truancy" (*New Challenge*, Fall 1937), he had not been "caught in the ego-centric predicament of aesthetic vanity and exhibitionism." Locke's conflict with McKay was one of the cornerstones of the Harlem Renaissance and, hence, merits some attention.

In his attack on McKay, Locke admitted that "one may not dictate a man's loyalties, but must, at all events, expect him to have some. For a genius maturing in a decade of racial self-expression and enjoying the fruits of it all and living into a decade of social issues and conflict and aware of all that, to have repudiated all possible loyalties amounts to self-imposed apostasy." Again, the kind of loyalty that Locke had in mind and wanted McKay to exhibit was a deep loyalty to the black folk masses. This comes out most clearly as he continues his attack on McKay, pointing out that

> In some sense these aberrations of spirit, this lack of purposeful and steady loyalty of which McKay is the supreme example has to a lesser extent vitiated much of the talent of the first generation of the "New Negro" writers and artists. They inherited, it is true, a morbid amount of decadent aestheticism . . . there was an unpardonable remainder of spiritual truancy and social irresponsibility. The folk have rarely been treated by these artists with unalloyed reverence and unselfish loyalty. The commitment to racial materials and "race expression" should be neither that of a fashionable and profitable fad nor of a condescending and missionary duty. . . . The task confronting the present younger generation of Negro writers and artists is to approach the home scene and the folk with high seriousness, deep loyalty, racial reverence of the unspectacular, unmelodramatic sort, and when necessary, sacrificial social devotion. They must purge this flippant exhibitionism, this posy but not

too sincere racialism, this care-free and irresponsible individualism.

Locke was, in other words, convinced that black writers must "become truer sons of the people, more loyal providers of spiritual bread and less aesthetic wastrels and truants of the streets."

As Clare Bloodgood Crane has noted, the relationship between Locke and McKay was one characterized from its very beginning by constant disagreement over the nature of black art. In a letter to McKay in 1927 (quoted in Crane), ten years before the writing of "Spiritual Truancy," Locke asserted: "The movement suffers—but that is your prerogative. I hope you will find the abstract (i.e., non racial) universal recognition you desire. My opinion is that your previous work and acceptance of racial representativeness and spokesmanship will follow you through life." McKay responded to Locke as follows:

> I must say that your letter's effect upon me is to destroy every vestige of intellectual and fraternal understanding that may have existed between us. . . . The movement suffers, you write. I won't comment on that except to say that perhaps the movement would suffer less, if the individuals who pretended they are leading it displayed a little more intellectual solidarity and disinterestedness. I never told you that I was seeking any 'abstract universal recognition' as a poet, but I think I may have my ambition without being catechized about them by Dr. Locke. . . . And as to your opinion concerning the ultimate appraisal of my life and work—keep it, my dear Dr. Locke. Keep your opinion, and forgive me, but I don't care a damn for it.

In light of Locke's own philosophy of relativism and pluralism, in the face of the plurality and relativity of the possible aesthetic attitudes, how could Locke try to force on McKay and other Harlem Renaissance writers his own attitude toward the work of art and its public? It seems that in conceptualizing about the cultural and artistic community of the Harlem Renaissance, Locke actually did capitulate to an axiology of positivism, with its monistic, objectivist, and even absolutist bent.

Nevertheless, it remains equally clear that despite his racial and ideological loyalties, Locke himself considered art too important to view as a mere racial and ideologically determined epiphenomenon. Because he viewed himself as a philosophical midwife to a generation of young writers, he

thought it was appropriate to stress ideology and propaganda in art throughout the 1920s and 1930s. After 1940, however, he never tired of pointing out that "no fiction can be great on mere courage and truthfulness" ("Black Truth and Black Beauty," *Opportunity*, November 1933). He became extremely critical of too detailed, overdocumented, and needlepoint realism, as revealed in his criticism of William March's *Boss Man*, a novel which was "true enough in detail, but packed so over-full with harrowing incidents that it fails both of conviction and social understanding. Such raw-document literature has its place, and has served a social purpose, but it has one great failing: it isn't literature. When this is fully realized we shall prefer tracts that are not fictionalized and fiction that is not tractarian" ("Dry Fields and Green Pastures," *Opportunity*, January 1940). In addition to excessive documentation, Locke became less tolerant of works in which characters were poorly drawn. Of George Henderson's *Ollie Miss* he said: "Too colorless in narrative style and too superficial in characterization, this character study barely rises above the plane of melodrama or breaks the shell of formula, thereby, proving an important point for the future work both of Mr. Henderson and all others,—that the mere novelty feature of Negro subject-matter has about vanished with the present-day audience, and only skillful characterization and projection can hope to succeed" ("Reason and Race," *Phylon*, 1948). Writers like Henderson, he concluded, "intent on moralizing in fiction, forget the basic essentials of good and effective art re-discovered by all incisive aestheticians since Aristotle,—that in a work of fiction, the truth must be more than possible or even probable, it must seem inevitable. The best sociological intentions often make the worse dramas and novels."

The rejection of ideology and sociology in black art signaled the decline of the Harlem Renaissance's popularity and Locke's disappointment with it. A note of frustration had become apparent in Locke's thought even before 1930, as revealed in his debate with McKay. By 1950, toward the end of his career, he could write with ease about the New Negro's failures: "All of us probably expected too much of the Negro Renaissance, but its new vitality of independence, pride and self-respect, its scoff and defiance of prejudice and limitations were so welcome and heartening" ("Self-Criticism," *Phylon*, 1950). Locke blamed most of the failure on "exhibitionism" and "racial chauvinism":

they made culture a market-place commodity and out of this shallow and sordid misunderstanding did it to death prematurely. Two childish maladies of the spirit—exhibitionism and racial chauvinism . . . became epidemic . . . Once the movement took on public momentum and offered that irresistible American lure of a vogue of success, a ready means of quick recognition, an easy, cheap road to vicarious compensation, this dangerous infection was on. True it was a typically American misapprehension, a characteristic American popular abuse but it brought about lamentably a Negro-American tragedy of the first magnitude.

American society during the period of the 1920s was highly diversified and quickly changing, a society in which black Americans' expectations outran the realities available to satisfy them. The Great Depression, which began in 1929 and lasted through much of the next decade, did much to deflate the first phase of the Harlem Renaissance which ended in the late 1920s. Even before the Depression began, the vast majority of urban blacks were already suffering economic hardships. The New Negro movement had been tumultuous and feverish but had obviously not produced the desired social and economic results. The Marxists, the numbers racketeers, the dope pushers, and the hustlers all helped to extinguish the New Negro's dreams during the 1920s, as, in perverse ways, they assimilated moments of the movement for their own personal advantage. In addition the New Negro writers and intellectuals themselves took various paths after the 1920s, with some joining the communists and others going into exile.

The dream of the New Negro was thus crushed not merely by the black artist's own doing but by the weight of an oppressive historical reality as well. But given the internal contradictions of the Harlem Renaissance and its ideological illusions, it is, as Locke has suggested, likely that the New Negro movement could not have realized its aesthetic, economic, and socioethical ideals in any case. The Harlem Renaissance vision of the New Negro was significantly flawed, weakened by an excessive individualism and messianic-rhetorical moralism which tried to recycle ideals of heart, spirit, brotherhood, and the like when crime, poverty, and misery were taking their toll on much of black American life and culture. Notwithstanding Locke's intense moral sense and his passionate love of the racial community from which he came, and

to which he continued to belong, his understanding of the black community during the Harlem Renaissance as an artistic and cultural entity, more real and more important than the individuals themselves, only distracted him from concentrating on those factors that prompted its members to be culturally active in the first place. In short, Locke concentrated on the "cake"; he did not realize that more interest should have been placed on the "bread." Locke himself later understood this. A few years before his untimely death in 1954 he wrote:

> I, too, confess that at one time of my life I may have been guilty of thinking of culture as cake contrasted with bread. Now I know better. Real, essential culture is baked into our daily bread or else it isn't truly culture. In short, I am willing to stand firmly on the side of the democratic rather than the aristocratic notion of culture and have so stood for many years, without having gotten full credit, however. I realize the inevitability of such misunderstanding: what price Harvard and Oxford and their traditional snobbisms!

Locke's confession here is but another way of acknowledging that the relationship of cultural products to the more fundamental social and economic realities of black America was much more complex than he had realized. As a social philosopher whose philosophy of art was not primarily an aesthetic system, but rather a social and political one, Locke could have applied his stupendous insights to this problem much more thoroughly than he did. He was held back at every point by his idealist heritage.

It is obvious that one who does not attach the importance Locke did to the achievement of cultural recognition will not accept his evaluation of the various modes of activities and forms of thinking during the Harlem Renaissance. Even if one does so, however, it seems that his discussion of the values, goals, and purposes of group life remain of considerable importance. They contain a great many insights concerning the possible ways of sensing, valuing, feeling, and living which are by no means inextricably bound up with his own convictions. It is, at least in part, for this reason that his thinking has exerted so great an influence, in spite of the fact that few, if any, have embraced the form of race loyalty to which he was so deeply committed. Still, like the Harlem Renaissance itself, there is no conclusion to Alain Locke's impact.

References:

Clare Bloodgood Crane, "Alain Locke and the Negro Renaissance," Ph.D. dissertation, University of California, San Diego, 1971;

S. P. Fullinwider, *The Mind and Mood of Black America* (Homewood, Ill.: Dorsey Press, 1969);

Abby Arthur Johnson and Ronald Maberry Johnson, *Propaganda and Aesthetics: The Literary Politics of Afro-American Magazines in the Twentieth Century* (Amherst: University of Massachusetts Press, 1979), pp. 69-70;

Richard A. Long, "Alain Locke: Cultural and Social Mentor," *Black World,* 20 (November 1970): 87-90.

Carl Van Vechten

(17 June 1880-21 December 1964)

Bruce Kellner
Millersville University

See also the Van Vechten entries in *DLB 4, American Writers in Paris, 1920-1939,* and *DLB 9, American Novelists, 1910-1945.*

BOOKS: *Music After the Great War and Other Studies* (New York: Schirmer, 1915);
Music and Bad Manners (New York: Knopf, 1916);
Interpreters and Interpretations (New York: Knopf, 1917); revised as *Interpreters* (New York: Knopf, 1920);
The Merry-Go-Round (New York: Knopf, 1918);
The Music of Spain (New York: Knopf, 1918; London: Kegan Paul, Trench & Trübner, 1920);
In the Garret (New York: Knopf, 1920);
The Tiger in the House (New York: Knopf, 1920; London: Heinemann, 1921);
Peter Whiffle: His Life and Works (New York: Knopf, 1922; London: Richards, 1923; revised edition, New York: Knopf, 1927);
The Blind Bow-Boy (New York: Knopf, 1923; London: Richards, 1923);
The Tattooed Countess: A Romantic Novel with a Happy Ending (New York: Knopf, 1924; London: Knopf, 1926);
Red: Papers on Musical Subjects (New York: Knopf, 1925);
Firecrackers: A Realistic Novel (New York: Knopf, 1925; London: Knopf, 1927);
Excavations: A Book of Advocacies (New York: Knopf, 1926);
Nigger Heaven (New York & London: Knopf, 1926; London: Knopf, 1926);
Spider Boy: A Scenario for a Moving Picture (New York & London: Knopf, 1928; London: Knopf, 1928);
Parties: Scenes from Contemporary New York Life (New York: Knopf, 1930; London & New York: Knopf, 1930);
Feathers (New York: Random House, 1930);
Sacred and Profane Memories (New York: Knopf, 1932; London, Toronto, Melbourne & Sydney: Cassell, 1932);
Fragments from an unwritten autobiography, 2 volumes (New Haven: Yale University Library, 1955);

The Dance Writings of Carl Van Vechten, edited by Paul Padgette (New York: Dance Horizons, 1975);
Portraits: The Photography of Carl Van Vechten, compiled by Saul Mauriber (Indianapolis & New York: Bobbs-Merrill, 1978);
"Keep A-Inchin' Along": Selected Writings of Carl Van Vechten about Black Art and Letters, edited by Bruce Kellner (Westport, Conn. & London: Greenwood Press, 1979);
The Dance Photography of Carl Van Vechten, edited by Padgette (New York: Schirmer/London: Collier Macmillan, 1981).

Carl Van Vechten (photo by Donald Angus; courtesy of Bruce Kellner)

Most of the readers—black as well as white—who made Carl Van Vechten's *Nigger Heaven* a best-selling novel in 1926 were unaware that his interest in the creative achievements of Afro-Americans had begun before the turn of the century. He had been writing essays, evaluating plays and books, and producing program notes and dust-jacket blurbs about black artists and for black artists for more than a decade when *Nigger Heaven* appeared, and he had delighted in the performances of black entertainers for more than thirty years. Van Vechten's support brought undeniably mixed results, as did the efforts of earlier sympathetic white reviewers and patrons. William Dean Howells, for example, had good intentions when he reviewed Paul Laurence Dunbar's poetry, but he solidified Dunbar's reputation as a dialect poet, a label Dunbar tried desperately and unsuccessfully to shake. In the 1920s the problem intensified; the black artist was torn between well-meaning encouragement from the white race to preserve his racial identity, usually by cultivating what some, though not Van Vechten, described as black "primitivism" (even to using blackface makeup on stage), and a misguided encouragement from his own race to emulate whites (by using, for example, products designed to straighten hair and lighten skin).

These complexities notwithstanding, the Harlem Renaissance would not so easily have progressed beyond Harlem without the intervention and support of white patrons. That such white support now seems patronizing is inevitable, but to deny its positive aspects is intellectually indefensible. White patrons were unavoidable in getting from the past to the present, and they made a strong supporting cast. Some were bad actors; Carl Van Vechten was a better one.

Yale University's James Weldon Johnson Memorial Collection of Negro Arts and Letters—which Carl Van Vechten founded—gives credence to his significance. He began it by donating his own vast collection of black literature and memorabilia, continued to contribute to it both materially and financially for the rest of his life, and specified in his will that money realized from reprints of his own books and photographs be donated to the collection's endowment fund. With the present interest in black studies, scholars will be increasingly grateful for this legacy. It is difficult to imagine books about the Harlem Renaissance or several recent biographies of black writers without it.

Moreover, Van Vechten's own writings about black arts and letters are of considerable value as well. During his life, most of his writings about

blacks—except *Nigger Heaven*—probably had little impact: those who most needed to become aware of black culture did not read the publications in which his articles were published. Gathered together in *"Keep A-Inchin' Along"* (1979), their sheer bulk is astonishing. Few people realize how much of his time and energy Van Vechten devoted to the advancement of Afro-American arts and letters.

His own involvement in black culture must have begun when he was about ten years old and heard Sissieretta Jones (known as "Black Patti" after the white opera singer Adelina Patti) in one of her opulent musical productions that played in his hometown, Cedar Rapids, Iowa, during a nationwide tour. By the turn of the century he had encountered many other black entertainers, including Bert Williams, who left him "trembling between hysterical laughter and sudden tears." Van Vechten would later identify the ability to command such contrary emotions simultaneously as the unique genius of black artists.

Although Van Vechten's initial exposure to Afro-Americans came through black performers often catering to the demands of white audiences, his private associations were more deeply rooted. A black washerwoman and a black yardman were the first adults he knew outside his immediate family, and he was reared to address them as "Mrs. Sercy" and "Mr. Oliphant," with the same respect due any other adult. His parents addressed them formally as well. Such civility hardly strikes one as unusual today, but the 1980s are far removed from the 1880s, and not only in years. By the time Van Vechten left for college, he was already inoculated against racial prejudice to whatever extent was possible in turn-of-the-century America. For three of his four years at the University of Chicago, he went with his fraternity's black housekeeper to the Quinn Chapel, where he played the piano for services and accompanied the singing. (The songs were more often Baptist hymns than the spirituals Van Vechten strove to popularize in later years.) His journal entries and essays of that period suggest that he adored the housekeeper, just as he had preferred the company of older people during his childhood, and he saw his new acquaintances at the chapel as "an intensely uncultured and uneducated race but just as intensely good hearted, humorous, . . . and even clever." They were "colored members of the human family," he concluded. At the present time such observations may suggest condescension, but in a twenty year old in 1900 they do not. The date at which his devotion developed refutes his critics' charges—particularly during the 1920s at the height of the notoriety of *Nigger Heaven*—that his views on the race were superficial because they were so new.

Van Vechten's first professional writings devoted exclusively to black entertainment appeared long before the sudden craze that began with the all-black musical comedy *Shuffle Along,* which opened on Broadway in 1921. Working as a cub reporter for the *Chicago American* in 1904, he wrote about black entertainers whenever he got the chance. In 1913, as drama critic for the *New York Press,* he wrote enthusiastically about *My Friend From Kentucky,* part of *The Darktown Follies,* at Harlem's Lafayette Theatre. That article—and his review in 1914 of *Granny Maumee,* a play by white writer Ridgely Torrence, in which black characters were played by white actors (it was revived with black actors three years later)—motivated Van Vechten's extended essay "The Negro Theatre," written in 1919 and first published in his *In the Garret* (1920). As early as 1914, in his *Granny Maumee* review, he had urged the formation of a Negro theater organization, with black actors and black playwrights. When, five years after "The Negro Theatre" was published, Van Vechten told Eric Walrond that he thought it was out of date, Walrond not only contended that its ideas and points were still pertinent, but that, had he not known of Van Vechten's authorship, he would have thought the essay had been written by a black because of its positive bias.

By the time *Nigger Heaven* appeared in 1926, he had become a self-proclaimed, unpaid press agent for Harlem's black intelligentsia, as well as for its cabarets. He had become, he later said, "violently interested in Negroes." In fact, the interest, he said, was "almost an addiction." His first black literary acquaintance was Walter White, whom he met through their publisher Alfred A. Knopf in 1924. Soon after, White introduced him to James Weldon Johnson, and he found the catalyst for his violent interest. Both men were firm believers in the idealistic theory of an articulate and educated "talented tenth"; each provided the other with an entrée to his race, and each named the other his literary executor. Also, through White, Van Vechten came to know Langston Hughes and Countee Cullen, and soon he had met Wallace Thurman and Zora Neale Hurston. (Hurston is responsible for having dubbed Van Vechten Harlem's first "Negrotarian.") In 1925 he arranged for some poems by Cullen and Hughes to appear in the popular magazine *Vanity Fair,* and through his instigation Knopf agreed to publish Hughes's first

collection of verse, *The Weary Blues* (1926), as well as books by black novelists Nella Larsen and Rudolph Fisher.

When Van Vechten wrote a series of articles on black subjects for *Vanity Fair* in 1925-1926 he dealt with singers Bessie Smith and Ethel Waters, spirituals, black theater, and the blues (the first serious consideration ever given this musical form). During that same period he financed in large part singer Paul Robeson's first programs of spirituals, as well as a recital of similar music by Taylor Gordon and J. Rosamond Johnson. Also, he reviewed at least a dozen books by black writers, frequently writing blurbs for their dust jackets and copy for their advertisements as well. Not surprisingly, a gossip column in 1925 declared that he was getting a heavy tan, and, as he only appeared in public after dark, he had to be acquiring it in a taxi, bound for the nightclubs in Harlem.

Indeed, Van Vechten devoted an inordinate amount of time to shabby pursuits—getting drunk in speakeasies, collecting Harlem sycophants, having dates with steamy sepia courtesans and assignations with handsome black callboys—that were common knowledge. But his intellectual admiration for black culture was genuine. His response to black music and writing was based on firm aesthetic values, developed over nearly a quarter century of broad experience as a serious, professional music and literary critic. Even a partial list of his other discoveries and enthusiasms is impressive. He endorsed the first performances in America of Isadora Duncan, Anna Pavlova, Mary Garden, Fyodor Chaliapin, Vaslav Nijinsky, Sergei Rachmaninoff, and the operas of Richard Strauss; he was the earliest American admirer of the music of Igor Stravinsky and Erik Satie and of George Gershwin as a serious composer. He advocated musical scores by classical composers for motion pictures; he was first to write extensively about Spanish music; he considered jazz and ragtime as fervently as he considered music by Rossini or any other composer popular in his own time. He was one of the first critics to rediscover Herman Melville's work; Ronald Firbank and Arthur Machen owe their American reputations to him; Henry Blake Fuller, Wallace Stevens, and Gertrude Stein all acknowledged their debt to Van Vechten's farsightedness and efforts on their behalf. Van Vechten's desire to share his latest discovery resulted in a cultural exchange unique at the time. In their glamorous apartment in Manhattan, Carl Van Vechten and his wife, actress Fania Marinoff, entertained frequently and lavishly and always with fully inte-

Advertisement for Van Vechten's controversial 1926 novel

grated guest lists. The parties were eventually reported as a matter of course in some of the city's black newspapers, and Walter White called the Van Vechtens' apartment "the mid-town office of the NAACP."

And then Van Vechten wrote *Nigger Heaven.* In "Moanin' Wid a Sword in Mah Han," published in the February 1926 issue of *Vanity Fair,* he discussed the black artist's reluctance to develop his unique racial qualities and the danger of white artists appropriating those qualities for their own work. A month later, in his answer to a *Crisis* magazine questionnaire called "The Negro in Art: How Shall He Be Portrayed?," Van Vechten posed a counter question: "Are Negro writers going to write about this exotic material while it is fresh or will they continue to make a free gift of it to white authors who will exploit it until not a drop of vitality remains?" (Actually Van Vechten had ghostwritten

the questionnaire, although it was sent out with a letter signed by *Crisis* editor Jessie Fauset.) Both observations create a disturbing irony that is either apt or cruel, since at that very time Van Vechten was writing *Nigger Heaven,* which employs this "exotic material." Furthermore, his response to the questionnaire, as well as *Nigger Heaven,* led to accusations that he encouraged the worst, rather than the best, efforts among young black writers who followed. Novels by Claude McKay, Wallace Thurman, and Rudolph Fisher would soon deal far more directly with Harlem's "untalented ninetieth." But the writers were black and young and virtually unknown both north and south of 125th Street in Harlem. Van Vechten proved a more visible target.

For many readers of *Nigger Heaven,* the black slang word for a white person—"fay" or "ofay," pig latin for "foe"—renewed its double meaning; but

Harlem knew Van Vechten as a regular customer in the cabarets jingling his bracelets when he tipped up his sterling-silver hip flask, as a white judge at the black transvestite balls at the Rockland Palace Casino, as somebody whose name turned up in black society columns, as a guest in black people's homes, as Nora Holt's escort, and as A'Lelia Walker's boon companion. At a Harlem party in Rudolph Fisher's novel *The Walls of Jericho* (1928), a black character says to a white one obviously patterned after Van Vechten, " 'you're the only fay I know that draws the color line on other fays.' 'It's natural,' " the white character replies fatuously. " 'Downtown I'm only passing. These,' he waved grandiloquently, 'are my people.' "

Most of the negative criticism of *Nigger Heaven* came from reviewers who contended that Van Vechten had made use of only the "primitive" aspects of Harlem life. A surprising number of present-day critics have agreed, some perhaps without having read the book. Nearly two-thirds of *Nigger Heaven* is given over to sociological and aesthetic discussions among black intellectuals and to a bloodless love affair between two dreary characters whose leaden encounters dominate the story line.

The other third of the novel—the lurid third—certainly does occur in cabarets and between the sheets. Any readers familiar with Van Vechten's four frivolous earlier novels would have been more surprised by his emphasis on a pathetic little love affair than by *Nigger Heaven*'s world of imaginatively drawn numbers racketeers, elegant demimondaines, strutting pimps, and plenty of sheiks and flappers doing the Charleston.

The real problem with *Nigger Heaven* is not its sensationalism but its conscious didacticism. A deliberate attempt to educate Van Vechten's already large white reading public, the novel presents Harlem as a complex society fractured and united by individual and social groups of diverse interests, talents, and values. The scandalous drinking and sleeping around in *Nigger Heaven* go on in all of Van Vechten's novels: such vagaries are hardly limited to one race. In his afterword to a 1951 edition, Van Vechten declared, "Negroes are treated by me exactly as if I were depicting white characters, for the very excellent reason that I do not believe there is much psychological difference between the races." *Nigger Heaven* is best understood as the Van Vechten novel in which his characters happen to be black.

Certainly the novel's sensationalism helped to sell it to white readers, but the same sort of elements

had helped the sales of its predecessors too, and those who accused the novel of exploiting black "primitivism"—a word Van Vechten never used—failed to consider that the sensational is not necessarily primitive, and vice versa.

"Primitivism," as Mark Helbling has suggested, should not be associated with any particular race or even with any particular culture. Rather, primitivism is an aesthetic point of view that has more to do with creativity. Picasso, Helbling has rightly observed, was not interested in Africans or in African "soul," but in their artifacts that could stimulate his own imagination. Van Vechten was no Picasso. His talents—and they were considerable—are not well illustrated in *Nigger Heaven*.

None of Van Vechten's friends seems to have misunderstood it, and he lost no friends of either color because of it. They were aware of his genuine concern for the race as well as his flamboyant behavior. They recognized his acute critical perception and stubborn adherence to a highly mannered style, on the one hand too analytical and discursive and on the other too arch and ornate. For many readers not personally involved with either his personality or his writing, *Nigger Heaven* has some serious troubles not remotely connected with the Harlem Renaissance. In another novel, *The Blind Bow-Boy* (1923), in quite another context, Van Vechten causes one of his characters to reflect: "A book . . . should have the swiftness of melodrama, the lightness of farce, to be a real contribution to thought. . . . How could anything serious be hidden more successfully than in a book which pretended to be light and gay?" Van Vechten's attempt at "a real contribution to thought" gets in the way of "a real contribution to thought." The observations of Harlem's intelligentsia may convey important information, but one tends to grow weary when a character stands stage-center and recites a canned speech. It created a large white readership for black writers, and it brought plenty of business into the cabarets north of 125th Street. Whether those two circumstances are close enough in value to be mentioned in the same sentence is open to question.

Whatever its limitations, however, the novel strengthened Van Vechten's ties with blacks and increased his loyalty. Through the rest of his long career he devoted his energies to a wider recognition of black achievements, primarily through photographing nearly every celebrated Afro-American and through his establishment of the James Weldon Johnson Collection at Yale, as well as through several other collections he started around the country. If the endeavor suggested sycophancy to some suspicious few who refused to be photographed, it was nevertheless as sincere as his "violent interest" was unflagging. Van Vechten admitted he was star-struck all his life, from the time he first met Bert Williams in 1906, until his last summer in 1964: "I am in my usual state of gaping enthusiasm. (Will it never end? Probably NOT.) I heard André Watts at the [Lewisohn] Stadium and sans doute he is the greatest living pianist. He has everything, including good taste and he will end in glory, as he has begun." Bert Williams died before Van Vechten began photographing, and Van Vechten himself died before he could get to André Watts, but hundreds of other subjects— white as well as black—came in between. The list of black subjects is staggering, and he photographed many of these people before their talents were generally recognized, when he sensed that same "glory" he predicted for André Watts: Chester Himes at thirty, Shirley Verrett at twenty-four, Leontyne Price at twenty-three, Lena Horne at twenty-one; and James Baldwin, LeRoi Jones, Alvin Ailey, Diahann Carroll, Harry Belafonte, and Arthur Mitchell more than thirty years ago.

With the passing of time, Carl Van Vechten's significance has been downplayed, on occasion, perhaps, on purpose. At best he has been given grudging acknowledgment for his role in the period now referred to as the Harlem Renaissance— which, in truth, he partly invented. All his life Van Vechten championed the avant-garde, writing seriously about scores of people and movements that later came into prominence, and he focused on Afro-American arts and letters early on. He made

integration fashionable in an attempt to introduce his own race to the pleasures he had discovered in another. Hindsight tells us, however, that the "untalented ninetieth" of either race rarely listens to the "talented tenth."

Nevertheless, James Weldon Johnson once wrote to Van Vechten, "Has anyone ever written it down—in black and white—that you have been one of the most vital forces in bringing about the artistic emergence of the Negro in America? Well, I am glad to bear witness to the fact." And George S. Schuyler, editor of the *Pittsburgh Courier*, unerringly suspicious but frequently given to overstatement, declared that "Carl Van Vechten has done more than any single person in this country to create the atmosphere of acceptance of the Negro."

These observations do not address the subtle distinction between patronage and patronizing which any consideration of Carl Van Vechten must confront. It is doubtless easy for the one to become the other, but it may be almost as easy for the one to seem to become the other because of black dismay over the circumstances that originally led to white patronage in the first place.

References:

Mark Helbling, "Carl Van Vechten and the Harlem Renaissance," *Negro American Literature Forum*, 10 (July 1976): 39-46;

Langston Hughes, "When Harlem Was in Vogue," *Town and Country*, 95 (July 1940): 49, 64-66;

Edward Lueders, *Carl Van Vechten* (New York: Twayne, 1965).

Books for Further Reading

Abramson, Doris E. *Negro Playwrights in the American Theatre, 1925-1959*. New York & London: Columbia University Press, 1969.

Adams, William, Peter Conn, and Barry Slepian. *Afro-American Literature*, 4 volumes. Boston: Houghton Mifflin, 1970.

Adams, ed. *Afro-American Authors*. Boston: Houghton Mifflin, 1972.

Allen, James S. *The Negro Question in the United States*. New York: International, 1936.

Anderson, Jervis. *This Was Harlem: A Cultural Portrait, 1900-1950*. New York: Farrar, Straus & Giroux, 1982.

Aptheker, Herbert, ed. *A Documentary History of the Negro People in the United States: 1910-1932*. Secaucus, N.J.: Citadel, 1973.

Baker, Houston A., Jr. *Long Black Song: Essays in Black American Literature and Culture*. Charlottesville: University Press of Virginia, 1972.

Ballard, Allen B. *The Education of Black Folk: The Afro-American Struggle For Knowledge in White America*. New York: Harper & Row, 1973.

Bardolph, Richard. *The Negro Vanguard*. New York: Rinehart, 1959.

Barton, Rebecca C. *Black Voice in American Fiction: 1900-1930*. Oakdale, N.Y.: Dowling College Press, 1976.

Barton. *Race Consciousness and the American Negro: A Study of the Correlation Between the Group Experience and the Fiction of 1900-1930*. Copenhagen: Arnold Busck, 1934.

Baskin, Wade. *Dictionary of Black Culture*. New York: Philosophical Library, 1973.

Bone, Robert A. *The Negro Novel in America*, revised edition. New Haven: Yale University Press, 1965.

Bontemps, Arna, ed. *The Harlem Renaissance Remembered*. New York: Dodd, Mead, 1972.

Brawley, Benjamin. *The Negro Genius; A New Appraisal of the Achievement of the American Negro in Literature and the Fine Arts*. New York: Dodd, Mead, 1940.

Brawley. *The Negro in Literature and Art*, second revised edition. New York: Dodd, Mead, 1929.

Bronz, Steven H. *Roots of Negro Racial Consciousness: The 1920's: Three Harlem Renaissance Writers*. New York: Libra, 1964.

Brown, Sterling A. *The Negro in American Fiction*. Washington, D.C.: Associates in Negro Folk Education, 1938.

Brown. *Negro Poetry and Drama*. Washington, D.C.: Associates in Negro Folk Education, 1937.

Butcher, Margaret J. *The Negro in American Culture.* New York: Knopf, 1956.

Clark, John Henry, ed. *Harlem, U.S.A., the Story of a City Within a City.* New York: Macmillan, 1964.

Clarke, John Henrik, ed. *Harlem: A Community in Transition.* New York: Citadel, 1964.

Coombs, Norma. *The Black Experience in America.* New York: Hippocrene, 1972.

Davis, Arthur P. *From the Dark Tower: Afro-American Writers, 1900 to 1960.* Washington, D.C.: Howard University Press, 1974.

Davis, Charles, and Daniel Walden, eds. *On Being Black, Writings by Afro-Americans from Frederick Douglass to the Present.* Greenwich, Conn.: Fawcett, 1970.

Emanuel, James A., and Theodore Gross, eds. *Dark Symphony: Negro Literature in America.* New York: Free Press, 1968.

Ferguson, Blanche W. *Countee Cullen and the Negro Renaissance.* New York: Dodd, Mead, 1966.

Ford, Nick Aaron. *Black Insights.* Waltham, Mass.: Ginn, 1971.

Ford. *The Contemporary Negro Novel, a Study in Race Relations.* Boston: Meador, 1936.

Fullinwider, S. P. *The Mind and Mood of Black America. 20th Century Thought.* Homewood, Ill.: Dorsey, 1969.

Gayle, Addison, Jr. *The Black Aesthetic.* Garden City: Doubleday, 1971.

Gayle, ed. *Black Expression; Essays By and About Black Americans in the Creative Arts.* New York: Weybright & Talley, 1969.

Gloster, Hugh M. *Negro Voices in American Fiction.* Chapel Hill: University of North Carolina Press, 1948.

Gross, Seymour, and John E. Hardy, eds. *Images of the Negro in American Literature: Essays in Criticism.* Chicago: University of Chicago Press, 1966.

Hemenway, Robert, ed. *The Black Novelist.* Columbus, Ohio: Merrill, 1970.

Hill, Herbert. *Anger and Beyond: The Negro Writer in the United States.* New York: Harper & Row, 1966.

Hoffman, Frederick J. *The Twenties; American Writing in the Post War Decade,* revised edition. New York: Free Press, 1969.

Huggins, Nathan I. *Harlem Renaissance.* New York: Oxford University Press, 1971.

Kellner, Bruce. *Carl Van Vechten and the Irreverent Decades.* Norman: University of Oklahoma Press, 1968.

Kellner, ed. *The Harlem Renaissance: A Historical Dictionary For The Era.* Westport, Conn.: Greenwood, 1984.

Kent, George. *Blackness and the Adventure of Western Culture.* Chicago: Third World Press, 1972.

Kerlin, Robert T., ed. *Negro Poets and Their Poems,* revised edition. Washington, D.C.: Associated Publishers, 1935.

Kornweibel, Theodore, Jr. *No Crystal Stair: Black Life and the "Messenger," 1917-1928*. Westport, Conn.: Greenwood, 1975.

Lewis, David Levering. *When Harlem Was In Vogue*. New York: Knopf, 1981.

Locke, Alain, ed. *Four Negro Poets*. New York: Simon & Schuster, 1927.

Locke, ed. *The New Negro Poets*. New York: Boni & Liveright, 1925.

Locke, and Montgomery Gregory. *Plays of Negro Life: A Source-book of Native American Drama*. New York: Harper, 1927.

Logan, Rayford, ed. *The New Negro Thirty Years Afterward*. Washington, D.C.: Howard University Press, 1956.

Loggins, Vernon. *The Negro Author: His Development in America*. New York: Columbia University Press, 1931.

Margolies, Edward. *Native Sons: A Critical Study of Twentieth Century Negro American Authors*. Philadelphia: Lippincott, 1968.

McPherson, James M., and others. *Blacks in America: Bibliographical Essays*. Garden City: Doubleday, 1971.

Miller, Ruth, ed. *Blackamerican Literature: 1760-Present*. Beverly Hills, Cal.: Glencoe, 1971.

Mitchell, Loften. *Black Drama: The Story of the American Negro in the Theatre*. New York: Hawthorn, 1967.

Olsson, Martin. *A Selected Bibliography of Black Literature: The Harlem Renaissance*. Exeter, U.K.: University of Exeter, 1973.

Perrett, Geoffrey. *America in the Twenties: A History*. New York: Simon & Schuster, 1982.

Perry, Margaret. *The Harlem Renaissance: An Annotated Bibliography and Commentary*. New York: Garland, 1982.

Redding, Saunders. *To Make a Poet Black*. Chapel Hill: University of North Carolina Press, 1939.

Scheiner, Seth M. *Negro Mecca: A History of the Negro in New York City, 1865-1920*. New York: New York University Press, 1965.

Schoener, Allon. *Harlem on My Mind*. New York: Random House, 1968.

Singh, Amritjit. *The Novels of the Harlem Renaissance: Twelve Black Writers, 1923-1933*. University Park: Pennsylvania State University Press, 1976.

Sochen, June, ed. *The Black Man and the American Dream: Negro Aspirations in America, 1900-1930*. Chicago: Quadrangle, 1971.

Thurman, Wallace. *Negro Life in New York's Harlem*. Girard, Kans.: Haldeman-Julius, 1928.

Turner, Darwin T, ed. *In A Minor Chord: Three Afro-American Writers and Their Search for Identity*. Carbondale: Southern Illinois University Press, 1971.

Turner, ed. *Black American Literature*. Columbus, Ohio: Merrill, 1969.

Wagner, Jean. *Black Poets of the United States: From Paul Laurence Dunbar to Langston Hughes,* translated by Kenneth Douglas. Urbana: University of Illinois Press, 1973.

Waldron, Edward E. *Walter White and the Harlem Renaissance.* Port Washington, N.Y.: Kennikat, 1978.

Whiteman, Maxwell. *A Century of Fiction By American Negroes, 1853-1952: A Descriptive Bibliography.* Philadelphia, 1955.

Williams, Kenny J. *They Also Spoke: An Essay on Negro Literature in America, 1787-1930.* Nashville: Townsend, 1970.

Young, James Owen. *Black Writers of the Thirties.* Baton Rouge: Louisiana State University Press, 1973.

Contributors

Schavi Mali Ali.. *Wayne State University*
Jay R. Berry... *University of Iowa*
Edward D. Clark .... *North Carolina State University at Raleigh*
Walter C. Daniel.............................. *University of Missouri, Columbia*
Thadious M. Davis .... *University of North Carolina at Chapel Hill*
Winona Fletcher.. *Indiana University*
Joyce Flynn .... *Harvard University*
Joanne V. Gabbin .... *James Madison University*
Eric Garber .... *San Francisco, California*
Sandra Y. Govan .... *University of North Carolina at Charlotte*
J. Lee Greene................................. *University of North Carolina at Chapel Hill*
Kathleen A. Hauke.. *Morris Brown College*
Lucy Kelly Hayden...................................... *Winston-Salem State University*
Burney Hollis.................................... *Morgan State University*
Lillie P. Howard .... *Wright State University*
Kirkland C. Jones .... *Lamar University*
Norma R. Jones .... *Alcorn State University*
Bruce Kellner.................................... *Millersville University*
Keneth Kinnamon................................ *University of Arkansas*
Phyllis R. Klotman .... *Indiana University*
Ernest D. Mason................................. *North Carolina Central University*
Nellie McKay .... *University of Wisconsin-Madison*
R. Baxter Miller .... *The Langston Hughes Society*
Emmanuel S. Nelson............................. *University of Tennessee*
Raymond R. Patterson................... *City College of the City University of New York*
Margaret Perry .... *Valparaiso University*
Patsy B. Perry.................................. *North Carolina Central University*
Alan Shucard .... *University of Wisconsin-Parkside*
Carolyn Wedin Sylvander .... *University of Wisconsin-Whitewater*
John Edgar Tidwell................................ *University of Kentucky*
Eleanor Q. Tignor .... *LaGuardia Community College, CUNY*
Sarah M. Washington....................... *South Carolina State College*
Allen Williams .... *Grambling State University*

Cumulative Index

Dictionary of Literary Biography, Volumes 1-51
Dictionary of Literary Biography Yearbook, 1980-1985
Dictionary of Literary Biography Documentary Series, Volumes 1-4

Cumulative Index

DLB before number: *Dictionary of Literary Biography*, Volumes 1-51
Y before number: *Dictionary of Literary Biography Yearbook*, 1980-1985
DS before number: *Dictionary of Literary Biography Documentary Series*, Volumes 1-4

A

E

F

G

H

Cumulative Index

Cumulative Index

K

M

O

P

Q

Cumulative Index

T

U

V

W

Y

Z

Cumulative Index

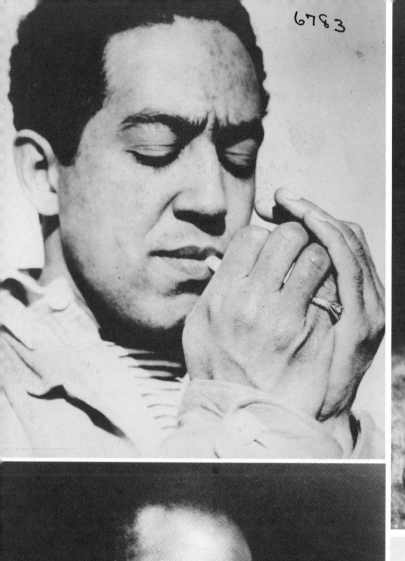

6783

To the students of
Crispus Attucks High School
in Indianapolis
Sincerely
(Bill)
Arthur